Contemporary French Cinema

A Student's Book

Contemporary French Cinema

A Student's Book

Alan Singerman
Davidson College
Emeritus

Michèle Bissière
University of North Carolina
at Charlotte

focus an imprint of
Hackett Publishing Company, Inc.
Indianapolis/Cambridge

A Focus book

Focus an imprint of
Hackett Publishing Company

Copyright © 2018 by Hackett Publishing Company, Inc.

21   20   19   18   1   2   3   4   5   6   7

For further information, please address
       Hackett Publishing Company, Inc.
       P.O. Box 44937
       Indianapolis, Indiana 46244-0937

       www.hackettpublishing.com

Cover design by Brian Rak
Composition by Integrated Composition Systems

Library of Congress Cataloging-in-Publication Data

Names: Singerman, Alan J., author. | Bissière, Michèle author.
Title: Contemporary French cinema : a student's book / Alan Singerman,
    Davidson College Emeritus ; Michèle Bissière, University of North Carolina
    at Charlotte.
Other titles: Cinéma français contemporain. English
Description: Indianapolis : Focus, 2018. | Includes bibliographical references
    and index.
Identifiers: LCCN 2018003364 | ISBN 9781585108930 (pbk.)
Classification: LCC PN1993.5.F7 S54413 2018 | DDC 791.430944—dc23
LC record available at https://lccn.loc.gov/2018003364

∞

For Carolee (who knows why)—AJS

For my parents—MB

Contents

Illustrations

Acknowledgments

We would like to express our gratitude to all those who have supported and helped us in such important ways throughout the preparation of this new textbook on contemporary French cinema. Our special thanks go out to Marc Buffat, emeritus of the Université de Paris VII, Brigitte Humbert of Middlebury College, Jonathan Walsh of Wheaton College, the Interlibrary Loan Services of both of our institutions—in particular Joe Gutekanst of Davidson College, who managed to ferret out every book, article, and film that we needed for this project—and Paul Brantley, technologist at Davidson College, who taught us how to make film excerpts available to our students. We also greatly appreciated the generosity of Agnès Varda, who provided important insights on her documentary masterpiece, *The Gleaners and I*.

We would like to thank also the students in our Contemporary French Cinema classes during the spring 2016 semester at Davidson College and at UNC Charlotte, where the French manuscript served as the textbook. We solicited and listened to their feedback and made important pedagogical adjustments in our chapters based on their suggestions. In addition, the inclusion of certain films was the result of a number of outstanding projects completed by UNC Charlotte students in previous courses, which were a constant source of inspiration for Michèle. Our thanks to them!

We have likewise greatly appreciated the constant support and encouragement from the editorial team at Hackett Publishing Company during the writing of this book, and especially that of Brian Rak and Laura Clark, as well as their copy editor Rebekah Cotton, whose meticulous work was invaluable during the final stages of this English-language manuscript preparation.

And finally, on a more personal note: Michèle is deeply grateful to Alan for his unremitting confidence in her throughout this remarkable adventure and for his firm hand on the tiller, moving us forward resolutely but with generosity and graciousness. She also thanks UNC Charlotte for granting her a semester sabbatical during the fall 2017 semester to be able to complete this long project on schedule. She is very aware, finally, of how much she owes to her daughters Carin, Audrey, and Lea and her friends Beth and Jean-Pierre, who supported her patiently and with great kindness throughout the writing of this book. Alan, for his part, would like to express his gratitude to Michèle, whose keen intelligence, finesse, and powerful work ethic were a constant source of encouragement during the long journey they embarked on together. Keeping the best for the last, he wishes to express his particular gratitude to his partner Véronique, not only for her unremitting moral support during these long months of research and writing, but also for her scrupulous readings of the text and invariably valuable insights.

Preliminary Remarks

First of all, what is "contemporary French cinema"? Is there a precise moment at which we can detect new trends that clearly indicate a break with what came before and mark the beginning of a cinema of our times? We hasten to note that there is no period in which a given tendency in the world of film suddenly disappears and yields to new fashions. Concepts of cinema, old and new, coexist over a long period of time, and certain currents, like social realism, may slip into the background for a moment only to reappear the following decade, albeit in new forms. With respect to the New Wave, which set traditional practices in cinema on their head at the end of the 1950s and beginning of the 1960s, and its heirs in the 1960s and 1970s, we believe that it is the beginning of the decade of the 1980s, with the spectacular arrival of both the *cinéma du look* and the **heritage film,** that inaugurates the contemporary era of the "seventh art" in France. It is likewise a period in which **women** begin to establish their presence behind the camera, and in which **Beur cinema** begins to make an impression with films made in the suburbs, phenomena that will both develop rapidly in the following decades.

We thus present in this textbook **twenty French films** among the most successful and critically acclaimed works from 1980 to the beginning of the second decade of the twenty-first century. The films are grouped in **six very broad categories** that reflect the major part (if not all) of the production of films in France during this period: I. Historical Films: The Occupation and the Colonial Period; II. Socio-Cultural Themes 1: Suburbs, Unemployment, and Exclusion; III. Socio-Cultural Themes 2: School, Immigration; IV. Thrillers and Crime Films; V. Personal Stories: Dramas and Documentaries; VI. Comedy. It is obvious that twenty films cannot be taught in a one-semester course, but we wanted to give fellow teachers a very wide choice to be sure that everyone could find a set of films that corresponds to their taste and interest—while knowing that whatever films are chosen, all of them are recognized as masterpieces of contemporary cinema by both the critics and the French public.

Each chapter of this book is organized in the same manner. The **Introduction** contains a **synopsis** (with no spoilers), followed by sections on the **director,** the **filming,** the **cast,** the **critical reception** of the film, and a segment that gives the **historical, economic, linguistic, or cinematographic context** of the film according to the need for explanation. This first section of the chapter is followed by a **Study Guide** in four parts. The first two, *What happens in this film?* and *True or False?,* both bear on the action of the film, which is essential to know well as a preparation for in-depth discussion, whereas *What did you learn in the Introduction?* is a quick check on how carefully the students read the important background information. In *Exploring the Film,* the culminating exercise, the students are encouraged to dig beneath the surface of the film with questions on the **characters, themes, motifs, and the most important cinematographic aspects of the work.** In this section the opinions of the students are often solicited on quotations from the film and on perspectives proposed by major film critics and scholars or by eminent theoreticians. To facilitate class discussion, we also single out in this section the particular **film excerpts** that students should watch again and study in detail. These excerpts are generally available on the **webpage of Hackett Publishing Company** devoted to this textbook.

Each chapter, finally, contains a **filmography** of the director of the film and a **bibliography** of works consulted in the preparation of that chapter.

Each instructor will decide, of course, what elements she or he wishes to emphasize in the discussion of a given film; it is normal to favor the elements of the introduction or the study guide that seem most important to that person. There is nothing prescriptive in our presentation of the films in this book. Our experience with the use of these chapters in class leads us to recommend, however, that an **initial class** be devoted to the discussion of the action of the film and the contents of the introduction. We've also found it useful to give short written quizzes in this first class to encourage students to pay attention to what happens in the film and to the circumstances surrounding its making. A **second class** should focus on the film's themes and techniques guided by the *Exploring the Film* section, and this in-depth discussion of the film could well extend into the following class as well. As this exercise represents a greater challenge to the students than the preceding ones, we recommend that the instructor ask certain students to take responsibility for the discussion of one or more topics in class, while all students are expected to prepare for discussion of the film in general.

Whether the course meets two or three times a week, it is important to schedule at least one week per film and often a day more according to the richness or complexity of the work involved.

In any case, we wish "Bon voyage" to all colleagues who choose to use this book. We hope that you and your students will take as much pleasure as we do in each stage of your cinematographic journey, whatever the itinerary may be. And please do not hesitate to share your travel notes with us!

Alan Singerman
Davidson College
Emeritus
Davidson, NC

Michèle Bissière
University of North Carolina
at Charlotte, NC

French Cinema:
A Rapid Overview

The Beginnings

French cinema ranks among the very earliest in the history of world cinema. French inventors, notably the Lumière Brothers, participated in the very creation of the medium in the last decade of the nineteenth century by producing technical innovations that permitted world cinema to go beyond Thomas Edison's kinetoscope, which limited the viewing of a film to one spectator at a time. It was **Louis Lumière** who discovered, in 1895, the way to project stable images onto a screen, opening the door to modern cinema, the public spectacle *par excellence*.

Not satisfied with inventing the **Cinematograph**, the first mobile camera—which served in fact as both a camera and a projector—Lumière likewise inaugurated one of the two principal genres of cinema, the documentary, as well as the newsreel, which sent cameramen all over the world to record important people and public events. We owe the initial development of the other principal genre, the fiction film, to another Frenchman, **Georges Méliès**. A magician and theater director in Paris, Méliès immediately understood the potential of this invention in the world of entertainment and soon began to adapt his most spectacular magic tricks to the cinematic medium before making the first fiction films, of which *The Trip to the Moon* (1902) remains the most famous. In the course of his experiments with silent film, he invented or popularized most of the special effects still used in cinema today: *stop-action photography* (in which the camera is stopped during a shot and a new subject placed before the lens), *superimpositions, fades to black, dissolves*, and *fast-* and *slow-motion shots*, among others.

Driven by the first great studios, those of **Charles Pathé** and **Léon Gaumont**, French silent cinema soon dominated screens throughout the world. The French school of comedy produced the first international superstar of the movies, **Max Linder**, who reached the summit of his career in 1910 and whose most celebrated fan was Charlie Chaplin. At the same time the fashion of serials, or episodic films, was on the rise, the most successful being *Nick Carter*, the first police series (beginning in 1908) by **Victorin Jasset**, and the serials by **Louis Feuillade**, *Fantômas* (1913–14), *Les Vampires* (1915–16), and *Judex* (1916). The First World War put an end to the domination of French cinema, and the American silent film industry took over with the Westerns of Thomas Ince, the comedies of **Mack Sennett**, and especially the films of **D. W. Griffith** and **Charles Chaplin**.

The 1920s

The postwar years and the 1920s brought a period of intense creativity and innovation to the cinema world. It is the period when silent movies blossomed, reached their maturity, and became an authentic art capable of mobilizing all of its resources. The first important European movements are born: **Expressionism** and the *Kammerspiel* in Germany (**Robert Wiene, F. W. Murnau,** and **Fritz Lang**) and the **montage school** in the Soviet Union (**Lev Koulechov, Dziga Vertov,** and **Sergei Eisenstein**). In Hollywood, **Charlie Chaplin** directed his first feature films, all enormous box-office successes: *The Kid* (1921), *The Gold Rush* (1925), and *City Lights* (1930). At the same time, the Westerns of **John Ford**, the film epics of **Cecil B. DeMille**, the comedies of the German-American filmmaker **Ernst Lubitsch**, and the naturalism of the Austrian American actor-director **Erich Von Stroheim** also pulled the crowds into the theaters.

In France, **Abel Gance** amazed spectators with his epic *Napoléon*, a vast fresco lasting more than nine hours in its original version (1925–27) that features some of the central episodes of the emperor's life and career in a flamboyant style that Prédal describes as "visual fireworks which mark one of the high points of the art of silent cinema" (1994, 55). Gance succeeded in creating a supercharged atmosphere through the use of multiple double exposures, blurred shots, camera movements, and fast editing. Like Eisenstein, he created striking metaphors by using parallel editing. He perfected the technique of combining point-of-view shots with tracking shots, as well as the use of the triple screen during the last segment of the film, the Italian campaign. If Gance's films stand out because of their narrative innovations, the **1920s in France** are remembered mostly as a period of **revolt, provocation,** and **formal experimentation**, which all fall outside the development of conventional narrative art in film. It is the period of **Impressionism, Dadaïsm,** and **Surrealism.**

Impressionism

For the moviemakers of the Impressionist school, the most "poetic" trend of the avant-garde, it was more important to **create an atmosphere or to depict a fantasy or a dream fragment** than to tell a story. They launched into **formal experiments** (visual and rhythmic) of all kinds. The most typical characteristics of the movement were the systematic utilization of fast editing and blurred images (both of which were relatively new to the movies), slow motion, superimpositions, light play, point-of-view shots, and various deformations of the image. The most prominent impressionist directors and films include one of the first female filmmakers, **Germaine Dulac** (*La Fête espagnole*, 1919; *The Smiling Madame Beudet*, 1922), as well as **Louis Delluc** (*Fever*, 1921; *The Woman from Nowhere*, 1922), **Marcel L'Herbier** (*Eldorado*, 1921), and **Jean Epstein** (*Faithful Heart*, 1923).

The experiments by the Impressionists resulted in a very abstract form of cinema whose ambition was to **approximate musical composition** by using moving shapes to achieve a visual representation of pure rhythm. In 1925 Germaine Dulac, the theoretician of "pure cinema," characterized this ambition quite aptly: "The ultimate film which we all dream of composing is a visual symphony made of rhythmic images that only an artist's sensitivity is capable of coordinating and projecting onto the screen" (quoted in Mitry, II, 444). Among the most noted directors of abstract films are **Fernand Léger** and **Dudley Murphy** (*Ballet mécanique*, 1924), **Jean Grémillon** (*Photogénie mécanique*, 1925), **Marcel Duchamp** (*Anemic cinéma*, 1925), **Henri Chomette** (*Five Minutes of Pure Cinema*, 1926), and **Germaine Dulac** (*Disque 957*, 1927).

Dadaism

Whether in poetry, theater, painting, or cinema, the Dadaists sought above all to surprise, shock, and provoke. The undisputed masterpiece of Dadaist cinema (and the only film produced by this movement still watched today) is *Entr'acte* (1924) by **René Clair**. Described as "liberated images" ("images en liberté") by Clair, *Entr'acte* is in fact a carefully calculated montage of shots intended to amuse the bourgeois public while simultaneously ridiculing what it venerated. In the main scene of the film Clair lampoons a religious ceremony, a funeral, by showing the audience a hearse pulled by a camel and followed by a gaggle of gentlemen in top hats and black suits running in slow motion. Later in the film the hearse breaks loose from the camel and goes out of control, followed by the whole crowd sprinting madly behind it in faster and faster motion.

In the process of creating this hallucinatory gag-filled work, Clair implemented the whole gamut of specifically cinematographic techniques, such as slow- and fast-motion shots, forward and backward tracking shots, swish pans, superimpositions, divided screens (masks), dissolves, reverse projections, stop-action shots, tilted camera shots, high- and low-angle shots, blurring, point-of-view shots, and fast editing. Unlike most of the other avant-garde films of the period, *Entr'acte* was highly successful, garnering praise from film critics and an enthusiastic reception from the public.

Surrealism

Surrealism was a politically left-leaning artistic movement founded by the poet-essayist **André Breton**. He defined the concept in 1924 in his first *Manifeste du surréalisme*: "A pure psychic automatism by which we propose to examine either verbally, by writing, or by any other manner how thought really functions. Dictates of thought in the absence of any rational control and with no aesthetic or moral considerations" (37). Inspired by the writings of **Freud** and the poet **Lautréamont**, Breton conceived of poetry as a form of **"automatic writing,"** the goal of which was to reproduce the content and functioning of unconscious thought by liberating its expressive power from the control of rational processes and morality. Like Freud's concept of dreams, poetry must become, according to Breton, the expression of the deep-rooted psychological reality of man.

However, few truly "surrealist" films were made, and the only ones that are still watched today are two works by the Spanish filmmaker **Luis Buñuel**, *An Andalusian Dog* (*Un chien andalou*, 1928), based on his own screenplay co-authored with the painter **Salvador Dalí**, and *The Golden Age* (*L'âge d'or*, 1930). Few films have provoked so much controversy as regards their interpretation as *An Andalusian Dog*, a short subject less than seventeen minutes long shot in two weeks in Le Havre. It has been the object of innumerable studies since it first came out, studies that propose interpretations of all stripes, often conflicting—not unlike the commentaries of the filmmaker himself. Buñuel takes pleasure in confounding the would-be exegetes, declaring, "Nothing in the film symbolizes anything," but adding immediately afterwards, "The only valid way of interpreting the symbols would perhaps be through psychoanalysis" (Buñuel 30). Buñuel nonetheless indicates several paths to pursue, remarking that "*Un chien andalou* is not an attempt to narrate a dream, but it develops a mechanism which is analogous to that of a dream" (Liebman 155) and "the protagonists' acts are determined by

subconscious drives" (Aranda 17), statements that rather clearly authorize psychoana-
lytic hypotheses on the meaning of the film.

Whatever the case may be, critics today agree more and more on the principle that
it is impossible to establish clearly the meaning of *An Andalusian Dog*. What is certain
is that Buñuel's film astonished everyone in its time, and that it continues to fascinate
the public today. By demonstrating that cinema was capable of treating the most serious
and complex subjects, of competing with the subtlest poetry, Buñuel helped to put the
"seventh art" on an equal footing with the classical literary and artistic genres.

The End of the Silent Film Era

The end of the 1920s coincides with the virtual end of silent cinema, its death knell toll-
ing with the opening of the first sound film, *The Jazz Singer* by the American **Alan
Crosland**, in 1927. The masterpiece by the Danish filmmaker **Carl Dreyer**, *La Passion
de Jeanne d'Arc* (1928), ranked among the "twelve best films of all time" in 1958, would
remain the definitive monument to the art of silent film. The decade of the 1930s ushered in the reign of the sound film and the progressive triumph of the great current of
the **"classical age"** of French cinema, its **"Âge d'Or,"** poetic realism.**

Poetic Realism

It has become customary to refer to the first great period of modern French cinema,
which stretched from the beginning of the talkies (1930) to the Liberation (1945), as
the **"French School,"** or, owing to one of its most pronounced tendencies, as "poetic
realism." Like the label "New Wave" thirty years later, poetic realism is in fact only a
general term tying loosely together a very heterogeneous group of filmmakers who
dominated a period in which French cinema distinguished itself as one of the finest in
the world, namely **René Clair, Jean Vigo, Jean Cocteau, Jean Grémillon, Julien Duvivier, Jean Renoir, Marcel Carné, Jacques Becker, Jacques Feyder, Marcel Pagnol,**
and **Sacha Guitry**. From the whimsical and slapstick comedy of the films of **René Clair**,
such as *Le Million* (1931), to the dark pessimism of **Marcel Carné** and his regular
screenwriter **Jacques Prévert** in *Port of Shadows* (*Quai des Brumes*, 1938) or *Daybreak*
(*Le Jour se lève*, 1939), and including the humanism of **Jean Renoir** in *Toni* (1934) or
Grand Illusion (1937), poetic realism encompassed the most disparate trends, the most
personal preoccupations, and the most diverse influences. In **Jean Vigo's films**, for instance, we note the traces of the surrealism of the 1920s, the strangeness and fantasy so
striking in *Zero for Conduct* (*Zéro de conduite*, 1933) and in *L'Atalante* (1934). **Renoir**'s
films, on the other hand, may bear the imprint of Impressionist painting, as in *A Day in
the Country* (*Partie de campagne*, 1936) or the mark of the literary populism and naturalism of Emile Zola in *The Human Beast* (*La Bête humaine*, 1938). For their part, **Carné**
and **Prévert** tended to propagate the tradition of expressionism, with the creation of
evocative scenery and the lugubrious atmosphere that dominate all of their films.

If we were to attempt to describe the major characteristics of this "school," we would
have to recognize first and foremost the **thematic richness** of its masterpieces. In poetic
realism reality is constantly used as a springboard for themes that are often expressed in
metaphors and symbols. We might refer to this as the "poeticizing" of reality. We may
think, for example—among a wealth of examples—of the theme of liberty in *Zero for*

Conduct, the metaphor of fishing in *A Day in the Country*, the theater motif in *Grand Illusion*, and the symbolic value of the toy bear and the broach in *Daybreak* or of the mechanical dolls in *Rules of the Game* (1939). However, the trademark of poetic realism may be located in the thematic nexus dominating the works of a particular group of filmmakers, beginning with Jacques Feyder. Feyder develops in his films (for example, **Pension Mimosas**, 1935) a **sordid and pessimistic social realism** that will later characterize the films of **Marcel Carné**, in which pessimism becomes **out-and-out despair** and a fundamental aspect of **man's fate**: his heroes, working-class people, are condemned to misfortune by a tenacious and malevolent fate: the search for happiness—through love—is always doomed to failure. Prédal characterized Carné-Prévert's poetic realism well when he observed that their films develop "a set of themes (the weight of destiny, unhappy love, failure), an atmosphere (oppressive, scummy surroundings, empty rain-splashed cities, gray nights), and a style (polished dialogue, lavish camera movements) which all seem made for cinema" (1994, 76). It is nonetheless above all the idea of the abjectness of a world in which the scum triumph over good people and in which escape through happiness is impossible that emanates from this collaboration.

To conclude, during the **Occupation** the movement that was still called poetic realism took on quite a different character. The filmmakers who continued to make films in France during this period—**Carné**, **Jean Delannoy**, and **Jean Cocteau**, for instance—labored under heavy censorship by the Germans and by the Vichy government, who forbade the treating of contemporary topics (except for light comedies). The filmmakers thus responded to the need of the French to find relief from their difficult daily existence under the Nazis by cultivating an escapist cinema that sometimes featured the fantastic situated in far-off periods and other times took refuge in aestheticism. With Jean Cocteau as his screenwriter, Delannoy made *The Eternal Return* (*L'Eternel Retour*, 1943), a modernized version of the medieval Tristan and Isolde myth, while Carné had major successes with *The Devil's Envoys* (*Les Visiteurs du soir*, 1942), whose action is set in a legendary Middle Ages, and with **Children of Paradise** (*Les Enfants du paradis*, 1945), considered by many to be his major work. The latter film is a story of unhappy love at the height of the romantic period (1820–40), combined with a reflection on the intimate relationship between theater and life. These are the most successful films, along with Jean Cocteau's **Beauty and the Beast** (*La Belle et la Bête*, 1946), in this final incarnation of poetic realism.

The 1950s

At the end of the 1940s, the French government began to use the Centre National de la Cinématographie (CNC, 1946) to promote the film industry in France, which had been severely repressed during the Occupation. The CNC thus created the *prime à la qualité* ("subsidy for merit") to underwrite films that highlighted French culture. This mainly concerned adaptations of famous French novels such as those by Stendhal, *The Charterhouse of Parma* (*La Chartreuse de Parme*, 1948) by **Christian-Jaque**, and *The Red and the Black* (*Le Rouge et le noir*, 1954) by **Claude Autant-Lara**, as well as *Gervaise* (1956), an adaptation of Emile Zola's novel *L'Assomoir* by **René Clément**. These big studio films, very expensive and highly polished aesthetically (albeit very conventional), are identified with what would later be called the "**tradition of quality**" in French cinema.

At the same time, influenced by the postwar **Italian Neo-Realism**, a new current of realism developed in France as well, first represented by **René Clément's** *The Battle of the Rails* (*La Bataille du rail*, 1946), followed by his masterpiece *Forbidden Games* (*Jeux interdits*, 1952), whose action begins at the time of the exodus of the French toward the south of France in June 1940, fleeing the German invasion. This movement will be exploited especially, in an extremely stylized and idiosyncratic manner, by one of the most iconoclastic French filmmakers, generally considered to be "unclassifiable," **Robert Bresson**. With films such as *A Man Escaped* (*Un condamné à mort s'est échappé*, 1956) and *Pickpocket* (1959), Bresson became a major figure in world cinema, and the films of many contemporary directors, certain of whom are represented in this book, bear the mark of his philosophy, which emphasizes **the specificity of film language** in relation to the medium of theater. He refused, for example, the use of professional actors in his films, preferring amateurs that he could shape exactly as he liked, calling them in fact "models" rather than actors. Seeking an ever-greater simplicity of expression, a form of totally neutral writing (écriture blanche), Bresson reduced the action of his films to the most essential words and gestures and paid meticulous attention to the editing of both the image and sound tracks. Mood music eventually disappeared completely from Bresson's films, a practice that, along with the use of nonprofessional actors, would have an important influence on many of the young French filmmakers who came of age in the 1990s.

The decade of the 1950s is marked likewise by the very innovative comedies of **Jacques Tati**. Just as original as Bresson, albeit in a completely different genre, Tati created in *Mr. Hulot's Holiday* (*Les Vacances de M. Hulot*, 1953) and *My Uncle* (*Mon Oncle*, 1958) a unique form of comedy, virtually impossible to emulate, with his protagonist Hulot, a naïve and likeable but incorrigibly bumbling character who unwittingly sows havoc among those around him. Like Bresson, Tati was obsessively concerned with the sound tracks of his films and demonstrated clear genius in their detailed, precise, and highly innovative editing.

We also see in this period the growing prominence, under the aegis of the great film theoretician **André Bazin**, of the young critics of the film journal *Cahiers du cinéma*, who revolted against the film industry in France, which was still bound by traditional practices in filmmaking. The tone is set by an incendiary article by **François Truffaut**, "**Une certaine tendance du cinéma français**," published in the *Cahiers* in January 1954, in which he violently attacks some of the most prominent and successful screenwriters for the big studios, **Jean Aurenche** and **Pierre Bost** notably. This revolt is nothing less than a call for the renewal of cinema in France that prepares the way for the **New Wave** (*La Nouvelle Vague*) that will dominate the end of this particular cinematographic age.

La Nouvelle Vague

French cinema seemed to run out of steam as it approached the end of the 1950s. The great directors of the "Golden Age" (1930–45) were at the end of their careers: Jean Renoir, René Clair, Sacha Guitry, Marcel Pagnol, and Jean Cocteau. Max Ophüls had already passed away, and both Jean Grémillon and Jacques Becker would leave us soon. Marcel Carné was still making films, but it was just more of the same. Those filmmakers who rose to prominence after the war—Claude Autant-Lara, Henri-Georges Clouzot, Jean Delannoy, and René Clément notably—had proved to be capable of little more than perpetuating the tradition of solidly conventional cinema. But others were waiting in the wings, growing impatient, demanding that they get their turn. They were the directors of the "New Wave" which was soon going to sweep over France.

So what was the New Wave?

It was first of all a term invented by the journalist Françoise Giroud (in *L'Express*) in October 1957 to describe the new generation of young Frenchmen and Frenchwomen who were beginning to grow impatient and rebel in the mid-1950s. This was the period when France was getting entangled in the Algerian War (1956–62), scarcely having had time to digest the painful defeat in Indochina in 1954. The expression "New Wave" was soon borrowed to designate a group of young filmmakers who stunned the film world, both the critics and the general public, in 1959 and 1960. They succeeded against all odds, thumbing their noses at the rules and at their elders in the film industry. We are speaking principally of **François Truffaut's** *The 400 Blows* (*Les Quatre Cents Coups*, 1959) and **Jean-Luc Godard's** *Breathless* (*A bout de souffle*, 1960), but also, in quite a different genre, of **Alain Resnais'** *Hiroshima mon amour* (1959). Between 1958 and 1962 no less than ninety-seven young French filmmakers made their first feature film before the "revolution" ran its course.

Far from being a "school" with a program, the New Wave referred to a group of filmmakers who were more different than alike. As Truffaut commented humorously, "Our only point in common was our attraction to the pinball machine." He added, however, "The New Wave is neither a movement, nor a school, nor a group; it is just a term invented by the press to group together fifty new names which erupted over a two-year period into a profession which normally only accepted three or four new names each year" (Douin 14). Where did these new filmmakers come from? First, let's not exaggerate the number of true talents among the new film directors. At best we may distinguish two small groups. One of them was associated with the young critics writing for the newly created film review *Cahiers du cinéma* (1952)—**Eric Rohmer**, **Claude Chabrol**, **François Truffaut**, **Jean-Luc Godard**, **Jacques Rivette**, and **Jacques Doniol-Valcroze**, notably. The others were seasoned directors of short subjects, like **Alain Resnais**, **Chris Marker**, **Georges Franju**, **Pierre Kast**, and **Jacques Demy**. This latter group, with which **Agnès Varda** was also associated, was often designated by the term "**Left Bank**" ("Rive Gauche"), because it was largely distinguished from the first group by its clearly left-wing political orientation, as well as by the literary character of its films.

What the "young Turks" of the *Cahiers du cinéma* had in common was, above all, the idea that **filmmaking is a form of "writing."** This elevated conception of cinema was formulated in a kind of manifesto-article written by **Alexandre Astruc** that clearly expresses their ambitions: "Little by little cinema [. . .] is becoming a language. A language, that is, a form in which and through which an artist can express his thought, no matter how abstract, or communicate his obsessions exactly as is done today in essays or novels. This is why I call this new age of cinema the age of the *Camera pen* [*Caméra stylo*]." The cinema, he continued, was in the process of becoming "a form of writing which is just as versatile and subtle as written language" (39). The directors of the New Wave thus considered themselves to be "authors" in every sense of the word, establishing a distinction between "**author cinema**" (*cinéma d'auteur*) and popular genre films (thrillers, comedies, horror films) for the broad public, a distinction that has lasted to the present day. In addition, they had in common a passionate love of cinema; they were all film buffs. They knew in depth all of the cinematographic traditions. While they criticized certain directors, they worshiped a group of filmmakers that they considered to be their models: Jean Renoir, Abel Gance, Max Ophüls, Jean Cocteau, and Robert Bresson in France; Alfred Hitchcock, Howard Hawkes, Orson Welles, and Nicholas Ray in the United States; Roberto Rossellini and Luchino Visconti in Italy. They were indignant at **the general sclerosis** of the works produced by the filmmakers in the "**French Quality**" tradition, films which were technically perfect but filled with thematic and stylistic clichés and all similar to each other. They wanted to rejuvenate French cinema, to help it find new paths, to make it more personal and sincere; in a word, to breathe new life into it.

The main problem for the young people who wanted to make different kinds of films was that it was extremely difficult at that time to become a film director. The National Center for Cinematography (CNC), the association that regulated the film industry, required an aspiring director to attend three workshops, work three times as second assistant director, and work three times as first assistant before being allowed to direct a film. And then, since all films were made in a studio—with a large technical staff and very expensive stars—the cost was prohibitive for newcomers. However, there was a foreshadowing of the revolt of the new generation. In 1955 **Agnès Varda** made her first film *La Pointe Courte* without the authorization of the CNC, just as would **Louis Malle** a few years later with *Elevator to the Gallows* (*Ascenseur pour l'échafaud*, 1957) and **Claude Chabrol** with *Handsome Serge* (*Le Beau Serge*, 1958). The financing of films by young filmmakers was facilitated, moreover, by the establishment of the "subsidy for merit" mentioned above and, beginning in 1959, a cash advance (created by the Minister of Culture, André Malraux) that the CNC began granting to new directors for film projects which were judged worthwhile.

The success of the New Wave was thus both an economic and aesthetic matter. The new directors rejected the burdensome and costly machinery of the studios. They took advantage of new technologies that provided light cameras that could be hand-held and extra-sensitive film that made artificial lighting unnecessary. They shot in natural light, both outdoors and indoors, and executed their tracking shots without rails. With the exception of Alain Resnais, who was a masterful director of short documentaries and an unparalleled film editor, the new filmmakers used largely makeshift methods. The images were less perfect and the actors less famous, but the films were made for only a quarter of the cost of a conventional studio film—and they exuded sincerity, authenticity, and originality. Some of the directors, like Godard, wrote their own screenplays and improvised during the shooting. They worked with a few friends out in the streets with curious passers-by staring into the camera.

The young directors of the New Wave liberated the cinema from corporatism (administrative and financial difficulties, the demands of the technicians' unions) and from academism (stylistic conventions), but also from the moral proprieties which had been rejected by the youth culture in France. **Roger Vadim** set the tone by daring to focus on female sexuality in *... And God Created Woman* (*Et Dieu ... créa la femme*), which revealed **Brigitte Bardot** to the public in 1956. The other new directors followed suit, ridding the cinema of its moral reticence, whether it be in **Louis Malle**'s *The Lovers* (*Les Amants*, 1958), **Claude Chabrol**'s *Les Cousins* (1959), *The Four Hundred Blows, Breathless,* or *Hiroshima mon amour.*

The success of the New Wave was short-lived. Its last great triumph would be *The Umbrellas of Cherbourg* by **Jacques Demy** (*Les Parapluies de Cherbourg*, 1964), an iconoclastic work whose dialogue (in everyday language) was sung to music composed by the jazz pianist Michel Legrand. After 1965, the revenues from the author films emanating from this movement waned dramatically, and producers became more and more reticent to finance new projects. However, if the New Wave itself only lasted a few years, its influence would far outlive it; cinema throughout the world bears its mark to various degrees.

After the New Wave: The End of the 1960s; the 1970s

1. Maurice Pialat and Bertrand Blier

Toward the end of the 1960s and the beginning of the 1970s, two highly original filmmakers would emerge in France and have a long-lasting influence on the world of cinema. We are speaking first of **Maurice Pialat**, "without a doubt the filmmaker of his generation who will have the greatest influence on younger authors" (Frodon 960), with his *Naked Childhood* (*L'Enfance nue*, 1968), *Graduate First* (*Passe ton bac d'abord*, 1978), and *Loulou* (1980). Pialat cultivates a **social realism**—indeed a form of **naturalism**—that will serve as a model for the major revival of this tendency in the 1990s. In step with his time, he features in his films strong women confronting rather fragile men. **Bertrand Blier** formed a sort of duo with Pialat while accentuating his naturalism. He set the film world on its heels with *Going Places* (*Les Valseuses*, 1974) and *Get Out Your Handkerchiefs* (*Préparez vos mouchoirs*, 1978), which won the Oscar for the Best Foreign Language Film, as well as with *Buffet froid* (1979) and *Ménage* (*Tenue de soirée*, 1986).

Blier's flms are **trenchantly satirical comedies** that often present triangular relationships while putting into question the virility of his masculine protagonists, if not simply their sexual identity. This **masculine anxiety** can be perceived beneath the surface of many films in the 1970s (Forbes 183), including *The Big Feast* (*La Grande Bouffe*, 1973) by **Marco Ferreri** and *Vincent, François, Paul et les autres* (1974) by **Claude Sautet**. This tendency would become even more acute in the following decade, leading one critic (Powrie) to devote a book to the "**crisis of masculinity**" in the French cinema of the 1980s.

2. The Heirs

The New Wave would have notable heirs among the filmmakers who began their career in the 1970s, beginning with **Jean Eustache**, who is considered by some to be the model "author" in this period, for both his highly innovative (and brutally realistic) documentaries and his several fiction films. Among the latter, his major work, *The Mother and the Whore* (*La Maman et la putain*, 1973), functions as a lengthy (three and a half hours) summary of the social and sexual preoccupations of the youth of this era. According to Forbes, this film is alone "a monument to a style of filmmaking and to a whole generation" (149). The aesthetic of the New Wave also influenced other important beginners in the 1970s, with very different works, like **Claude Miller**'s *The Best Way to Walk* (*La Meilleure Façon de marcher*, 1976), *Garde à vue* (1981), and *The Little Thief* (*La Petite Voleuse*, 1988); the very iconoclastic **Philippe Garrel**'s *Un ange passe* (1975), *L'Enfant secret* (1983), and *Regular Lovers* (*Les Amants réguliers*, 2005); **Jacques Doillon**'s *The*

Little Gangster (*Le Petit Criminel*, 1990) and *Ponette* (1996), notably; and **André Téchiné**, a former critic of the *Cahiers du cinéma*, whose film **Wild Reeds** (*Les Roseaux sauvages*, 1992) is the subject of a chapter in this book.

3. Historical and Socio-political Cinema

The cinema of the 1970s is characterized above all by forays in all directions without any clear trend dominating the field. In addition to extreme social realism, as well as a tendency toward intimism concerned with the young and their problems related to sexuality, we note, in the historical and socio-political register, the **retro fashion** in film (*la mode rétro*) that appears at the beginning of the 1970s. This tendency attacks the vogue of "résistancialisme" in France, best represented by **Jean-Pierre Melville**'s *L'Armée des ombres* (1969), dedicated to the heroism of the Gaullist Resistance during World War II. In the anti-establishment spirit of May 1968, filmmakers blew up the myths that masked the true behavior of many of the French during the Occupation by the Germans. **Marcel Ophüls**, for example, revealed the broad support for Vichy, as well as out-and-out collaboration with the occupiers, in his very lengthy documentary *The Sorrow and the Pity* (*Le Chagrin et la pitié*, 1971). The following year **André Harris** and **Alain de Sédouy**, taking advantage of the disappearance of General de Gaulle from the political scene, called into question the merits of Gaullism itself in their documentary *Français si vous saviez*—which, like Ophüls' work, also contributed to the renewal of the form of documentary films. **Louis Malle** then proceeded to confront the anger of public opinion with *Lacombe Lucien* (1974), a film featuring a minor member of the French *milices* (Gestapo) in rural southwest France and a whole group of French *miliciens* representative of the type of individuals who participated in this type of extreme collaboration with the enemy.

The "Events" of May 1968 also inspired **political films**, brilliantly represented by *Tout va bien* by **Jean-Luc Godard** and **Jean-Pierre Gorin** and *Coup pour coup* by **Marin Karmitz**: both of these films, appearing in 1972, focus on the strikes of the month of May. As Forbes remarks, they reveal to the public a segment of the population rarely shown on the screen, demonstrating the interest exhibited by the cinema of the 1970s in marginal or minority groups of all kinds (25).

Likewise in the domain of the socio-political film, **Costa-Gavras** drew considerable attention with his political trilogy (always starring **Yves Montand**), **Z** (1969), *The Confession* (*L'Aveu*, 1970), and *State of Siege* (*Etat de siège*, 1973). He followed these films with one of the most hard-hitting examples of the *mode rétro*, **Section spéciale** (1975), which targets the collaborationist behavior of the French system of justice during the Occupation. We note also the astringent works of **Yves Boisset**, which denounce political assassination in *The Assassination* (*L'Attentat*, 1972), racism in *The Common Man* (*Dupont Lajoie*, 1974), the Algerian War in *Nothing to Report* (*R.A.S.*) the same year, and both the system of justice and the police in *Le Sheriff* (*Le Juge Fayard, dit "Le Sheriff*," 1976).

As regards historical films, including those of a political bent, the works of **Bertrand Tavernier** are particularly notable. This anti-New Wave author returned to the psychological realism popular in the 1950s in a first film located in the middle of May 1968, *The Clockmaker of St. Paul* (*L'Horloger de Saint-Paul*, 1974), before turning to the French Revolution in *Let Joy Reign Supreme* (*Que la fête commence*, 1975) and to a serial killer at the end of the nineteenth century in *Le Juge et l'assassin* (1976). In this register, we note, finally (among many other films) **Alain Resnais'** *Stavisky* (1974), **André Téchiné**'s *French Provincial* (*Souvenirs d'en France*, 1975), which touches on the most important moments of the political and economic history of France from WWI to the 1970s, and **René Allio**'s *The Calvinists* (*Les Camisards*) and *I, Pierre Rivière, Having Slaughtered My Mother, Sister, and Brother . . .* (*Moi, Pierre Rivière, ayant égorgé ma mère, ma soeur et mon frère . . .*), both appearing in 1976.

The historical current would have strong echoes in the 1980s and 1990s, and we present four remarkable examples in the present volume, *The Last Métro* (*Le Dernier Métro*, 1980) by **François Truffaut**, *Au revoir les enfants* (1986) by **Louis Malle**, *Chocolat* (1988) by **Claire Denis**, and *Indochine* (1992) by **Régis Wargnier**. The film by Wargnier belongs, moreover, to the specific category of "heritage films" that were a major genre in this period (see below, as well as the chapter on *Indochine*).

4. Women behind the Camera

As regards women, the aftermath of May 1968 saw the rise of the Movement for the Liberation of Women (MLF) in France, which is not unrelated to the growing number of female film directors at that time. As Frodon observes (321), fourteen women filmmakers appeared between 1968 and 1975. In addition to the veterans, like **Agnès Varda** with *One Sings, the Other Doesn't* (*L'une chante, l'autre pas*, 1977) and **Marguerite Duras** with *Nathalie Granger* (1972) and *India Song* (1975)—the most venerated among the women directors—**Yannick Bellon** made a series of feminist films such as *Jean's Wife* (*La Femme de Jean*, 1974), *Rape of Love* (*L'Amour violé*, 1978), and *Naked Love* (*L'Amour nu*, 1981), this last film treating the subject of breast cancer. **Coline Serreau**, for her part, directed her feminist documentary *But What Do They Want?* (*Mais qu'est-ce qu'elles veulent?*, 1975), the very bold *Why Not?* (*Pouquoi pas?*, 1978), on the theme of the love triangle (but inverted—two men and a woman), and her greatest success, *Three Men and a Cradle* (*Trois hommes et un couffin*), which won the César for the Best Film in 1986. This is only a small sample, and we will return to the subject of "women's films" in the chapter devoted to the work by **Diane Kurys**, *Coup de Foudre/ Entre nous* (1983). The arrival of women behind the camera is a phenomenon that became more and more common in the following decades: the average number of films made by women each year goes from thirteen in the 1980s to seventeen in the 1990s, and then to twice that number since 2000—and it is in France that we find today the highest percentage of first films that were made by women (Rollet 402, 413).

5. Popular Genre Films: Thrillers and Comedies

In all periods, thrillers and comedies thrive. **Jean-Pierre Melville** lends a new style to the *polar* (police film) in his famous trilogy with **Alain Delon**, *Second Breath* (*Le Deuxième Souffle*, 1966), *The Red Circle* (*Le Cercle rouge*, 1970), and *The Cop* (*Le Flic*, 1972). Liberating himself from his American models, Melville launched the "*thriller à la française* that will see a spectacular proliferation in the seventies" (Prédal, 1984, 53). Following Melville, **Robin Davis** shot a series of highly successful police films such as *The Police War* (*La Guerre des polices*, 1979), *The Shock* (*Le Choc*, 1982), and *I Married a Shadow* (*J'ai épousé une ombre*, 1983), while an American filmmaker working in France,

Bob Swaim, virtually transformed the polar/film noir genre with his ethnographic approach in *The Nark* (*La Balance*, 1982).

However, year in year out, half of the films made in France are comedies, and one of the most popular films of all times is *La Grande Vadrouille* (roughly, "On the Road," 1966), a comedy on the Resistance by Gérard Oury. Oury dominated the comic genre in the 1970s and met huge popular success with Louis de Funès' burlesque character in *Les Aventures de Rabbi Jacob* (1973), but the top comic hit of the decade was indisputably *La Cage aux folles*, the hilarious if caricatural portrait of a gay couple by **Edouard Molinaro** in 1978. As Moine notes, the comedy, using laughter, is the best way to "shine light, more powerfully than other genres," on social shifts and resistance in the areas of gender, class, and ethnicity (235). For a more in-depth look into French comedies, see the introduction to Section VI ("Comedy").

The 1980s

"Cinéma du look" and Heritage Films

In the 1980s, unlike the preceding decade, two new types of films stand out clearly, the so-called *cinéma du look*, with its unrepentant aestheticism (represented in this book by **Jean-Jacques Beinex**'s thriller, *Diva*, 1981), and the **heritage films** (*films patrimoniaux*), works that highlight national identity and appeal to nostalgia for the past in France (represented herein by Régis Wargnier's *Indochine*, 1992). In addition to *Diva*, several other films popularized the *cinéma du look* in this period, in particular Leos Carax's *Bad Blood* (*Mauvais Sang*, 1986) and Luc Besson's *Subway* (1985) and *Nikita* (*La Femme Nikita*, 1990).

However, Austin calls the 1980s, purely and simply, the "decade of the heritage film" (168), a fashion that is launched in 1982, in his opinion, by two films, *The Return of Martin Guerre* (*Le Retour de Martin Guerre*) by Daniel Vigne and *That Night in Varennes* (*La Nuit de Varennes*) by the Italian filmmaker **Ettore Scola**. The trend is then consolidated, he believes, by **Claude Berri**'s diptych, *Jean de Florette* and *Manon of the Spring* (*Manon des sources*), both in 1986, and the films of **Bertrand Tavernier** like *A Sunday in the Country* (*Un dimanche à la campagne*, 1984), *Béatrice* (*La Passion Béatrice*, 1987), and *Life and Nothing But* (*La Vie et rien d'autre*, 1989).

Determined to support French films, which had seen a serious drop in attendance during the 1980s, and to promote the national culture and identity, the Minister of Culture Jack Lang encouraged and subsidized big budget heritage films that could compete with Hollywood's products—which explains the series of blockbusters that appeared at the beginning of the following decade, like **Jean-Paul Rappeneau**'s *Cyrano de Bergerac* (1990), **Wargnier**'s *Indochine* (1992), **Claude Berri**'s *Germinal* (1993), and **Patrice Chéreau**'s *La Reine Margot* (1994).

The 1990s (and Beyond)

Parallel with the short-lived spate of heritage films, we remark during the 1990s and in the new century renewed interest among the young (and not so young) French filmmakers in **social realism** (often tending toward a very hard and quasi-documentary naturalism) and in the **excluded members of society** (*les marginaux*). We see it especially in the suburb films (*films de banlieue*) like **Hate** (*La Haine*, 1995) by **Mathieu Kassovitz**, but concern with the excluded is a focus that would be increasingly prominent in this period, as witnessed, each in its own manner, by many films that are presented, in addition to **La Haine**, in the present volume: **The Life of Jesus** (*La Vie de Jésus*, 1997) by **Bruno Dumont**, **The Dreamlife of Angels** (*La Vie rêvée des anges*, 1998) by **Erick Zonca**, the documentary by **Agnès Varda**, **The Gleaners and I** (*Les Glaneurs et la glaneuse*, 2000), **Games of Love and Chance** (*L'Esquive*, 2003) by **Abdellatif Kechiche**, **The Class** (*Entre les murs*, 2008) by **Laurent Cantet**, and **Welcome** (2009) by **Philippe Lioret**. We would be remiss not to mention also in this category the films of **Robert Guédiguian** such as **Marius et Jeannette** (1997), **The Town Is Quiet** (*La Ville est tranquille*, 2000), and **The Snows of Kilimanjaro** (*Les Neiges du Kilimandjaro*, 2011), which feature the life of people of very modest means in L'Estaque, a suburb city of Marseilles.

As regards marginality, finally, it is important to note the deep interest that French cinema, like other national cinemas, shows in homosexuality and lesbianism in the contemporary period. We present three examples in this book by devoting chapters to the films of **Diane Kurys**, **Coup de foudre/Entre nous** (1983), of **André Téchiné**, **Wild Reeds** (1992), and of **Josiane Balasko**, **French Twist** (*Gazon maudit*, 1994). See the introduction to Section V, "Personal Stories: Dramas and Documentaries," for additional information on this subject.

The New Century

At the dawn of the twenty-first century, the taste for the documentary style that is so palpable in the naturalistic films of the new generation is evident also in a new current of high-quality documentaries, beginning with **Varda**'s **The Gleaners and I** in 2000. The following decade features a series of other documentaries for the big screen that drew a broad public, like **To Be and to Have** (*Etre et avoir*, 2002) by **Nicolas Philibert**, **March of the Penguins** (*La Marche de l'empereur*, 2005) by **Luc Jacquet**, and **Océans** (2010) by **Jacques Cluzaud** and **Jacques Perrin**—without forgetting the remarkable documentary **Her Name Is Sabine** (*Elle s'appelle Sabine*, 2007) by the actress **Sandrine Bonnaire**, who worked behind the camera to film her autistic sister.

The pornographic film, which had its moment of glory in the 1970s, virtually disappeared from the commercial circuit at the end of the following decade. Some of its characteristics, however, beginning with unsimulated sex on-screen, have left their mark on contemporary French films. One can detect a "major contemporary trajectory" in the "**cinema of the body**" (Palmer 424), which features either simple explicit sexual activity or violent sex acts like rape or some other form of perversity. In this category we find, for example, the films of **Bruno Dumont**, such as **The Life of Jesus** (1997), **L'Humanité** (1999), and, especially, **Twenty-Nine Palms** (2003), as well as **Romance** (1999) and **Fat Girl** (*A ma soeur*, 2001) by **Catherine Breillat**, **Criminal Lovers** (*Les Amants criminels*, 1999) by **François Ozon**, **Screw Me** (*Baise-moi*, 2000) by **Virginie Despentes** and **Coralie Trinh Thi**, **Trouble Every Day** (2001) by **Claire Denis** (an extreme case in which sexual desire is expressed through cannibalism), **Irréversible** (2002) by **Gaspar Noé**, and, much more recently, in the areas of lesbianism and homosexuality respectively, **Blue Is the Warmest Color** (*La Vie d'Adèle*) by **Abdellatif Kechiche**, and **Stranger by the Lake** (*L'Inconnu du lac*) by **Alain Guiraudie**, both in 2013.

Popular genre films, *polars* and comedies, are still just as successful at the box office in the twenty-first century, and certain thrillers, such as **Hidden** (*Caché*, 2005) by **Michael Haneke** and **Un prophète** (2009) by **Jacques Audiard** (2009), both presented in this volume, are astonishingly original. As for comedy, after a decade of genial filmmakers such as **Jean-Marie Poiré**, **Michel Blanc**, **Claude Zidi**, **Etienne Chatiliez**, and **Francis Veber** (to mention some of the most successful), the comedic vein scarcely slows down in the new century—much to the contrary, as we see in the various chapters in this book devoted to **The Taste of Others** (*Le Goût des autres*, 2000) by **Agnès Jaoui**, **Amélie** (*Le Fabuleux Destin d'Amélie Poulain*, 2001) by **Jean-Pierre Jeunet**, and **Intouchables** (2011) by **Eric Toledano** and **Olivier Nakache**, the last two works attracting audiences worldwide at unheard of levels for French films. The box office champion for a French film in France, however, with more than twenty million tickets sold, is still **Welcome to the Sticks** (*Bienvenue chez les Ch'tis*, 2008) by **Dany Boon**. Nonetheless, the even more recent dramatic comedy by **Michel Hazanavicius**, **The Artist** (2011), a "silent" film, stunned the world of the seventh art by earning five Oscars and three Golden Globes in the United States, as well as six Césars in France.

Certain films mentioned in this introduction are the very substance of the present book, which presents twenty masterpieces of French cinema from 1980 to the present period. We will go into much greater depth as regards the cinematographic traditions and socioeconomic or historical contexts of the films, as is appropriate, within each chapter. But we make no claim to offer a complete survey or, of course, to give a precise definition of contemporary French cinema in this volume. Indeed, as Frodon observes, the extreme richness and diversity of the works involved discourage any attempt at reducing them to any over-arching cinematic trend.

Works Consulted

Note: The sections on the evolution of French cinema from its beginnings to the New Wave are adapted from Alan Singerman's earlier cinema textbook, *French Cinema: The Student's Book* (Indianapolis: Hackett Publishing), 1–17, 37–38, 229–31. Original edition (2006) by Focus Publishing/R. Pullins.

Aranda, Juan Francisco. "La Réalisation d'*Un chien andalou*." *Revue belge du cinéma* 33–35 (1993): 17–21.

Astruc, Alexandre. "Naissance d'une nouvelle avant-garde: la Caméra-stylo." *L'Ecran français* 144 (30 Mar. 1948): 39–40.

Austin, Guy. *Contemporary French Cinema.* Manchester, England: Manchester UP, 2008.

De Baecque, Antoine. *La Nouvelle Vague. Portrait d'une jeunesse.* Paris: Flammarion, 1998.

Betton, Gérard. *Histoire du cinéma.* Paris: PUF, 1984.

Breton, André. *Manifeste du surréalisme.* Paris: Gallimard, 1977.

Buñuel, Luis. "Notes on the Making of *Un chien andalou*." *Art in Cinema.* Ed. Frank Stauffacher. San Francisco: San Francisco Museum of Art, 1947. 29–30.

Daney, Serge. "La Nouvelle Vague—essai d'approche généalogique." *D'un cinéma l'autre*. Ed. Jean-Loup Passek. Paris: Centre Georges Pompidou, 1988. 72–74.

Douin, Jean-Luc, ed. *La Nouvelle Vague 25 ans après*. Paris: Editions du Cerf, 1983.

Fox, Alistair, Michel Marie, Raphaëlle Moine, and Hilary Radner, eds. *A Companion to Contemporary French Cinema*. Malden, MA: Wiley Blackwell, 2015.

Forbes, Jill. *The Cinema in France after the New Wave*. Bloomington: Indiana UP, 1992.

Frodon, Jean-Michel. *Le Cinéma français, de la Nouvelle Vague à nos jours*. Paris: Cahiers du cinéma, 2010.

Gillain, Anne. *Le Cinéma selon François Truffaut*. Paris: Flammarion, 1988.

Jeancolas, Jean-Pierre. *Histoire du cinéma français*. Paris: Nathan, 1995.

Liebman, Stuart. "Le Traitement de la langue." *Revue belge du cinéma* 33–35 (1993): 155–61.

Marie, Michel. "The Veterans of the New Wave, Their Heirs, and Contemporary French Cinema." *A Companion to Contemporary French Cinema*. Ed. Alistaire Fox, Michel Marie, Raphaëlle Moine, and Hilary Radner. Malden, MA: Wiley Blackwell, 2015. 163–83.

Mitry, Jean. *Histoire du cinéma*, II. Paris: Editions universitaires, 1969.

———. "Le réalisme poétique en France." *Histoire du cinéma*, IV. Paris: Delarge, 1980. 325–52.

Moine, Raphaëlle. "Contemporary French Comedy as Social Laboratory." *A Companion to Contemporary French Cinema*. Ed. Alistair Fox, Michel Marie, Raphaëlle Moine, and Hilary Radner. Malden, MA: Wiley Blackwell, 2015. 234–55.

Palmer, Tim. "Modes of Masculinity in Contemporary French Cinema." *A Companion to Contemporary French Cinema*. Ed. Alistair Fox, Michel Marie, Raphaëlle Moine, and Hilary Radner. Malden, MA: Wiley Blackwell, 2015. 419–38.

Passek, Jean-Loup, ed. *D'un cinéma l'autre*. Paris: Centre Georges Pompidou, 1988.

Powrie, Phil. *French Cinema in the 1980s. Nostalgia and the Crisis of Masculinity*. Oxford: Oxford UP, 1997.

Prédal, René. *Histoire du cinéma*. Courbevoie: CinémAction-Corlet, 1994.

———. *Le Cinéma français contemporain*. Paris: Cerf, 1984.

Radner, Hilary. "The Historical Film and Contemporary French Cinema. Representing the Past in the Present." *A Companion to Contemporary French Cinema*. Ed. Alistair Fox, Michel Marie, Raphaëlle Moine, and Hilary Radner. Malden, MA: Wiley Blackwell, 2015. 289–313.

Revault d'Allonnes, Fabrice. "Genèse d'une vague bien précise." *D'un cinéma l'autre*. Ed. Jean-Loup Passek. Paris: Centre Georges Pompidou, 1988. 76–92.

Rollet, Brigitte. "French Women Directors since the 1990s. Trends, New Developments, and Challenges." *A Companion to Contemporary French Cinema*. Ed. Alistair

Fox, Michel Marie, Raphaëlle Moine, and Hilary Radner. Malden, MA: Wiley Blackwell, 2015. 399–418.

Sadoul, Georges. *Histoire du cinéma mondial des origines à nos jours*, 9th ed. Paris: Flammarion, 1949.

———. *Le Cinéma français*. Paris: Flammarion, 1962.

Truffaut, François. "Une certaine tendance du cinéma français." *Cahiers du cinéma* 31 (January 1954): 15–28.

"Reading" a Film*

In their *Introduction to Film Analysis*, Vanoye and Goliot-Lété remind us that film is "**a cultural product inscribed in a socio-historical context**" (43). As regards the precise character of the relationship between a film and its context, they add:

> In a film, whatever its goal (to describe, entertain, criticize, denounce, or militate), society is less *shown* than staged. In other words a film makes choices, organizes elements, borrows from both reality and the imagination, and constructs a virtual world which entertains complex relations with the real world [...]. Whether a reflection or a rejection, a film constitutes a *viewpoint* on this or that aspect of the contemporary world. It represents society in the form of a spectacle or drama (in the broadest sense of the word), and it is this representation that is the analyst's object of study. (44–45)

This very apt conception of the object of film analysis implies of course the description by the analyst of the type of representation that is presented in the film. This may be the depiction of society or of a character's inner life or of any fictional universe posited by the director. While it is generally agreed that "the analysis of films is above all descriptive" (Aumont and Marie 11), this undertaking is not a simple affair. As many theoreticians, including Aumont and Marie, recognize, **description is also an interpretative activity**. To describe a film—that is, to analyze it—it is first necessary to break it up into its component parts. This critical first step is then followed by an attempt to understand the relationship between those parts in order to gain an appreciation of the manner in which the film produces its various meanings. This second activity, which is reconstructive in nature, itself produces meaning, to such an extent that the film reader's perspective (informed by his/her personal culture, opinions, and biases) tends to be superimposed on the viewpoint that is inscribed in the film. We mention from the outset this particular complication in order to emphasize both the role of description in film analysis and the importance of keeping constantly in mind the perspectives that are developed in the film itself, so as not to substitute our personal preoccupations. Aumont and Marie propose the following general rule: "Never perform an analysis which loses sight of the film being analyzed; to the contrary, always return to the film whenever possible" (56). Vanoye and Goliot-Lété concur completely, formulating the same principle slightly differently: "The film is thus the point of departure and the destination of the analysis" (10). This being said, what do we mean precisely by the "description" of a film?

*Note: This chapter is adapted from Alan Singerman's earlier cinema textbook, *French Cinema: The Student's Book* (Indianapolis: Hackett Publishing), 19–36. Original edition (2006) by Focus Publishing/ R. Pullins. The examples given here are drawn from some of the most famous classical French films.

Film "Language"

Let's discuss immediately the notion of "film language." For some theoreticians like André Bazin or Marcel Martin, the cinematographic medium is an authentic language to the extent that it disposes of "innumerable means of expression that it uses with the flexibility and effectiveness of a verbal language" (Martin 15). Martin goes on to state (quoting Alexandre Arnoux) that **"cinema is a language of images with its own vocabulary, syntax, inflections, ellipses, conventions, and grammar"** (*loc. cit.*). He recognizes nonetheless that film language most closely resembles poetic language, a realm where the image reigns supreme also. For linguists, however, the basic elements of cinematographic representation are not equivalent to the elementary units of meaning in natural languages—phonemes, morphemes, or even words—because of the analogical character of images and the "continuity" of the visual signifier. Since a natural language, like English or French, is neither analogical (in general, words do not physically "resemble" what they signify) nor continuous (it is a concatenation of discrete phonemes), **we can only refer to film as a "language" in a metaphorical sense.**

Understood literally or metaphorically, the notion of "film language," referring to the whole gamut of techniques used in cinema, is extremely useful in discussing how one "reads" a film. Like verbal narrative language, which can be divided into units of meaning from a single word to sentences, paragraphs, chapters, and even a whole novel, a film lends itself to a similar segmentation—called *découpage*—into signifying units. This is where the description of a film must begin.

The Filmic Image

Martin is right to insist on the following point: "*You must learn to read a film*, to decipher the meaning of images just as you decipher the meaning of words and ideas, to understand the subtleties of cinematographic language" (29). Film is like any other area of knowledge (mathematics, biology, psychoanalysis, linguistics, etc.): to understand it, you must learn its language, because you learn its fundamental concepts along with its language. The basic element of film is the *image*. In narrative terms, the image is the (metaphorical) equivalent of the word, and the film will be built on images combined with sound. We note immediately that the filmic image has its own specific character. It is always **"in the present"**—in movies the past is constructed mentally by the spectator, aided by the temporal context or by technical indications, as we shall see below. It is **"realistic"**—that is, it creates through movement, as the semiotician Christian Metz notes, an "impression of reality" (16–19). It is **polysemous** (i.e., it contains multiple meanings) and lends itself therefore to diverse interpretations, although its significance is anchored, at least partially, by its context, by the soundtrack, and by its combination with other images (film "montage," which we will discuss below). Given the polysemous nature of the image, it is generally agreed that the analysis of a film is never "over," its meaning never exhausted by a given interpretation.

To finish this introduction to the image, we note that the filmic image is always circumscribed by a *frame*, just like a photograph. When the director of photography (or the cameraman) "frames" a space, this space (corresponding to the image we see on the screen) is called a *shot*. When we discuss an image, we speak of what is in the shot and, conversely, what is *off-screen*. The off-screen space is an imaginative continuation of the visible space of the shot; it is the invisible space where are located "all of the elements (characters, settings, etc.) that, not being included in the shot, are nonetheless attached to it by [the spectator's] imagination" (Aumont et al., *Esthétique du film* 15). In a film the *voice-over* (a voice that we hear without seeing the person speaking on-screen), for example, often belongs to a character located off-screen.

Shot, Sequence, Scene

If we pursue the comparison with the linguistic model, just as words combine to make a sentence, individual images combine to create a larger unit that is also called a *shot*. A shot is the portion of film that is recorded between a single starting and stopping of the camera. A series of shots that form a distinct dramatic unit (like a "scene" in a play) is called a *sequence*, which may be compared also to a paragraph or a chapter in a written narrative text. A single shot, on the other hand, may constitute by itself a dramatic unit of a film: this is called a *sequence shot* (or a lengthy take), a technique perfected by Jean Renoir in the 1930s. Christian Metz's reflections on film language permit us to make a useful technical distinction between a sequence and a *scene*. The latter refers, in Metz's taxonomy, to a type of sequence which takes place in real time, whereas the term "sequence" is reserved for sequences which contain temporal ellipses (130–31). All of the sequences and scenes taken together constitute the entire film, as the set of chapters constitutes the novel.

To understand the dramatic structure of a film, **one needs to know how to analyze its *découpage*, that is, how to identify in a film the various sequences which compose it and the manner in which they are connected.** To be able to appreciate the nuances of a filmmaker's style, **you also have to be able to identify the shots in a given sequence and know how to describe them, as well as how they are linked together.** In the following paragraphs we will speak of the fundamental characteristics of the various types of shots, including the relative size and the length of the shots, the camera angles and movements, the types of transitions between shots, and finally the use of deep focus.

Shot Lengths and Sizes

Though the average length of a shot is eight to ten seconds, a shot can vary from a fraction of a second to a whole reel (the latter being of course extremely rare!). **The various lengths of the shots determine the rhythm of the film.** A series of very short shots creates, for instance, a tense, nervous, or even violent atmosphere, whereas a very lengthy shot that emphasizes the passage of time may give an impression of calm, reflection, or monotony—or it may create suspense. A professional film analyst, working on an editing table, may go so far as to time each shot to be able to draw conclusions as to the rhythmic style of a film.

Among the important characteristics of a shot, the spectator needs to be sensitive to **its relative size**, which is generally determined by the distance between the camera and its subject, although size can also be determined optically by varying the focal length of the lens (see "zoom" below). Shot sizes range from the extreme close-up to the vast establishing shot. The conventional "rhetoric" of film formulated very early in the history of cinema dictated the use of an extremely long shot, or *establishing shot*, at the beginning of the film to reveal the geographic context of the action. In a Western, for example, this could be a wide plain dotted with buttes. This initial shot was then followed by a *long shot* which normally depicted people in a setting; e.g., a Western town with people in the streets. This would be followed by a *medium shot* framing characters in a precise décor, such as the interior of a saloon. It was not unlike the description of the physical and social environment at the beginning of a Balzac novel in the nineteenth century, although considerably more cursory. This convention is no longer widely respected in cinema. We see numerous films that do not begin with a long shot, like Jean Renoir's *Grand Illusion* (1937), for instance, which begins with a close-up of a record spinning on a turntable.

The scale of shots closer than the long shot is best illustrated in relation to the characters in the film. In descending order we move from the long shot, in which we see characters from head to toe, to the medium shot, in which they are framed from the knees up. The French refer to the medium shot as an *American shot* because it is the typical shot in American comedies from the 1930s. According to André Bazin, it is also the shot which "best corresponds to the spontaneous gaze of the spectator" (72). A *near shot* frames the upper body of the actor, whereas a *close-up* focuses on the actor's face and the *extreme close-up* (or *insert*) on a small detail of the actor's body, such as the tearful eye of Henriette in a famous shot near the end of Renoir's *A Day in the Country* (1936, 1946). It should be understood that the range of shots just described (with the exception of the "American shot") applies to settings and objects as well as to characters.

Among the various shot sizes it is important to note the particular character and role of the **long shot** and the **close-up**, the two most specifically cinematographic shots insofar as there is no real equivalent in the theater. The long shot serves above all to situate the character in the world, to objectify it and reduce it to its proper proportions. At the same time, it creates a wide range of atmospheres: pathetic or threatening, dramatic or comical, lyrical or epic, to name a few. The long shot often sets the tone for the film. **The close-up, on the other hand, is one of the most powerful and expressive devices of cinema.** As Martin remarks, "It is in the close-up of the human face that the psychological and dramatic significance of a film are depicted most powerfully" (42). When the camera moves forward until it frames a character's face in close-up, we have the impression that we are coming into contact with the character's inner being. As a corollary, **the close-up of a face often suggests "a high degree of mental stress in the character"** (44), if not out and out anguish. We see this clearly in the case of François in Marcel Carné's *Daybreak* (1939), just before the besieged factory worker begins to search his memory to understand the murder he has just committed. Likewise, **very close shots and close-ups produce tension in the spectator.** Alfred Hitchcock's films have amply demonstrated that the suspense rises as the camera approaches a character (especially if it is in the middle of the night in a forest or in a dark basement. . .)! In the case of an object, the close-up dramatizes its presence and endows it with meaning—even if we do not understand immediately what meaning—as in the case of the twitch in the Japanese lover's hand in Alain Resnais' *Hiroshima mon amour* (1960).

Camera Angles

In addition to the shot size, the director must choose the camera angle which best suits the subject, that is, the particular perspective from which he or she is going to show the subject. If the camera is positioned above the subject (above the normal level of the eyes), so that we are looking downwards, the director is producing a *high-angle shot* or a *"down shot."* Conversely, if the camera is placed below the subject, we are seeing a *low-angle shot* or an *"up shot."* Although it is not a general rule, camera angles that are not at normal eye level may have a specific psychological function. An **up shot** which frames a character **gives that person a dominant position** in relation to whomever he or she is looking at. The object of the character's gaze (as well as the spectator, who is in a similar position) feels diminished. On the other hand, in the case of the **down shot, it is the character being filmed who feels dominated and diminished** by the gaze; the spectator is on the side of the character who is in the superior position. In extreme cases, to produce a striking effect, we may see vertical up or down shots. In the famous dormitory sequence in *Zero for Conduct* (1933), for example, Jean Vigo places his camera near the ceiling to shoot from above, nearly vertically, the children running wildly across the beds. In *Entr'acte* (1924), René Clair films a female dancer from below, in a vertical up shot through a glass floor, to provoke the bourgeois public.

In the area of camera angles, finally, we should mention two sparingly used angles, *tilts* and what Martin calls *"disorderly shots."* In the first, the camera is tilted on its side to the left or the right. If we are dealing with a point-of-view ("subjective") shot, a tilt may suggest a psychologically or morally aberrant state of mind, as in the case of a drunken or deranged individual. In the case of "disorderly shots," the camera is turned every which way, such as the scene in *Napoleon* (1925–27) where Abel Gance puts his portable camera inside a soccer ball and then throws it into the air to simulate the viewpoint of a soldier who is tossed end over end by an exploding artillery shell.

Camera Movements

At the beginning of cinema, the camera rarely moved. It simply recorded action taking place in front of it. According to the theoretician Alexandre Astruc, "The history of cinematographic technique, reduced to its simplest terms, is the history of the liberation of the camera" (Martin 32). Liberation means movement: the camera has become mobile and can henceforth represent the spectator's gaze as well as the viewpoint of a character in the film. There are two principal types of camera movements: the *panning shot* (or **pan**) and the *tracking* (or *traveling*) *shot*. A *pan* is a rotation of the camera around its vertical or horizontal axis without moving the tripod on which it is mounted. In other words, when the camera pans, it simply pivots toward the right, toward the left, upwards, or downwards. While pans often just accompany the movement of a character, vehicle, or object, they can also have an important descriptive function. This function may be purely objective, as when the camera's eye sweeps across Von Rauffenstein's room at Wintersborn in Renoir's *Grand Illusion*, or subjective, as when it represents Antoine's gaze as the adolescent examines the police station through the bars of his cell in François Truffaut's *The 400 Blows* (1959).

The tracking shot (also called a "dolly shot" or a "crane shot," depending on the method used) involves moving the camera, which leaves its horizontal or vertical axis to move closer to or farther away from its subject, or to accompany its movement. If the camera approaches the subject, we say that it *is **tracking forward***; if it moves away from it, it is ***tracking backward***. If the camera moves parallel to a motionless subject, we speak of a *lateral tracking*; if the tracking shot follows a moving person or object, it is, quite logically, a *follow shot*. In the case of tracking both forward and backward, the camera movement can be simulated, as we mentioned above, by optical means, allowing the cameraman to approach or move away from the subject without the camera moving physically. This is called a *zoom*. Like the pan, a tracking shot can be objective or subjective. When the camera represents a character's point of view, which occurs frequently in films, we may speak of a *subjective (or point of view) tracking shot*. Tracking shots of all sorts—including vertical dolly shots—have invaded the cinema, for both descriptive and dramatic reasons. As we saw in the case of François in *Daybreak*, tracking forward to a close-up of a character's face materializes his state of mind and suggests unusual psychological stress. Tracking backward produces various effects depending on the context, including an impression of solitude or alienation. A striking example of this may be found in the famous paddy wagon sequence in *The 400 Blows* in which Antoine stares out the back window as the vehicle drives through and away from the Pigalle neighborhood where he lived, on the way to prison.

Finally, we note that panning and tracking shots may be combined in relatively complicated movements, as we often see at the beginning of a film (during the credits for example) to introduce us to the diegetic (fictional) world in which the action is going to take place. At the beginning of *The 400 Blows*, the camera tracks rapidly through the streets of Paris while panning over the fronts of the buildings, before sweeping around the Eiffel Tower and panning upward to look at the tower in a low-angle shot. In Renoir's films pans are often choreographed with tracking shots in complicated sequences like the rehearsal scene for the prisoners' show in *Grand Illusion* or the celebrated "Danse macabre" scene at the marquis' castle in *The Rules of the Game* (1939).

Film Editing

As Gérard Betton states, "**Editing is the element most specific to cinematographic language**" (72), to the extent that it presides over the organization of the film's component units. In its most elementary acceptation editing is the assembling of the shots of a film in the order decided by the director. In conventional *narrative editing*, the most common type of editing, it involves ordering the shots in such a way that the logical progression of the action is assured. If the shots and sequences are presented in chronological order, we are dealing with *linear editing*. Linear editing may include *cross-cutting*, in which shots of two different actions are alternated to suggest simultaneity. We see this often, for example, in Westerns where, in order to create suspense, shots of the fort under attack by Indians are alternated with shots of the cavalry galloping to the rescue. In other cases the chronological order of the action may be interrupted by a series of flashbacks that mix the past with the present.

In addition to narrative coherence, **editing creates the rhythm of the film through the choice of the size and length of the shots.** As we suggested above, the shorter the shots, the greater their intensity and dynamism. Accordingly, series of short shots tend to dominate action films, while lengthy shots are more characteristic of psychological films, insofar as they emphasize the characters' state of mind (sadness, boredom, introspection, etc.). The level of intensity varies similarly according to the size of the shots— the closer the shot, the higher the psychological tension.

It is generally agreed that the American filmmaker **D. W. Griffith** is the principal pioneer in narrative editing. More than anyone else in his time, Griffith exploited the potential of editing, giving the art its modern form by varying the length and size of shots for expressive and narrative purposes. As regards expressivity, however, it is above all the Soviet school which led the way by showing the entire world of cinema that editing is not simply the logical organization of shots to tell a story. Referred to as *montage* (the French term for editing), it is also the art of juxtaposing shots to produce emotions and ideas. As the most famous Soviet theoretician and filmmaker **Sergei Eisenstein** says, "*Montage is the art of expressing or signifying through the juxtaposition of two shots such that their combination gives rise to an idea or expresses something which is not contained in either of the two shots alone. The whole is superior to the sum of the parts*" (quoted in Betton, *Esthétique* 75). More simply put, "montage produces an idea which is born of the shock created by bringing together two distinct elements" (Eisenstein 49).

The discovery that the confrontation of two shots can produce a meaning that is not in either of the shots separately belongs however to one of Eisenstein's teachers, **Lev Koulechov**, who conducted a now famous experiment. In one of the several versions of the story, Koulechov edited a series of shots together alternating close-ups of the actor Ivan Mosjoukine with a blank look on his face and shots depicting a bowl of steaming hot soup, a revolver, a child's casket, and an erotic scene. The spectators invited to view this short sequence were amazed at how subtly Mosjoukine's facial expressions (his face was blank, we remember) conveyed the feelings of hunger, fear, sadness, and desire. Specific meanings were thus produced solely by the juxtaposition of the shots: this is the now famous "*Koulechov Effect.*"

Eisenstein elaborates a complete theory of montage in which he describes the different methods of editing at the filmmaker's disposal. Explaining the precise effect that each is intended to have on the spectator, he distinguishes between *metric montage*, based on the length of the shots, *rhythmic montage*, based on both the length of the shots and movement within the frame (the content of the shot), *tonal montage*, based on the "emotional resonance," the "general tone" of the shot, and, finally, *intellectual montage*. This last form of editing, which Eisenstein described somewhat abstrusely as "the conflicting combination of concomitant intellectual affects" (71), is the basis for the *ideological montage* for which the Soviet director is most famous. This type of editing shots together produces either an emotion or a precise idea through the shock of their juxtaposition. *Parallel editing* is a particular case of ideological montage in which the combination of two or more shots produces a symbolic or metaphorical effect. One of the best-known examples of this is found in the first film by Eisenstein, *Strike* (1924). A shot of workers being mown down by Cossacks is followed by a shot of animals being killed in a slaughterhouse. The spectator draws the obvious conclusions. In this case the parallel editing of the two shots creates a metaphor, which explains why it is sometimes referred to as *metaphorical montage*. As J. Aumont et al. note, this classification of editing techniques and the theory surrounding it is "generally outmoded" today (49). It nonetheless remains important as regards the discovery of the specifically cinematographic techniques that are available to narrate a story, provoke emotional responses, produce meaning, and create atmosphere.

Transitions (Continuity Editing)

To be able to speak about the editing of a given film, an analyst needs to understand how the transition is effected from one shot to the next and between sequences. Such transitions constitute the *continuity editing* of a film, and the techniques used for this purpose are tantamount to the "punctuation" of the film. As regards the transition between shots, the simplest and most common type is a *cut*, where two shots are simply set side by side, the second replacing the first. In principle the cut is neutral; it does not in and of itself add any meaning to the passage from one shot to the next. But cut editing, because of its abrupt nature, may produce a shock. It is not by chance that Eisenstein's films, in which the shock of images produces meaning, are dominated by simple cuts between both the shots and the sequences.

In the case of editing between sequences, several types of transitions are commonly used in classic cinema. When the linkage between two sequences is effected by a particular technique, the technique is always chosen (at least in the better films) with the goal of producing a particular effect and a certain meaning. For example, to indicate the end of a sequence, filmmakers often use a *fade-out*, that is, the progressive disappearance of the image until the screen becomes black. This is a very strong punctuation mark that tells the spectator that it is the end of a segment of the narrative. Conversely, a *fade-in*, the progressive appearance of an image beginning with a black screen, indicates the beginning of a new action following the one that has just ended.

In old films, especially in silent cinema, the *iris in* and the *iris out* were frequently used. This is a particular type of fade-in in which the image appears or disappears by means of a circle of light which expands or shrinks, from or to the black screen. The iris shot was frequently used to focus attention on a particular detail of the image. Rarely seen in cinema today, this technique is sometimes used in modern films when the director wants to allude to the origins of cinema or emphasize cinema as a theme. In *Breathless* (1960), for example, Godard uses an iris in, focusing on a few coins in the palm of Michel's hand to emphasize his urgent need for money.

One of the most frequently used and most expressive transition techniques in classic cinema is the *dissolve*, in which an image fades out as the following image fades in, the second image superimposed for a moment on the first. The dissolve most frequently indicates the passage of time between two sequences. It is normally a simple moving forward in time (with an ellipsis), but when the dissolve is drawn out, it may signal the beginning of a flashback, as in the case of François at intervals throughout *Daybreak*. The dissolve may also be used inside a sequence, as in the train episode in *Grand Illusion* where the long series of dissolves signifies both the passing of time and the transfer of the French officers from prison to prison. We see a similar use of the dissolve in Antoine's interview with the psychologist at the juvenile delinquent facility, where a series of dissolves on the boy's face implies temporal discontinuity (jumping ahead in time) in spite of the apparent continuity of the dialogue.

We note, finally, the use of *sound dissolves*, in which the linkage of two sequences is accomplished by music or sound effects which gradually replace the sound accompanying the preceding image. An exceptionally successful example of this transition technique may be seen at the end of the sequence in *Daybreak* where François, lost in the memory of his first confrontation with Valentin at the cabaret, returns slowly to the present.

Deep Focus

When we speak of "*depth of field*" in photography, we are referring to the range of distances, from close to far, at which the subject framed by the camera remains in focus. If there is very little depth of field, the characters or objects which are in the foreground or background of the shot will be blurry. **To shoot in deep focus (with depth of field) means therefore that everything that is in the shot will be in focus.** In use since the very beginning of cinema, depth of field will take on a new significance with the move from the aesthetics of silent film to the techniques of the talkies in the 1930s and 1940s. If we are to believe **André Bazin**, "the talkies are the death knell of a certain kind of aesthetics of film language" (78). Silent film had perfected the art of montage, and the nature of montage is fragmentation of space. **Bazin insists that fragmentation is inimical to the principal goal of cinema, which is the realistic representation of the world.** To the extent that it preserves unity of space, deep focus, often combined with camera and actor movements, "places the spectator in a relationship with the image that is similar to the one he has with reality" (75).

Bazin considers moreover that deep focus has a liberating effect on the spectator, whereas liberty is lost in the process of classical découpage, which constantly directs the spectator's attention and imposes certain meanings. In this perspective montage takes away an essential aspect of reality, its fundamental ambiguity. **Roland Barthes** conjectures, in fact, that Eisenstein's cinema, which is based on montage, tends to destroy the ambiguity of reality (quoted in Aumont et al. 59). Depth of field and its corollary, the sequence shot, would thus grant the spectator greater liberty, while at the same time soliciting his active participation in the construction of the meaning of the film.

There is no unanimity, however, on the concept of the liberating function of deep focus. Marcel Martin, for instance, expresses strong reservations about the real liberty offered by depth of field (197–98). Many techniques—words, movements, objects, sound effects, music, organization of space—serve in fact to focus the spectator's attention and anchor certain meanings, as we see in the servants' meal sequence in *Rules of the Game*, which is analyzed at the end of this chapter. Martin nonetheless points out other advantages of deep focus, such as **the possibility of representing several actions at the same time (in both the foreground and the background, for instance) and of highlighting the psychological drama by framing characters in a given decor in lengthy fixed shots** (194). But the importance of depth of field in the evolution of cinema is clear to everyone, for "it implies a whole concept of staging and even of cinema itself" (Martin 189). In the hands of a great filmmaker, such as Jean Renoir or Orson Welles, the conscious use of deep focus tends to create "a cinematographic narrative that is capable of expressing everything without cutting up the world; it is capable of revealing the hidden meaning of beings and things without destroying their natural unity" (Bazin 78).

Whatever position one takes, the opposition between Bazin's aesthetic bias (based on the representation of reality) and Eisenstein's (based on the construction of meaning) represents one of the most important ideological debates in the history of world cinema. It is about the very conception of cinema, for Bazin's theory promotes the notion of the "transparency" of the filmic narrative—the spectator's attention is focused wholly on the illusion of reality—whereas Eisensteinian montage foregrounds cinema itself, drawing the spectator's attention to the techniques which are specific to the seventh art (Aumont et al. 52).

Sound

The great masters of silent film attacked the talkies violently at the end of the 1920s when they first appeared on the scene, accusing them of having a negative impact on the most specifically cinematographic techniques. Chaplin accused them, for instance, of ruining the art of pantomime, which was a fundamental part of silent film, while Eisenstein and his Soviet colleagues claimed that it destroyed the art of montage. Today everyone agrees that sound is an essential and fundamental component of cinema that has transformed its very aesthetics.

There is little doubt **that the soundtrack contributes greatly to the impression of reality** that characterizes cinema in general, just as it reinforces the impression of the continuity of the visual representation (which, we remember, is a series of discrete photographs). The use of sound effects and talking permitted filmmakers to do away with the title cards containing dialogue or explanations that were part and parcel of silent cinema. It also obviated the need to use certain visual metaphors or symbols to communicate ideas—like the hands vigorously shaking the mixer to represent the sound of the doorbell in *An Andalusian Dog*. In addition, the technique of **voice-over** "opens up to cinema the rich domain of in-depth psychology by making it possible to exteriorize the most intimate thoughts" (Martin 130). Voice-over enriches cinematographic representation in general by greatly increasing the relevance of off-screen space in comparison to silent cinema.

Music, finally, plays a critical role in sound cinema—provided that it is not a simple paraphrasing of the image, as is too often the case. In the best of scenarios the music either has a dramatic function, since it creates an atmosphere that supports the action, or it constitutes an additional source of meanings that complements those that are located in the images. Examples of **music that is absolutely essential to the success of a given scene** are numerous in French cinema. One need only consider the famous music by **Maurice Jaubert** in the dormitory scene in **Jean Vigo**'s *Zero for Conduct*, the music by the same composer in **Marcel Carné**'s *Daybreak*, the music by **Joseph Kosma** in **Jean Renoir**'s *A Day in the Country*, the use of **Saint-Saëns**' *Danse macabre* in the party sequence in Renoir's *Rules of the Game*, or **Giovanni Fusco**'s score for Alain **Resnais**' *Hiroshima mon amour*—to mention only a few of the most famous examples of remarkable film music.

Commentaries of Selected Sequences

We offer here two examples of analyses of film sequences in which we put into practice some of the concepts presented in the foregoing discussion of how to read a film. Excerpts from two major films are featured: Renoir's *Rules of the Game* (1939), one of the greatest works in the vein of poetic realism, and Godard's *Breathless* (1960), the film that is the most emblematic of the New Wave. The excerpt from *Rules of the Game*, the servants' meal sequence, is a striking example of a sequence shot (lengthy take), a technique for which Renoir is famous and in which deep focus and camera movements play a principal role. On the other hand, in *Breathless* we have chosen an excerpt in which the dominance of *montage* reaches a kind of apogee in French film: the sequence toward the beginning of the film in which the protagonist, Michel, shoots and kills one of the policemen who had been chasing him for a traffic violation. Unless otherwise indicated, the transitions between shots are simple cuts.

Sequence 1. *The Servants' Meal in* Rules of the Game

The beginning of the servants' meal shows that their world is homologous to that of their masters, insofar as it is structured by a similar hierarchy. The majordomo Corneille reigns over this world, while Lisette, as chambermaid to Madame (the wife of the marquis de la Chesnaye), is second in line. Lisette even answers in English (with consummate snobbism!) when one of the servants asks for mustard. Her "If you please" recalls the conversation in English between the two aristocrats Boëldieu and Rauffenstein in *Grand Illusion*, by the same director. The servants' conversation at the table, before the beginning of the excerpt we will discuss here, reflects moreover the same concern for social proprieties—and the same prejudices—that characterize their employer's society. Their conversation revolves around the impropriety of the presence of André Jurieu, whom everyone assumes to be Madame's former lover, and expressions of prejudice toward the marquis, who is of German Jewish extraction. This is the context for the remarkable sequence shot lasting nearly two minutes which begins with the arrival of the marquis' game warden Schumacher, Lisette's husband. During the following sequence Schumacher's departure marks the arrival of Marceau, a poacher whom the warden detests but whom the marquis has just hired to work as a domestic in the castle. The attraction between Marceau and Lisette becomes quickly apparent.

The large table at which the servants are dining is located in the foreground of a spacious hall adjacent to the kitchens, which we can see far off in the background. During most of the scene in question, which takes place in real time, Renoir plays on the great depth of field to integrate the action more effectively into the world of the servants, which is precisely the world of kitchens and work.

Shot 1 (1 min. 50 sec.): Medium up shot on Schumacher as he stops on a short stairway to answer a question someone has asked him. Schumacher: "*I don't know what you're talking about; I just got here.*" **Pan downwards and to the right** following Schumacher's descent into the hall. **Slight tracking forward** to meet the head chef who stops in a **near shot** just behind the two servants sitting at the table. Behind the chef, as he speaks, we can see from time to time a cook moving in the kitchens in the far background, emphasizing the great depth of field. The chef: "*Speaking of Jews, before coming here I was in the service of the baron d'Epinay. I can assure you that there are no Jews there. But I can also assure you that they ate like pigs. And that's why I left them.*" While the chef moves toward the rear, **short pan toward the right** to frame Schumacher in a **near shot** just behind Lisette. Schumacher: "*Will you be long, Lisette?*" Lisette: "*I don't know. Madame needs me a while longer.*" **Pan in the opposite direction** to frame the chef, who returns and stops again in a **near shot** in front of the table and begins to speak again: "*La Chesnaye, even though he's a foreigner, summoned me the other day to bawl me out for a potato salad. You know, or rather you don't know, that for this salad to be edible you have to pour the white wine on the potatoes when they are boiling hot—which Célestin hadn't done because he doesn't like to burn his fingers. Well, the boss caught that immediately! You can say what you will, but that's a real connoisseur.*"

While the chef is speaking, Schumacher moves away from the table to go back up the stairs. When the chef leaves again, **the camera pans toward the left** to accompany Schumacher's departure just as the warden passes Marceau coming down the stairs. **The two men (and the camera) stop briefly**; they exchange glances before **the pan resumes** accompanying Marceau's descent. Marceau then moves back toward the camera and stops in a **medium shot** behind the servants seated at the table. During Marceau's arrival we hear a servant say in voice-over: "*Who's that guy?*" Marceau: "*I'd like to speak to M. Corneille.*" Corneille: "*How may I help you, my good fellow?*" Marceau: "*I'm the new servant. The marquis must have told you about me.*" Corneille: "*What do you know how to do, my good fellow?*" Marceau: "*What do I know how to do? Oh, I don't know . . . a little bit of everything.*" Corneille: "*Do you know how to polish boots?*" Marceau: "*Yes, indeed, M. Corneille. For anything concerning clothes and all, I'm a real specialist.*" Corneille: "*Good. Tomorrow morning you'll go get the boots outside the rooms and do them.*" Marceau: "*Very well, M. Corneille.*" During this exchange the domestic who is serving the other servants at the table comes up from the back of the hall. **We can see the chef and the other cook moving back and forth in the kitchens in the background.** As we mentioned above, Renoir is clearly emphasizing the unity of space in order not to cut the action off from its socio-cultural context.

Leaning toward Corneille, Marceau asks, "*Is this where we eat?*" Corneille: "*Yes, my good fellow.*" **Pan toward the right** stopping on the male servant seated beside Lisette. He gets up, saying, "*I've got to get back to work.*" **Slight pan toward the left** to greet Marceau as he stops beside Lisette, who asks the servant to set a place for Marceau before asking him, "*What's your name?*" Marceau: "*Marceau. And you, Mademoiselle?*" Lisette: "*Madame. My name is Lisette. I'm Mme Schumacher.*" Marceau is taken aback and begins to walk away. Lisette calls him back, laughing: "*Oh, don't let that stop you from sitting down!*" At this moment **the space is divided into three parts, again drawing attention to its depth, by the arrival of the female servant from the right side**, midway between the foreground where Lisette and Marceau are placed and the background occupied by the chef and the kitchens. Marceau comes back to the table and sits down. Voice-over of two male servants speaking of the coming hunt provides the transition to the following shot.

Shot 2 (7 sec.): Near shot of the two male servants seated at the table, who continue to speak, but on-screen now. **Slight tracking forward, then short pan to the left** to frame Lisette, who is smiling at Marceau, whose head is cut by the left edge of the frame, in the foreground.

Shot 3 (10 sec.): Reverse angle near shot of Marceau, with Lisette's head cut by the right edge of the frame in the foreground this time. Marceau leers at her as he eats.

Shot 4 (3 sec.): A **close-up of the face of a radio** followed by a **dissolve to a clock** on the mantelpiece upstairs returns us to the world of the marquis and his guests.

This two-minute ten-second sequence, which is dominated by the **long sequence shot lasting a minute fifty seconds** at the beginning, only includes four shots. To appreciate Renoir's feat here, and the aesthetics of the sequence shot, one must understand that in a conventionally edited film (that is, most films at that time), shots only last five to ten seconds. A sequence such as this, shot by a conventional director, would have been composed of around twenty shots, continually fragmenting the space. Insofar as possible Renoir refuses this fragmentation, for the reasons we have indicated in the section on **deep focus** above. His technique is nonetheless quite risky, for it implies a precise choreography of movements and dialogues, entries and departures of characters, and camera movements that highlight this "ballet." If there is the slightest misstep, you have to start all over again—and that is expensive. For Renoir it is worth the risk because his principal goal is to represent reality as a unified whole: the fewer the shot changes (reminding the spectator that it is a film), the more realistic the impression.

This doesn't stop him of course from using classical editing when necessary. We see a good example of this in the **conventional angle-reverse angle shot** at the end of the sequence shot, where he highlights the mutual attraction between Marceau and Lisette that is going to provoke the circumstances leading to Jurieu's death.

Sequence 2. *The Death of the Motorcycle Policeman in* Breathless

The death of the policeman comes at the end of the second sequence of the film, in which Michel, having stolen a car in Marseilles, is driving toward Paris on Highway 7. In the first part of the sequence Michel's character is established: he's an arrogant, pretentious little punk, but sentimental and likable. At the beginning of the film he says to the girl who has helped him steal the car, "*I gotta run, Hon.*" He is, in fact, a character who never stops "running"; he seems obsessed by speed. But speed leaves him no time to think about what he is doing. It seems that the whole murder episode, the editing style of which emphasizes speed, occurs with no reflection on Michel's part, as if a malevolent destiny were dictating his actions.

The excerpt of nineteen shots that interests us here is preceded by a momentary slowing of the action. Michel has to slow down because of roadwork. But he is chafing at the bit, and at the first opportunity he passes, despite the solid line.

Shot 1 (1 sec.): In the very brief shot that begins this sequence, we see in a **near shot** the front of the car crossing the solid line on the highway. This detail is important because it is this act that materializes Michel's status as an "outlaw." He "crosses the line" and moves both outside the law and into the public domain. He will remain in this situation until his death at the end of the film.

Shot 2 (2 sec.): Point of view shot through the windshield: Michel sees two motorcycle policemen on the side of the road. Michel: "*Oh shit, the cops!*"

Shot 3 (4 sec.): Michel's car passes **a truck framed in a near shot and accompanied by a rapid lateral pan.**

Shot 4 (1 sec.): Long shot of the truck through the back window of Michel's car.

Shot 5 (3 sec.): Long shot of the two policemen who begin the chase. The transition from the previous shot is a **jump cut**, an abrupt cut that startles because it violates the classical principle that the continuity editing should not be perceived by the spectator. At the end of the shot **the camera pans laterally from the back window to Michel's back.**

Shot 6 (1 sec.): Medium shot of Michel's car, accompanied by a **pan from left to right** as it passes another car.

Shot 7 (2 sec.): Long shot, with a pan, of the two policemen speeding from right to left—in the *opposite direction* **of the preceding shot**, again violating conventional editing principles.

Shot 8 (5 sec.): Close shot of Michel's car as it turns off the highway into a small side road (**with an accompanying pan**) and stops. Michel: "*Oh! The wire's come off.*" (He had hotwired the car to steal it.)

Shot 9 (1 sec.): Long shot of the highway, seen from the side road. A policeman speeds by.

Shot 10 (4 sec.): Medium shot of Michel, who opens the hood of the car. Michel: "*Piece o' crap!*"

Shot 11 (1 sec.): Repeat of shot 9 (long shot of the highway): the second policeman speeds by.

Shot 12 (4 sec.): Medium shot of Michel trying to repair the wire he used to steal the car.

Shot 13 (3 sec.): Same long shot of the highway, but this time the policeman has turned around and come back to the side road where Michel's car is parked.

Shot 14 (3 sec.): Near shot of Michel followed by a lateral pan accompanying him to the car door. Framed from behind, he leans through the open window into the car. The **voice-over of the policeman** provides a **sound transition** to the following shot in which the sentence is ended: *"Don't move or you're a dead man!"*

Shot 15 (1 sec.): In a **close-up of Michel's profile, the camera pans from his hat to his arm.**

Shot 16 (1 sec.): Jump cut followed by an **extreme close-up of Michel's arm and a lateral pan to his hand,** which is holding a revolver.

Shot 17 (1 sec.): Extreme close-up of the cylinder of the revolver. Loud click followed by a **pan to the barrel of the gun.** Loud detonation of the revolver that provides the transition to the following shot.

Shot 18 (2 sec.): Medium shot of the policeman falling beside a tree. We note that this shot is introduced by a clearly **faulty transition** (probably intended by Godard), since the pistol shot is accompanied by a pan to the right, whereas the policeman falls to the left (Marie 82).

Shot 19 (14 sec.): Long shot, angled slightly downward, with a pan accompanying Michel as he runs across a field. **The camera comes to a stop and maintains a fixed shot** as Michel runs off into the twilight. **Fade out.** On the soundtrack we hear **loud jazz music** underlining the dramatic nature of the event.

It would be difficult to take the aesthetics of fast editing any further than this. We note that these **nineteen shots,** eleven of which are **no longer than two seconds,** last only **fifty-four seconds in all.** The combination of **fast editing, camera movements, jump cuts, and reverse movements** has a **dizzying effect on the spectators** that draws them into Michel's sphere of experience. We identify with Michel, seeing the action largely through his eyes from the beginning of the sequence. The rapidity and intensity of the action create the impression of a hellish moment in which, as we indicated above, reflection is impossible. Michel is not thinking about what he is doing. He just reacts to the situation he provoked by yielding to his desire to go faster, to live "breathlessly." The death of the motorcycle policeman is the sign of Michel's destiny; the rest of the film is the chronicle of an unavoidable fate that will track him down until it finishes him off.

Works Consulted

Aumont, Jacques, and Michel Marie. *L'Analyse des films*. Paris: Nathan, 1989.

Aumont, Jacques, Alain Bergala, Michel Marie, and Marc Vernet. *Esthétique du film*. Paris: Nathan, 1983.

Bazin, André. *Qu'est-ce que le cinéma?* Paris: Editions du Cerf, 1981.

Betton, Gérard. *Esthétique du cinéma*. Paris: Presses universitaires de France, 1983.

Eisenstein, S. M. *Le Film: sa forme, son sens*. Paris: Christian Bourgeois, 1976.

Gillain, Anne. *Les 400 Coups*. Coll. "Synopsis." Paris: Nathan, 1991.

Marie, Michel. *A bout de souffle*. Coll. "Synopsis." Paris: Nathan, 1999.

Martin, Marcel. *Le Langage cinématographique*. Paris: Les Editeurs Français Réunis, 1977.

Metz, Christian. *Essais sur la signification au cinéma*, I. Paris: Klincksieck, 1978.

Vanoye, Francis, and Anne Golio-Lété. *Précis d'analyse filmique*. Paris: Nathan, 1992.

Film Terms

Auteur: A director ("author") who imposes a recognizable personal style on his or her films.

Camera Angle: The position of the camera in relation to the subject being filmed (for example, an upward or a downward angle—see **Shot** below).

Cast: The actors and actresses in a film (or play).

Cinéaste: A filmmaker.

Cinemascope: A wide-screen process.

Cinéma Vérité: Refers generally to documentary-style filmmaking; originally associated with the New Wave style of hand-held cameras, small crews, and interviews.

Continuity: Smoothness of transition between shots (the responsibility of the **continuity supervisor**—see below).

Continuity Supervisor: The person who is responsible, during the shooting of a film, for all the links between the shots, that is, for the film's "**continuity**" (see above). This person (formerly referred to as the "script girl") also usually times all the shots to keep track of the length of the film.

Credits: The beginning and end of a film that show the title of the film and the names of the actors, the director, and everyone who participated in making the film.

Cross-Cutting: An editing technique in which shots of two actions are alternated regularly for a certain time to suggest the simultaneity of the two actions; often used to create suspense.

Cut: A simple transition between two shots accomplished by simply joining two pieces of film together (see also **Editing**).

Découpage: Last stage in the preparation of the shooting script. The screenplay is cut into sequences and numbered shots, usually with detailed notes regarding the specific camera angles and movements. It refers to the general arrangement of the shots in a film.

Deep Focus: A type of photography in which the focal length and the light permit objects or characters in both the foreground and the background to be in focus at the same time. Also referred to as **depth of field**, this shooting technique facilitates dramatic effects that depend on the interplay between actions in the foreground and background of the **field** (see below).

Dissolve: Link between two shots in which the first image disappears progressively while the second appears superimposed on the first and remains alone when the first image has disappeared completely (see also **Transition** and **Superimposition**).

Dubbing: Technique that involves replacing the original soundtrack with another that contains the dialogue in a different language. The new soundtrack is coordinated with the images so that the words correspond as closely as possible to the lip movements of the actors.

Editing: Process in which the finished shots of a film are assembled according to the narrative thread. Special attention is paid in this stage of post-production to the **links** between shots and the rhythm of the film (the respective lengths of the shots). There are various editing styles, for instance, fast, slow, cut, parallel, cross-cutting, etc. (see separate entries for "**Parallel Editing**" and "**Cross-Cutting**").

Fade-Out: An editing technique in which the image disappears progressively until the screen is completely black. It is usually a form of punctuation used to end a sequence. The opposite technique, a **Fade-In**, is primarily used to begin a new sequence: the image appears progressively, beginning with a black screen.

Fast Motion: An effect obtained by projecting at normal speed (twenty-four frames per second) images that have been shot at a slower speed. If the cameraman shoots at eight frames per second, for example, the action will be three times faster than normal when projected.

Field: The portion of space that is framed by the cameraman during a take. Characters may enter or leave the field (i.e., the image on the screen) during a shot.

Flash: A very short shot used for special effect (e.g., brusqueness, brutality, rapidity).

Flashback: a shot or sequence of shots that represent a return to an earlier time in the chronological narrative.

Flash-Forward: a shot or sequence of shots that represent a jump forward in time with respect to the chronological narrative.

Frame: Refers to a single photograph of the twenty-four photographs (frames) that are shot in one second. The same term also refers to the space of the entire image (the field) that the spectator sees on the screen. The cameraman **frames** a portion of space. The **framing** of a shot involves the camera angle and the arrangement of everything (characters and objects) that is in the field.

Freeze Frame: A single frame is reproduced a certain number of times and then spliced into the film, creating the effect of a photograph or of frozen action.

Insert: Usually a close-up of an object or character that is added during the editing process to clarify the action or make a special point.

Iris: A special type of shot used at the end of a sequence in which the image disappears by means of a black circle that progressively fills the screen until there is only a point of light left at the center, which then also disappears. This shot is referred to as an **iris out**. The opposite shot, in which the image appears as a widening circle, is called an **iris in**. This type of shot was common in the silent film era but is rarely used today, except as a reference to early cinema.

Jump Cut: Abrupt "jump" from one shot to the next by removing a small segment of the film and thereby breaking the normal continuity of the action. It is actually a cut within a scene rather than between scenes. It is normally used to create a special effect, as in J. L. Godard's *Breathless* (see also **Editing**).

Maquette: Scenery built in miniature that is intended to be taken for an authentic setting.

Mask: A shield that is put in front of the camera lens while shooting. Part of the surface of the shield is opaque, while part is transparent, permitting the recording of an image on a specific part of the film only. A mask is often used to present multiple images, side by side, in the same **field** (see above).

Match Cut: A shot that is similar in size and composition to the preceding shot.

Mise en scène: The staging (overall organization) of a shot.

Mixing: Post-production process which involves "mixing" together the several sound tracks of a film (dialogue, music, sound effects) and varying the volume of each according to its importance at a given moment. The result of the mixing is the final sound track, synchronized with the images.

Off-Camera: Refers to the invisible space that is adjacent to the field that appears on the screen in a given shot. This space is an extension of the field and exists in the spectator's imagination.

Panning: A movement in which the camera pivots horizontally around its vertical axis while the tripod remains stationary. The **pan** is used most commonly to "describe" a setting by sweeping over it or to follow the movement of a character or object. A **swish pan** is a type of link between shots that consists of an extremely rapid pan that produces a blurred horizontal movement on the screen.

Parallel Editing: An editing technique in which shots are juxtaposed to suggest a metaphorical or symbolic connection between them.

Post-Synchronization: A post-production technique that consists of adding the dialogue and sound effects after the film has been shot.

Rear Screen Projection: Projection of a moving image on a screen behind the actors in a studio, giving the impression that the scene was shot on location (in a moving car, for example).

Reframing: Using camera movements (**pans** and **tracking shots**) instead of beginning a new shot to change the framing or the camera angle (typically used during **sequence shots**).

Screenplay: The written script, also called the **scenario**, which is cut up into scenes and includes the dialogue.

Sequence: A series of shots that constitutes a narrative unit. It is the loose equivalent of a scene in a play or a chapter in a novel.

Shot: The basic unit of a film. A shot includes any continuous series of images recorded between the moment when the camera is started ("Camera!") and when it is stopped ("Cut!") each time.

Sizes of Shots:

Close-Up: Shot that features a character's face or singles out an object. An ***extreme close-up*** is a shot that frames a small detail, either an object or a part of the face.

Establishing Shot: Very long shot in which the general locale of the film is established (e.g., a prairie or a city).

Long Shot: Shot encompassing a large space (e.g., a street) in which characters can be identified; they must be framed full length.

Medium Shot: Shot in which characters are framed from the knees up; called an "*American shot*" by the French because of its wide use in American films of the 1930s.

Near Shot: Shot in which the characters are framed from the waist or from the chest up.

Types of Shots:

Down Shot: Shot in which the camera is placed above the subject being filmed and angled downward (also called a **high-angle shot**). An *up shot* is the opposite of a **down shot**: the camera is placed below the subject being filmed and angled upward (also called a **low-angle shot**).

Iris Shot: See entry above.

Point-of-View Shot: Shot which represents the viewpoint of a character in the film (also called **subjective camera**).

Sequence Shot: Also referred to as a **long take**, this is an unusually lengthy shot that constitutes an entire sequence by itself. It commonly includes a number of camera movements and the use of **deep focus** photography (see separate entry).

Shot-Reverse Shot: A technique generally used to film dialogue. In a sequence in which two characters A and B exchange remarks, the camera frames A and B alternately, the angle changing each time to show one or the other character. These shots are also called **match cuts** (see above), since they are similar in size and composition.

Static Shot: Shot in which the camera does not move in any way.

Tilt: Shot in which the camera is tilted up or down around its horizontal axis. In the "Dutch tilt" shot, the camera is slanted to the side and was often used to represent an aberrant psychological state in Expressionist films.

Tracking Shot: See entry below.

Two Shot: A shot which frames two people; a ***three shot*** includes three people.

Slow Motion: An effect obtained by projecting at normal speed (twenty-four frames per second) images that have been shot at a faster speed. If the cameraman shoots at ninety-six frames per second, for example, the action will be four times as slow as normal when projected.

Soft Focus: Shot in which the image is slightly blurred.

Special Effects: Any unusual effect achieved through cinematographic or theatrical means or devices. A good example is **stop-action photography,** in which the camera is stopped after filming a shot, then a new subject is placed before the camera or the first subject is simply removed. When the film is projected, the spectator is given the impression, in the first case, that the subject has been suddenly transformed; in the second case one has the impression that the subject has suddenly disappeared as if by magic.

Superimposition: A technical procedure that involves recording a second image over a first one, so that the two images are visible at the same time (for example, titles appearing over a moving background, supernatural events, phantoms). The superimposition is an integral part of a **dissolve** (see above).

Synchronization: Refers to the coordination of the soundtrack with the images of a film. "Synch sound" refers to sound that is recorded at the time of the filming of a movie; see also **Post-Synchronization** above.

Synopsis: A short summary of the action of a film.

Title Card: Written text placed between shots. In silent films the dialogue was presented on title cards, but the title card may also contain information to clarify the action.

Tracking Shot: Camera movement that usually involves placing the camera on a dolly (which is then rolled on tracks) or on a crane or holding the camera in the hands while moving in various directions. Cameras may track forward, backward, vertically, or laterally. Also referred to as a **traveling, trucking,** or **dolly shot.** A tracking shot can be simulated by varying the focal length of the lens (see **Zoom** below).

Transition: Any means of going from one shot to the next. This is normally accomplished in such a way that the transition, or link, seems natural to the spectators. Links must take into consideration such things as scenery, costumes, the actors' movements, the general rhythm of the film, etc. When any of the above elements are not respected, a transition is considered to be bad. The most common types of transitions include **cuts, fades,** and **dissolves** (see separate entries and **Editing**).

Voice-Over: The voice of a character who is off-screen or who is visible on-screen but is not speaking. Voice-over is thus often used to express the thoughts of a character or as a narrative voice.

Wipe: A technique in which one image is pushed off the screen by another (with a vertical line moving horizontally across the screen). A wipe normally indicates a change in subject, place, or time.

Zoom: A simulated **tracking shot** (see above) achieved by use of a lens with variable focal length while the camera remains stationary.

Historical Films: The Occupation and the Colonial Period

François Truffaut, *The Last Metro* (1980)

Louis Malle, *Goodbye, Children* (1987)

Claire Denis, *Chocolat* (1988)

Régis Wargnier, *Indochine* (1992)

In this first section we present a significant sample of historical films: two films on the Occupation, *The Last Metro* and *Goodbye, Children*, followed by two films on the colonial period, *Chocolat* and *Indochine*, the latter being one of the most successful **heritage films** (*films patrimonaux*). To understand these films more fully and better appreciate their importance, it is useful to know their historical and cinematographic contexts. The following remarks provide broad outlines of both the Occupation period and that of colonial France. The reader will find more specific information in the chapters devoted to each film.

The Occupation (1940–44)

The German army invaded France on May 10, 1940. In less than a week, overwhelmed by the rapid tank attacks (*Blitzkrieg*) and the superior aircraft of the Germans, France was defeated. It was a complete debacle and horrendously costly: 85,000 dead, two million prisoners, nine million refugees on the highways fleeing toward the south. In addition, as Paxton remarks, "France is economically strangled and financially exhausted by the stringent demands of Germany" (145), which imposed an Occupation tax of 400 million francs a day after the armistice on June 22 (Prost 49). France was divided into an occupied zone—the northern half of the country and the whole Atlantic coast—and a "free" zone that was under the authority of the government of Maréchal Pétain, established on July 1 in Vichy.

A hero of World War I, Pétain was an arch-conservative who rapidly took the side of the Nazi victors and fully subscribed to the "New Order" they promised. The French Republic was abolished and replaced by the "French State," which functioned like an absolute monarchy. The official Collaboration began on October 24, 1940, with a handshake, now infamous, between Pétain and Hitler. In London, General de Gaulle began the Resistance officially with his famous "Appeal of 18 June," in which he exhorted the

French people to continue the fight against the enemy. He marched down the Champs-Elysées as a national hero at the Liberation of Paris in August 1944 that put an end to the Occupation and the Vichy regime.

In 1946 René Clément's film *The Battle of the Rails* (1946), which depicts the heroic actions of French railroad workers during the Occupation, inaugurated a long tradition of films in praise of the Resistance. As we mentioned in the survey of French cinema at the beginning of this book (p. xxiv), the myths regarding the Resistance were attacked and debunked in the 1970s with the appearance, in particular, of Marcel Ophül's monumental documentary *The Sorrow and the Pity* (1971) and Louis Malle's film *Lacombe Lucien* (1974). Soon after, French cinema also began to show interest in an aspect of the Occupation that had been absent from the big screen: the fate of the Jews. This is one of the principal themes of the two films devoted to this period, which treat the question in two completely different universes, that of the Parisian theater (*The Last Metro*) and that of a provincial Catholic middle school (*Goodbye, Children*).

France and Colonialism

Colonialism has been an integral part of the history of France since the sixteenth century. At the beginning, there was an extensive French presence in North America (Canada, Newfoundland, and Louisiana, for example), in India, and in the Caribbean (Martinique, Guadeloupe, Saint-Martin, and Saint-Domingue), most of which France had to cede at the end of the French and Indian War, won by England in 1763. It built a second colonial empire in the nineteenth century, largely during the reign of Napoléon III (1852–70), by colonizing North Africa, beginning with Algeria in 1830 and later adding Morocco and Tunisia, as well as Indochina, a large part of West Africa (Mauritania, Senegal, Ivory Coast, Niger, etc.), Oceania (especially Polynesia, including Tahiti), and New Caledonia.

The French colonial empire, the second largest in the world after the British Empire, crumbled after the Second World War. In 1947 Indochina requested a measure of autonomy. France's categorical refusal provoked a war of independence that the Vietnamese won by defeating the French forces at the battle of Diên Biên Phú in 1954. The Geneva Accords that marked the end of hostilities that same year divided Vietnam in two parts, the North and the South. No sooner had the war ended in Indochina than the Algerian people also began to revolt against French domination. This developed into a long and bloody conflict culminating in the independence of Algeria in 1962. Two years earlier France had already granted independence to Morocco, Tunisia, and the eight colonies in East Africa. Of the vast former French empire, there only remains today the few departments and territories of Martinique, Guadeloupe, French Guyana, Reunion, Mayotte, Tahiti, New Caledonia, and Saint Pierre and Miquelon, two tiny islands near Newfoundland.

Despite severe government censorship, the contemporary colonial wars were already on the screens in France in the 1960s. Films bearing on the Algerian War included, for example, *Muriel, or the Time of Return* (*Muriel ou le temps d'un retour*, 1963) by Alain Resnais, *The Battle of Algiers* (*La Bataille d'Alger*, 1966) by the Italian filmmaker Gillo Pontecorvo (authorized, finally, in 1971), *To Be Twenty in the Aures* (*Avoir vingt ans dans les Aurès*, 1972) by René Vautier, *Nothing to Report* (*R.A.S.*, 1974) by Yves Boisset, and *The Honor of a Captain* (*L'Honneur d'un capitaine*, 1982) by Pierre

Schoendoerffer. Other films by Schoendoerffer, like *La 317e Section* (1965), *Drummer-Crab* (*Le Crabe-Tambour*, 1977), and *Diên Biên Phú* (1992), all treat aspects of the war in Indochina. Many French films of the 1980s and 1990s focus on the colonial period in Africa or in the Caribbean, such as *Coup de torchon* (1981) by Bertrand Tavernier, *Sugar Cane Alley* (*Rue Cases-Nègres*, 1983) by Euzhan Palcy, *Fort Saganne* (1984) by Alain Corneau, and *Overseas* (*Outremer*, 1990) by Brigitte Roüan.

Claire Denis' film *Chocolat* takes place in a French colony in West Africa shortly before the decolonization in 1960. Régis Wargnier's *Indochine* plunges us back into the 1930s, when Indochinese nationalism was just raising its head. In both cases the spectators share a retrospective viewpoint, for these films are based on flashbacks, and their protagonists live in the postcolonial era.

Works Consulted

Paxton, Robert O. *La France de Vichy 1940–1944*. Paris: Seuil, 1973.

Prost, Antoine. *Petite Histoire de la France au XXe Siècle*. Paris: A. Colin, 1979.

François Truffaut

The Last Metro (*Le Dernier Métro*)

(1980)

François Truffaut, *The Last Metro*: Marion Steiner (Catherine Deneuve) defends her theater at the Nazi headquarters.

Director. . . . . François Truffaut
Screenplay. . . . . François Truffaut, Suzanne Schiffman
Dialogue . . . . François Truffaut, Suzanne Schiffman,
. . . . Jean-Claude Grumberg
Director of Photography . . . . Nestor Almendros
Film Editor. . . . . Martine Barraqué
Sound . . . . Michel Laurent
Art Director . . . . Jean-Pierre Kohut-Svelko
Music. . . . . Georges Delerue
Costumes . . . . Lisele Roos
Continuity . . . . Christine Pellé
Administrator . . . . Jean-Louis Godfroy
Producer . . . . Jean-José Richer
Length. 2h11

Cast

Catherine Deneuve (*Marion Steiner*), Gérard Depardieu (*Bernard Granger*), Jean Poiret (*Jean-Loup Cottins, the director*), Heinz Bennent (*Lucas Steiner, famous Jewish director, hiding in the theater cellar*), Andréa Ferréol (*Arlette Guillaume, costumes*), Paulette Dubost (*Germaine Fabre, dresser*), Jean-Louis Richard (*Daxiat, theater critic and collaborator*), Maurice Risch (*Raymond Boursier, stage manager*), Sabine Haudepin (*Nadine Marsac, young careerist actress*), Marcel Berbert (*Merlin, administrator of the theater*), Martine Simonet (*Martine, black marketeer*), Franck Pasquier (*little Jacquot*), Jean-Pierre Klein (*Christian, Resistance fighter*), Alain Tasma (*Marc, property man*)

Story

We are in Paris in October 1942. Like the whole northern half of France, the city is occupied by the Nazis. Marion Steiner, a former film star and model for Chanel, has taken over the direction of the Théâtre Montmartre in the absence of her husband Lucas Steiner, a German Jew and famous theater director who has been forced to flee to avoid deportation to a concentration camp. He is believed to be in South America, but in reality he is hidden in the theater cellar where his wife, the only person who knows he is there, comes to see him every night before returning to the hotel where she lives.

The theater has begun rehearsals for a new play starring Marion and novice actor Bernard Granger, who has come over from the Théâtre du Grand Guignol (a popular theater specializing in horror shows), as well as a young, very ambitious actress, Nadine Marsac. The director of the play, Jean-Loup Cottins, a gay man who seems to have relationships with both the occupiers and the occupied, is following the instructions that Lucas Steiner gave him upon "leaving." Since the theater exists under the ever-present threat of being requisitioned by the German authorities, Marion and her colleagues are forced to put up with and cultivate Daxiat, the theater critic of the collaborationist newspaper *Je suis partout* (*I Am Everywhere*), who holds the fate of the Parisian theaters in his hands. Hiding in the cellar, Lucas is on the verge of a nervous breakdown when he discovers that he can listen to the rehearsals of the new play through a heating shaft, which gives him the opportunity to offer his wife advice on the staging each evening. But he could be discovered at any moment; Bernard, involved in the Resistance, could be arrested by the French police; Daxiat, a virulent anti-Semite, could have the theater closed out of pure malice; the new play could fail. So many pitfalls that could mean the end of the existence of a theater under the Occupation.

The Director

François Truffaut will forever be known as one of the *enfants terribles* of the *Cahiers du cinéma* who ravaged the cinema of the previous generation. Participating in the creation of the cult of the *author* in the 1950s, he distinguished himself at the beginning of his career as a young hothead producing dazzling, incisive film reviews. His first feature film, *The 400 Blows* (*Les Quatre Cents Coups*, 1959), an autobiographical film, was the first big success of the New Wave. It earned him a Best Director prize at the Cannes Film Festival and a load of other prestigious awards throughout the world, as well as a nomination for an Oscar in Hollywood. This first triumph would be followed shortly by two other films belonging clearly to the New Wave, *Shoot the Piano Player* (*Tirez sur le pianiste*, 1960) and *Jules et Jim* (1962). The latter film, adapted from a novel, was a big risk on Truffaut's part, given his virulent condemnation of the practice of adapting novels that had dominated conventional French cinema during the preceding decades. Featuring a love triangle widely perceived as scandalous (one woman, two men), the film was censured in several countries (Italy and Canada, for instance), but it was highly praised by the critics and popular with the general public, turning Jeanne Moreau, the star, into one of the most famous actresses in France.

In the course of a long career, Truffaut made four more films that depict the life of Antoine Doinel, the protagonist of *The 400 Blows* (played by Truffaut's alter ego, Jean-Pierre Léaud), as he grows up and discovers love (the short subject *Love at Twenty* [*Antoine et Colette*, 1962] and the feature film *Stolen Kisses* [*Baisers volés*, 1968]), gets married (*Bed & Board* [*Domicile conjugal*, 1970]), and, having divorced, reflects on the history of his love life while beginning a new sentimental adventure (*Love on the Run* [*L'Amour en fuite*, 1979]). Between the various episodes of the "Doinel cycle," Truffaut shot a variety of films with variable success but which made of him one of the most respected and admired French filmmakers (see "François Truffaut's Filmography" at the end of this chapter). His thirteenth feature film, *Day for Night* (*La Nuit américaine*, 1973), which earned the Oscar for the Best Foreign Language Film, tells the story of the making of the film that is embedded in the framing narrative, and whose subject serves as a mirror of the themes in the main film.

Day for Night reveals the normally hidden tricks of cinema, beginning with "day for night" itself, which refers to the use of a special lens to shoot nighttime scenes during the day. The film highlights the contributions of all the participants in the undertaking, but especially the complicated relationships that develop between them: the director, the actors, and the technical crew. It is easy to understand why critic after critic points out that *The Last Metro* functions as a counterpart to *Day for Night* by introducing the spectators into the wings of a theater and allowing them to witness the inner workings of a theater troupe and all the aspects of the preparation of a play. As Truffaut himself said, "In writing the screenplay for *The Last Metro* with Suzanne Schiffman, my intention was to do for the theater what I had done for cinema with *Day for Night*: the chronicle of a company at work" (1983, 4). Here too the show being prepared is embedded in another show (a play in a film), but Truffaut doubles down on the *mise en abyme*, because the plays that are embedded reflect certain elements of both framing devices, life in the theater on the one hand and the film itself on the other.

Truffaut only made two films after *The Last Metro*—*The Woman Next Door* (*La Femme d'à côté*, 1981) and *Confidentially Yours* (*Vivement Dimanche*, 1982)—both with Fanny Ardant (nominated each time for the Best Actress prize at the Césars), who would become his partner. Truffaut died of a brain tumor on October 21, 1984, at the age of fifty-two.

The Origin and Making of the Film

Truffaut had long yearned to make a film whose action was situated in the Occupation period, through which he had lived as a young adolescent in Paris (he was thirteen at the Liberation in 1945). The Occupation was long a taboo subject in France, but a few French films on this period had begun to appear, such as *Lacombe Lucien* (1974) by

Louis Malle and the documentary *Chantons sous l'Occupation* (*Singing during the Occupation*, 1976) by André Halimi, after Marcel Ophüls' epic documentary *The Sorrow and the Pity* (1969) was finally allowed onto the screens in 1971. Ophüls' film burst the myths about the behavior of the French during this period by showing, contrary to most of the preceding films touching on the Occupation, that the French hadn't all been heroic members of the Resistance. As far back as 1976, Truffaut knew the general outline of the film that he would make, a film on the life of a Parisian theater during the Occupation. He had only two peremptory principles: "a film on the Occupation should take place almost entirely at night and in confined spaces" and "as the only cheerful element, it had to include, in their original recordings, a few of the songs that people heard at that time in the streets and on the radio" (1983, 5). Thus, several times in the film we hear hit songs from the period such as "Mon amant de Saint-Jean" sung by Lucienne Delyle, "Sombreros et mantilles" by Rina Ketty, and "Zumba, zumba," in addition to "Bei mir bist du schön" sung by Renata.

Truffaut and Schiffman got down to work on the screenplay between May and August 1979, following extensive research during the preceding year. Both having lived part of their youth under the Occupation in Paris, they enriched their scenario with personal memories of daily life in that period. It was Truffaut's mother, for example, who forced him to return home immediately to wash his hair—like Jacquot in the film—after a German soldier had patted him on the head in the street. It was an uncle of Truffaut's in the Resistance who, like the Resistance fighter Christian in the church, was captured by the police but "managed to get off a signal to a friend coming to meet him so that he could avoid arrest" (Gillain, *Cinéma* 394). It was Suzanne Schiffman (whose mother was deported and did not return) who inspired the character of the young Jewish girl who hid her yellow star with a scarf to be able to go to the theater in the evening. The co-screenwriters remembered the people who grew tobacco in their vegetable gardens illegally, given the scarcity of this substance during the Occupation. And they remembered, like everyone, the fluctuating hours of the curfew (11:15 p.m. at the beginning, 8:30 p.m. toward the end) that made it imperative not to miss the last metro so as to be able to get back home in time.

Without really being a "film à clef," *The Last Metro* features certain characters who are transparently based on well-known figures of the Occupation period, beginning with Daxiat, who represents unambiguously Alain Laubreaux. Laubreaux had a disproportionate influence on the French theaters under the Nazis as the anti-Semitic theater critic of the newspaper *Je suis partout*. The episode in which Bernard Granger punishes Daxiat, in the rain outside the restaurant, for the insults he had published concerning Marion, is a virtually unvarnished rendering of an incident in which the actor Jean Marais, then Jean Cocteau's lover, punished similarly but still more harshly Laubreaux for having insulted Cocteau in an article concerning his play *The Typewriter* (*La Machine à écrire*) in 1941. The theater and stage director Lucas Steiner recalls clearly the famous theater director Louis Jouvet, who took his troupe on tour in South America to escape the Nazis (at the beginning of Truffaut's film, people think that Lucas Steiner has gone to South America). Truffaut admits, moreover, "the idea for this film probably came to me initially in thinking of Louis Jouvet [...]. One day I imagined that he hadn't gone to South America during the Occupation but that he had stayed in France, directing his theater secretly" (Montaigne, "François Truffaut"). The character of Jean-Loup

Cottins, who replaces Lucas as director of the Norwegian play, is associated both with Jean Cocteau, also homosexual, and with Sacha Guitry, one of the most celebrated directors, actors, and filmmakers in France who was likewise arrested—twice—by the Free French Forces (FFL) at the Liberation and led away in his pajamas, suspected of collaborating with the enemy for continuing to exercise his profession in the theater during the Occupation. As for Marion Steiner, Truffaut modeled her on a whole group of female theater directors in Paris in this period, notable Alice Cocéa at the Théâtre des Ambassadeurs, Yvonne Printemps at the Théâtre de la Michodière, Simone Berriau at the Théâtre Antoine, and Marguerite Jamois at the Théâtre Montparnasse (Fechner; Rochu). It was Printemps "who, one evening when the electricity went out, found a way to light the stage at her theater using automobile lights charged by batteries" (Fechner). As for Bernard Granger, a novice actor torn between his pride at being hired at a great theater and his desire to fight for his country, Truffaut cited the cases of Louis Jourdan and Jean-Pierre Aumont ("Pourquoi" 5), two great French actors who fought the Nazis, the former in the Resistance, the latter with the Free French Forces.

The shooting of the film started on January 28, 1980, and finished on April 21. It began at the Théâtre Saint-Georges in Paris, where all the sequences of the staging of *La Disparue* (literally, "The Woman Who Had Disappeared"), the Norwegian play produced in *The Last Metro*, are filmed. Most of the scenes of the film are shot, however, on sound stages installed in the vast abandoned Moreuil chocolate factory in Clichy. The only sequences that are shot on location are the flight of Daxiat, the scenes with him at the offices of *Je suis partout*, the action in Marion's hotel room, the scene at the restaurant, and the brief scene inside the church when Bernard's friend from the Resistance is arrested by the Gestapo (de Baecque and Toubiana 699–701). The first scene in the "street," when Bernard hassles Arlette, is clearly (blatantly) shot on a stage in a studio, which stresses from the outset the theatrical character of the action and highlights the theme of theater itself.

To evoke the dark atmosphere of the Occupation, many scenes take place in semi-darkness—at night, in fact, during the first forty-five minutes of the film. As for the colors, Nestor Almendros, the Director of Photography, only used browns, ochres, and reds. "This precise work on the color," de Baecque and Toubiana observe, "gives the film both an artificial and a gentle atmosphere: all of French society under the Occupation thus appears to be a theater stage" (700). Truffaut and Almendros chose a Fuji film that is duller than that offered by Eastman Kodak, producing streets that are "gray and wonderfully lugubrious, like in the films in the poetic realism vein in this period" (Boujut 45; Salachas). In addition, Alemendros used two different types of lighting, one for the action of the framing film (realistic), another for that of the play being presented (artificial), "a shifting light, symptomatic of an often ambiguous film. . ." (Bouteiller).

Since the denouement of the film is a big surprise for the spectators, and rumors about the film had begun to circulate, Truffaut barred any journalists from the shoot—which annoyed certain of them: "Before the age of fifty, our friend François Truffaut, a former journalist and film critic, has just been struck by a stupefying affliction: a sudden attack of allergy to the press" (Montaigne, "Truffaut: metro"). The editing of the film took four months. In the end it would be the most expensive film Truffaut had made, approaching eleven million francs, funds that he scraped together with great difficulty.

The Actors

Truffaut wrote the role of Marion Steiner for Catherine Deneuve and that of Bernard Granger for Gérard Depardieu, both of them already well known in French cinema and in the process of becoming superstars. Deneuve was a big hit in Jacques Demy's *The Umbrellas of Cherbourg* (*Les Parapluies de Cherbourg*, 1964), a film whose everyday dialogue is sung instead of spoken, as well as in two films by the famous Spanish director Luis Buñuel, *Belle de jour* (1967) and *Tristana* (1970). In Truffaut's *Mississippi Mermaid* (*La Sirène du Mississippi*, 1969), she plays a *femme fatale*, blond and cold (à la Hitchcock, Truffaut's favorite filmmaker). In *The Last Metro*, according to the film critic at *Le Monde*, she is "mysterious and simmering, bending without breaking, a vision of an *eternal feminine* that is hardened by the footlights and the accidents of life while remaining, as the theater would have it, unpredictable" (Siclier). Owing to her classical beauty, Deneuve was chosen to embody Marianne, the symbol of France, from 1985 to 1989. She was nominated for an Oscar for her performance in Régis Wargnier's *Indochine* (1992), which is also presented in this book.

Depardieu played a principal role in two other films also appearing in 1980, Maurice Pialat's *Loulou* and Alain Resnais' *My American Uncle* (*Mon oncle d'Amérique*). This latter film was nominated for an Oscar and awarded the Best Foreign Film prize by the New York Film Critics in 1980. He would also be the hero of Truffaut's next-to-last film, *The Woman Next Door* (*La Femme d'à côté*, 1981), before starring in numerous additional films that received awards, including Andrzej Wajda's *Danton* (1983), Claude Berri's *Jean de Florette*, Bruno Nuytten's *Camille Claudel* (1988), and Jean-Paul Rappeneau's *Cyrano de Bergerac* (1990), for which he was nominated for a Best Actor Oscar.

The role of Jean-Loup, a homosexual with suspicious connections, is played by Jean Poiret, a somewhat unusual choice since Poiret normally played comic roles. He is the only member of the cast who actually acted in Paris during the Occupation, having begun to play minor roles in the theater in 1943 (Milhaud). Finally, the role of Daxiat is played by Jean-Louis Richard, a filmmaker, former member of Louis Jouvet's company in the 1950s, and friend of Truffaut's, whose performance is remarkable. He manages to give an ambiguous quality to the sinister character he embodies: "He confers on Daxiat a troubling personality, with his soft voice, his childlike yet imposing physique, his gazes that suggest madness" (de Baecque and Toubiana 695). For the role of Lucas Steiner, Truffaut chose Heinz Bennent, one of the greatest actors of the German theater. Bennent had appeared recently in two major films by Volker Schloendorff, *The Lost Honor of Katharina Blum* (1975) and the adaptation of the famous novel by Günter Grass, *The Tin Drum* (1979), which received the Oscar for the Best Foreign Language Film. Bennent was awarded a prize for Best Actor for his performance in the film by Ute Wieland *Year of the Turtle* (1988).

The Reception

The Last Metro hit the theaters on September 17, 1980. It was a huge success with both the critics and the general public, drawing a record number of spectators in the first week for a film by Truffaut. The following January, *The Last Metro* won ten awards at the Césars, the most ever by a film—Best Film, Best Director, Best Actress (Deneuve), Best Actor (Depardieu), Best Screenplay, Best Photography, Best Sound, Best Editing,

Best Scenery, Best Music—to which many additional prizes would be added in France and abroad during the year. In Paris alone, the film drew over a million spectators in 1981, and the French press showered constant praise on it. For example: "*The Last Metro* is one of most fascinating films by Truffaut" (Pérez); "At a time when power is shared between so many false gods devoid of magic, François Truffaut is the revolutionary that French cinema needs" (Baignères); "The Occupation between comedy and tragedy. With a subtle balance, Truffaut revives a whole age. And produces a superb film that will be an important date in his work" (Billard 129); and finally, "This time everyone agrees about François Truffaut: the critics and spectators who saw *The Last Metro* all call it perfect, the masterpiece of a filmmaker who nonetheless already has remarkable films to his credit . . ." (Hamel). In the United States, the film was nominated for the Best Foreign Film at both the Golden Globes and the Oscars.

Intertextuality

Like all the New Wave directors, Truffaut was a notorious cinephile. His film is filled with references to fellow filmmakers, beginning with the transparent allusion to the famous American comedy by Ernst Lubitsch *To Be or Not to Be* (1942), which is about a theater company that dupes the Nazis during their occupation of Warsaw. The intertextuality of *The Last Metro* is an integral part of the film and enriches its content considerably. The very first sequence, for example, in which Bernard tries to pick up Arlette in the street, is a clear reference to the beginning of Marcel Carné's *Children of Paradise* (*Les Enfants du paradis*, 1945). The allusion is all the more obvious in that the star of this film, pursued by one of the protagonists in the first scene, is named "Arletty," one of the most famous film actors of her time. *Children of Paradise* is also a film on theater life seen from the wings and shot, moreover, during the Occupation, making it doubly relevant to *The Last Metro* (Affron and Rubinstein 18). The allusion to Carné's film is all the more interesting in that the music and set of the film were created, respectively, by Joseph Kosma and Alexandre Trauner, two Jewish professionals who had to hide out in a little mountain inn near Nice (like Lucas in his cellar) during the shooting of *Children of Paradise*, while accomplices lent their names to conceal the participation of the two famous artists—as was also the case for the other great film by Carné under the Occupation, *The Devil's Envoys* (*Les Visiteurs du soir*, 1942).

The presence of Paulette Dubost in the role of Germaine, the dresser, is a subtle allusion to Jean Renoir, one of the filmmakers Truffaut admired the most (along with Lubitsch and Hitchcock), and in particular to his film *Rules of the Game* (*La Règle du jeu*, 1939) in which Dubost plays the role of Lisette, the chambermaid of the heroine. Moreover, the confusion of play and reality, theater and life, is one of the most important themes of Renoir's film. Likewise, the casting of Sabine Haudepin in the role of Nadine is an allusion to Truffaut's own *Jules and Jim* (1962), in which she plays Sabine, the little daughter of Jules and Catherine. As in *The Last Metro*, *Jules and Jim* is about a love triangle (one of the most famous), with Jeanne Moreau in the middle.

In addition, the final lines of *La Disparue*, the Norwegian play, are borrowed word for word from the denouement of *Mississippi Mermaid* (1969) in which Catherine Deneuve, as we noted above, is also the heroine: "You are beautiful. When I look at you, it is agony." "But yesterday you said that it was a joy." "It's both joy and agony." The paradoxical opposition between joy and agony is an apparent allusion to the pleasure/

pain antithesis developed by Alain Resnais in *Hiroshima mon amour* (1960), just as the exchange at the end of the new play in the epilogue clearly recalls the theme of Forgetting (of the lover) at the end of Resnais' film, one of the most important works of the New Wave period, and which also evokes the horrors of World War II.

The Theater and Censorship under the Occupation

A severe censorship was exercised both by the Nazi occupiers and by the Vichy government as regards films and plays that were proposed to the French public. Any work that touched upon the current socio-political situation in France or that was the slightest bit patriotic was blocked, which resulted in the production of a large number of comedies and mediocre dramas, in the cinema as well as in the theater, intended solely for entertainment. The most talented film directors thus took refuge, on the one hand, in the distant past, as is the case of Carné's *The Devil's Envoys*, whose action takes place in the fifteenth century, and his most famous film, *Children of Paradise*, whose action is situated in the Romantic period between 1820 and 1840. On the other hand, some directors turned to mythology—as we see in *Love Eternal* (*L'Eternel Retour*, 1943) by Jean Delannoy and Jean Cocteau, which is a modern version of the medieval myth of Tristan and Isolde—or to fairytales, as in Cocteau's *Beauty and the Beast* (*La Belle et la Bête*, 1946).

In the theater, the best directors staged plays from the classical repertory, comedies by Molière or tragedies by Corneille and Racine, as well as tragedies from antiquity and plays by Shakespeare and by Scandinavian playwrights such as Strindberg and Ibsen (which explains the choice of a play by a female Norwegian author in Truffaut's film). Nonetheless, as Truffaut remarks, this did not prevent theaters from presenting during this period the best plays by Sartre, such as *The Flies* (*Les Mouches*, 1943) and *No Exit* (*Huis clos*, 1944), Paul Claudel's *The Satin Slipper* (*Le Soulier de satin*, 1943), and, in 1944, Jean Anouilh's *Antigone* (Gillain, *Cinéma* 392).

Despite the general mediocrity of most of the shows, the theaters, like the cinemas, were nearly always full during this period. As René Rocher, the president of the Paris theater committee in 1944, remarks, "The current prosperity of the theater is miraculous: you can put on anything by anyone, wherever and whenever—all the seats are taken, all the records broken" ("Le Théâtre français sous l'Occupation"). The theater, like the cinema, was a way to flee the painful reality of the Occupation, including very difficult living conditions. Since there was a lack of coal, the inhabitants went to the shows partly in search of a little warmth, be it only body heat. Indeed, the venues were scarcely heated, if at all, and it is said that during the performance of Claudel's *The Satin Slipper*, the spectators, huddling under blankets, applauded with their feet . . . . Going to a show became more dangerous after September 1942 with the publication by Vichy of the law creating the Compulsory Work Service (*Service du Travail Obligatoire* or STO). As Truffaut recounts, policemen began to watch the doors of the theaters and cinemas to grab recruits for the "French Workers in Germany" (Bazin 17). Bernard, in *The Last Metro*, describes humorously the trick he used to elude them.

The problem of the lack of food and gasoline, like that of coal for heating homes, was part of daily life in Paris during the Occupation. Everything was rationed, and the black market flourished. This aspect of life in this period is represented by the character of Martine, the black marketeer who, at the beginning of Truffaut's film, brings Marion the seven-kilo ham costing 4,200 francs. In order to understand the cost of black market goods at this time, consider that the average monthly salary of a worker at the beginning of the 1940s was 2,500 francs—also the price of a bicycle, the principal means of travel by Parisians at this time. This explains the extreme distress of Raymond, the stage manager, when his bike is stolen.

The Status of Jews under the Occupation

Pétain's government hadn't waited for the official Collaboration to begin to publish, on October 3, 1940, new laws concerning the status of Jews in France. From this day forward, Jews were forbidden to "belong to elected bodies, occupy positions of responsibility in any public service, the judiciary, and the army, and exercise any activity having an influence on cultural life (teachers, business leaders, managers or editors of newspapers, directors of films or radio programs)" (Paxton 171–72). Beginning in July 1942, it was even forbidden for Jews to go to theaters, which explains the sequence in *The Last Metro* in which the young Jewish girl Rosette insists that she can go to the theater by hiding beneath her scarf the yellow star she has been forced to wear, like all Jews in France since June 1942. As for Jewish theater owners, the German or Vichy authorities simply requisitioned their theaters to "aryanize" them. The whole team of film and theater critics of the newspaper *Je suis partout*—including, notably, Alain Laubreaux, Lucien Rebatet (writing under the name "François Vinneuil"), and Robert Brasillac—ranted and raved about the Jewish presence in that world. Laubreaux's anti-Semitic tirade on the radio in Truffaut's film is taken literally from a book by Rebatet published in 1941, *Les Tribus du cinéma et du théâtre* (*The Tribes of Cinema and Theater*). The humorous remark by Lucas Steiner, "the Jews take our most beautiful women," is a sentence repeated obsessively, Truffaut tells us, by Rebatet (Boujut 45).

In November 1942, following the landing of the Americans in North Africa, the Occupation of France was extended to the Free Zone, that is, to all of France, which explains why the escape of Lucas Steiner becomes so perilous that Marion has to persuade him to stay hidden in the cellar while she directs the theater in his place. Around half of the 300,000 Jews living in France at the beginning of the Occupation are, like Lucas and Rosette's father, foreigners who arrived in France in the 1930s to flee the Nazis in Germany, Austria, and Poland (Paxton 167). They thus still have a very strong accent, making it very dangerous for them to be caught in public in Paris. At the beginning of the Occupation, the policy of deportation or internment of Jews, carried out primarily by Vichy, targeted foreign Jews above all; this is the explanation for the allusion to the problem of the heavy accent ("à couper au couteau") of Rosette's Polish father.

STUDY GUIDE

What Happens in This Film?

1. Why is the director of the Théâtre Montmartre, Lucas Steiner, absent? Where is he hiding?

2. What does Bernard Granger have to sign before he can be hired by Marion?

3. Why does Marion have to be nice to Daxiat, the anti-Semitic theater critic of the far-right newspaper *Je suis partout* (*I Am Everywhere*)?

4. When Bernard tells his story of the stolen bicycle, in which he refers to a guy who calls him a faggot, he apologizes to Jean-Loup. Why?

5. What does Marion discover when she goes looking for Nadine in her dressing room during the electrical outage? What is Arlette's reaction?

6. Bernard had shown the actors' dressing rooms to Martine, the black marketeer. What is the consequence?

7. What indicates Marion's extreme apprehension before the opening of *La Disparue*?

8. At the restaurant, how does Bernard react to the vile review that Daxiat writes on the play after opening night? Did Truffaut make this episode up?

9. After the visit of the cellar by the two French Gestapo members, what surprising observation does Lucas make to Bernard? What question does he ask him?

10. What is the fate, at the Liberation, of Nadine, Jean-Loup, and Daxiat?

11. What does the epilogue of the film lead the spectators to think regarding the situation of Lucas, Bernard, and Marion at the Liberation?

12. What does Marion do onstage, with Bernard and Lucas, at the very end of the film? Why?

True or False?

If the statement is false, correct it!

1. Jean-Loup is going to direct the Norwegian play *La Disparue* all alone.

2. Marion spends each evening alone in the hotel where she lives.

3. Arlette rejects Bernard's advances because she prefers more refined men.

4. Lucas Steiner is going to be able to participate in the directing of *La Disparue* by using an old heating shaft to listen to the rehearsals and performances.

5. Lucas advises Marion to be less obviously in love in her scenes with Bernard.

6. Bernard works on a record player in the theater to prepare it for an act of terrorism by the Resistance.

7. Bernard leaves the cabaret with his date because he wants to go to the movies, whereas Marion heads back to her hotel.

8. Delighted with the success of the opening night of *La Disparue*, Marion shakes Bernard's hand after the curtain falls.

9. To attempt to save her play after the incident in the restaurant, Marion is forced to go to the Propagandastaffel (which is in charge of censorship) to speak to a German officer.

10. The two men from the Gestapo cannot see Lucas Steiner's furniture in the cellar of the theater because of the lack of light.

11. When Bernard tells Marion that he is leaving the theater to join the Resistance, she slaps him in the face.

12. At the end of the film, it is clear that Marion is now again living normally with her husband while maintaining a professional relationship with Bernard.

What Did You Learn in the Introduction?

1. Who is the protagonist of the cycle of five films by Truffaut that begins with *The 400 Blows?*

2. What is the relationship between *The Last Metro* and *Day for Night?*

3. What is the importance of Marcel Ophüls' documentary *Sorrow and Pity?*

4. What is the origin of many of the memories of the Occupation that are found in *The Last Metro?*

5. What is *Je suis partout?* What is the position of Daxiat and his colleagues toward Jews in the theater world?

6. Where does Truffaut shoot most of the sequences of his film, on location or on a sound stage in the studio? Why?

7. Which actors in this film became extremely famous in France?

8. What famous film by Marcel Carné is alluded to in the first sequence of *The Last Metro?* What aspects of this film are particularly relevant to Truffaut's film?

9. What is the stunning fate of *The Last Metro* at the Césars in January 1981?

10. What is the effect of the law of October 3, 1940, on the status of Jews in France?

11. Describe the policy of the Germans and Vichy toward the cinema and the theater.

12. How would you describe the attendance figures of movie houses and theaters in France during the Occupation? What is the explanation for this?

Exploring the Film

1. The Prologue

Bernard Granger approaches Arlette in the street and tries to pick her up. What is striking in this initial scene as regards the set? **Is the scene shot on location (in a real street) or on a studio set?** What is the importance of Truffaut's choice here? *Review this sequence* (Excerpt 1, 3'07–4'57). **What is your first impression of Bernard?** Why does Arlette reject his advances?

2. The Title of the Film

What metro is being referred to, precisely, as the "last metro"? Why is this important in the context of the film? Does the title suggest anything as regards the ambiance of the Occupation, whether it be for the theater and the cinema or for the population in general?

3. The Characters

+ *Lucas*

Why is it particularly difficult for Lucas Steiner to leave France with the help of a smuggler? What are the dangers? Why is his foreign accent a problem? *Review the scene in which Marion joins him in the cellar at the beginning of the film* (Excerpt 2, 27'45–29'30). What shocking statistic do we learn here?

   What metaphorical value does Lucas have as regards the situation of the Jews under the Occupation? Could his "hidden presence" also have a meaning in relation to the director of a film (or of a play)?

   Review the sequence in which Lucas puts on a false nose and wonders aloud, "What does 'look like a Jew' mean?" and in which we hear the song "Mon amant de Saint-Jean" at the end (Excerpt 3, 41'45–43'30). **How do you understand Lucas' query in its historical context?** When Lucas and Marion listen to "Mon amant de Saint-Jean," there is a very lengthy close-up of Marion's face. **How do you interpret this shot?**

+ *Marion*

What sort of woman is Marion? Why does Bernard say to Christian, his friend in the Resistance, "There is something troubling about this woman. Something isn't clear"? What is it, in fact (that the spectator knows before Bernard)?

   Is it realistic that Marion, a woman, is the director of a big Parisian theater during this period?

   In speaking of his films toward the end of the 1960s, Truffaut says, "What all my films have in common is that the women direct the events, faced with men who are not as strong" (Gillain, *Cinéma* 189). **Is this the case in *The Last Metro*?**

+ *Bernard*

What is Bernard involved in other than his work as an actor? *Review the scene of the record player that he gives to his friend Christian* (Excerpt 4, 59'54–1h00'13). To what use will this record player be put? What does Bernard do in the cabaret when he sees all the German officers' caps in the cloakroom?

✦ Nadine

How would you describe Nadine? What is the most important thing in her life? *Review the scene in which she arrives late for the rehearsal* (Excerpt 5, 23'58–25'15). Does she lack principles? Who drops her off at the theater that day? How does Raymond the stage manager react? What is her attitude toward Daxiat, for example? **How may her ambition be related to the scene in which Marion surprises her in Arlette's arms?** Does Nadine's character seem realistic or caricatured to you?

✦ Daxiat

Truffaut wholeheartedly subscribes to Hitchcock's maxim that "The better the bad guy is, the better the film is" (Toubiana). **Is this true, in your opinion, in the case of Daxiat?** Does his character contribute significantly to the success of this film? If so, in what way?

What essential aspects of the film are related to Daxiat? How would you describe him? **Is he an ambiguous character?** Daxiat tells Marion that he is a "living paradox." What did he mean by that? *Review his conversation with her* (Excerpt 6, 1h03'15–1h05'48). What piece of "news" does he bring her? What advice does he give her concerning her husband? Why, in your opinion? **How would you describe Daxiat's attitude toward Marion Steiner?**

Jean-Pierre Richard accepted the role of Daxiat with the understanding that he could give a certain class to the character. Did he succeed in this regard? **How does he behave during the incident at the restaurant** in which he is severely punished by Bernard? Is he simply a coward? *Review this sequence* (Excerpt 7, 1h40'20–1h42'20).

4. Bernard and Marion

How would you describe the relationship between Bernard and Marion during most of the film? What does Marion think of Bernard's behavior toward women? How do we know that Marion is hiding her true feelings for Bernard? *Review the cabaret sequence* (Excerpt 8, 1h16'53–1h19'45). **Why does Marion go out with René Bernardin?** Simply for fun? What does Marion do behind the curtain at the end of the opening of their play? *Review this scene* (Excerpt 9, 1h31'02–1h32'00). Later on, what is the effect of Bernard's violent treatment of Daxiat at the restaurant on his relationship with Marion? Explain.

Why, in your opinion, does Marion give Bernard a slap when he tells her that he is going to leave the theater to join the Resistance? What do you think of the reversal in their relationship that occurs as Bernard is preparing to leave? Do you think that Marion's behavior is reprehensible?

5. Lucas and Bernard

Lucas tells Marion to be more "sincere" in the only love scene she plays with Bernard in the play they are rehearsing. Later, after the Gestapo's visit to the cellar, he declares to Bernard that his wife Marion is in love with him (with Bernard). **Do you think that Lucas is pushing Bernard into his wife's arms?** Explain. *Review the sequence of the* *visit of the cellar* (Excerpt 10, 1h57'27–1h59'35). How do you interpret **the last shot** in the film? *Review the end of the epilogue* (in Excerpt 11, below) as regards the relationship between the three characters.

6. Secretive Characters

Lynn Higgins remarks that in this film "everyone is an actor who is constantly hiding behind a role" (153). It is also true that many characters in this film are duplicitous: they are hiding something, a secret side of themselves. **How does this apply to Marion, Bernard, Jean-Loup, Arlette, and Nadine?** One critic, Carole Le Berre, even contends that this is "a film governed by secrecy" (284) and suggests that the act of hiding a ham in the cello case, then in the closet, as Marion does, is emblematic of the whole film (272). **Do you agree with this interpretation?**

Le Berre also points out the importance of the gaze in this film (282): Truffaut constantly emphasizes the fact that the characters are keeping an eye on each other, as Marion observes the behavior of Bernard. **What might this aspect of the film, as well as the motif of the secret, have to do with the Occupation period?**

7. The Epilogue

The spectators are generally duped by the epilogue of the film, in which Bernard alludes to the death of Marion's husband, then rejects her, denying that he had ever loved her. What we take for reality is in fact only a theatrical illusion, highlighting the confusion between play and reality throughout the film. **How does Truffaut succeed in deceiving the public by the manner in which he shoots this scene?** Why do the spectators believe that they are seeing a further development of the principal action in the film? *Review the epilogue* (Excerpt 11, 2h06'26–2h10'25), paying close attention to the **scenery and background** during this sequence. What change do you notice? **How does Truffaut play here on the difference between cinema and theater?**

8. The Songs

Truffaut gave great importance to the songs in *The Last Metro*, like "Mon amant de Saint-Jean" ("My Lover in Saint-Jean"), which we hear during the beginning credits and several other times during the film. **Why did he consider the songs to be essential to a film on the Occupation?** (What do these songs add to the film? What spectators do they target in particular?)

9. The Mise en Abyme of the Play

How might we interpret the relationship between the main film (the preparation of the play by the whole company) and the role of the actors in the play they are rehearsing? Since the actors play their roles in the film just as the actors play their roles in the play, how do we distinguish between playacting and reality, between being and appearance? Is illusion less an integral part of "real life" than of theater? **In other words, what metaphorical value does Truffaut seem to give to theater in this film?**

10. Homosexuality

Truffaut himself reminds us, "It is not sufficiently known that the pro-Nazi French, who proclaimed their cult of virility (for them victorious Germany was *male* and defeated France *female*), showered the same hate on both Jews and homosexuals" ("Pourquoi" 6). They particularly detested the "effeminate theater" of Jean Cocteau. **What role do homosexuality and homophobia play in this film?** What does Daxiat criticize in the staging of Jean-Loup in his review of *La Disparue*?

11. The Socio-Political Context

It is well known that Truffaut has little interest in socio-political issues in his films. Some critics have nonetheless felt that the image he gives of the Occupation is much too mild considering the horrors of the Holocaust. What do you think about that? **Do you feel that Truffaut gives a false image of the period he represents in his film?** What aspects of the Occupation, and in particular the situation of the Jewish population during this time, did you note in the film? **Why, in your opinion, are there so few Germans in *The Last Metro*?** What might that imply regarding the greatest source of danger for Parisians during the Occupation?

Truffaut himself asserted, "the Occupation is not a theme in and of itself but simply a background" ("Pourquoi" 4). **If this is the case, what does this "background" contribute to the film in particular?**

12. The Performing Arts and the Collaboration

Jean-Loup receives a little black casket with a noose inside. This is how the French Resistance put on notice those that it suspected of collaborating with the Nazis. At the Liberation, the "purification committees" criticized certain directors and actors, such as Sacha Guitry, Marcel Carné, Jean Cocteau, and Pierre Fresnay, for "collaborating" with the enemy by continuing to exercise their profession during the Occupation. **How do you feel about that? Should people in the performing arts have refused to practice their trade to protest against the presence of the occupiers? Or were they right, on the contrary, to contribute to the survival of French culture and provide the French people a means of entertainment despite the Occupation?**

A former theater director under the Occupation speaks frankly of the "compromise" that was necessary to enable a theater to survive during this period (Voisin). And Truffaut adds, "Deneuve and Depardieu embody antiheroes, compromised characters, because during the Occupation people just had to live with compromise" (Gillain, "Cinéma" 399). **How do you interpret these statements?**

François Truffaut's Filmography

1958   *The Brats (Les Mistons, short subject)*

1959   *The 400 Blows (Les Quatre Cents Coups)*

1960   *Shoot the Piano Player (Tirez sur le pianiste)*

1962   *Antoine et Colette (second episode of the Doinel cycle, short subject in the collective film, Love at Twenty [L'Amour à vingt ans])*

1962 *Jules and Jim*

1964 *Soft Skin (La Peau douce)*

1966 *Fahrenheit 451*

1967 *The Bride Wore Black (La Mariée était en noir)*

1968 *Stolen Kisses (Baisers volés, third episode of the Doinel cycle)*

1969 *Mississippi Mermaid (La Sirène du Mississippi)*

1970 *Bed & Board (Domicile conjugal, fourth episode of the Doinel cycle)*

1970 *The Wild Child (L'Enfant sauvage)*

1971 *The Two Englishwomen and the Continent (Les Deux Anglaises et le continent)*

1972 *A Beautiful Girl like Me (Une belle fille comme moi)*

1973 *Day for Night (La Nuit américaine)*

1975 *Histoire d'Adèle H.*

1976 *Small Change (L'Argent de poche)*

1977 *The Man Who Loved Women (L'Homme qui aimait les femmes)*

1978 *The Green Room (La Chambre verte)*

1979 *Love in Flight (L'Amour en fuite, end of the Antoine Doinel cycle)*

1980 *The Last Metro (Le Dernier Métro)*

1981 *The Woman Next Door (La Femme d'à côté)*

1983 *Confidentially Yours (Vivement Dimanche)*

Works Consulted

Affron, Mirella Jona, and E. Rubinstein, eds. *The Last Metro*. New Brunswick, NJ: Rutgers UP, 1985.

Babert, Caroline. "Heinz Bennent le saltimbanque." *Le Matin*, 20 Sept. 1980: 26.

Baignères, Claude. "En ce temps-là . . . ." *Le Figaro*, 17 Sept. 1980: n. pag.

Bazin, André. *Le Cinéma de l'Occupation et de la Résistance*. Preface by François Truffaut. Paris: Union générale des éditions, 1975.

Billard, Pierre. "Truffaut sans restriction." *Le Point*, 15 Sept. 1980: 129–30.

Boujut, Michel. "L'auteur du *Dernier Métro*: 'Je suis un cinéaste de l'extrême centre'!" *Nouvelles littéraires* (18 Sept. 1980): 45.

Bouteiller, Pierre. "Entre chagrin et pitié." *Le Quotidien*, 19 Sept. 1980: n. pag.

Cervoni, Albert. "Le théâtre dans le film. *Le Dernier Métro* de François Truffaut." *L'Humanité*, 17 Sept. 1980: n. pag.

De Baecque, Antoine, and Serge Toubiana. *François Truffaut*. 2nd ed. Paris: Gallimard, 2001 (original edition 1996).

Delain, Michel. "Truffaut: théâtre, mon amour." *L'Express*, 20–26 Sept. 1980: n. pag.

Fechner, Elisabeth. "Le dernier métro des années noires." *VSD*, 11 Sept. 1980: n. pag.

Fonvieille Alquier, F. "Les deux réponses." *Nouvelles littéraires*, 18 Sept. 1980: 44.

Frodon, Jean-Michel. "Le Dernier Métro. An Underground Golden Coach." *A Companion to François Truffaut*. Ed. Dudley Andrew and Anne Gillain. Oxford: Blackwell, 2013. 571–83.

Gillain, Anne. *Le Cinéma selon François Truffaut*. Paris: Flammarion, 1988.

———. *Le Secret perdu*. Paris: Hatier, 1991.

Hamel, Bernard. "Le Dernier Métro . . . et le Premier Truffaut." *La Nouvelle République du Centre Ouest*, 26 Sept. 1980: n. pag.

Hanoteau, Guillaume. "Dans son *Dernier Métro* Truffaut ressuscite Alain Laubreaux qui pendant l'Occupation terrorisait le théâtre." *Journal du dimanche*, 28 Sept. 1980: n. pag.

Higgins, Lynn A. *New Novel, New Wave, New Politics*. Lincoln: U of Nebraska P, 1996.

Holmes, Diana, and Robert Ingram. *François Truffaut*. Manchester, England: Manchester UP, 1998.

Insdorf, Annette. "How Truffaut's *The Last Metro* Reflects Occupied Paris." *François Truffaut. Interviews*. Ed. Ronald Bergan. Jackson: UP of Mississippi, 2008. 142–46.

Lachize, Samuel. "Conversation avec François Truffaut." *L'Humanité Dimanche*, 26 Sept. 1980: n. pag.

Le Berre, Carole. *François Truffaut au travail*. Paris: Cahiers du cinéma, 2004.

Léon, Céline. "Truffaut: la disparue du *Dernier Métro* et de *Jules et Jim*." *The French Review* 84.1 (Oct. 2010): 82–98.

Milhaud, Sylvie. "Poiret n'a pas raté son dernier métro." *Les Nouvelles littéraires*, 25 Sept. 1980: n. pag.

Montaigne, Pierre. "François Truffaut le sourire de la nostalgie." *Le Figaro*, 13–14 Sept. 1980: n. pag.

———. "Truffaut: métro, boulot, huis clos." *Le Figaro*, 25 Feb. 1980: n. pag.

Paxton, Robert O. *La France de Vichy 1940–1944*. Paris: Seuil, 1973.

Pérez, Michel. "*Le Dernier Métro* de François Truffaut." *Le Matin*, 17 Sept. 1980: n. pag.

Prost, Antoine. *Petite Histoire de la France au XXe Siècle*. Paris: A. Colin, 1979.

Rochu, Gilbert. "Jules et Jim sous l'Occupation, version théâtre filmé." *Libération*, 17 Sept. 1980: n. pag.

Salachas, Gilbert. "*Le Dernier Métro*. Les quatre cents coups d'un théâtre sous l'Occupation." *Télérama*, 17 Sept. 1980: n. pag.

Siclier, Jacques. "Le Théâtre des années noires." *Le Monde*, 18 Sept. 1980: n. pag.

Smith, Alan K. "Incorporating Images in Film: Truffaut and Emblems of Death." *Mosaic: A Journal for the Interdisciplinary Study of Literature* 32.2 (June 1999): 107–22.

"Le Théâtre français sous l'Occupation." Web. 4 Jan. 2014. <Theatrefrancais-tpe.blogs pot.com>.

Toubiana, Serge. "Les passions avant le couvre-feu." *Libération*, 17 Sept. 1980: n. pag.

Truffaut, François, dir. *Le Dernier Métro*. Alliance Atlantis Vivafilm (Canada), 2005.

———. "Pourquoi et comment *Le Dernier métro?*" *L'Avant-Scène Cinéma* 303–4 (1–15 Mar. 1983): 3–9.

Voisin, François. "Quand spectateurs et comédiens prenaient 'le dernier métro.'" *Le Matin*, 4 Oct. 1980: n. pag.

2

Louis Malle

Goodbye, Children
(Au revoir les enfants)

(1987)

Louis Malle, *Goodbye, Children*: The children at the Saint-Jean-de-la-Croix middle school during the Occupation.

Director.	Louis Malle
Screenplay.	Louis Malle
Director of Photography	Renato Berta
Sound	Jean-Claude Laureux
Film Editor.	Emmanuelle Castro
Music.	Franz Schubert, Camille Saint-Saëns
Art Director	Willy Holt
Costumes	Corinne Jorry
Continuity	France La Chapelle
Producer	Marin Karmitz
Length	1h43

Cast

Gaspard Manesse (*Julien Quentin*), Raphaël Fejtö (*Jean Bonnet/Kippelstein*), Francine Racette (*Mrs. Quentin*), Stanislas Carré de Malberg (*François Quentin*), Philippe Morier-Genoud (*Father Jean*), François Berléand (*Father Michel*), François Négret (*Joseph*), Peter Fitz (*Herr Müller*)

Story

Winter 1944, during the Occupation. Julien Quentin, eleven years old, is taking leave of his mother with a heavy heart to go back to the Catholic middle school where he is a boarder. A harsh, disciplined life is waiting for him there: mass on an empty stomach early in the morning, washing up with cold water, vitamin-enriched biscuits to make up for nutritional deficiencies, and, for this introspective boy who loves books, not a single spot to read in peace except in bed at night—with a flashlight.

This year Julien's life is about to change with the arrival of three new students, among them Jean Bonnet, his dormitory room neighbor. Jean is nice and loves books too, but Julien, the top student in his class, finds him a little too brilliant for his taste, and Jean also acts weird at the refectory and at prayer and does not like to talk about himself. A mystery to solve for Julien, who is a born detective!

The two boys are going to play cat and mouse for a while before getting to know each other. The fear they share during a treasure hunt in the forest at night will bring them closer . . . and remind them that war is in full swing beyond the walls of the boarding school. One day, the Gestapo storms into the classroom unannounced. . . .

The Director

Louis Malle, born in 1932, is one of the most prolific directors of the second half of the twentieth century. Like Julien, one of the two protagonists of *Goodbye, Children*, he comes from a Parisian upper-middle-class Catholic family. During the Second World War his parents sent him to the Avon middle school near Fontainebleau, where he had an experience that changed his life: the head priest of the school and three of his classmates were arrested by the Gestapo. Malle explains that his desire to become a film-maker stems back to this event: "I told my parents, shortly afterwards, that I wanted to make movies. They were shocked. I don't know if it was a rational decision on my part, but I really wanted to find a path, a job, a position that would allow me to look for a certain truth, to investigate" (Heymann, "Entretien").

After studying business and political science, he attended the film school Institut des Hautes Etudes Cinématographiques (IDHEC) in 1951–52 and then started his film career as an assistant to Jacques Cousteau in 1952–55. In tandem with Cousteau he made his first documentary, *The Silent World* (*Le Monde du silence*), which won the Palme d'Or, the highest prize at the Cannes Film Festival, in 1956. Subsequently, Louis Malle built an eclectic oeuvre that includes around forty short and feature-length films, a veritable "patchwork of situations and genres" (Péretié 105). Indeed, starting with his early films he worked in all genres: the crime thriller (*Elevator to the Gallows* [*Ascenseur pour l'échafaud*], Louis-Delluc Prize in 1957), drama (*The Lovers* [*Les Amants*, 1958]; *A Very Private Affair* [*Vie privée*, 1962]; *The Fire Within* [*Le Feu follet*, 1963]), comedy

(*Zazie dans le métro*, 1960), and the musical (*Viva Maria!*, 1965, which he considers his only entertainment film). He also made two acclaimed documentaries during a trip to India in 1969, *Calcutta* (three nominations at the Cannes Festival) and *Phantom India* (*L'Inde fantôme*). Back in France he proceeded to make *Murmur of the Heart* (*Le Souffle au cœur*, 1970), which received two nominations at Cannes, and *Lacombe, Lucien* (1974), two films that confirmed his reputation as a scandalous filmmaker. Indeed, his films shocked bourgeois, Catholic, conservative France. *The Lovers* portrays an adulterous middle-class woman and *Zazie*, an outspoken teenager; *Murmur of the Heart* deals with incest between a mother and son, and Malle films a French Nazi collaborator in *Lacombe, Lucien*, at a time when the myth of "*résistancialisme*" still prevailed—the theory that most of the French had supported the Resistance during the Occupation.

Lacombe, Lucien received a nomination for the Oscar for Best Foreign Language Film and two nominations for the BAFTA awards in Great Britain, but its negative reception in France, combined with a desire to expand his world, led Louis Malle to try his luck in the United States. He met considerable success there with *Pretty Baby* (1978), a film about child prostitution that was nominated for four awards at Cannes, *Atlantic City* (1980), a film noir about an old disillusioned gangster, and *My Dinner with Andre* (*Mon dîner avec André*, 1981), a long conversation between two friends. *Atlantic City* was his greatest hit in America, garnering nominations at the Oscars and the Golden Globes. It also won the Best Director Award at the BAFTAs and the Golden Lion at the Venice Film Festival.

Malle's enthusiasm for America started to wane when he undertook a studio film, *Crackers* (1985), another gangster film that, along with *Alamo Bay* (1983), the story of Vietnamese immigrants in a small fishing town in Texas, was a complete flop. Utterly disgusted by Hollywood cinema, which he considered to be "in a deplorable state, corrupted by merchants, obsessed by the high-concept film, the 'formula,'" and where "the director is reduced to nothing" (Heymann, "Entretien"), Malle decided to go back to France after about a decade in the United States. With thirty years of experience as a director behind him, Malle was ready to make the movie whose context had triggered his desire to become a filmmaker, *Goodbye, Children* (1987). This film, the peak of his career, would be followed by three other successful features, *May Fools* (*Milou en mai*, 1990), about a carefree family reunion gone bad at the time of the events of May 1968, *Damage* (*Fatale*, 1992), a politico-erotic drama, and *Vanya on 42nd Street* (*Vanya, 42e rue*, 1995), which depicts the production of a play by Chekhov at a New York theater.

A contemporary of the filmmakers of the New Wave, Louis Malle shared their "immense admiration for American cinema and their desire to make films that were closer to real life," but he considered himself on the fringes of this movement. As he explained, "Cliques have never been my thing," and it is known that he had a predilection for the directors of the "tradition of quality" in French cinema who were vilified by Truffaut and his cohort of critics at the *Cahiers du cinéma*, filmmakers like Autant-Lara, Clément, and Clouzot (Schidlow 20). Daniel Toscan du Plantier, then President of the *Académie des arts et techniques du cinéma* (the French Motion Picture Academy), nevertheless considered Malle the worthy successor of Truffaut at the helm of French cinema. He applauded his decision to come back to France thus: "The very day when François Truffaut died [in 1984], I told [Malle] how much we needed him: a leader had fallen, he alone could take his place, the top one. He has done it" (Toscan du Plantier).

The Origin and Making of the Film

Louis Malle had mulled over the idea of *Goodbye, Children* for a long time, but he could not bring himself to make the film because the memory of the arrest and deportation of his classmates by the Gestapo was too painful. He considered including this story as the prologue of *Lacombe, Lucien* (1974), his other film set during the Occupation, but he was not ready. "Making this film took me a long time," he explained in an interview. "I was full of anxiety when I made it, and terribly afraid to fail [. . .]. It could have been my first film because it was based on the most vivid, the most indelible memory of my childhood, but I was probably not mature enough" (Tranchant). According to Péretié, Malle began taking notes to avoid being bored on Sundays in the small fishing town where he was shooting *Alamo Bay* (105). It soon became obvious to him that he had to go back to France to make the film. He wrote the first draft of his screenplay in ten days without listening to the reservations of his French friends, who thought that he was out of touch with his native country, and that the Occupation and the Holocaust were no longer popular at the movies. Ironically, several events revived the interest of the public in this dark period before the film was released, as we will see in "The Reception" below.

Like Truffaut in *The 400 Blows* and *The Last Metro*, Malle found inspiration for his screenplay in his childhood memories, but he also left a lot up to his imagination. The characters and the story are based on reality. Julien has a lot in common with the director, as Malle recalls: "I was raised like Julien in the film. Like him I went to mass [. . .]. Like him I dreamed of great callings and said that I wanted to become a missionary in the Congo" (Heymann, "Entretien"). Like Julien, Malle was a good student, and he felt that his prestige was threatened by Hans-Helmut Michel (Jean Bonnet in the film), a tall, multi-talented young man who shared his passion for music and literature. On the other hand, Malle did not know that his classmate was Jewish, and he did not have time to become friends with him before his arrest, something he felt guilty about later. He admitted that, as a result, he took some liberties with the story of their friendship and imagined "how I would have liked things to happen" (Audé 34). Toward the end of the film, he also added Julien's gaze that revealed Bonnet's Jewish identity to Herr Müller. In fact, Malle felt so guilty about this fateful event that he believed for years that the scene had occurred this way until he realized after talking with other witnesses that his imagination had deceived him (Toubiana 22).

The other important characters (Father Jean, Joseph, Mrs. Quentin, François, Herr Müller) are also based on real people. The middle-school students were mean to the kitchen boy, as in the film, but Malle added his own touch by turning Joseph into an informer. In fact, no one ever found out who had betrayed the Jewish children and the school principal to the Gestapo (Pascaud). Malle paid attention to other sociological features that he considered the most accurate aspect of the film. He carefully portrayed the middle class, epitomized for the most part by Julien's mother, and he laced his story with references to the Occupation period (some of which will be clarified below in "The Occupation in *Goodbye, Children*").

The shoot took place from January to March 1987 in a middle school that was in session, the Sainte-Croix institution in Provins, in the Seine-et-Marne department east of Paris. Malle wanted a film shot in low light and cold tones, without sun (Toubiana 22), and he instructed the costume designer not to use warm colors in order to stay faithful to the hostile environment he remembered. Fortunately for him the weather cooperated. The temperature fell below -12° (10°F), and the children went back to school after the takes completely frozen!

Louis Malle admits that he was anxious during the shoot because it brought back painful memories of his past, but retrospectively he was satisfied with the experience. He liked working with children—whom he sometimes asked to rehearse a scene up to ten times—and he was moved to tears when the actor portraying Bonnet was able to follow his instructions and look Herr Müller in the eye for fifteen seconds. It was the first time, he said, that he had felt so much emotion on a shoot (Péretié 106). Finally it is worth noting that the art director Willy Holt, who won the César Award for Best Production Design for this film, was a former Resistance fighter who had been arrested by the Gestapo in 1943 and deported to Auschwitz, like the Jewish children in the movie.

The Actors

Louis Malle wanted to work with unknowns to increase the authenticity of his film. He received 3,000 applications for the children's roles but fairly quickly cast the actor who portrays Julien (Gaspard Manesse), who impressed him with his liveliness and intelligence. For his two leads, he was looking for a striking gaze rather than a physical resemblance, and Manesse's immediately reminded him of his childhood: "He looked at me, and I felt eleven again" (Attali). Malle hired locals to play the adults in the film, for example the principal of the Collège Sainte-Croix as the physical education teacher.

The director also turned to a few professionals. Francine Racette, a Canadian actress cast as Julien's mother, had played in a few films and received a nomination for the César for Best Actress in a Supporting Role in Jeanne Moreau's *Lumière* (1977). François Négret (Joseph) had already acted in three films. He was nominated for the César Award for Most Promising Actor for his performance in *Goodbye, Children*. François Berléand (Father Michel) also appears in the film. He is a well-known theater and film actor who has won several prizes and nominations.

The Reception

Goodbye, Children was a popular and critical hit. With more than 3.6 million tickets sold, it belongs to the five or six French films that attract more than two million spectators every year. It earned seven Césars, including for Best Film and Best Director, the Louis-Delluc Prize, the Golden Lion at the Venice Film Festival, and the British BAFTA for Best Director. It also received many nominations, including for Best Foreign Language Film at the Golden Globes and the Oscars.

Everyone agrees that *Goodbye, Children* is Malle's best work, "a great auteur film, a masterpiece that raises the reputation of French cinema to great heights" (Toscan du Plantier), "one of his most beautiful films, perhaps the most perfect" (Chazal). The critics praise above all the personal side of the story, which they find deeply moving. For Baignères, "This film is not only an all-time cinematographic masterpiece; with its depth, its emotion, its sobriety, it is also a story that ranks first among the most fundamental expressions of the human heart and spirit." As in this last comment, the words "emotion," "sobriety," "heart" abound in reviews of the film, together with "restraint," "modesty," "moving," and "poignant."

Most critics laud the depiction of adolescence and the natural and authentic performance of the actors, but a few disagree and criticize "all these clichés about childhood, from the age-old fights in the courtyard to the obligatory discussions on women" (Bernard), as well as Bonnet's portrayal, a little too perfect for their taste. Malle is also blamed for having his characters act and speak like rebellious teenagers at the end of the twentieth century (Pérez, "Un heureux retour"), to which the director responds that "middle-class boys were not afraid of cursing" in the period depicted, even though their straight-talk was rarely heard in the movies (Gasperi).

The critics also commend the film for its excellent representation of history. It is "the strongest and most truthful testimony on the Occupation and its persecutions," notes Elgey, a historian. Malle is praised for describing the tragedy without pathos by intensifying the threatening atmosphere and the vague fear that surround Julien's gradual discovery of Jean's identity. Critics laud Malle for his gift of observation, "his realistic details, and his patient re-enactment of atmosphere" (Toubiana 20). For Maupin, "Louis Malle is truly one of the few French filmmakers who uses the camera like a surgical knife. He has never refrained from broaching topics that others have kept under the rug [like incest or collaboration with the Nazis]." Several critics make positive references, we note, to *Lacombe, Lucien* (1974), his story of a young French collaborator, even though they prefer the more nuanced message of *Goodbye, Children*. Elgey, for example, prefers the characters' complex motivations in the latter film: "In *Goodbye, Children* [...] we find everything, madness, cowardice, courage, abjection, heroism [...]. No civics course can match its beauty and efficiency."

The public and critical interest in *Goodbye, Children* increased sharply owing to several events that happened between the end of the shoot in March 1987 and the release of the film at the beginning of October. Klaus Barbie, head of the Gestapo in Lyon during the Occupation, was tried from May to July and found guilty of crimes against humanity for the deportation of hundreds of French Jews. During the trial of "the butcher of Lyon," as he came to be known, the television channel TF1 scheduled for the first time a screening of *Shoah* (1985), Claude Lanzmann's acclaimed documentary on the extermination of the Jews, which drew millions of viewers. This period also saw the rise of "negationism," cultivated by revisionist historians who refuted the existence of the Jewish genocide by Nazi Germany.

Given this context, it comes as no surprise that people went to see *Goodbye, Children* in droves, and that the press evaluated the film in light of the contemporary situation. For Jamet, Malle "responds to revisionist lies and reminds us of the crime. This film was not just necessary, it was urgently needed." Garcia, for his part, sees in the film "France's retrospective look, at the time of the Barbie trial, at its past attitude toward collaboration and the deportation of Jews." For Macia, "*Goodbye, Children* is as essential as *Shoah*, relatively speaking, for our collective memory, which has been attacked of late by lesser [revisionist] historians." The reviews of the film sometimes include stories of people who witnessed the roundups or survived the camps. Gastellier, for example, quotes a testimony by Maurice (Moreau in the film), who explains how he managed to escape the Gestapo by hiding in an attic.

The Occupation in *Goodbye, Children*

The story of *Goodbye, Children* takes place during three weeks in January 1944, toward the end of the Occupation. Eager to stay true to history, Malle depicted the attitude of the population toward contemporary events through small details in the children's games and conversations. They repeat their parents' opinions in favor of De Gaulle or, more often, Pétain. When they come back from the public baths, for example, some are heard to say that "if we didn't have Pétain, we would be in deep shit" or that "Jews and communists are much more dangerous than Germans." Like most members of the upper middle class, Malle's parents supported Pétain. It makes sense, then, that Julien should start singing "Marshal, here we are," a patriotic song honoring Pétain, to overcome his fear when he and Jean are lost in the forest.

The Catholic bourgeoisie backed Pétain largely because of his opposition to the Popular Front, a left-wing coalition government that had ruled France in 1936–38. French people on the political right disapproved of the social policies of this government and held it responsible for France's moral decline and defeat in 1940. In particular, they felt a strong hatred for Léon Blum, the head of the Popular Front government, who moreover was Jewish (he was sentenced to prison under the Vichy Regime and transferred to a German prison in March 1943). Julien's mother says about him at the restaurant, "Note that I have nothing against Jews—except for Léon Blum, of course. They can go hang that guy!"

Malle reveals that middle-class support for the Vichy government had already declined at the time of the events shown in the film. When François asks his mother if his father still sides with Pétain, she replies, "No one supports Pétain anymore!" We also hear children say that "Pétain is senile" and Laval (Pétain's Prime Minister) "has sold out to the Germans." Indeed, many French people did not agree with the policy of collaboration with Germany, which required that France assist the occupying forces in identifying and deporting Jews and supply French workers to support the German war effort. The French Militia, a Nazi-associated paramilitary group created in 1943, took part in these initiatives by helping the Gestapo track down Jews, Resistance fighters, and those who tried to avoid the Compulsory Work Service (Service du Travail Obligatoire, or STO), the enlistment of twenty- to twenty-three-year-olds as forced labor for Germany. In the film Moreau, the schoolyard supervisor, is in hiding because he refuses to join the STO, and we see the black-uniformed Militia twice, in the courtyard and at the restaurant.

In January 1944, when the story takes place, the Allied forces had reconquered North Africa (which was then French), and the Soviet allies were advancing on the Eastern Front, as the math teacher explains to his students by pinning small flags on a map. The Allied forces were about to invade France—D-Day would take place six months later—and they were intensifying their strategic strikes on industrial sites around Paris, which had been requisitioned by Germany. Mrs. Quentin refers to these bombings in a letter to Julien, and the students have to seek shelter on several occasions to avoid them.

To retaliate against these enemy advances as early as 1942, Germany increased its tracking down of Jews by imposing additional restrictions (including the mandatory display of the yellow star, worn by a man who is coming out of the public baths in the film) and by organizing roundups (*rafles*). After the surrender of Italy in September 1943, German troops had also invaded the Free Zone, until then theoretically under Vichy control, occupying most of French territory by January 1944, the period of the film. This is why Julien responds, "There's no more free zone!" when Jean tells him that his own mother is safe in Marseilles. At the end of the war, living conditions were more and more difficult, and the French had to use ration tickets to buy food (as at the restaurant in the film) and other necessities. To find a way around these restrictions or to take advantage of the situation, some used the black market—like Joseph, who sold back the provisions that he stole from the school and the food items that the students exchanged with him.

Finally the film calls for a few remarks on the attitude of the Catholic Church toward the Vichy Regime and the Holocaust. The Church remained relatively silent about the extermination of Jews, and French bishops actively supported the Vichy government. But some priests, like Father Jean in the film, criticized the policies of Vichy in their sermons and opposed them by hiding Jewish children. His model in real life, Father Jacques de Jésus, the founder of the middle school that Malle attended, also belonged to a Resistance network. In June 1985, he was awarded the Medal of the Righteous, an honor bestowed by the State of Israel on those who put their lives in danger to save Jews.

STUDY GUIDE

What Happens in This Film?

1. In what city does the first scene take place, and where specifically? Where is Julien going, and how does he feel?

2. At the middle school, what do the children have to do every morning before breakfast?

3. Why is the math class interrupted?

4. What does Joseph, the kitchen boy, do for the students? How do they behave toward him?

5. Why is Julien intrigued by Jean, the new student, and what does he discover a little later when he rummages through his locker?

6. What were the children doing in the forest? What happened? How did the two boys get back to the school?

7. Why did Jean and Julien fight in the infirmary?

8. Why did one of the parents leave the chapel during Father Jean's sermon?

9. What happened at the restaurant?

10. What film did the children and adults watch together?

11. Why did Father Jean dismiss Joseph, and how did he explain this decision to the children?

12. How did the Gestapo learn that Jewish students were hidden at the school?

True or False?

If the statement is false, correct it!

1. As he is about to get on the train at the beginning of the film, Julien tells his mother how much he loves her.

2. The children reenact the wars of religion between Muslims and Christians when they play on stilts in the schoolyard.

3. At the boarding school the children are allowed to eat the provisions sent by their families without sharing them with the other students.

4. The big boys taunt Joseph by making fun of a photo of his mother.

5. Jean is jealous of Julien because his gift for playing the piano attracted the attention of the music teacher.

6. In his office Father Jean encourages Julien to pursue his desire to become a priest.

7. When they are together, Jean and Julien like to talk about the political situation and Marshal Pétain.

8. When the children ask Bonnet why is he not preparing for his (Catholic) confirmation, he replies that he is too young.

9. Mrs. Quentin ate fish in a white butter sauce at the restaurant.

10. The militiamen left the restaurant because a Jew was dining there.

11. One of the Jewish children managed to escape the Gestapo by fleeing by the roof.

12. At the end of the film we hear the director explain in voice-over that forty years have passed since this tragic episode of his childhood.

What Did You Learn in the Introduction?

1. What event inspired Malle to become a filmmaker?

2. Why did some of his films create a scandal?

3. What did Malle achieve during the time he spent in the United States, and why did he go back to France?

4. Why did Malle wait about forty years before making *Goodbye, Children*?

5. What did Malle like about the actor whom he cast as Julien?

6. Where does *Goodbye, Children* rank in Louis Malle's filmography?

7. What aspects of the film were particularly praised by critics?

8. To which other film by Malle was *Goodbye, Children* compared? Who is the protagonist of this other film?

9. What events renewed public interest in the Occupation and the Shoah when Malle was making *Goodbye, Children*?

10. Why did the pro-Pétain French middle class hate the Popular Front and Léon Blum?

11. How did the Vichy government collaborate with Nazi Germany?

12. What did some priests do to oppose the support of the Catholic Church for the Vichy Regime during the Occupation period?

Exploring the Film

1. The Prologue

Review the opening sequence (Excerpt 1, 00'00–3'20). How do you know that the scene at the train station takes place during the Occupation?

What do we learn about Julien's family and social class? Why does Julien address his mother with "vous" (you) instead of the less formal "tu"? Why does he tell his mother that he hates her? What is the true relationship between Julien and his mother? What does François insinuate when he tells his mother to be good?

2. The Setting: A Catholic Boarding School during the Occupation

Louis Malle said during an interview: "It was important for me that the story start like a mere chronicle of the period, to show what it was like being a child at the time, at a middle school. And then that it turn into a drama" (Audé 35). He also said about the relationships between children in the middle school that he attended that "there was a near Darwinian notion of the power relations in a social group; they let the stronger ones have their way. There were victims and persecutors" (Audé 33). Did he manage to show this in his film?

What impact do the Occupation and the war have on life at the school?

Discuss how the children's Catholic background influences their games and their conversations. What is their attitude toward other religions? What historical events do they allude to when they play on stilts? *Review the battle scene on the playground* (Excerpt 2, 11'50–13'20). Whom does Laviron represent? Why did Malle cast Négus/Lafarge as the Muslim black knight? (Note that Laviron uses the pejorative word "moricaud" instead of "noir" (black) to address Négus.) Which character do the majority of the children cheer for? Were you surprised by the priests' hands-off attitude in this scene?

How does one of the children behave toward Jean after he made them believe that he was Protestant?

How can we consider the school a microcosm of French society during World War II?

3. The Characters

✦ Julien Quentin

Describe Julien's personality and interests. What embarrassing problem does Julien have at night sometimes? Why do you think Malle included this in the film?

How does Julien's life change when Jean arrives at the school? What are Julien's initial feelings toward his classmate? What does he learn through his interactions with him?

Malle suggests a similarity between Julien and Sherlock Holmes, whom the two protagonists consider to be one of their heroes, when he depicts his gradual discovering of Jean's identity. **How does Malle foreground Julien's curiosity, and what clues help the boy solve the mystery surrounding Jean?**

✦ Jean Bonnet/Kippelstein

What do we know about Jean's life prior to his arrival at the school? How does his behavior show that his past life was difficult? **Through his character, how does Malle make us understand what it meant to be Jewish at that time?**

Describe some of the ways in which the students behave toward him. How do you explain their hostility? Is it because he is a new student, or do you agree with Southern's suggestion that Jean's attitude invites persecution (269)?

How do you interpret his attempt to take Communion?

✦ Jean and Julien

What do the two boys have in common? **How does Malle show the development of their friendship?** (What scenes are important in this regard?) What role does music play in the evolution of their relationship?

✦ Father Jean

In general, how does Father Jean treat the students?

What ideas does he express in the sermon that the parents attend? *Review the sermon scene* (Excerpt 3, 1h02'00–1h04'00).

Father Jean fired Joseph because he stole provisions from the school and sold them on the black market. **Were Joseph's actions more reprehensible than the students'?** How were *they* punished? Do you think there is a double standard here? If yes, how do you explain Father Jean's behavior?

In your opinion, why does Father Jean refuse to give Communion to Jean Bonnet? This decision was interpreted variously as a moral mistake on his part (Higgins) or, on the contrary, as a sign of integrity, especially since some of the priests who protected Jewish children during the Occupation tried to convert them (Craft-Fairchild 84). **Which interpretation appeals to you the most?**

Malle, who admitted harboring "long-held anticlerical feelings," said that in *Goodbye, Children* he showed for the first time "priests that were admirable" because this was true to his experience in real life, even though he was aware that part of the clergy had collaborated (Audé 35). How are the priests in this school admirable?

+ *Joseph*

What social class does he come from? How do the students treat him? *Review one of the scenes between Joseph and the students* (Excerpt 4, 16'55–18'35). In this sequence, why does he tell Julien, "You are a real Jew, you know"? What anti-Semitic stereotype does this comment reveal?

It is clear that Joseph is the person who betrayed Father Jean to the German authorities. Malle said in an interview that he prefers to try to understand rather than condemn people that he disapproves of, like Joseph (Schidlow 19). **How is Joseph depicted in the film?** Is he a likeable or unpleasant character? How do you judge him?

+ *Mrs. Quentin*

Mrs. Quentin is inspired by the filmmaker's mother, but Malle has often reiterated that she is different from his mother in several ways. With this character, he wanted above all to portray a woman who belonged to the Catholic middle class of the time. **Where does Mrs. Quentin stand politically?**

As we have already seen, Malle focuses on the relationship between Julien and his mother in the first scene of the film. One of his previous films, *Murmur of the Heart* (1971), had created a scandal because it depicted an incestuous relationship between a mother and her son. Critics saw in *Goodbye, Children* a reminder of Malle's interest in mother-son relationships, but "without the blasphemous emphasis on the oedipal feelings" (Benayoun). Do you agree with the critical opinion here? **When viewing the film, did you find Julien's relationship with this mother unhealthy? Justify your opinion.**

+ *François Quentin*

How does François differ from his brother Julien? Does he have the same type of relationship with their mother?

When Julien questions him about Jews, François replies by citing a popular cliché about Jews among French people. What is this cliché, and what does Julien think about it? *Review their conversation* (Excerpt 5, 47'00–47'45). What is Malle's intention in inserting this dialogue?

What is François' attitude toward the Vichy Regime and the Germans?

+ *The Germans*

Malle said in an interview, "It's very ironic. It seems to me that many of the Germans who were in France were not very influenced by Nazi ideology" (Audé 33). Is this opinion perceptible in the way he represents the Germans in the film? **How are the German characters depicted** in the scene at the public baths, in the episodes in the forest and at the restaurant, and in the scene where the children are arrested at the end of the film?

4. The Sequence at the Public Baths

Review the sequence at the public baths (Excerpt 6, 32'40–35'25). What do we learn about the situation of the Jews at that time (at the end of the sequence)? In addition to this general context, what threats hang over Jean in this scene?

Whom is Julien thinking about in his bathtub?

5. The Scene of the Treasure Hunt in the Forest

How do Julien and Jean end up alone in the forest? **What do you think Julien feels in this long sequence, perhaps for the first time? What is the significance of this scene for his relationship with Jean?**

This scene is inspired by real treasure hunts in which Malle took part in middle school and that evoke bad memories. He remembers that the head priest sent the students in the forest past the curfew in order to build their character, unbeknownst to their parents (Audé 33). **How does Malle create a threatening atmosphere in this scene?** *Review this episode* (Excerpt 7, 54'00–56'30).

6. The Restaurant Scene

Review the scene at the restaurant (Excerpt 8, 1h08'35–1h11'25). Comment on the militiaman's change of attitude when he realizes that Mr. Meyer is Jewish. How does Mr. Meyer react? Why did Malle decide to have him wear a red rosette, which means that he has received the Legion of Honor, the highest French honor, bestowed on people who have rendered "eminent services" to the nation?

The waiter explains to the militiaman that Mr. Meyer has been a patron for twenty years. In the scene at the public baths (where Jews were not allowed), we see a man come out who is wearing a yellow star on his coat. What do these two scenes suggest?

How do the restaurant customers react during this incident? What does the woman mean when she screams out, "Send all the Jews to Moscow!"? What is Mrs. Quentin's opinion of the Jews and of Léon Blum in particular?

How does Malle convey the tension in the restaurant and Jean's and Julien's emotions?

Why did the German officer put an end to the situation? What outcome might one have expected instead?

What do you think of François' reaction? Is he courageous or reckless? According to Stanley Hoffmann, a political scientist, his attitude is not realistic because, given the circumstances, one would expect the guests to be scared and remain silent instead (Greene 89). How do the reactions of François and other customers affect our perception of how the French behaved during the Occupation?

How do you interpret the way Jean looks at Mrs. Quentin at the end of this sequence? Malle insisted on Mrs. Quentin wearing bright red lipstick in contrast to the subdued colors used in the rest of the film. Why do you think he made this exception?

7. The Movie Night

British and American films were banned from French screens during the Occupation, but they were distributed on the sly. The Germans had a particular aversion to Charlie Chaplin because they suspected him of being Jewish, and he had made a satirical comedy about Adolph Hitler, *The Great Dictator*, released in October 1940. Malle said that he had always loved Chaplin, the first filmmaker that made him laugh, and that he included excerpts from *The Immigrant* (1917) in his film as a form of homage (Schidlow 20). The *mise en abyme* of Chaplin's film, which depicts the voyage of European immigrants to the United States, signals the importance of this scene in the film. *Review the scene of the film screening* (Excerpt 9, 1h14'50–1h18'10).

What may have been the reasons for the priests to show *The Immigrant* to their students? When are the children particularly moved during this very funny film? When does the camera focus on the Jewish children and why, in your opinion? How is this film by Chaplin on immigration relevant to the period represented in *Goodbye, Children*?

In this scene we see the children, the priests, Joseph, and other school employees together. **What happens here that could be compared to a "religious experience"? What is Malle suggesting as to the function of cinema?**

8. The Arrest of the Jewish students

Why does Julien feel responsible for Jean's arrest?

In your opinion, why did the nurse show the Gestapo where Négus was hiding, and why did she not betray Moreau, the supervisor? *Review an excerpt of the infirmary scene* (Excerpt 10, 1h35'00–1h36'25). What (highly criticized) aspect of the behavior of the Catholic Church in France during the Occupation does this scene evoke? When the German soldier asks where the Jew is hiding, Julien replies that they have not seen anyone. Why does the German soldier respond by ordering him to drop his pants?

How does Julien react in the following scene when he understands that Joseph is the informer? *Review the final scene between Julien and Joseph* (Excerpt 11, 1h36'50–1h38'20). How has Joseph's appearance changed? What arguments does he use to justify his action? How does Malle convey Julien's state of mind here, in addition to his silence? **This scene ends on a static shot of the door that closes behind Julien after he has left without saying a single word to Joseph. What does Malle suggest by ending the scene this way?**

9. The Last Scene

Louis Malle said that he wanted to avoid pathos in his film: "I wanted a film full of modesty and restraint, which required an austere cinematography" (Tranchant). How does the *mise en scène* in the last scene (the action and the performance of the actors in particular) contribute to the "modesty" and the "restraint" that Malle mentions? *Review a part of the last scene* (Excerpt 12, 1h41'15–1h43'00).

To achieve this "austerity," Malle suppressed things that occurred in real life. For example, he explains that he and his classmates applauded when the Jewish children and the head priest left their school, but that he decided not to include the applause in the film (Tranchant). Do you think it was a good idea? How would adding applause have changed the scene?

Father Jean's last words, "Goodbye, Children, see you soon," are found in the film's title, except "see you soon." Why does he say "see you soon"? **How does the omission of these words affect the meaning of the title?**

At the end of the film there is a very slow tracking shot that ends on a close-up of Julien's face. Why does the camera move so close to him? **What is the ultimate purpose of this close-up combined with the director's voice-over?** How did you react when you heard this voice-over? In an earlier version of the screenplay Malle had included the last sentence in voice-over at the beginning of the film (Andreu). **How did the change in location affect the character of his film?**

After the three Jewish children and Father Jean have left with the German soldiers, there is a long static shot on the school gate that has remained open. What do you think Malle intended here? What does he want to emphasize?

In your opinion, **who is responsible for the tragic fate of Father Jean, Jean Bonnet, and the other Jewish children:** the Nazis? The Vichy government? Joseph? The Catholic Church? The children themselves (because they did business with Joseph)?

Louis Malle's Filmography

1955 *The Silent World (Le Monde du silence,* documentary)

1957 *Elevator to the Gallows (Ascenseur pour l'échafaud)*

1958 *The Lovers (Les Amants)*

1960 *Zazie dans le métro*

1962 *A Very Private Affair (Vie privée)*

1963 *The Fire Within (Le Feu follet)*

1965 *Viva Maria!*

1967 *The Thief of Paris (Le Voleur)*

1969 *Calcutta* (documentary)

1971 *Murmur of the Heart (Le Souffle au cœur)*

1974 *Lacombe, Lucien*

1975 *Black Moon*

1978 *Pretty Baby (La Petite)*

1980 *Atlantic City*

1981 *My Dinner with Andre (Mon dîner avec André)*

1983 *Crackers*

1985 *Alamo Bay*

1987 *Goodbye, Children (Au revoir les enfants)*

1990 *May Fools (Milou en mai)*

1992 *Damage (Fatale)*

1994 *Vanya on 42nd Street (Vanya, 42e rue)*

Works Consulted

Andreu, Anne. "Louis Malle signe son chef-d'œuvre et, déjà, les politiques rappliquent. . . ." *L'Evénement du jeudi,* 1–7 Oct. 1987: 96–97.

Attali, Danielle. "Louis Malle, le cinéma souffle au coeur." *Le Journal du dimanche,* 4 Oct. 1987: 11.

Audé, Françoise, and Jean-Pierre Jeancolas. "Entretien avec Louis Malle sur *Au revoir les enfants.*" *Positif* 320 (Oct. 1987): 32–39.

Austin, Guy. "The Occupation, Colonial Conflicts, and National Identity." *Contemporary French Cinema*. 2nd ed. Manchester, England: Manchester UP, 2008. 17–54.

Baignères, Claude. "Au plus profond de l'être." *Le Figaro*, 7 Oct. 1987: n. pag.

Benayoun, Robert. "Un ailleurs infiniment proche sur *Au revoir les enfants*." *Positif* 320 (Oct. 1987): 29–32.

Bernard, René. "L'enfance nue de Louis Malle." *L'Express*, 9 Oct. 1987: n. pag.

Chazal, Robert. "Au revoir les enfants: l'innocence assassinée." *France-Soir*, 7 Oct. 1987: n. pag.

Craft-Fairchild, Catherine. "Do We Remember? The Catholic Church and the Holocaust." *Logos: A Journal of Catholic Thought and Culture* 9.2 (2006): 68–106.

Elgey, Georgette. "Le sens du drame." *Le Quotidien de Paris*, 7 Oct. 1987: n. pag.

Garcia, Jean-Pierre. "Louis Malle: l'exil et l'enfance." *Différences* 71 (Oct. 1987): 26–27.

Gasperi, Anne de. "Le Chagrin et la piété." *Le Quotidien de Paris*, 7 Oct. 1987: n. pag.

Gastellier, Fabian. "Le seul rescapé de la rafle témoigne." *Le Quotidien de Paris*, 7 Oct. 1987: n. pag.

Greene, Naomi. "Battles for Memory: Vichy Revisited." *Landscapes of Loss: The National Past in Postwar French Cinema*. Princeton, NJ: Princeton UP, 1999. 64–97.

"Hans-Helmut Michel." *Anonymes, Justes et persécutés durant la période nazie*. Web. 21 July 2016. <http://www.ajpn.org/personne-Hans-Helmut-Michel-(Jean-Bonnet) -685.html>.

Heymann, Danièle. "L'ami perdu." *Le Monde*, 2 Sept. 1987: n. pag.

———. "Un entretien avec Louis Malle; la blessure d'une amitié perdue." *Le Monde*, 4 Oct. 1987: n. pag.

Higgins, Lynn A. "If Looks Could Kill: Louis Malle's Portraits of Collaboration." *Fascism, Aesthetics, and Culture*. Ed. Richard J. Golsan. Hanover, NH: UP of New England, 1992. 198–211.

Jamet, Dominique. "Moi, mon remords, ce fut. . . ." *Le Quotidien de Paris*, 7 Oct. 1987: n. pag.

Leclère, Marie-Françoise. "Au revoir les enfants." *Le Point*, 5 Oct. 1987: n. pag.

Lefort, Gérard. "Le malaise Malle." *Libération*, 8 Oct. 1987: n. pag.

Macia, Jean-Luc. "La mémoire brûlée." *La Croix*, 8 Oct. 1987: n. pag.

Malle, Louis, dir. *Au revoir les enfants*. Criterion Collection, 2006.

Maupin, Françoise. "Au revoir les enfants: re-bonjour Louis Malle." *Le Figaro Magazine*, 3 Oct. 1987: 36.

New, Elisa. "Good-bye, Children; Good-bye, Mary, Mother of Sorrows: The Church and the Holocaust in the Art of Louis Malle." *Prooftexts* 22 (2002): 118–40.

Pascaud, Fabienne. "Qu'avez-vous fait de mon enfance? Entretien." *Télérama*, 1 Apr. 1987: 24–25.

Péretié, Olivier. "Un petit 'détail' sans importance." *Le Nouvel Observateur*, 2 Oct. 1987: 104–6.

Pérez, Michel. "Au revoir les enfants." *Le Nouvel Observateur*, 16 Oct. 1987: n. pag.

———. "Un heureux retour aux sources." *Le Matin*, 7 Oct. 1987: 16.

Rouchy, M-E. "Louis Malle: 'Le passé m'envahit.'" *Le Matin*, 7 Oct. 1987: 16–17.

Schidlow, Joshka. "L'ami retrouvé. Entretien." *Télérama*, 7 Oct. 1987: 18–20.

Shorley, Christopher. "History, Memory and Art in Louis Malle's *Au revoir les enfants*." *The Seeing Century: Film, Vision, and Identity*. Ed. Wendy Everett. Amsterdam, Netherlands: Rodopi, 2000. 49–59.

Southern, Nathan, et al. *The Films of Louis Malle: A Critical Analysis*. Jefferson, NC: McFarland, 2006.

Toscan du Plantier, Daniel. "Louis Malle: le retour de l'enfant prodigue." *Le Figaro Magazine*, 3 Oct. 1987: 37.

Toubiana, Serge. "Regards d'enfants." *Cahiers du cinéma* 400 (Oct. 1987): 18–22.

Tranchant, Marie-Noëlle. "*Au revoir les enfants*. Louis Malle: l'œuvre d'une vie." *Le Figaro*, 7 Oct. 1987: n. pag.

3

Claire Denis

Chocolat

(1988)

Claire Denis, *Chocolat*: France as a child (Cécile Ducasse) and Protée the houseboy (Isaach de Bankolé) in Cameroon.

Director. . . . . .Claire Denis
Screenplay. . . . . Claire Denis, Jean-Pôl Fargeau
Director of Photography . . . . .Robert Alazraki
Camera Operator . . . . Agnès Godard
Sound . . . . Dominique Hennequin, Jean-Louis Ughetto
Film Editor. . . . . Claudine Merlin
Music. . . . . .Abdullah Ibrahim
Art Director. . . . . .Thierry Flamand
Producer . . . . Marin Karmitz
Length. 1h45

Cast

Mireille Perrier (*France as an adult*), Emmet Judson Williamson (*Mungo Park*), Isaach de Bankolé (*Protée*), Cécile Ducasse (*France as a child*), Guilia Boschi (*Aimée Dalens*), François Cluzet (*Marc Dalens*), Jean-Claude Adelin (*Luc*), Jacques Denis (*Joseph Delpich, the coffee planter*), Kenneth Cranham (*Jonathan Boothby, the Dalens' English friend*), Didier Flamand (*Captain Védrine*), Jean-Quentin Châtelain (*Courbassol, the navigator*), Laurent Arnal (*Machinard, the colonial administrator*), Emmanuelle Chaulet (*Mireille Machinard*), Jean Bediebe (*Prosper, the African doctor*), Clementine Essono (*Marie-Jeanne*), Essindi Mindja (*Blaise*)

Story

France, around thirty years old, goes back to Cameroon where she lived with her parents before independence. After a few days in the south, she plans to travel by plane to her childhood home, far off in the bush in the northern part of the country. A black man and his son whom she met by chance offer to drive her to the airport.

In the car that is taking her toward Douala, France remembers her life as a child, punctuated by the long absences of her father, a colonial administrator, during which she and her mother tilled the dry soil of their garden, paid visits under a scorching sun, and spent many tense nights listening to the hyenas nearby. A solitary life brightened by the presence of Protée, the handsome, faithful servant who asked her riddles and graciously participated in her games, humoring her authoritarian ways that mimicked the attitudes of her elders.

France also remembers the unexpected visit of a group of Europeans whose plane had broken down nearby, an event that disturbed the fragile equilibrium of her well-ordered life. In the same period she recalls Luc, a young seductive French vagabond who was crossing the country on foot and identified with the natives—but mocked and mistreated Protée.

For unspoken but obvious personal reasons, her mother eventually had Protée dismissed from his houseboy duties and relegated to the outbuildings, a decision that left France marked for life....

The Director

Claire Denis, born in 1946, spent her childhood in different African countries (Cameroon, Burkina Faso, Djibouti), where her father was a colonial civil servant. She went back to France as a teenager and experienced the loneliness that affects former expatriates when they come back home. She also discovered cinema, her knowledge of which was up to this point confined to American war films that were popular when she lived in Africa.

After a stint as a photographer, she studied cinema at the prestigious IDHEC (Institut des Hautes Etudes Cinématographiques) film school, then made a few short films and worked as an assistant for Robert Enrico and Jacques Rivette. She had revered Rivette as a student and says that he "bequeathed her his filmmaker's eye" (Macia, "Claire Denis"). Enrico's *The Old Gun* (*Le Vieux Fusil*) introduced her to the difficulties of the filmmaking milieu, including its machismo. She said about her work on this film,

"It's a very physical job, a guy's job, I was told. Many tried to discourage me" (Rousseau). Nevertheless, she subsequently became First Assistant to directors such as Jacques Rouffio, Costa Gavras, Jim Jarmusch, and Wim Wenders, a filmmaker who played a decisive role in her career.

After working on two films by Wenders that won awards at Cannes, *Paris, Texas* (1984) and *Wings of Desire* (*Les Ailes du désir*, 1987), she presented *Chocolat* at the festival in 1988. This first feature, well received by the public and nominated at the Césars the following year, inaugurated a long list of fiction films and documentaries on a variety of topics. Among Denis' early feature films were two documentaries of note, *Man No Run* (1989), about the Cameroonian band Les Têtes Brulées (whose music she had considered including in *Chocolat*), and *Jacques Rivette, the Watchman* (*Jacques Rivette, le veilleur*, 1990), made for a television series titled *Cinema of Our Times*.

According to Denis, her next two fiction films and *Chocolat* make up a trilogy on the themes of colonization, immigration, and assimilation into a new society (Mayne 20). *No Fear, No Die* (*S'en fout la mort*, 1990), with Isaach de Bankolé (who plays Protée in *Chocolat*) and Alex Descas, is the tragic story of two friends from Benin and Martinique who hope to make a fortune by organizing illegal cock fights for a shady restaurant owner in the Parisian suburbs. *I Can't Sleep* (*J'ai pas sommeil*, 1994), also set in the capital, deals with migrants and people of modest means who live alongside each other without interacting. One of them, Camille, a transvestite from Martinique, is also the serial killer of old ladies that the police finally arrest at the end. Based on a news story of the 1980s, this film was part of the Official Selection at the Cannes Film Festival.

In her next films Denis focuses more on white characters, even though the postcolonial context is never totally absent. *U.S. Go Home* (1994), a contribution to the television series *Tous les garçons et les filles de leur âge* on the transition to adulthood, is centered on a brother and sister eager for sexual experiences who return from a party accompanied by a GI stationed nearby. The siblings of *U.S. Go Home* are also the protagonists of *Nénette and Boni* (awarded the Silver Lion in Venice in 1996), played again by Alice Houri and Grégoire Colin. In this film Denis examines the relationship between two young quasi-orphans who lead lives on the edge in Marseilles. It is likewise from this city that a warrant officer dismissed from the Foreign Legion (Denis Lavant) describes his downfall in flashback in *Good Work* (*Beau Travail*, 2000), a film inspired by Melville's novel *Billy Budd* and winner of the César for Best Cinematography in 2001. This story set in the Djibouti desert confirms Denis' predilection for the representation of the male body and simmering desire (homosexual here).

Sexuality is at the center of her next two feature films. *Trouble Every Day*, presented out of competition at Cannes in 2001, angered its many critics owing to its graphic violence. The film is about a strange disease that a scientist contracted in French Guyana and that triggers cannibalistic tendencies during sexual relations. *Friday Night* (*Vendredi soir*) the following year describes a one-night stand between a young woman who is engaged and a hitchhiker (Vincent Lindon) who invites himself into her car during a huge traffic jam in Paris.

In *The Intruder* (*L'Intrus*, 2004), inspired by philosopher Jean-Luc Nancy's book of the same title, the protagonist is an old man who has received a heart transplant and must handle both the fear of death and the strange feeling of having a foreign body part inside himself. *35 Shots of Rum* (*35 Rhums*, 2008) represents a change of tone because it depicts the strong love between a single father from Guadeloupe who makes a living driving suburban trains and his daughter who is about to leave the nest. The film is an homage of sorts to the relationship between Denis' mother and her mother's father.

More than twenty years after *Chocolat*, Denis filmed another African story in *White Material* (2010). She depicts a country ravaged by civil war where orphaned child soldiers are sowing terror. Amidst the chaos Maria (Isabelle Huppert), a white coffee planter, strives to finish the harvest. Denis' last film to date, *Bastards* (*Les Salauds*, 2013), presented in the Un Certain Regard section at Cannes, is a film noir dealing with the revenge of a man whose brother-in-law was driven to suicide by the failure of his business, and whose niece was a victim of sexual abuse—with shady financial dealings and severe moral turpitude as a backdrop.

Denis is thus a true "vagabond," according to the title of Sébastien Lifshitz's documentary about her. She has worked in many genres—drama, dramatic comedy, chronicle, thriller, horror film, film noir—whose codes she often subverts by adding her personal touch. Jean-Michel Frodon (*Claire Denis*) sums up her originality as a filmmaker and the main characteristics of her œuvre as follows: "Following the highly unusual paths we have mentioned, even rarer in French cinema where rationality, psychology and powerful discourse so often prevail, she allows us to feel and understand from the sensations she produces the great issues of our time. Convergences and clashes of civilizations and cultures, individual anguish and solitude, the destabilizing effect of migrations, the renewal and evolution of the great oppressions."

The Origin and Making of the Film

Deeply affected by her childhood in Africa, Claire Denis wished to dedicate her first film to this continent and felt compelled to "face the colonial problem" (Frodon, "Claire Denis"). She began making a documentary about a community of African-American soldiers who had settled in Senegal after the Vietnam War. However, while scouting locations for the film she felt uncomfortable when she realized that she was being treated like a tourist in Africa and decided to explore her connection to the country of her childhood through a fiction film instead. From the documentary project she kept the idea of the African-American character, Mungo (Strauss 31).

According to Judith Mayne (35), Denis found part of her inspiration for *Chocolat* in a novel that made a big impression on her as a teenager, *Houseboy* (*Une vie de boy*, 1956), by Cameroonian writer Ferdinand Oyono. This book is the diary of Toundi, the black servant of a colonial civil servant who, like Marc in the film, is often away on official business. Toundi, who was educated by a priest, records his experience of colonial relations and describes his difficult relationship with his master's wife, who resents him for knowing her secrets, beginning with her unfaithfulness. We recognize some elements of the film here, but Denis invented the reciprocal attraction between Protée and Aimée.

Denis also drew inspiration from her own childhood to write the screenplay, but she did not want to make a purely autobiographical piece. She wanted rather to make "a film on the memory of childhood, based on the particular situation of a French girl in Africa" (Tranchant) and use a framed narrative to show the connections between past and present. Those who read the screenplay recommended that she delete the contemporary part and only keep the flashback on her childhood in Africa, but she insisted on including images of modern Africa. She wanted to prove wrong those who did not believe that the continent could survive independence: "I did not want to talk only about Africa in the past because, when colonization came to an end, people said 'It's the end of an empire, this world is over.' Even if the economy is bad in Africa, the countries continue to exist independently, and this needs to be shown" (Strauss 31).

Denis created the characters of France and her father from her personal history, and Protée and Aimée were born of her memories of books and films. After writing a first draft of the story she took her co-screenwriter, Jean-Pol Fargeau, to Cameroon to introduce him to the country. His contribution can mostly be felt in the characters' behavior and ways of speaking (Gili 14–15).

Denis received an "advance on ticket sales" (financial support from the Centre National de la Cinématographie) to make *Chocolat*. Nevertheless, she had difficulty finding enough funding, which is not surprising for a first film, and had to work with eight producers. Some of them wanted her to include an affair between Aimée and Protée, but she refused. To avoid their pressuring her too much, she shot several key scenes early, knowing that they would be too expensive to revisit.

The shoot took place in Mindif, a small town in northern Cameroon known for a strange mountain formation called Mindif Peak (literally Mindif Tooth, "la dent de Mindif"). This choice of setting was inspired by Denis' readings of Jules Verne. She said in an interview that "Jules Verne spoke of this mountain that he had never seen but wanted to include in the setting of *Five Weeks in a Balloon* [*Cinq Semaines en ballon*]" (Gili 15). Denis had a house built in the bush because she wanted "to avoid the tourist brochure look with its luxuriant scenery and emphasize instead the constricted setting of the story" (Rousseau). The shoot lasted nine weeks in rather difficult material conditions but in a congenial summer camp atmosphere because Denis already knew many members of the crew, with whom she had worked as an assistant on another film (Gili 16). She also hired technicians from Cameroon to ensure a variety of viewpoints. "Working with them was non-negotiable," she said. "I needed their black gaze in addition to my white gaze. I think that the significance of the film lies here, in this subtle blending of viewpoints" (Trenchant).

The Actors

France as a child is embodied by Cécile Ducasse, who is only known for her role in *Chocolat*. Denis found her by visiting French schools in Cameroon and was immediately drawn to her "marvelous seriousness" (Rousseau). France as an adult is played by Mireille Perrier, a theater actress who began her film career in a film by Leos Carax, *Boy Meets Girl* (1983). She has since appeared in many auteur films and worked with young directors.

Protée is played by Isaach de Bankolé, an actor from Ivory Coast who studied mathematics and subsequently drama in Paris. He received the César for Best Promising Actor in 1987 for his role as a marabout in Thomas Gilou's first film, the comedy *Black Mic Mac*. Denis noticed him on the stage in plays directed by Patrice Chéreau. After *Chocolat* he portrayed an organizer of cockfights in Denis' *No Fear, No Die* (*S'en fout la mort*, 1990) and a fallen leader in *White Material* (2010). Altogether he has played in over fifty films and television series with renowned filmmakers like Jim Jarmusch, Michael Mann, or Lars von Trier.

Giulia Boschi (Aimée Dalens) is an Italian actress who retired from cinema in 2001 after a short but successful career. Like Mireille Perrier, she chose to act primarily in auteur films and first films. Denis spotted her in the role of a drug addict in Francesca Comencini's *Pianoforte* (1984), a first role that earned her several international awards. She chose her to portray Aimée because she had "the strength and at the same time the youthfulness and the beauty of the character" (Gili 15), and her face expressed "a touch of disillusionment" (Rousseau).

As for François Cluzet, who impersonates Marc Dalens, he was already well known as an actor when Denis made her first film. She would not have dared to offer him this supporting role, but Cluzet himself contacted her when he heard about her plans to make *Chocolat* (Gili 15). Cluzet made his cinema debut in a film by Diane Kurys, *Cocktail Molotov*, in 1980. He has since played around a hundred roles, including many for Claude Chabrol, his favorite director. He has earned over twenty nominations and several prestigious awards, including the Jean Gabin Prize in 1984 and the César for Best Actor for his performance in *Tell No One* (*Ne le dis à personne*, 2006), a thriller by Guillaume Canet. Recently he distinguished himself as the wealthy quadriplegic in *The Intouchables* (*Intouchables*, 2011), beside Omar Sy (see Chap. 20).

The Reception

Chocolat was part of the official selection at Cannes in 1988, which is rather rare for a first film. It was nominated for six different awards at this festival and for the César for Best First Film the following year.

The critical reception was positive overall. Commentators found the film "magical and secretive" (Grainville), "evocative and attentive to detail" (Grousset), "grave and sensitive" (Trémois), unusually high praise for a first film. Lefort (*Libération*) is the only one who disagreed, as he often does with the critical consensus, describing *Chocolat* as "an adolescent film, written as if by a fifteen-year-old."

Most of the comments deal with the treatment of the colonial theme. Critics praise Denis for broaching this topic from the point of view of a child and indirectly. "If the [colonial] problem is at the heart of the film," Ferenczi notes, "it is hidden with rare ingenuity, as if covered, softened by the tone of the chronicle." Many critics commend the director for avoiding the pitfalls of this type of subject, "terrible dangers," according to Leclère, that include "nostalgia, autobiography of course, the white man's guilt, racism, and even the setting, whose magnificence can become overpowering." They praise Denis' original gaze, the fact that she does not try "to 'understand' black people, to step into their shoes, since it is impossible," (Heymann) and shows a side of Africa "freed from these pseudo mysteries that burden our traditional viewpoint" (Baignères).

Some mention the political aspect of the film, even though they consider it secondary. Grousset speaks of "the characters whose despicable behavior toward blacks explains why whites were driven out of Africa." The critic for *La Vie ouvrière* (i.e., "Blue-Collar Life") deplores the fact that Denis did not "confer a more obvious political dimension to a topic that cried out for it" but encourages people to go to the theaters to see "everything that was hidden from us for several decades" (Anon.).

Most critics also appreciate the very personal style of this first film, its "disconcerting slow pace" and its sensuality (Toscan du Plantier) that allow it to "bring to the surface the underlying principles, the unspoken truths of this colonial Africa" (Macia,

"*Chocolat*"). Borel observes that "*Chocolat* relies on understatement to express a maximum number of emotions with minimal means." For Jousse one of the strengths of the film is that "it does not explain anything but circles around these two characters [Protée and France], faithfully recording what remains unsaid, vague, latent between them" (132).

Finally, critics generally agree on the quality of the characters and the performance of the actors. They praise the leading duo, a "magnetic couple" according to Lefort, for whom it is the only positive aspect of the film. The actor who portrays Protée, in particular, draws praise. Rousseau sees in Isaach de Bankolé "the African Brando" and describes him as an actor with "miraculous restraint, quasi-silent presence, and subtle intelligence."

On the other hand, the secondary characters are deemed mediocre. Lefort finds them too reminiscent of literary characters, like "the plane pilot that seems to come straight out of Saint-Ex[upéry]" and the "Rimbaud-like wanderer," Luc. For Jousse, "the supporting actors all lack density and gradually become weak extras (except Jacques Denis as the highly amusing racist planter)" (133), an opinion shared by Le Morvan, among others.

Surprisingly, at a time when the concept of women's literature was widely discussed in academia, few critics commented on *Chocolat* as a "woman's film." Toscan du Plantier was an exception when he predicted—with over-the-top hyperbole—the rise of a new type of cinema: "Here finally is a cinema rich in emotions," he says. "It anticipates at last the true revolution that will probably transform women into the leaders of tomorrow's film production. Beyond boring feminism—a sad response to our exacerbated machismo—we see rising everywhere the harbingers of a new world, a continent of new, deep sensations, inhabited by these women who are laying claim to the cameras that soon will no longer be a tool reserved for the expression of the male worldview. Finally!"

The Historical Context: French Cameroon

The story of France's childhood takes place in northern Cameroon in the mid-1950s, a few years before that country's independence in 1960. The film alludes to the colonial history of Cameroon through small details. We learn that it was first a German colony (from 1884 to 1916) owing to a plaque on the Dalens' house explaining that a German administrator used to live there and to the nearby graves of German soldiers. The territory was then divided between the British (in the south) and the French (in the north) after the First World War. This explains why a British administrator, Jonathan Boothby, visits the Dalens, and why Enoch, the cook, speaks English and prepares traditional British dishes.

Starting in the 1940s France launched a program to modernize the territory by building an electric grid and a transportation network and developing new crops like coffee and cotton. The characters in the film represent different facets of this project. As an administrator, Marc Dalens promotes economic development (he speaks of building a new road at the beginning of the film). Delpich, the coffee planter, is in Cameroon to exploit its natural resources.

As in the rest of the French colonial empire, an anticolonialist sentiment grew in Cameroon in the middle of the twentieth century and reached its climax around 1955, at the time of the story, when the pro-independence movement turned to violence. The film alludes to the rise of nationalism in the episode with the doctor at night. During the meal that precedes his visit, the Dalens' guests also mention rebellions and the beheading of colonists in Mbanga, a southwestern town where Machinard is about to be stationed. The gathering of villagers at the school that night is probably a political meeting. Nevertheless, Cameroon's access to independence occurred peacefully in 1960, as in most territories colonized by France (except for Algeria and Indochina).

STUDY GUIDE

What Happens in This Film?

1. How was France planning to go to the beach in Limbé and on to Douala? Finally, with whom did she travel?

2. Where and with whom is France the first time we see her in the past? What does she eat for lunch?

3. What unique geographical feature is found near the Dalens' home? Where did we see it before?

4. What are Marc Dalens' responsibilities in north Cameroon, and why does he travel away from home for long periods?

5. Why did Aimée ask Protée to spend the night in her room with a gun? What did he do instead?

6. What happened to the animals of the Norwegian neighbors of the Dalens family? What did Protée do with the blood of a dead chicken?

7. How did Aimée spend the evening with her English visitor, Johnathan Boothby?

8. Who are the passengers of the plane that landed near the Dalens' house? Why did they have to stay there a good while?

9. Why did Delpich sneak food out of the kitchen before retiring to his bedroom?

10. Where does Luc Sigalen sleep and shower? Who is offended by this?

11. Where was Protée transferred to when he was fired from his houseboy position? What happened when France went to see him one night?

12. What do we learn about Mungo's identity at the end? Why does he want to read France's palm?

True or False?

If the statement is false, correct it!

1. During the car ride, Mungo's son teaches his father the names of body parts in his African language.

2. France helps her mother clean the tombs of French soldiers who died during the war.

3. One day Protée went to pick up France at school after her classes.

4. An old man whom Marc is visiting tells him that blacks are more efficient than whites at getting rid of the lions that attack their herds.

5. Aimée advises her Norwegian neighbor, Nansen, to leave Cameroon because Muslims frown upon his work as an evangelist.

6. Aimée criticizes Enoch, her cook, for putting too much salt in his dishes.

7. People say that the German administrator who lived in the house before the Dalens committed suicide because he was too lonesome.

8. France and Protée watched Johnathan Boothby as he was undressing and made fun of his physical appearance.

9. Marc drew the pictures of the mountain that France was looking at in Mungo's car.

10. During a meal, the Dalens' guests reassure Mrs. Machinard by describing to her the advantages of Mbanga, the town where her husband is about to start his job as administrator.

11. People think that Luc Sigalen is a former seminarian who is crossing the African continent on foot.

12. Luc left the Dalens' house because Marc asked him to stop sleeping on the veranda.

What Did You Learn in the Introduction?

1. According to Denis, what do her first three films have in common? Where do their main characters come from?

2. What does *Beau Travail* have in common with *Chocolat*?

3. Why can one say that Denis is a "vagabond" filmmaker?

4. What film by Denis is the closest to a thriller? Which one has some of the characteristics of a horror film?

5. Why did Denis want to make *Chocolat*, and where did she draw inspiration for her story and characters?

6. What aspects of *Chocolat* was she asked to change?

7. Why did Denis insist so much on using a flashback and showing France as an adult?

8. How did Denis choose the setting for her film?

9. Among the main actors of *Chocolat*, who has worked the most with Denis? Who has earned the most awards?

10. What aspects of the film received positive reviews from critics? Which one received the harshest criticism?

11. Why did Toscan du Plantier have such high praise for Denis' film?

12. What elements of Cameroonian history are present in the film?

Exploring the Film

1. The Title of the Film

What meanings can we give to the title of the film? The expression "*être chocolat*" (to be *chocolat*) means "to be taken by surprise, duped, mistaken, deprived of something one expected." Claire Denis said that she used to hear this expression when she was young and that "the little girl of the film could make it her own" (Bernard). **In what respect(s) does the expression apply to France? Can it be applied to other characters as well?**

2. The Beginning of the Film: France and Mungo

According to some critics, like Danièle Heymann, Africa is one of the main characters of the film, on the same level as France and Protée. **How may the beginning of the film give this impression?**

Why do you think Claire Denis spends so much time showing Mungo and his son? **Can we establish a connection between them and the main story, that of France's childhood?** What scene is particularly significant in this regard (and also suggests that Mungo is not from Cameroon)?

When Mungo drops off France in Limbé, where she plans to take a bus to Douala, we see a church and a Texaco station. **What do these places represent in the African context of the 1950s?**

Finally, Mungo drives France to Douala. **During the trip, what predisposes the young woman to remember her past?** *Review the scene in the car* (Excerpt 1, 6'20–8'20). **How does Denis transition from the present to the past visually and through the sound track?**

3. *The Characters*

+ *France*

The first name "France" was very common among the women of Denis' generation, but it is obvious that it has an allegorical meaning in the film. When France tells him her name, Mungo exclaims, "Long live France!" Beside the fact that this first name was fashionable, **why might Aimée and Marc have chosen it for their daughter?**

How does France's attitude toward Protée reproduce the colonial model that she witnessed as a child? How does she behave, for example, in the sequence where she is waiting for him in front of the school and then plays with him at home? *Review this sequence* (Excerpt 2, 19'20–21'36). Why do the children follow Protée, screaming, "Protée, it's time to go home"? **Whom are they making fun of?** Denis said of her past life in the colonies, "As a child, I must have suffered from the situation and at the same time taken advantage of it. I was the master's daughter, white and yet close to the servants, as is the case with very young children. In reality, sometimes, when I remember this, I am ashamed" (Rousseau). **Do you think France (as a child) is ashamed here or in other scenes?**

What aspects of African culture does France learn from Protée? Can you point out some scenes where there is evidence of a close connection between them?

According to Denis, the camera represents France's viewpoint in the film. Rather than an autobiography, she considers *Chocolat* "a film on the memory of childhood." "I wanted to use memory like a magnifying glass, to show small details of life," she says. "But from these tiny elements I tried to ask broader questions" (Tranchant). **What "broader questions" are addressed by the film?**

+ *Protée*

Claire Denis describes the status of the houseboy in colonial society as follows: "The black servant shares the intimate lives of the household [. . .]. But he has to stay in his inferior position not because of racism, but because it was the law, the very principle on which colonization was built. For these reasons he had to be treated like a minor and an asexual being, the equivalent of a child" (Macia, "Claire Denis"). **Comment on the second sequence of Excerpt 2, where France feeds Protée.** What does she reduce him to, in effect? (What comparisons come to mind?) What are Protée's responsibilities at the Dalens' house? **In particular, what role does he play when Marc is away?**

Edson argues that Denis subverts colonial discourse by suggesting that Protée's servile manner is just a veil over his individuality. **How does Protée's behavior in the episode with the hyena and the scenes with Luc differ from what is expected of him?** Are there other episodes that highlight his strong individuality? For example, how does he react when Aimée is angry with the cook and the latter threatens to resign? What is the significance of this scene for the portrayal of his character?

Protée is usually silent and seems emotionless. Denis says that he "reflects, through his silences, the dignity of the land," and that she chose actor Isaach de Bankolé for his "iceberg side" because she wished "to reveal what lay under the surface" (Schidlow). **In your opinion, what is Protée hiding beneath his opaque exterior?** In what circumstances does he show emotions? *Review for example the scene with Aimée, followed by the shower scene* (Excerpt 3, 43'13–46'16). Why do you think he kicks the water buckets, and why does he start crying with rage while taking a shower?

✦ *The Dalens Couple*

What are Marc's responsibilities as the administrator of the Mindif region? What types of situations does he have to face in the film, for example?

Denis said about the character of Aimée, "I especially did not want the kind of dissatisfied, useless beautiful woman that is typically found in colonial literature" (Schidlow). **How does Aimée spend her time when her husband is away?** What aspect of her personality comes through when she gardens? When she talks to the cook about his English dishes?

Denis remembers that when she lived in Africa as a child it was not uncommon for wives of colonists to feel so useless that they became depressed and had to be sent back to France, "whereas the male colonist lived a romantic adventure, a life full of escapades of all kinds" (Strauss 32). **How does Denis' mise en scène show the difference between Marc's life and Aimée's?** *Review the scene showing Aimée and France while Marc is going away* (Excerpt 4, 14'20–15'45). What contrasts do you notice between the way Denis films Marc and his retinue on the one hand, and Aimée and France on the other (as regards the setting, colors, camera movements, and the characters' actions)? What sensation does the dining room create? Why do you think Denis films vultures, birds of prey associated with death? What activity of Aimée's (involving grooming the grounds) also has something to do with death?

How do France's parents behave toward their servants and the local population? **What aspect of colonization do they represent?**

✦ *The Dalens' Neighbors and Guests*

Denis expands on her description of colonial society through her portrayal of the secondary characters. Beside Machinard, who, like Marc, represents French administration, **what characters illustrate other rationales for colonization?**

How does the arrival of the plane passengers break the harmonious relationship between blacks and whites in Mindif? For example, how does Delpich treat the man who has brought Aimée a goat for her guests? *Review this scene* (Excerpt 5, 56'14–57'54). How does he behave toward Enoch, the cook, and what taboo does he break in his relationship with his housekeeper, Thérèse?

How do Machinard and his wife treat the native doctor Prosper? *Review the episode of the doctor's visit* (Excerpt 6, 1h14'45–1h16'32). What role does Luc play in this scene? **What unspoken aspects of colonial relations does he explicitly reveal?** How does the doctor behave? This scene comes after a gathering of black men at the village school in the middle of the night. What type of meeting is it? Proper's visit is followed by a conversation between Marc and Luc during which Marc reaches a conclusion that Denis considers the most important sentence of the film. **What does Marc say to Luc? In this whole episode with the doctor, what is Claire Denis' viewpoint on the French presence in Africa?**

✦ *Luc*

How did Luc arrive in Mindif? **How does his attitude toward the blacks differ from that of the other white characters?** What does Protée tell Luc when the latter is showering in the servants' quarter? Why is this comment surprising coming from Protée, and what does it reveal about his principles?

In addition to racial tensions in the scene with Prosper, what other taboo subject does Luc reveal? Why does he read these words from a nineteenth-century explorer to Aimée: "I found white skin unnatural compared to the delicious plenitude of black skin"? **Why does he invite her to come and eat with the servants?** *Review the servants' meal* (Excerpt 7, 1h21'00–1h23'00). Why does Protée stay away from the group? How does he react when Luc provokes him? Compare his reaction to Aimée's when Luc insinuates that she is attracted to Protée.

Given Luc's preference for black people, how do you explain his hostility toward Protée? What is Luc trying to do when he tells the latter, "Get lost. Go lick your bosses' boots. You are worse than the priests who tamed you"? In which ways does Protée show himself superior to Luc in this scene?

4. Protée and Aimée

In colonial society, sexual relations between the races were taboo, especially between black men and white women. But novels and films set in this period are replete with fantasies of interracial sexual unions, and the bodies of colonized people are highly eroticized. In the film the camera highlights Protée's beauty, and the sexual attraction between him and Aimée is more than obvious before Luc hints at it. **In what scenes in particular did you feel the desire between the two characters?** How does it express itself most of the time? *Review, for example, the scene where Aimée is getting ready for the evening with Johnathan Boothby* (Excerpt 8, 35'50–36'43). How does Aimée play with fire in this scene? What happens to the power relations between boss lady and servant here?

After the scene where Protée throws Luc off the veranda, we see Aimée sitting on the floor next to a door as Protée arrives to draw the curtains. **How does Aimée transgress taboos at this moment? How does Protée react?** *Review this intimate scene between them* (Excerpt 9, 1h25'13–1h26'21). How do you interpret the fact that Protée is standing and Aimée sitting on the floor? **How do you explain Protée's abruptness when he lifts her to her feet?**

Claire Denis mentions in some interviews, as noted above, that the film producers wanted her to include an affair between Aimée and Protée. She declined because, she said, "Protée's refusal was the purpose of the film" (Petrie 67). **What does she mean by that? Can we read a broader comment on colonial relations here?**

After the scene in Excerpt 9, Marc talks to France about the horizon line that recedes when one tries to approach it, never to be reached. **What metaphorical meaning can we give this (imaginary) line with regard to the scene between Aimée and Protée?** The next morning Aimée tells Marc that she no longer wants Protée as a houseboy. Since Protée is a competent servant, Marc does not understand but agrees to Aimée's request without asking questions, watching her intently. **What do you think Marc is wondering at this point?**

5. The Garage Scene

How do you interpret Protée's decision to let France burn her hand and the fact that both he and France are marked for life? *Review the garage scene* (Excerpt 10, 1h31'05–1h32'54). This scene recalls an earlier scene where France was hiding in the garage to see

Protée. What is different here? **What is the significance of the silence and the looks between the two characters (that serve as a final example of the theme of the unspoken that runs through the film)?** Before this scene, could you imagine such cruelty on Protée's part? Why (not)? **How does the meaning of his name become obvious here?**

6. *The Last Scenes*

✦ *France and Mungo*

What personal information does Mungo share with France in the car on their way to Douala? France, too, starts talking about herself. She tells him, among other things, "I've been hanging around Douala for two weeks. I should head north. I already have my plane ticket." What does her choice of words ("hanging around," "I should") betray about France's state of mind? **What do Mungo and France have in common?**

When France steps out of Mungo's car in Douala, she invites him for a drink. Why, in your opinion? **Why does Mungo refuse the invitation?** When he attempts to read her palm to help her decide whether to go to her childhood home, he remarks, "Your hand is very strange, there is nothing to see, no past, no future." **How can we interpret this observation?** What is the connection with what happened in the garage thirty years or so earlier? Why does he advise her to go back to France before being "eaten up"?

✦ *The Airport Scene*

What catches France's attention at the Douala airport? *Review the scene at the airport* (Excerpt 11, 1h39'25–1h42'36). Whom is she probably thinking about when a hint of a smile crosses her face? (Denis encouraged this association when she cast Isaac de Bankolé as one of the baggage handlers, although she carefully avoided showing him facing the camera.) **What does Denis suggest when she focuses on the African artifacts that are being loaded in the cargo hold of the plane?** Where are these objects probably going?

What scene at the beginning of the film echoes the one where the three men are seen from the back in front of a field? What has changed? (Who has disappeared, along with what he stood for?) What type of music do we hear? Are the men motionless or animated? **What do these changes suggest regarding the present situation of Cameroon and its people when compared to the past (the time of France's childhood)?**

Do you think France will go and visit her childhood home?

Claire Denis' Filmography

1988   *Chocolat*

1989   *Man No Run* (documentary)

1990   *Jacques Rivette, the Watchman* (*Jacques Rivette, le veilleur* [documentary])

1990   *No Fear, No Die* (*S'en fout la mort*)

1994   *I Can't Sleep* (*J'ai pas sommeil*)

1994   *US Go Home*

1996   *Nénette and Boni*

1999   *Good Work* (*Beau Travail*)

2001   *Trouble Every Day*

2002   *Friday Night (Vendredi soir)*

2004   *The Intruder (L'Intrus)*

2008   *35 Shots of Rum (35 Rhums)*

2008   *White Material*

2013   *Bastards (Les Salauds)*

Works Consulted

Anon. "*Chocolat.*" *La Vie ouvrière*, 23 May 1988: n. pag.

Austin, Guy. "Women Filmmakers in France." *Contemporary French Cinema, an Introduction*. 2nd ed. Manchester, England: Manchester UP, 2008. 98–117.

Baignères, Claude. "*Chocolat*, de Claire Denis. Souvenirs, souvenirs." *Le Figaro*, 17 May 1988: n. pag.

Bernard, René. "Y'a bon *Chocolat*." *L'Express*, 13 May 1988: n. pag.

Beugnet, Martine. *Claire Denis*. Manchester, England: Manchester UP, 2004.

Borel, Vincent. "Y'a bon les noirs." *7 à Paris*, 18 May 1988: n. pag.

Denis, Claire, dir. *Chocolat*. MGM Home Entertainment, 2001.

Edson, Laurie. "Planetarity, Performativity, Relationality: Claire Denis' *Chocolat* and Cinematic Ethics." *The Planetary Turn: Relationality and Geoaesthetics in the Twenty-First Century*. Ed. Amy J. Elias and Christina Miraru. Evanston, IL: Northwestern UP, 2015. 107–24.

Ferenczi, Aurélien. "*Chocolat* de Claire Denis. La tendre fable du boy et de l'enfant." *Le Quotidien de Paris*, 16 May 1988: n. pag.

Frodon, Jean-Michel. *Claire Denis*. Paris: Institut français, 2012. Web. 22 Feb. 2018. <http://www.institutfrancais.com/sites/default/files/livret_claire_denis.pdf>.

———. "Claire Denis: une enfance africaine." *Le Point*, 9 May 1988: n. pag.

Gili, Jean A. "Entretien avec Claire Denis sur *Chocolat*." *Positif* 328 (June 1988): 14–16.

Grainville, Patrick. "*Chocolat*." *V-S-D*, 19 May 1988: n. pag.

Grousset, Jean-Paul. "*Chocolat*." *Le Canard enchaîné*, 18 May 1988: n. pag.

Hayward, Susan. "Filming the (Post-)Colonial Landscape: Claire Denis' *Chocolat* (1988) and *Beau Travail* (1998)." *Cinema and Landscape*. Ed. Jonathan Rayner and Graeme Harper. Bristol, England: Intellect, 2009. 163–75.

Heymann, Danièle. "Amitié sans issue." *Le Monde*, 18 May 1988: n. pag.

Hottell, Ruth A. "The Cinema of Claire Denis: Post-Colonial Configurations." *French/Francophone Culture and Literature through Film*. Ed. Catherine Montfort and Michèle Bissière. *Women in French Studies* (2006): 220–36.

Jousse, Thierry. "Jeux africains." *Cahiers du cinéma* 407–8 (May 1988): 28–33.

Leclère, Marie-Françoise. "L'adieu à l'Afrique." *Le Point*, 16 May 1988: n. pag.

Lefort, Gérard. "Claire d'Afrique." *Libération*, 17 May 1988: n. pag.

Le Morvan, Gille. "Flash Black. *Chocolat* de Claire Denis." *L'Humanité*, 17 May 1988: n. pag.

Lifshitz, Sébastien, dir. *Claire Denis, la vagabonde*. FEMIS, 1996.

Macia, Jean-Luc. "*Chocolat* de Claire Denis. African Spleen." *La Croix*, 18 May 1988: n. pag.

———. "Claire Denis: l'Afrique couleur chocolat." *La Croix*, 8 May 1988: n. pag.

Mayne, Judith. *Claire Denis*. Urbana: U of Illinois P, 2005.

Murray, Alison. "Women, Nostalgia, Memory: *Chocolat, Outremer*, and *Indochine*." *Research in African Literatures* 33.2 (2002): 235–44.

Petrie, Duncan. *Screening Europe: Image and Identity in Contemporary European Cinema*. London: British Film Institute, 1992.

Rousseau, Nita. "Regard noir." *Le Nouvel Observateur*, 13 May 1988: n. pag.

Schidlow, Joshka. "Une enfance africaine. Entretien." *Télérama*, 18 May 1988: n. pag.

Strauss, Frédéric. "Mémoires d'exil. Féminin colonial." *Cahiers du cinéma* 434 (July–Aug. 1990): 28–33.

Toscan du Plantier, Daniel. "Les caméras ne sont plus des attributs virils." *Le Figaro Magazine*, 28 May 1988: n. pag.

Tranchant, Marie-Noëlle. "Claire Denis ou la saveur de l'Afrique." *Le Figaro Magazine*, 16 May 1988: n. pag.

Trémois, Claude-Marie. "Maîtres et serviteurs." *Télérama*, 18 May 1988: n. pag.

"Une enfance africaine. *Chocolat* de Claire Denis" [par A.C.]. *Les Echos*, 18 May 1988: n. pag.

4

Régis Wargnier

Indochine

(1992)

Régis Wargnier, *Indochine*: Eliane (Catherine Deneuve) and her adopted daughter Camille (Linh Dan Pham) learn to dance the tango.

Director. . . . . Régis Wargnier
Screenplay. . . . . .Catherine Cohen, Louis Gardel,
. . . . Erik Orsenna, Régis Wargnier
Director of Photography . . . . François Catonné
Sound . . . . .Guillaume Sciama and Dominique Hennequin
Film Editor. . . . . Geneviève Winding
Music. . . . . .Patrick Doyle
Art Director . . . . .Jacques Bufnoir
Costumes . . . . Gabriella Pescucci, Pierre-Yves Gayraud
Continuity . . . . .Jean-Baptiste Filleau
Producer . . . . .Eric Heumann
Length. 2h40

Cast

Catherine Deneuve (*Eliane Devries*), Vincent Perez (*Jean-Baptiste Le Guen*), Linh Dan Pham (*Camille, Eliane's adopted daughter*), Jean Yanne (*Guy Asselin, Chief of Police*), Dominique Blanc (*Yvette, the wife of Eliane's foreman Raymond*), Henri Marteau (*Emile, Eliane's father*), Eric Nyugen (*Tanh, nationalist fighter, Camille's husband*), Carlo Brandt (*Castellani*), Gérard Lartigau (*the admiral*), Hubert Saint-Macary (*Raymond*), Andrzej Seweryn (*Hebrard*)

Story

In the 1930s in Indochina, beautiful Eliane Devries runs with an iron hand the family rubber plantation, along with the plantation of her friends, an aristocratic Vietnamese couple whose daughter Camille she adopted when they died. She is raising her in a protective cocoon, hiding the worrisome political situation from her—the rise of Vietnamese nationalism and its harshly repressed uprisings. An independent woman, Eliane prefers love affairs to the earnest courtship of her friend Guy, the Chief of Police. Her meeting with a naval officer, Jean-Baptiste, is going to disturb her well-ordered life and break her close bonds with Camille, as both fall in love with the young man. Emboldened by her love, Camille becomes more independent, escapes her mother to join Jean-Baptiste, now stationed on a small remote island in the Tonkin, and discovers during her trip the harsh realities of colonization and the poverty of her people. She will come to be known as the "red princess," figurehead of the nationalist cause. Eliane, for her part, will spend years trying to find her and rebuild the mother-daughter connection while raising Etienne, Camille and Jean-Baptiste's son.

Personal and political history blend in this melodrama told in flashback at the time of the Geneva Accords (1954) that ended French colonization in Indochina.

The Director

After literary studies and a stint as a photographer, Régis Wargnier, born in 1948, started his film career as a crew member for French and international directors from 1973 to 1984 (Claude Chabrol, Francis Girod, Patrice Leconte, Alexandre Arcady, Valerio Zurlini, Volker Schlöndorff, Margarethe Von Trotta, and Andreï Tarkovsky, among others). He stepped behind the camera in the mid-1980s and made a few documentaries, as well as nine fiction films for which he also wrote the screenplays.

His first films were intimist dramas: *The Woman of My Life* (*La Femme de ma vie*, 1986), winner of the César for Best First Film, is about an alcoholic musician, while *I'm the King of the Castle* (*Je suis le seigneur du château*, 1988) deals with a rich widowed industrialist and his son's governess and focuses on the difficult cohabitation between their respective children. This film alludes to the French war with Indochina (1946–56)—the governess's husband is missing in action there—and anticipates Wargnier's interest in this conflict and his predilection for historical dramas. He received worldwide acclaim with *Indochine* (1992), winner of both the Oscar and Golden Globe for Best Foreign Film.

Indochine inaugurates in his filmography a series of heroic stories centered on strong, independent women. *A French Woman* (*Une femme française*, 1994), an homage to his mother, recounts the tumultuous love life of a young woman whose husband is fighting in World War II and also touches upon colonial conflicts in Indochina and Algeria. *Est-Ouest* (1998), one of his most successful works (four nominations at the Césars and one at the Oscars and the Golden Globes in the Best Foreign Film category), tells the romantic story of a Franco-Russian couple in the USSR at the time of the Cold War. In 2004 Wargnier revisited the theme of colonialism—British this time—in a "humanist fable," *Man To Man*. In this film set in 1870, an anthropologist wants to prove to his scientific peers that pygmies are true human beings and prevent "specimens" brought back to Scotland by the British authorities from being exhibited at freak shows.

After a change of genre with the thriller *Have Mercy on Us All* (*Pars vite et reviens tard*, 2006) and a film about track, one of his passions (*The Straight Line* [*La Ligne droite*], 2010), the director made another film set in Southeast Asia, *The Gate* (*Le Temps des aveux*, 2014), adapted from a novel by ethnologist François Bizot, in which the latter describes his capture and detention by the Khmer Rouge in the Cambodian jungle in the 1970s.

Régis Wargnier's interest in colonial and postcolonial matters manifests itself in other areas of his professional life. From 2006 to 2008 he presided over "Fonds Sud" (the "Southern Fund"), a commission that awards grants to help fund the production of feature films made by filmmakers from emerging nations and shot primarily in those countries. He was elected to the Académie des Beaux-Arts (Academy of Fine Arts) in 2012 in recognition of his filmmaker career and service to the profession.

The Origin and Making of the Film

Régis Wargnier made *Indochine* at the request of producer Eric Heumann, who enjoyed Puccini's opera *Madame Butterfly* (1904) and wished to use it as the basis for a great romantic film set in Indochina. Wargnier was the perfect choice to make this particular film. As a high school student he skipped class to watch Hollywood adventure films of the 1940s and 1950s. Later he developed a passion for David Lean's films, especially *Lawrence of Arabia* (1962), his "absolute reference" (Roth-Bettoni, "Entretien" 36). Wargnier's personal history also explains his interest in the project, because his father had fought in Indochina: "My initial motivation was the word 'Indochina' that marked my childhood because my father, a military man, was fighting there, and I heard over and over again, like a leitmotiv, that 'We have to keep Indochina, we should never lose Indochina...'" (Andreu 113).

To accomplish this ambitious project and find the right balance between a romantic story and recorded history, Heumann and Wargnier surrounded themselves with historical consultants and writers known for their colonial stories. One of the co-screenwriters, Erik Orsenna, a civil servant at the Ministry of Foreign Affairs, had worked in Ho Chi Minh City (previously Saigon) and won the prestigious Prix Goncourt for his novel *The Colonial Exhibition* (*L'Exposition coloniale*) in 1988. Louis Gardel, for his part, was the author of *Fort Saganne*, 1980 winner of the equally famous *Grand Prix du roman* awarded by the French Academy, the story of a soldier in the Sahara at the beginning of the twentieth century, adapted to the screen by Alain Corneau in 1984. The four screenwriters worked together for a year and divided the characters among themselves (Royer). Régis Wargnier, in charge of Eliane, drew some of his inspiration from *The Indochina Night* (*La Nuit indochinoise*), a series of seven novels written by Jean Hougron between 1950 and 1958. To prepare Catherine Deneuve for this role, he recommended that she read one of the volumes of this saga, *Asians* (*Les Asiates*), about the failure of a family of settlers in Saigon (Andreu 113).

The film attracted exceptional resources, in part owing to subsidies given to top heritage films by the Ministry of Culture under Jack Lang: a budget of close to 120 million francs, equivalent to that of five regular French films, 120 participants, and funds for the 7,000 kilometers covered while scouting the film. The shoot in Vietnam and Malaysia lasted eighteen weeks in difficult conditions and with some memorable incidents, including when part of the set was swept away by a hurricane and when a market that was to be used in the film was plundered by famished extras (Lacharrière). The shoot benefited from Wargnier's prior experience with directors of colonial movies filmed in far-away lands, like Valerio Zurlini's *The Desert of the Tartars* (*Désert des Tartares*, 1976).

The Actors

Catherine Deneuve played her seventieth movie role in *Indochine*. An actress since 1957, she made a breakthrough in 1964 in Jacques Demy's musical melodrama, *The Umbrellas of Cherbourg* (*Les Parapluies de Cherbourg*), and has since appeared in leading roles in both popular and auteur films by great French and international filmmakers like Roman Polanski, Luis Buñuel, Claude Lelouch, François Truffaut, Raoul Ruiz, Lars Von Trier, François Ozon, and André Téchiné (the director of *Wild Reeds* [*Les Roseaux sauvages*], presented later in this volume). She accepted the role of Eliane because she liked the lyricism of Wargnier's first two films and the blend of fiction and history in the screenplay of *Indochine*, written especially for her: "In *Indochine* there was emotion, passion, fragility, humor, too. I was spoiled" (Stouvenot).

Deneuve has played in over 140 films to date (2016)—including Wargnier's *Est-Ouest* in 1999—and received twenty-four nominations and seven awards in international festivals, such as the César for Best Actress in François Truffaut's *The Last Metro* (*Le Dernier Métro*; see Chap. 1) in 1981 and *Indochine* in 1993, a nomination at the Oscars for *Indochine*, and an Honorary Palme d'Or in recognition of her whole career at the Cannes Film Festival in 2005. She was the first woman to win the prestigious Prix Lumières in 2016 honoring an influential personality of the seventh art.

Since the 1980s Catherine Deneuve has been regarded as an ambassador of French fashion and culture and has also embodied "Marianne," the symbol of the French Republic, which is pertinent to an allegorical interpretation of *Indochine*, as we will see in "Exploring the Film" below.

Camille is portrayed by Linh Dan Pham, an eighteen-year-old Parisian high school student born in Saigon, whom Wargnier found by placing an ad at a restaurant in the thirteenth *arrondissement* of the capital. This role allowed her to get to know the country that she had left as an infant: "The journey of Camille, my character, is a little like mine: like her I discovered my country and my people" (Gianorio). In spite of a nomination for the Most Promising Actress César for *Indochine*, Pham took a break from acting for over ten years to devote herself to her studies and a business career. She reappeared in Jacques Audiard's *The Beat That My Heart Skipped* (*De battre mon cœur s'est arrêté*, 2005), for which she received the Most Promising Actress César. She has since played in both French and foreign films, including Wargnier's *Have Mercy on Us All* in 2007 and her first film in Vietnam, *Adrift* (*Vertiges*), in 2011.

Vincent Perez plays Camille's lover, Jean-Baptiste. A theater and film actor from Switzerland, Perez debuted in 1986 and has played in around sixty French and American films. He made a big impression beside Gérard Depardieu as Roxanne's awkward lover in Jean-Paul Rappeneau's *Cyrano de Bergerac* (1990), which earned him a nomination for the Most Promising Actor César. In 1993, one year after *Indochine*, he won the Jean Gabin Prize, awarded yearly to a promising actor in French or Francophone films.

The supporting actors also received popular and critical acclaim. Dominique Blanc (Yvette) is sometimes compared to French actress Arletty and to Bette Davis (Pascal). Long passed over by casting directors because of her out-of-the ordinary looks, she made her debut in two films by Régis Wargnier, playing an alcoholic in *The Woman of My Life* in 1986 and a governess in *I'm the King of the Castle* in 1988, roles which earned her two nominations for the Most Promising Actress César. She also won three Best Supporting Actress Césars for *May Fools* (*Milou in mai*) by Louis Malle in 1991, *Indochine* in 1993, and *Those Who Love Me Can Take the Train* (*Ceux qui m'aiment prendront le train*) by Patrice Chéreau in 1999, as well as a Best Actress César for Roch Stéphanik's *Stand-by* in 2001.

For his part, Jean Yanne (Guy) had many occupations—as a journalist, writer, singer, radio and television host—before launching his film career in 1964. He attracted early attention for his role as a grouch in Jean-Luc Godard's *Week-End* (1967) and as a psycho serial killer in Claude Chabrol's *The Butcher* (*Le Boucher*, 1970). Yanne has appeared in around a hundred films and has worked as a composer, screenwriter, and director for films that are often wacky and satirical. He received the Best Actor award at Cannes in 1972 for his performance in Maurice Pialat's *We Won't Grow Old Together* (*Nous ne vieillirons pas ensemble*).

The Reception

Indochine had resounding success in France and abroad, receiving multiple awards around the world, including five Césars—Best Actress (Catherine Deneuve), Best Supporting Actress (Dominique Blanc), Best Photography, Best Cinematography, and Best Sound—the Oscar and the Golden Globe for Best Foreign Film, and a nomination for the Best Actress Oscar for Catherine Deneuve.

Critics, on the other hand, were divided. The most positive among them credited the film with renewing French cinema and allowing it to compete with Hollywood blockbusters. Daniel Toscan du Plantier, then President of Unifrance, an organization in charge of promoting and distributing French cinema abroad, welcomed the fact that the film broke with the intimist tradition inherited from the New Wave: "*Indochine* [...] carries us far away and makes us dream of *Madam Butterfly* and *Gone with the Wind* [...]. This film, we understand, illustrates perfectly the renaissance of French cinema, with the opening of a window toward the outside world, a resolve to avoid the narrow, egocentric stories of the New Wave [...]. We should not let Hollywood have a monopoly on super productions and settle for a cinema focused solely on our private emotions." Like him, other critics praise "the brilliance of its fictional world [...], its inspiring force and dramatic power reminiscent of the most sumptuous Hollywood films" (Roth-Bettoni, "*Indochine*" 20), "its exalted atmosphere, emotions, feelings, passions, adventures, individual fates determined by a social, economic, and political environment that is factually correct but fictionalized to the highest degree" (Siclier).

Critics who applaud the film grant that it has a lot in common with a photo-novel but, like Génin, are willing to overlook the fact: "Photo-novel dialogue? Of course. *Indochine* is nothing but a photo-novel. But with a masterful, seductive story" (34). Copperman agrees: "Yes, it is a pulp novel à la Delly. With an implausible plot, annoying ellipses, and clichés galore, but also magnificent images and a tone befitting the depiction of the colonial atmosphere." For its harshest critics the only appeal of the film lies in its stunning images, "incredibly exciting incitements to travel" according to Baignères, while Vallée adds, "The big winner is the Vietnam tourist office. When the film is over, all we think about is buying a ticket to Saigon."

Critics also disagree on the representation of colonialism. Some commend Wargnier for trying to convey the colonial atmosphere and showing the negative effects of colonization. Jeancolas is at another end of the critical spectrum on this point when he calls *Indochine* "the first pro-communist film of French cinema," adding, "*Indochine* is like *Gone with the Wind*, but it is a leftist *Gone with the Wind* [...]. We don't shed tears over defeated Southerners; the colonists and their guard dog police play the bad guys; nationalists and the people on the whole are the salt of the earth" (90).

Other commentators argue on the contrary that the film throws a positive light on colonization. The more nuanced among them agree that Wargnier takes a critical stance toward the topic. Roy, a journalist for the communist daily *L'Humanité*, describes *Indochine* as "a colonial film that had to take the course of history into account." According to Lefort's scathing review in *Libération*, on the other hand, the film looks back nostalgically on "the good old days of the colonies" and glorifies colonialism instead of questioning it: "Any fiction film (worthy of the name) that deals with the French 'presence' in Vietnam should spark controversy, raise a storm, or at least cause embarrassment." His most pointed criticism is directed at the portrayal of the Chief of Police, who is both brutal and likeable: "In order to avoid Manichaeism, as some would argue? Not at all: it is pure cowardice [on Wargnier's part]. This cowardice ends up eliciting if not respect, at least empathy for a historically questionable character" (43).

Finally, critics ponder the filmmakers' sudden interest in Vietnam—Pierre Schoendoerffer's *Diên Biên Phû* and Jean-Jacques Annaud's *The Lover* (*L'Amant*) were released the same year as *Indochine*. They offer several explanations: the end of the grieving process that started over thirty years before with the loss of Indochina and the rest of the colonial empire, the vogue of heritage films (see "The Cinematic Context" below), the opening of the borders of formerly colonized countries, and, in the case of Vietnam, the issuing of permits to make films in the country. Historian Benjamin Stora is favorable to the latter explanation: "Fundamentally, by allowing the former colonizers to come back, the ex-colonized were calling upon France to go further, to assume its historical responsibility."

The Historical Context: Indochina

Geographically, Indochina is the name given to the Southeast Asia peninsula located between India and China that includes Burma, Laos, Thailand, Cambodia, Vietnam, and part of Malaysia. Historically, the term Indochina (or French Indochina or the Indochinese Union) was applied in 1884 to the Indochinese territories colonized by France:

Cochinchina, Annam, Tonkin (all three part of modern Vietnam), and Cambodia. Laos was annexed to French Indochina in 1893.

The French colonized Indochina to protect their commercial interests and Catholic missionaries. At the beginning of the twentieth century, Indochinese intellectuals who had been educated at French universities began to oppose French rule, and dissenters became more radical after the creation of the Vietnamese Communist Party in 1930. The Communist Party led the fight against both the French colonization and the Japanese occupation during World War II. The people of Vietnam proclaimed their independence on September 2, 1945, and called themselves the Democratic Republic of Vietnam. However, France refused to give up Cochinchina, in the southern part of current Vietnam, starting their ill-fated Indochinese war the following year. After the defeat of its army at the battle of Diên Biên Phú in 1954, France signed the Geneva Accords. These declared the independence of Laos and Cambodia, divided Vietnam temporarily into two zones, and planned an election to reunify them. But ideological differences led to a war between communist North Vietnam and the government of South Vietnam, the latter backed by the United States. The reunification of the country finally took place in 1976, after the end of the Vietnam War.

The story of the film is told in flashback at the time of the Geneva Accords (1954). The story itself takes place from around 1928 to 1932, a period marked by the rise of nationalism and an increasing number of peasant revolts in the northern and central regions of the country, where poverty had worsened during the Great Depression. In a scene at the café at the beginning of the film, the Chief of Police mentions the Yen-Bay uprising of 1930, when Indochinese soldiers killed their French officers. The French army executed the rebel soldiers and destroyed the village where they had sought refuge. To protest against this harsh repression, Indochinese nationalists who lived in Paris organized a demonstration in front of the Élysée Palace. Camille's fiancé Tanh took part in this solidarity march as a student and was expelled from France.

We also witness a brief scene set in 1936 when the Popular Front, a left-wing coalition government, came to power in France and ordered the liberation of Indochinese political opponents who had been detained at a penal colony on the island of Poulo Condor. Camille is released from prison on this occasion and briefly reunited with her mother. We also learn that the Chief of Police was fired by the Popular Front and left Indochina.

The Heritage Film Genre

Indochine is a "heritage film," which refers to a corpus of big-budget films released in England and France in the 1980s and 1990s that draw their inspiration from history or literature and are characterized by a classical narrative and visual style, an elaborate mise en scène, and major stars (Austin 167). These films are very diverse but can be grouped into a few key categories: literary adaptations like *Jean de Florette* (Claude Berri, 1986), *Cyrano de Bergerac* (Jean-Paul Rappeneau, 1990), *Germinal* (Claude Berri, 1993), and *Madame Bovary* (Claude Chabrol, 1991); biopics about historical figures and artists, like *Danton* (Andrzej Wajda, 1983), *Camille Claudel* (Bruno Nuytten, 1989), or *Lucie Aubrac* (Claude Berri, 1997); historical dramas mostly centered on the French Revolution, World War II, and colonial conflicts. *Indochine* belongs to the last group, along with *Fort Saganne* (Alain Corneau, 1984).

Critics ascribe the emergence of heritage films in the 1980s to a crisis of national identity. Indeed, many socioeconomic changes were altering the way of life and outlook of French people at that time. Domestically, the economic downturn after the boom of *les Trente Glorieuses* (the "thirty glorious years," an expression coined by economist Jean Fourastié to describe the period of prosperity between 1945 and 1975) led to rising unemployment and, consequently, resentment against foreign workers and the appearance of the immigration issue on the political scene. Externally, the French felt threatened by the growth of the European Union, globalization, and the economic and cultural hegemony of the United States. Heritage films, which highlighted French culture, the rural way of life, and France's glorious past were a strong antidote to this crisis of identity. The production of blockbusters was encouraged by subsidies from the Ministry of Culture (as mentioned above for *Indochine*), moreover, as a way to compete with Hollywood and halt the steep decline in movie ticket sales for French films in the 1980s.

Although the socialist governments of the 1980s and 1990s promoted heritage films, these are often considered reactionary because they offer a nostalgic and one-sided perspective on the national past by foregrounding white characters from the privileged class and their viewpoints. In her reevaluation of the genre, Oscherwitz distances herself from this interpretation, however. She argues that these films also invite us to interrogate the relation between past and present and inscribe colonial history into French history, helping to legitimate the presence of descendants of colonized peoples in French society. It should also be noted that heritage films feature great female roles that allow actresses to compete with their male counterparts on a more level playing field.

STUDY GUIDE

What Happens in This Film?

1. What type of plantation does Eliane run? What does the work on the plantation consist of?

2. What happened at the auction?

3. What was Jean-Baptiste doing when he got lost and ended up at Eliane's plantation?

4. Why is Guy worried about the political situation, and what offer does he make to Eliane during their first meeting at the café?

5. Who burst into the house where Jean-Baptiste and Eliane had spent the night? Why?

6. Who is Tanh? Why did he come back from Paris? How does his mother hope to "tame" him?

7. How did Camille meet Jean-Baptiste? Why was he transferred to Dragon Island?

8. How did Camille manage to free herself to join Jean-Baptiste on Dragon Island? What happened there?

9. How did Jean-Baptiste and Camille manage to survive after their escape from Dragon Island?

10. How was Eliane treated by the French community after Camille's arrest?

11. What happened to Camille and Guy when the Popular Front came to power in 1936?

12. What did Camille reply when Eliane told her that the whole plantation was being kept for her? What did she ask Eliane to do?

True or False?

If the statement is false, correct it!

1. The film begins with the funeral of Eliane's husband.

2. The French crew led by the marine officer won the rowing race.

3. There was opium in the sampan (flat-bottomed boat) that Jean-Baptiste had set afire.

4. Eliane congratulated Raymond, Yvette's husband, for his courage during the factory fire started by nationalists.

5. Indochinese peasants go to Dragon Island in the hopes of finding work on plantations in the southern part of the country.

6. Tanh tells his mother that he learned the words "freedom" and "equality" by reading Karl Marx.

7. The goal of the "Operation Molière" was to perform Molière's plays in the villages of northern Indochina.

8. Guy tells Eliane that the only way for Camille to survive the penal colony is by collaborating with French authorities.

9. The Indochinese nicknamed Camille "the Joan of Arc of Indochina."

10. Jean-Baptiste committed suicide in the house of Eliane's father.

11. Camille belonged to the Vietnamese delegation that attended the signing of the Geneva Accords.

12. The reunion between Etienne and his mother was very moving, and Etienne decided to go back to Vietnam with her.

What Did You Learn in the Introduction?

1. What films by Régis Wargnier deal with Southeast Asia?

2. Why did Wargnier agree to make *Indochine*?

3. What role did literature play in the origin and making of the film?

4. Why was Catherine Deneuve interested in *Indochine*, and why was the role of Eliane perfect for her?

5. What are some of the similarities between actress Linh Dan Pham and her character, Camille?

6. How do critics assess the representation of colonialism in the film?

7. How can one explain the renewal of interest in Indochina in French cinema of the early 1990s?

8. When, why, and how long did France colonize Indochina?

9. Who were the Indochinese nationalists, and what examples of nationalist fights are mentioned in the film?

10. What are some of the characteristics of heritage films?

11. What explains the release of many heritage films in the 1980s and 1990s?

12. What are some of the criticisms of the heritage genre?

Exploring the Film

1. The Prologue

Watch the beginning of the film again (Excerpt 1, 00'20–4'00). What impression do the first images create—the mist on the river and boats gradually appearing? **What themes of the film are introduced in the prologue (up until the voice-over stops)?** What types of music do we hear? When does the music change? How is the music related to the themes and to the narrator's comments?

How is the passage of time depicted in the film when Camille arrives on the plantation in the luxury car driven by the Hindu chauffeur? How much time do you think has passed since the prologue? What differences do you notice in Camille's clothing?

What characteristics of the heritage film are found in this sequence?

2. The Voice-Over

What is the role of the voice-over at the beginning of the film? When do we understand that it is part of a flashback and that Eliane is telling her story to Etienne, her Indochinese adopted son? What did you think the first time you saw Eliane with him, before his identity was revealed?

3. The Setting: Scenes of Colonial Life

Review the sequence at Eliane's house (Excerpt 2, 4'20–6'00). How do Eliane and her father relate to their Vietnamese female employees? What is Eliane's reaction to her father's behavior with the young Indochinese servant? What do you think of it?

Review the rowing race (Excerpt 3, 6'00–8'50). What characters and groups are introduced in this scene? What are these colonists' different opinions of the Indochinese? What is the symbolic meaning of the race and its outcome?

In the auction scene, what painting does Jean-Baptiste Le Guen want to buy and why? **What facets of his personality and of his future relationship with Eliane are revealed in this scene?**

4. The Characters

+ *Eliane*

How long has Eliane lived in Indochina? What shows that she is well integrated into Indochinese society?

Describe Eliane's personality and her role on the plantation. *Review the scene where she has just flogged her coolie* (Excerpt 4, 14'10–14'40). Why does Wargnier not show the flogging? What does Eliane compare herself to in this scene, and how do you interpret the worker's response?

What type of mother is Eliane for Camille? Can you find similarities in her roles as plantation boss and mother?

What are Eliane's relationships with the men around her? What type of relationship does she have with her father? How is she implicitly presented when she punishes her worker and when she dances the tango with Camille in Excerpt 2 (especially through the parallel with the Emile-Hoa couple)?

Do you agree with critics who, like Humbert, think that Eliane emasculates the men around her?

How do you explain her passion for Jean-Baptiste?

Do you agree with Yvette when she says that Eliane does not know how to love? And with Jean-Baptiste, who believes that she and the whole planter class use people the way they "bleed" their trees?

How does Eliane evolve in the film? What aspect of her life is highlighted at the end?

+ *Camille*

What sort of life does Camille lead at the beginning of the film? What does she know about her country? How can we interpret the fact that she is often seen inside, behind doors or windows (as in the car in the opening sequence or during the Christmas party, when Guy makes her dance with him)?

What can we make of the scene after her accident when, covered with blood, she opens her eyes and asks Jean-Baptiste if she is alive?

What did Camille learn from her trip through Vietnam, and how did this influence her political evolution? *Review the scene where she is eating with the peasant family* (Excerpt 5, 1h17'50–1h18'50).

Why did Camille kill the French officer on Dragon Island?

Why did Camille become a communist at the penal colony? How do you understand her decision to cut all ties with her family when she was released? Why do you think she asked her adoptive mother to take Etienne to France when she herself wanted to devote herself to her country?

+   *Jean-Baptiste*

What are Jean-Baptiste's values at the beginning of the film? *Review in particular the scene where he has the sampan burned* (Excerpt 6, 11'45–13'00). How do you explain his sudden change in attitude the next day, when he is looking for the Indochinese man and his son who were aboard the boat? Does it have something to do with his personality, or is it an inconsistency in the story?

How does Jean-Baptiste evolve? Compare the sampan scene and the scene at the slave market. *Review this latter scene* (Excerpt 7, 1h25'00–1h26'30).

In your opinion, how did Jean-Baptiste die? Did he commit suicide? Was he murdered? If yes, by whom? By the communists? By Guy and the police? By the Navy?

+   *Guy*

What methods does Guy use as Chief of Police (for example to find the people who set fire to Eliane's plant)? Do you agree with Lefort who criticizes this character for eliciting empathy and even respect? Do you find Guy likeable?

+   *Monsieur Emile*

How does Eliane's father spend his time (when he is not with the Indochinese servant)? What do you think of his intrusion into Eliane's love life? Is Jean-Baptiste's violent reaction justified?

+   *Tanh*

What is Tanh's social class? After being deported from France, he tells Camille, in the scene at the café, "Now it's over. I was bad, and I'm taking the consequences." What are his true feelings, in fact? *Review the scene with his mother* (Excerpt 8, 1h18'40–1h19'20). What does he plan to do? How do Tanh's revolutionary ideas also apply to the personal sphere (his relations with Camille)?

5. Colonial Relations

Academic critics, like journalists, focused on the representation of colonial relations in the film, often by comparing *Indochine* with other fiction films on the same theme. Given the absence of the Indochinese conflict from the big screen until the release of *The Lover*, *Diên Biên Phú*, and *Indochine* in 1992, Wargnier's film has been mainly compared to movies made before decolonization and the access of African countries to independence in the 1960s, like *Zouzou* (Marc Allégret, 1934), *Princess Tam-Tam* (Edmond Gréville, 1935), or *Pépé le Moko* (Julien Duvivier, 1937). Commentators reach different conclusions, but some of the characteristics of colonial cinema can still prove useful for an in-depth discussion of *Indochine*.

Colonial films depict the sweetness of life in the colonies by emphasizing the exotic scenery (Loufti) without paying much attention to local cultures. **What is the situation in *Indochine* in this regard?** Does the film highlight the scenery, or does Wargnier avoid "aestheticism for aestheticism's sake," as he argues (Brantes)?

What aspects of Vietnamese culture are presented, and are they treated with respect? As we mentioned earlier, some critics consider the film as nothing but a series of beautiful images. Do you agree? Do you share the opinion of a commentator for whom, "When the film is over, all we think about is buying a ticket to Saigon"? Did the film make you want to visit Vietnam?

Traditional colonial films also focus on adventure and overlook the reality of colonial life. **Do you think that the colonial context in *Indochine* is just a backdrop for the romantic story?** Jeancolas considers that "*Indochine* is the first French commercial film that takes apart the mechanism of colonialism with calculated but convincing innocence [. . .]" (89). What does the film teach us about the way colonialism worked in Indochina?

Do you believe, like Lefort (*Libération*), Rollet, and Norindr, among others, that the film sings the praises of colonialism by glorifying its agents, such as planters, the police, or the Navy? Or do you favor the opinion of Jeancolas, for whom "colonists and their guard dog police play the bad guys; nationalists and the people on the whole are the salt of the earth" (90)?

One justification for colonialism was the "civilizing mission," the idea that France was bringing progress to inferior and uncivilized peoples. From this perspective the relation between colonizers and colonized was often paternalistic, reproducing hierarchical family relations with the father as head of the family, in charge of his children's education. **Are there references to this civilizing mission in the film?**

Another aspect of the colonial imaginary is the **eroticization of colonized people, women in particular.** At the same time, interracial relationships were taboo in colonial societies, especially those involving white women. According to Sherzer, films dealing with colonialism since the 1980s depict the Other in a much more positive light and feature mixed couples, but she notes that their relationships are bound to fail and have negative consequences. **Are the Vietnamese women of the film, including Camille, eroticized? How are interracial relationships portrayed?**

Finally, colonial films tell their stories from the viewpoint of the colonizer. **What viewpoint dominates in *Indochine*?** Is it completely plausible, given some of the events that take place? Is the action sometimes presented from the viewpoint of Indochinese characters? If yes, when?

6. Eliane and Camille: An Allegorical Interpretation?

Most critics argue that the relationship between Eliane and Camille mirrors that of France and Indochina, an observation reinforced by the fact that **Catherine Deneuve has served as model for the representation of "Marianne," the symbol of the French Republic.** Wargnier himself said that this idea helped him make progress on the screenplay: "The big break came the day we found a metaphor for the film. We needed two characters to embody France and Vietnam. We chose the mother-daughter pair, and we imagined adoption as a metaphor for colonization" (Andreu 113).

What parallels can you find between Eliane and Camille on one side, and France and Indochina on the other? Analyze the stages in Eliane and Camille's relationship, and link them to changes in the relation between France and Indochina. For example, what might the following events stand for: Eliane's adoption of Camille, the conflict between the two, and their separation at the end?

7. The Last Sequence

What does the scenery around Lake Geneva call to mind at the beginning of the sequence? What other elements of the setting reinforce this parallel? What does this parallel reveal about Eliane's state of mind?

As in the opening sequence, Eliane is dressed in black, as if in mourning. What is she grieving here? Is the ending of the film totally dark?

8. Etienne

Can you understand Etienne's refusal to reunite with his mother in Geneva? He tells Eliane, "You are my mother," and there is no doubt that he is going to return to France with her. What **allegorical interpretation** could we give of this comment by Etienne with regard to the integration of second-generation Vietnamese immigrants into French society? What might be its implications concerning the prospect of integrating Franco-Maghrebis successfully, an important debate at the time of the release of the film in 1992?

Régis Wargnier's Filmography

1986   The Woman of My Life (La Femme de ma vie)
1988   I'm the King of the Castle (Je suis le seigneur du château)
1992   Indochine
1995   A French Woman (Une femme française)
1999   Est-Ouest
2005   Man to Man
2006   Have Mercy on Us All (Pars vite et reviens tard)
2010   The Straight Line (La Ligne droite)
2014   The Gate (Le Temps des aveux)

Works Consulted

Andreu, Anne. "Cinéma français: la reconquête de l'Indochine." L'Evénement du jeudi, 16–22 Apr. 1992: 112–13.

Austin, Guy. Contemporary French Cinema. 2nd ed. Manchester, England: Manchester UP, 2008.

Baignères, Claude. "Indochine de Régis Wargnier. Mélodrame exotique." Le Figaro, 16 Apr. 1992: n. pag.

Brantes, Emmanuel de. "La légende de la congaï." Le Quotidien de Paris, 15 Apr. 1992: n. pag.

Coppermann, Annie. "Indochine de Régis Wargnier. D'un romanesque flamboyant." Les Echos, 15 Apr. 1992: n. pag.

Génin, Bernard. "Indochine." Télérama, 15 Apr. 1992: 33–34.

Gianorio, Richard. "Linh Dan Pham, la tonkiki-tonkinoise. . . ." *France-Soir*, 15 May 1992: n. pag.

Grousset, Jean-Paul. "Indochine." *Le Canard enchaîné*, 15 Apr. 1992: n. pag.

Humbert, Brigitte E. "Filming France's Colonial Past: Women 'Wearing the Pants' in *Outremer* and *Indochine*." *Studies in French Cinema* 12.1 (2012): 59–74.

Jeancolas, Jean-Pierre. "*Indochine*. Avant la guerre." *Positif* 375–76 (May 1992): 89–91.

Lacharrière, Marc Ladreit de. "Discours prononcé par M. Marc Ladreit de Lacharrière pour l'installation de M. Régis Wargnier à l'Académie des beaux-arts, le mercredi 1er février 2012." Web. 16 Feb. 2018. <http://www.academiedesbeauxarts.fr /upload/reception/2012/discours_marcdelacharriere_2012.pdf>.

Lefort, Gérard. "La France occupée par l'Indochine." *Libération*, 15 Apr. 1992: 42–43.

Loufti, Martine. "Film Industry and Colonial Representation." *Cinema, Colonialism, Postcolonialism: Perspectives from the French and Francophone World*. Ed. D. Sherzer. Austin: U of Texas P, 1996. 21–29.

Murray, Allison. "Women, Nostalgia, Memory: *Chocolat, Outremer*, and *Indochine*." *Research in African Literatures* 33.2 (2002): 235–44.

Nicholls, David. "Indochine." *History Today* 46.9 (1996): 33–38.

Norindr, Panivong. "Filmic Memorial and Colonial Blues: Indochina in Contemporary French Cinema." *Cinema, Colonialism, Postcolonialism: Perspectives from the French and Francophone World*. Ed. D. Sherzer. Austin: U of Texas P, 1996. 120–46.

Oscherwitz, Dayna. "Family Pictures: Ancestry, Nostalgia, and the French Heritage Film." *Past Forward: French Cinema and the Post-Colonial Heritage*. Carbondale, IL: Southern Illinois UP, 2010. 33–63.

Pascal, Michel. "Parfums d'Asie." *Le Point*, 11 Apr. 1992: n. pag.

Rollet, Brigitte. "Identity and Alterity in *Indochine* (Wargnier, 1992)." *French Cinema in the 1990s: Continuity and Difference*. Ed. Phil Powrie. Oxford, England: Oxford UP, 1999. 37–46.

Roth-Bettoni, Didier. "Entretien avec Régis Wargnier." *Revue du cinéma* 482 (May 1992): 36–37.

———. "*Indochine*. Le temps d'aimer, le temps de mourir." *Revue du cinéma* 481 (Apr. 1992): 20–21.

Roy, Jean. "*Indochine*, film français de Régis Wargnier. Pour l'amour de Catherine." *L'Humanité*, 17 May 1992: n. pag.

Royer, Philippe. "Un roman écrit à quatre mains. Un entretien avec Régis Wargnier." *La Croix*, 16 Apr. 1992: n. pag.

Sherzer, Dina. "Race Matters and Matters of Race. Interracial Relationships in Colonial and Postcolonial Films." *Cinema, Colonialism, Postcolonialism: Perspectives from the French and Francophone World*. Ed. Dina Sherzer. Austin: U of Texas P, 1996. 229–48.

Siclier, Jacques. "Indochine, ton nom est femme." *Le Monde*, 17 Apr. 1992: n. pag.

Stora, Benjamin. "Rebonds. Indochine, Algérie, autorisations de retour." *Libération*, 30 Apr. 1992: n. pag.

Stouvenot, Michèle. "Deneuve, l'Indochine et l'amour." *Le Journal du dimanche*, 12 Apr. 1992: n. pag.

Toscan du Plantier, Daniel. "*Indochine*." *Le Figaro Magazine*, 11 Apr. 1992: n. pag.

Tranchant, Marie-Noelle. "Régis Wargnier: 'Sous l'Indochine, j'ai découvert le Vietnam.'" *Le Figaro*, 15 Apr. 1992: n. pag.

Vallée, Didier. "*Indochine*." *V-S-D*, 16 Apr. 1992: n. pag.

Vincendeau, Ginette. "Un genre qui fait problème: le Heritage film. La critique face à un genre populaire des deux côtés de la Manche." *Le Cinéma français face aux genres*. Ed. Raphaëlle Moine. Paris, France: Maison des sciences de l'homme, 2005. 131–40.

Wargnier, Régis, dir. *Indochine*. Sony Pictures Classics, 1999.

II

Socio-Cultural Themes 1: Suburbs, Unemployment, Exclusion

Mathieu Kassovitz, *Hate* (1995)

Bruno Dumont, *The Life of Jesus* (1997)

Erick Zonca, *The Dreamlife of Angels* (1998)

Agnès Varda's film *Vagabond* (*Sans toit ni loi*, 1985), which is about a young woman who roams around southern France in the winter living from hand to mouth and meeting a tragic end, inaugurated a new focus in French cinema that asserted itself more and more clearly during the 1990s. Related to the crude realism of the 1970s (the films of Jean Eustache, Maurice Pialat, and Bertrand Blier, for example), this trend is represented primarily by young filmmakers who, like the directors of the three films in this section, made their first feature film in this decade—although it also includes more seasoned filmmakers like Bertrand Tavernier, Claire Denis, Robert Guédiguian, and Benoît Jacquot.

As many commentators have observed, this brand of cinema is characterized particularly by its "ex-centrism," that is, the fact that the films are made outside Paris, whether it be in the suburbs, as in Matthieu Kassovitz's *Hate* (1995), or in the provinces, like Manuel Poirier's *Western* (1997), the action of which takes place in Brittany, Sandrine Veysset's *Will It Snow for Christmas?* (*Y'aura t'il de la neige à Noël?*, 1996), filmed on a farm in the south of France, Laetitia Masson's *To Have (or Not)* (*En avoir [ou pas]*, 1995) placed in Lyon, or all of Robert Guédiguian's films, like *'Til Death Do Us Part* (*A la vie, à la mort!*, 1995) and *Marius et Jeannette* (1997), which take place in the disadvantaged neighborhoods of Marseille.

Suburb films like *Hate* occupy a particularly important place in contemporary French cinema. The worrisome situation in the French suburbs had been portrayed for decades, beginning with Jean-Luc Godard's film *2 or 3 Things I Know about Her* (*Deux ou trois choses que je sais d'elle*, 1967), in which he criticizes the conception of the huge low-income housing project at La Courneuve, the Cité des 4000, north of Paris. For a good dozen years before the release of *Hate*, the representations of the Parisian suburbs had become more and more troubling. After the depiction of juvenile delinquency in Serge Le Péron's *Forget It* (*Laisse béton*, back slang for "Laisse tomber," 1984) and of North African families in the suburbs in Mehdi Charef's *Tea in the Harem* (*Le Thé au harem d'Archimède*, 1985), Claude Brisseau's film *Sound and Fury* (*De bruit et de fureur*, 1988) served up "a convulsive, quasi-apocalyptic vision of these same suburbs" (Jousse 37).

In the United States, after the huge success of Spike Lee's *Do the Right Thing* (1989), multiple films came out on the black ghettos of Los Angeles (the "hood"), such as John Singleton's *Boyz n the Hood* (1991) and the Hughes Brothers' *Menace II Society* (1993), providing encouragement to French directors. Malik Chibane's *Hexagone*, for instance, follows the lives and reveals the ambitions of five adolescents of North African descent (Beurs) seeking their identity in a suburb twenty kilometers from Paris.

Then, in 1995, we witnessed an explosion of films on the suburbs, soon perceived as a new genre, the "suburb film" (*film de banlieue*): along with *Hate*, the prototype, were released, one after the other, Thomas Gilou's *Raï*, Jean-François Richet's *Inner City* (*Etat des lieux*), and Malik Chibane's second film *Sweet France* (*Douce France*), followed in 1997 by Richet's hyper-violent film *Crack 6-T* (*Ma 6-T va crack-er*).

The successive French governments were not unaware of the problems facing suburb dwellers, and grand "suburb plans" to improve the situation came one after the other. In autumn 1995 the president of the Republic Jacques Chirac even announced a "Marshall Plan" for the suburbs. That did nothing to prevent the long-suffering suburbs from exploding throughout France in 2005, ten years after the release of *Hate*, as if to confirm the predictions of Kassovitz's film. During several weeks of rioting in the projects in September 2005, thousands of cars were burned in a surge of anger against the living conditions in the suburbs, the rampant unemployment, the lack of hope for a better life—in short, the exclusion from French society. Miraculously, no deaths resulted from the weeks of violent demonstrations.

Despite the importance of the suburb films, it is primarily the North of France, a region that was suffering severely from the economic crises of the period, that attracted the attention of this "New New Wave," as certain critics called it. A whole series of films were thus shot either in Lille, like Erick Zonca's *The Dreamlife of Angels* (*La Vie rêvée des anges*, 1998) and Gaspar Noé's *I Stand Alone* (*Seul contre tous*—the first part, at least—1998), or in the small towns of the Nord-Pas-de-Calais region, like Xavier Beauvois' *North* (*Nord*, 1991), Bertrand Tavernier's *It Begins Today* (*Ça commence aujourd'hui*, 1999), and Bruno Dumont's *The Life of Jesus* (*La Vie de Jésus*, 1997) and *L'Humanité* (1999). All of these films, one critic remarks, "choose as their subject 'another' France, non-Parisian, non-intellectual, a France of 'little people,' small merchants in provincial towns of little interest, underprivileged social classes, the excluded, unemployed, street people, products of the famous 'social divide' (*fracture sociale*) . . . , a whole world of people who had been excluded from the French screens for a very long time" (Konstantarakos 2). Since the cinema of the 1930s, more precisely.

Konstantarakos was referring, in particular, to the poetic realism of the 1930s, the films of Marcel Carné and his regular screenwriter, the poet Jacques Prévert, works like *Port of Shadows* (*Quai des brumes*, 1938) and *Daybreak* (*Le Jour se lève*, 1939). It was a deeply pessimistic cinema that depicted little people in gray working-class neighborhoods, but a cinema that was rich in symbolism, metaphors, and themes. Similarly, the hard-core realism of the films of the 1990s is often tempered by a lyrical side that has led some critics (Beugnet, Vassé, Konstantarakos, Singerman, for example) to associate them with a "new poetic realism." The metaphysical contours of *The Life of Jesus* and *Humanity* are often cited as examples, and, indeed, Dumont constantly refers to "poetry" when speaking of his films. The introduction of forms of poetry into the grimmest realism, a phenomenon that we observe in numerous films of this period, is one of the defining features of the French cinema of the 1990s.

Works Consulted

Beugnet, Martine. "Le Souci de l'autre: réalisme poétique et critique sociale dans le cinéma français contemporain." *Iris* 29 (Spring 2000): 53–66.

Jousse, Thierry. "Le Banlieue-film existe-t-il?" *Cahiers du cinéma* 492 (June 1995): 37–39.

Konstantarakos, Myrto. "Retour du politique dans le cinéma français contemporain?" *French Studies Bulletin* 68 (Autumn 1998): 1–5.

Singerman, Alan. "Le Cinéma français de nos jours: pour un réalisme poétique *frontal*." *France in the Twenty-First Century. New Perspectives.* Ed. Marie-Christine Weidemann Koop and Rosalie Vermette. Birmingham, AL: Summa, 2009. 317–40.

Vassé, Claire. "*En avoir (ou pas).* La girafe et son prince." *Positif* 419 (Jan. 1996): 22–23.

5

Mathieu Kassovitz

Hate (La Haine)

(1995)

Mathieu Kassovitz, *Hate*: The three urban ghetto buddies (Vinz, Hubert, and Saïd).

Director. .... Mathieu Kassovitz
Screenplay.. Mathieu Kassovitz
Director of Photography .... Pierre Aïm
Camera ....Georges Diane
Film Editors .... Mathieu Kassovitz, Scott Stevenson
Sound .... Vincent Tulli
Art Director ....Giuseppe Ponturo
Music... Assassin
Costumes ....Virginie Montel
Continuity ....Nathalie Vierny
Producer .... Christophe Rossignon
Length.. 1h38

Cast

Vincent Cassel (*Vinz*), Hubert Koundé (*Hubert*), Saïd Taghmaoui (*Saïd*), Karim Belkhadra (*Samir*), Edouard Montoute (*Walmart*), François Levantal (*Snoopy*), Solo Dicko (*Santo, Vinz's friend, in Paris*), Arash Mansour (*Arash, Santo's friend*), Marc Duret (*Inspector "Notre Dame"*), Héloïse Rauth (*Sarah*), Rywka Wajsbrot (*Vinz's grandmother*), Tadek Lokcinski (*Monsieur Toilettes in Paris*), Choukri Gabteni (*Nordine, Saïd's older brother*), Philippe Nahon (*police chief*), Nabil Ben Mhamed (*Sam, young boy who tells a joke*), Félicité Wouassi (*Hubert's mother*), Fatou Thioune (*Hubert's sister*), Zinedine Soualem, Bernie Bonvoisin, Cyril Ancelin (*plain-clothes policemen in Paris*), Karine Viard, Julie Mauduech (*young women at the art gallery*), Vincent Lindon (*drunk man in the street*), Mathieu Kassovitz (*the skinhead who is beaten and threatened with death*)

Story

Abdel, a young Frenchman of North African descent (a *Beur*), is lying in a coma in the hospital owing to excessive force used by the police while he was being interrogated in a police station in the Paris suburbs. Violent riots have broken out in the Cité des Muguets where Abdel lived. The young men in the neighborhood, furious, have confronted the police all night long, burning cars and a school, as well as centers that were created for them, including a gymnasium where Hubert, a young black man, worked on his boxing skills. The following morning Hubert is met there by his two buddies, Vinz, a working-class Jew, and Saïd, a wise-cracking young Beur, who had both participated in the events of the night before. Vinz, who loathes the police, had picked up a service revolver dropped by a policeman during the skirmishes. If their pal Abdel dies from his wounds, he swears, he is going to "blow away a cop." The spectator is going to live this whole day with the three friends, twenty-four hours that are punctuated by the posting of the precise time of day on the screen at various intervals. Life in the projects is revealed in bits and pieces, as are the relations between the three friends, who eventually take a run into Paris—alien territory—to get some money owed to Saïd. Then things get complicated . . .

The Director

Mathieu Kassovitz was born on August 3, 1967, in Paris. His father was a filmmaker (a Jewish refugee from Hungary at the time of the 1956 Revolution) and his French mother a professional film editor. There was thus little doubt about his destiny. As he said himself, "My father is a cineaste . . . my mother is a film editor; if they had been bakers, I probably would be making baguettes somewhere today" (Ferenczi, "Kassovitz"). As a young boy he spent much of his time on his father's shoots and began to play small roles at the age of twelve. While he was still in high school, he did internships in filmmaking during the summer, then left school without receiving his diploma when he was offered a spot on a film project during the school year. Following this experience, he worked as assistant director on several films before undertaking a series of short subjects, the second of which, *White Nightmare* (*Cauchemar blanc*, 1991), won a prize at Cannes.

Before achieving fame as a filmmaker, Kassovitz had already drawn considerable attention as a film actor by winning two major acting awards, a César as the Most

Promising Actor and the Jean Gabin Prize, for his role across from Jean-Louis Trintignant in *See How They Fall* (*Regarde les hommes tomber*, 1993) by Jacques Audiard. Encouraged, he launched into his first feature film, *Café au lait* (*Métisse*, 1993), which earned him plaudits from the critics and two awards at the Paris Film Festival, the Special Jury Prize, and a Best Actor prize. We also see in this film, in his first big role, Hubert Koundé, who two years later played the role of Hubert, the young black man, in *Hate*— the film that made Mathieu Kassovitz a major film director at the age of twenty-seven.

Kassovitz continued his double career of actor and director in the following years. He played starring roles in *A Self-Made Hero* (*Un héros très discret*, 1996) by Jacques Audiard and *Amélie* (2001) by Jean-Pierre Jeunet, while at the same time directing several thrillers, *Assassin(s)* in 1997, *The Crimson Rivers* (*Les Rivières pourpres*, 2000), which won another Best Director award, and *Gothika* (2003), made in Hollywood with two big stars, Hally Berry and Penelope Cruz. Trying his hand at nearly everything, he made a commercial for the celebrated Parisian department store Le Printemps, then turned himself into a male model to serve as the image for Lancôme's perfume "Miracle." The following year, however, we found him nominated again for a Best Actor prize for his performance in the multi-award-winning Holocaust film by Costa Gavras, *Amen* (2002).

The Origin and Making of the Film

Hate was shot from September to November 1994 in Paris and in the Cité de La Noé in Chanteloup-les-Vignes in Ile-de-France (less than an hour northwest of Paris). This site was chosen in part because it was a "normal" *cité* (housing project in the suburbs) and, as the director explains, "not a slum, like we see too often in the media. Because what is interesting is to show that things can blow up anywhere," not only in the toughest suburbs (Bernard 113). In fact, Kassovitz didn't have much choice. As Eric Pujol, the first assistant director, confides, they had proposed their film project to a dozen suburb cities, and "eleven of them threw us out" (Bernard 106). Since the police would not dare set foot in the Cité de la Noé, security was provided during the shooting of the film by The Messengers, a group of around fifteen "big brothers," between twenty and thirty years of age, who belonged to an organization in the suburb city (from the commentary of the producer, Christophe Rossignon, on the Bonus DVD).

Kassovitz chose his three principal actors six months ahead of time and informed them that he was writing his screenplay with them in mind. He even kept their real first names in the film: Vinz, Hubert, and Saïd. Knowing that it would be difficult to film in the projects, the director and his three protagonists lived for three months in the *cité* itself—"in a three-room apartment, to have a minimum of credibility" ("Spécial Cannes" 141)—including a whole month before the beginning of the shoot. "The young people in the suburbs are understandably sick and tired of the image of them in the media. Some of them refused to have anything to do with us. But we were able to grow their comfort level with us little by little" (Remy 44). Kassovitz knew that it was essential to create relationships well ahead of time with the neighborhood youth to avoid problems with them during the filming. The risk involved in making a film in the projects surrounded by aggressive, disrespectful young men was considerable: "The *cité*," said Kassovitz, "has to be managed carefully. All one person has to do is slap a kid once because he's sick of being insulted by him, and the shoot is over. We were all aware of it.

There was a lot of tension, but it was healthy. We knew that we were making a 'different kind' of film" ("Spécial Cannes" 141). Ultimately, around 300 young people from the Cité de la Noé would serve as extras in *Hate*, some of them in police uniforms . . .

It is not indifferent that the idea for the film was triggered by a real event: the murder of a young man from Zaïre, Makome M'Bowole, by a police inspector on April 6, 1993, during an interrogation in a police station of the 18th arrondissement for the theft of a carton of cigarettes. "I wondered," the director muses, "how a guy could get up in the morning and die at night in this manner" (Remy). This tragic event set off a week of demonstrations and violent confrontations in the streets between the angry youths and the police, both of which Kassovitz witnessed personally. The following day, he went to his producer and told him that he wanted to make a film on what had just happened.

Kassovitz first made *Hate* in color (to avoid alienating the television channels that were financing the project) but used a copy in black and white as the finished product "to emphasize the stark character of the film," he said. This produced a documentary tone as well as a kind of hyperrealism that fit well with the asphalt environment in which the action takes place and with the underlying violence, always ready to burst out. As the director explained, "Film in black and white recalls the newsreels during the war. You can't be more realistic than images of war. . . . A film in black and white always has a rather exceptional side, because it shows things in an unusual light, and that is why it produces more realism" (Levieux 20). From an aesthetic viewpoint, he adds elsewhere, black and white film highlights the particular beauty of the *cité* by making it more graphic.

Contrary to the practice of many filmmakers, and doubtlessly to go more quickly, Kassovitz reduced dramatically the number of takes, limiting himself to a maximum of four per shot. This was a big risk if one considers that certain filmmakers, like Robert Bresson, would do twenty or thirty takes of a single shot that might last ten seconds. Kassovitz also attempted by purely cinematographic means to create a contrast between the scenes in the suburbs and those that take place in Paris, since these are two different worlds with different atmospheres. In the sequences filmed in the suburbs, for example, he used numerous dolly shots, whereas he shot in Paris with a tripod and a hand-held camera—although many of the scenes were shot with a Steadicam in both places. In the *cité* he did many shots with a short focal lens (and thus with considerable depth of field) "to better integrate the people into their environment," whereas in Paris he generally used a long focal lens to separate the three "intruders" from the urban milieu (by creating a blurred background).

Following the example of Bresson this time, Kassovitz refused to use any background (mood) music in his film. Only diegetic music is permitted—music coming from a radio, for example, or from a recording in the fictional universe of the film (funk, rap, and soul especially). As the director explained, "The elimination of music allows us to do a better job with the sound track. We put in sounds from the city, which became *our* music" (Bourguignon and Tobin 13); "Everything is based on the natural rhythm of language and gestures" (Tranchant). "The dialogue," a critic observes finally, "is like the musical accompaniment" of the film (Chemineau).

For another commentator, *Hate* is "a film on the pleasure of speaking and the permanent invention of language, on the enjoyment of glibness, and on energy as a channeling of distress" (De Bruyn 16). It is a film in which, indeed, the youth of the suburbs talk endlessly, using over and over again certain basic expressions, using their own particular slang—*verlan* especially—the very special language (see below in the Study Guide) that emanates from their oral culture and highlights their existential specificity, as it does their anchorage in the suburbs. The role of language in the film is perhaps best summed up as follows: "Contrary to expectations, there is little or no music in Mathieu Kassovitz's film, but on the other hand people talk all the time and on every topic. [There is] an avalanche of words, expressions, stories, the infernal rhythm of the dialogue, an astonishing invention of language. . . . It is this language that gives its beat to the film, through the accents, the inflections, the musicality composed of syncopation and fluidity, the torrent of insults, the accelerations . . . " (Jousse 34). The rhythmic character of the dialogue is thus not a matter of chance. As Kassovitz states, in speaking of his three protagonistes, "They are good actors. I worked incessantly with them on the rhythm; they have it naturally, but we tried to develop it to the maximum" (Boulay and Colmant).

The Actors

The actors embodying the three young suburb dwellers had all acted already in other films. Hubert Koundé, who is not from the suburbs (and who had obtained a college degree in philosophy), played one of the main roles in Kassovitz's first feature film, *Café au lait* (1993), as noted above. Saïd Taghmaoui, a Beur, is the only one of the three actors who came from a tough neighborhood, "the 3,000" in Aulnay-sous-Bois (a northeastern suburb of Paris). He attracted attention for his performance in a film for television by Olivier Dahan (*Frères*, 1994) and an episode of *All the Boys and Girls of Their Age . . .* (*Tous les garçons et filles de leur âge. . .*, 1993), before being nominated for the Most Promising Actor award at the 1996 Césars for his role in *Hate*.

But the great revelation of the film was Vincent Cassell, the son of the famous French actor Jean-Pierre Cassell. In *Hate* Cassell plays, as Kassovitz describes it, the role of a "little jerk" (*petit con*), which the actor has some difficulty assuming. He nonetheless manages to embrace brilliantly the obnoxious, tormented character. "With his character Vinz, Hate personified," marvel the critics at *Libération*, "[Cassell] has established himself as a physical, electrifying, astonishingly graceful, ethereal actor" (Boulay, "Vincent"). With *Hate* Cassell began a remarkable career in the cinema, playing beside Jean Reno in Kassovitz's following film *The Crimson Rivers* (2000), then main roles in Christophe Gans' extremely successful *Brotherhood of the Wolf* (*Le Pacte des loups*, 2001), Jacques Audiard's *Read My Lips* (*Sur mes lèvres*, 2001), and Gaspar Noé's *Irréversible* (2002), before winning numerous Best Actor awards for two films by Jean-François Richet on Jacques Mesrine, *Mesrine Part I: Killer Instinct* (*L'Instinct de mort*) and *Mesrine Part II: Public Enemy #1* (*L'Ennemi public No. 1*), both in 2008. He also played an important role in Darren Aronofsky's *Black Swan* (2010), which garnered around one hundred awards, including a Best Actress Oscar for Nathalie Portman.

The Reception

Hate was selected for the Cannes Film Festival in 1995. The day before the screening of the film at Cannes, an adolescent was severely beaten in a Paris suburb by the police and was lying in a critical state—as if reality were imitating fiction. Whether or not this incident had an effect on the reception of the film, *Hate* was a huge hit with the audience and the critics, winning the Best Director prize for Mathieu Kassovitz and a nomination for the grand prize (the Palme d'Or), before receiving the Félix for the Best Young European Film in Berlin in November. At this time, with two million seats already sold, *Hate* was one of the five most commercial successful films of the year (Campion). The following spring brought a complete consecration: three Césars, including Best Film, Best Producer, and Best Editing—although both Kassovitz and Cassell refused to attend the ceremony (to protest against the type of films that normally win awards at the Césars). The same year, Kassovitz walked away with the Best Film and Best Director prizes at the Lumière Awards. Critics began to compare him to the iconic American filmmakers Martin Scorsese (*Mean Streets*, 1973, *Raging Bull*, 1980) and Spike Lee (*Do the Right Thing*, 1989), noting an important revival of the influence of American cinema (especially ghetto films) on French cinema.

With rare exceptions, *Hate* was widely praised by the cinema press, which recognized Kassovitz's originality and talent as a director: "A *tour de force*" and "a brilliant piece of cinema," says *Le Figaro* (Baignères), while the film magazine *Positif* proclaims, "With *Hate*, the suburbs finally come out of the ghetto to take the Cannes Festival by storm" ("Mathieu Kassovitz" 4). *L'Avant-Scène du Cinéma* follows suit: "This film gives the floor to people we have never heard from before in French cinema" (Rebouillon 128). The *Cahiers du cinéma* calls it "the film event of the Cannes Festival, turned into a social phenomenon" (Sibony 30), and *Le Nouvel Observateur* goes even further: "Mathieu Kassovitz has just succeeded in making, with *Hate*, the film that we were all awaiting on contemporary life. A truly seminal work of an absolutely modern cinema, as *A bout de souffle* was in its time" (Riou). The critic of *InfoMatin*, finally, strongly concurs: "Mathieu Kassovitz has made an exceptionally mature film; with linguistic fireworks and constant innovation in the filming, this flaming work in black and white, alternately funny and frightening, demonstrates a rare perfection. . . . Mathieu Kassovitz is already an important filmmaker whose film points the way to a new future for French cinema" (Ferenczi, "La Compétition" 18).

The Prime Minister of France, Alain Juppé, alerted by the uproar in the media, organized a private screening for his whole cabinet and with Charles Pasqua, the Minister of the Interior, watched the film several more times to try to understand better what was happening in the suburbs. Ghetto teens went en masse to the Parisian cinemas to see the film, and in Saint-Denis teachers brought whole classes—especially after two nights of rioting on June 8 and 9 (a gymnasium and three schools were burned down) following the death of a young Arab, gunned down by the police at Noisy-le-Grand for stealing a motorcycle. . . . Some evenings the crowd of adolescents from tough neighborhoods was extremely tense: "The cashiers were insulted, people smoked in the cinema, and screenings became volcanic"; fighting broke out at the end of the film. In Marseilles, there were incidents in the cinemas, damaged seats, vociferous spectators: "Electric atmosphere, as if at any moment, because of a gesture or a look, conflicts were going to break out in the room" (Le Leurch).

As for all films, and especially those that have a social or political bent, critical opinion is virtually never unanimous, and the right-wing press drew its own conclusions about *Hate*. The young dropouts from the suburbs were, according to *Le Figaro Magazine*, "a dangerous class," "a virtual danger for French society, which they refused to integrate." The three heroes of Kassovitz's film were "tragic products of a society that has shown itself incapable, at least up until now, of turning its mass of immigrants into French people." If we are to believe this school of thought, the true victims of the suburbs, the true "outcasts," aren't the immigrants; it is the "native-born French" (*Français de souche*) who do not have the financial means to live elsewhere and "who have the impression that the State has forgotten them" (Plunkett 19).

This is not, however, the viewpoint of Kassovitz, who is known for speaking his mind. He declares in the dossier for the press, "This is a film against the cops, and I wanted it to be understood as such." *Hate* is to some extent a response to the then recent film of Bertrand Tavernier, *L.627* (1992), which emphasizes the difficult working conditions of the French police, who are poorly equipped, badly paid, and insufficiently supported. The comment by Kassovitz was poorly received by the police, and the officers assigned to form the honor guard at the Cannes Film Festival expressed their displeasure by turning their backs on the *Hate* team when it came out after the official screening of the film (Séguret). Apparently, the director had second thoughts, for he walked his statement back in the following interviews, where he was regularly bombarded with questions about his remark: "No, let me be clear: this film is not against the cops; it is a film against police action that spirals out of control and produces blunders" (Ferneczi, "Kassovitz"). What he condemns, therefore, are the police blunders and the system that produces them, a system that is criticized, according to Kassovitz, by the police itself: "The cops are against the police system. I try to explain why there are cops who are so exhausted that, at night, they lose it and blow a guy away" (Levieux 20). "Like the people in the projects, there are good and bad cops," he added in another interview (Pantel), stating that his film "doesn't denounce anyone individually. Because even the cop who commits a blunder is not necessarily a potential killer . . . " (Boulay).

What concerned Kassovitz the most, in fact, was how his film would be perceived by the ghetto teens who are its subject. With all the media hype around the film, he feared that *Hate* would become a simple "object of consumption," a commercial product, and that the suburbs would feel betrayed: "Unfortunately for the film, I'm not an Arab. That is, I have no street creds, and I risk provoking bitterness among the people that the film is about. . . . There are people who are always hard up in the suburbs, who are going to see that and say to themselves, that guy is making bread on our backs" (Boulay and Colmant).

On the other hand, Kassovitz confronts aggressively the journalists who question his right to make a film on the suburbs since he doesn't come from there: "But I felt that I had the right to treat this subject: if you had to be black to denounce apartheid or Jewish to recall the Holocaust, in short, if you could only be concerned with your own situation, that would be horrible" ("Spécial Cannes" 142). Kassovitz insists, moreover, on the advantage he has by not coming from the suburbs: "I'm fortunate not to be blinded by hate and to observe that from far away. I have the distance necessary to be able to say, 'There are good cops and kids who are jerks, like there are good kids and rotten cops'" (Bernard 110).

The "Tough" Suburbs

Mathieu Kassovitz's film shows a representative slice of the daily life of the youth in a "tough" suburb, Parisian in this case. What do we know of this milieu? Do such suburbs only exist around Paris? Who lives in them, native-born French or immigrants? In fact, it is both groups. What we know is that there was a big wave of immigration in France at the turn of the century, followed by a new and even greater wave after the First and

Second World Wars, when France had an urgent need of workers to rebuild the country. In addition, the flight from the countryside in the 1950s brought millions of French to the cities in search of work, at the same time as the massive arrival of immigrants from North Africa (Algeria, Morocco, Tunisia). This quickly created a serious problem as regards lodgings: hundreds of thousands of immigrants, as well as a large number of poor French workers, piled into filthy slums on the outskirts of the major cities (Paris, Lyon, Marseille, and Lille, for example).

To deal with this situation, the French government established, in the 1960s, what they called "priority urbanization zones" (the ZUP) in which 500,000 new lodgings would be built each year (Condé 13). Of course, these "major housing developments" (*grands ensembles*) would not be built in the inner city. They are apartment blocks (*cités*) for workers built in the suburbs, like the Cité des 4000 at La Courneuve, a commune in the Seine-Saint-Denis department, or the Cité des 3000 in Aulnay-sous-Bois northeast of Paris (where Saïd Taghmaoui comes from, we remember). We are speaking of enormous structures made of concrete, containing thousands of "rabbit cages" (*cages à lapin*), as they are sometimes called, and surrounded by broad expanses of asphalt. While shoddily built, these "towers" have all the modern conveniences—water, electricity, heating, toilets—but virtually nothing to promote social life: few meeting rooms, sports venues, or cultural centers, for example, and few shops or cafés, as well as minimal means of mass transit.

At the beginning of the 1970s a serious economic crisis hit France, like many other countries, causing a sharp rise in unemployment. This problem was aggravated in France by a crisis in both the steel and automobile industries. The population of the suburbs, composed in large part of immigrants, was the hardest hit, and the gap between the French in the cities and the "excluded"—the fringe groups (*marginaux*) or "exiled" people of the suburbs—grew ever wider. In 1993, the "Pasqua laws" (named after Charles Pasqua, the right-wing Minister of the Interior from 1993 to 1995) increased the power of the police, redoubled racial profiling in the streets, and tightened the laws governing immigration, naturalization, and the residence of foreigners in France. These new policies increasingly poisoned the relations between the residents of the *cités* in the suburbs and the authorities, beginning with the police. Since there were more than 300 police blunders in France leading to death between 1981 and 2005 (Vincendeau, *La Haine* 12), the problem is far from negligible. One journalist frankly called *Hate* a "pamphlet against the Pasqua laws" (Ferenczi, "La Compétition" 18).

In 1994 around three million people were living in underprivileged suburbs, around 6 percent of France's population. The rate of unemployment in the hardest-hit *cités* was twice the national average, and among the eighteen- to twenty-five-year-olds, 25 percent were unemployed, compared to 15 percent among the general population. Nonetheless, the rise in unemployment was accompanied by an increase in racism, some native-born French blaming the immigrants for their lack of a job and encouraged in this by the extreme-right in France. As Michel Condé observes in a study of the suburbs, this resulted in a social crisis in the disadvantaged suburbs: "continual deterioration of the environment, delinquency, drug trafficking that provided illegal resources for the unemployed youth, conflicts with the police, quarrels among neighbors, an increase in racial remarks (and sometimes racial acts), a general feeling of insecurity, etc." (14). There were outbreaks of violence, riots in the suburbs of Lyon in 1981, then again in 1990

(Vaulx-en-Velin), in Paris in 1991 (Mantes-la-Jolie), and in Avignon in 1994, in which angry adolescents burned cars and pillaged stores. As we mentioned above, there were additional riots in the Paris suburbs in June 1995 (after the Noisy-le-Grand incident), and again in July, scarcely a few months after the screening of *Hate* in Cannes. The tension was high in all of the deprived suburbs in France, including at Chanteloup-les-Vignes where *Hate* was shot, and the relations between the youths hanging out in the streets and the neighborhood police could not have been worse. This is the explosive situation that existed in the period in which the action of *Hate* takes place.

STUDY GUIDE

What Happens in This Film?

1. Where does the action of this film take place, and in what period?

2. Who are the three protagonists of the film? Describe them briefly.

3. What did Vinz scoop up the previous night during the confrontation with the police?

4. What are the kids doing on the roof of the building? Why is there a confrontation with the police?

5. Why have the TV journalists come to the *cité*? What kind of a reception do they get from the boys? Why does Hubert say, "This isn't Thoiry here"?

6. Who is arrested by the police at the hospital? Why? Where do they take him?

7. In the sequence with the young deejay who does "scratching" in his room, what sort of music does he play? What theme is emphasized the most?

8. Why do the three friends go to Paris?

9. Why is there a conflict between Hubert and Vinz in the public bathroom? What does Vinz again threaten to do?

10. What happens in the police station in Paris?

11. Who do the three friends fight with in the street? What does Hubert exhort Vinz to do? What does Vinz do in the end?

12. At the end of the film, what does "Notre Dame" the plainclothes policeman do (the one who was involved in the argument on the roof of the building earlier in the day)?

True or False?

If the statement is false, correct it!

1. "Up until now, everything is fine" is a sentence repeated over and over by a TV journalist.

2. The riots of the night before were provoked by a police blunder.

3. The film lasts around forty-eight hours, with title cards posting the exact time at various intervals.

4. When the three friends go to the hospital to see their friend Abdel, who is still in a coma, Vinz brings the police service revolver hidden in his trousers.

5. Samir, the French Moroccan (Beur) policeman, takes Hubert and Vinz to the police station to arrest them.

6. Hubert earns money selling drugs, but he dreams of getting out of the projects.

7. Saïd criticizes his little sister over her behavior in public; in his culture, he has authority over her.

8. The elder Jewish man in the public bathroom tells the story of his deportation to Siberia.

9. When the three friends leave Snoopy's building, they meet some friends and go to the movies with them.

10. When Vinz sees on the television screen at the Forum des Halles that Abdel has died, he shoots and kills two policemen.

11. When he is back home, Vinz throws the revolver in a trash can.

12. At the end of the film, we hear two shots, so we know that both Hubert and the policeman have fired their weapons.

What Did You Learn in the Introduction?

1. In which films by Jacques Audiard and Jean-Pierre Jeunet did Kassovitz play starring roles after the appearance of *Hate*?

2. Where was *Hate* shot? Why was this location chosen?

3. What did Kassovitz and his three actors do to smooth the way for filming in the *cité*?

4. What true event inspired this film?

5. Why didn't Kassovitz use background music in *Hate*? What "replaces" it?

6. What actor began a huge career in cinema with his role in *Hate?*

7. What kind of reception did Kassovitz's film receive in Cannes and at the Césars the following year?

8. What did *L'Avant-Scène du Cinéma* have to say about *Hate?*

9. What did Kassovitz say about his film as regards the police?

10. Who lives in the disadvantaged suburbs in France—only immigrants?

11. Why did they build huge apartment blocks in the suburbs throughout France in the 1960s?

12. What was the effect of the high unemployment, the racism, and the bad relations with the police in the suburbs in France? What feeling did this produce for the residents? What did this situation provoke in certain suburbs, beginning in particular with the decade of the 1990s?

Exploring the Film

1. The Prologue

At the beginning of the film, we hear Hubert saying, in voice-over, "This is the story of a guy who falls from a fifty-story building. At each floor, as he goes down, he repeats, as if to reassure himself, 'Up to now, everything is fine; up to now, everything is fine; up to now, everything is fine. . . .' What counts is not the fall, it's the landing." At the end of the film, the same anecdote will be repeated, but "the story of a guy" is replaced by "the story of a society." **How do you interpret this anecdote?**

During his whole presidential campaign in 1994 and 1995, Jacques Chirac, the candidate of the classical conservatives in France, spoke of "social fracturing." **How does Kassovitz's film reflect the same theme?**

Kassovitz said that he wanted his film to be a "fable," not simply a specific story in a specific suburb city. What did he mean by this, in your opinion? How does Hubert's anecdote add to the "fable" aspect of the film?

What does the first part of the film consist of, before we meet the main characters? *Review the whole first segment of the film* (Excerpt 1, 1'40–6'15). **What does the shot of the Molotov cocktail mean for you?** In the confrontation between the young demonstrators and the police, does the director take sides in any way? **What might be the role of the Bob Marley song, "Burnin' and Lootin'," in relation to the real riot (archival footage) that is occurring before the spectator? What image does television give of the suburbs?** Can this representation in and of itself provoke violence? How does it contribute to the marginalization of this population? Further along in the film, are the TV journalists presented in a positive or negative manner? **How do you explain the abrupt cutting off of the television news program? Whose gaze is the spectator sharing here?**

2. The Title of the Film

The original title of the film was *Right to Belong* (*Droit de cité*), which was later replaced by *Hate*. Why do you think this change was made? What meaning does "hate" have in this film? **What relationship is there between "*droit de cité*" and the suburbs (*la* "*banlieue*").** To help answer this, look up the meaning of the French expression "mettre au ban."

3. The Characters

+ *The Three Friends from the Cité des Muguets*

Why, in your opinion, did Kassovitz choose for his film a working-class Jew (Vinz), a Beur (Saïd), and a black man (Hubert)—in other words, a "black-white-Beur" trio? In American films on urban ghettos, racism against blacks is a major theme. **Is racism the principal problem in *Hate*?** Explain your answer.

Why did the director choose to have the most intense hate embodied by the white Jewish boy, Vinz? **How are Vinz and Hubert opposed in the film? What is the role of Saïd in this context?**

We see little of the family environment of the three friends. Aside from the mothers and sisters of Vinz and Hubert, there are hardly any women in *Hate*, and particularly not in important roles. **Why do you think this is so?** And how do you explain the absence of the fathers? **What is the probable consequence of the latter fact for the young men of the suburbs?**

+ *Vinz and* Taxi Driver

When Vinz speaks to himself in the mirror—"You talkin' to me?"—he is imitating Travis Bickle (Robert de Niro) in a famous scene from *Taxi Driver* (1976) by Martin Scorsese. **How do you interpret this scene? What does it tell us about Vinz's character?**

+ *Samir, the Beur Policeman*

Why did Kassovitz include a Beur policeman (detective) in his film? Does this policeman play a positive or negative role? What does Hubert say when Samir says to him (in the car on the way to the police station), "The cops in the street are there to protect you"? What does Saïd answer when Samir tells the trio (upon leaving the police station), "A young cop who begins full of good intentions doesn't last more than a month"? **What do these responses demonstrate?**

4. The Policeman's "Piece" Lost in the Riot

What is the effect in the film of the presence of the Smith and Wesson .44 Magnum revolver that Vinz scooped up during the riot the night before? Kassovitz said in an interview that the whole film was built around this weapon. What do you think about that? In addition, is the well-known Freudian (phallic) symbolism relevant here? Is the masculinity of the ghetto adolescents an issue in this film? Explain.

5. The Technique: Some Key Scenes

Kassovitz's camera is sometimes very mobile (pans and tracking shots), often with a hand-held camera, and sometimes fixed in place, with long static shots. There are many close-ups, especially of the faces of the trio, but also many long shots in which the boys move away from the camera, which does not move. How do you explain these technical choices by Kassovitz? **What is the effect of the quick camera movements, especially the close-ups?** In general, at what points in the film do they occur?

Review the first sequence of the film in which Saïd is looking at the policemen (C.R.S.) standing in front of their vans (Excerpt 2, 6'18–7'32). Describe how Kassovitz films first Saïd, then the police. From what viewpoint do we see the police? How is this perspective changed at the end of the sequence? What effect does that have on the spectator's position? What is the function of the tagging done by Saïd here?

Review the sequence in which Samir takes Hubert and Vinz into the police station to get Saïd, who had been arrested (Excerpt 3, 32'30–34'25). What is particularly striking in the manner in which this is filmed, beginning with the arrival in the car? Kassovitz prefers long takes (*plans-séquences*) when possible, rather than editing together a series of shots (that is, he prefers mise en scène to montage). **Describe the long take inside the police station and the effect the director attempts to produce here.**

Review the two sequences in which the police arrest Abdel's brother who had shot at them, and in which they pursue the young men in the basement of one of the buildings (Excerpt 4, 48'08–49'50). What can you say about the relative length and size of these shots and the editing of this sequence?

6. The "Scratching" Sequence and the Drone

This scene in an inner courtyard of the *cité* begins in Hubert's room where he is smoking some grass, then moves to the room of the deejay who does scratching, a technique used in hip-hop music. *Review this sequence* (Excerpt 5, 40'45–43'23). **Try to interpret what happens here. What is being shown?** Are we dealing with a representation of reality or a poetic vision—or both? How do you understand the combination of a song by Edith Piaf (a famous French torch singer of the 1940s and 1950s) and a piece by Suprême NTM, with its anti-police rhetoric ("F— the police")? What cultural opposition seems apparent here? What relationship may be perceived between the music and the aerial tracking shot?

7. The Arrival in Paris

When the three boys arrive in Paris, we suddenly find them on the terrace of the Montparnasse railroad station overlooking a large boulevard (the Rue de Rennes). The camera effects what is called a "dolly zoom" (*traveling compensé*) composed of a tracking-out combined with a zoom-in. *Review this short scene* (Excerpt 6, 50'40–51'20). Note that the dolly zoom maintains the focus on the trio, whereas the background (Paris) becomes blurred. **What impression is Kassovitz trying to create?** Here, as elsewhere in the film, aesthetics seems to supercede realism; why, in your opinion, did the director choose to film in this manner?

The pretext for the trip into Paris is that someone (Snoopy) owes some money to Saïd. Is this the real reason for the Parisian escapade? **Why did Kassovitz set half of the action of the film in Paris?**

8. *The Scene in the Public Bathroom in Paris*

There are several scenes involving mirrors in *Hate*. What can you say about the role of the mirrors that fragment the image in the public bathroom scene in Paris? **What does the mirror play "reflect" as regards the relationship between Hubert and Vinz here?** What does Vinz reply when Hubert says, "If there is one thing that history has taught us, it's that hate begets hate"? What did "the street" teach Vinz? *Review this scene* (Excerpt 7, 51'21–53'56).

In the same sequence, an elderly Jewish man relates the story of his friend Grunwalski who freezes to death on the way to exile in Siberia during the time of Stalin's goulags. The three friends look at each other dumbfounded, and Saïd asks twice, "But why did he tell us that story?" Saïd clearly serves here as a spokesman for the spectator, who certainly is asking the same question. **What answer would you suggest? What is Kassovitz suggesting here?** Why does he bring up the theme of exile? Is there a relationship between the train that Grunwalski misses and the train to the suburbs that the three protagonists miss later that night?

9. *In the Police Station in Paris*

What is the purpose of the scene in which the two policemen insult and torture Hubert and Saïd in the police station? Is racism involved in this scene? What importance should be given to the fact that one of the policemen who is mistreating the two friends is a French Arab himself (played by a well-known Beur actor in France, Zinedine Soualem)? **What is the attitude of the novice policeman who watches them at work?** Do you think that he is going to resign from the police? What do you think his future holds for him?

10. *The Scene at the Opening at the Art Gallery*

What image does this scene give of the three ghetto dwellers? What does it suggest? Why do you think Kassovitz put it in his film? *Review this sequence* (Excerpt 8, 1h15'51–1h19'45).

11. *Violence*

It is clear that violence is one of the major themes in *Hate*. **Does this concern only the violent relationship between the youths of the suburbs and the police?** Discuss, in this context, what happens in Snoopy's apartment in Paris, as well as the episode with the skinheads in the street.

Why do the adolescents in the suburbs think that violence might be an appropriate response to police abuse and social injustice in *Hate*? **How is Vinz's real relationship to violence suggested in the nightclub scene** in which his black buddy shoots a bouncer through the door's peephole? Is this a realistic scene or a nightmarish fantasy of Vinz? *Review this scene* (Excerpt 9, 1h12'24–1h13'12).

How does Vinz's character become clearer, as regards violence, in the sequence at the Forum des Halles, when Vinz sees on TV that Abdel has died, and, especially, in the scene in which Hubert incites him to blow away the skinhead (played by Kassovitz)? *Review the sequence at the Forum des Halles* (Excerpt 10, 1h29'46–1h31'18). How do you interpret this scene?

12. Style

+ **Black and White**

In 1995 hardly anyone made films in black and white anymore. **Why do you think Kassovitz preferred black and white to color for his film?** What is the effect on the spectator (you)? What does black and white suggest in films? Is this important here? In fact, color is more "realistic," more "natural" than black and white, although black and white can evoke reality also. **Why would Kassovitz have wanted his film to be realistic at the same time that he distances himself from realism?** Are there other stylistic elements in the film that work against realism?

+ **The Posting of the Time**

We see at varying intervals throughout the film title cards that give the exact time of day, accompanied by a loud "tick-tock." **What is the effect on the spectator of this posting of the time? What might the "tick-tock" evoke?** Like French classical tragedies, those by Racine in particular, the film spans twenty-four hours. How do you think that might be relevant here?

13. The Role of Language

The *cité* dwellers often use *verlan*, a form of slang, in their comments. **The word "verlan" comes from "l'envers," because the syllables or the consonants are reversed.** A "flic" (cop) becomes a "keuf," a "mec" (guy) a "keum," a "Juif" (Jew) a "feuj," a "black" a "keubla," and an Arab a "Beur." "Bête" (dumb) becomes "teubé," "dégage" (beat it) "gagedé," "copains" (buddies) "paincos," "pourris" (rotten, corrupt) "ripoux," "racaille" (scum) "caillera," "cité" "téci," and much more. *Verlan* has become so common that "beur" has become "rebeu" or *verlan* verlanized! (See "Language in *L'Esquive*," Chap. 16, for a more extensive discussion of *verlan*.)

If we consider the relationship between the residents of the *banlieue* and the members of the dominant culture, what may be the role of *verlan* in the suburb culture? As a sort of "foreign language," how does *verlan* contribute to the image of the suburbs in the minds of the French in the cities? **Verlan or not, what role does language as such play in the daily existence of the youth in the suburbs?**

14. Humor

In what form does humor appear in this film? **What role does it appear to play in the life of the *cité*? What character in particular, among the three buddies, is associated with humor in the film?** Why this one? **What are we to think of the somewhat** surrealistic scene in which Vinz "sees" a cow in the *cité* (the same cow that he thought he glimpsed during the riots the night before)? The director explained that the cow was an homage to his anarchist grandfather. The slogan of the anarchists was "Death to the cows" ("Mort aux vaches"), the "cows" being the police—much as they have been referred to derogatorily as "pigs" in American contemporary culture. **This notwithstanding, might the appearance of the cow lend itself to other interpretations?**

15. *The Denouement*

Review the final sequence of the film (Excerpt 11, 1h35'19–1h37'47). **In what respect is the denouement ironic?** How does it change the respective positions of Vinz and Hubert in the film? We only hear a single shot fired, so only one person pulled the trigger. **Who, in your opinion?** Saïd closes his eyes just before we hear the shot. Why? How does that bring the film full circle? Is it significant that the denouement takes place beneath a huge portrait of the famous French poet Charles Baudelaire?

One critic wrote that the denouement of the film is an "ending that strongly resembles a call to the suburbs to revolt against the cops" (Jousse, "Prose combat" 35), and the press later suggested that the riots of June 8 and 9, 1995, at Noisy-le-Grand had been inspired by *Hate* ("Noisy-la-haine"). . . . Another commentator added that Kassovitz's film risked encouraging the young men of the suburbs to view the police as their enemy (Condé 23). **Do you feel that the denouement could serve as a justification of the use of violence by the young residents of the suburbs?**

As we saw earlier in this chapter, for certain Frenchmen the disenfranchised youth of the suburbs are simply a "dangerous class," "a potential danger for French society, which they refuse to integrate" (Plunkett 19). **What do you think? If this is the case, what can be done?** Reinforce the security measures in the suburbs? Seek out more effective means to assimilate the populations of the suburbs into French society? If this is your opinion, **how would you go about it?**

Mathieu Kassovitz's Filmography

1991   *White Nightmare (Cauchemar blanc, short subject)*

1993   *Café au lait (Métisse)*

1995   *Hate (La Haine)*

1997   *Assassin(s)*

2000   *The Crimson Rivers (Les Rivières pourpres)*

2003   *Gothika*

2008   *Babylon A.D.*

2011   *Rebellion*

Works Consulted

Baignères, Claude. "Une Vérité qui fait mal." *Le Figaro*, 29 May 1995: n. pag.

Bernard, Jean-Jacques. "Les Enfants de *La Haine*." *Première* (June 1995): 104–13.

Bosséno, Christian. "Immigrant Cinema: National Cinema. The case of beur film." *Popular European Cinema* (1992): 47–57.

Boulay, Anne, and Marie Colmant. "*La Haine* ne nous appartient plus." *Libération*, 31 May 1995: n. pag.

———. "Vincent à tout Cassel." *Libération*, 29 May 1995: n. pag.

Bourguignon, Thomas, and Yann Tobin. "Entretien avec Mathieu Kassovitz." *Positif* 412 (June 1995): 8–13.

Campion, Alexis. "*La Haine*, la tournée." *Le Journal du dimanche*, 12 Nov. 1995: n. pag.

Celmar, Rep and David Dufresne. "De la Croisette à La Villette, *La Haine* navigue." *Libération*, 5 June 1995: n. pag.

Chemineau, Sophie. "*La Haine*, chronique d'une errance en noir et blanc." *La Tribune Desfossés*, 31 May 1995: n. pag.

Condé, Michel. *La Haine, un film de Mathieu Kassovitz*. Liège: Le Centre Culturel des Grignoux et le centre de documentation du C.T.L., 1996.

Darke, Chris. "La Haine." *Sight and Sound* 5.11 (Nov. 1995): 43.

De Bruyn, Olivier. "Trois garçons dans le vent." *Les Inrockuptibles*, 31 May 1995: 16.

Favier, Gilles, and Mathieu Kassovitz. *Jusqu'ici tout va bien . . . Scénario et photographies autour du film "La Haine."* *Un film de Mathieu Kassovitz*. Paris: Actes Sud, 1995.

Ferenczi, Aurélien. "Kassovitz: 'Je ne veux pas qu'on trouve mon film sympa . . .'" *Info-Matin*, 31 May 1995: n. pag.

———. "La Compétition Made in France." *InfoMatin*, 29 May 1995: 18.

Higbee, Will. "Screening the 'Other' Paris: Cinematic Representations of the French Urban Periphery in *La Haine* and *Ma 6-T va crack-er*." *Modern and Contemporary France* 9.2 (2001): 197–208.

———. "The Return of the Political, or Designer Visions of Exclusion? The Case for Mathieu Kassoitz's 'fracture sociale' Triology." *Studies in French Cinema* 5.2 (2005): 123–35. <http://www.tandfonline.com/doi/abs/10.1386/sfci.5.2.123/1?journal Code=rsfc20>.

Jousse, Thierry. "Prose Combat." *Cahiers du cinéma* 492 (June 1995): 32–35.

Kassovitz, Mathieu, dir. *La Haine*. Criterion Collection, 2007. Bonus: Interviews with the director, producer, director of photography, actors, etc.

Konstantarakos, Myrto. "Which Mapping of the City? *La Haine* (Kassovitz, 1995) and the *cinéma de banlieue*." *French Cinéma in the 1990s. Continuity and Difference*. Ed. Phil Powrie. Oxford: Oxford UP, 1999. 160–71.

Le Leurch, Vincent. "Pastaga [mess] sur la Canebière." *Télérama*, 28 June 1995: n. pag.

Levieux, Michèle. "Mathieu Kassovitz: le noir et blanc draine plus de réalisme." *L'Humanité*, 29 May 1995: 20.

"Mathieu Kassovitz." *Positif* 412 (June 1995): 4–13.

Murat, Pierre. "La Haine." *Télérama* 31 May 1995: 40–42.

Oscherwitz, Dayna. "La Haine/Hatred." *The Cinema of France*. Ed. Phil Powrie. London: Wallflower, 2006. 223–35.

Pantel, Monique. "Kassovitz le surdoué." *France Soir*, 26 May 1995: n. pag.

Perron, Bernard. "Chute libre." *Cinébulles* 14.3 (Autumn 1995): 10–11.

Plunkett, Patrice de. "*La Haine*, la France et les municipales." *Le Figaro Magazine*, 10 June 1995: 19.

Reader, Keith. "After the Riot." *Sight and Sound* 5.11 (Nov. 1995): 12–14.

Rebouillon, Lawrence. "*La Haine* de Mathieu Kassovitz." *L'Avant-Scène du Cinéma* 445 (Oct. 1995): 128.

Remy, Vincent. "Ce n'est pas interdit de parler aux mecs des banlieues." *Télérama*, 31 May 1995: 42–46.

Reynaud, Bérénice. "Le 'hood. *Hate* and Its Neighbors." *Film Comment* 32.2 (March–April 1996): 54–58.

Riou, Alain. "Tout est clair, rien n'est simple." *Le Nouvel Observateur*, 25–31 May 1995: n. pag.

Sadock, Johann. "L'origine dévoilée du discours sur la violence et sur les relations inte-rethniques dans le cinéma de Kassovitz." *Contemporary French and Francophone Studies* 8.1 (2004): 63–73.

Séguret, Olivier. "M. ta n." *Libération*, 29 May 1995: n. pag.

Sharma, Sanjay, and Ashwani Sharma. "So far so good . . . : *La Haine* and the Poetics of the Everyday." *Theory, Culture & Society* 17.3 (2000): 103–16.

Sibony, Daniel. "Exclusion intrinsèque. A propos de *La Haine*." *Cahiers du cinéma* 493 (July–Aug. 1995): 30–31.

Spécial Cannes 1995. "Kassovitz et le droit des cités." *L'Express*, 11 May 1995: 140–42.

Tarr, Carrie. "Ethnicity and Identity in the *cinéma de banlieue*". *French Cinéma in the 1990s. Continuity and Difference*. Ed. Phil Powrie. Oxford: Oxford UP, 1999. 172–84.

Toubiana, Serge. "L'effet 'Itinéris.'" *Cahiers du cinéma* 493 (July–Aug. 1995): 32–33.

Tranchant, Marie-Noëlle. "Mathieu Kassovitz: le discours armé." *Le Figaro*, 27 May 1995: n. pag.

Vassé, Claire. "*La Haine*. Un regard métisse." *Positif* 412 (June 1995): 6–7.

Vindendeau, Ginette. "Designs on the *Banlieue*. Mathieu Kassovitz's *La Haine* (1995)." *French Film: Texts and Contexts*. Ed. Susan Hayward and Ginette Vincendeau. London: Routledge, 2000. 310–27.

———. *La Haine [Hate]*. (Mathieu Kassovitz 1995). London: I.B. Tauris, 2005.

Zisserman, K., and C. Nettlebeck. "Social Exclusion and Artistic Inclusiveness: The Quest for Integrity in Mathieu Kassovitz's *La Haine*." *Nottingham French Studies* 36 (1997): 83–98.

6

Bruno Dumont

The Life of Jesus (La Vie de Jésus)

(1997)

Bruno Dumont, *The Life of Jesus*: Freddy (David Douche) and his gang loaf in front of the town hall: nothing to do.

Director	Bruno Dumont
Screenplay	Bruno Dumont
Director of Photography	Philippe Van Leeuw
Film Editors	Guy Lecorne, Yves Deschamps
Sound	Eric Rophe, Mathieu Imbert, Olivier de Nesles
Art Director	Frédérique Suchet
Music	Richard Cuvillier
Costumes	Nathalie Raoul, Isabelle Sanchez
Continuity	Virginie Barbay, Isabelle Le Grix
Producer	Jean Bréhat, Rachid Bouchareb
Length	1h36

Cast

David Douche (*Freddy*), Marjorie Cottreel (*Marie*), Geneviève Cottreel (*Yvette, Freddy's mother*), Kader Chaatouf (*Kader*), Sébastien Delbaere (*Gégé*), Sébastien Bailleul (*Quinquin*), Samuel Boidin (*Michou*), Steve Smagghe (*Robert*)

Story

Freddy, a twenty-year-old kid out of work, lives in Bailleul, a dreary little town in French Flanders where he and his buddies spend their time loafing and roaring through the city streets and country roads on their souped-up mopeds. Suffering from epileptic seizures, Freddy lives with his mom, owner of a little café with a sparse clientele, and makes no effort to find work. Aside from his moped rides, the only things that interest him are his girlfriend Marie, with whom he frequently makes love, the finch he is training for the town's trilling contest, and the town's brass band in which he and his buddies play drums.

Idle and immature, Freddy and his group of dropouts seek to escape their boredom one day by sexually molesting one of the majorettes of the band. In addition, frustrated by their hopeless existence, they find an outlet in racism, harassing a local couple of North African origin. One day Kader, the couple's adolescent son, begins to hit on Marie, who rejects his attentions. When Freddy becomes aware of Kader's actions, he seeks an opportunity to punish him. . . .

The Director

Born on March 4, 1958, in Bailleul in French Flanders (Nord-Pas-de-Calais), son of a doctor, Bruno Dumont was drawn to the cinema very early in his life. Having failed the entrance exam to IDHEC (School for Advanced Studies in Cinema) after finishing high school, he completed a master's degree in philosophy with a thesis on film aesthetics at the Sorbonne. He began teaching philosophy in a lycée in Lille but soon left to teach French and general culture to students who were preparing a BTS (Advanced Technical Diploma, a two-year program following high school), a population with whom he had a greater affinity.

At the same time, Dumont began to make commercials and films for businesses—around forty in ten years—becoming an experienced filmmaker in the process. Industrial films, he says, are "a very concrete manner to become involved with the cinema," and "even when I was filming a candy factory, I found ways to create emotion, to get directors of marketing excited over a machine. This experience taught me to film little things, nothings, and not necessarily scripts and extraordinary events" (Garbarz, "*L'Humanité*" 12). Retrospectively, he was happy that he hadn't studied in the School for Advanced Studies in Cinema, since, according to him, this school only offers technical training, and "a filmmaker is first and foremost an intellectual, someone who has a particular way of seeing the world, of seeing others, and who attempts, through film, to express what he feels" (Lavoie 19). His philosophy studies taught him to see the world more clearly, although he denies that he makes "intellectual" films. What he aspires to make, he says, are deep but simple films: "You go much deeper when you use a very simple story. The approach of the artist is to give a form to the quest for the universal.

What interests me is to descend into human nature all the way to the bottom, if possible" (Boulay). He discovered that the best place to probe human nature was the desolate countryside where he had grown up, a milieu whose access is not obstructed, he adds, by "the varnish of culture" that one finds in the big cities.

It is in Bailleul that he places the action in his first films, *The Life of Jesus* (1997) and *Humanity* (*L'Humanité*, 1999). The second film goes more deeply into Dumont's favorite themes, that is, the difficulty of human relations, the brutal, animalistic character of people in the area of sexuality, the harshness of life in general. Despite its shocking character, *Humanity* was awarded the Grand Prize of the Jury (Grand Prix du Jury) at the Cannes Film Festival as well as Best Actor awards for both of the stars, simple inhabitants of Bailleul, and a nomination for the Palme d'Or (the highest award for a film in France). Four years later, as if to demonstrate his thesis that "we are all ignoble creatures subject to bizarre drives" ("Dumont"), Dumont brought out *Twentynine Palms* (2003), which pushes violence—sexual and other—to its extreme. This rather controversial film was followed by *Flandres* (2006), a war film that, like *Humanity*, won the Grand Prize of the Jury and a nomination for the Palme d'Or. In *Hadewijch* (2009), a fable on religious fanaticism (whether it be Christian or Islamic), a young novice nun is drawn into terrorism by a group of Islamic jihadists. In his following film, *Outside Satan* (*Hors Satan*, 2011), Dumont presents a sort of parable that bears once again on human relations, the existence of good and evil in the world, violence, and spirituality. In his most recent film, however, *Camille Claudel 1915* (2013), he changes genres completely, offering an intense intimate portrait of the last years of the famous sculptor (played by Juliette Binoche), which she spends in a secured mental facility.

The Origin and Making of the Film

Strongly attracted to paintings that represent the life of humble country dwellers, such as certain landscapes of Braque like *Fields, Low Sky* (*Les Champs, ciel bas*, 1956) or *The Plow* (*La Charrue*, 1960), Dumont decided to make a very down-to-earth work for his first feature film, "a film as simple as possible, very physical and bare" (Frodon, "Il faut" 32). It would be a film on the life of the youth of Bailleul, the little town where he grew up, near Lille. His decision was motivated in particular by his experience as a high school teacher, his contact with students of modest potential who often demonstrated racist attitudes and a certain resistance to moral principles: "I wanted to confront the life, the pain, and the misery of these young people who had been more or less abandoned by adults and no longer had any direction in their lives" (Royer). He is interested "in simple people, in direct contact with life and the problems of today's society—joblessness, insecurity, idleness, violence, sex, AIDS, and racism" (Baudin)—but his true subject, he insists, is human nature rather than the social context.

In fact, Dumont wanted originally to make a film on the life of Christ inspired by the famous work of the philologist Ernest Renan, *History of the Origins of Christianity* (*Histoire des origines du christianisme*, 1864), in which Jesus is presented as a simple human being with his vices and virtues, like everyone else. Dumont received a Catholic education in private schools, and although by his own admission he is not a believer, he was fascinated by the personage of Christ and its diverse representations. He was struck by the complete lack of interest of his young students in Christ and his whole story and wanted to show them that the story of Christ and its signification were still very relevant in the world today: "I wanted to make a film for them, to show them what, to me, seems magnificent and powerful in Christianity: Man" (Danel).

Dumont thus conceived his film as "a contemporary version of the story of Christ" (Frodon, "Il faut" 32). "It's not what happened 2,000 years ago that interests me but what is happening now," he says. "I am trying to find a contemporary echo of his teachings" (Lavoie 19). He told a story located in a place that he knew well, Bailleul, with characters who resembled his students.

If Dumont shot his film in Bailleul, it was also because he was charmed by the topography of the region where he was born: "I find the landscape of Flanders grandiose, flat, powerful, and humble. It puts man in his place" (Lavoie 20). There is such an intimate relationship between the people and their land that the filmmaker shot his film in Cinemascope in order to integrate his characters more fully into their physical environment: "Cinemascope is a difficult format to the extent that an enormous number of things are included in the image [...]. From whatever angle, the décor is always present; you can't separate the characters from it. Cinemascope constantly forces me to preserve a harmony between the characters and the landscapes" (Garbarz, "*L'Humanité*" 12). "My characters speak very little," he adds, "because the landscape is preponderant within the comprehension of emotions. I try to work like an artist, which means to photograph landscapes which are ways of expressing the emotions of my characters" (Peranson and Picard 70).

To present his images as simply as possible, he framed his characters systematically "in the center of the image, facing the camera, to avoid any stylistic effect" (Frodon, "Il faut" 32). To reinforce the austerity of his film—in the manner of Robert Bresson, whom he greatly admires—he refused to use any background music: "For me, cinema is rhythm and melody, and adding music on top makes no sense. When I edit a film, with the voices and noises, I'm already seeking a form of harmony" (Garbarz, "*L'Humanité*" 12). It is a film, in any case, in which silence is preeminent, despite the deafening noise of the mopeds of Freddy's gang, and especially when the boys find themselves together with nothing to do or to say, and during the intimate scenes between Freddy and Marie, always wordless.

The Actors

To find his actors, Dumont put up flyers everywhere in Bailleul—to little avail at first. He looked for ten months before finding his cast . . . in the list of unemployed persons at City Hall. People often speak of the quality of an actor's creation of his or her character. Dumont wanted nothing to do with this. Like Bresson, he sought an actor who *was* the character, an actor who essentially played himself. "When I chose David Douche to play Freddy," he said, "he was what I wanted. I wanted to film his body, his eyes [...]. There was no question of his 'creating' a character, since he is not an actor. On the other hand, what he does very well is being himself" (Lavoie 21). Dumont's approach as regards the relationship between an actor and his or her character is thus contrary to normal practice: "As a rule, you ask the actor to resemble the character, but I do just the opposite. Consequently, there is a subtle interplay between the story and the character. David Douche, who plays Freddy, must find it hard to watch the film, because it is he, himself, that he sees on the screen. But, at the same time, it is not he, since I draw him into the fictional universe" (Boulay).

The use of nonprofessional actors is part and parcel of Dumont's conception of filmmaking. He doesn't even give the text to the actors ahead of time. The morning of the shoot, he explains to them the scene in which they are going to play, what they are going to say or reply, the gestures they need to do. He has them rehearse once or twice, just to see how they behave, and then he shoots. He also refuses to film on studio sound stages, preferring to shoot on location: "I don't shoot in studios. I shoot trees with real trees, houses with real houses, and therefore I shoot real people. It's the same thing" (Peranson and Picard 70–71). With the same logic, but contrary to Bresson's practice, Dumont does not post-synchronize his films; he records the voices in synch sound (simultaneously with the images) and does not rework the sound track afterwards. On the other hand, for the sex scenes in the film, Dumont used doubles in place of his amateur actors (a fact that he is careful to mention in the credits at the end of the film), in the interest of the actors: "I did it for them, for their life, for the people they frequent" (Garbarz, "*L'Humanité*" 12). The mother of Marjorie Cottreel (Marie), who plays the role of Freddy's mother in the film, commented in fact that her daughter was severely criticized by certain acquaintances for the intimate scenes in the film. . . .

Many critics have noted the similarities between Dumont and Robert Bresson, who also practiced a bare, austere type of cinema and rejected professional comedians in favor of inexperienced amateurs—whom he called "models," since he molded them as if they were made of clay to obtain the precise performance he was seeking. However, again contrary to Bresson, who reduced his actors to nothing and then reshaped them according to his fancy, Dumont does not tyrannize his cast. Since he chooses them for how they are, he respects their individuality, he says, and takes their own reactions into consideration: "If one of them told me, 'I can't say that, it's dumb, I'd never say it like that in reality,' I would take that into account, and we would change the text together. My only concern was that they be genuine" (Danel). Furthermore, as regards the shooting of the film, far from imitating Bresson, who would often do dozens of takes for the simplest shots, Dumont never needed, he tells us, to do more than two takes (Campion), convinced, in any case, that he obtained in this manner a maximum of authenticity and truth. The results bear him out. One critic finds his actors "unbelievably convincing and troubling" despite the fact that they are all novices (Campion), and the three protagonists, David Douche, Marjorie Cottreel, and Kader Chaatouf, all received acting awards in international film festivals.

The Reception

The Life of Jesus received the Prix Jean Vigo, awarded each year to a French filmmaker distinguished by her or his "independence of mind and the quality of the direction of the film," as well as a special mention for the Golden Camera (*Caméra d'or*) at the Cannes Film Festival. It also met considerable success in film festivals around the world—London, Avignon, Edinburgh, Chicago, Alexandria, São Paulo, Valencia, among others—where it won fifteen prizes and several nominations. It appeared in theaters on June 4, 1997, with a limited distribution owing to its relatively modest budget (8.4 million francs, around $1.5 million at the time).

Despite a few reservations on the title of the film, the reviews were generally very favorable. Critics spoke not only of Bresson but also of Maurice Pialat and Pier Paolo Pasolini, extremely flattering comparisons for a filmmaker who had just brought out his first feature film. One of the commentators notes that "*The Life of Jesus* [...] is one of the best illustrations of the renewal of French cinema" (Frodon, "A bras" 32), another that "*The Life of Jesus* remains above all an experience of intense and truly poignant cinema for the spectator who agrees to be led into the tragic reality of this universe" (Sivan). And Landrot goes even further in the same sense:

> In shots that are short and dense like sighs in music, Bruno Dumont succeeds in capturing the interminable.... With the precision of a calligrapher, he nourishes his images with the energy that the children of Bailleul deploy to fill their void. This produces poignantly beautiful sequences composed like paintings by Magritte, with his mixture of livid realism and powerful onirism.

Several critics marvel at Dumont's technical mastery, one of them calling him a "virtuoso of the camera" (Baignères), another remarking that he "surprises us by his mastery, an astonishing mixture of crude and sensitive images" (Campion), and yet another declaring that "*The Life of Jesus* captivates us completely, thanks to such a convincing conformity of style and content that one has the impression of contemplating a mystery" (Mandelbaum).

STUDY GUIDE

What Happens in This Film?

1. How is Freddy introduced to the spectators at the beginning of the film?

2. How does Freddy's mother spend her time in the café?

3. What happens to Freddy after making love to Marie?

4. What happens after the parade, in the café where Kader and his parents are sitting?

5. What happens to Freddy after the episode in which he and his buddies play their macho moped game by driving straight toward an oncoming car?

6. What dominates almost completely the relationship between Freddy and Marie?

7. What do Freddy and his friends do to help Michou get over his brother's death?

8. What is Freddy interested in, apart from Marie and his moped rides with his buddies?

9. What happens after the rehearsal of the town band with the majorettes?

10. How does Marie shock Kader, who had followed her into the park?

11. How does Freddy take revenge after seeing Kader speak to Marie in the street?

12. What does Freddy do after leaving the police station?

True or False?

If the statement is false, correct it!

1. When Freddy gets back home at the beginning of the film, he stops his moped, parks it on the sidewalk, and goes into the café.

2. Freddy and his gang go to the hospital to see a friend's brother who is dying from AIDS.

3. There is a parade with the town's brass band and its majorettes to celebrate November 11, Armistice Day.

4. When Kader arrives in front of the house where the group of friends are repairing a car, he greets them cordially and chats with them.

5. Kader goes to the supermarket to introduce himself to Marie, who works at a cash register there.

6. At the snack wagon, Freddy's gang sees Kader go by on his moped. They try to catch him, but he hides in an underground garage.

7. When Freddy and his friends are sitting in front of the town hall, they spend their time telling jokes.

8. Marie is highly amused by the story of the sexual molesting of the chubby majorette.

9. Freddy's mother is very happy with the life he is leading and doesn't offer any advice.

10. When Freddy sees Kader stop and speak to Marie in the street, he kicks the wall violently and drives off on his moped.

11. Marie apologizes to Kader for the behavior of Freddy's gang.

12. At the police station, after his arrest, Freddy breaks down and cries.

What Did You Learn in the Introduction?

1. What kind of work does Bruno Dumont do before becoming a filmmaker?

2. What kind of films does he make at the beginning? How does this experience help him as a filmmaker?

3. What interests Dumont the most as a filmmaker?

4. What are his favorite themes?

5. What did Dumont hope to accomplish, as regards the youths of Bailleul, in making this film?

6. Why did he want to film a contemporary version of the story of Christ?

7. Why did Dumont shoot his film in Cinemascope? What role do the landscapes play in his film?

8. What does *The Life of Jesus* have in common with the films of Robert Bresson (as regards the music and the actors)?

9. Why did Dumont prefer nonprofessional actors in his film? How does his manner of working with them differ from the way a director normally works with professional actors?

10. What differences can we note between Bresson's and Dumont's style of filmmaking?

11. What award did *The Life of Jesus* win at the Cannes Film Festival?

12. What great compliment did the prominent film critic for *Le Monde*, Jean-Michel Frodon, pay to Dumont's film?

Exploring the Film

1. The Title of the Film

Dumont chose *The Life of Jesus* as the title of his film. What do you think of this choice? Does it suit his film well? **To what extent can one see in this film a version of the life of Christ?** The protagonist of the film is Freddy. **Is he a Christ-like figure?** Explain your opinion. Is there another figure in the film who could be compared to Christ? Christ is often considered to be the prototypical "scapegoat," the victim chosen to save the human race. **Is there a scapegoat in the film? If you think there is, scapegoat for what?**

2. The Beginning of the Film

What impression does the beginning of the film give us of Freddy? Where does he go on his moped? **What are we supposed to think of his fall when he arrives at the café?** Does he fall on purpose? If you think he does, why? *Review the first sequence of the film, until Freddy comes back home* (Excerpt 1, 0'07–2'00).

3. The Characters

+ *Freddy*

Freddy's epileptic attacks are called "grand mal" seizures (in earlier times, they were even referred to as "sacred mal" ("le mal sacré"). **Might this detail be important in this film?**

    Could there be a relationship between Freddy's epilepsy and his tendency to take falls with his moped?

    How does Freddy react to his frequent examinations at the hospital for his epilepsy? Is there any relationship to his aggressive behavior in other instances? **The hospital naturally brings to mind the idea of sickness. Does this notion have metaphorical** contours in the film that go beyond Freddy? One critic suggests that Freddy's encephalogram is a metaphorical way to "try to see what these young people have in their heads" (Mandelbaum). What do you think of this interpretation?

What meaning should we assign to Freddy's frequent kicks of walls?

What do the finch and the trilling contests represent for Freddy? Might the bird in the cage have a metaphorical dimension? Are there other elements—symbolic or metaphorical—in this film that justify the "new poetic realism" label that is often attached to Dumont's films?

+ *Freddy's Mother*

How may we characterize the relationship between Freddy and his mother? Is she a good mother? And is Freddy a good son? How would you describe the communication between them?

Freddy's mother spends her days watching television. **What does television represent for her?** Does television have a particular role in the film as regards life in Bailleul?

+ *Freddy and Marie*

What can we say about the manner in which the intimate relations between Freddy and Marie are presented in the film? Is a critic justified in saying, as regards sex between two people in love (Freddy and Marie), that Dumont "only shows the purely animalistic side" (Garbarz, "*Vie de Jésus*" 117)? **Why, in your opinion, does the director emphasize to such an extent the sexual relations between Freddy and Marie?**

How would you describe the attitude of Freddy's friends toward his relations with Marie? Are they jealous or just impressed? One critic asserts, as regards the group, that "this girl is above all [. . .] the clearest proof of its virility" and that Freddy is the leader of the gang because he is "the only one who is sleeping with a girl" (Lounas 77). **Do you agree with this interpretation?** Does Marie have this particular role in the film, in your opinion?

What difference may we note between **Freddy's and Marie's attitudes toward Bailleul** in the sequence of the ride on the chairlift? *Review this sequence* (Excerpt 2, 14'45–17'00).

+ *Freddy and his buddies*

How would you characterize Freddy's group of friends? What do they have in common? **Why do they spend their time riding around aimlessly on their mopeds?** Could the deafening noise they make have a thematic function in the film?

What role does the scene at the hospital (when the group of friends visits Cloclo) play in the film? What importance may we give to the picture of Lazarus on the wall? Is there any other episode in the film where the group of friends shows sensitivity? *Review the scene at the hospital* (Excerpt 3, 5'50–8'45).

Is there any relationship between the macho game with the cars and Freddy's epileptic seizure that follows? How do you imagine Freddy's feelings after such an episode? *Review this sequence* (Excerpt 4, 32'00–33'55).

What do these boys have to say to each other, in general? What kind of future can they hope for in Bailleul? Why? *Review the scene in which the boys are sitting on the steps of City Hall* (Excerpt 5, 59'40–1h02'25). *Discuss how they are filmed and the level of conversation between them.* What is their main concern?

+ *Kader*

How is Kader presented in the film? Does he resemble Freddy and his friends? What do we know about his relationship with his parents? **How does he behave with Marie?**

Why does Kader make an obscene gesture toward the boys when he stops his moped in front of the house where they are repairing the car (and calls them "French sons of bitches")?

Later, when the gang chases Kader on their mopeds in the streets of the city, Kader hides in a cemetery (whose entrance is watched by a North African guard). **How do you interpret this scene? Is it a kind of foreshadowing?** *Review this sequence* (Excerpt 6, 57'50–59'40).

When Kader follows Marie in the street a second time, she warns him that Freddy's gang "wants to beat him up." When he continues to follow her, she turns around suddenly and thrusts his hand into her underpants, saying, "Is this what you want?" Kader is shocked, exclaiming, "Are you nuts?" **How do you interpret this scene?** What is the director suggesting here?

In the last scene between Marie and Kader, she apologizes for her behavior with him. While he is holding her in his arms, he looks up toward the sky through the pointed arch of a Gothic cathedral in ruins. *Review this scene* (Excerpt 7, 1h19'00–1h20'20). **How do you interpret this scene? Is there any relationship between it and the last shot of the film in which Freddy also looks up toward the sky?**

4. *The Town Band (La Fanfare)*

What role does the town band play in the life of Freddy's gang? Does it have a "cultural" function for them? How would you describe the quality of its music? To show off by driving your moped straight at cars is an example of bluster (*fanfaronade*). **Is there a thematic relationship here with the "fanfare" in which the boys play drums?**

Is there any irony in the parade on November 11, a patriotic holiday that celebrates the Armistice at the end of World War I?

5. *Racism*

How do you explain the mocking, mean treatment of the North African family by the boys in the café? *Review this sequence* (Excerpt 8, 22'25–24'05). Why does Marie apologize to Kader when he introduces himself to her at the supermarket where she works at a cash register? **Is the murder committed by Freddy and his friends an act of racism, or is it rather a crime of passion born out of spite?** Is this distinction important here?

6. *The Majorette Episode*

As regards the sexual molestation of the chubby majorette by the gang, one critic notes "their stupefaction when accused of rape. For them, the fact that they 'felt up a fatty' can not in any case constitute a crime and be considered a rape" (Garbarz, "*Vie de Jésus*" 117). *Review the scene where the girl's father castigates the gang, followed by their exit into the street* (Excerpt 9, 1h05'30–1h07'00). How would you explain the attitude of the boys? Why don't they take their actions seriously?

What are the consequences of this incident on the relationship between Freddy and Marie? And how does this situation prepare what follows, as well as the ending of the film?

7. Nudity and Crudeness

Why did Dumont put in his film the rapid but very crude close-up of Freddy and Marie's genitals (including penetration) when they make love in the field? And why did he include the shot of the withered nude body of Freddy's mother as she steps out of the bathtub?

Certain critics consider the nudity in this film completely gratuitous and think that the nude scenes "didn't seem to belong to the film" (Louanas 76). Dumont, for his part, claims that the sex scenes are an integral part of his film and that it was essential to show them in all their crudeness (Danel). His films have also been criticized as vulgar. In one interview (Peranson and Picard 70), he rejects this criticism, remarking that "rawness is a way to bring the viewer closer to primary matter, to emotions and relationships with others, to what really exists." He seeks to produce a physical shock because "physicality is the beginning of the spirit/mind. What comes first is the body, so I keep to this," adding that words do not interest him: "I think that someone who speaks is simply expressing what his body feels. . . . " **Do you think that Dumont is right as regards the body, nudity, and sex scenes in his film?** Is the body the favored and most important object of cinema?

8. Time

Dumont said (after many others) that "cinema is the art of time" (Lavoie 20), and that this art is practiced above all on the editing table after the shooting of the film. **How do Dumont's shots (long static shots, for example) contribute to the representation of time?** Do the frequent fades to black have any signification as regards the representation of time? **What importance does the representation of time have in the film?** What is its thematic value?

9. Masochism

We see Freddy naked to the waist several times, sometimes with the bruises and scrapes caused by his falls (on purpose) with his moped. **Is Freddy a masochist?** If you think so, why? **Could the desire to hurt oneself (to whip oneself in a certain sense) have a metaphorical function here?** What would that be? Bowles suggests that Freddy's "incessant self-mutilation can be read as an expression of what Freud calls Thanatos: the unconscious attraction toward death experienced by those who have suffered cataclysmic trauma" (50). **What do you think of this interpretation?**

Bowles also suggests that "the scars that cover Freddy's torso function as a physical signifier of his torment" (50). Numerous critics also speak of "stigmata," suggesting a Christian interpretation. **What is your opinion here?**

10. The Denouement

The denouement of the film contains several parts: the murder of Kader, the arrest of Freddy, and the last sequence in which Freddy is in the field alone after fleeing the police station. **How do you interpret the murder? Did Freddy intend to kill Kader, or did he just go too far without realizing it?** Is the savage character of his act comprehensible in the context of the film? *Review this sequence* (Excerpt 10, 1h22'20–1h23'50). Note how it is filmed. **How is the violence presented? Why?**

When Freddy is led away by the police, Marie is there, close to the police van, her face filmed for a long time in close-up. **Does she feel responsible, in some sense, for Kader's death?** Later, at the police station, the policeman wonders in front of Freddy, "Are you even responsible?" **Is Freddy's burden of guilt lessened here? Who then would be responsible for the murder?**

How do you understand Freddy's actions when he runs out of the police station? Does he think that he can escape the police like that, or is it just an irrational act?

How do you interpret the very last sequence of the film, where Freddy throws himself on his back on the ground and looks up at the sky, his eyes full of tears? *Review this last sequence* (Excerpt 11, 1h26'50–1h29'00). Is this ending optimistic or pessimistic? **Does it suggest that Freddy is finally repenting for his act—or is he just feeling sorry for himself?** Do you feel, like certain commentators, that Freddy is "a character torn between the fall and the mystery of redemption," that this film is the product of a "Christian humanism whose tendency is always to study human nature and its failings" (Grugeau 48)? **Does the sunlight play a symbolic role in this scene as regards what Freddy is experiencing?**

It has been said of Dumont's films that "as seen by him, the reality of beings and things [...] is transformed into a metaphysical space" (Gabarz, "*L'Humanité*" 5). Dumont claims, indeed, in speaking of *The Life of Jesus*, that "the film is the birth of morality, that arrives at the very end. It is the story of Freddy's ascension. Christ realizes the greatest possible spiritual ascension; little Freddy is at the very bottom, and suddenly there is a little something that ascends at the end. And you have to believe in that" (Boulay). **Do you agree with this interpretation of the last scene of the film? Do you see there a parallel between Freddy and Christ?**

Dumont admits that "what this film recounts is absolutely monstrous," but he asserts that "it is up to the spectator to marshal his humanity when confronted with this spectacle" (Danel). **Are you able to sympathize with Freddy and give him the benefit of the doubt despite his horrible act?** One critic maintains that if spectators condemn Freddy, they are condemning themselves and rejecting, implicitly, their faith in humanity. By judging him, he claims, we are judging ourselves, whether we like it or not (Bowles 53). **Do you agree with this viewpoint?**

11. Confronting the spectator

Dumont says that art is war and that he likes to fight with the spectator; he isn't afraid of confrontation (Peranson and Picard 71). He adds, moreover, "My films attempt to confront the spectator, not to amuse him" (Sivan). Do you think that Dumont is right? **Is the goal of a work of art to challenge its public?**

In addition, he admits that he likes "incomplete characters and visions of the world and to confront the spectator with that," because "the spectator arrives with his own story, his own life, and his own sensitivity; as a result, something unpredictable is going to happen" (Gabarz, "*L'Humanité*" 11). How do you understand this position of the director? **What role does this imply for the spectator as regards the meaning of the film?**

Bruno Dumont's Filmography

1997   *The Life of Jesus (La Vie de Jésus)*

1999   *Humanity*

2003   *Twentynine Palms*

2006   *Flandres*

2009   *Hadewijch*

2011   *Outside Satan (Hors Satan)*

2013   *Camille Claudel 1915*

2014   *Li'l Quinquin (P'tit Quinquin)*

Works Consulted

Baignères, Claude. "Premières Réussites." *Le Figaro*, 5 June 1997: n. pag.

Baudin, Brigitte. "Bruno Dumont, l'ennui et la rédemption." *Le Figaro*, 9 May 1997: n. pag.

Beaulieu, Jean. "Trois films et un seul Nord." *Cinébulles* 18.2 (1999): 10–13.

Benhaim, Safia, and Damien Cabrespine. "Calvaire." *Vertigo* 18.18 (1999): 96.

Beugnet, Martine. "Le Souci de l'autre: réalisme poétique et critique sociale dans le cinéma français contemporain." *Iris* 29 (Spring 2000): 53–66.

Boulay, Anne. "Au fond de la nature humaine." *Libération*, 12 May 1997: n. pag.

Bowles, Brett. "The Life of Jesus (La Vie de Jésus)." *Film Quarterly* 57.3 (Spring 2004): 47–55.

Buchet, Jean-Marie. "La Vie de Jésus." *Ciné-Fiches de Grand Angle* 210 (Dec. 1997): 47–48.

Campion, Alexis. "La Vie de Jésus ou de Freddy?" *Journal du Dimanche*, 1 June 1997: n. pag.

Camy, Gérard. "La Vie de Jésus." *Jeune Cinéma* 244 (Summer 1997): 44–45.

Danel, Isabelle. "C'est au spectateur de devenir humain." *Télérama*, 4 June 1997: n. pag.

Dumont, Bruno. "Notes de travail: sur La Vie de Jésus." *Positif* 440 (Oct. 1997): 58–59.

———, dir. La Vie de Jésus. Fox Lorber, 1997.

"Dumont pharaon des Flandres." *Le Nouvel Observateur*, 12 May 1999: n. pag.

Dupont, Joan. "In France, the Focus Shifts from Paris." *New York Times*, 5 Oct. 1998: 19, 31.

Frodon, Jean-Michel. "A bras le corps dans l'enfer du Nord." *Le Monde*, 5 June 1997: 32.

———. "Il faut donner au spectateur la possibilité de penser par lui-même." *Le Monde*, 5 June 1997: 32.

Garbarz, Franck. "*La Vie de Jésus.* Etre dans la norme, naturellement." *Positif* 437/438 (July–Aug. 1997): 117–18.

———. "*L'Humanité.* Consoler la souffrance du monde." *Positif* 465 (Nov. 1999): 5–13.

Grugeau, Gérard. "La Résurrection de Freddy." *24 Images* 90 (Winter 1998): 48–49.

Hardwick, Joe. "Fallen Angels and Flawed Saviours: Marginality and Exclusion in *La Vie de Jésus* and *La Vie rêvée des anges.*" *Studies in French Cinema* 7.3 (2007): 219–30.

Hoberman, J. "Fits and Starts." *The Village Voice* 43 (19 May 1998): 132.

Konstantarakos, Myrto. "Retour du politique dans le cinéma français contemporain?" *French Studies Bulletin* 68 (Autumn 1998): 1–5.

Landrot, Marine. "*La Vie de Jésus.*" *Télérama*, 4 June 1997: n. pag.

Lavoie, André. "Je suis un cinéaste qui n'aime pas le cinéma." *Cinébulles* 16.3 (1997): 18–22.

Lefort, Gérard. "Les Pieds dans le cru. Dans le Nord, des adolescences cabossées: *La Vie de Jésus*, de Bruno Dumont." *Libération*, 4 June 1997: n. pag.

Lounas, Thierry. "Seuls les anges ont des ailes." *Cahiers du cinéma* 514 (June 1997): 75–77.

Mandelbaum, Jacques. "Un bloc de beauté et d'horreur." *Le Monde*, 11–12 May 1997: n. pag.

Maslin, Janet. "Tragedy Waiting to Happen, and the Sad, Brutish Youth at Its Center." *New York Times*, 15 May 1998: E10.

Peranson, Mark, and Andréa Picard. "A Humanist Philosophy: Interview(s) with Bruno Dumont." *CineAction* 51 (2000): 69–72.

Royer, Philippe. "Les Flandres servent de cadre à une *Vie de Jésus* assez particulière." *La Croix*, 4 June 1997: n. pag.

Singerman, Alan. "Le Cinéma français de nos jours: pour un réalisme poétique *frontal.*" *France in the Twenty-First Century. New Perspectives.* Ed. Marie-Christine Weidemann Koop and Rosalie Vermette. Birmingham, AL: Summa, 2009. 317–40.

Sivan, Grégoire. "*La Vie de Jésus.*" *24 Images* 88/89 (Autumn 1997): 41.

Tinazzi, Noël. "La Rédemption de Freddy, jeune paumé." *La Tribune Desfossés*, 4 June 1997: n. pag.

Vassé, Claire. "*En avoir (ou pas)*. La girafe et son prince." *Positif* 419 (Jan. 1996): 22–23.

7

Erick Zonca

The Dreamlife of Angels
(La Vie rêvée des anges)

(1998)

Erick Zonca, *The Dreamlife of Angels*: Isa (Elodie Bouchez) and Marie (Natacha Régnier) share thoughts.

Director	Erick Zonca
Screenplay and Dialogue	Erick Zonca, Roger Bohbot
Director of Photography	Agnès Godard
Film Editor	Yannick Kergoat
Sound	Jean-Luc Audy
Art Director	Jimmy Vansteenkiste
Music	Yann Tiersen
Costumes	Françoise Clavel
Continuity	Maureen Meyer
Producer	François Marquis
Length	1h53

Cast

Elodie Bouchez (*Isa*), Natacha Régnier (*Marie*), Grégoire Colin (*Chriss*), Patrick Mercado (*Charly*), Jo Prestia (*Fredo*)

Story

Isa, a young backpacker, arrives in Lille broke. She finds work sewing in a sweatshop where she meets Marie, a worker who is angry about her social and economic condition. When Isa is fired for incompetence, Marie leaves the shop also, out of solidarity. She agrees to share with Isa a nice apartment where she is living temporarily to keep an eye on it following an automobile accident that left the owner of the apartment dead and her daughter in a coma.

Isa and Marie quickly become close friends, living together in desperate financial straits, with no regular jobs or any clear future. However, they experience their marginality in radically different ways, Marie in a permanent state of revolt against a social order that she considers unjust and humiliating for her, Isa consistently generous and optimistic, accepting any job she can find just to survive. They become friends with Charly and Fredo, two congenial bouncers at a nightclub.

Marie tries to find a way out of her social position through a love affair with Chriss, an affluent young bourgeois whose father owns a large brasserie in the center of Lille, and who is himself the owner of the nightclub where Charly and Fredo work. For her part, Isa becomes more and more interested in the fate of Sandrine, the girl in a coma. Their different perspectives, as well as their individual needs, will soon create unbearable tension between the two friends.

The Director

Zonca did not rise quickly in the world of cinema. Born in Orléans in 1956, he left high school at the age of sixteen without his diploma and went to Paris. He enrolled in acting school there and took whatever jobs he could find to survive financially. Since he was only interested in American cinema at that time, he went to New York where he worked in various Greenwich Village restaurants and spent the rest of his time at the famous art house cinema Bleeker Street Cinema in order to improve his knowledge of independent American and foreign cinema. He married an American dancer, but they divorced a few years later. After three years he returned to Paris where he earned a GED, permitting him to enroll in the university where he studied philosophy for several years. At the age of thirty he abandoned his studies in favor of internships in television, where he eventually became an assistant in the production of commercials, sitcoms, and news shows before he was able to try his hand at directing.

Before attempting a feature film, Zonca made three shorts, all of which won prizes at international film festivals: *Shores* (*Rives*, 1992) at the Film Shorts Festival of Clermont-Ferrand; *Eternelles* (1993), the Grand Prize in 1995 at Clermont; and *Alone* (*Seule*, 1995), winner of the Musidora Best Actress Prize in 1997 and nominated for the Best Short Subject at the Césars in 1998. *Seule*, whose action is situated in Paris, already contains some of the essential themes of *The Dreamlife of Angels*: joblessness and despair.

A notable fact: all three films won prizes for acting, which indicates Zonca's particular talent for casting and working with actors.

The Dreamlife of Angels was an immediate success with both the general public and the critics and won prizes in a variety of international festivals. This first feature film by Zonca was followed by another successful drama, *The Little Thief* (*Le Petit Voleur*, 1999), which he directed and co-authored with Virginie Wagon. The roles were reversed the following year for *The Secret* (*Le Secret*, 2000), a steamy tale of adultery directed by Wagon and co-written with Zonca that won a prize at the Deauville Film Festival. Zonca's next film, *Julia* (2008), is a thriller featuring the British actress Tilda Swinton that won her multiple Best Actress prizes, confirming once again Zonca's talent in working with his cast. The most recent film by Zonca at the writing of this book, *White Soldier* (*Soldat blanc*, 2014), made for television, is a drama that takes place during the war in Indochina.

The Making of the Film

Zonca shot *The Dreamlife of Angels* from February 3 to March 29, 1997, followed by several months of editing. At the end of the year, the film was submitted to Gilles Jacob, the official in charge of selecting films for the Cannes Film Festival at that time (and subsequently president of the festival since 2000), who accepted it with some slight modifications. *The Dreamlife of Angels* won the César for the Best Film in 1998, an event that suddenly covered Zonca with glory at the age of forty-one, a rather advanced age for a first feature film. His mastery was a source of astonishment for everyone, especially considering the fact that he made his film with extremely modest funding, spending less than $1.5 million, a third of the average budget for a French film. To economize (and also to obtain the more granular images he wanted), he shot the film in Super 16, which allowed him to make multiple takes of certain shots, "ten, twelve, up to twenty-four sometimes" (Mérigeau 146), emulating Robert Bresson, one of his idols. A certain number of shots were made with a hand-held camera, an approach that he admired in the works of the American filmmaker John Cassavetes, who also exercised considerable influence on him. As Théobald observed, Zonca is an "author" in every sense of the word, a director who co-authors his scenarios.

The Actors

The principal roles in *The Dreamlife of Angels* are played by Elodie Bouchez and Natacha Régnier. Bouchez had already won a Most Promising Actress César for her performance in André Téchiné's *Wild Reeds* (*Les Roseaux sauvages*) in 1995 (see Chapter 15) and is considered by certain filmmakers to be "the most talented actress of her generation" (Douin 25). It is the first major role for Régnier, born in Belgium and already twenty-five years old, but the following year (1999) she played the title role in François Ozon's *Criminal Lovers* (*Les Amants criminels*). At the Cannes Film Festival in May 1998, the two actresses shared the Best Actress prize and were both highly praised by the press. Zonca's film was recognized not only for their brilliant performances, but also for those of the rest of the main cast, all excellent in their roles. Grégoire Colin, who plays Chriss, had already been nominated, in 1993, for the Most Promising Actor award for his role in Agnieszka Holland's *Olivier, Olivier*, and he had won a special prize for his performance in Claire Denis' *Nénette et Boni* in 1996. Colin would become a favorite actor of Denis, playing the main role in her following film, *Good Work* (*Beau Travail*, 1999), as well as minor roles in *Friday Night* (*Vendredi soir*, 2002), *The Intruder* (*L'Intrus*, 2004), *35 Shots of Rum* (*35 rhums*, 2008), and *Bastards* (*Les Salauds*, 2013).

The Reception

Pascal Mérigeau gives us a good idea of the public reception awaiting *The Dreamlife of Angels* by remarking at Cannes "the ovations that hailed each of its screenings" and adding, "Impossible to recall a first French film greeted at Cannes with such enthusiasm" ("La Vie" 102). The film, its director, and the two stars won awards at festivals throughout the world, and it is one of the French films that drew the greatest number of spectators in Great Britain in 1998. When the film came out in French theaters on September 16, it was an immediate success. The distributor tripled the number of venues originally planned, programming the film in around thirty Parisian cinemas and in more than 150 in metropolitan France.

Despite a few divergent opinions, the film was acclaimed by a large majority of French film critics: "an exceptionally successful little film" (Tobin 109); "a first film of astonishing vitality" (Pascal 88); "This film, both funny and bitter, is one the most successful of the last few years" (Rousseau 5). Although they express some reservations about the originality of the subject and Zonca's technique, Kaganski and Bonnet are clearly charmed by the exceptional dynamism of the film: "Each shot seems to be charged with TNT, each event leads naturally to the next, each sequence seems dictated by the previous one, each image seems to be printed onto the film as if it were the last one" (20, 22). Guérin adds, finally,

> "Always a balancing act, an interplay of contrary forces nourishes a narrative that just cannot be adequately described: a mixture of feverishness and hard-heartedness, of harshness and tension, all of which is to the credit of the director. Composed of bonds that form, the story winds together trajectories and confronts paths that are filled with destitution, economic insecurity, and despair, but also with confidence in life and with grace." (251)

The Dreamlife of Angels and Marginality

The Dreamlife of Angels is part of the current of social (and often "poetic") realism that is very prominent in French films of the 1990s, which are often concerned with ordinary people suffering from the social divide (*fracture sociale*) in its diverse forms, such as exclusion, joblessness, exploitation, and racism or other forms of discrimination. It is, in particular, one of the best French films on marginality, foregrounding both the voluntary and involuntary versions of this phenomenon. The two young women barely get by, with no regular work and no economic future. Isa, however, has chosen this lifestyle, content to backpack around, surviving on temporary jobs and by selling in the street little greeting cards that she creates from pictures cut out of magazines. Although a trifle androgynous, she recalls Mona, the backpacker in Agnès Varda's, *Vagabond* (*Sans toit ni loi*, 1985), although without Mona's off-putting side. Marie, for her part, is in revolt against her social and economic status, while refusing temporary work, which she considers humiliating. She has not chosen her marginality and only dreams of escaping it.

In Zonca's film the working world plays an important role, even if it is only in relation to the problem of unemployment, which is the focal point of so many films of this period like *To Have (or Not)* [*En avoir (ou pas)*, 1995] by Laëtitia Masson, *Nothing to Do* (*Rien à faire*, 1999) by Marion Vernoux, or *Time Out* (*L'Emploi du temps*, 2001) by Laurent Cantet, among others. The Nord-Pas-de-Calais, whose principal city is Lille, has been particularly hard hit by joblessness since the end of the last century, the number of people receiving unemployment benefits being well above the average in France. Economic insecurity among women is particularly acute, contributing to an increase in shoplifting and a highly worrisome number of suicide attempts by both women and the young—social phenomena that are both reflected in Zonca's film.

By its uncompromising realism, *The Dreamlife of Angels* is typical of the renewal of French cinema in the 1990s. As we see in other films of this period, such as *North* (*Nord*, 1991) by Xavier Beauvois, *En avoir (ou pas)* by Masson, *The Life of Jesus* (*La Vie de Jésus*, 1997; see Chapter 6) and *L'Humanité* (1998) by Bruno Dumont, *I Stand Alone* (*Seul contre tous*, 1998) by Gaspar Noé, or *It All Starts Today* (*Ça commence aujourd'hui*, 1999) by Bertrand Tavernier, this realism is solidly anchored in the socioeconomic context of the northern region of France. It is generally characterized by a tenacious pessimism as well as by the unrestrained and unromanticized representation of relations between people, including sexual relationships.

STUDY GUIDE

What Happens in This Film?

1. How does Isa get to Lille?

2. In general, how does she survive financially?

3. How do Isa and Marie come to live together?

4. How do the two young women meet Charly and Fredo, the two bouncers?

5. How is Marie's behavior different from Isa's as regards the two new friends?

6. Who is Chriss? How did Isa and Marie meet him?

7. How does Marie come to know Chriss personally? Describe the evolution of their relationship.

8. How does Isa become interested in Sandrine, the girl in a coma at the hospital?

9. What does Isa do when she visits Sandrine at the hospital?

10. Where does Chriss take Marie?

11. What happens when Isa tries to warn Marie about Chriss?

12. What dramatic event takes place when Isa returns to the apartment the next morning?

True or False?

If the statement is false, correct it!

1. Isa comes to Lille to look for work.

2. Isa finds work in an automobile factory.

3. Marie lives in an apartment owned by a woman who died in a car accident.

4. Isa and Marie are both willing to accept any old job to survive.

5. Charly and Fredo hire Isa and Marie to work in the nightclub where they are employed.

6. Marie steals a handbag in the department store.

7. When Marie goes looking for Chriss in his father's brasserie, she violently attacks one of his bourgeois friends who talked down to her.

8. Isa begins to write in Sandrine's diary.

9. Chriss waits for Isa at the apartment door to tell her that he is in love with Marie and wants to marry her.

10. After her argument with Marie, Isa spends the night in the hospital cafeteria.

11. When Isa learns that Sandrine has come out of her coma, she goes into her room to tell her how happy she is.

12. At the end of the film, Isa hits the road looking for new adventures.

What Did You Learn in the Introduction?

1. What did Zonca do in New York for three years?

2. Why did he abandon his university studies at the age of thirty?

3. What success did Zonca have as a film director before making *The Dreamlife of Angels*?

4. What particular talent does Zonca possess as regards the actors in his films?

5. What very important prize did *The Dreamlife of Angels* win?

6. What shows the influence of the French filmmaker Robert Bresson on this film?

7. What shows the influence of the American filmmaker John Cassavetes?

8. What do the two stars of this film, Elodie Bouchez and Natacha Régnier, receive at the Cannes Film Festival in 1998?

9. How is this film received by most of the French film critics? What does Nita Rousseau say about it?

10. To what current of filmmaking does *The Dreamlife of Angels* belong? What sort of people are usually represented in this type of film?

11. What socioeconomic problem is at the center of this film? In which region of France is this problem particularly acute?

12. How is *The Dreamlife of Angels* typical of the renewal of French cinema in the 1990s?

Exploring the Film

1. The Social Question

The Dreamlife of Angels poses many questions, beginning with the lifestyle of the two protagonists. They live in dire economic straits, but is their socioeconomic state inescapable? **Is society alone responsible for their marginal status, or are they, themselves, responsible to a certain extent?** *Review the scene in which Isa is fired from the sweatshop* (Excerpt 1, 16'00–16'55). Is she a victim of injustice on the part of the boss? Why does Marie leave her job at the same time? Why did Marie leave her previous job?

2. The Characters

✦ *Isa and Marie*

How would you describe the respective characters of Isa and Marie? How would you explain their lifestyle? In this respect, Zonca said in an interview, "I wanted to confront two different manners to be opposed to society." What do you think about that? **In what way is Isa "opposed to society," if we consider how she is living at the beginning of the film?** What (metaphorical) meaning might we lend to the attractive apartment where the two girls are squatting? **Could there be a relationship with the theme of "dreamlife" here?**

✦ *Marie and Chriss*

Marie is a particularly complicated character. She agrees to sleep with Charly, one of the nightclub bouncers, although she seems to look down on him. Later she will have intimate relations with Chriss whom she despises, calling him a "filthy little bourgeois asshole." **What image does Marie have of herself and of her social position? How might this image explain her behavior with both Charly and Chriss?**

Marie is clearly ambivalent with regard to Chriss, who belongs to a social class that is economically superior to hers. **What does he eventually come to represent for her? (What "dream"?)**

+ *Isa and Sandrine*

The relations between Isa and Sandrine, the girl in the coma, are rather unusual. **How do you explain the interest that Isa shows in her? Why does she take the liberty of writing in her diary? Why does she visit her regularly in the hospital?** Does this behavior reveal anything about Isa's character, her particular mentality, and her personal needs? **Does Isa identify with Sandrine?** If so, on what level?

3. The Scene at the Brasserie

Review the scene at the brasserie that Chriss' father owns (Excerpt 2, 1h05'15–1h06'45), where we see the violent encounter between Marie and Chriss' bourgeois girlfriend. **How do you interpret this scene?** Is it an allusion to "class struggle"? If you do not think so, why not?

4. Donjuanism

Are you familiar with the Don Juan myth? **Find the meaning of this myth on the internet. Could it explain, at least in part, Chriss' behavior with Marie?** What does she represent for him? On another tact, may we speak of "sado-masochism" in the relationship between these two characters? **How important are the themes of humiliation and victimization in this film?**

5. The Quarrel

How do you understand the violent quarrel between Isa and Marie? *Review this scene* (Excerpt 3, 1h34'00–1h37'20). Marie screams at Isa, "All you know how to do is latch onto other people like a parasite!" **Is Marie right to accuse Isa of being too dependent on others?** Is this accusation ironic given Marie's own situation? **What does Isa reproach Marie?** At the hospital Isa discovers Sandrine "with her eyes open." **Could this scene have a metaphorical meaning in relation to Marie's situation?**

6. The Scene in the Chapel

How do you interpret the night that Isa spends in the hospital chapel after her quarrel with Marie? *Review this scene* (Excerpt 4, 1h40'15–1h43'20). **What do Isa (and the spectators) think about Sandrine's fate at this point in the narrative? Do you think that Zonca is developing a religious theme here?** Does the candle have a symbolic function? **Why does Isa decide not to see Sandrine the next morning when she learns that she has come out of the coma?** Do you think that there is a connection between Isa's behavior with Sandrine and the girl's return to life?

7. The Denouement

+ *Marie's Suicide*

Marie's final act is shocking. *Review this scene* (Excerpt 5, 1h47'30–1h48'25). Were you expecting this? **How do you interpret it? What might this act reveal about Marie's character?** Is there a thematic relationship between Sandrine's fate and Marie's?

Is there a connection between Marie's suicide and the situation of Isa at the end of the film?

◆ *Isa in the Factory*

The last shot of the film has lent itself to a variety of interpretations. *Review this scene* (Excerpt 6, 1h49'50–1h50'50). **Has Isa abandoned her previous outsider lifestyle and resigned herself to becoming part of the socioeconomic system—or is the factory job only a brief hiatus in her life?** Do you agree with the following conclusion of a film critic: Isa, in the electronics factory at the end of the film "is sitting there, serious, concentrating on her job, resolved this time to join the working world, to face her future" (Toscan du Plantier 75). Here is what another critic thinks: "This shot of Isa, a minimum-wage earner among other minimum-wage earners, learning a mechanical, repetitive job under the scrutiny of the foreman, who remarks, 'You look like you've been doing this your whole life; just continue like that.' A terrible phrase that announces a dreary existence, followed by a long dolly shot of the other women workers riveted to their machines" (Théobald 51).

Zonca has quite a different opinion of Isa's future: "She has lost her carefree attitude.... But she is not going to remain in this factory for long.... It is revolting" (Garbarz 39). **What do you think?** Do we have to agree with the director as regards the interpretation of his film? **If we assume that Isa is really going to be integrated into the workplace, is this denouement optimistic or pessimistic, in your opinion?**

In any case, as regards the last shot of the film Zonca declares, "By filming all of these women, I wanted to generalize Isa's character." **What does Zonca mean here?**

In a political film by Jean-Luc Godard, *All's Well* (*Tout va bien*, 1972), which may have influenced Zonca's film, a very long take near the end of the film includes a long continuous tracking shot on a row of cashiers in yellow overalls, filmed from behind in a big-box store; they remain anonymous. Compare the last shot of *The Dreamlife of Angels*. **What difference do you note? Why did Zonca choose to film the workers in this way?**

8. *The Music*

As regards the music in this film, Zonca again shows the important influence of Bresson, who increasingly refused background music in his films as his career developed. You may have noticed that there is only one piece of extradiegetic music (that is, music that is not produced within the fictional universe) in this film, and that it accompanies the final shot. *Review this shot again* (Excerpt 6, 1h49'50–1h50'50). Originally, Zonca did not intend to put music here, but, according to him, this long scene did not work at all until the music was added. **Why, in your opinion? What is the effect of this music, placed at the very end of the film?** Look up the words to the song "In Cascade Street" on the internet. **Are these words important here?**

In addition, Zonca had included a piece of music in the scene where Marie and Chriss are together on the beach, before eliminating it at the request of Gilles Jacob, in charge of the selection of films for Cannes. Zonca later confessed that Jacob was right (Ferenczi 30). *Review this sequence* (Excerpt 7, 1h29'10–1h30'05). **Why does this scene work better without music, whereas the last scene works much better with the music?**

9. Cinematography

Regarding the cinematographic technique in *The Dreamlife of Angels*, we note in this film **many reframing camera movements (instead of new, separate shots), as well as lateral pans accompanying movement or espousing the gaze of a character.** There are multiple short forward and backward tracking shots following or preceding Isa or Marie (in the apartment, the brasserie, or the hospital corridor), as well as during the episode at the shopping center where the two girls make a game of approaching various men. However, Zonca's camera remains generally very discrete. The most important tracking shots that attract the spectator's attention are found at the beginning and end of the film, that is, when Isa arrives in Lille with her backpack (a following shot made with a hand-held camera), and when we see her at her workstation with the other factory workers at the end. *Review the beginning of the film to compare the two tracking shots* (Excerpt 8, 0'30–01'10 and Excerpt 6, 1h49'50–1h50'50). **Do the two shots have the same function? If not, what is the difference? Why does the dolly shot at the end stop a moment, in a near shot, on each worker?** Aside from these two shots, the film seems to be dominated by static shots, especially close-ups or near shots of faces. **What aspect of the film is foregrounded in this way?**

10. The Title of the Film

Finally, to finish with the beginning, **what does the title of the film, *The Dreamlife of Angels*, mean to you?** Its meaning is not obvious, and one film critic calls it an "enigmatic title, fluid and dancing like a fragment of a poem" (Soullard 266). Nonetheless, the notion of "dreaming" appears several times in the film. Marie says to Isa, for example, toward the end of the romantic story she tells in the big bed they share, "You dream a lot," and Isa writes in the note she leaves for Marie at the end of the film, "I hope you will find the life you are seeking, the one you dream of." The notion of "angels," however, is more difficult to apprehend. Some critics take refuge in metaphors, observing that the two girls "break their wings," or that they are "angels with ruffled wings," or, again, that they are "angels whose wings are leaded by life." Zonca explains his title a little differently, giving two different versions of the allusion to "angels": (1) "The film is called *The Dreamlife of Angels* because Marie and Isa constantly delude themselves, dreaming their relationships with others. Angels because I see them as virgin characters, not yet tainted by life" (Rousseau 5); (2) "*Dreamlife* refers to the dream of absolute love that Marie, one of the heroines, entertains; it is also the dream of idyllic relations between Isa (her friend) and others. *Angels* also suggests poetry, even if the film has little to do with that" (Schwab 6). Another critic notes, nevertheless, "These characters may be called angels, but it's hard to tell why; they're stuck in an extremely harsh social reality. . . " (Mérigeau 146). **What do you think? May Isa and Marie be considered "angels" in some way?**

Finally, can you identify with either of these two young ladies? **Are you sympathetic with them, or do you have a bad opinion of them?**

Erick Zonca's Filmography

1992   *Shores (Rives, short subject)*

1993   *Eternelles (short subject)*

1995   *Alone (Seule, short subject)*

1998   *The Dreamlife of Angels (La Vie rêvée des anges)*

1999   *The Little Thief (Le Petit Voleur, film for television)*

2008   *Julia*

2014   *White Soldier (Soldat blanc, film for television)*

Works Consulted

Baudin, Brigitte. "Erick Zonca: l'amitié pour tout bagage." *Le Figaro*, 16 May 1998: 24–25.

Beugnet, Marie. "Le Souci de l'autre: réalisme poétique et critique sociale dans le cinéma français contemporain." *IRIS* 29 (2000): 53–66.

Coppermann, Annie. "Une justesse miraculeuse." *Les Echos*, 17 Sept. 1998: 55.

Douin, Jean-Luc. "Elodie Bouchez fait scintiller les étoiles de jadis." *Le Monde*, 17–18 May 1998: 25.

Ferenczi, Aurélien. "Le Cas Zonca." *Télérama*, 16 Sept. 1998: 26–32.

Frodon, Jean-Michel. "Une œuvre au noir." *Le Monde*, 17 Sept. 1998: 27.

Garbarz, Franck, and Yann Tobin. "Erick Zonca." *Positif* 451 (Sept. 1998): 36–40.

Gonzalez, Christian. "Nouvelles Muses du cinéma français." *Madame Figaro*, 26 Sept. 1998: 64–66.

Grassin, Sophie. "Deux anges passent." *L'Express*, 10 Sept. 1993: 92.

Guérin, Nadine. "Entretien avec Erick Zonca." *Jeune Cinéma* 251 (Sept.–Oct. 1998): 20–22.

Hardwick, Joe. "Fallen Angels and Flawed Saviours: Marginality and Exclusion in *La Vie de Jésus* and *La Vie rêvée des anges*." *Studies in French Cinema* 7.3 (2007): 219–30.

Harris, Sue. "Dispossession and Exclusion in *La Vie rêvée des anges*." *Possessions; Essays in French Literature, Cinema, and Theory*. Ed. Julia Horn and Lynsey Russell-Watts. Oxford, UK: Peter Lang, 2003. 183–98.

Kaganski, Serge, and Sophie Bonnet. "Une nouvelle vie." *Les Inrockuptibles*, 16 Sept. 1998: 20–25.

Leclère, Jacques. "*La Vie rêvée des anges*." *L'Avant-Scène Cinéma* 475 (Oct. 1998): 105–6.

Maillochon, Florence. "Penser l'initiation sexuelle à la fin du siècle." *Critique* (June 2000): 531–42.

Mérigeau, Pascal. "La Révélation Zonca." *Le Nouvel Observateur*, 14 May 1998: 146.

———. "La Vie rêvée de Zonca." *Le Nouvel Observateur*, 10 Sept. 1998: 102.

Murat, Pierre. "*La Vie rêvée des anges.*" *Télérama*, 16 Sept. 1998: 24–26.

Orr, Christopher. "A Working Class Hero(ine) Is Something to Be." *Film Criticism* 27.1 (2002): 36–49.

Pascal, Michel. "Les Anges vont en enfer." *Le Point*, 12 Sept. 1998: 88.

Rousseau, Nita. "Deux anges à la dérive." *TéléObs*, 10 Feb. 2000: 4–5.

Schwaab, Catherine. "Erick Zonca" (interview). *Match de Paris*, 17 Sept. 1998: 6–7.

Smith, Gavin. "*La Vie rêvée des anges.*" *Sight and Sound*, 8 Nov. 1998: 64.

Soullard, Catherine. "*La Vie rêvée des anges.*" *Etudes* (Sept. 1998): 266–68.

Stigsdotter, Ingrid. "British Audiences and 1990s French New Realism: *La Vie rêvée des anges* as Cinematic Slum Tourism." *Je t'aime . . . moi non plus: Franco-British Cinematic Relations*. Ed. Lucy Mazdon and Catherine Wheatley. New York: Berghahn Books, 2010. 169–81.

Théobald, Frédéric. "Zonca ouvre les cœurs." *La Vie* 2768 (Sept. 1998): 50–51.

Tobin, Yann. "*La Vie rêvée des anges.*" *Positif* 449/450 (July–Aug. 1998): 109–10.

Toscan du Plantier, Daniel. "Les Enfants perdus du paradis." *Le Figaro Magazine*, 12 Sept. 1998: 75.

Vassé, Claire. "*La Vie rêvée des anges.* Entre terre et ciel." *Positif* 451 (Sept. 1998): 34–35.

Zonca, Erick, dir. *La Vie rêvée des anges.* Sony Pictures Classics, 1999.

III

Socio-Cultural Themes 2:
School, Immigration

Abdellatif Kechiche, *Games of Love and Chance* (2003)
Laurent Cantet, *The Class* (2008)
Philippe Lioret, *Welcome* (2009)

While the filmmakers in the first decade of the twenty-first century continued to explore the socio-cultural themes that so engrossed their predecessors of the previous decade—poverty, unemployment, immigration and its consequences, particularly in the suburbs—they sought out new approaches. In this section we present three major contemporary French films that treat the issue of immigration, two of them through the prism of schools.

The theme of immigration has occupied an important place in French cinema since the birth of "Beur" cinema in the 1980s. The first films by French filmmakers of North African origin featured Beur characters in main roles, whereas such characters were formerly either totally absent from films or complete stereotypes—the most often delinquents. In the 1980s and 1990s these films were largely low-budget social realism pieces set in the suburbs, like those of Mehdi Charef (*Tea in the Harem* [*Le Thé au harem d'Archimède*, 1985]) and Malik Chibane (*Hexagone*, 1994; *Sweet France* [*Douce France*, 1995]). Their characters are often young people raised in France but who are seeking their identity because, while they do not share their parents' traditional culture, they also feel rejected from French society and have trouble finding work. Some lapse into delinquency, which is presented as a consequence of the exclusion they experience rather than as a basic trait of immigrants. Since the action of most of the Beur films takes place in the suburbs, these films are often identified as "suburb films"—like *Hate*—in the 1990s, even if the director and the characters of a typical suburb film are not necessarily the offspring of immigrants, and even if violence is more prevalent in suburb films than in most Beur films.

Since the end of the 1990s, films dealing with the suburbs and immigration have become diversified as regards genres, aesthetics, and themes, and Beur cinema has become less "marginal" (and even this latter expression is used less and less in this context). Social realism, for example, has given way to comedy and history, and the setting of choice is no longer limited to the Paris suburbs, some of the films being located in provincial cities and rural communities or even in the native countries of the immigrants. A dozen comedies (in particular those of Djamel Bensalah) that have North African French directors and actors met considerable success at the box office between

1999 and 2010, and a handful of actors, like Jamel Debbouze, Roschdy Zem, and Gad Elmaleh, have joined Isabelle Adjani as major movie stars with immigrant origins.

Among the historical films, one might point to high-budget productions like Rachid Bouchareb's *Days of Glory* (*Indigènes*, 2006) and *Outside the Law* (*Hors-la-loi*, 2010) and more personal immigration stories like Yamina Benguigui's *Inch' Allah Sunday* (*Inch' Allah dimanche*, 2001) or Mehdi Charef's *Summer of '62* (*Cartouches gauloises*, 2007). Some North African French directors, like Abdellatif Kechiche and Rabah Ameur-Zaïmeche, gradually moved away from the immigration theme and have even abandoned it in their latest films, *Blue Is the Warmest Color* for the first (*La Vie d'Adèle*, 2013), *Smugglers' Songs* (*Les Chants de Mandrin*, 2011) and *Story of Judas* (*Histoire de Judas*, 2015) for the second.

It is in the preceding context of the evolution of the filmic representation of the suburbs and of immigration that we need to place Abdellatif Kechiche's *Games of Love and Chance* (*L'Esquive*) and Laurent Cantet's *The Class* (*Entre les murs*). The two films approach these two subjects from the perspective of schools, another favorite theme of French cinema. Since Jean Vigo's *Zero for Conduct* (*Zéro de conduite*) and Jean Benoit-Lévy and Marie Epstein's *Children of Montmartre* (*La Maternelle*), both from 1933, there have been innumerable films featuring the educational system in France. Some give a negative image of the teacher, like *Zero for Conduct*, Marcel Pagnol's *Topaze* (1951), or François Truffaut's *The 400 Blows* (*Les 400 Coups*, 1959). Others, however, depict teachers who believe sincerely in their vocation, like Jean Dréville's *A Cage of Nightingales* (*La Cage aux rossignols*, 1945), Louis Malle's *Goodbye Children* (*Au revoir les enfants*, 1987), Bertrand Tavernier's *It All Starts Today* (*Ça commence aujourd'hui*, 1999), Nicolas Philibert's *To Be and to Have* (*Etre et avoir*, 2002), or Christophe Barratier's *The Chorus* (*Les Choristes*, 2004), a remake of Dréville's film featuring both the negative and positive models.

Since the 1990s many films on schools have been set in the suburbs. Some of them, like the popular comedy *The Best Job in the World* (*Le Plus Beau Métier du monde*, 1996) by Gérard Lauzier or the telefilm *Skirt Day* (*La Journée de la jupe*, 2009) by Jean-Paul Lilienfeld—for which Isabelle Adjani won both the Best Actress César and Lumière Award—convey an alarming image of the schools on the periphery of the large cities. *Games of Love and Chance* and *The Class* both break with this type of representation by offering a reflection on the role of education as a means of social promotion. A certain number of subsequent films that met with some success, like the documentary *School of Babel* (*La Cour de Babel*, 2013) by Julie Bertuccelli and *Once in a Lifetime* (*Les Héritiers*, 2014) by Marie-Castille Mention-Schaar, focus on the most promising pedagogical approaches to promote socio-cultural integration and success in school.

The theme of the last film in this section, Philippe Lioret's *Welcome*, is illegal immigration. This topic had made headlines in France since the 1990s but had scarcely appeared on the screen before the release of Lioret's film. The context of illegal immigration will be explored in the chapter devoted to *Welcome*.

Works Consulted

Durmelat, Sylvie, and Vinay Swamy, eds. *Screening Integration: Recasting Maghrebi Immigration in Contemporary France*. Lincoln: U of Nebraska P, 2012.

Higbee, Will. *Post-Beur Cinema. North African Emigré and Maghrebi-French Filmmaking in France since 2000*. Edinburgh, UK: Edinburgh UP, 2013.

Vincendeau, Ginette. "The Rules of the Game." *Sight and Sound* 19.3 (2009): 34–36.

8

Abdellatif Kechiche

Games of Love and Chance (L'Esquive)

(2003)

Abdellatif Kechiche, *Games of Love and Chance*: The students rehearse Marivaux's *The Game of Love and Chance* in the classroom.

Director .... Abdellatif Kechiche
Adaptation and Dialogue.......... Ghalya Lacroix, Abdellatif Kechiche
Screenplay....................................... Abdellatif Kechiche
Director of Photography ....Lubomir Bakchev
Sound ....Nicolas Washkowski
Film Editor .... Ghalya Lacroix
Art Director.................................Michel-Ange Gionti
Costumes..................................... Mario Beloso-Hall
Continuity ....Ghalya Lacroix
Producer... Jacques Ouaniche
Length.. 1h59

Cast

Osman Elkharraz (*Krimo*), Sara Forestier (*Lydia*), Sabrina Ouazani (*Frida*), Nanou Benhamou (*Nanou*), Hafet Ben-Ahmed (*Fathi*), Aurélie Ganito (*Magali*), Carole Franck (*the French teacher*), Hajar Hamlili (*Zina*), Rachid Hami (*Rachid*), Meriem Serbah (*Krimo's mother*), Hanane Mazouz (*Hanane*), Sylvain Phan (*Slam*)

Story

In a housing project (*cité*) in the suburbs of Paris, Krimo, a gloomy teenager, slips away from his buddies, who are planning reprisals against another neighborhood gang. His father is in prison, and Magali, his girlfriend, dumps him soon after. Then appears Lydia, parading around in the neighborhood in a magnificent vintage dress because she is going to play Lisette in Marivaux's play *The Game of Love and Chance* (*Le Jeu de l'amour et du hasard*, 1730) at the end-of-year middle school celebration. Krimo agrees to attend a rehearsal at a small outdoor amphitheater at the foot of the towers, but this does not meet the approval of Frida, the other main actress. Love-struck, Krimo decides to act in the play in order to get closer to Lydia, and he takes advantage of a rehearsal to declare his flame in a very awkward way. Lydia, surprised, asks for time to give it some thought.

Since Lydia cannot decide if she likes Krimo and wants to go out with him, her peers in the *cité* gang up on her to make her decide, with painful consequences. Meanwhile, Krimo drops his part because he is clearly not good at acting, and he is also pressured by his friends, who would like him to reconcile with Magali. As for Magali, she is mad at Lydia for stealing her boyfriend—even though *she* dumped Krimo. So many complications! How can all this possibly end?

The Director

Born in Tunisia in 1960, Abdellatif Kechiche grew up in the Cité des Moulins in Nice, next to the Victorine studios, where he saw stars and limousines come and go. He studied acting at the Nice Conservatory in 1977–78 and appeared in a few plays, including at the Avignon Theater Festival, while working as a film extra. He played his first important role in *Mint Tea* (*Le Thé à la menthe*,1985), by Abdelkrim Bahloul, in which he portrays a young Algerian immigrant who lives off minor drug trafficking. Then he played gigolos in *Les Innocents* (1987) by André Téchiné and *Bezness* by Nouri Bouzid, a role that earned him the Best Male Actor award at the Namur Francophone Festival in 1992.

Kechiche started his career as a filmmaker with *Poetical Refugee* (*La Faute à Voltaire*, 2000), the story of a Tunisian illegal immigrant who makes ends meet by moonlighting in Paris. Jallel frequents big-hearted ordinary people who are filmed with humanity, like Lucie, a young street person whom he meets at a mental hospital (played by Elodie Bouchez, one of the two main actresses of *The Dreamlife of Angels* [*La Vie rêvée des anges*]; see Chapter 7). Unlike other directors of immigrant background, Kechiche avoids painting an overly bleak picture of the immigrant population and prefers to film matters of the heart. In fact, he claims that he became a filmmaker to break with the stereotypical depiction of immigrants in films of the 1980s: "At that time there was a way to talk about the immigrant, a representation of the immigrant in French cinema with which I did not agree, rather negative and often false [. . .]. I felt that I had to express my own views" (Fontanel 4).

Poetical Refugee received the Golden Lion for Best First Film at the Venice Festival, but this did not stop Kechiche from struggling to make *Games of Love and Chance*, his second feature film, whose screenplay he had begun writing in the early 1990s. This film, which received sixteen awards—including four Césars—in 2004, propelled him to the forefront of film directors. It was followed by the equally successful *The Secret of the Grain* (*La Graine et le mulet*, 2007), which depicts the family and professional life of an old Tunisian immigrant settled for many years in Sète, in the south of France. Fired for economic reasons, he undertakes to restore an old boat that he dreams of converting into a couscous restaurant. Kechiche's next film, *Black Venus* (*Vénus noire*, 2010) was a commercial failure. It tells the tragic life of Saartjie Baartman, also called the Hottentot Venus, a well-endowed young African woman who was exhibited at fairs in England before being displayed at the Musée de l'Homme in Paris after her death in 1815. Kechiche met high critical acclaim again thanks to *Blue Is the Warmest Color* (*La Vie d'Adèle*), which earned numerous prizes and nominations, including the Palme d'Or (the top award at the Cannes Film Festival) in 2013. With this story of a passionate love affair between two women of different social backgrounds, Kechiche moved away from the (post)colonial themes of his previous films.

In sum, Kechiche has a unique trajectory for a director of his generation. He turned to filmmaking to offer a new perspective on the immigrant condition, then he progressively distanced himself from this topic by showing characters who are more and more rooted in France, from an illegal immigrant to young Beurs (adolescents of North African descent) who live in Parisian suburbs, to a multigenerational family settled in the provinces, before finally depicting non-immigrant protagonists.

The Origin and Making of the Film

Kechiche faced many difficulties in making *Games of Love and Chance*. About fifty producers and television channels refused the first version of his screenplay because Kechiche intended to shoot with unknown actors, and his approach did not match their expectations about how to film the suburbs: he was asked, for example, to add a scene in which Krimo would visit his father in prison (Aubenas). Kechiche explains the situation as follows: "Paradoxically, I think that the screenplay suffered from the fact that I wanted to shed a different light on the *cités*. Low-income neighborhoods in the suburbs have been so stigmatized that it's considered quasi revolutionary to film anything there without including gang rapes, drugs, veiled girls or forced marriages" ("Dossier de presse"). Finally he met producer Jacques Ouaniche, who was looking for a story with a personal and innovative perspective on the projects that could be filmed on a small budget.

Funds were also in short supply (3.5 million euros instead of the 12 million Kechiche had hoped for), which led to economy measures: no lighting, no makeup for the actors, working with a digital camera to save on film and developing, six and a half weeks of shooting instead of ten in the Cité de Franc-Moisin in Saint-Denis, cuts on meals, salaries and costumes—the actors had to wear their own clothes (Mélinard). Sara Forestier

(Lydia) remembers these drastic conditions: "We rehearsed more than two months in a squat without getting paid. We shot for two months on a tiny budget," but this did not prevent her from appreciating her work on the film (90). As for Kechiche, he says that making the film with so few resources was "akin to a miracle" (Mélinard).

The Actors

The cast of *Games of Love and Chance* is composed primarily of beginning actors. Only a few adult characters are played by professionals: Carole Franck (the French teacher), the best known, has performed about fifty roles; Olivier Loustau, one of the policemen, has acted in about thirty films; Meriem Serbah (Krimo's mother) has appeared in a few. These three actors, incidentally, had already played in *Poetical Refugee*, Kechiche's first feature film.

The two lead actresses, Sara Forestier, born in 1986, and Sabrina Ouazani, two years younger, were revealed to the broad public in *Games of Love and Chance*, and each received a nomination for the César for Most Promising Actress, awarded to "the mind-boggling Sara Forestier, a sort of language juggler" (Mélinard). Forestier, who grew up in Paris, had appeared in a television film for the Arte channel and played small parts in movies before Kechiche discovered her. She dropped out of high school to devote herself to cinema. For Sabrina Ouazani, born to Algerian parents and raised in a neighborhood similar to the one in the film (the Cité des 4 000 in La Courneuve, north of Paris), it was a first role. The two actresses have since had brilliant careers in the movies. Sara Forestier has acted in about forty films by directors such as Claude Lelouch, Michel Deville, Bertrand Blier, Thomas Gilou, and Alain Resnais. She earned the César for Best Actress for her role in the comedy *The Names of Love* (*Le Nom des gens*, Michel Leclerc, 2010) and a second nomination for this prize for her performance in *Suzanne* by Katell Quillévéré (2013). After *Games of Love and Chance*, Sabrina Ouazani appeared in about fifty films, including *The Secret of the Grain* by Abdellatif Kechiche (2007), *Paris* by Cédric Klapisch (2008), *The Source* (*La Source des femmes*, 2009) by Radu Mihaileanu, and *Of Gods and Men* (*Des Hommes et des dieux*, 2010) by Xavier Beauvois.

The other actors were also nonprofessionals recruited in schools in and around Paris. Osman Elkharraz (Krimo), for example, was an unmotivated student well known to the social workers of Colombes, who deemed him incapable of succeeding as an actor (they were proved wrong, because he received a nomination for the César for Most Promising Actor!). Like many young people from the suburbs, he was subjected to a police check during an evening with friends while the shoot was in progress (Grassin 86). According to Kechiche, "his life experience has given him great sensitivity as well as incredible strength of character for his age [he was only fourteen]" ("Dossier de presse").

The Reception

Released in theaters on January 7, 2004, the film was a huge success with the critics. It was re-released in March 2005 following its unexpected consecration at the Césars, where it came in ahead of the favorites, *The Chorus* (*Les Choristes*) by Christophe Barratier, and *A Very Long Engagement* (*Un Long Dimanche de fiançailles*) by Jean-Pierre Jeunet. The film was awarded four Césars (Best Film, Best Director, Most Promising Actress for Sara Forestier, Best Original Screenplay) and two other nominations for

Most Promising Actor (Osman Elkharraz) and Most Promising Actress (Sabrina Ouazani). It also received the Louis Delluc Prize in 2004 (a prestigious award given to the Best French film of the year) as well as, among other recognitions, the Lumières Award of the international press in the Best Original Screenplay or Adaptation category. *Games of Love and Chance* has sold over 637,000 tickets to this day, a good score for an auteur film.

François Bégaudeau, a critic for the *Cahiers du Cinéma* who later wrote the script of the phenomenally successful film *The Class* (*Entre les murs*, 2008; see Chap. 9), sums up its impact as follows: "*Games of Love and Chance*, the French film of the year? The most talked about, in any case. Since its release in January (cf. *Cahiers* n° 586), it continues to occupy center stage in the debates, by critics but not only. For once, a film is the topic of conversation: in the newspapers, at school, everywhere" (78).

The film was screened in several high schools in the suburbs, where it elicited mixed reactions from instructors. Some did not appreciate the pedagogical message that they detected in the film, while others recognized themselves in the character of the teacher. One instructor, for example, remarked: "I had to hold back my tears ten times. It's so real, so true, the children's distress, their boredom, their solitude, their shame, sometimes, when they come onstage" (Fajardo). As for the young people of the suburbs, they identified primarily with the character of Fathi, the tough guy of the neighborhood who is faithful in friendship, rather than Krimo, the lover. They were also sensitive to the arrest scene, which is part of their daily reality.

The critics praised first and foremost the novelty of Kechiche's approach to the suburbs: "For the first time, a director does not point a camera like a gun on the *cité* nor depict it as a scary place inhabited by picturesque or threatening creatures" ("La banlieue côté cœur"). The critics are grateful that the director avoided both "the predictable rituals of the suburb film" of the *Hate* type (Thabourey 43) and the naive optimism of some Beur films of the 1980s: "One would have to be blind to see [. . .] in Abdellatif Kechiche's film nothing more than an ode to Seine Saint-Denis, replete with good feelings, old-fashioned slang, and an atmosphere reminiscent of social comedy in the '80s, totally cut off from its time" (Maussion 6).

Like Jean-Philippe Tessé, who wrote, "Abdellatif Kechiche dodges. We expected a film on the suburbs, but the main focus is adolescence" (52), the critics emphasize Kechiche's subtle analysis of first love and cite his kinship with directors who are well known for their depiction of adolescence, like Jean Vigo, Jacques Doillon, and especially Maurice Pialat. They praise the original way in which Kechiche conveys the young people's feelings by means of Marivaux's theater and also suggests that it is possible to have a classical education in the suburbs. They particularly praise him for putting language at the center of his film. Guillaume Massart skillfully sums up Kechiche's original take on the suburbs by subtitling his article "Chat 6-T" ("MA 6-T VA TCHATCHER"), a variation on the title of a hard-hitting film by Jean-Francois Richet, *Crack 6-T* (*MA 6-T VA crack-er*, 1997). "Tchatcher," which means to talk incessantly, characterizes the relationship between young people in the suburbs, as we have seen in the chapter on *Hate* by Mathieu Kassovitz.

Even though Kechiche merely uses the *cité* as background and refrains from any kind of advocacy, some critics see his film as a political statement. For Colombani, there is a political subtext under all the love talk, and the film is subversive "because it foregrounds the Arlequins and Lisettes of today." Kaganski concurs: "If

Games of Love and Chance is political, it is not because it condemns injustices known to all or proposes solutions to heal the divisions in French society, but rather because it casts young people of immigrant stock in a play on subtle matters of the heart and allows them to escape the prison of identity and social class, if only while the film is playing." The only negative comments come from critics who accuse Kechiche of giving in to clichés by filming a police check, but this scene is sometimes considered subversive because the director, unlike Kassovitz in *Hate*, for example, does not show the outcome of this episode. Instead, he uses an ellipsis (leaving the outcome to the spectator's imagination) and jumps without any kind of transition to the end-of-year school performance. This happy scene has also come under fire. Some, like Thabourey and Bégaudeau, blame Kechiche for depicting an idyllic suburb where people of different cultures and generations coexist a little too peacefully.

Theater in Kechiche's Film: Marivaux's *The Game of Love and Chance*

The characters of *Games of Love and Chance* are rehearsing *Le Jeu de l'amour et du hasard* (1730), a play by Marivaux (1688–1763). Marivaux is an eighteenth-century author who wrote very long novels like *The Life of Marianne* (*La Vie de Marianne*, 1731–41) and *The Upstart Peasant* (*Le Paysan parvenu*, 1735) but who is known mostly as a playwright. His comedies, like *Le Jeu de l'amour et du hasard* and *Les Fausses Confidences* (1737), explore the psychology of love. Marivaux is especially interested in the initial moment of attraction and the way feelings evolve, and he analyzes the many obstacles (such as pride, doubt, fear, self-love) that delay the blossoming of love. This minutely detailed analysis of feelings was called *marivaudage* (Voltaire, for his part, described *marivaudage* as the art of "weighing flies' eggs in cobweb scales"). Language plays a key role in expressing subtle shades of feelings in his plays. Marivaux was also interested in the influence of social class on behavior, and he was considered subversive because characters from different backgrounds often mingled in his works. In *Le Jeu de l'amour et du hasard*, a three-act play, Sylvia and Dorante are two young aristocrats who are about to have an arranged marriage. Both ask their respective fathers to let them dress up as their servants in order to better observe their future spouse. The roles are thus reversed, with Sylvia and Dorante passing themselves off as Lisette and Arlequin and vice versa. In spite of the disguises and class prejudice, each character falls in love with the person who belongs to his/her own social class, and order is restored.

    Games of Love and Chance focuses on the rehearsal of a few excerpts from the play that feature the servants disguised as their masters, with Lydia playing Lisette and Krimo as Arlequin. Frida, for her part, is cast as Sylvia, the aristocrat who pretends to be a servant. The young people rehearse the play in the *cité* and in class before performing it in front of their friends and families at the end of the film. Asked why he included Marivaux's play in his film, Kechiche responded that he wished to analyze feelings and throw light on the creativity of Marivaux's language and the language of the suburbs:

> I wanted to talk about theater in a *cité*. I wanted my characters to experience a *marivaudage* [. . .]. I was happy to mix the two types of language. I love Marivaux's language, but I also love the way the young people talk, it is very

inventive. It is a cultural blend [. . .]. I was not trying to compare the relative merits of each culture. Both cultures can live together. In any case, one can go back and forth between the two." (Mélinard)

The title of the film comes from Act III, Scene 6, in which Arlequin tries to get closer to Lisette, who dodges (*qui esquive*, in French) verbally to get away from him (this takes place in the scene where Lydia first rehearses with Rachid, then Krimo). At this point, Arlequin says: "Finally, my Queen, I see you again and will not be separated from you anymore, because it hurt too much to be away from you, and I thought that you were avoiding me (*esquiviez*)." The word *esquiver* appears several times in the dialogue of the film, including in its "verlanized" form (in reverse) when Lydia tells her friends that she has "vesqui" ("odgdayed" [dodged]) Krimo.

Language in *Games of Love and Chance*

Games of Love and Chance is striking for its original use of several language registers: formal (Marivaux's literary language), neutral (the language spoken at school or with adults, including the police), and the informal language and slang (*verlan*) used by the young people of the *cité*. It is this aspect of the film that the critics most raved about: "*Games of Love and Chance* is a film about speech. Fiery speech, phenomenal for its energy and creativity" (Kaganski), "a film that speaks two languages at once. A language of today, inventive, funny, moving, that one can explore, decipher, and intuit with incredible pleasure while enjoying its abrupt and jubilant poetry [. . .], and an older language, that of Marivaux, which, surprisingly, rings so true when it is rediscovered and spoken by these youth from the suburbs" (Fansten).

Deciphering the language of the adolescents of the film is no easy task because it is the language of the *cités*, a creative mix of *verlan*, foreign words, neologisms, images, common phrases, all pronounced with intensity and at a fast pace. Kechiche was "fascinated by the relationship of young people to language in the suburbs," and he associated that language with "freedom, invention, pleasure, sensuality" (Regnier). Because he had written his screenplay fifteen years before making *Games of Love and Chance*, he spent time at McDonald's to listen to young people talk and see how their language had evolved (Porton). By using "suburb talk" in his film, Kechiche was following a trend of the 1990s popularized by the success of *Hate* in the media and at the box office in 1995.

What is "suburb talk"? *Verlan*, a type of slang, is a major component. Renaud, a well-known singer, brought it to the attention of the general public with his song "Laisse béton," the reverse of "Laisse tomber" ("Forget it"), in 1977. Filmmakers like Claude Zidi and Josiane Balasko followed suit in their popular comedies about the police (*Les Ripoux*, *verlan* for "pourris" [rotten], in 1983, and *Les Keufs*, *verlan* for "les flics" [cops] in 1987, respectively). In its simplest form, *verlan* consists in inverting the syllables of a word (the word *verlan* itself results from the permutation of the two syllables of the word "l'envers," which means "the reverse side"). The verlanized word can be a common word (like "café" [coffee], which becomes "féca") or a slang word ("mec" [guy], which turns into "keum"). In *Games of Love and Chance*, for example, the following words are heard: "cimer" (merci [thank you]), "chelou" (louche [suspicious]), "eins" (sein [breast]), "guedin" (dingue [crazy]), "oim" (moi [me]), "ouf" (fou [crazy]), "secla" (classe [class]), "téma" (mater [to stare at]), "vénère" (énervé [angry]). The inversion of syllables some-times comes with other changes, as is the case for "Beur" (Arabe [Arab]), "meuf" (femme [woman]), and "keuf" (flic [cop]).

Little by little, some *verlan* words have appeared in colloquial French (and in some dictionaries, like *Le Petit Robert*) and have as a result lost their subversive or self-defining character. To make up for it, people sometimes resort to "re-verlanization," a technique that turns "meuf," "keuf," and "beur," for example, into "feum," "feuk," and "rebeu," with slight differences in meaning. *Verlan* is thus an extremely creative language that is constantly changing.

Verlan serves different purposes. It is a way to play with language, mark one's iden-tity, and build a positive self-image—and to subvert authority when addressing adults, teachers, and other people in charge. *Verlan* is primarily comprised of words associated with life in underprivileged neighborhoods, and terms linked to drugs and violence are very common. But the language of the suburbs is not limited to *verlan*. In *Games of Love and Chance*, we also find words borrowed from Parisian slang (Krimo mentions his "daron" [his father]), Arabic words ("bsarh tik," "mabrouk" [congratulations, bravo], "ouallah" ["I swear by Allah/God"]), Arabic words absorbed into French ("kiffer" [to like]; "niquer" [to screw]), adjectives used as adverbs ("mortel," "grave," which both mean "a lot"), emphatic expressions ("sur la tête de ma mère" [on my mother's grave], "sur la tête de oim" [on my life], "sur le Coran de la Mecque" [on the Koran of Mecca], "sur la vie de ma race" [on the life of my race]), and vulgar images and expressions ("je m'en bats les couilles" [I don't give a f--k]), "il pue la merde" [he stinks]).

For example, this is how Hanane and Rachid answer Lydia when she asks what they think of her dress:

> HANANE: Na, ouallah, elle est trop belle mabrouk! [I swear by God, it is too beautiful, congrats!]
>
> LYDIA: Sérieux? Elle est belle? [You mean it? It's beautiful?]
>
> RACHID: Bsarh tik! [Good for you!]
>
> LYDIA: Ça fait bien ou quoi? [Looks good or what?]
>
> RACHID: Mortel! [Out of this world!]
>
> LYDIA: Ouais? Ça fait bien? [Yeah? Looks good?]
>
> RACHID: Ouais, moi je kiffe! [Yeah! I dig it!]

The female characters of *Games of Love and Chance* use the same language as the males, even though it is often sexist. They call each other "mon frère" [Bro], refer to girls as "putes" [whores], and speak loudly and aggressively like the boys. This marks a change when compared to a film like *Hate* about ten years before, in which the female characters were less visible and spoke more properly. This change reveals the girls' desire to appro-priate the language of the boys in order to earn more respect. As Lalanne puts it, "Per-haps it shows how much tougher the girls need to be in the *cité*. When they call each other "Bro," they are no longer girls but on a par with guys, they are no longer victims."

We should mention, finally, another characteristic of the language of the suburbs, which consists in talking loudly and quickly, using exaggeration, without pause, as if participating in a boxing or fencing match. For Sabrina Ouazani, who plays Frida, talking loud is the only way to prove one's existence in the difficult environment of the suburbs: "In the cités, people don't have much of a future, she says. They are so used to being looked down upon.... If we don't talk loud, if we don't scream, no one will listen to us, no one will hear us" (Regnier).

Language, in this film, also "dodges": its violence should not be taken at face value, but viewed as a covert way to express feelings of love and friendship, because doing it directly would be an admission of weakness and go against the macho codes of the *cité*. Kechiche says that he wanted to "demystify this verbal aggressiveness and show it for what it is, a true mode of communication. A sort of superficial aggressiveness that very often hides a degree of modesty, and sometimes even real fragility, rather than violence for its own sake" ("Dossier de presse"). Sara Forestier (who plays the Lydia character) shares the critics' enthusiasm for the special place accorded to language in *Games of Love and Chance*: "In the film, the teacher wants her students to discover lots of new horizons; Abdellatif, for his part, wants to reveal the richness of the language of the suburbs. He has drawn attention to it like no one else before by highlighting its musical rhythm, its very own metaphors, far from the clichés spread by television. For once the reality of the suburbs is presented from an aesthetic angle [. . .]. People come and ask if we really speak like this when we are together: it's a sure sign of our success" (Regnier).

STUDY GUIDE

What Happens in This Film?

1. What do the young people talk about at the beginning? What does Krimo do instead of joining them?

2. What is Lydia doing when Krimo sees her in the basement of an apartment block of the *cité*?

3. Where do the young people rehearse a scene from Marivaux's *Le Jeu de l'amour et du hasard*? Why is Frida mad at Lydia?

4. What is Krimo's family situation?

5. Why does Krimo want to replace Rachid in the role of Arlequin? Why does Rachid let him have the part?

6. What does Magali accuse Lydia of? What does she threaten to do?

7. How does Krimo play Arlequin? How do his classmates and the teacher react when he plays the role?

8. What dramatic event occurs during the rehearsal between Lydia and Krimo in the amphitheater?

9. Why does Fathi assault Frida and take away her cell phone?

10. What happens when Krimo and Lydia are talking in the car by the road?

11. Where does the end-of-year show take place? Who attends it? Who is outside looking in?

12. What does Lydia do at the end of the film? And Krimo?

True or False?

If the statement is false, correct it!

1. Lydia wears her eighteenth-century dress everywhere because she is proud to have made it herself.

2. Krimo's father likes to paint animal pictures.

3. Krimo's mother likes to watch American films on television and listen to rock music on the radio.

4. In Marivaux's play Lisette and Arlequin are servants who pretend to be masters.

5. Fathi is the "boss" of the young people in the *cité*. He is the one who deals with problems.

6. Fathi and his friends admire boys who act in plays.

7. Fathi learns from his friend that Krimo is in love with Lydia.

8. Lydia cannot decide if she is going to go out with Krimo, because she is afraid of Magali's reaction.

9. Frida is afraid that her mother will get mad if she comes back home without her cell phone.

10. The policewoman is gentler with the young people than her male colleagues.

11. During the end-of-year celebration, the show put on by the children talks about birds that have traveled a long way.

12. Magali and Krimo reconciled and attended the performance together.

What Did You Learn in the Introduction?

1. What role did the representation of immigrants in the movies play in Kechiche's decision to become a filmmaker?

2. What is the general evolution of his films?

3. What difficulties did he face when making *Games of Love and Chance*?

4. What types of actors did he cast, mostly? What did Sara Forestier receive for her performance in *Games of Love and Chance*?

5. What aspects of *Games of Love and Chance* were particularly praised by the critics?

6. Why did some critics consider *Games of Love and Chance* a political film?

7. What is "marivaudage"? What is the origin of this term?

8. Why did Kechiche integrate Marivaux's play, *Le Jeu de l'amour et du hasard*, into his film?

9. What is the language called *verlan*? Give a few examples.

10. Besides *verlan*, what are other characteristics of the language spoken in the *cités*? For example, what does one find in the dialogue between Hanane, Rachid, and Lydia?

11. Why can it seem surprising (in the light of previous suburb films) that girls speak the language of the *cités*? How can we explain this?

12. How can one interpret the violence of "suburb talk"?

Exploring the Film

1. The Title and Prologue of the Film

According to the *Petit Robert* dictionary, an *esquive* is "an evasive move to dodge an attack," as practiced by a boxer, for example. By extension, this term means avoiding a person or situation. **To whom or to what do you think this term applies in the film? Which character(s) dodge(s)?**

According to critic Jean-Philippe Tessé, "Abdellatif Kechiche dodges. We expected a film on the suburbs, but the main focus is adolescence." How do you interpret this comment? How do the first two sequences of the film, which are separated by the opening credits and the title *Games of Love and Chance*, illustrate Tessé's remark? (What do we expect during the first sequence, the conversation between the boys? What happens next instead?) *Review the first two sequences* (Excerpts 1 and 2, 0'30–02'15, 02'5–04'20).

2. The Characters

+ **Krimo**

We know that Krimo's father is in prison and that his mother is raising him alone and working at the same time. Why does Kechiche choose to show us Krimo's family and his home and not the home environment of the other characters?

Why does Krimo decide to act in a play? Given what his group of friends think about boys who perform in theater, what does this decision tell us about his state of mind?

Why doesn't Krimo succeed as Arlequin?

✦ *Lydia and Krimo*

In your opinion, when does Krimo fall in love with Lydia, his childhood friend? When does Lydia realize that Krimo has feelings for her? **Why does it take her so long to respond when he asks if she wants to go out with him?** Is she a "tease," as Magali and Frida say?

3. Groups and Individuals

Fathi is clearly the leader of the group of boys in the *cité*. Does the group of girls work the same way?

What "code" prevails in the *cité* when it comes to romantic relationships? What role does the group play regarding matters of the heart?

4. The Boys and the Girls

How do the two groups, the boys and the girls, talk among themselves? **Is there a difference in the way these two groups express themselves?** For example, *review the first sequence* (Excerpt 1, 00'30–02'15) **and one of the scenes where the girls are talking** (Excerpt 3, 33'03–35'00). What do the young people talk about? What is striking in both cases?

How are the roles of the girls within the family different from the boys' roles? Consider, for example, the case of Zina, to whom Lydia is showing her dress at the beginning of the film. *Review this scene* (Excerpt 4, 11'00–11'50).

Except for this example, are the girls on an equal footing with the boys?

5. Spaces

Which spaces of the *cité* are shown? Which ones are not? Why? **How does Kechiche depict the reality of life in the suburbs in his film?**

In what scenes do the characters leave the *cité*? What happens then? **How does this influence our perception of the *cité* as a place to live?** For example, does it make the *cité* appear as a place of freedom or confinement? Both?

6. Language

When do the young people speak the language of the suburbs? When do they speak standard French? What does Kechiche want to show by using both? For example, compare the following scenes to illustrate your answers:

✦ *Review the scene where Fathi talks to his buddies at the beginning of the film (Excerpt 1, 00'30–02'15), and then the scene where he talks to Krimo's mother (Excerpt 5, 40'50–41'50).*

✦ *Review the scenes where Lydia and Frida discuss how to impersonate the rich and the poor (Excerpts 6 and 7, 18'10–19'10, 26'50–27'25).*

7. Theater

What parallels can you find between theater (in general) and Kechiche's film? Where does most of the action take place? How do we get from one scene to the next (what type of transitions does Kechiche use)? At the theater, we always see the whole stage, as in a static long shot (the camera does not move). What is the situation in *Games of Love and Chance*? How does Kechiche's cinematographic style compensate for the relatively static (theatrical) character of his sequences? *Review, for example, the scene where the girls are talking among themselves, and pay attention to the way Kechiche reframes and edits his shots* (Excerpt 3, 33'03–35'00).

What parallels do you notice between Marivaux's *Le Jeu de l'amour et du hasard* and *Games of Love and Chance* as regards the themes and the characters' motivations? For example, how could we apply the notion of "marivaudage" to the romantic difficulties of Krimo and Lydia?

During a classroom scene, the teacher reads aloud and assigns the following question as a reflection topic: "To what extent do you think that Marivaux meant to focus on the analysis of feelings rather than the plot in Act I, Scene V?" How could we ask the same question about Kechiche's film? How do his shots reinforce the psychological aspect of the film? *Review the sequence where Lydia and Krimo rehearse their parts* (Excerpt 8, 58'05–1h02'20).

What role does the play have in the film? For example, what is its impact on the sentimental plot and on the life of the *cité*?

The inclusion of Marivaux's play in the film gave rise to many different interpretations. Some critics read it as Kechiche's homage to the theater (he started his career as an actor). For others, like Nettelbeck (314), it shows that French culture helps teenagers in the *cités* to integrate better into French society. Others yet, like Kaganski, interpret it as Kechiche's desire to avoid stereotypes about the suburbs by filming the typical preoccupations of adolescents (love, friendship, school). **Which interpretation do you find the most convincing?**

8. The School System

In France, public school is seen as an institution with universal values that can remedy class and cultural differences and ensure equal opportunities for all. Given the extent of discrimination against young people in the suburbs and their poor school performance, achieving this republican ideal seems less and less likely, and reforms are considered to ensure that education truly promotes upward social mobility.

Let's analyze the teacher's remarks through the lens of this republican ideal. **What does she think of the impact of social class on the individual?** For example, how does she interpret the fact that Lisette and Arlequin fall in love with each other even though they are disguised as masters? Is her interpretation limited to eighteenth-century society, or does it also apply to her own time? *Review this sequence* (Excerpt 9, 27'25–28'38). According to the teacher, **what role can theater play,** in particular when she tells Krimo: "Have fun [. . .] try to play someone who has power [. . .]. There must be pleasure in being someone else, enjoy yourself, change the way you talk, have fun!"? *Review her advice to Krimo* (Excerpt 10, 1h08'15–1h11'40).

Taking into account the teacher's comments and her interaction with the class, **do you think she believes in her mission as a representative of republican education?** Or rather, does she consider that her students' future is predetermined by their social class?

For Serge Kaganski, the rehearsal scene in the classroom (Excerpt 10) is a "brilliant scene because the spectator sides at the same time with Krimo [...] and with the teacher [...], and also because it sums up in a few minutes the complexity of the problems facing French society." Do you agree with this comment? **How can the spectator side with Krimo and the teacher at the same time? Do you?**

For some critics (Williams, for example), Krimo's leaving the classroom and his failure at acting result from the teacher's (or the school system's) inability to adapt their methods to the students' culture. Do you think that an eighteenth-century play like *Le Jeu de l'amour et du hasard* is a bad choice for the twenty-first-century classroom, especially given the backgrounds of the students in the film? Does literature contribute to social exclusion in this film or, on the contrary, does it enrich the students' lives and promote social integration? **Can we interpret Krimo's failure at play acting as a failure of the republican school?**

9. Violence

What types of violence are found in the film, and who are the victims?

Kechiche was accused of yielding to clichés by including a scene of police violence. Why did he do that, in your opinion? *Review an excerpt from this scene* (Excerpt 11, 1h 42'05–1h44'50).

How did Kechiche portray the police? How does Fathi behave during this scene? What contrast does Kechiche draw between the police and the young people?

What happens when the policewoman discovers *Le Jeu de l'amour et du hasard* in Frida's pocket? Why is she suspicious? How does violence evolve from that point on? **How and why does Kechiche insist on Marivaux's play in this scene?**

10. The School Celebration and the Denouement

During the school celebration, the spectators attend a play performed by young children before watching *Le Jeu de l'amour et du hasard*. Kechiche's focus on this scene —it lasts four minutes, almost as long as the scene devoted to Marivaux's play—raises questions about its presence in the film. The piece is an Islamic poem by Farid al-din Attar titled "The Conference of the Birds" in which the different birds of the world, tired of their never-ending conflicts, go on a long journey to find a king who can unite them. The most courageous reach their destination and realize that the purpose of the trip was personal discovery (Sachs 138–39). As little Abdelkrim says in the film, "We made a long journey to find ourselves." **What connections can you make between this poem and the film? Whom do the birds bring to mind? How can we interpret the sentence spoken by Abdelkrim?** Is it related to the situation of the young people in the suburbs? Why do you think Kechiche juxtaposed an Islamic poem and a classical French play?

A few commentators found the school celebration too positive. According to Thabourey, Kechiche depicts "an idyllic suburb where the community center presents a happy show which is to everyone's taste, transgenerational, and transcultural." **Who** reconciles with whom after the performance? What kinds of people attend the celebration? How do they relate to each other? What types of music do we hear? **Review an excerpt of this scene** (Excerpt 12, 1h 54'30–1h56'03). **What does this blend of music suggest regarding the story of Games of Love and Chance?** Do you agree with Thabourey that this aspect of the denouement is too positive? If yes, do you think that Kechiche should not have included it in his film? What is the significance of the school celebration in the film, in your opinion?

Finally, what do you think of the outcome of the relationship between Krimo and Lydia? Do you think it is positive or negative? What do you think Lydia wants to say to Krimo at the end of the film, when she calls him from the bottom of his apartment block? Why doesn't Krimo respond? Could the fact that Magali has a new boyfriend (as we saw during the school performance) explain his reaction?

Abdellatif Kechiche's Filmography

2000   *Poetical Refugee (La Faute à Voltaire)*

2004   *Games of Love and Chance (L'Esquive)*

2007   *The Secret of the Grain (La Graine et le mulet)*

2010   *Black Venus (Vénus noire)*

2013   *Blue is the Warmest Color (La Vie d'Adèle)*

Works Consulted

Aubenas, Florence. "La Banlieue par la Bande." *L'Avant-Scène Cinéma* 542 (2005): 4–5.

"La banlieue côté cœur." *Le Figaro*, 7 Jan. 2004: n. pag.

Bégaudeau, François. "Esquives (retour sur un film dont on parle)." *Cahiers du cinéma* 592 (July–Aug. 2004): 78–81.

Black, Catherine, and Larissa Sloutsky. "Evolution du verlan, marqueur social and identitaire, comme vu dans les films: *La Haine* (1995) et *L'Esquive* (2004)." *Synergies Canada* 2 (2010): 1–14.

Blatt, Ari J. "The Play's the Thing: Marivaux and the *banlieue* in Abdellatif Kechiche's *L'Esquive*." *French Review* 81.3 (Feb. 2008): 516–27.

Boujut, Michel. "*L'Esquive*: un film d'Abdellatif Kechiche." *L'Avant-Scène Cinéma* 542 (2005): 3–91.

Colombani, Florence. "Entre les dalles de béton, une parole qui jaillit." *Le Monde*, 7 Jan. 2004: n. pag.

"Dossier de presse." Web. 13 May 2017. <www.histoire-immigration.fr/sites/default /files/musee-numerique/documents/ext_media_fichier_611_DP_esquive_1 .pdf>.

Fajardo, Isabelle. "Cités dans le texte." *Télérama*, 10 Jan. 2004: n. pag. [Interview with Abdellatif Kechiche and Cécile Ladjali, a French teacher].

Fansten, Jacques. "*L'Esquive*." *L'Avant-Scène Cinéma* 542 (May 2005): 3.

Fontanel, Rémi. "*L'Esquive* d'Abdellatif Kechiche. Dossier pédagogique." Web. 13 May 2017. <www.clermont-filmfest.com/03_pole_regional/newsletter/img/sept07/pdf 31.pdf>.

Forestier, Sarah. "Comment *L'Esquive* a changé ma vie." *Première* 323 (Apr. 2005): 90–91.

Grassin, Sophie. "*L'Esquive* d'Abdellatif Kechiche." *Première* 323 (Jan. 2004): 84–87.

Higbee, Will. *Post-Beur Cinema. North African Émigré and Maghrebi-French Filmmaking in France since 2000.* Edinburgh: Edinburgh UP, 2013.

Kaganski, Serge. "*L'Esquive*, un film subtil and *électrisant*." *Les Inrockuptibles*, 7 Jan. 2004: n. pag.

Kechiche, Abdellatif, dir. *L'Esquive*. Aventi, 2004.

Lalanne, Jean-Marc. "*L'Esquive*: entretien avec Abdellatif Kechiche." *Les Inrockuptibles*, 7 Jan. 2004: n. pag.

Massart, Guillaume. "*L'Esquive*." Web. 30 Dec. 2016. <http://www.filmdeculte.com /cinema/film/Esquive-L-751.html>.

Maussion, Yves. "*L'Esquive*. Dossier pédagogique complémentaire." Rectorat de Nantes. Web. 30 Dec. 2016. <yjmauss.fr/cinemauss/cinemauss/Lesquive_files/ l'esquive .pdf>.

Mélinard, Michaël. "'Cette jeunesse n'a pas de place dans le paysage audiovisuel': Abdellatif Kechiche, *L'Esquive*." *L'Humanité*, 7 Jan. 2004: n. pag.

Nettelbeck, Colin. "Kechiche and the French Classics: Cinema vs. Subversion and Renewal of Tradition." *French Cultural Studies* 18.3 (2007): 307–19.

Porton, Richard. "Marivaux in the 'Hood': An Interview with Abdellatif Kechiche." *Cineaste* 31.1 (2005): 46–49.

Regnier, Isabelle. "Les tirades musicales et politiques de la banlieue." *Le Monde*, 6 Jan. 2004: n. pag.

Sachs, Leon. *The Pedagogical Imagination: The Republican Legacy in Twenty-First Century French Literature.* Lincoln, NE: U of Nebraska P, 2014.

Sanaker, John Kristian, and David-Alexandre Wagner. "Hétérolinguisme filmique. L'exemple du film de banlieue." *Alienation and Alterity: Otherness in Modern and Contemporary Francophone Contexts.* Ed. Helen Vassalo and Paul Cooke. Oxford: Peter Lang, 2009. 155–80.

Shea, Louisa. "Exit Voltaire, Enter Marivaux: Abdellatif Kechiche on the Legacy of the Enlightenment." *French Review* 85.6 (May 2012): 1136–48.

Sloutsky, Larissa, and Catherine Black. "Le Verlan, phénomène langagier and social: récapitulatif." *French Review* 82.2 (Dec. 2008): 308–24.

Strand, Dana. "Etre et Parler: Being and Speaking French in Abdellatif Kechiche's *L'Esquive* (2004) and Laurent Cantet's *Entre les murs* (2008)." *Studies in French Cinema* 9.3 (2009): 259–72.

Swamy, Vinay. "Marivaux in the Suburbs: Reframing Language in Kechiche's *L'Esquive* (2003)." *Studies in French Cinema* 7.1 (2007): 57–68.

Tarr, Carrie. "Class Acts: Education, Gender, and Integration in Recent French Cinema." *Screening Integration: Recasting Maghrebi Immigration in Contemporary France.* Ed. Sylvie Durmelat and Vinay Swamy. Lincoln, NE: U of Nebraska P, 2012. 127–43.

———. "Reassessing French Popular Culture: *L'Esquive.*" *France at the Flicks: Trends in Contemporary French Popular Cinema.* Ed. Darren Waldron and Isabelle Vanderschelden. Newcastle: Cambridge Scholars, 2007. 130–41.

———. *Reframing Difference: Beur and Banlieue Filmmaking in France.* Manchester, England: Manchester UP, 2005.

Tessé, Jean-Philippe. "*L'Esquive* d'Abdellatif Kechiche." *Cahiers du cinéma* 586 (Jan. 2004): 52–53.

Thabourey, Vincent. "*L'Esquive*, une banlieue si sensible." *Positif* 515 (Jan. 2004): 43–44.

Williams, James S. "Open-Sourcing French Culture: The Politics of Métissage and Collective Reappropriation in the Films of Abdellatif Kechiche." *International Journal of Francophone Studies* 14.3 (2011): 397–421.

9

Laurent Cantet

The Class (Entre les murs)

(2008)

Laurent Cantet, *The Class*: Discussion with the students.

Director . . . . Laurent Cantet
Screenplay . . . . Laurent Cantet, François Bégaudeau, Robin Campillo
Director of Photography . . . . Pierre Milon
Sound . . . . Jean-Pierre Laforce, Olivier Mauvezin, Agnès Ravez
Film Editors . . . . Robin Campillo, Stéphane Léger
Art Directors . . . . Sabine Barthélémy, Hélène Bellanger
Costumes . . . . Marie Le Garrec
Producers . . . . Caroline Benjo, Carole Scotta
. . . . Barbara Letellier, Simon Arnal
Length 2h08

Cast

François Bégaudeau (*François Marin*), Franck Keïta (*Souleymane*), Esméralda Ouertani (*Esméralda*), Rachel Régulier (*Khoumba*), Louise Grinberg (*Louise*), Wei Huang (*Wei*), Carl Nanor (*Carl*), Burak Özyilmaz (*Burak*), Boubacar Touré (*Boubacar*), Arthur Fogel (*Arthur*), Nassim Amrabt (*Nassim*), Cherif Bounaïdja Rachedi (*Cherif*), Angélica Sancio (*Angélica*), Rabah Naït Oufella (*Rabah*), Damien Gomes (*Damien*), Henriette Kasarhuanda (*Henriette*), Justine Wu (*Justine*), Jean-Michel Simonet (*the principal*), Frédéric Faujas (*Frédéric*)

Story

It's the first day of school at the *collège* Dolto in Paris, a middle school located in a Priority Education Zone (*Zone d'éducation prioritaire*, or ZEP). One last cup of coffee to get his courage up, and François Marin, an eighth-grade French teacher, walks up to his classroom—or rather gets into the arena. The students are unruly and well below grade level. "What does *l'argenterie* [silverware] mean?" "The inhabitants of Argentina," Damien answers. Patiently, Mr. Marin asks questions, tries hard to come down to the students' level: "I'm sure you watch soccer on TV. What are the players of the Argentina national team called?" "Soccer players." It is time to move on, but Souleymane doesn't have his class materials, Esméralda speaks too much *verlan* (back slang), Khoumba inexplicably refuses to read, and a lesson on the imperfect tense turns into questions about . . . the teacher's sexual orientation. In the teachers' lounge, a colleague breaks down and cries. Fortunately Wei is a good student, and Carl, who arrived in the middle of the year, doesn't seem as tough as they say. . . .

The school year continues, with its close readings, self-portraits, parent-teacher conferences . . . and a fateful teachers' meeting. Louise and Esméralda, the student representatives, break the rules and report everything to their classmates. Souleymane is angry to learn that the teachers "dissed" him. The representatives go too far and the teacher loses it, calling them "pétasses" (bitches). Souleymane goes ballistic and accidentally injures Khoumba while bolting out of the classroom. He will face a disciplinary hearing.

The Director

Laurent Cantet, born in 1961, started his career with a bang (he was admitted to the top film school *Institut des hautes études cinématographiques*) after studying photography in hopes of becoming a reporter. During his film studies he founded a production company, Sérénade (now defunct), with a circle of friends who would later participate in the writing of his screenplays. Sérénade produced his first shorts, *Let's all join the demonstration* (*Tous à la manif*, 1994), in which we already recognize his interest in social cinema, and *Beach Games* (*Jeux de plage*, 1995), both featuring a future star, Jalil Lespert, in his first movie roles. Cantet caught the attention of the producers of the independent company Haut et court, who invited him to contribute to a collection of ten television films on the theme of the transition to the year 2000, "2000, Seen by . . ." ("2000 vu par . . ."). His film, *The Sanguinaire Islands* (*Les Sanguinaires*), is about a group of buddies who retire to a Corsican island to avoid the millennium celebrations. Cantet has remained loyal to this company, which produces and distributes all his films.

Cantet rose to fame with *Human Resources* (*Ressources humaines*, 1999), the first in a series of feature films that deal with the impact of capitalism on the individual and the family. The film tells the story of an ambitious young man, played by Lespert, who has just graduated from a top business school and is hired as an intern in the Human Resources department of the factory where his father has worked a blue-collar job for over thirty years. When a strike breaks out upon the implementation of the thirty-five-hour workweek, he discovers social conflict and the underhanded methods of management, which forces him to pick sides. *Human Resources* won the Louis Delluc Prize, the César Award for Best First Feature Film, and the César Award for Most Promising Actor for Jalil Lespert.

Cantet continued exploring the workplace in *Time Out* (*L'Emploi du temps*, 2001), based on a true story. In this film, which won awards at the Venice and the Montreal film festivals, a man does not want to tell his family that he has been fired. Instead he pretends to be working for the United Nations and sinks deeper and deeper into deception until it all blows up in his face. Cantet's next film, *Heading South* (*Vers le sud*, 2005), looks at the power relations between North and South from the angle of sexual tourism. The story is about Western women past their prime who spend their vacations in Haiti to treat themselves to the services of young local gigolos. With *The Class*, winner of the Palme d'Or (the top award at the Cannes Film Festival), Cantet broaches the sensitive topic of education in the suburbs, where issues of integration and equal opportunity are even more urgent than elsewhere. *Foxfire* (*Foxfire, confessions d'un gang de filles*, 2012), adapted from a novel by Joyce Carol Oates, revisits themes from his two previous films, adolescence and women's desire for independence. The film is about a group of young women who rebel against male oppression in 1950s America.

More recently, the director also contributed to a film anthology, *7 Days in Havana* (*7 jours à la Havane*, 2012), presented in the Un Certain Regard section at Cannes, where it received six nominations. In the spirit of *Paris, je t'aime* (2006) or *New York, I Love You* (2008), the film is a compilation of shorts that pay homage to the Cuban capital and its population. Cantet directed one of the seven segments, a comedy for a change, centered on Sunday. This short forms the basis of his next project, *Return to Ithaca* (*Retour à Ithaque*, 2014), a film in Spanish also located in Havana. The story brings together a group of former friends upon the return of one of them after a self-imposed exile of about twenty years. Through their long discussions they recall the dreams of their youth and share their feelings about the evolution of their country. The director departed here from his earlier films by working with Cuban stars rather than nonprofessionals.

In sum, Cantet has built an eclectic oeuvre, often halfway between fiction and documentary, in which we find recurring favorite themes such as "the idea of the group confronting the world" (Burdeau 11) and power relations at work and at home. He has brought the camera into places rarely shown in cinema before him, like the factory and the classroom. For Douin, what matters to the director is "to be anchored in reality, immersed in social relations, to study power relations and anything that generates violence and exclusion," and his films depict above all "the fight of people who have not given up hope to make a place for themselves."

The Origin and Making of the Film

Cantet began writing *The Class* because of a delay in the shooting of *Heading South*, which was postponed for a year due to political chaos in Haiti. From the outset it was a story set in a middle school and centered on a struggling student already named Souleymane. The rest of the film took shape after Cantet's meeting with François Bégaudeau during a radio show upon the release of *Heading South*. Bégaudeau, a French teacher turned writer and literary critic, was invited to talk about his book *The Class* (2006), the chronicle of the year he had spent teaching French at a tough middle school in Paris. Cantet was immediately impressed by Bégaudeau's enthusiasm for the teaching profession and the fact that "for once, a teacher was not writing to settle scores with teenage students depicted as savages or morons" (Mangeot). The book gave him the documentary background that he was missing and his main character, François.

Cantet was interested in the school system for personal reasons—both his parents were teachers, and he had two children in middle school—and because he considered middle school "one of the last places where social mixing can occur" and "a sounding board, a small environment that can tell us about the state of the world, as in *Human Resources*" (Burdeau 15). However, he did not want to make an ideological statement about schools but merely "show its contradictions and the complexity of decision making, without seeking to give answers nor illustrate a thesis" (Raspiengeas, "*Entre les murs*"). Cantet and Bégaudeau identified and reworked the situations of the book that could enrich Souleymane's story, and they condensed the portraits of some of the students to turn them into characters in the film. At that stage of the project, Bégaudeau was a "documentary watchdog" in charge of verifying if the episodes made sense in a real school situation; it soon became obvious that he was the best casting choice for the male lead, Mr. Marin.

Cantet decided to shoot in the twentieth arrondissement of Paris because he liked its diversity. He promptly received permission to work with the staff and the students of the Collège Dolto, a "mixed" but "trouble free" school according to the principal, located in a ZEP like the middle school of the book (Laffeter). For five months the director organized weekly theater workshops attended by volunteers—about ten teachers and fifty students. He jotted down their conversations to write the film dialogues, and he consulted with the parents to better understand their expectations of the school and of their children.

The shoot lasted for seven weeks during the summer of 2007 at a nearby vocational high school because the college Dolto was under renovation. Cantet used a simple arrangement for the set which, combined with the casting of nonprofessional actors, resulted in a low-budget film (2.5 million euros). He built a hallway along the classroom where he positioned three cameras: one focused on the teacher, a second one on the teenagers, and the third on the student who was supposed to talk, the idea being "to film the classes like tennis matches—which required that the teacher and the students be on equal terms" (Mangeot). The digital cameras ran continuously for twenty minutes at a time so that the students could forget their presence and be more spontaneous. Besides, most of them only had a vague idea of what was going to happen, and they played the game by following the teacher's directions. The students who anchored the scene followed the script but were also asked to improvise (Borde).

Cantet proceeded in the above manner—a first for him—to "make room for surprise and chance" (Grassin), and he was pleased with the outcome: "The verbal jousting that occurred could only be achieved by shooting without a break. We could not have caught Esméralda's or Franck's elan on camera by saying 'Action'" (Burdeau 13). The final version included a number of elements absent from the screenplay because Cantet insisted on "doing justice to the students' spot-on performances." Khoumba's shouting out that the imperfect subjunctive is "bourgeois," for example, was accidental, and so was Angelica's questioning the teacher's sincerity when he insists that he is interested in the feelings expressed in the self-portraits (Bégaudeau, Cantet, and Campillo 52). These improvised remarks by the students also increased the teacher's spontaneity, which allowed Cantet to film the classroom in a new light: "We knew what we did not want to do: *Dead Poets Society*, or even *Half Nelson*, a film that, incidentally, I liked a lot, but where the teacher has it easy—always brilliant, faultless, able to give the right answer at the right time. François had to be able to mess up" (Domenach 30).

Cantet ended up with over 170 hours of rushes to edit. He decided to eliminate the most routine classroom scenes and to highlight the episodes of confrontation because, as he says, "a class, like a love story, is only interesting for fiction when it gets bogged down, dysfunctional, out of hand" (Bégaudeau, Cantet, and Campillo 33). However, except for Esméralda there were not a lot of strong personalities and troublemakers among the student volunteers. To help them overcome their natural modesty and get them to say things that were out of character without fear of being judged, Cantet taught them to hide behind their roles, and he was surprised to see how capable they were of letting go, as in the scene with the imperfect subjunctive. Nevertheless, Bégaudeau noted in his journal of the making of the film that the students told jokes that they would not have made in a real classroom, and that he sometimes had trouble "maintaining the illusion of a class" without bursting out laughing (Attali; Lipinska; Perucca).

The Actors

As was his normal practice, and even more so in *The Class*, Cantet cast nonprofessional actors, with the exception of the person who portrays Souleymane's mother, who had acted in a few minor roles before the film.

As we saw above, François Bégaudeau was well known in intellectual circles as a writer and film critic before he played Mr. Marin. A teachers' son like Cantet, Bégaudeau studied literature in Nantes while indulging two of his passions, soccer and rock music (he founded a punk rock band, Zabriskie Point, and recorded four albums with them in the 1990s). In addition to teaching, he wrote books, essays, and chronicles on varied subjects like sports, education, politics, cinema, and music. He has been an editor for the film journal *Cahiers du cinéma* since 2003 and has codirected a few documentaries, most of them on political themes.

His fourth book, *The Class* (2006), awarded the France Culture-Télérama Prize, and his participation in Cantet's film as actor and co-screenwriter (receiving the César for Best Adaptation), brought him to the attention of the general public. Thanks to his success, he was able to take a leave from the Ministry of National Education and devote himself to writing. He has published a variety of works since the film, including comics and plays in addition to numerous essays and novels.

Bégaudeau made his first and only foray into acting in Cantet's film. It became obvious that he should play Mr. Marin when he and the director were conducting workshops with the students of the Collège Dolto. For Cantet, Bégaudeau's involvement marked the true beginning of the film: "The day that I offered him the role and he accepted is when the film took shape in my mind" (Burdeau 11). Bégaudeau created his role but says that he stayed true to his teaching methods in a few scenes, in particular when Souleymane asks if he is homosexual. He answered this question to honor the "egalitarian contract" that he had set up for himself in his interactions with the students and which allowed them, like him, to ask delicate questions.

The other teachers, some of the adolescents, and the students' parents play themselves, and most have the same names in the film as in real life (Wei, for example, is played by Wei Huang, and his parents by Lingfen and Wenlong Huang). The principal, for his part, is played by the assistant principal of the Collège Dolto. In their interviews Cantet and Bégaudeau insist on the fact, mentioned above, that the students played characters that were sometimes very different from them. Of all the teenagers, Franck Keïta was the furthest removed from his character, Souleymane, because he was a gentle, reserved boy in real life. Wei, on the other hand, and especially Esméralda, were very similar to their characters: "As for Esméralda, she *is* Esméralda: monolithic, perfectly at ease in power relations and conflict" (Mangeot). A disruptive student, she was even expelled from the middle school before being readmitted for the shoot (Borde). Along with her classmates, she had to learn "suburb talk" because she had always lived in the nineteenth arrondissement and was not familiar with the suburbs (Bégaudeau, Cantet, and Campillo 29).

All the teenage actors were proud and surprised when the film received the Palme d'Or, "a crazy thing" according to Franck Keïta ("Grande émotion"). They had walked the red carpet amid general indifference on the last day of the festival, and their bus was already headed back to Paris (they had school the next day) when they learned the news—and turned around to accept the prize. After receiving the award, they had to deal with the photographers and journalists who invaded their neighborhood, but once the media frenzy died down they resumed their student lives. Franck Keïta (Souleymane) acted in another film in 2010. Louise Grinberg and Rabah Naït Oufella became actors and have appeared in several feature films (Grinberg played the lead role in *17 Girls* [*17 filles*] in 2011).

The Reception

The awarding of the Palme d'Or to *The Class* was a huge surprise to everyone. It was the first time for a French film since *Under the Sun of Satan* (*Sous le soleil de Satan*) by Maurice Pialat in 1987. The president of the jury, Sean Penn, had announced that the prize would go to "a filmmaker who is deeply aware of the state of the world," and he justified the unanimous decision to recognize Cantet's film thus:

> We were won over by the cinematography of the work, its wholeness. The performances by the young actors are all magical, and so is the writing. We never see the seams of the editing. *The Class* meets all our expectations of cinema in a world that is hungry for education. It's a gift for the young generations. (Raspiengeas, "Le message universel")

The film was sold in over fifty countries and selected for the opening of the New York Film Festival even before it was released in French theaters in late September 2008. It represented France at the Oscars the following year and received many prizes and nominations throughout the world.

Given the importance of everything that pertains to education in France, *The Class* was the object of intense media and political hype. When it was released in Cannes, politicians seized the opportunity to express satisfaction or criticism regarding the state of French society and its school system. On the right, which was then in the majority, President Nicolas Sarkozy and his Minister of Culture, Christine Albanel, praised the vitality of French cinema and paid homage to the teachers and the school system while acknowledging the difficulties they had to face. Albanel, for example, declared that "this film sheds light on the complex relationships at play in a classroom that reflects the diversity of French society" ("Grande émotion"). For his part Jean-Marie Le Pen, the President of the National Front, hostile to diversity and immigration, denounced the "leftist" bias of the festival but sarcastically welcomed the fact that the award shed light on the multiethnic student body of Parisian middle schools (Strand 270). Jack Lang, a socialist legislator and former Minister of Culture, took advantage of the situation to attack the right-wing government: this excellent film, he said, "could not have come out at a more opportune time, when [. . .] the government cares so little and acts so lamely about school" (Cédelle). The film had no impact on educational policy, but it led to the legalization of a student's (Boubacar's) immigrant mother, thanks to the involvement of Laurent Cantet, an advocate for the undocumented through the Without Borders Educational Network.

The titles of two articles, by Luc Cédelle and Jean-Claude Raspiengeas respectively, "The Palme d'Or reactivates the national debate on education" ("La Palme d'Or réactive le débat national sur l'école") and "*Entre les murs*, a disturbing film" ("*The Class*, une œuvre qui dérange"), sum up well the avalanche of often contradictory reactions that greeted the film upon its release at Cannes and in theaters. With its stories of academic failure, its moments of grace, and its impartial approach, this film has given rise to debates of all kinds about how to promote academic success and integration in schools that educate students from very diverse social and ethnic backgrounds. The critics, philosophers, and teachers who have commented on the film agree on at least one point: the students' level in French and their ability to express sophisticated thoughts leave a lot to be desired.

Commentators disagree on the teacher's pedagogy and the instructional content of his classes. Proponents of a traditional education consider the film a failure and even "a pedagogical fiasco" (Brizard 46) because Mr. Marin, they argue, loses his authority by trying to place himself on an equal footing with the students. Instead of imparting knowledge, he wastes his time managing his class, and his constant attempts to provoke the students lead him to talk nonsense when he says, for example, that he is not proud to be French. His students, who are already underprivileged, sink deeper and deeper into ignorance, thus validating the clichés about them. Mr. Marin is also criticized for not teaching literature—he chose the *Diary of Anne Frank* over a more classical text by Voltaire and, instead of analyzing it, he uses it as a pretext to make the students talk about themselves (Audoubert; Debril, "Pour Xavier Darcos"). Those who have a more positive view of the school system emphasize the vitality and creativity of the students and the productive rapport—but in need of constant reinvention—that Mr. Marin sometimes manages to establish with them, proof that "with individual effort, a collective will, and unrelenting effort, one can achieve encouraging results" in underprivileged schools (Guillaume; Kaganski).

The testimonies of middle and high school teachers more or less reproduce the critics' arguments. A literature instructor in a ZEP says that she is appalled by the image of the profession conveyed by the film, for example the teachers' petty argument over the coffee maker and their lack of involvement in unions (Sultan). Others recognize themselves in Mr. Marin and praise the film for showing the difficulty of their jobs as well as their dedication and deep loneliness (Pascal-Moussellard). Most voice their fear that the prestige of the profession might suffer as a result of *The Class*, and that the film might be recuperated to show the nefarious influence of immigration or the *collège unique*—a single-track system in effect in middle schools since the 1970s where students of different ability levels are mixed together (Peiron). All these comments show that *The Class* was perceived by many as a documentary on the state of French education rather than a fiction film on the experience of an individual teacher in his class.

Not much is said about film as an art form in the majority of the reviews of *The Class*, but there are a few exceptions, like Kaganski's comments below:

> [B]efore being a film "on" something (school, education, youth, *métissage*, immigration, integration, authority, transmission [. . .], *The Class* is an intelligent and sensitive piece of cinematography, well written, with good dialogue [. . .], remarkably acted [. . .], a film whose mise en scène is dense and sparse in the details of each scene and elegant and consistent overall.

Like Roy, for whom "the film is also an exceptional work on language," Kaganski sees as a stroke of genius the fact that everything starts unraveling because of a language issue, the unfortunate and ironic use of the word *pétasse* by the teacher, who is supposed to master the French language. To compensate for the general tendency to read the film as a documentary, Lefort, for his part, stresses its fictional side by describing the students as "born performers, perfect at playing out their made-up lives."

Although debates on the educational and social context of *The Class* dominated the critical reception of the film, the reviews also lavished praise on the film in more general terms. Of particular note are the allusions to its energy: the film is described as a "sporty" film (Wachthausen) that "captivates thanks to its physical energy" (Péron) and gives rise to metaphors of all kinds related to tennis, soccer, boxing, and equestrian jousting ("choreographed like a boxing ring," "The Constant and Perilous Jousting between a Teacher and his Students," Widemann), as well as war ("Saving Student Suleyman," Bas). Icing on the cake for Cantet: this last critic considers *The Class* "the best French film on school since *Zero for Conduct (Zéro de conduite)*," a film by Jean Vigo released in . . . 1933.

The Educational Context of *The Class*

1. *"Priority Education"*

In France the school system is very centralized and, theoretically, all schools are equal. The Ministry of National Education decides on the curriculum and hires the secondary public school teachers, who have national diplomas. In actual fact, there are substantial differences in the students' level owing to the dissimilar social, economic, and cultural backgrounds of their families. To address this inequality, the government created "priority education zones" (ZEP) in the 1980s. The at-risk elementary, middle, and high schools located in these zones (which were relabeled ÉCLAIR in 2012 and REP/REP+ later) are allocated a higher budget, among other benefits, which allows them to offer smaller classes (twenty-five students at most in middle school), differentiated pedagogical approaches, and individualized instruction for struggling students. It is estimated that about 20 percent of French students attend schools in priority education zones.

The collège Françoise-Dolto, where the story of The Class takes place, was among the twenty-three Parisian middle schools located in priority education zones when the film came out (the number was higher still if we include the suburbs and reached 831 overall in France). This middle school is in the twentieth arrondissement, on the eastern side of Paris. According to Debril ("Entre les murs"), "50% of the [Dolto] students come from a disadvantaged background. Many belong to the 15% of primary school students who are notorious for entering sixth grade with an inadequate command of reading and writing."

2. School Life

The Class shows with quasi-documentary faithfulness vignettes of the life of a class over a school year. Since these moments are condensed in the film, some clarification on French school life is in order.

To start with, the students are in eighth grade at a public middle school (French middle schools educate students eleven to fourteen/fifteen years old from the sixth to the ninth grades). At each grade level, the students belong to groups (classes) that take most of their courses together (except perhaps a couple of electives) and have the same teachers for a whole school year, from September to June.

The school year is divided into three trimesters that each end with a "class council" (conseil de classe) during which the performance and behavior of each student and questions related to the life of the whole group are discussed. Participants include the principal, the teachers, a guidance counselor (called CPE, or conseiller principal d'éducation), and representatives of the students and their parents who are elected by their peers at the beginning of the year. At the end of the discussion on each student and based on his/her grade point average for the term, the teachers may decide to include a commendation on the report card, such as les félicitations (to congratulate an excellent student), les encouragements (to encourage a student who is improving), or a warning (for a student with academic or behavioral issues). The principal makes the final call if teachers cannot reach a consensus, and he/she is responsible for writing a general comment on each report card.

In the film we witness the second-trimester class council. Louise and Esméralda are present as class representatives (but we do not see the parent representatives in this scene). Their role is to participate in the discussion and share any information that can shed light on the academic performance or the behavior of their classmates. For example, Esméralda points out that Souleymane has improved because his GPA has increased from 6.75 to 7.25 (out of 20) since the first semester. . . . It should be noted that grading is rather strict in France. A passing grade is 10 out of 20, and grades above 14 are considered excellent.

The class council at the end of the last term also decides about promotion to the next grade level. It is particularly important at the end of ninth grade when the council determines whether the student will attend a regular high school (a *lycée général* that prepares students for a national exam, the *baccalauréat*, required to pursue university studies) or a vocational high school (a *lycée professionnel* that leads to a professional degree and to the workplace). Most students wish to attend a regular high school because their reputation is better, and they can appeal if they do not agree with the decision of the class council. At the end of the film Henriette, who is just finishing eighth grade, is already worrying about the decision that the council will make the following year. That is why she tells Mr. Marin that she does not want to go "the professional route" (it should be noted that some of the teachers who were asked to comment on the film did not approve of this "disparagement" of the vocational track by Cantet in the scene with Henriette).

Some of the deliberations of the class council are confidential, especially those on individual students. After the meeting the representatives are allowed to share information on the general level of the class with their classmates, as well as the teachers' suggestions for improving student learning in general and the atmosphere of the class. In the film, Louise and Esméralda make a serious faux pas when they reveal the students' GPAs before report cards are sent out. And they certainly should never have reported to the class Mr. Marin's comment about Souleymane being "academically challenged."

Each class council is followed by parent-teacher conferences (we see the first-trimester conference in the film). Teachers who wish to communicate with parents at other times can do so in the student's *carnet de correspondence*, a special notebook that the student must ask his/her parents to sign to acknowledge reception. In the film, Mr. Marin adds a comment in Khoumba's notebook concerning her behavior in class that day. He wonders why Souleymane's parents are not aware of their son's behavioral issues, since he mentioned them several times in his *carnet*. Because his mother does not understand French, it may be that Souleymane lied to her regarding the content of the messages. Or perhaps he simply forged her signature. . . .

The film also shows a disciplinary hearing. The committee is made up of the principal, a guidance counselor, representatives from the administration, the teaching staff, the student body, and the parents, all elected yearly by their peers. It considers serious disciplinary problems and issues sanctions that range from warnings to permanent exclusion.

STUDY GUIDE

What Happens in This Film?

1. What is the purpose of the meeting between the teachers and the staff at the beginning of the film?

2. What comments do the students make when Mr. Marin writes on the board: "Bill is enjoying a delicious cheeseburger"?

3. What do the students think of the imperfect subjunctive?

4. What happens to the technology instructor in the teachers' lounge?

5. Why are the students hesitant to write their self-portraits?

6. Why does Mr. Marin write a comment in Khoumba's notebook (which she must show her parents)?

7. During the class council, what do the parent representatives think of the discussion on the best way to penalize students?

8. Who joins the class in the middle of the term? Why? What did the students have to do when the principal walked into the classroom with this student?

9. Why is the meeting between Mr. Marin and Souleymane's mother difficult?

10. What is Wei's family situation? How do the teachers decide to help him?

11. How do Louise and Esméralda behave during the class council? What confidential information do they share with their classmates? What happens afterwards, in the classroom?

12. What decision is reached at the disciplinary hearing? What does Souleymane's mother say in support of her son?

True or False?

If the statement is false, correct it!

1. A math teacher introduces himself to his colleagues as a teacher of multiplication tables.

2. When Esméralda says that she is not proud to be French, Mr. Marin responds that *he* is.

3. Boubacar asks Mr. Marin if he is homosexual in front of the whole class.

4. Mr. Marin chooses a famous novel called *The Diary of a Country Priest* as a reading for his class.

5. During the class council, the teachers discuss developing a disciplinary protocol based on the driver license point system.

6. Wei's parents think that he spends too much time playing sports.

7. A student's mother finds the level of the middle school too low, and she would like her son to continue his studies at the prestigious Lycée Henri-IV.

8. Mr. Marin takes Souleymane to the principal's office because he disrespected him by insulting his (Mr. Marin's) mother.

9. Khoumba is afraid that the French authorities will expel Souleymane to Mali.

10. Mr. Marin agrees with his colleagues that Souleymane must face a disciplinary hearing.

11. Wei read Plato's *Republic* outside school.

12. Mr. Marin gives his students a copy of *The Diary of Anne Frank* as an end-of-the-year present.

What Did You Learn in the Introduction?

1. What is Cantet's first feature film about, and what famous actor had his debut role in this film?

2. What are the recurrent themes of Cantet's films?

3. Why did Cantet want to make a film about school?

4. Why did he use three cameras and let them run continuously?

5. What choices did Cantet make as regards the portrayal of the teacher and the scenes to be included in the final version?

6. What challenges did Cantet and Bégaudeau face in their work with students as actors?

7. Besides his role as Mr. Marin, what are some of François Bégaudeau's other professional activities?

8. Which actor is the most different from the character he plays in *The Class*? Which actress is the closest to her character?

9. What indicates that many spectators considered the film a documentary on the French school system?

10. What explains the big gap in achievement levels among French students? What did the government create to remedy this problem?

11. When in the school year are class councils scheduled? What purpose do they serve? What follows each class council?

12. What is the role of the class representatives?

Exploring the Film

1. The Title of the Film

In your opinion, why did Cantet choose *Entre les murs* ("Within the Walls") as the title of his film? What takes place inside the school, and in which spaces in particular? What do we know about the characters' lives "outside the walls"?

What are some of the challenges when making a film centered on the classroom? Which aspects of the academic experience would not be interesting for the viewers? How does the story differ from life in a real classroom? (Which moments does the director insist on?)

2. The Preamble: The Beginning of the School Year

Review the teachers' meeting and the students' arrival in Mr. Marin's classroom (Excerpt 1, 3'45–6'30). What adjective does an instructor use to describe students to Frédéric, the new social studies teacher? What other adjective might one expect from a teacher?

What are the backgrounds of Mr. Marin's students? Compare the students and the teaching staff when it comes to diversity.

What arguments does Mr. Marin use to persuade the students to get to work? Which one, in particular, causes Khoumba's strong reaction?

What are your expectations of the film after watching the teachers' meeting and the first scene in the classroom?

3. Language

As in Kechiche's *Games of Love and Chance*, language is of paramount importance in *The Class*. We hear formal and standard French, slang, *verlan* (back slang), some Arabic, and Bambara in the scenes with Souleymane's mother. There is also a lot of *tchatche* or fast talk (See the section "Language in *Games of Love and Chance*," Chap. 8.)

Mr. Marin's main concern is to teach standard (and even formal French) to his class. He takes advantage of a reading to explain the words that the students do not recognize, like "condescendance," "argenterie" (silverware), "autrichienne" (Austrian), "trompeur" (deceptive), or "désormais" (henceforth). In your opinion, why is Wei not familiar with the word "Austrian"? And why has Damien never heard the term "silverware"? **How can the school difficulties of some of the students be explained from these two examples?**

What kinds of obstacles does Mr. Marin face when he attempts to explain the word "succulent" (delicious)? What theme is introduced when Khomba and Esméralda protest against his use of the first name Bill? *Review this scene* (Excerpt 2, 11'30–13'40). Why does the teacher ask Esméralda "Aren't you French?" and how does she respond? How do you interpret her answer?

On what grounds do the students argue against the use of the imperfect subjunctive? What does Mr. Marin reply? *Review this scene* (Excerpt 3, 17'00–20'10). To what specific language issue does he draw the students' attention in the course of this discussion?

The lack of understanding of other people's language causes important conflicts in the film. **For example, how may the fact that his mother did not speak French have contributed to Souleymane's problems?** In Mr. Marin's discussion with Esméralda and Louise regarding their behavior during the class council, **how do their different interpretations of the word "pétasse" intensify the conflict?** (This scene will be discussed in more detail in Question 7 below.)

4. The Students

Mr. Marin chose to have the students read *The Diary of Anne Frank* to prepare them to write their self-portraits. Are there parallels between the students and Anne Frank that could lead the class to identify with her and be more interested in reading her *Diary*?

When the students explain their hesitation to write their self-portraits, they mention shame as one of the reasons. Rabah tries to define shame by sharing with the class his experience at a party. What happened to him? Whom is he referring to when he speaks of "jambons-beurre" (people who eat ham and butter sandwiches)? Why was he ashamed? *Review Rabah's comments* (Excerpt 5, 35'50–36'45).

What do we learn about Esméralda's and Wei's personal lives and interests? *Review their self-portraits* (Excerpt 5, 50'00–52'00). Why does Mr. Marin congratulate Wei and not Esméralda? Do you think there is a significant difference between their self-portraits? What does Rabah blame Mr. Marin for when he says, "Of course, it's good because *he* wrote it. When it comes from us, it's never good"? **Whom does he mean by "us"?** Is he right in suggesting that Mr. Marin only criticizes him and his "group"?

What do Mr. Marin's conferences with the students' parents tell us about the young people's family backgrounds, their parents' hopes, and the reputation of the school? *Review the scenes with the parents of Wei, Nassim, Arthur, and Burak* (Excerpt 6, 58'50–1h02'45).

5. Mr. Marin's Pedagogy

Cantet was fascinated by François Bégaudeau's pedagogy in his book *The Class*, and that is why he decided to use the book as the basis for his film and cast its author in the role of Mr. Marin. Cantet said of Bégaudeau, "There is some Socrates in this man." He added that his pedagogy "consists in always 'going after' the students, even though it sometimes hurts, and always when their reasoning comes up a little too short to be valid or acceptable as is. If one can speak of democracy at school, that's where it is" (Mangeot).

What is the Socratic method? Do you think Mr. Marin's pedagogy is Socratic? *Review the scene where Esméralda tells him that she has read Plato's* **Republic** (Excerpt 8, 2h01'55–2h03'30). In your opinion, why did Cantet include this scene in his film (besides the fact that François Bégaudeau had had the same experience in one of his classes and encouraged him to do so)? **Also examine the way in which Mr. Marin responds when Souleymane goes off on a tangent and asks if he is homosexual.** *Review this scene* (Excerpt 9, 21'45–23'30). How might another teacher have answered? What does Mr. Marin ask Souleymane to think about? What do you make of his comment on Souleymane's "psychological issues" at the end? Does he go too far here and in other circumstances, as Khoumba sometimes contends (*Vous charriez trop!*)?

Why did Mr. Marin encourage Souleymane to do another type of self-portrait? How does his relationship with Souleymane in this scene differ from their other interactions? What does this suggest concerning best pedagogical practices?

As we saw in "The Origin and the Making of the Film," Cantet used three cameras to show a "democratic" classroom in which all points of view are equal (Mangeot).

Did you get this impression when you watched the film and reviewed some of the excerpts?

6. Disciplinary Problems

What types of situations involving the students among themselves and in their relationship with Mr. Marin generate tension?
During a meeting of the class council, the teachers discuss developing a disciplinary protocol based on the driver's license point system. *Review a portion of this meeting* (Excerpt 9, 43'30–45'30). Why does a parent representative criticize this approach, and what does she suggest instead? What does the guidance counselor think of her proposal?

What is François Marin's philosophy about discipline, as shown in this scene? How does it differ from his colleague Frédéric's views? **Do you believe, like Frédéric, that the approach advocated by Mr. Marin is arbitrary?** In practice, do you find that his dealings with the students are arbitrary or that they depend on the circumstances of each case? Is he unfair to some of the students?

Students can face disciplinary hearings in cases of serious offenses. **What is the typical outcome of a disciplinary hearing in this middle school?** Mr. Marin and his colleagues express opposing points of view on the responsibilities of members of the hearing panel, who must issue sanctions. *Review the teachers' informal discussion about disciplinary hearings* (Excerpt 10, 1h45'25–1h47'50). What point in particular do they address? What is the main difference of opinion? Do you think that a student's personal situation should not be taken into account when a sanction is issued?

7. The Confrontation in the School Courtyard

According to Cantet, Mr. Marin takes risks in order to achieve his dream of "establishing an equality of sorts with the students [...], which can make him say things that he later regrets" (Domenach 30). *Review the scene where Mr. Marin goes down to the courtyard to confront Esméralda and Louise* (Excerpt 11, 1h38'25–1h41'25). **Visually, how does this scene show him on an equal footing with his students?** (From what angle is the courtyard usually shot? How is it filmed in this scene?)

Why is the argument over the meaning of the word "pétasse" ("bitch" or "whore") ironic (given Mr. Marin's focus on vocabulary work in the classroom)?

Mr. Marin had criticized the two student representatives for sharing confidential remarks made during the class council with their peers. **What is ironic, in this regard, in Mr. Marin's interaction with Carl?**

Carl uses the word "enculé" ("a—hole" or "motherf—er") to describe teachers who expel students from school. Mr. Marin objects, but **Esméralda argues that there is no difference between using the terms "pétasse" and "enculé."** How does the teacher respond? How does he fight back? What becomes of his ideal of "democracy" in this scene? Mr. Marin got "into the arena" with the students. What happened to his authority as a result?

8. *Souleymane's Fate*

How did Souleymane's behavior in French class worsen throughout the school year? What do the other teachers say about him at the class council?

Review the scene where Souleymane injures Khoumba by accident (Excerpt 12, 1h32'45–1h36'00). In this scene, which takes place after the class council, the representatives Louise and Esméralda divulge information that should have remained confidential, like the students' GPAs. Rabah and Souleymane interrupt the poetry class to ask questions about their personal situations. Mr. Marin is surprised and replies sarcastically that the representatives have at least "done part of their job" in spite of their lack of attention during the meeting.

In your opinion, why did Louise and Esméralda report Mr. Marin's remark about Souleymane being "academically challenged"? Had Mr. Marin been harsh on Souleymane during the class council? **How does the situation degenerate?** At what point do the students intervene in support of the teacher? How do you explain Souleymane's sudden bolt from the classroom?

Review an excerpt from the disciplinary hearing (Excerpt 13, 1h56'45–1h58'15). What impression does the camera create when it focuses almost exclusively on Souleymane and his mother, in a frontal position, after displaying several points of view in the previous scene? A critic wrote about this scene: "It is one of the most powerful scenes ever created in French cinema showing a young black man facing white government employees" (Renzi 19). Did this thought occur to you as you watched the film? **In your opinion, is the scene a confrontation between a black man and white people? Is Cantet making a statement about race?**

Why do you think Souleymane does not say anything in his own defense? How does his attitude contrast with his mother's?

Why does Cantet focus on anonymous hands depositing their votes in the big transparent box?

After Souleymane's exclusion has been announced, there is a close-up on Mr. Marin's face. **What is he thinking, in your opinion?**

Who do you think is responsible for Souleymane's exclusion? Souleymane himself? Mr. Marin? The school system?

9. *The End of the School Year*

Why is Mr. Marin taken aback when Henriette comes to talk to him after the other students have left? Why do you think Cantet includes this scene with her? How does it contrast with the following scene, the soccer game between the teachers and students?

How do you interpret the last images, which show the empty classroom with a focus on the desks (first the teacher's and then the students') while the cries of the soccer players and the spectators are heard off-screen?

According to the screenplay, the film was supposed to end on a scene showing Souleymane in Mali. Cantet cut this scene at the editing stage. **Was it a good idea to eliminate it? How would its inclusion have changed the film?**

Cantet and Bégaudeau find the film fairly optimistic. For Cantet, "the film says something rather uplifting: school is indeed very chaotic sometimes, let's face it. There are periods of discouragement, but also great moments of grace, of intense happiness."

Bégaudeau agrees that the tension between failure and success is what makes a film about school interesting, *The Class* in particular, and he concludes: "Some will see in the film a story of failure; others on the contrary will remember true moments of utopia" (Mangeot). **What are the failures represented in the film? What are the moments of grace? What will you remember most, the failures or the moments of grace?**

Laurent Cantet's Filmography

1997   *Les Sanguinaires*

1999   *Human Resources (Ressources humaines)*

2001   *Time Out (L'Emploi du temps)*

2005   *Heading South (Vers le sud)*

2008   *The Class (Entre les murs)*

2012   *Foxfire (Foxfire, confessions d'un gang de filles)*

2012   *7 Days in Havana (7 jours à la Havane)*

2014   *Return to Ithaca (Retour à Ithaque)*

Works Consulted

Attali, Danielle. "Laurent Cantet. Entretien." *Le Journal du dimanche*, 25 May 2008: n. pag.

Audoubert, Sophie, et al. "Professeures de zones sensibles entre les murs." *Libération*, 9 Oct. 2008: n. pag.

Bas, Frédéric. "Il faut sauver l'élève Suleyman." *Charlie Hebdo*, 24 Sept. 2008: n. pag.

Bégaudeau, François. *Entre les murs*. Paris: Gallimard, 2006.

———, Laurent Cantet, and Robin Campillo. *Le scénario du film* Entre les murs. Paris: Gallimard, 2008.

Borde, Dominique. "Laurent Cantet à l'école de la vie." *Le Figaro*, 24 Sept. 2008: n. pag.

Brizard, Caroline. "Zéro pointé. Huit profs notent *Entre les murs*." *Le Nouvel Observateur*, 25 Sept. 2008: 44–46.

Burdeau, Emmanuel, and Antoine Thirion. "Entretien avec Laurent Cantet." *Cahiers du cinéma* 637 (Sept. 2008): 8–18.

Cantet, Laurent, dir. *Entre les murs*. Haut et Court, 2009.

Cédelle, Luc. "La Palme d'Or réactive le débat national sur l'école." *Le Monde*, 28 May 2008: n. pag.

Debril, Laurence. "Entre les murs d'*Entre les murs*." *L'Express*, 18 Sept. 2008: n. pag.

———. "Pour Xavier Darcos, *Entre les murs* est 'l'histoire d'un échec pédagogique.'" *L'Express*, 26 Sept. 2008: n. pag.

Domenach, Elise, and Grégory Valens. "Entretien avec Laurent Cantet: une envie d'accidents." *Positif* 571 (Sept. 2008): 28–31.

Douin, Jean-Luc. "Laurent Cantet, cinéaste de classe." *Le Monde*, 26 May 2008: n. pag.

"Grande émotion après l'attribution de la Palme d'Or à *Entre les murs*." *Le Nouvel Observateur*, 26 May 2008: n. pag.

Grassin, Sophie. "Cantet. Luttes dans la classe." *Le Monde*, 15 May 2008: n. pag.

Gueye, Abdoulaye. "The Color of Unworthiness: Understanding Blacks in France and the French Visual Media through Laurent Cantet's *The Class* (2008)." *Transition: An International Review* 102 (2009): 158–71.

Guillaume, François-Régis. "Prendre acte du rapport positif aux élèves." *L'Humanité*, 4 Oct. 2008: n. pag.

Hecht, Emmanuel. "Une palme démagogique." *Les Echos*, 24 Sept. 2008: n. pag.

Heymann, Danièle. "Une palme amplement méritée. *Entre les murs*: ni angélique, ni démago, intègre!" *Marianne*, 31 May 2008: n. pag.

Kaganski, Serge. "*Entre les murs*." *Les Inrockuptibles*, 23 Sept. 2008: n. pag.

Laffeter, Anne. "Quelques jours après leur rentrée scolaire, on retrouve les élèves/acteurs d'*Entre les murs*, Palme d'Or à Cannes." *Les Inrockuptibles*, 29 Sept. 2008: n. pag.

Lefort, Gérard. "Bonne note." *Libération*, 22 Sept. 2008: n. pag.

Levieux, Michèle. "Rabah, une aventure humaine." *L'Humanité*, 24 Sept. 2008: n. pag.

Libiot, Eric. "L'école buissonnière." *L'Express*, 29 May 2008: n. pag.

Lipinska, Charlotte. "Grande classe." *Le Nouvel Observateur (TéléObs)*, 25 Sept. 2008: n. pag.

Mangeot, Philippe. "Entretien avec Laurent Cantet et François Bégaudeau." *Commeaucinema.com*. Web. 16 Aug. 2016. <http://www.commeaucinema.com/notes-de-prod/entre-les-murs,87210>.

O'Shaughnessy, Martin. *Laurent Cantet*. Manchester, England: Manchester UP, 2015.

Pascal-Moussellard, Olivier. "Qu'en pensent les profs?" *Télérama*, 17 Sept. 2008: n. pag.

Peiron, Denis. "Des enseignants décernent au film la palme du malaise." *La Croix*, 23 Sept. 2008: n. pag.

Péron, Didier. "Captation d'énergie scolaire." *Libération*, 22 Sept. 2008: n. pag.

Perucca, Brigitte. "De septembre 2006 à juin 2007, François Bégaudeau a raconté dans *Le Monde de l'éducation* le tournage du film tiré de son roman, qui vient d'obtenir la Palme d'Or. Excerpts." *Le Monde*, 28 May 2008: n. pag.

Raspiengeas, Jean-Claude. "*Entre les murs*, une œuvre qui dérange." *La Croix*, 23 Sept. 2008: n. pag.

———. "Le message universel de la Palme d'Or." *La Croix*, 27 May 2008: n. pag.

Renzi, Eugénio. "A égalité." *Cahiers du cinéma* 637 (Sept. 2008): 19–21.

Rigoulet, Laurent. "Retour sur un cas d'école." *Télérama*, 17 Sept. 2008: n. pag.

Roy, Jean. "Précis d'anatomie." *L'Humanité*, 24 Sept. 2008: n. pag.

Strand, Dana. "Etre et parler: Being and Speaking French in Abdellatif Kechiche's *L'Esquive* (2004) and Laurent Cantet's *Entre Les Murs* (2008)." *Studies in French Cinema*, 9.3 (2009): 259–72.

Sultan, Valérie. "On a peine à se reconnaître." *L'Humanité*, 4 Oct. 2008: n. pag.

Tarr, Carrie. "Class Acts: Education, Gender, and Integration in Recent French Cinema." *Screening Integration: Recasting Maghrebi Immigration in Contemporary France*. Ed. Sylvie Durmelat and Vinay Swamy. Lincoln, NE: U of Nebraska P, 2012. 127–43.

Vincendeau, Ginette. "The Rules of the Game." *Sight and Sound* 19.3 (2009): 34–36.

Wachthausen, Jean-Luc. "Sportif! Palme d'Or à Cannes." *Le Figaroscope*, 24 Sept. 2008: n. pag.

Widemann, Dominique. "La Constante et Périlleuse Joute entre un prof et ses élèves." *L'Humanité*, 26 May 2008: n. pag.

Williams, James S. "Framing Exclusion: The Politics of Space in Laurent Cantet's *Entre Les Murs*." *French Studies: A Quarterly Review* 65.1 (2011): 61–73.

10

Philippe Lioret

Welcome

(2009)

Philippe Lioret, *Welcome*: Bilal (Firat Ayverdi) contemplates swimming across the English
Channel despite the warnings of Simon, his swimming instructor (Vincent Lindon).

Director . . . . Philippe Lioret
Screenplay. . . . . Philippe Lioret, Emmanuel Courcol, Olivier Adam
Director of Photography . . . . Laurent Dailland
Sound . . . . Pierre Mertens, Laurent Quaglio, Eric Tisserand
Music . . . . Nicolas Piovani, Wojciech Kilar, Armand Amar
Film Editor. . . . . Andréa Sedlackova
Costumes . . . . Fanny Drouin
Art Director. . . . . Yves Brover
Continuity . . . . .Béatrice Pollet
Producer. . . . . .Christophe Rossignon
Length. 1h55

Cast

Vincent Lindon (*Simon Calmat*), Firat Ayverdi (*Bilal*), Audrey Dana, (*Marion*), Derya Ayverdi (*Mina*), Selim Akgül (*Zoran*), Firat Celik (*Koban*), Murat Subasi (*Mirko*), Olivier Rabourdin (*the police lieutenant*), Yannick Renier (*Alain*), Mouafaq Rushdie (*Mina's father*), Behi Djanati Ataï (*Mina's mother*), Patrick Ligardes (*Simon's neighbor*), Thierry Godard (*Bruno*)

Story

Bilal, a young Kurd who has just arrived from Iraq on foot, reconnects with a friend and some fellow countrymen at a soup kitchen run by a refugee aid organization near the port of Calais. He hides with them in the back of a truck in a failed attempt to sneak into England, where he wants to find his girlfriend, Mina, who has settled there with her Kurdish family. Meanwhile Simon, a lifeguard at the Calais swimming pool, leads a routine life giving swimming lessons and dining alone. His wife Marion, a volunteer for the organization that feeds the illegal immigrants, has filed for divorce, but Simon is still in love with her. Marion has just chastized him for his indifference toward the eviction of migrants from a supermarket when Bilal arrives at the pool and inquires about swimming lessons. Simon is suspicious at first but soon sees in this encounter a way to regain Marion's love. Little by little, he gets involved in the project of the young man, who clearly intends to try his luck again and get to England by . . . swimming the Channel. Simon will have to overcome his natural passiveness but also the determination of the government officials who track down the migrants and those who help them. This moving human adventure will turn his life upside down.

The Director

Philippe Lioret, born on October 10, 1955, in Paris, worked as a sound engineer on around thirty films before becoming a screenwriter and director. He has made seven feature films in different genres since 1993. *Lost in Transit* (*Tombés du ciel*, 1993) and *Proper Attire Required* (*Tenue correcte exigée*, 1996) are comedies in which we already recognize the social themes of his later films: the protagonist of *Lost in Transit*, for example, has been robbed and is stranded at Roissy Airport like other undocumented people, refugees, and illegal immigrants, whose stories he learns. Lioret also directed more intimate films like *Mademoiselle* (2000), a sentimental comedy, and the dramas *The Light* (*L'Equipier*, 2003) and *Don't Worry, I'm Fine* (*Je vais bien, ne t'en fais pas*, 2006), all starring excellent actors (Sandrine Bonnaire, Jacques Gamblin, Philippe Torreton, Kad Merad, Mélanie Laurent) and well received by the general public and some of the critics. *Welcome* (2009) and *All Our Desires* (*Toutes nos envies*, 2010), intimate dramas laced with social themes, mark another turning point in his filmography and the beginning of his association with the actor Vincent Lindon. In both films Lindon plays an ordinary man who is transformed by his respective encounters with migrants and people in debt and stands ready to fight for more social justice. Lioret also collaborated on compilations of short films on social issues, such as *3,000 Scenarios to Combat a Virus* [AIDS] (*3 000 scénarios contre un virus* [*le SIDA*], 1994) and *Don't Make Trouble! 12 Looks at Racism in Daily Life* (*Pas d'histoires! 12 regards sur le racisme au quotidien*, 2001).

Given the social character of his films, Lioret has earned the reputation of "censor of the flaws of modern society," "moral activist," or "thesis filmmaker" (Marsa), and critics often compare him to the British director Ken Loach. Some find, however, that the mise en scène of his films lacks originality, and Chapuys refers to them as "very innocuous and a little mawkish," while nonetheless considering them "heads and shoulders above the average French popular film." More indulgent, Jean Roy, a movie critic for *L'Humanité* (a communist newspaper that appreciates socially engaged cinema), praises his unobtrusive cinematography and regrets that Lioret does not win more prizes at festivals: "People have always liked this unassuming director, often a finalist, rarely a winner at festivals, because he so deliberately avoids a flashy mise en scène [. . .]. This auteur-director is modest enough not to reveal his presence, leaving the limelight to his characters and the plot."

The Origin and Making of the Film

Lioret began thinking of making *Welcome* during a conversation with the writer Olivier Adam, whose novel *Don't Worry, I'm Fine* he had adapted to the screen in 2006. Adam had just written *Nowhere Safe* (*A l'abri de rien*, 2007), the story of a woman who neglects her family to take care of migrants in a town in northern France, and his evocation of the lives of refugees stuck in Calais while waiting to cross into England triggered Lioret's interest: "It's as if he were describing the Mexican border to me. I decided to go there with the scriptwriter, Emmanuel Courcol. We spent several days and several nights there, in the cold, with the volunteers and the migrants. We discovered a shameful reality and witnessed what these men and women, many of whom were very young, were made to endure. As we were about to leave, a volunteer told us that several of them had tried to swim the Channel. One of them had disappeared. No one knew what had become of him. We were obsessed by these illegal immigrants who had tried to swim across to England. We started working around this idea" (Raspiengeas, "Philippe Lioret").

In making this film, Philippe Lioret also wished to protest against a law that severely punished people who helped illegal aliens—with a five-year prison sentence and a 30,000-euro fine. This law, originally conceived to sanction handlers, was being used more and more against ordinary citizens—given the influx of migrants in Calais—by right-wing governments during the second term of Jacques Chirac (2002–7) and the presidency of Nicolas Sarkozy (2007–12).

Lioret decided to film this story "at a human level" by focusing on an ordinary citizen who shows an interest in migrants in order to win back his wife. He wrote the role of Simon for Vincent Lindon, who, uncharacteristically, accepted it without even reading the screenplay. Before shooting, Lindon and Lioret went to Calais to live with volunteers and migrants. They were regulars at the "soup kitchen wharf" and had the opportunity to transport refugees in their car, like Simon in the film. Lioret had qualms about making a commercial product out of situations of human misery, but the associations convinced him that a fiction film was necessary to sensitize the public to the migrants' situation (Lemercier, "Des gamins"). The director did a lot of research because, he says, "I had to be just right on everything: the screenplay, the actors, the images. To be careful not to be clumsy nor reinforce conventional reflexes, avoid contrasting nice migrants with mean public authorities" (Raspiengeas, "Philippe Lioret"). According to him, "There is not a single image in my film whose truthfulness I can't vouch for" (Rouden).

The shooting lasted eleven weeks. It took place on location in Calais and in studios in Roubaix. Lioret chose Calais rather than a port city in the Third World, which would have been less expensive, because "identification and embodiment would not have been strong enough somewhere else" (Lemercier, "Des gamins"). Asked about the impact of the shooting on him, Lioret replied that he discovered "an unfamiliar world 200 kilometers from Paris. A most unlikely place," and that he was appalled by the treatment inflicted on the migrants: "I started the film as a filmmaker; I ended it as an outraged citizen" (Raspiengeas, "Philippe Lioret").

The Actors

Vincent Lindon (Simon) worked as assistant costume designer for the film *My American Uncle* (*Mon oncle d'Amérique*, Alain Resnais, 1980) and pursued a brief career as a journalist before becoming an actor in 1983. Since then he has played in more than seventy films by respected directors such as Jean-Jacques Beineix, Bertrand Blier, Claire Denis, Tony Gatlif, Benoît Jacquot, Claude Lelouch, Claude Sautet, and Coline Serreau, among others. A versatile actor, he is just as comfortable with comedy as with psychological or social dramas. He became known to the general public for his role in *L'Etudiante* by Claude Pinoteau; the film earned him the Prix Jean Gabin in 1989, a prize given to the most promising actor of the year. In 1993 he received his first nomination for the Best Actor César for playing a fired executive who strikes up a friendship with a homeless man in *La Crise*, a comedy by Coline Serreau. He received four additional nominations for this César for his performance in films with a strong social component such as *My Little Business* (*Ma petite entreprise*) in 2000, *Those Who Remain* (*Ceux qui restent*) in 2008, *Welcome* in 2010, and *A Few Hours of Spring* (*Quelques heures de printemps*) in 2013. Lindon earned the ultimate accolade with the Best Actor Award at the Cannes Film Festival in 2015 and at the Césars the following year for his role in *The Measure of a Man* (*La Loi du marché*). In this second collaboration with Stéphane Brizé, the director of *A Few Hours of Spring*, he portrays a long-term unemployed man who faces a moral dilemma when he takes a job as a supermarket security guard.

Despite his upper-middle-class origins—he stems from a long line of industrialists and intellectuals—Lindon has become the embodiment of the average Frenchman. He has "the extraordinary ability to impersonate ordinary heroes," Guillemette Odicino writes. Sébastien Chapuys, for his part, remarks: "Who else besides Lindon, nowadays, in France, could portray with as much subtlety and accuracy a nice ordinary guy overwhelmed by dramatic events that he faces with a mix of resignation and mild opposition?" François-Guillaume Lorrain more or less agrees with Chapuys' observation: "Who has this depth, this density, in French cinema? Bacri, Amalric, Darroussin, Auteuil—when he wishes—and then him."

Audrey Dana, who plays Marion, is well known in the world of entertainment as well. Originally a theater actress, she made her breakthrough on the big screen in a film by Claude Lelouch, *Crossed Tracks* (*Roman de gare*), for which she received a nomination for Most Promising Actress at the Césars in 2008 in addition to the Prix Romy Schneider, awarded to the most promising actress of the year. She has appeared in about twenty films and directed a few short and feature films. Her comedy *French Women* (*Sous les jupes des filles*, 2014) brings together eleven famous French actresses who represent different facets of the contemporary woman.

Among the other professional actors of the film, Olivier Rabourdin plays the policeman. Rabourdin is a prolific and versatile actor accustomed to supporting roles on the big screen and in TV series, where he often portrays policemen. Since the end of the 2000s he has appeared in more important roles in dramas (*Animal Heart* [*Cœur animal*, 2009], *Of Gods and Men* [*Des hommes et des dieux*, 2010]), comedies (*My Father's Guests* [*Les Invités de mon père*, 2010]) and thrillers (*Love Crime* [*Crime d'amour*, 2010]).

The migrants of the film are played by many nonprofessional actors, like Firat Ayverdi (Bilal) and his sister Derya (Mina). Philippe Lioret and his casting director combed the cities where the Kurdish diaspora has settled (Berlin, Istanbul, London, Stockholm) before finding Firat Ayverdi in France. He received a nomination for Most Promising Actor at the Césars for his performance.

One should also mention the presence of co-scriptwriter Emmanuel Courcol as the supermarket director and a cameo appearance à la Hitchcock by Philippe Lioret himself as the man walking his dog on the beach.

The Reception

Welcome came out in 2009 at the Berlin International Film Festival, where it was awarded the Prize of the Ecumenical Jury. It was well received by the public upon its theatrical release in March 2009, with over one million spectators in its first month and around 1.3 million overall. Chapuys explains this popular success by the choice of Vincent Lindon in the lead role: "With this wise but safe casting choice, one can sense a will to reach a larger audience, which would not necessarily have wanted to follow the ups and downs of a young Kurdish refugee if there hadn't been the opportunity to identify with a French actor who was both dignified and popular."

The controversy that preceded the release of the film also contributed to its notoriety. During an interview, Philippe Lioret had criticized a law that penalized assistance to illegal aliens (see the section "The Origin and Making of the Film") and compared the treatment of those who helped migrants to that of individuals who assisted the Jews under the Vichy Regime during the German Occupation (1940–44). This elicited a very strong reaction from Eric Besson, the Minister of Immigration, Integration, National Identity, and Socially Cohesive Development, who found this parallel "unacceptable, unpleasant, unbearable" and accused Lioret of resorting to provocation in order to better promote his film. The latter responded in an open letter published in *Le Monde*, concluding thus: "Today, in our country, there is no respect for basic human values. That's what you should find 'unacceptable'" (Lioret).

The socialist caucus in the National Assembly, which was preparing a bill to remove the "délit de solidarité" or "solidarity crime" (the name given by its detractors to the article of the law that penalizes assistance to illegal aliens) organized a screening at the National Assembly with the director in attendance in March 2009 in order to rally the maximum number of lawmakers to its cause; to no avail, however, because the law was not passed. The film was also screened at the European Parliament, where the Eurodeputies awarded it the Lux Prize. Created in 2007, this prize rewards a film that encourages reflection on European identity. It consists of a subsidy of 87,000 euros to subtitle the film in the official languages of the European Union and to distribute it to member countries. Lioret was very pleased with the political impact of this award: "I am proud of the film when I see an important European body embracing its subject matter, especially since the proposal to amend article L622-1, which was rejected in France, is about to be considered by the European Court of Justice" (Lemercier, "Des gamins"). On the other hand, he was disappointed by the results of the screening of *Welcome* in the countries of origin of migrants. He had hoped that his film would discourage young people from trying to emigrate, but he was struck by their reactions at showings in Kurdistan, for example, where they were indifferent to the dangers represented in the film and mostly inquired about how to get to England (Bosquet). *Welcome* received many other prizes and nominations, including the Audience Award at the Los Angeles Film Festival in 2009 and, in 2010, the "Prix lycéen du cinéma" (given by high school students), the Lumières Prize for Best Film, a nomination for the Louis Delluc Prize, and ten nominations at the Césars.

The reactions of the film critics confirm this success. Most consider *Welcome* halfway between popular cinema and auteur film and appreciate the way in which Lioret mixes the personal story and the social context: "The difficult lives of the illegals who dream of England enrich the plot of a sensitive story" (Roy); "Philippe Lioret excels at blending the intimate melodic line of human relationships with the syncopated rhythm of the social and political thriller" (Tranchant); "*Welcome*, by Philippe Lioret, is deeply moving in its humanity and combines a documentary-like description of a disturbing situation in contemporary France [. . .] and two wonderful love stories" (Raspiengeas, "*Welcome*"). Some commentators stress the film's ability to elicit the spectator's empathy and raise his/her consciousness. For Roy, "when leaving the theater, we know more, and above all more intimately, about these people, who now have names and lives." Clara Dupont-Monod considers the film "An engaged, political, disturbing masterpiece [. . .]. In a word: indispensable!" Thomas Sotinel finds it original "in its goal, successfully achieved, to place the spectator on the side of the aspiring traveler and compel him to ask himself the question of the day: 'What would *I* do if I were in Simon's shoes?'"

Among the less admiring critics, Kevin Prin considers the film too heavy in its demonstration: "Unfortunately, Philippe Lioret's film is so eager to take sides that it becomes a caricature and, above all, a tearjerker" (through its music, in particular). For him, *Welcome* "is closer to a moral lesson than to the hard-hitting social denunciation it could and should have been." Jean Baptiste Morain also blames the director for minimizing the social aspect of the film by focusing on Simon's story: "[The film has] a very strong theme that revolves around an illegal alien trapped in a northern town but sacrificed at the altar of a star-studded French conjugal psychodrama." He regrets that Bilal disappeared "when the story no longer needed him to promote the national hero." Chapuys shares this point of view on the migrants' instrumentalization: "The Other [Bilal] is domesticated, reduced to his least disturbing aspect, transformed into an ideal adoptive son for a depressive, childless Westerner." However, he considers the film as a precursor in the representation of illegal immigrants. If the combination of a "social melodrama à la Ken Loach" and of "the typical French sentimental drama" is only partially successful according to him, he finds that "the graft [. . .] was worth trying, and—who knows?—may pave the way for other stronger and more socially engaged stories." Thanks to the film, he concludes, "now the 'undocumented' is no longer unrepresented: for this alone, and for shedding light on the national shame associated with the tracking down of migrants by the French State, Philippe Lioret's film deserves recognition."

Parallels with Ken Loach's social films, as noted above, are found in the writings of several critics. Chapuys, for his part, also notes a resemblance with the fiction films of the Dardenne brothers in the first thirty minutes of *Welcome*, which are shot like a documentary with "great sobriety and no naive optimism." Finally, Pierre Murat suggests a link with Italian Neorealism when he compares the effect of the film to that of Vittorio De Sica's *The Bicycle Thief* (1948), without naming it: "As in these old Italian masterpieces where a child sliding his hand into that of his humiliated father is enough to rekindle hope, fragments of fraternity is what we take away."

The Situation of the Migrants in Calais

The story of *Welcome* takes place in Calais in the first decade of the 2000s in a very particular socio-political context. Since the Schengen Agreement of 1985 and its gradual implementation in the 1990s, it has been possible to move freely within most of the countries of the European Union. The United Kingdom is an exception: it is not part of the Schengen area, and therefore a passport is necessary to go there. The migrants who have managed to enter a European country illegally and wish to go to England try to cross from Calais, the most important French city with a direct link to England, thanks to its port and the Channel tunnel. The opening of the tunnel in 1994 led to an increase in the number of migrants in the city and its surroundings. These migrants were mostly Afghans, Iranians, Iraqis, Kurds, and Kosovars who were trying to escape the war or persecution in their countries (they have since been joined by refugees from Somalia, Sudan, Eritrea, and Syria, among others). According to the 1951 Geneva Convention relative to the status of refugees, people from countries where their lives are in danger can seek asylum in the country where they live in voluntary exile. If their applications are approved, they obtain refugee status; otherwise, they must go back to their countries or stay in the host country illegally. Many migrants wish to go to England rather than the Schengen area because they speak English or have community or family networks in that country. Some have been denied refugee status in the Schengen zone and wish to try their luck again in England, where the immigration policy is more liberal—or at least *was* until the 2016 vote in favor of "Brexit," the future departure of the United Kingdom from the European Union, which may well result in a tightening of immigration policies.

To respond to the influx of migrants, Lionel Jospin's socialist government (during President Chirac's first term) opened a shelter run by the Red Cross in Sangatte, near Calais, in 1999. This center, which could not meet demand—it was designed for 200 people and welcomed as many as 1,600—was closed by Nicolas Sarkozy in 2002 (Sarkozy was then Minister of the Interior in Jean-Pierre Raffarin's right-wing government, during President Chirac's second term). The migrants then settled in makeshift dwellings in the region, including a zone that was nicknamed the "Calais jungle." The presence of these illegal campsites created public health issues and caused conflicts with the local population. To remedy them, the French authorities, pressured by the British government, organized raids to dismantle the jungle on several occasions starting in 2002, and several times under the presidency of Nicolas Sarkozy, who made the fight against illegal immigration one of the focal points of his term in office. Philippe Lioret includes a direct allusion to Sarkozy's policies in a scene of the film where the latter appears on television.

To discourage migrants from coming, the government also put pressure on the private citizens and associations that helped them, in accordance with Article L622-1. As we saw in the section "The Reception," the release of *Welcome* intensified opposition to this law, which had led to demonstrations for several years, but without any concrete results. It was not until 2013 and the coming to power of a left-wing government that acts of solidarity of this sort were decriminalized. Since that date, individuals and associations that help illegal aliens without financial gain—by providing "legal advice or food, accommodations, or health care with the aim of insuring dignified and decent living conditions"—are no longer subject to penalties. It is worth noting that the problem of migrants in Calais has worsened with the Syrian conflict. According to *Le Monde*, their numbers have risen from 2,000 in the spring of 2015 to about 6,000 in October of the same year (Pauwels). In October 2016, the "Calais jungle" was destroyed by the authorities and most of its residents transferred to other reception centers on French territory.

Cinema and Politics

Welcome is one of many films released in the 1990s that show an interest in contemporary social reality and express a more or less explicit message about it. According to Martin O'Shaughnessy, the rebirth of committed cinema in France in that decade can be explained by a growing social divide and the return of mass demonstrations—a quarter of a century after May 1968—to protest against capitalism and the increasing erosion of social protection. Filmmakers rallied to the defense of certain causes, in particular that of the "sans papiers" (undocumented workers). Indeed, following the rise of the National Front and its xenophobic discourse in the 1980s, the immigration issue was at the forefront of the political stage. The right-wing governments, worried about losing votes to Jean-Marie Le Pen's party, passed restrictive immigration laws, the "Pasqua laws" of 1986 and 1993. They took spectacular action to fight against illegal immigrants, like the highly publicized removal, in August 1996, of about 300 Africans who had sought refuge in Saint-Bernard's Church in Paris.

This event mobilized artists and intellectuals, and they continued to express their points of view on the state of society through their works or their public statements. In the area of cinema, for example, a group of directors signed a call for civil disobedience to protest against the treatment of people who came to the help of migrants. "The call of the 66 filmmakers," published in *Le Monde*, *Libération*, and *Les Inrockuptibles* on February 12, 1997, opposed a bill (the Debré bill) requiring that people who hosted illegal aliens declare them to the local government (Bantman). Some of the directors included in the present textbook belonged to this group, like Jacques Audiard (*A Prophet*), Claire Denis (*Chocolat*), Mathieu Kassovitz (*Hate*), and Philippe Lioret (*Welcome*).

Before *Welcome*, there was no French fiction film focused solely on illegal immigrants, except for *Eden Is West* (*Eden à l'Ouest*, Costa-Gavras, 2009) and *Nowhere, the Promised Land* (*Nulle part, terre promise*, Emmanuel Finkiel, 2009), two road movies released the same year, but which went virtually unnoticed (whereas Swiss cinema, for example, had produced a major work on this theme, *Journey of Hope* [*Voyage vers l'espoir*] by Xavier Koller in 1990). As Chapuys noted when Lioret's film came out, "French cinema, too little concerned with world events, is less vocal on the topic, except for a handful of documentaries [. . .], a few auteurist fictions (*The Wound* [*La Blessure*]), and other weak and decontextualized fables (*Eden Is West*). We hoped, without expecting much, that a French director would tackle the issue and finally come up with a film that would be bold and mainstream at the same time. With *Welcome*, this wish has been fulfilled."

Indeed, *Welcome* ushered the illegal alien into mainstream French cinema. Several films, like *Looking for Hortense* (*Cherchez Hortense*, Pascal Bonitzer, 2012) or *Little Lion* (*Comme un lion*, Samuel Collardey, 2013) took up its central plot, the growing awareness and rebirth of an ordinary citizen after meeting a migrant. Other works follow a similar pattern but confront groups, rather than individuals, to the presence of illegal aliens. That is the case of *Hands Up* (*Les Mains en l'air*, Romain Goupil, 2010) and *Le Havre* (Aki Kaurismaki, 2011), two films by left-wing filmmakers that are heartfelt hymns to solidarity (Bissière 224–29).

STUDY GUIDE

What Happens in This Film?

1. How did Bilal and the group of Kurds try to reach England? What happened?

2. Why did Bilal go to the swimming pool? What did Simon understand the next time they met?

3. What is the relationship between Simon and Marion? What is Marion's profession?

4. What happened at the supermarket? How does Marion's reaction differ from Simon's?

5. What did Simon learn about Bilal and Zoran when he put them up at his place? How did they arrive in France, for example? What was Bilal known for in his village in Iraq? What are his ambitions?

6. Why were there trophies at Simon's apartment?

7. Why did the police come to Simon's home early one morning, and what did they find?

8. What did Simon do when he understood that Bilal had begun to swim the Channel (the first attempt)?

9. Why did Simon admit to the policeman that he had helped an illegal alien? What were the consequences of this confession?

10. Where did Simon see Bilal again for the last time? What message from Mina did he relay to the boy?

11. How did Bilal die? Who told the news to Simon, and what objects did that person give back to him?

12. Why did Simon go to England at the end of the film?

True or False?

If the statement is false, correct it!

1. Marion works for an association that shelters migrants at night.

2. At the beginning of the film, Bilal calls his family, which has remained in Iraq.

3. Bilal paid a trafficker 500 euros to go to England.

4. After the failure of the passage to England, the judge assigned Bilal to a shelter because he was a minor.

5. The migrants followed Bilal to the swimming pool to learn how to swim.

6. According to Simon, it takes ten hours to swim the English Channel, and the currents are very strong.

7. During the night Simon found Bilal breathing in a plastic bag.

8. Bilal stole one of Simon's medals.

9. His neighbor insinuates that Simon has a homosexual relationship with Bilal.

10. Simon passes himself off as Bilal's uncle when he asks a rescue crew to search for him at sea.

11. When Mina talks to Simon on the phone, she asks him to tell Bilal to come to England as soon as possible.

12. While driving through the city, Simon sometimes sees migrants who are being brutalized by the police.

What Did You Learn in the Introduction?

1. What is Philippe Lioret's reputation as a director? What types of critics appreciate his films the least and why?

2. Why did Lioret wish to make a movie about migrants? What did he discover while shooting the film?

3. Why did Lioret choose Vincent Lindon for the lead role?

4. What was the controversy that erupted when the film was released?

5. How was *Welcome* received by French and European political officials?

6. According to the critics, what are the positive aspects of the film? What was the film criticized for?

7. Why does the city of Calais often make the newspaper headlines when immigration is discussed?

8. What explains the rebirth of committed cinema in the 1990s?

9. Why was immigration at the center of political discussions at that time?

10. What were the "Pasqua laws" of 1986 and 1993?

11. What was the "call of the 66 filmmakers," in which Philippe Lioret took part?

12. What is *Welcome*'s particular contribution to French cinema?

Exploring the Film

1. The Title

In your opinion, why did Lioret choose *Welcome* as the title of his film? Where is this word found in the film? To which word in the French national motto ("Liberty, Equality, Fraternity") does the film title refer? Why did Lioret defer the appearance of the title until the closing credits?

2. The Characters

+ *Simon*

What do we know about Simon? What is his marital status? **Why does he work at a swimming pool?** What is his attitude toward Bilal at the beginning? How does his attitude evolve? What impresses Simon about Bilal?

Which aspects of his personal life does Simon experience again through Bilal? **What type of relationship do they finally develop?** What does Simon say in this respect to the coast guard the first time Bilal tries to cross the English Channel?

+ *Bilal*

Why does Bilal want to go to England, and what are his ambitions? Why can't he tolerate the plastic bag over his head in the truck during the attempted crossing? What is the effect of this revelation on the spectator and Zoran? Why does one of the Kurds demand that Bilal give him 500 euros? Why is the scene in the telephone booth important? What is the meaning of the short sequence in which Bilal is playing with the soccer ball? *Review pertinent scenes* (Excerpt 1, 21'30–23'20).

+ *Marion*

What is Marion's attitude toward the migrants? What does she criticize Simon for after the incident at the supermarket? Why did Marion leave Simon, in your opinion?

What do you think of the scene in which Simon and Marion make love in the kitchen? What does this scene reveal about Marion's feelings for Simon? *Review this scene* (Excerpt 2, 1h17'00–1h19'50).

+ *The Migrants*

Where do the migrants of the film come from? **Why did they leave their countries?** Why does the director insist on Zoran's experience in Calais when Bilal meets up with him at the beginning of the film? Why does Zoran say that it is impossible to cross over to England by boat or train? *Review the scene where Bilal meets Zoran in the food line* (Excerpt 3, 4'00–6'30).

What contrasts does Lioret draw between the world of the migrants and that of the Calais residents? **In what places are the migrants shown?** At what time of the day, usually? Why, in your opinion? What are the migrants implicitly compared to when they are in the truck at the beginning of the film?

    ✦   *Character Portrayal*

In his open letter to the Minister of Immigration, Philippe Lioret writes that his work consists in paying attention "to events that are taking place today, in our country, to their impact and their consequences for the human spirit, while trying not to be Manichean" ("De simple valeurs"). Some commentators agree that he managed to film his story "without ever succumbing to Manicheism" (Lemercier, "Welcome"). **What do they mean by this?** Do you agree with them? On another subject, is there too much caricature in the depiction of the characters, as some critics claim, or is the characters' portrayal, on the contrary, true to life?

3. Parallels with the Occupation Period

As we saw in the section on "The Reception," the release of the film stirred up controversy because the Minister of Immigration did not appreciate some comments by Philippe Lioret, who, during an interview, compared the situation of the Calais migrants and volunteers to that of the Jews and the Just (the people who helped them) in France during the Second World War. Some critics (Deandrea, Fevry) have noted that one can find this parallel in *Welcome*.

    For your part, what allusions to this historical period did you notice in the dialogue and the situations of *Welcome*? Which aspects of the film are reminiscent of the treatment of the Jews during the Second World War? (Think about *Goodbye, Children* and *The Last Metro*, two films in this book which deal with that period). *For example, review the scene at the supermarket* (Excerpt 4, 28'30–29'40) *and the police raid on Simon's apartment* (Excerpt 5, 1h11'18–1h13'00). In the first scene, what was Marion alluding to when she said to Simon: "You know what it means when one starts to bar certain people from entering stores? Do you want me to buy you a history book?" In the second, how does Lioret show his disapproval of the policemen's and the neighbor's actions? What type of events of the Second World War do they call to mind?

4. Social and Political Criticism

Lioret includes several scenes that examine immigration policy and the population's attitude toward the migrants. What is the attitude of the authorities (the police, the judicial system) toward the migrants? *Review the scenes where Bilal is at the police station and at the courthouse* (Excerpt 6, 15'40–17'50). *In addition, review a scene of police violence* (Excerpt 7, 1h01'40–1h02'00). In this last scene, how does the director elicit the spectator's sympathy and indignation? How do you explain this violence on the part of the police?

How do some of the Calais residents, like Simon's neighbor, view the migrants? *Review the scene with the neighbor* (Excerpt 8, 1h07'00–1h07'47). Why is this scene ironic, given Bilal's physical appearance?

How does Lioret's opposition to Nicolas Sarkozy's immigration policy express itself when Simon switches channels to find a television program? Where does Simon go next? Why, according to you? *Review this scene* (Excerpt 9, 58'00–59'20).

Since the Declaration of the Rights of Man and the Citizen of 1789, France has been called "the homeland of human rights," and it likes to consider itself a "country of asylum." For one critic, Marion is an embodiment of France (Labibi). **If we agree with this idea, what does the film say about France's attitude toward foreigners?** Consider this question with Simon in mind also. Do you feel he has become more politically conscious? Is he going to continue the fight? Do you think that the film limits itself to exposing the migrants' situation, or does it also seek to influence the spectator in some way? How?

Beyond the French situation, **what statement does the film make about the expectations of the migrants who perceive Europe as a Promised Land?** How are the lives of the Kurds in England depicted? Is Mina's family well integrated? (What work did her brother find in London? How is he treated by his boss? Whom is Mina going to be forced to marry?)

5. *The Languages of the Film*

We hear four languages in the film: French, English, Kurdish, and Pashto. The presence of so many different languages in a film is unusual. **What aspect of the film is reinforced by this multiplicity of languages?** Why do Bilal and his Kurdish friends speak English? What do you know about the history of Iraq in this regard?

What language do Mina's family members speak at home in London? Could that also suggest something as to their integration into English life?

Simon and Bilal speak English together most of the time. In the scene where Simon tends to Bilal, who has been attacked and wounded by his Kurdish countryman, Bilal utters a word in French for the first time ("Merci"). **Why is Simon so pleased to hear this?**

6. *Symbolic Objects*

There are many symbolic objects in the film, such as the doormat, the plastic bag, Mina's photo, the medal, the ring. **Explain when these objects appear in the film and what their function is.** (Do they move the plot forward? Do they symbolize something in particular? Are they used for foreshadowing?)

7. *Structure and Style*

The film includes numerous parallels and oppositions, for example the scenes where Bilal, then Simon, are questioned by the police or appear before a judge. Note other parallels and oppositions. **Why did Lioret choose to structure his film in this way?**

The style of the film is very elliptical. Philippe Lioret uses juxtapositions, symbolic objects and other significant elements (like television), rather than words, to make us understand the thoughts and feelings of the characters. ***Review the following scenes and explain what they teach us about the protagonists:*** (a) Bilal on the beach and at the swimming pool (Excerpt 10, 18'25–19'15). **What do we understand about his intentions?** (b) Simon with Marion, then at the restaurant (Excerpt 11, 30'15–31'00). **What do we learn about his social life?** What is he probably thinking about while watching television?

A key scene in the film is the one that crosscuts Simon at the swimming pool and Bilal swimming the English Channel. ***Review this scene*** (Excerpt 12, 1h28'40– 1h35'10). **Does Simon know that Bilal is swimming across?** In your opinion, why does Simon start swimming all of a sudden? What is he thinking about when he watches the young boy swimming in the pool? **What role does music play in this sequence?** When does the music stop completely in this sequence? Why? **Why does Lioret not show Bilal's death (in keeping with his elliptical approach)?**

8. The Denouement

What do you think of this tragic denouement? Is it a predestined outcome, in a way? Would you rather Lioret had let Bilal cross the English Channel successfully? How would this have changed the effect of the film on the spectators?

What is the purpose, in your opinion, of the episode where Simon goes to London to meet Mina?

How do you interpret the final phone call between Simon and Marion, during which Simon promises to return to Calais? How important is the allusion to the ring that has been found? How do you think the relationship between Simon and Marion will evolve?

Philippe Lioret's Filmography

1993   *Lost in Transit* (*Tombés du ciel*)

1994   *3,000 Screenplays to Combat a Virus [AIDS]* (*3 000 scénarios contre un virus [le SIDA]*)

1996   *Proper Attire Required* (*Tenue correcte exigée*)

2000   *Mademoiselle*

2001   *Don't Make Trouble! 12 Looks at Racism in Daily Life* (*Pas d'histoires! 12 regards sur le racisme au quotidien*)

2003   *The Light* (*L'Equipier*)

2006   *Don't Worry, I'm Fine* (*Je vais bien, ne t'en fais pas*)

2009   *Welcome*

2010   *All Our Desires* (*Toutes nos envies*)

2015   *A Kid* (*Un garçon*)

Works Consulted

Bantman, Béatrice. "Immigration: appels à la désobéissance. Associations et cinéastes lancent le boycott de la loi Debré." *Libération*, 12 Feb. 1997: n. pag.

Bissière, Michèle. "L'immigration dans le cinéma français: Quelques tendances depuis la fin des années 2000." *Contemporary French Civilization* 40.2 (July 2015): 215–33.

Bosquet, Sarah. "Philippe Lioret: *Welcome*: un lien entre romanesque et politique." *Le Petit Journal*, 7 May 2010. Web. 23 Feb. 2018. <lepetitjournal.com/valence/actualites /interview-philippe-lioret-welcome-un-lien-entre-romanesque-et-politique -18251>.

Chapuys, Sébastien. "*Welcome*. Éloge de l'insoumission tranquille." *Critikat*, 10 Mar. 2009. Web. 23 Nov. 2015. <www.critikat.com/actualite-cine/critique/welcome .html>.

Deandrea, Pietro. "The Spectralized Camp: Cultural Representations of British New Slaveries." *Interventions: International Journal of Postcolonial Studies* 17.4 (2015): 488–502.

Dupont-Monod, Clara. "*Welcome*." *Marianne*. Web. 23 Nov. 2015. <www.allocine.fr /film/fichefilm-111722/critiques/presse/>.

Fevry, Sébastien. "Mémoires en dialogue: Shoah et sans-papiers dans le cinéma français contemporain." *Image (&) Narrative* 14.2 (2013): 51–62.

Higbee, Will. "Hope and Indignation in Fortress Europe: Immigration and Neoliberal Globalization in Contemporary French Cinema." *Substance: A Review of Theory and Literary Criticism* 43.1 (2014): 26–43.

Konstantarakos, Myrto. "Retour du politique dans le cinéma français contemporain?" *French Studies Bulletin* 68 (Autumn 1998): 1–5.

Labibi, Imed. "*Welcome*: An Insight into the Landscape of Contemporary French Consciousness." *Senses of Cinema: An Online Film Journal Devoted to the Serious and Eclectic Discussion of Cinema* 59 (2011). Web. 23 Nov. 2015. <sensesofcinema .com/2011/feature-articles/welcome-an-insight-into-the-landscape-of-contem porary-french-consciousness/>.

Lemercier, Fabien. "Des gamins vivant comme des animaux domestiques." Entretien avec Philippe Lioret. 10 Sept. 2009. Web. 23 Nov. 2015. <cineuropa.org/it.aspx?t =interview&l=fr&did=112474>.

———. "*Welcome*." 10 Sept. 2009. Web. 23 Nov. 2015. <cineuropa.org/nw.aspx?t=ne wsdetail&l=fr&did=112473>.

Lioret, Philippe. "De simples valeurs humaines ne sont pas respectées." *Le Monde*, 10 Mar. 2009: n. pag.

———, dir. *Welcome*. Film Movement, 2010.

Lorrain, François-Guillaume. "Lindon, à hauteur d'homme." *Le Point*, 5 Mar. 2009: n. pag.

Marsa, Julien. "Toutes nos envies. Tous nous envient." *Critikat*, 8 Nov. 2011. Web. 23 Nov. 2015. <www.critikat.com/actualite-cine/critique/toutes-nos-envies.html>.

Morain, Jean-Baptiste. "*Welcome*." *Les Inrockuptibles*, 6 Mar. 2009. Web. 23 Nov. 2015. <www.lesinrocks.com/cinema/films-a-l-affiche/welcome/>.

Murat, Pierre. "*Welcome*." *Télérama*, 11 Mar. 2009: n. pag.

Odicino, Guillemette. "Toutes nos envies." *Télérama*, 13 Sept. 2014: n. pag.

O'Shaughnessy, Martin. "Post-1995 French Cinema: Return of the Social, Return of the Political?" *Modern & Contemporary France* 11.2 (2003): 189–203.

Pauwels, David. "Dans la 'jungle' de Calais." *Le Monde*, 14 Oct. 2015: n. pag.

Powrie, Phil. "Heritage, History and 'New Realism.'" *French Cinema in the 1990s: Continuity and Difference.* Ed. Phil Powrie. Oxford: Oxford UP, 1999: 1–21.

———, ed. *French Cinema in the 1990s. Continuity and Difference.* Oxford: Oxford UP, 1999.

Prin, Kevin. "*Welcome*." *Filmsactu.* Web. 23 Nov. 2015. <cinema.jeuxactu.com/critique -cinema-welcome-1-5692.htm>.

Rascaroli, Laura. "On the Eve of the Journey: Tangier, Tbilisi, Calais." *Open Roads, Closed Borders: The Contemporary French-Language Road Movie.* Bristol, England: Intellect, 2013. 21–38.

Raspiengeas, Jean-Claude. "Philippe Lioret: 'J'ai terminé *Welcome* en citoyen révolté.'" *La Croix*, 11 Mar. 2009: n. pag.

———. "*Welcome*, une approche empreinte d'humanité." *La Croix*, 11 Mar. 2009: n. pag.

Renault, Gilles. "*Welcome*, la nage de vivre." *Libération*, 11 Mar. 2009: n. pag.

Rime, Claudine. "Sortie du film *Welcome* au cinéma à partir du 11 mars 2009." *Bouvignies demain*, 17 Jan. 2009. Web. 23 Nov. 2015. <www.bouvigniens.org/Sortie-du -film-Welcome-au-cinema-a.html>.

Rouden, Céline. "Le film *Welcome* relance le débat sur l'aide aux réfugiés." *La Croix*, 18 Mar. 2009: n. pag.

Roy, Jean. "*Welcome*." *L'Humanité*, 11 Mar. 2009: n. pag.

Sotinel, Thomas. "*Welcome*: le maître-nageur dans le grand bain des migrants." *Le Monde*, 10 Mar. 2009: n. pag.

Thomas, Dominic. "Into the Jungle: Migration and Grammar in the New Europe." *Multilingual Europe, Multilingual Europeans.* Amsterdam, Netherlands: Rodopi, 2012. 267–84.

Tranchant, Marie-Noëlle. "*Welcome*." *Le Figaroscope*, 11 Mar. 2009: n. pag.

IV

Thrillers and Crime Films

Jean-Jacques Beineix, *Diva* (1981)

Michael Haneke, *Caché* (2005)

Jacques Audiard, *Un prophète* (2009)

In France there is a long tradition of crime films, that is, *polars*, including thrillers and other types of films noirs, largely commercial products for the broad public. Most frequently adapted from popular crime novels, thrillers are today (along with comedies) "the most widely produced and distributed genre in France" (Philippe 24). These two forms of fiction have been closely linked since the earliest periods of cinema, beginning with Louis Feuillade's *Fantômas* (1912) and *Judex* (1915), two series that would "seal the sacred union between crime novels and films, never to be divorced from one another" (Lebrun and Schweigenhaeuser 36). With the exception of the dark years of the Occupation (1940–44), the crime genre, especially the Anglo-American films, has always enjoyed the favor of the French public, beginning with a sort of golden age in the 1930s and continuing its success up to the present day. Certain authors like Georges Simenon (after Maurice Leblanc and his gentlemen burglar Arsène Lupin, and Gaston Leroux and his amateur detective Rouletabille) long dominated the French crime novel: there are eighty-four novels in the series featuring Maigret, Simenon's police inspector, beginning in 1931. Many Maigret novels were quickly turned into movies—eight, for example, during the Occupation alone. In the 1950s, despite the persistent Anglo-American domination of this genre, the Boileau-Narcejac tandem (Pierre Boileau and Thomas Narcejac) enjoyed great success among the French writers of crime novels, and some of their masterpieces like *Diabolique* (*Les Diaboliques*, 1954) and *Vertigo* (*Sueurs froids*, 1958) would be adapted to the big screen by Georges Clouzot and Alfred Hitchcock respectively. The American director Jules Dassin produced a great classic of French film noir, *Rififi* (*Du rififi chez les hommes*, 1955), adapted from the Auguste Le Breton novel of the same name. During the same period, other crime film classics were adapted from novels by Albert Simonin, including *Hands Off the Loot* (*Touchez pas au grisbi*, 1954) by Jacques Becker and *Monsieur Gangster* (*Les Tontons flingueurs*, 1963) by Georges Lautner, whose screenwriter-in-chief was Michel Audiard, the father of the director of *Un prophète* (see Chapter 13).

Beginning in the 1950s, the crime genre gained increasing respectability in France with the films of Jean-Pierre Melville, among which *Bob le Flambeur* (1956), *Second Wind* (*Le Deuxième Souffle*, 1966), *Le Samouraï* (1967), and *The Red Circle* (*Le Cercle rouge*, 1970) are the best known. Robin Davis also contributed a collection of well-made crime thrillers such as *The Police War* (*La Guerre des polices*, 1979), *Contract in Blood* (*Le Choc*, 1982), and *I Married a Dead Man* (*J'ai épousé une ombre*, 1983). Bob Swaim (an

183

American) virtually transformed the genre in 1982 with his sociological approach in *The Nark* (*La Balance*), winner of Césars for both Best Film and Best Actress (Nathalie Baye). The preceding year Jean-Jacques Beinex had adapted the second thriller by the Swiss novelist Delacorta, *Diva*, the film that inaugurated the nascent trend of the *cinéma du look* (see Chapter 11).

Along with *Diva* we present in this section two other thrillers: Michael Haneke's film *Caché*, an entirely different kind of work in which the psychological and social dimensions are given priority, and Jacques Audiard's *Un prophète*, a prison film that may be viewed as a sub-genre of the *polar* (see the commentary on this particular type of film in the section "The Prison Film" in Chapter 13).

Works Consulted

Lebrun, Michel, and Jean-Paul Schweighaeuser. *Le Guide du "polar."* Paris: Syros, 1987.

Philippe, Olivier. *Le Film policier français contemporain.* Paris: Cerf, 1996.

11

Jean-Jacques Beineix

Diva

(1981)

Jean-Jacques Beineix, *Diva*: Cynthia Hawkins (Wilhelmenia Wiggins Fernandez) and Jules (Frédéric Andréi) in the Luxembourg Gardens in Paris.

Director	Jean-Jacques Beineix
Adaptation	Jean-Jacques Beineix, Jean Van Hamme
Director of Photography	Philippe Rousselot
Film Editors	Marie-Josèphe Yoyotte, Monique Prim
Sound	Jean-Pierre Ruh
Art Director	Hilton McConnico
Music	Vladimir Cosma
Costumes	Claire Fraisse
Continuity	Sylvie Koechlin
Producers	Irène Silberman, Ully Pickard
Length	1h57

Cast

Frédéric Andréi (*Jules*), Wilhelmenia Wiggins Fernandez (*Cynthia Hawkins*), Richard Bohringer (*Gorodish*), Jacques Fabbri (*Police Commissioner Saporta*), Thuy An Luu (*Alba*), Gérard Darmon (*l'Antillais* [the *West Indian*]), Dominique Pinon (*Curé* [*Priest*]), Anny Romand (*Paula*), Patrick Floersheim (*Zatopek*), Chantal Deruaz (*Nadia, the white prostitute*), Roland Bertin (*Weinstadt, Cynthia Hawkins' manager*), Jean-Jacques Moreau (*Krantz*)

Story

Jules, a young Parisian mailman, is a passionate fan of a black American opera singer, Cynthia Hawkins. Since Cynthia stubbornly refuses to have recordings made of her performances to sell records, Jules makes a clandestine high-quality recording of one of her recitals at the Paris Opera for his personal pleasure. Two shady Taiwanese businessmen who want to force Cynthia to sign a record contract with them spot Jules making the recording and set out to find him and steal the cassette.

Soon after, Nadia, a prostitute on the run, slips a compromising audiocassette into the saddlebag of Jules' moped just before being assassinated by a couple of killers in front of the Gare Saint-Lazare. In the cassette she denounces Saporta, a corrupt police commissioner who is at the head of a prostitution and white slave trade ring. Police officers and the gangsters who work for Saporta both head out to find Jules to recover the cassette.

At the same time Jules meets a pretty Vietnamese adolescent, Alba, who indulges in regular shoplifting. She lives with a mysterious man, Gorodish, an unusually resourceful individual given to Zen philosophy who has vague contacts in the underworld, and who will come to Jules' aid. Despite the extreme danger he is in, Jules begins a kind of idyll with Cynthia Hawkins, with whom he is also in love. . . .

The Director and the Making of the Film

Born in 1946, Jean-Jacques Beineix abandoned medical school after the May 1968 "events" to try to make his way in filmmaking. He spent nine years as an assistant in studios, working as a delivery boy, clapman, boom operator, decorator, and photographer. He served as an assistant to Jerry Lewis, René Clément, Claude Zidi, and Claude Berri before shooting his first film, a short subject titled *Mister Michel's Dog* (*Le Chien de Monsieur Michel*) that won prizes at several film festivals in 1977. When he decided to stop working as an assistant and try to direct his first feature film, he had the good fortune of making a strong impression on the producer Irène Silberman. Silberman gave him the opportunity to make a film adaptation of *Diva*, a crime novel by Delacorta (the pen name of the Swiss novelist Daniel Odier), but with a six-month probation period to prove himself. Six months, he says, "during which I endured interrogations, lectures, and dinners in which I shared my ideas on the film and my plans for adaptation to prove that I was capable of doing it, to reassure everyone" (Cornet 5). Ultimately he spent two months in Brussels working out the final screenplay for the film with the Belgian screenwriter Jean Van Hamme.

The Actors

Diva was shot in ten weeks on a very modest budget, around $1.5 million. Since most of the cast was completely or relatively unknown at the time, the actors' paychecks were very modest, which allowed Beineix and his Director of Photography, Philippe Rousselot, to devote the major part of the budget to the cinematography, which is dazzling. Among the novice actors, however, two of them would have long and successful careers and receive several acting awards. Dominique Pinon ("Curé") was given a Most Promising Actor award at the Césars in 1983 for his performance in Daniel Vigne's *The Return of Martin Guerre* (*Le Retour de Martin Guerre*) before becoming a favorite actor of Jean-Pierre Jeunet, playing important roles notably in *Delicatessen* (1991), *The City of Lost Children* (*La Cité des enfants perdus*, 1995), *Alien: Resurrection* (1997), and *Amélie* (*Le Fabuleux Destin d'Amélie Poulain*, 2001; see Chapter 19). Richard Bohringer (Gorodish), for his part, played in Luc Besson's *Subway* (1985) and won a Best Actor César in 1988 for his performance in *The Grand Highway* (*Le Grand Chemin*) by Jean-Loup Hubert. He also played main roles in Peter Greenaway's *The Cook, the Thief, His Wife & Her Lover* (1989) and in Claude Miller's *The Accompanist* (*L'Accompagnatrice*, 1992).

The Reception

Diva appeared in theaters in mid-March 1981 and was immediately massacred—"shot down in flames," one commentator said—by the film critics. The film was vilified for "the pretentiousness of its conception, its attempt to be grandiose and lyrical, the outrageous hyperrealism of the sets, the frenzied character of the chase scenes and the violence" (Siclier). Rousselot's virtuosity with the camera, although admittedly "remarkable," was called "flashy," with no other purpose than to dazzle the spectators. The director was criticized for "artistic megalomania," his style called blatantly "over-aestheticized," the photography too perfect, the decors too aggressive and artificial, the characters unconvincing, the action trite, the dialogue poor, and so on. Crippled by the negative criticism, the film was taken off the screens nearly everywhere after two weeks.

If the critical reception of *Diva* was largely negative, however, this was not a unanimous position. Many specialists, among the best, recognized the extreme originality of Beineix and applauded it:

> On this improbable plot, nonetheless full of twists and turns and creating a constant tension that excludes any possibility of boredom, Jean-Jacques Beineix constructs a magical universe by combining in an extravagant cocktail the comic book style that fits the plot, the lyrical solemnity of opera, and a hyper-realistic treatment of the image. Improbabilities are of little importance here; do we demand common reality of fairytales? But by endowing the clichés of a crime novel with flamboyant photographic images, the director has invented a modern baroque style that casts a strange spell. (Billard)

Or again:

> What a crazy story! And what audacity, for a new director, to mix genres in such a way! But also, what a successful film, so different from most first films

that are more or less self-absorbed and pale. . . . Here, at least, not only are we not bored, but we are constantly astonished, delightfully bounced back and forth between the wildest romanticism, the most sophisticated surrealism, and the most mischievous humor. Not so bad for a beginning. . . . (Coppermann)

A Cult Film

Defying the film's numerous detractors, a few theaters continued to show it, and word of mouth began to take effect. The public, the young and not so young, began little by little to fill the seats. A year after the film came out, at the 1982 Césars, the critics finally bowed to the spectators' plebiscite: *Diva* won four prizes: Best First Film, Best Photography, Best Sound, and Best Music. The film took off in Paris (800,000 tickets sold), as well as in Belgium, Canada, and the United States, where it hauled in $4.5 million in profits, placing it third on the list of successful French films in the U.S. since 1975. When *Diva* was shown on French television two years later, it was hailed as a masterpiece. Ten years after its premiere, when *Diva* was consecrated by the publication of its screenplay in *L'Avant-Scène Cinéma* (1991), Jacques Leclère remarked, "The youth recognized itself in the taste for the outrageous, in the bizarre decors, in its obsession with recording. And the others? The over twenty-five-year-olds who liked this film were fascinated by the intertwined plots, the perfection of the photography" (205). This was a film, one critic observed retrospectively, that was "particularly in sync with its times" (Parent 196).

Diva and the "Cinéma du Look"

The expression "cinéma du look" was originally meant to denigrate Beineix's film by suggesting a complete lack of depth, supposedly sacrificed to the flashy visual effects. Many film critics, especially those writing for the *Cahiers du cinema*, only had praise for films with political and social messages, films dominated by the naturalism and strong dose of psychological realism that had characterized French cinema during the 1970s; it had become the traditional filmic mode in France.

What was one to make of a film that seemed to thumb its nose at these serious preoccupations, that insolently mixed genres, combining the worlds of opera and pop art, lyrical music and a crime thriller, a little white Parisian mailman and a famous black opera singer? And for this film to be shot superbly, with highly sophisticated camera work, upbeat editing, dazzling images, hyper-saturated colors (blues especially), evoking television commercials and video clips—that took the cake. It was only later in the 1980s that people would clearly understand that Jean-Jacques Beineix had inaugurated a new aesthetics, a new film language in some sense, a cultural mishmash that broke with past practices and reached out, like *Breathless* (*A bout de souffle*) in 1960, to a new generation of young people.

Diva and the "Neo-baroque"

In 1989, in an article since become famous, Raphaël Bassan summarized this decade by showing that Beineix was simply opening the way to a new current of filmmaking that he baptized "neo-baroque" and which includes primarily Beineix and two other film-makers of the 1980s and 1990s, Luc Besson and Leos Carax. Beineix himself made several other films during this period—*The Moon in the Gutter* (*La Lune dans le caniveau*, 1983), *Betty Blue* (*37°2 du matin*, 1986), and *Roselyne and the Lions* (*Roselyne et les Lions*, 1989)—while developing his particular style, attempting to "create the total poetic cinema" that he dreamed of (Parent 256). What all of his films have in common, as many have observed, is the heterogeneity of the registers he uses and the primacy of the visual, whose "neo-baroque" side consists of bizarre and surrealist effects, unusual and futuristic sets in strong colors, or in the confrontation of incongruous elements such as classical music and pop art in *Diva*.

It is false to claim, in any case, that these films lack substance; what has really happened is that "the manner of creating meaning has changed" (Bassan 46). Beineix summarized this renewal of French cinema, sometimes referred to as the "New New Wave," by observing, "For such a long time cinema has been dominated by naturalism.... Well, today ... this reality has been increasingly transcended by color, outsized decors, and a new approach (that is no longer about truth). The author no longer speaks the 'truth,' he just speaks in a different way" (Parent 241). The works of the so-called "cinéma du look," despite their excessive and unrealistic emphasis on aesthetics, are not lacking in substance; all the critics have to do is "peek under the surface, for there is hidden below a very (overly) pessimistic vision of the society of the 1980s" (Bassan 48).

What really rankled the critics about these films, however, as suggested above, is their lack of political content. This is an intolerable failing in certain eyes, since the decade of the 1980s is also the time of Mitterrand, the first socialist president of the Fifth Republic, a period in which the political divide between left and right was particularly deep. Nonetheless, the universe of the "cinéma du look" is loaded with timely social themes. It is peopled by eccentrics, alienated individuals living on the fringes of society, like those who have taken up residence in the tunnels under the Parisian subway in Luc Besson's *Subway* (1985) or the couple in Leos Carax's *The Lovers on the Bridge* (*Les Amants du Pont Neuf*, 1991). It is a world both dreamlike and playful, a world of couples that are either impossible, damned, or in dire straits of some kind, as we see in Beineix's *The Moon in the Gutter* and *Betty Blue* or Carax's *The Lovers on the Bridge* and *Bad Blood* (*Mauvais Sang*, 1986)—a world, finally, in which the police are exceedingly suspect, as in Besson's *Leon: The Professional* (1994) and, of course, *Diva*.

Postmodernism, Politics, and Feminism

In any case, Bassan considered *Diva* to be the "model film, containing all of the themes as well as their aesthetic translation" in the quasi-movement that it had inaugurated (46). A few months after the film's triumph at the Césars in 1982, while the French critics were coming to grips with the fact that they had been sorely mistaken about this film, one of the most influential American literary critics, Frederic Jameson, published an article titled "*Diva* and French Socialism" that begins by calling *Diva* "the first postmodern French film." Jameson relates the release of *Diva* in 1981 to the election of the socialist François Mitterrand the same year and sees in Beineix's film a sort of political allegory in which Jules represents traditional France, while Gorodish embodies post-industrial France. Along with the Gorodish character, the film's postmodernism is expressed, according to Jameson, in the foregrounding of technological reproduction, of surfaces, of hyper-saturated colors, and "postmodern" urban spaces like Jules' loft and Gorodish's vast studio. Bassan elaborates on Jameson's reflections by noting that post-modernism, just as in *Diva*, "puts on the same level lowbrow culture—comic strips, graffiti, commercials—and the elite modes: painting, classical music and films" (46).

Jameson's article focused the attention of the American critical community on Beineix's film, and a swarm of articles soon appeared in journals in the United States, dissecting the film and emphasizing, for example, its pastiche character, its clichés and various caricatures, and its ironic, ludic allusion to earlier films (its intertextuality). In addition, the American feminist critics (Silverman, Dagle, Yervasi, for example) brought their gaze to the film, pillorying the patriarchal nature of the society portrayed in the film, as well as the particular roles played by women. The two critical communities, American and French, thus came together in the course of the decade to reach a consensus on the important innovative role of Beineix's film in the evolution of contemporary cinema.

STUDY GUIDE

What Happens in This Film?

1. What does Jules do during Cynthia Hawkins' performance at the Paris Opera? Who is seated just behind him?

2. Where does Jules live? What does he do when he gets back home that evening?

3. What happens to Nadia, the prostitute? What does she do just before that happens?

4. Where does Jules meet Alba, the young Vietnamese girl? With whom does she live?

5. What revelations did Nadia want to make (according to Krantz, the informer) on the international drug and white slave trade ring? Whose identity does she know?

6. What piece of information essential to the film's plot does Krantz give to the police?

7. What use does Jules make of the Diva's white evening gown when he goes out that evening?

8. Why does the Diva refuse to make records? What does she think of bootlegged recordings?

9. Where does the chase scene involving Jules and the police take place at the end of that sequence?

10. Who comes to the rescue of Jules in the telephone booth? Where do they take Jules into hiding?

11. How is Jules captured by the assassins who work for Saporta? Where do they take him? Who saves his life when the killers are about to push him into the elevator shaft?

12. What does Jules do at the end of the film as an apology to Cynthia?

True or False?

If the statement is false, correct it!

1. Right after getting the opera singer's autograph, Jules steals her evening gown.

2. Jules sees Alba steal a book in a store.

3. While Alba and Jules listen to *La Wally* by Catalani, Krantz works his job in a carnival and then goes home.

4. While Jules is with the prostitute, the Taiwanese men ransack his loft looking for the tape of Cynthia Hawkins' concert.

5. During their "date," Jules and Cynthia walk around Paris, then Jules spends the night on the couch in her apartment.

6. Weinstadt, the Diva's manager, advises her not to make records, even though a recording has been made of her concert.

7. Jules seeks refuge in a prostitute's room, but he leaves abruptly after listening to Nadia's cassette.

8. Gorodish meets the two henchmen of Saporta to offer to give Nadia's cassette to the police commissioner.

9. Saporta burns the photo in the cassette box because it was the only real proof of his guilt.

10. The two Taiwanese take the cassette from Saporta, thinking that it is the tape of Cynthia Hawkins' concert. They leave in Gorodish's white Citroën.

11. When Saporta arrives at Jules' loft, he kills his henchman, l'Antillais, whom he had incriminated in the doctored cassette.

12. Paula and Jules are saved from certain death by the arrival of the police at the last moment.

What Did You Learn in the Introduction?

1. What permits Beineix and his Director of Photography, Philippe Rousselot, to devote most of their budget to the cinematography of their film?

2. How is *Diva* received when it comes out in 1981? What do numerous critics reproach the film and its director?

3. What qualities do the more prescient critics nonetheless recognize in Beineix's work?

4. How does the general public receive this film? What happens at the Césars in 1982?

5. Why was Beineix's film described as the "cinéma du look" when it came out?

6. What kind of films dominated French cinema during the 1970s?

7. What does *Diva* mix together, to the astonishment of many critics?

8. What does *Diva* have in common with Jean-Luc Godard's film, *Breathless* (*A bout de souffle*, 1960)?

9. What did the critic Raphaël Bassan call the new current of filmmaking that Beineix created, along with Luc Besson and Leos Carax? What characterizes this trend, from a stylistic viewpoint?

10. What is lacking in particular in *Diva*, for critics like those of the *Cahiers du cinéma*, at the beginning of the 1980s? Why?

11. What originality does the American literary critic Frederic Jameson attribute to *Diva*?

12. What artistic modes of expression does postmodernism put on the same level, according to Bassan?

Exploring the Film

1. The Beginning of the Film

In a film we distinguish between diegetic music (that emanates from the film's universe) and non-diegetic music (or background music that come from the outside). How would you categorize, in this respect, the classical music that we hear at the very beginning of the film, as Jules arrives at the Opera on his moped? *Review the scene with the film's opening credits and our first view of Jules* (Excerpt 1, 0'20–1'10). When do we understand the source of the music? **How does this affect the viewpoint in the film?** (You will note the same technique when Jules returns home on his moped the first time.)

What camera movements do you note inside the Opera, and how are they also related to the point of view in the film? *Review this sequence* (Excerpt 2, 1'10–5'00). **How are the male gaze and the object of its desire emphasized here?** How is an important element of the plot prepared in this sequence?

2. *The Characters*

+ *Jules and Cynthia Hawkins*

What is surprising about Jules, a young mailman? How may we characterize the relationship that develops between Jules and Cynthia? From what viewpoint is it incongruous? How do you explain it? Is their relationship purely platonic, based solely on Jules' passion for opera and Cynthia's voice in particular? May we speak, as certain commentators do, of a mother-son relationship? Why? Is the fact that Cynthia rehearses *Ave Maria* in Jules' presence significant here? Cite events in the film that justify your opinion. *Review the nocturnal stroll that Jules and Cynthia take through Paris, then the scene the following morning* (Excerpt 3, 53'40–56'40).

Do you think that there is a parallel created between the crime plot, which is about the desire to possess a recording (the voice of Nadia, Saporta's former mistress), and the story of Jules' desire to "possess" the object of his passion through a recording? **What would be the meaning of such a parallel?**

Cynthia tells the reporters that bootlegged recordings are "a theft, a rape!" **What may be the importance of this allusion to sexual violence as regards Jules?**

+ *Gorodish*

How would you describe Gorodish? What aspect of his character is exhibited in the scene where he demonstrates "the Zen in the art of buttering bread": "There is no more knife, no more bread . . . a void!" *Review this scene* (Excerpt 4, 43'50–45'29). **How may we tie this scene to the importance Beineix grants aesthetics (the form) in this film?** Are there any other important elements in this scene?

Beineix said that he saw in Gorodish "the white Knight," and that the white Citroën was "a white horse." **Does this description fit Gorodish?** Why? In ancient theater, an impossible situation sometimes found a happy solution through the use of a special machine that lowered from the heavens a god who solved the problem. This divine character was referred to as a *deus ex machina*. **In what sense may we consider Gorodish to be a *deus ex machina*?**

+ *Alba*

In Delacorta's novel Alba is a very young (thirteen-year-old) white French vamp. In Beineix's film she becomes a somewhat older Vietnamese girl, although no less a little nymph than her literary model. **Why do you think that Beineix changed Alba's character in this manner?**

How would you describe Gorodish's relationship with Alba (he is around forty, she fifteen or sixteen)?

What would you say about Alba's character? **Why does she shoplift all the time?** What trick does she use to steal records? *Review this episode* (Excerpt 5, 13'26–14'30). Does she feel guilty when she steals? Is there any thematic connection between her thefts and other thefts in the film?

In the episode of the lighthouse where they take Jules to recover from his wound, **what aspect of Alba's character is emphasized?** What shot in particular, in the first part of this sequence, only serves to foreground the aesthetic side of the film (visual pleasure)? *Review this sequence* (Excerpt 6, 1h25'00–1h27'45). Why did Beineix choose to put his characters in a lighthouse near the end of the film? (What is the function of a lighthouse?)

3. Living Spaces

✦ Jules' Loft

Review the sequence in which we see Jules' loft for the first time (Excerpt 7, 8'00–10'00). Is there a parallel created with the manner in which the beginning of the Opera sequence is filmed? Describe Jules' loft. **What is striking about its decor? How would you explain Beineix's choice of decor here?** Jules' loft contains very expensive electronic equipment, while Jules, as a young mailman, cannot be earning a lot of money. How do we interpret that? What meaning may we assign to the wrecked luxury cars in the garage next to Jules' loft?

✦ Gorodish's Studio

Review the first sequence in Gorodish's studio (Excerpt 8, 49'20–51'35). Compare Gorodish and Alba's studio to Jules' loft. What is unusual about it? Gorodish is on the floor doing a gigantic puzzle, and we also see a large glass tank filled with water seesawing back and forth, creating little waves. **What might be, in your opinion, the connection between these objects and Gorodish's character?** What auditory and visual elements create a connection between Jules' and Gorodish's lodgings, so different in most respects. **What color is dominant?** Why?

Alba is roller-skating around the studio. **What does this activity seem to emphasize, as regards both the space and Alba's character?**

4. Means of Transport

What are the various means of **transport** that we see in this film? **What is the effect of this proliferation as regards the world that is represented?** The car chase scene is a cliché in police thrillers. **How does Beineix create a pastiche of this cliché?**

What is the function of Jules' moped in the definition of his character? How does it also become a symbol of his passion for Cynthia Hawkins?

What is the symbolism of the white Citroën Traction Avant (front-wheel drive) in this film as it relates to Saporta? *Review the scene in which Saporta drives Gorodish's car* (Excerpt 9, 1h31'10–1h32'20). What else is there in this scene that emphasizes the aesthetic side of the film (provoking the indignation of some film critics)?

5. Morality

How are good and evil presented in this film? Are there characters who represent untainted good or absolute evil? Try to place the various characters on a moral spectrum. Where would you place Jules on this spectrum? And Gorodish? Explain your viewpoint.

6. The Status of Women

How are women represented in *Diva*, particularly in relation to men? Are they living in a clearly patriarchal universe? If you think so, how is male domination expressed in this film? **Could Cynthia Hawkins' refusal to have her voice reproduced (to make records) be an expression of her refusal of women's exploitation by men?** Could the separation of her voice from her body represent a loss of integrity (physical and moral) for her? **Does prostitution become a metaphor in the film?** Does the theme of prostitution make Cynthia's position clearer?

What importance, if any, may we give to the fact that the two female protagonists of this film—Cynthia and Alba—are not white European women? **Does the race of the various women play a role in *Diva*?**

7. Diva *and Fetishism*

Jules steals both Cynthia Hawkins' voice and silk evening gown. The sexual fetishism of silk garments (among other fabrics) has been one of the commonplaces of psychoanalysis since the beginning of the twentieth century as regards male fantasies and the erotic pleasure attached to certain objects. **Where does fetishism play a clear role in Beineix's film? What do these sequences tell us about the nature of Jules' feelings toward Cynthia?**

May one suspect here an allusion to the opposition of "the mama and the whore" (or the Madonna and the whore), like certain feminist critics do? **In what sense is the black prostitute the link between the two main threads of the plot?**

8. *Unreality and Humor*

In the 1970s, harsh social realism was very much in fashion in French cinema. **Many commentators criticized Beineix's film severely, when it first came out, for its lack of "realism," its lack of "seriousness." Do you agree with this criticism? If not, why?**

Beineix said in an interview, "What shocked a lot of people about *Diva* was that we were playing with archetypes" in a humorous, mocking way that was in sync with its times, with "modernity" (Sablon 50). **What are the clichés (stereotypes) and caricatures in this film that signal Beineix's intention to turn his film into a pastiche, if not a parody?** Think of the murders, for example, and of Curé's character. *Review the sequence of the murder of Krantz at the carnival* (Excerpt 10, 27'18–28'25). What may be said about Gorodish in this same context?

9. *The Color Blue*

Beineix admitted that he was inspired, in the making of *Diva*, by the paintings of Jacques Monory (the most prominent artist of the narrative figuration movement in France), and in particular by a series of paintings titled "Icy Operas" ("Opéras glacés," 1974–75). What characterizes the paintings of Monory is the use of the color blue, on the one hand, and, on the other, the representation of scenes and fragments that evoke the American gangster film of the 1930s, such as Howard Hawks' *Scarface*. These works were sometimes referred to as "cinematographic narratives on canvas." His works are bathed in violence and include a series of twenty-eight paintings titled "The Murders" ("Les Meurtres," 1968–69). These canvasses, some of them gigantic, often show a gangster brandishing a revolver or machine gun, a large American car from the 1950s or 1960s ("une belle Américaine"), rooms, women in a state of panic, wild beasts, etc.—most of them painted in an iridescent blue. Some art critics think that blue represents dreams in Monory's painting and serves to moderate the cruelty of the world that is shown in his works. As for Monory, he suggests that the blue provides a sort of unity to an otherwise very fragmented body of work. **Look up "Jacques Monory" on the internet to see an example of his paintings.**

Where do we see the color blue in *Diva***?** In your opinion, what is the function (or meaning) of this color in the film? **With which character is this color most closely associated? Why?** What connection might Beineix's film have with Monory's painting, which is often tied to the pop art movement in Europe?

10. The Work of Art and Its Reproduction

The German philosopher Walter Benjamin wrote a now famous essay titled "The Work of Art in the Age of Mechanical Reproduction" (1939). In this text he shares some ideas on the status of the reproduction of a work of art—painting, statues, structures—in relation to the original object: a photograph, for example, or a recording. Benjamin asserts, notably, that the reproduced version of an artwork loses the "authenticity" of the original, as well as its uniqueness; we see the "withering" of the "aura" of this work, which is devalued, desacralized even, by the limitless copies that can be made of it. On the other hand, this proliferation favors the development of art for the masses, the general public.

What connection might there be between Benjamin's thesis and *Diva* **(whether or not Beineix was aware of it), especially concerning Cynthia and Jules?** Cynthia maintains that "the concert is an exceptional moment for the artist and for the spectator. It is a unique moment." Given the growing importance of technology in the modern world, is Cynthia's position just a diva's whim, as one of the journalists suggests at the press conference in the film? **What effect does Cynthia's attitude have on the film's plot?**

11. The Denouement

How do you interpret the denouement of the film? At the end of Delacorta's novel, Jules and Cynthia make love on the floor while listening to the bootlegged recording. **Does the film suggest that Jules and Cynthia are going to become lovers or, rather, that their relationship is purely "spiritual"?** *Review the denouement* (Excerpt 11, 1h51'00–1h55'30). Is Cynthia united with Jules solely as the spectator (listener) of her own voice? **Does the ending suggest anything as regards Cynthia's attitude toward the recording of her voice and the production of records?** The singer's voice (just like a book, a painting, a symphony, etc.) is a work of art. **What is the fate of any work of art once it is made public?** Has Cynthia become aware of this?

Jean-Jacques Beineix's Filmography

1981   *Diva*

1983   *The Moon in the Gutter (La Lune dans le caniveau)*

1986   *Betty Blue (37°2 le matin)*

1989   *Roselyne et les Lions*

1992   *IP5: The Island of Pachyderms (IP5: L'île aux pachydermes)*

1994   *Otaku* (documentary)

2001   *Mortel Transfert*

2002   *Loft Paradoxe* (television documentary)

2013   *The Gauls beyond Myth* (*Les Gaulois au-delà du mythe*, television documentary)

Works Consulted

Bassan, Raphaël. "Trois néobaroques français: Beineix, Besson, Carax, de *Diva* au *Grand Bleu*." *La Revue du cinéma* 448 (1989): 44–50.

Bates, Robin. "Alienation in *Diva*: Two Kinds of Rape." *Holding the Vision: Essays on Film*. Proceedings of the First Annual Film Conference of Kent State University. Kent, OH: International Film Society, 1983. 27–31.

Beineix, Jean-Jacques, dir. *Diva*. Meridian Collection, 2008.

———. *Diva* (screenplay). *L'Avant-Scène Cinéma* 407 (1 Dec. 1991): 9–85.

Benjamin, Walter. *The Work of Art in the Age of Mechanical Reproduction*. Accessed 2 June 2017.<http://berk-edu.com/VisualStudies/readingList/06b_benjamin-work%20of%20art%20in%20the%20age%20of%20mechanical%20reproduction.pdf>.

Bescos, José-M. "Diva." *Pariscope*, 25 Mar. 1981: n. pag.

Billard, Pierre. "Ne ratons pas le premier métro." *Le Point*, 23 Mar. 1981: 23.

Bosseno, Christian. "Diva." *Revue du cinéma* 361 (May 1981): 30.

Carcassonne, Philippe. "Diva." *Cinématographe* 66 (Mar.–Apr. 1981): 76.

Coppermann, Annie. "La Diva." *Les Echos*, 17 Mar. 1981: 19.

Cornet, Philippe. "Entretien avec Jean-Jacques Beineix." *Amis du film, cinéma et télévision* 312–13 (1982): 5–6.

Cuel, François. "Diva." *Cinématographe* 66 (Mar.–Apr. 1981): 76.

Dagle, Joan. "Effacing Race: The Discourse on Gender in *Diva*." *Post Script* 10.2 (Winter 1991): 26–35.

Delacorta [Daniel Odier]. *Diva*. Paris: Seghers, 1979.

Devarrieux, Claire. "La Métaphore de l'alpiniste." *Le Monde*, 9 Apr. 1981: n. pag.

Figgis, Mike. "Jean-Jacques Beineix: Interview." *Hollywood Film-Makers on Film-Making*. Ed. Mike Figgis. London: Faber & Faber, 1999. 68–76.

Forbes, Jill. *The Cinema in France after the New Wave*. Bloomington: Indiana UP, 1994.

Garrity, Henry. "Pop-Culture Love in *Diva*; Objects as Icon, Index, and Syntagma." *Sex and Love in Motion Pictures*. Proceedings of the Second Annual Film Conference of Kent State University (11 Apr. 1984). Kent, OH, Romance Languages Dept. 47–51.

Hagen, W. M. "Performance Space in *Diva*." *Literature and Film Quarterly* 16.3 (1988): 155–59.

Higbee, Will. "Diva." *The Cinema of France*. Ed. Phil Powrie. London: Wallflower, 2006. 152–62.

Jameson, Frederic. "Diva and French Socialism." *Signatures of the Visible*. New York: Routledge, 1992 (original article: "On Diva." *Social Text* 6 [Autumn 1982]: 55–62).

Kael, Pauline. "Rhapsody in Blue." *The New Yorker*, 19 Apr. 1982: 165–68.

Kelly, Ernece B. "*Diva*. High Tech Sexual Politics." *Jump Cut* 29 (Feb. 1984): 39–40.

Kurk, Katherine. "When Orpheus Met *Diva*." *Kentucky Philological Review* 19 (2005): 30–35.

Leclère, Jacques. "Chant et Contrechamp." *L'Avant-Scène Cinéma* 407 (1 Dec. 1991): 205.

Leirens, Jean. "*Diva*." *Amis du film, cinéma et télévision* 312–13 (1982): 4.

Parent, Denis. *Jean-Jacques Beineix. Version originale*. Paris: Barrault-Studio, 1989.

Powrie, Phil. *French Cinema in the 1980s*. Oxford, UK: Clarendon, 1997.

Sablon, Jean-Luc. "Entretien. Jean-Jacques Beineix. L'adversaire, c'est soi." *La Revue du cinéma* 448 (1989): 49–53.

Saint Angel, Eric de. "Diva chez soi." *Le Matin*, 25 Dec. 1984: n. pag.

Sarran, Patrice de. "*Diva*. Belles images sur écran glacé." *La Nouvelle République du Centre-Ouest* 12 June 1981: n. pag.

Siclier, Jacques. "*Diva* de Jean-Jacques Beineix." *Le Monde*, 18 Mar. 1981: n. pag.

Silverman, Kaja. *The Acoustic Mirror: The Female Voice in Psychoanalysis and Cinema*. Bloomington: Indiana UP, 1988.

Tranchant, Marie-Noëlle. "La Passion au cinéma selon Jean-Jacques Beineix." *Le Figaro*, 8 Mar. 1982: n. pag.

Vaugeois, Gérard. "Diva." *L'Humanité*, 20 Mar. 1981: n. pag.

White, Mimi. "They All Sing . . . : Voice, Body, and Representation in *Diva*." *Literature and Psychology* 34.4 (1988): 33–43.

Yervasi, Carina L. "Capturing the Elusive Representations in Beineix's *Diva*." *Literature Film Quarterly* 21.1 (Jan. 1993): 38–46.

Zavaradek, Mas'ud. "Diva." *Film Quarterly* 36.3 (1983): 54–59.

12

Michael Haneke

Hidden (Caché)

(2005)

Michel Haneke, *Caché*: The confrontation between Georges (Daniel Auteuil) and the cyclist (Diouc Koma).

Director. . . . . Michael Haneke
Screenplay. . . . . Michael Haneke
Director of Photography . . . . Christian Berger
Film Editors . . . . Michael Hudecek, Nadine Muse
Sound . . . . Jean-Paul Mugel
Art Directors . . . . Emmanuel De Chauvigny, Christoph Kanter
Original Music . . . . Ralph Rieckermann
Costumes . . . . Lisy Christl
Continuity . . . . .Jean-Baptiste Filleau
Producers . . . . Margaret Ménégoz, Veit Heiduschka
Length. 1h57

199

Cast

Daniel Auteuil (*Georges Laurent*), Juliette Binoche (*Anne Laurent*), Maurice Bénichou (*Majid*), Annie Girardot (*Georges' mother*), Lester Makedonsky (*Pierrot Laurent*), Daniel Duval (*Pierre, the Laurents' best friend*), Nathalie Richard (*Mathilde, Pierre's wife*), Walid Afkir (*Majid's son*), Bernard Le Coq (*Georges' editor-in-chief*), Denis Podalydès (*Yvon, a friend of the Laurents*), Hugo Flamigni (*Georges as a child*), Malik Nait Djoudi (*Majid as a child*), Diouc Koma (*the cyclist*)

Story

Georges and Anne Laurent, a hip Parisian bourgeois couple, live quietly with their twelve-year-old son Pierrot in an elegant house in the eighteenth arrondissement. He is the star of a weekly literary program on television (think Bernard Pivot), while she works for a book publisher. They have a group of cultivated, intelligent, witty friends. One day they receive an anonymous videotape that shows the front of their house as if it were filmed by a surveillance camera placed in the middle of the little street that is just across from their abode. A second cassette arrives, accompanied by a very rough sketch, as if drawn by a small child, showing a head with blood gushing from the mouth. Other cassettes soon arrive, featuring the property where Georges grew up, then a street, a hall in a low-income housing building, and a door in this hall. At the same time, there are also anonymous telephone calls that disturb the couple's life and add to their anxiety.

Since the police refuse to intervene, Georges leads his own investigation, discovering in the process childhood memories that had been buried for decades—since the period of the Algerian war more precisely—very painful, shameful memories that he is now forced to face. But who is the author of the videotapes and the telephone calls? What does this individual want? This vague and apparently gratuitous threat creates persistent tension in the Laurent home, and the formerly solid couple begins to come apart. Their son Pierrot, a well-behaved tranquil adolescent up to now, begins to act up, inexplicably. Suspicion pervades the home, both as regards the outside threat from the tapes as well as between the members of the family.

The Director

Born on March 23, 1942, in Munich, his father German and his mother Austrian, Michael Haneke grew up in a little town near Vienna. Although as an adolescent he had a passion for literature and classical music, he revolted against school (against everything, he says), which did not prevent him from toying with the idea of becoming a pastor, earning his high school diploma, and enrolling in philosophy at the University of Vienna where he also studied psychology. Near the end of his studies, he began to write book reviews for the radio, as well as radio plays and film reviews for the newspapers, before finding a full-time position in German television assisting in the selection and production of telefilms (Cieutat and Rouyer 26). It is there in Baden-Baden that Haneke began to direct plays, and he would spend the next twenty years as a theater director while at the same time making films (around ten of them) for television.

At the age of forty-six, in 1989, he directed his first film for the big screen, *The Seventh Continent* (*Le Septième Continent*), the first installment of what would come to be known as the "trilogy of emotional glaciation." Haneke's films often feature, indeed, people who seem to be devoid of any kind of human sentiment, which allows them to commit horrifying acts. *The Seventh Continent*, shot on an exceedingly spare budget, tells the true story of a family—father, mother, and small daughter—that falls victim to a deep malaise that deprives them of any taste for life and leads them to a collective suicide after the systematic destruction of their home (with a sledgehammer, axe, and chainsaw). The husband and wife are named Georg and Anna, their daughter Evi. Haneke would give roughly the same names to the characters in several of his following films, Frenchifying them when necessary into Georges Laurent, Anne Laurent, and Eve. If there is a son, he is most often named Ben (or Benny). Haneke explains this rather curious practice by saying, simply, "I have little imagination. I choose short, simple names because cinema, for me, is a realistic art. . ." (Widemann).

Haneke followed *The Seventh Continent* with two other films of the same tenor: *Benny's Video* (1992) and *71 Fragments of a Chronology of Chance* (1994). The first film is about a teenager obsessed with videos who films the slaughter of a pig on a farm, then uses it as a source of inspiration to kill in cold-blood a girl he had invited to his home, "just to see how it felt to do that." Like the members of the family in *The Seventh Continent*, he seems devoid of emotion, insensitive to the horror of his act. In the third film of the "trilogy" Haneke shows an aggravated student who calmly shoots down a crowd of people in a bank before blowing his own brains out in his car. All of these films are shot through with audiovisual images, especially television news concerning, for the most part, foreign wars and other forms of violence and human suffering in the Third World.

It is however with his fourth film, *Funny Games*, a grotesque and vaguely Brechtian parody of Hollywood horror films, that Hanecke began to be seriously noticed in the world of cinema. Selected for the Cannes Film Festival in 1997, *Funny Games* is the story of a bourgeois Austrian family that is held prisoner and tortured in its vacation home by a pair of psychopaths, themselves bourgeois, who force them to participate in sadistic games. To break the codes of the genre, Haneke has the leader of the psychopathic couple occasionally look directly into the camera (that is, directly into the eyes of the spectators), as if he were putting the spectator on his side and associating him or her with his revolting acts. Although at the extreme limit of what is bearable, this film on gratuitous violence was nominated for the Palme d'Or at Cannes and won several important awards in other international film festivals. Ten years later, in 2007, Haneke himself directed an American remake of *Funny Games* starring Naomi Watts and Tim Roth.

After becoming a film professor at the University of Vienna (where he tries, notably, to teach his students how images can manipulate spectators), Haneke then began his career in France with a film promoted zealously by the actor Juliette Binoche, a top star of French cinema who was dying to make a film with the Austrian director. This film would be *Code Unknown* (*Code inconnu: récit incomplet de divers voyages*, 2000), whose background is the war in Kosovo; it was the beginning of a new cycle of films that Haneke calls "the world war" (Gutman 5). Likewise nominated for the Palme d'Or at the Cannes Film Festival, where it won the Prize of the Ecumenical Jury, *Code Unknown* features the personal stories of several people of different nationalities and cultures who are brought together around a banal incident that changes their respective lives. The international consecration of Haneke will not come, however, until his next French film, *The Piano Teacher* (*La Pianiste*, 2001), based on the novel of the same name by the Austrian novelist Elfriede Jelinek, the future winner of the Nobel Prize for literature. The protagonist, a piano teacher in Vienna, is played by another top star of French cinema, Isabelle Huppert. The film won numerous prizes at Cannes, including the Grand Prix du Jury, and throughout the world, as well as a Best Supporting Actress César for Annie Girardot, who would play Georges' mother in *Caché* a few years later. As for Huppert, her performance in the main role of *La Pianiste* would be rewarded with a dozen Best Actress prizes, including at Cannes, and a Best Actress nomination at the Césars.

Haneke's following film, also starring Huppert, *Time of the Wolf* (*Le Temps du loup*, 2003), is a dystopian thriller in which the action takes place in a future world whose environment has been completely destroyed. It was the next film, however, *Caché* (*Hidden*, 2005), featuring two of the biggest stars in France—Daniel Auteuil and Juliette Binoche—that definitively established Haneke's international reputation as a filmmaker. The film won prizes everywhere it was shown, dozens of awards and nominations, including a Best Director prize and two additional prizes at Cannes, as well as numerous awards for Best Film, Best Foreign Film, and Best Screenplay (written by Haneke himself, as he does all of his films). A few years later, with his success growing ever greater, Haneke won the Palme d'Or at Cannes for both *The White Ribbon* (*Le Ruban blanc*, 2009) and *Love* (*Amour*, 2012).

Haneke has been interviewed many times, and the questions and answers virtually always focus on the same subjects: representation of violence, the manipulative role of audiovisual images in contemporary life, the emotional void of his characters, and the deep pessimism of his films. Haneke does not deny a certain fascination with violence and cruelty, but he is, as he says, "more moved by pain and suffering. I feel compelled as an 'artist' to keep my eyes open. All the more so since ninety-eight percent of films have the opposite objective of anaesthetizing the spectator" (Allion 8). Hanecke wants the spectator to keep her/his eyes open too, to make a personal effort to lend meaning to the film: "The ideal is for spectators to finish the film in their head as they see fit. It is essential that the film ask more questions than it answers, otherwise it is of no interest" (Allion 10).

The Origin and Making of the Film

Haneke's original plan was, as he tells it, to "tell the story of a boy who had denounced another boy out of jealousy before being confronted with his past [as an adult] and feeling even more guilty than before" (Cieutat and Rouyer 239). To this story of individual culpability was attached another story which is about collective culpability and bad conscience. On October 17, 2001, when he was writing the screenplay of his film, Haneke saw on Arte (the Franco-German television channel) a British documentary from 1992, *Drowning by Bullets*, by Philip Brooks and Alan Hayling. This film was broadcast on the fortieth anniversary of the tragic events of October 17, 1961, that occurred toward the end of the Algerian War (1956–62; on this conflict, see "The Context: the Algerian War," Chapter 15) and in which numerous Algerians—estimates of the number of victims vary from 30 to 200—died or disappeared.

Called by the National Liberation Front (FLN) that represented the revolutionaries in Algeria to demonstrate in Paris against a curfew imposed on the Algerians by the now infamous Police Commissioner Maurice Papon, tens of thousands of Algerians dressed in suits and ties marched peacefully in the streets. Thousands of policemen opened fire on the crowd of demonstrators, throwing the bodies of the victims in the Seine near the Saint-Michel Bridge and in the Canal Saint-Martin. In addition, 200 Algerians simply disappeared and 12,000 were arrested, 2,000 of whom were deported and interned in a concentration camp in Algeria (Celik 64, Crowley 277).

This massive attack on immigrants (*ratonnade*) was virtually hidden from the public at the time owing to the censorship of the press during the war in Algeria. The police publicly announced only two deaths and 164 wounded among the demonstrators, and the truth of the massacre was only disclosed by the French government more than twenty-five years later, in 1988. A public survey published the same day as the program on Arte showed that the majority of the French knew nothing about this event (Crowley 269). The questions of guilt and responsibility, however, remained under the carpet: hidden. A documentary film made in 2011 by Yasmina Adi for the fiftieth anniversary of this event, *Here We Drown Algerians: October 17, 1961* (*Ici on noie les Algériens, 17 octobre 1961*, nominated for the Best Documentary César), offers an additional perspective on all of the circumstances of this horrific incident.

Haneke understood that he could put this national tragedy to use in his film: "I saw that this could be a basis for the traumatism I needed" (Allion 11), that is, a collective traumatism that would be related to the personal one that had been repressed by his protagonist. However, he adds, "it was essential that no one think that the film was attacking France in particular, since it was meant to be universal. Every country has its shameful secrets. And Austria has much blame to accept concerning the Nazi period" (Allion 11). That would not prevent certain critics from raking Haneke over the coals for daring, as a foreigner, to recall this ignominious national memory. (See "Critical Reception" below.)

Caché is Haneke's fourth French film. Like *Code Unknown*, it was filmed in Paris, but in high-definition video, the first time that the Austrian cineaste had used a digital camera for the big screen. This choice was dictated by the subject of his film, which involves videotapes whose goal is to harass the protagonist and ruin his career. Since the director wanted to create confusion (to "dupe the spectator," as he says) between the images that are part of the film's principal narrative level on the one hand and those of the video recordings on the other, he was forced to use video for both: the difference in texture between celluloid film and digital recordings would have been too easy to spot by the spectators. He said, moreover, that filming digitally "presented enormous technical problems," given the limitations of the medium at that time (Champenois). It was as if they had returned to the beginning of the talkies, when cameras had to be enclosed in a separate chamber to mute the noise they made: "For example, the digital camera's fan made a terrible racket. We had to put a blanket over it, but then it got too hot, so we had to stop shooting regularly to let it cool down" (Cieutat and Rouyer 244).

When you make a film, you have to choose between the fragmentation of the action into relatively short shots in which editing (*montage*) plays a primary role (as in Jean-Luc Godard's 1960 classic *Breathless/À bout de souffle*) or into lengthier takes in which the organization of the action within the shot (mise en scène) takes precedence over the editing (as in Jean Renoir's films). Michael Haneke, for his part, prefers lengthy takes (*plans-séquences*), sometimes extremely lengthy, and it is a dominant formal trait of his films. In *Caché* we see a considerable number of lengthy takes—beginning with the very first shot, a static shot of the front of the Laurent house.

Haneke has often spoken of this preference in his interviews. He explains that the length of the shots is one of the essential elements that constitute the difference between television and cinema. Television commercials, for instance, tend to be very rapid; the goal is not to lead spectators to reflect but to beguile them, to entice them to buy such and such a product. The aesthetics of commercials has, moreover, pervaded television programs in general. The lengthy take, on the other hand, gives time to reflect and to understand what one is seeing, not only on the intellectual level, Haneke insists, but also on the emotional plane (Sharrett). Haneke's long static shots are thus intended to highlight not only what is being filmed but also the element of time, which is necessary in his opinion to allow the spectators' emotions to play out—and to trouble the spectators, since they are not accustomed to this slow rhythm.

Although a past master in the art of manipulating the spectator, Haneke also prefers the *plan-séquence*, paradoxically, because it is less manipulative insofar as it tinkers less with time than does the *montage* approach: the action takes place in "real" time. Generally, Haneke's concept of the lengthy take is consistent with the positions of the famous film theorist André Bazin. An apostle of the *plan-séquence* and depth of field, Bazin saw therein, using as an example the Italian Neorealists, a way to render the spectator more responsible and to help cinema better represent reality—while at the same time emphasizing the very ambiguity of that "reality," which is one of the most striking traits of Haneke's films (73–80).

As regards film music, Haneke rejects the use of background (mood) music, whose only goal, in his opinion, is to manipulate the spectators' emotions and hide certain weaknesses in the film. Following the example of Robert Bresson, and in the interest of realism, he only uses diegetic music in his films (as when a character turns on the radio, for example), and he follows this practice in *Caché*, where music is virtually absent.

The Actors

Haneke could have made *Caché* in any country he chose, but he preferred shooting in France, he said, because he wanted to "benefit from the quality of the French actors and their international fame" (Cieutat and Rouyer 240). He states frankly, for instance, that he made *Caché* in large part to be able to work with Daniel Auteuil, and that he wrote the role of Georges expressly for him. It was his first collaboration with Auteuil (born in French Algeria in 1950), and he sings his praises endlessly: "He is extraordinary in every genre, always has this secretive reticent style and never overplays his part. He produces a great effect with minimal apparent effort" (Campion). For Haneke, he is simply "the best French actor of his generation" (Cieutat and Rouyer 241). Like many directors, Haneke likes to work regularly with the same actors: "When we know each other and get along well, we begin a film with the same level of understanding" (Borde). He had already worked with Juliette Binoche in *Code Unknown*, with Annie Girardot (Georges' mother) in *The Piano Teacher*, and twice with Maurice Bénichou (the older Majid) in *Code Unknown* and *Time of the Wolf*.

When they were chosen to play the protagonists of *Caché*, Auteuil and Binoche were already among the most famous actors of their generation in France. Auteuil's activity was stupifying—three films the same year he made *Caché*, another ready to be released in the first few months of the following year, and still another in preparation—and he already had acted in seventy films. He won two Best Actor Césars for *Jean de*

Florette (1986) and *The Girl on the Bridge* (*La Fille sur le pont*, 1999), a Best Actor prize at Cannes in 1996 for *The Eighth Day* (*Le Huitième Jour*), and numerous best actor awards in other festivals for *A Heart in Winter* (*Un coeur en hiver*, 1992), *Sade* (2000), *The Widow of Saint-Pierre* (*La Veuve de Saint-Pierre*, 2000), and *The Closet* (*Le Placard*, 2001). For his performance in *Caché* he received the Best Actor prize at the European Film Awards of 2005.

Born in 1964, Binoche was already, well before *Caché*, a *monstre sacré* of French cinema, the best-paid actor in France. To work with Haneke again, she accepted a modest check for 150,000 euros instead of the usual 800,000 or 900,000 that she received for most of her films at this time. She had received a Best Actress nomination at the Césars for her very first important role, in André Téchiné's *Rendez-vous* (1985). Soon known as "la Binoche" to the French public, she finally won this prize at the European Film Awards of 1991 for her role in Leos Carax's *The Lovers on the Bridge* (*Les Amants du Pont-Neuf*) before earning the Best Actress César in 1993, as well as the same awards at the Venice and Berlin film festivals, for Krzystof Kieslowski's *Three Colors: Blue*. She achieved worldwide fame three years later with the Best Supporting Actress Oscar for the British film *The English Patient* (1996), directed by Anthony Minghella. The awards continued to rain down on Binoche for her performances in Lasse Halström's *Chocolat* (2000), Abbas Kiarostami's *Certified Copy* (*Copie conforme*, 2010, another Best Actress prize at Cannes), and, more recently, Olivier Assayas' *Clouds of Sils Maria* (2014)—in all around thirty prizes and as many additional nominations.

Annie Girardot, who passed away in 2011, had been a major star of French cinema since the 1960s, having played in around 150 films and earned a dozen acting prizes, including three Césars—most recently for the Best Supporting Actress in *The Piano Teacher* by Michael Haneke in 2001. Maurice Bénichou, born in Algeria like Daniel Auteuil (but of North African origin), was a theater actor and director and one of the favorite actors of the famous British director Peter Brooks. From the beginning of the 1970s, he played around seventy roles in films and television series. Generally restricted to minor roles—like Dominique Bretodeau, the owner of the little tin box of souvenirs found by the heroine of Jean-Pierre Jeunet's *Amélie* (2001; see Chap. 19)—he has a natural style of acting that struck Haneke: "What he liked about me," remarks Bénichou, "was not that I was such a brilliant actor, but rather that he got the impression that I wasn't acting at all, that I behaved like I was at home. He really liked that" (Rouchy). To play the role of Majid, he thought of his own father, a "humble" immigrant like Majid: "Majid is the type of fellow that we meet everywhere around here, near the Bouffes du Nord theater, along the Boulevard de La Chapelle: a poor sap, a good guy to be sure, intelligent, but who doesn't have the financial means to do anything" (Rouchy). Bénichou received a Best Supporting Actor nomination at the 2006 Césars for his performance in *Caché*, his third film with Haneke.

The Reception

After meeting a huge success—twenty-nine awards, twenty-five nominations—in international festivals throughout the world, *Caché* was released in theaters on October 5, 2005. Even before its presentation at the Cannes Film Festival in May, the opinions in the press were varied. Haneke's films, which pick at scabs on modern Western society, rarely leave spectators indifferent. The critics are in agreement, however, on one point:

the remarkable mastery of Haneke and the meticulousness of the direction of *Caché*. These are terms that are repeated over and over again. Gorin says, for example, that Haneke is "a filmmaker who shows mastery," adding that "his talent lies in injecting into sophisticated situations an elementary, if not to say primary, malaise that hits you in both the mind and the gut."

The critical commentaries, while generally positive, betray a certain ambivalence, as we see in Mérigeau's observations: "Haneke persists in revealing the mechanisms of a modern society obsessed with its own fears, with a mastery that puts some off and charms others" ("Obsessionnel Haneke"). Tranchant exhibits the same reservations, despite her admiration: "Haneke has a pure geometric spirit. He ferrets out of Georges' childhood a repressed, hidden wrong that becomes an emblem of a collective misdeed committed by France against Algeria. . . . The extremely precise direction yields a theoretical demonstration rather than a human truth. Haneke has great mastery, but God is it dry!"

Some commentators are nonetheless much less ambivalent, like Douin, who praises Haneke's work unreservedly: "This splendid, vertiginous film is rich in reflections on eternally gaping childhood wounds, the solitude experienced when confronted by internal demons, the ravages of secrets on the relationship of a couple, the way in which guilt gnaws at a person, the revenge of the repressed"; "*Caché* emphasizes the necessity for an individual to undertake a therapeutic flashback and, by extension, for a people to look its past squarely in the eye. This poignant individual drama takes on a universal dimension." And Quenin adds, "This is M.H.'s forte: revealing by cinema what we do not wish to see. What is fascinating in this work (and here we should also mention *The Piano Teacher* and *Code Unknown*) is the way the treatment of reality is turned into an artistic, philosophical, and moral endeavor. Moral especially" (16).

The unabashed detractors are often aggressive and ironical, criticizing the Austrian filmmaker either for the cruelty of the film or for its form (the extremely lengthy static shots), if it is not for a foreigner having the nerve to bring up a memory that is extremely painful for France: "But more than a meticulous directing job, it is the admission of a cineaste who revels in puerile cruelty, in framing shots, in playing with time, and in multiplying mirrors" (Rehm 14); "Anti-France, did you say anti-France? Trussed up in the hyper-cerebral manipulations and ultra-political correctness of their director, the actors, with the exception of Maurice Bénichou, strive to show as little emotion as possible. Yes, that's right—if you want to put up with bouts of indignation alternating with interminable stretches of boredom, *Caché* is a film for you" (Laurent 15–16); and to finish, this ironic comment, a trifle nasty, from Emmanuel Hecht: "It is a film on guilt and the manipulation of images. In Vienna Haneke teaches his students the tricks of the propaganda film trade, from Eisenstein to Riefenstahl. He will certainly be grateful to the spectators for not falling victim to his own tricks, that is, his attempt to transform Austrian bad conscience into whining over the tribulations of the Third World."

STUDY GUIDE

What Happens in This Film?

1. What does the first shot of the film show? Who is watching here (and where) at the same time as the spectators?

2. What drawing is in the envelope with the second videotape?

3. What is striking about the very brief shots in which we see the little North African boy (Majid young)?

4. What do the Laurents see on the videotape that arrives during the dinner with their friends?

5. What nightmare does Georges have during the night he spends at his mother's house.

6. What does the last videotape show?

7. Why does Anne become angry when Georges refuses to reveal the identity of the person he suspects of having made the tapes?

8. Of what is Georges convinced when he visits Majid?

9. Why is Georges forced to tell his wife the truth about his visit with Majid?

10. Why does Georges lead the police to Majid's apartment?

11. What did Majid do the last time Georges went to his apartment?

12. Who comes to see Georges at his place of work?

True or False?

If the statement is false, correct it!

1. The first videotape arrived in the mail.

2. Georges is the star of a variety show on television.

3. Upon leaving the police station, Georges has an argument with a taxi driver.

4. Pierrot receives a videotape at his school.

5. The third tape is accompanied by a child's drawing of a rooster whose neck is bloody.

6. By deciphering the name of a street, Georges and Anne succeed in locating the neighborhood of the housing project shown on the tape.

7. Majid tells Georges that he knows why he has come to see him.

8. The editor-in-chief of Georges' television show is worried about the latter's career if the story of the tapes is made public.

9. Pierrot sleeps over at a friend's house without telling his parents.

10. Georges' parents sent little Majid away because Georges had lied about him.

11. At the end of the film there is a flashback in which we see the scene where Georges lies about Majid to his parents.

12. In the final shot of the film, before the beginning of the end credits, Pierrot only talks to his friends before leaving.

What Did You Learn in the Introduction?

1. How did Haneke learn to direct before beginning to make films for the cinema?

2. What label was given to his first three films, *The Seventh Continent, Benny's Video*, and *71 Fragments of a Chronology of Chance*? Why were they given this label?

3. What names does Haneke repeatedly give his main characters?

4. What parody of horror films was remade subsequently in the United States, by Haneke himself?

5. What does Haneke make a special effort to teach his students at the University of Vienna?

6. What two very big stars of current French cinema have played in Haneke's films? What stars have won Best Actress prizes at the Cannes Film Festival for their roles in a Haneke film (and for which film)?

7. What are the constant themes of Haneke's films, including those he made in France?

8. What documentary did Haneke see on the Franco-German television channel Arte that gave him material for the screenplay of *Caché*? What tragic event took place in October 1961?

9. Why did Haneke feel obliged to make his whole film in high definition digital video rather than with normal film?

10. Why does Haneke prefer lengthy takes rather than shorter shots and more editing? What difference does he point out in this respect as regards cinema and television?

11. What award brought worldwide fame to Juliette Binoche, and for which film?

12. What do most critics admire about Haneke's work, even if they have reservations about the content of his films? What do they reproach him for?

Exploring the Film

1. The Title of the Film

What does the title of the film *Caché* refer to? **What is "hidden"?** Are there several possible interpretations of this title?

2. The Beginning of the Film

How does the director trick—or manipulate—us in the first shot? What may we say about the dialogue in this shot (and in the following shot) as regards the image we are watching? What do we hear? Where is this voice-over coming from? *Review this scene* (Excerpt 1, 0'12–3'06).

In speaking of the first shot, Haneke says, "From the very beginning, I wanted the spectator to realize to what extent he could be a victim of images" (Allion 11). What does he mean? When and how do we understand clearly the nature of the images we are watching? **What is the effect of this deceptive shot on our attitude toward the other images in the film?** (What kind of attitude does Haneke seem to wish to foster?) *Review the shot in which we see the front of the Laurent home at night* (Excerpt 2, 9'20–11'56). Can we know if we are watching images of the film or if it is a videotape? When do we learn the truth about this? **Are there other shots in this film that deceive the spectator or leave us in doubt?**

3. The Characters

+ *Georges and Anne Laurent: the family*

What are Georges' and Anne's professions? How would you describe their cultural level? *Review the scene in which Georges and Anne sit down to dinner* (Excerpt 3, 6'40–7'00). **What elements of the decor of this home indicate the cultural level of its inhabitants?** Is bourgeois culture a target in this film? Is it presented in a positive or negative manner—or neutrally? What relationship may we observe between the decor of the Laurents' dining room and that of the set of Georges' television program? **What may be implied here?**

Ever since the period of his Austrian films, Haneke has kept the same names for his couples (Georges and Anne) and their children. What explanation might we give to this practice? For certain critics (Niessen 192), it targets the spectator to some extent. How, in your opinion?

Try to describe Georges' character. Does he behave like a normal adult? Does he show particular courage or cowardice in the film? **What do you think of the incident with the cyclist, when Georges and Anne leave the police station?** Does it reveal anything about Georges' character? Is he guilty of racism here? *Review this scene* (Excerpt 4, 16'50–17'55).

In typical films for the general public, the spectators tend to identify with the main character, the "hero" of the film. **Do you identify with Georges, or do you find yourself inclined to judge or condemn him?** Explain.

How would you describe the relationship between Georges and Anne? Affectionate? Hostile? Indifferent? Is Anne an unfaithful wife? In his films Haneke often depicts families in crisis, couples falling apart. He maintains that the family, at least in Western society, is at the origin of all conflicts, that it is the theater of a "miniature war" that can be as murderous as what we normally refer to as war (Sharrett). **Do you think that this negative reflection on the family is relevant to the family that is shown in** *Caché? Review the scene in which Georges refuses to share with Anne his suspicions regarding the author of the videotapes* (Excerpt 5, 43'30–46'03).

+ *Pierrot*

How would you describe Pierrot's behavior in general? And his relationship with his parents? Does he seem to have any preference concerning his father and mother?

Why does Pierrot sleep over at a friend's house without letting his parents know? What does he seem to reproach his mother for when he returns the next morning? Do you think he is right? Why? *Review the scene in which Anne confides in Pierre* (Excerpt 6, 1h09'21–1h10'16) *and the scene with her son* (Excerpt 7, 1h22'40–1h25'45).

Anne's boss is named "Pierre," and her son is named "Pierrot." Haneke tells us that "it is not by chance that Pierrot has the same name as Pierre" (Toubiana). What does he mean by that? **Why would he choose this name for the Laurents' son (rather than "Ben," the name of most of the sons in his films)?**

+ *Majid*

Why did Georges' parents want to adopt Majid when he was little? Where did Majid grow up after being sent away? What did that mean for Majid's upbringing, for his chances of social and financial success in life?

How would you describe Majid as an adult? **How does he treat Georges when the latter shows up at his home and accuses him of harassment?** Do you think Majid is sincere in his denials? Why?

What importance do you grant Majid's remarks when he tells Georges that he (Georges) had "too much to lose" if he beat him (Majid) to death—adding, "What isn't a person capable of doing to avoid losing anything?" **Why does Haneke say that this is "the key sentence in** *Caché*" (Guichard and Strauss)?

It is well known that Haneke does not like to emphasize psychology in his films, preferring to remain on the moral plane. As a result, we know very little of Majid's inner life. For Crowley, Majid is "reduced to a screen on which the white European's anxiety is projected" when faced with the surfacing of the repressed memory of the wrongs that it has perpetrated against its former colonies (274). **Do you see this perspective developed anywhere in Haneke's film? If so, where?**

+ *Majid's Son*

Why does Majid's son go to see Georges at his place of work? What does he want from him? What does he mean when he says, "I wanted to know how someone feels when he has a man's life on his conscience. . . . Now I know"?

Why does Georges attack the politeness that Majid's son exhibits in this confrontation? Why is he so irritated by it? **Why, in your opinion, does Majid's son try to provoke Georges, inviting him to strike him?** What would it prove if Georges were to assault him physically?

Right after this confrontation, there is another long static shot at night showing the front of the Laurent house. **Are we to understand that the recordings are going to continue, that this story is not over?**

4. Majid's Suicide

How do you explain Majid's tragic act when Georges comes back to his home (at Majid's request)? Why does Majid say to him, "I wanted you to be present"? *Review this scene* (Excerpt 8, 1h27'51–1h29'53). Haneke says that Majid's suicide is "an act of aggression against Georges" (Porton 51). What does Majid hope to accomplish? **What effect can this act have on Georges?** Is Georges' distress, not to speak of the disintegration of his couple, a form of "poetic justice," as has been suggested (Wood 40)?

Is there any connection (metaphorical or other) between the scene in which little Majid cuts off the rooster's head and the later one in which Majid, the father, cuts his own throat?

What are we watching in the suicide scene, action in the present or a videotape? It has been noted that the placement and angle of the camera here are the same as they were in Georges' first visit to Majid's apartment (Gibson 34). If it is a videotape, with whom are we watching it?

5. Themes

+ **Intrusion**

In several of Haneke's films (*Funny Games* and *Time of the Wolf*, for example), the family is the victim of a home invasion, with tragic consequences. The Laurents live in a house that resembles a "fortress," with an iron gate in front and bars on the windows. **What are they protecting themselves from?** Is the idea of paranoia suggested here?

What kind of reflections might one make on the notions of intrusion and victimization as regards the two families, that of Georges and that of Majid, in *Caché*? **Who intrudes really on whom? Who are the real victims here?**

Does the film suggest that immigrants are considered to be "intruders" in France?

+ **Guilt**

In an interview, Haneke suggests that his film is a "moral tale about the problem of guilt" and how to deal with it (Niessen 183). What is the role of the inserts in which we catch brief glimpses of little Majid? *Review these shots* (Excerpts 9 and 10, 13'23–13'26, 20'30–20'42). **What is the connection between these shots, in which we see the child's face covered with blood, and Georges' feelings of guilt?**

In general, people associate childhood with innocence. **In your opinion, do people remain responsible for acts they committed when they were small children?** Could Georges have understood, at the age of six, the consequences of his lies? What do you think of Georges' remark to Majid: "You were older and stronger than I was. I didn't have any choice"? **What does he mean? Why does he feel it necessary to say that?**

When Majid's son visits him at his place of work, Georges tells him, "I'm not responsible," alluding to the death of the father. He had said the same thing to Anne in speaking of Majid's removal from Georges' parents' home. This statement has been made famous (and infamous) by the denouement of Alain Resnais' 1955 documentary film *Night and Fog (Nuit et brouillard)* about the Nazi death camps, when everyone repeats, "I'm not responsible." **Does Georges as an adult nevertheless have some responsibility for Majid's fate in life?** Could he have acted differently with him to compensate somewhat the wrong he did him as a child? Does he in fact have a debt toward Majid?

Why did Georges speak of Majid to his mother? **What nightmare does he have when sleeping over in his mother's home?** *Review the nightmare sequence* (Excerpt 11, 38'08–38'54). What is the meaning of this bad dream? Haneke emphasizes that this sequence "begins like a flashback. It is the memory of an event that took place: Majid as a child had indeed cut off the rooster's head. But, little by little, the editing and framing of the shots transform this realistic flashback into a nightmare" (Cieutat and Rouyer 250). **How do the montage and framing of this scene effect this transformation?**

How does Haneke relate individual guilt to collective guilt in his film? One critic maintains that Haneke sacrifices Majid in order to lead the public to recognize its own guilt stemming from its indifference and the repression in the French collective subconscious of the violence committed by France against the Algerians (Celik 60–61, 76). The blood that squirts on the wall when Majid cuts his throat would be intended, in this interpretation, to shock the spectators, to force them to open their eyes, to see this stain on their country's history, and to provoke at least a feeling of responsibility if not of moral duty. **What do you think of this "allegorical" interpretation of the film, which is supported by many other critics as well** (Niessen 197 and Speck 98, for example)?

Haneke has often asserted that every country has "dark stains," shameful memories that the country has repressed to some extent: "I think that each country has skeletons in its closet. . . . You will find hardly any country in Europe, indeed any in the world, that hasn't been affected by this phenomenon" (Silverman 59). He could have very well chosen a country other than France to make his film. **If Haneke had wanted to make his film in the United States, for example, is there a "dark stain" that he could have used in his film? Which one (or ones)?**

✦ *Lies*

What role did lying play in the traumatic removal of Majid by Georges' parents? Are there other examples of lies in the film? What does Georges reply, for example, when Anne asks him who is familiar with the property where he spent his childhood? **Why does Georges lie to his wife about his visit to Majid?** He tells her that the door was locked, and that it was a door to "a storage room or something like that." **Are we dealing with a metaphor here?** What is the function of a storage room?

Some critics say that "*Caché* is thus a film on lying as a means for human survival" (Cieutat and Rouyer 245). **In what sense may we consider that Georges uses lies to "survive"?** More generally, is lying, in fact, a necessity in life?

6. Media and Drawings

✦ *Television*

What role does television play in this film? In the Laurent home we see images of wars in Iraq and the Middle East. What sentiment might these images produce in the middle-class Western spectator who is living in complete material and psychological comfort?

What relationship does television have to reality? What does Georges do with the segment of his television show that he finds a little too theoretical? **What is Haneke** trying to tell us here about the reality of the audiovisual images that are offered to the public?

+ *The Videotapes*

Haneke made the shots on the outside of the Laurent house in a neighborhood of the eighteenth arrondissement of Paris that is referred to as the "flower quarter," and the little street where the video camera had to have been set is named "la rue des Iris." The word "iris" necessarily calls to mind the eye, and thus the gaze. **Is this allusion important in the film?** What, moreover, is an "iris shot" in cinema (closing or opening a shot with an iris)? Is this a simple wink at cinephiles, or is there a more important reference here to the act of filming?

The video camera that was necessarily placed in the middle of the rue des Iris had to remain motionless in the same spot for at least two hours during the morning. Is this possible without anyone noticing it?

This static shot is similar to those produced by a surveillance camera. What is the normal function of a surveillance camera? Who or what are these cameras trying to get on film? **What does that imply about the Laurents? Why are these images so troubling for them?**

Describe the progression of the content of the videotapes received by the Laurents. **What might be the intention of the individual(s) who made them?**

Georges is filmed by a hidden camera when he first visits Majid. **What is problematic here?** Did Majid know that Georges was coming to see him?

In your opinion, who made the video recordings? Both Majid and his son deny having made them. Is one or both of them lying? If not Majid or his son, who else would have had an interest in making them and sending them to various people, including Georges' boss? Might the entity hiding behind the video camera be Haneke himself, as Niessen suggests (185)? **What effect is Haneke attempting to produce on the spectator by refusing to identify the person who is responsible for the videos?** Is it possible to conclude, like many critics, that the origin of the tapes is of no importance, that the only thing that counts here is their effect on the protagonist and his family: their terror before the unidentified foreign Other who wishes to do them harm and is always capable of bursting into their privileged space?

+ *The Drawings*

What is the function of the drawings that accompany the videotapes? If there hadn't been drawings, would the tapes have had a different effect on the Laurents? **Why did the sender include a child's drawing of a face that seems to be spitting blood? Why a rooster with a bloody neck?**

7. Majid's Removal

Discuss the manner in which the next to last scene of the film is shot, when little Majid is sent away from Georges' parents' home to spend his childhood in an orphanage. *Review this scene* (Excerpt 12, 1h50'40–1h54'00). What do we call this type of shot? **Why is the camera so far from the action? With whom are we watching this traumatic scene?** What are we seeing here, a dream (nightmare) of Georges, an event that he is recalling as he lies on his bed, or a flashback offered to us by the filmmaker? **Why** does Haneke place this scene at the end of his film—like Alain Resnais places the flashback of the traumatic scene of the death of the German soldier, the French girl's lover, toward the end of *Hiroshima mon amour?*

8. The Last Shot

What happens in the last shot of the film, a long static shot that recalls the beginning of the film? **Review this scene** (Excerpt 13, 1h54'02–1h56'05). Why does Haneke have a preference for very lengthy takes like this one? What is his goal? **What obligation do these shots create for the spectator?**

Did you see, at your first viewing of this scene, the meeting between Pierrot and Majid's son? Haneke tells us that half of the spectators to whom he has put this question answered "no" (Toubiana). **What are we to think about that?**

What might Majid's son have said to Georges' son? How do you interpret this scene?

In speaking of this last shot, Cieutat and Rouyer propose a metaphorical interpretation of the camera: "This rather particular framing could nonetheless either suggest that the shot was made by the author of the videotapes or that it symbolizes an atemporal and universal gaze on mankind" (246). **Is it possible that this last shot, like the first, is a recording made by the author of the tapes? If you think so, by whom and to what end?** What do you think of the metaphorical interpretation suggested here?

According to Haneke (Toubiana), as well as several critics, we could read this sequence as either a scene of reconciliation between the two sons (and a sign of hope for their generation), or as a scene of collusion and conspiracy against Pierrot's father—but the film doesn't help us to decide. **What do you think personally?**

9. Interpreting a Film

Haneke asserts that **the interpretation of a film, its integration into a system of values and beliefs, is always the role of the spectator.** As regards the interpretation of *Caché*, Haneke says, as we saw in the introduction, "I make sure, in general, that my films lend themselves to the greatest number of different interpretations. . . . The ideal is for spectators to finish the film in their head, as they see fit. It is essential that the film ask more questions than it answers, otherwise it is of no interest" (Allion 10). **Do you agree with this conception of the interpretation of a film and the role of the spectator?**

Michael Haneke's Filmography

1989   *The Seventh Continent (Le Septième Continent)*

1992   *Benny's Video*

1994   *71 Fragments of a Chronology of Chance (71 Fragments d'une chronologie du hasard)*

1997   *Funny Games*

2000   *Code Unknown (Code inconnu: récit incomplet de divers voyages)*

2001   *The Piano Teacher (La Pianiste)*

2003   *Time of the Wolf (Le Temps du loup)*

2005   *Caché*

2009   *The White Ribbon (Le Ruban blanc)*

2012   *Amour*

Works Consulted

Adi, Yasmina. *Ici on noie les Algériens*. Agat Films, 2011.

Aknin, Laurent. "Haneke's Video." *L'Avant-Scène Cinéma* 558 (Jan. 2007): 12–14.

Allion, Yves. "Entretien avec Michael Haneke." *L'Avant-Scène Cinéma* 558 (Jan. 2007): 7–11.

Bazin, André. *Qu'est-ce que le cinéma?* Paris: Editions du Cerf, 1981.

Borde, Dominique. "La Longue Traque de Michael Haneke." *Le Figaro*, 5 Oct. 2005: n. pag.

Brunette, Peter. *Contemporary Film Directors: Michael Haneke*. Champaign: U of Illinois P, 2010.

Campion, Alexis. "Comme un coup de couteau." *Le Journal du Dimanche*, 2 Oct. 2005: n. pag.

Celik, Ipek A. "'I Wanted You to Be Present': Guilt and the History of Violence in Michael Haneke's *Caché*." *Cinéma Journal* 50.1 (Autumn 2010): 59–80.

Champenois, Sabrina. "Cannes 2005." *Libération*, 16 May 2005: n. pag.

Cieutat, Michel, and Philippe Rouyer. *Haneke par Haneke*. Paris: Stock, 2012.

Crowley, Patrick. "When Forgetting Is Remembering. Haneke's *Caché* and the Events of October 17, 1961." *On Michael Haneke*. Ed. Brian Price and John David Rhodes. Detroit, Ml: Wayne State UP, 2010. 267–79.

Douin, Jean-Luc. "Regard forcé sur les démons de l'enfance pour un homme filmé à son insu." *Le Monde*, 17 May 2005: n. pag.

Ezra, Elizabeth, and Jane Sillars. "Hidden in Plain Sight: Bringing Terror Home." *Screen* 48.2 (Summer 2007): 215–21.

Gibson, Brian. "Bearing Witness. The Dardenne Brothers' and Michael Haneke's Implication of the Viewer." *CineAction* 70 (2006): 24–38.

Gorin, François. "Caché." *Télérama*, 8 Oct. 2005: n. pag.

Grønstad, Asbjørn. *Screening the Unwatchable. Spaces of Negation in Post-Millennial Art Cinema*. New York: Palgrave Macmillan, 2012.

Grossvogel, D. I. "Haneke: The Coercing of Vision." *Film Quarterly* 60.4 (Summer 2007): 36–43.

Guichard, Louis, and Frédéric Strauss. "Nous baignons dans la culture de la culpabilité." *Télérama*, 5 Oct. 2005: n. pag.

Gutman, Pierre-Simon. "Michael Haneke, le provocateur idéaliste." *L'Avant-Scène Cinéma* 558 (Jan. 2007): 3–6.

Haneke, Michael, dir. *Caché*. Sony Pictures Classics, 2006.

Hecht, Emmanuel. "De la manipulation des images." *Les Echos*, 5 Oct. 2005: n. pag.

Jacobowitz, Florence. "Michael Haneke's *Caché* (*Hidden*)." *CineAction* 68 (2006): 62–64.

Laurent, Patrick. "Revues de presse." *L'Avant-Scène Cinéma* 558 (Jan. 2007): 14–16.

Mérigeau, Pascal. "Obsessionnel Haneke." *Le Nouvel Observateur*, 12 May 2005: n. pag.

———. "Rencontre avec Michael Haneke. Le manipulateur." *Le Nouvel Observateur*, 19 Sept. 2005: n. pag.

Niessen, Neils. "The Staged Realism of Michael Haneke's *Caché*." *Cinémas: revue d'études cinématographiques* 20.1 (2009): 181–99.

Osterweil, Ara. "*Caché*." *Film Quarterly* 59.4 (Summer 2006): 35–39.

Porton, Richard. "Collective Guilt and Individual Responsibility: An Interview with Michael Haneke." *Cineaste* 31.1 (Winter 2005): 50–51.

Quenin, François. "Revues de presse." *L'Avant-Scène Cinéma* 558 (Jan. 2007): 16.

Rehm, Jean-Pierre. "Revues de presse." *L'Avant-Scène Cinéma* 558 (Jan. 2007): 14.

Riemer, Willy. "Beyond Mainstream Film. An Interview with Michael Haneke." *After Postmodernism. Austrian Literature and Film in Transition*. Ed. Willy Riemer. Riverside, CA: Ariadne Press, 2000. 159–70.

Rouchy, Marie-Elisabeth. "Le Petit Prince." *Le Nouvel Observateur*, 6 Oct. 2005: n. pag.

Seshadri, Kalpana Rahita. "Spectacle of the Hidden: Michael Haneke's *Caché*." *Nottingham French Studies* 46.3 (Autumn 2007): 32–48.

Sharrett, Christopher. "The World That Is Known. Michael Haneke Interviewed." *Kinoeye. New Perspectives on European Film* 4.1 (8 Mar. 2004). Accessed 20 Dec. 2016. <http://kinoeye.org/04/01/interview01.php>.

Silverman, Max. "The Violence of the Cut: Michael Haneke's *Caché* and Cultural Memory." *French Cultural Studies* 21.1 (2010): 57–65.

Speck, Oliver C. *Funny Frames. The Filmic Concepts of Michael Haneke*. New York: Continuum, 2010.

Thoret, Jean-Baptiste. "'*Caché*' de Michael Haneke." *Charlie Hebdo*, 5 Oct. 2005: n. pag.

Tinazzi, Noël. "Les Taches noires du passé." *La Tribune*, 5 Oct. 2005: n. pag.

Toubiana, Serge. "*Caché*: Entretien avec Michael Haneke par Serge Toubiana." Bonus sur le DVD de *Caché*, sorti en 2006.

Tranchant, Marie-Noëlle. "Logique punitive." *Le Figaro*, 16 May 2005: n. pag.

Welcomme, Geneviève. "Dès qu'on pose une caméra quelque part, on manipule." *La Croix*, 5 Oct. 2005: n. pag.

Widemann, Dominique. "Parfois, le tapis bouge." *L'Humanité*, 5 Oct. 2005: n. pag.

Wood, Robin. "Hidden in Plain Sight: Robin Wood on Michael Haneke's *Caché*." *Artforum International* 44.5 (Jan. 2006): 35–40.

13

Jacques Audiard

A Prophet (Un prophète)

(2009)

Jacques Audiard, *A Prophet*: Malik (Tahar Rahim) sitting beside the Corsican gang boss César (Niels Arestrup) in the prison courtyard.

Director . . . . Jacques Audiard
Screenplay . . . . Jacques Audiard, Thomas Bidegain
Original Screenplay. . . . . Abdel Raouf Dafri, Nicolas Peufaillit
Director of Photography . . . . Stéphane Fontaine
Sound . . . . Francis Wargnier, Brigitte Taillandier,
. . . . Jean-Paul Hurier, Marc Doisne
Film Editor . . . . Juliette Welfing
Music. . . . . Alexandre Desplat
Art Directors.. . . . . .Michel Barthélémy, Etienne Rohde, Boris Piot
Costumes . . . . .Virginie Montel
Continuity . . . . Nathalie Vierny
Producer . . . . Martine Cassinelli
Length 2h35

Cast

Tahar Rahim (*Malik El Djebena*), Niels Arestrup (*César Luciani, leader of the Corsican clan*), Adel Bencherif (*Ryad, Malik's friend*), Reda Kateb (*Jordi the Gypsy, the prison drug dealer*), Hichem Yacoubi (*Reyeb, the witness assassinated by Malik*), Jean-Philippe Ricci (*Vettori, Luciani's lieutenant*), Gilles Cohen (*Prof*), Pierre Leccia (*Sampierro*), Antoine Basler (*Pilicci*), Foued Nassah (*Antaro*), Jean-Emmanuel Pagni (*Santi*), Frédéric Graziani (*Ilbanez, the head guard*), Leila Bekhti (*Djamila, Ryad's wife*), Slimane Dazi (*Lattrache, the Arab gang leader in Marseilles*), Rabah Loucif (*Malik's lawyer*)

Story

Malik El Djebena, a nineteen-year-old delinquent, finds himself sentenced to six years in prison for assaulting a policeman. Illiterate, penniless, alone in the world, physically and psychologically fragile, he is soon at the mercy of the prison gangs, especially the Corsicans. The boss of the latter, César Luciani, threatens to kill him if he doesn't agree to assassinate another prisoner, an Arab like Malik, who is getting ready to testify in court against a member of the Corsican mafia. Although much against his will, Malik goes through with it and, as a result, benefits from the protection of the Corsicans in the prison. He becomes their flunky, doing the dishes, mopping the floor, serving coffee, swallowing all sorts of humiliations without complaint.

Although uneducated, Malik is far from stupid. He learns the codes necessary for survival in prison, takes French courses to learn to read and write, and even learns Corsican by listening to the members of the gang chat among themselves. Eventually he gains César's confidence and is sent on confidential missions when he has leaves from prison. He waits for the opportunity to reverse the power relationship, and when it comes he seizes it.

The Director

Born on April 30, 1952, in Paris, the son of Michel Audiard, a famous screenwriter of police thrillers, Jacques Audiard at first rejected the idea of pursuing a career in film and enrolled in literature and philosophy at the University of Paris. He abandoned his studies, however, and began to learn to edit films before discovering that he had a singular talent for the adaptation of texts for the theater and cinema and especially thrillers like Claude Miller's *Deadly Circuit* (*Mortelle Randonnée*, 1983) and Michel Blanc's *Dead Tired* (*Grosse Fatigue*, 1994).

With these successes to his credit, Audiard was able to obtain financing for his first film, *See How They Fall* (*Regarde les hommes tomber*, 1994), a thriller featuring a major star, Jean-Louis Trintignant, and a newcomer who would not remain unknown for long: Mathieu Kassovitz. The latter won the Most Promising Actor César for his performance in the film, an award that was added to the César for the Best First Work for Audiard and a César for Best Editing for Juliette Welfling (who also edited *Un prophète*). This was a most promising debut, and Audiard showed that it was no fluke with his following film *A Self-Made Hero* (*Un héros très discret*, 1996), whose hero was again played by Kassovitz just a year after his directing of *Hate* (*La Haine*; see Chap. 5) and a few years before his prize-winning role in *Amélie* (*Le Fabuleux Destin d'Amélie Poulain*,

2001; see Chap. 19) by Jean-Pierre Jeunet. *A Self-Made Hero* is the story of a false hero that takes place in France at the end of the Second World War. It won the Best Screenplay award at Cannes in 1996 and a half dozen nominations at the Césars the following year.

Audiard's success continued with his third feature film, *On My Lips* (*Sur mes lèvres*, 2001), another thriller that is, this time, a love story between a nearly deaf secretary (Emmanuelle Devos) and a little hoodlum (Vincent Cassel—Vinz in *Hate*) who attempt to scam some gangsters. The film was awarded three new Césars: Best Actress (Devos), Best Sound, and Best Screenplay. It is Audiard's next film, however, that guaranteed his reputation internationally: *The Beat That My Heart Skipped* (*De battre mon coeur s'est arrêté*, 2005), a remake of James Tolback's American film *Fingers* (1978), with rising star Roman Duris in the title role. The film won the BAFTA Prize (British Academy of Film and Television Arts—the British Oscars) for the Best Film in a Foreign Language, eight Césars, including Best Film, Best Director, and Best Actor, four Etoiles d'or for the Best Film, Best Director, Best Actor, and Best Original Music—twenty-one major awards in all. It was the consecration of Audiard as the best director of thrillers in France.

Incredible as it may seem, the success of *A Prophet* exceeded that of *The Beat That My Heart Skipped*, barely missing the Oscar for the Best Film in a Foreign Language and winning the Grand Prize at Cannes, nine Césars, the Lumière Prize, the Louis Delluc Prize, forty-seven awards and forty additional nominations—an absolute triumph that would lead the critic Jean-Michel Frodon to observe that Audiard occupied "a central position in French cinema at the end of the first decade of the twenty-first century" (1001). Audiard's success would continue with his following film, *Rust and Bone* (*De rouille et d'os*, 2012), a love story between a tough ex-boxer, now a nightclub bouncer, and a whale trainer in a theme park who loses her legs in a freak accident with an orca. The film was nominated for the Palme d'Or at Cannes, Best Film and Best Actress prizes at both the Golden Globes, and the BAFTA Awards, and won four Césars, two Lumière Prizes, five Etoiles d'or, thirty-two prizes, and seventy nominations in all. Audiard's most recent film, *Dheepan* (2015), is the story of a former Tamil fighter in Sri Lanka who manages to flee the civil war by emigrating to France where he tries to make a new life in the Parisian suburbs despite the violence he has to confront there. *Dheepan* won the Palme d'Or at Cannes in 2015 and was nominated at the BAFTA Awards for the Best Film Not in the English Language as well as for nine Césars.

The Origin and Making of the Film

It took Audiard and his co-screenwriter, Thomas Bidegain, three years to write the screenplay for *A Prophet*, working from another screenplay written by Abdel Raouf Dafri and Nicolas Peufaillit. The project of the latter two was nonetheless quite a different film, based on Brian De Palma's thriller *Scarface* (1983). In their scenario the North African hero resembled Tony Montana, the main character of the De Palma film played by Al Pacino, "a psychopath, a madman whose principal pleasure and goal was killing people" (Mérigeau 64). This is not what Audiard had in mind: his project, from the beginning, was to "create a kind of anti-Tony Montana" (Mérigeau 64). Audiard and Bidegain thus "adapted" the Dafri-Peufaillit screenplay just as they would have adapted a novel, and only the broad outline of the original remains: the prison, the gang of Corsican inmates, a young Arab delinquent—who, in the original, leaves prison soon after the beginning of the story. If their hero, like Montana, comes out of nowhere and ends up in power, he more greatly resembles the character played by Denzel Washington in a 2007 crime thriller by Ridley Scott: "El Djebena belongs to another race of gangsters, that of the hero of Ridley Scott's *American Gangster*, who owes his success largely to his role as an underling" (Tessé 20). He kowtows and keeps his head down until he finds the opportunity to raise it up.

In Audiard's film the hero Malik serves out his sentence but learns to survive by adapting to circumstances and by relying on both intelligence and luck. Audiard and Bidegain wanted to create a new sort of hero who would not be a big tough guy but rather a defenseless, fragile young man, played by a virtually unknown actor: "We wanted to make heroes from unfamiliar figures who were not recognizable heroic types from other films," says the director. It is for this reason that Audiard chose for the role of the young Arab inmate Tahar Rahim, a young actor he had seen in *La Commune*, a 2007 television series on Canal+ in which Rahim played the role of a little punk in "a tough housing project riven by communitarian strife and crime," whose screenplay was also written by Abdel Raouf Dafri (Tessé 19).

The film was shot over a four-month period at Gennevilliers in the northwestern suburb of Paris. For 2.5 million euros (out of a total budget of eleven million) Audiard turned a set of vacant apartment buildings into a prison. As Audiard explains, his crew built the prison yard, four hallways, and around ten cells (Mérigeau 66). To magnify the feeling of confinement, the cells, hallways, showers, etc., are all life size; in addition, the cells were built with thick walls and real ceilings to make them seem as authentic as possible (B 20). In these narrow spaces there was little extra room, and it was impossible to put down tracks for dolly shots (this was only done twice in the whole film), which explains both why the film was shot principally with a hand-held camera favoring close-ups or very near shots, primarily of faces. Audiard had quickly understood that in these conditions the success of the film would depend mostly on the acting and not on the camerawork (Widemann, "Le cinéma").

To add to the authenticity of the sets, the art director, Michel Barthélemy, tells us, they "recuperated furniture and lamps from the former Avignon prison, and used the same type of locks that were in use in French prisons in general" (Monnin). For the meticulously constructed soundtrack, they mixed noises recorded in the Fleury-Mérogis prison (the largest in Europe) in the southern suburb of Paris. Audiard thus succeeded in recreating, according to a former inmate, "the unbearable background noise that, day and night, permeates the prisoners' existence" (Korber). To increase yet further the realism of the décor, they hired many former inmates as extras; these people dominate the population of the prison yard and hallways where much of the main action of the film takes place.

Generally, if we are to believe the prison directors who were invited to a special screening reserved for penitentiary administrators, the representation of the prison universe is remarkably true to life in *A Prophet*: " . . . the decor, the noises, the language, the rhythm of prison life. Everything is there: the schemes to get a few cigarettes or chocolate cookies, the stealthy exchange of tennis shoes under the table in the visiting room, the trafficking of drugs and cell phones, the 'soft music' of the porno videos in the evening. . ." (Des Déserts). Korber, the former inmate, also notes the realism of the tiniest details of the decor, "such as the repeated shots of the can of Ricoré [chicory coffee]—evocative of all prisons—the need to have a cup of 'coffee' ten times a day, a mechanical ritual to kill time. . . . It's visceral; I can't stand the sight of a can of Ricoré any more" (Korber).

The Actors

For the most part, the characters of A Prophet are played by relatively unknown actors, often only seen before in television series or, in the case of the extras, by nonactors. The only exception, and it is an important one, is Niels Arestrup, who plays the role of César Luciani, the sinister Corsican boss in the film. Arestrup is well known to the French public, having acted in dozens of films, telefilms, and television series since 1974. Born in France to a French mother and Danish father, with a reputation as a brute, the "ogre of French cinema," an "uncontrollable" actor—which put off many filmmakers (Lorrain)—Arestrup nonetheless won three Best Actor in a Supporting Role Césars, the only actor to have accomplished this. He won this prize both for A Prophet and for the preceding film of Audiard, The Beat That My Heart Skipped (2005), in which he plays a shady, disturbing father, as well as for his role in Quai d'Orsay (2013), a comedy by Bertrand Tavernier. He also won a Best Actor prize and a César nomination for his performance in Volker Schlöndorff's Diplomatie in 2014. The exceptional quality of his acting in A Prophet, his embodiment of the old Mafioso lion who loses little by little his grip on power, was unanimously applauded by the film press.

The great revelation of the film, however, was the unknown twenty-seven-year-old actor Tahar Rahim, who plays Malik El Djebena, the young ignorant and illiterate Arab who falls prey to the Corsican boss in the Brécourt Penitentiary. Having no experience on the big screen, Rahim met Audiard by pure chance one day as they both were leaving the set of La Commune. Rahim caught the filmmaker's attention at the precise moment he was seeking an actor for the role of the helpless young delinquent in A Prophet. As Audiard remembers it, "What attracted me to Tahar Rahim was his juvenile charm, an absence of aggressiveness, his ideal son-in-law side that was going to force him to compromise and to secrete violence" (Widemann, "Le cinéma").

Audiard's judgment is exceptional in the choice of actors, and the excellence of the casting in A Prophet is widely recognized by the critics, who lavish praise on Rahim's performance: "Tahar Rahim, a new arrival, is brilliant. While extremely physical, his acting neglects no nuance of his character's psychology. . ." (Widemann, "Le triomphe"); "There is no doubt that we will hear from this young actor again, a veritable comet in the sky of French cinema. In his very first film he is dazzling, like De Niro in Scorsese's Taxi Driver or Al Pacino in De Palma's Scarface. We can't wait to see what comes next" (Delcroix, "La Bonne Etoile"). Other comparisons, over-the-top flattering, soon follow: "We see in this rank novice the virility of Marlon Brando in On the Waterfront, the sensual fragility of Alain Delon in Rocco and His Brothers, the power of Vincent Cassel in Mesrine, the impulsiveness of Al Pacino in Scarface" (Théate, "Naissance").

We must mention, finally, the critical importance of all the supporting roles in a film whose success depends so much on the quality of the acting. All of the actors who play these roles, described as a "gang of brilliant, immensely talented actors" (Fontaine), are all unknown to the general public, which is surprising given the excellence of the performances by, for example, Hichem Yacoubi (Reyeb, the phantom), Adel Bencherif (Ryad, Malik's friend), Reda Kateb (Jordi the Gypsy), or Slimane Dazi (Lattrache, the Marseilles gang boss), and Jean-Philippe Ricci (César Luciani's right-hand man).

The Reception

A Prophet was released on August 26, 2009, in 280 theaters across France. For once a French film enjoyed virtually unanimous applause from film critics in France as well as abroad, receiving "rave reviews" everywhere (Delcroix, "Jacques Audiard"). As noted above, Audiard's film was nominated for the Oscar for the Best Film in a Foreign Language in 2010 after having earned numerous awards in France and in the most prestigious film festivals in the world. The critical consensus is extraordinary, as Eric Libiot observes in *L'Express*, referring to *A Prophet* as "the best French film of the present, past, and future": "I will not be the only one who will write this. There may even be a surfeit of praise in the press. So extremely rare at Cannes . . . the French and foreign journalists, hand in hand, all opened up their dictionaries of compliments. An exceptional unanimity such as we've never seen before. . . ."

Libiot proves to be right, and the praise rains down: "With *A Prophet* Jacques Audiard confirms his reputation as one of the most brilliant French filmmakers of his time" (Melinard); "With this masterly incursion into the prison film genre, Jacques Audiard rises to the level of the greatest filmmakers" (Raspiengeas); and "Admirable, masterful, mind-boggling, deeply moving, complex, subtle, disturbing. . . . One runs out of adjectives to describe this incredible voyage into prison hell that Jacques Audiard takes us on" (Théate, "Au bout"). Comparisons with the greatest directors of thrillers—including Scorsese, Coppola, and De Palma, of course—are rampant, not to speak of the references to Kafka and Balzac. . . . And numerous critics, like the following one, evoke the most famous French prison film before *A Prophet*, the last and perhaps best work by Jacques Becker, *The Hole* (*Le Trou*, 1960): "The film moves constantly back and forth between the pointillist realism of Jacques Becker when he was filming *Le Trou* and the lyrical unrealism of Coppola in his Mafia trilogy" (Murat).

The only important false note in this symphony, apart from the wrath of the critic of *Témoignage chrétien*, clearly offended by the blatant immorality of the film, stemmed from the Corsican proponents of independence, who protested vigorously the negative image of the Corsican community conveyed in *A Prophet*, a film that has a "racist character" and promotes a "confusion between political militants and thugs" ("Début de polémique"). One can only sympathize; the image of the Corsicans in this film is indeed not very flattering.

Prison Films

In 1960, as mentioned above, Jacques Becker made his final film, *The Hole*, an adaptation of a novel by José Giovanni. After Jean Renoir's *La Grande Illusion* (1937), which is about prisoners of war in Germany during the First World War, and Robert Bresson's *A Man Escaped* (*Un condamné à mort s'est échappé*, 1956), whose action takes place in a Gestapo prison in Lyon during the Occupation (1940–44)—and if we do not take into account Eric Valette's *Maléfique* (2002), an eccentric horror film—Becker's film is the only notable French prison film until *A Prophet*. For whatever reasons, the prison film has remained since the 1930s an American specialty, beginning with George W. Hill's *The Big House* (1930), which won two Oscars, followed by Howard Hawks' *The Criminal Code* (1931), Mervyn LeRoy's *I Am a Fugitive from a Chain Gang* (1932), and Lloyd Bacon's *San Quentin* (1937). In the following decades we also note Jules Dassin's *Brute Force* (1947), John Frankenheimer's *Birdman of Alcatraz* (1962), Stuart Rosenberg's *Cool Hand Luke* (1967), Franklin J. Schaffner's *Papillon* (1973), and, closer to the present period, Frank Darabont's two blockbusters, *The Shawshank Redemption* (1994) and *The Green Mile* (1999).

What virtually all of these classic prison films have in common (*The Green Mile* is an exception) is a plot focused on an escape attempt, successful or not. The heroes are convicts who are perceived as the "good guys," while the prison guards are the "bad guys"—antipathetic characters if not sadistic brutes. Just as in police films, the heroes of prison films are played by major stars: Burt Lancaster, Burt Reynolds, Steve McQueen, Paul Newman, and Clint Eastwood, for example, in the United States, and Jean Gabon, Lino Ventura, Alain Delon, and Jean-Paul Belmodo in France.

In the more recent prison films (still mostly American), the above is no longer true. Whether it be *American Me* (1992), *Slam* (1998), *Undisputed* (2002), *Felon* (2008), *Dog Pound* (2010), or the Brazilian film *Carandiru* (2003), the focus is now on the struggle between the inmates themselves. While there are still corrupt and brutal guards, the principal enemy is the other prisoners: "The priority is no longer to escape but to succeed in surviving in a universe governed by the survival of the fittest" ("Une évolution"). Moreover, the stars have disappeared: the main characters are played by unknowns who may become stars because of the film, as happens with Tahar Rahim in *A Prophet*, a film which is also not about escaping but just adapting, surviving, and, in this particular case, coming out on top.

STUDY GUIDE

What Happens in This Film?

1. What happens to Malik the first time he goes out into the prison yard?

2. What mission does César Luciani, the Corsican boss, give to Malik? And if he refuses to carry it out, what will happen to him?

3. What do the spectators learn about the head guard?

4. Why does Malik kick the inmate down on the floor in the textile workshop?

5. How does Malik's life change after the murder of Reyeb? What does he begin to learn? How does his relationship with the Corsicans evolve?

6. Where does Malik meet Ryad? Why is Ryad going to get out of prison soon?

7. How does Malik's situation change when he informs César that he understands Corsican?

8. What is the role of Jordi the Gypsy in the prison? What does he propose to Malik?

9. What mission does César give Malik during his first short leave from prison?

10. How does Malik convince Latif the Egyptian to let Ryad go and return the drugs he took from them?

11. Where does César send Malik to meet Brahim Lattrache? What does Malik do for the first time in his life?

12. Why does Lattrache ask Malik if he is a prophet?

13. What does Luciani ask Malik to do as regards the Lingherris and Jacky Marcaggi?

14. How long does Malik spend in solitary confinement? What happens during that time?

15. What is Malik's situation when he leaves prison?

True or False?

If the statement is false, correct it!

1. The authorities bring in a prisoner named Reyeb who is going to testify in a trial of a member of the Corsican clan.

2. After speaking to César, Malik complains to the head guard, who promises to help him.

3. Malik has to hide a razor blade in his sleeve in order to kill the Arab inmate.

4. After killing Reyeb, Malik completely forgets him.

5. Malik begins to learn Corsican by himself; he follows various courses in the prison school.

6. César is very pleased at the idea of many of the Corsican prisoners leaving for prisons in Corsica to be closer to their families.

7. When César learns that Malik has the right to daylong leaves from prison, he decides to put him to work on the outside.

8. Before being arrested, Jordi hid a large package of hash in a service station's store.

9. Malik and Ryad, along with Jordi, are going to begin a drug trafficking business between Spain and Paris.

10. César becomes suspicious of Malik and his personal business; he injures his arm to keep him in line.

11. In a nightmare Malik sees horses running on the road ahead of his car.

12. Malik reaches an agreement with Brahim Lattrache, who also invites him to work with him.

13. Malik reaches an agreement with the Arabs in the prison by giving money to the guards.

14. Malik returns to the prison late on purpose, because he wants to spend more time with Ryad, his wife Djemila, and their baby.

15. Upon leaving solitary confinement, Malik joins the group of Muslims, who now protect him from César.

What Did You Learn in the Introduction?

1. Audiard gives main roles in his first three films to three actors who will become big stars in French cinema. Who are they?

2. What remake of an American film catapulted Audiard into the forefront of cinema in France and in the world? How many Césars did it receive?

3. In what respect is Malik El Djebena a new kind of hero in a thriller?

4. Why did Audiard choose Tahar Rahim to play the hero of *A Prophet*?

5. Why did Audiard have to shoot his film mostly with a hand-held camera with many close-ups of the characters' faces?

6. What guaranteed the authenticity of the sets for this film?

7. What approach did Audiard use to make the soundtrack (to replicate the real atmosphere of a prison)?

8. In his casting Audiard chose little-known actors, with one exception. Which one?

9. To which famous American actors did the critics compare Tahar Rahim?

10. What important prizes did *A Prophet* win in France? In what sense was the critical reception of this film really exceptional?

11. What country has always dominated the production of prison films? What were the only important French prison films before *A Prophet*? Who made them?

12. How are recent prison films different from traditional prison films?

Exploring the Film

1. The Title of the Film

How would you explain the title of this film? In what sense could Malik El Djebena be considered a "prophet"? One commentator said, "The title of the film is absurd. . . . 'A model' would have been preferable, because this is the first time in a long time that a

French film has attempted to create a new paradigm. . ." (Tessé 22). If you do not find the title of the film appropriate, **what title would you propose?**

2. *The Subheadings*

We see large subheadings at certain moments in the film, beginning with "Reyeb," then after the first appearance of his phantom, "1 Year." **What is, in your opinion, the function of the subheadings in the film?**

3. *The Beginning of the Film: The Viewpoint*

How does the beginning of the film (including the beginning titles) establish the dominant point of view? **What kind of shots does Audiard choose here? What effect is he trying to achieve?** What is the role of the soundtrack and the lighting? *Review the beginning of the film* (Excerpt 1, 0'18–1'30).

4. *Money*

Malik tries to hide **a fifty-franc bill** in his shoe when he goes into the prison. Since money is forbidden in prison, his bill is confiscated until he has served his sentence. The iconography of the fifty-franc bill is well known in France: it is **Antoine de Saint-Exupéry, as well as the eponymous hero of his famous tale *Le Petit Prince*.** The Saint-Exupéry Prize has been awarded every year since 1987 to a book for children that expresses the values of Saint-Exupéry's work. **Check out the description of this prize on the internet.** Based on what you learn, explain why one of the commentators of Audiard's film believes that the allusion to Saint-Exupéry's values serves to emphasize certain aspects of *A Prophet* (MacDonald 565). Do you agree with this interpretation?

   If money as such is forbidden inside the prison, what serves as "currency" in this world?

   How does the reference to money in the film serve to establish its chronology? **Find out on the internet what year the euro was put into circulation for the general public.**

5. *The Characters*

   ✦ *Malik El Djebena*

How would you describe Malik's character at the beginning of the film? What are his deficiencies, his most apparent weaknesses? **What do we know of his personal life before he arrives at the Brécourt Penitentiary?** Two inmates beat him up in the prison yard and take his shoes. **Why is this incident important for the subsequent action of the film?** What are Malik's most important qualities (which are going to help him survive in prison)? Do you agree with the following opinion of one critic: "Malik is a hero whose principal quality is his endurance, his ability to absorb punishment" (Tessé 22)?

   Many critics have pointed out that Malik owes his success, his rise to the top of the "social" ladder, to his stay in prison. **Do you agree? What kind of life could Malik have hoped for if he hadn't gone to prison?**

In a certain sense *A Prophet* may be considered to be a *film d'apprentissage*, similar to a *roman d'apprentissage* (or *Bildungsroman*) in which a young person learns about life and, in some cases, how to succeed on the social and economic levels. **How does Malik's "apprentissage" ("apprenticeship") begin in prison? What are the main stages afterwards?** May the society of the prison world be taken for a microcosm of society in general? Is the formula for socioeconomic success the same in both cases? If not, what are the differences?

+ *César Luciani*

Describe César Luciani's character. What are his defining characteristics? **What kind of relationship develops between him and Malik?** In Audiard's preceding film, *The Beat That My Heart Skipped*, the (very difficult) father-son relationship is at the heart of the story. **May we speak of a father-son relationship here?**

Malik learns Corsican by listening to the Corsicans speak among themselves and with the help of a Corsican grammar. Why is this important? **What does that tell us about Malik's character?**

Why does César attack Malik so violently later in the film, injuring his eye, at a time when Malik seems to have finally gained his confidence?

Why, in your opinion, does Malik continue to serve as a flunky for the Corsicans, even after he's been promoted to higher functions by César?

Why is Malik surprised when César asks him to assassinate Jacky Marcaggi? How does Malik turn this plan to his advantage?

+ *Reyeb*

Describe this character. What is the importance of the advice he gives to Malik (as regards the prison school) before the latter assassinates him: "The whole idea is to leave prison a little less stupid than when you came in"? **How do you explain the appearances of Reyeb's phantom beside Malik? What is the function of these appearances in the film?** Discuss the scene at the prison school and the one in which Reyeb's phantom appears for the first time. *Review these scenes* (Excerpt 2, 31'33–33'49). What is the connection between these two scenes? **How do you interpret the struggle in the bed? Why is Reyeb's finger burning?**

As regards Malik's evolution, what meaning would you give to Reyeb's religious discourse that finishes with the title "recite" (what God said to Mohammed), in French and Arabic just before the episode in which Malik and Ryad attack Jackie Marcaggi and his bodyguards in Paris? *Review this shot* (Excerpt 3, 2h07'04–2h07'52). MacDonald explains that the word "recite" (*iqra* in Arabic), which begins this chapter of the film, refers to the first word revealed to the prophet Mohammed by Allah, and that the text that Reyeb recites is the sura 96 (chapter 96) of the Qur'an that begins with this word (570). **Search for "sura 96" on the internet. Is there anything in this text that seems relevant to Audiard's film?**

+ *Ryad*

Describe this character and his initial relationship with Malik. **How does Ryad become more and more important?** Why is his family (his wife Djemila and their child) important in the film?

✦ *Jordi the Gypsy*

What is Jordi's role in the prison? What is his function in the film as regards Malik's evolution? *Review the scene in which Malik talks with Jordi, as well as the following two short scenes* (Excerpt 4, 52'30–55'02). Discuss these last two scenes. **What do they tell us about Malik?**

✦ *Latif the Egyptian*

What role does Latif the Egyptian, who kidnapped Ryad and stole his shipment of drugs, play in the ascent of Malik (without realizing it, of course)? To whom does Malik have to appeal to settle the Latif problem definitively? **What qualities does Malik show in taking care of the Latif matter?**

✦ *Brahim Lattrache*

Who is Brahim Lattrache? How does Malik get out of trouble when Lattrache, suspicious of him, puts his revolver to his head and interrogates him? *Review and discuss this scene, as well as the scene with the deer that follows it* (Excerpt 5, 1h43'12–1h45'00).

How does his meeting with Lattrache represent an important new stage in Malik's journey?

6. The Corsicans and the "Beards" (les Barbus)

Who are the guys with the beards? Who dominates in the prison, the Corsicans or the "Beards"? Why? *Review the scene in the yard where Malik sees the group of Beards arrive* (Excerpt 6, 34'04–35'28). What is the function of this scene? **What choice does Malik, who is an Arab, have to make here? How is the balance of power between the two groups going to change in the course of the film, and why?**

Why does Malik advise César, later in the film, to have the "screws" (the guards) hassle the Beards? Of what use is that to Malik? How do you interpret Malik's remark, "I'm just another Arab who thinks with his balls"? What does this remark express? *Review the sequence where Malik meets Hassan for the first time* (Excerpt 7, 1h21'20–1h22'22). What is the importance of this sequence?

7. The Imam Moussab and the Beards

Why does Malik ask Ryad to give a large sum of money (from the drug traffic) to the Imam Moussab? What is the upshot of that, ultimately?

8. The Deer

Malik has a dream the night following the scene in which César injures his eye and then chastizes him. He sees a herd of deer running on the highway in his car headlights at night. *Review this sequence* (Excerpt 8, 1h32'18–1h33'34). In a later scene, when Malik is with Brahim Lattrache, their car has a violent collision with a deer right after Malik warns Lattrache that it is going to happen. **How do you interpret the deer in this film?** It has been suggested that the deer are an allusion to Sufism, because the Sufi Saint Ibrahim ibn Adham underwent a conversion while hunting a deer, leading him to renounce material wealth and devote his life to God (Oscherwitz 260–70). **Do you agree** that it is possible to apply this idea to Audiard's film? How would it be relevant? What role does religion play in this film?

9. Cinematography

In the scene introduced by the title "the eyes and the ears," after César learns that Malik understands Corsican, there is a series of shots that show Malik's activities in the prison. **What is the function of the music here?** How has Malik's life changed? *Review this sequence* (Excerpt 9, 49'50–51'26).

Discuss the cinematography of *the scene where Malik delivers the attaché case full of money to the gangsters* to buy the freedom of César's henchman (Excerpt 10, 1h06'50–1h08'42).

Discuss the scene in which César berates Malik after injuring his eye, followed by the delirious dream and the shot with Rayeb whose T-shirt is burning (Excerpt 11, 1h31'30–1h32'14). In the first scene (as in the beginning sequence of the film), the Director of Photography, Stéphane Fontaine, puts his hand in front of the lens, darkening part of the frame. **What effect is he trying to produce here?**

Discuss the sequence where Malik and Jordi get high and then attend the party, as well as the following scene with Reyeb (Excerpt 12, 2h02'46–2h04'32). What can you say about the representation of Malik's (subjective) viewpoint?

Discuss, from the viewpoint of the image and soundtrack, *the sequence in which Malik attacks Jackie Marcaggi's bodyguards in Paris* (Excerpt 13, 2h12'42–2h14'30).

10. The Denouement

How does **the scene with Ryad's family,** the day after the event in Paris, play into the denouement of the film?

How do you interpret the subheading "40 days, 40 nights"? What is it alluding to? One critic feels that this reference indicates "an ungraspable Christ-like dimension of the character," adding that it is a "bizarre bifurcation, all the more so since the universe of the film is secular" (Tessé 21). What do you think? **What role does this allusion seem to assign to Malik? And to César?** What does it suggest regarding Malik's destiny?

The shots of Malik in solitary confinement alternate with those in which Ryad becomes sicker and sicker. Why?

While he is in solitary, Malik asks Reyeb twice if he is there. There is no answer. **What might that mean?**

How does the relationship between César and Malik change at the end of the film? Prison is a place where, in principle, justice is done. **Of what kind of "justice" may we speak here?** *Review the last scene in the prison yard, after Malik is released from the punishment cell* (Excerpt 14, 2h23'04–2h25'50).

Discuss the final sequence in which Malik gets out of prison. *Review this sequence* (Excerpt 15, 2h27'08–2h29'00). **What is the meaning of the three big black Mercedes that follow the couple while they walk toward the bus stop?** Djamila, Ryad's widow, teaches the words "cat" and "tayyara" ("airplane" in Arabic) to Issam, her baby. **Could the baby have a symbolic role here as regards the future?**

At the end of the film and during the end credits we hear the song "Mack the Knife." Where does this song come from? **Look for information about this song and its words on the internet. Why, in your opinion, does Audiard use it in his film?** What does the song suggest? Do you think that Berthold Brecht's *Verfremdungseffekt* ("alienation effect") is at work in this film, as has been suggested (Oscherwitz 272)? If yes, where? Look up information, if necessary, on this famous principle of Brechtian dramaturgy.

Jacques Audiard's Filmography

1994   *See How They Fall (Regarde les hommes tomber)*

1996   *A Self-Made Hero (Un héros très discret)*

2001   *On My Lips (Sur mes lèvres)*

2005   *The Beat That My Heart Skipped (De battre mon cœur s'est arrêté)*

2009   *A Prophet (Un prophète)*

2012   *Rust and Bone (De rouille et d'os)*

2015   *Dheepan*

Works Consulted

Audiard, Jacques, dir. *Un prophète*. Sony Pictures Home Entertainment, 2010.

B, Benjamin. "A Self-Made Man." *American Cinematographer* (Mar. 2010): 18–22.

Blumenfeld, Samuel. "Audiard. Les Seconds Couteaux crèvent l'écran." *Le Monde*, 22 Aug. 2009: n. pag.

"Début de polémique en Corse." Secrets de tournage sur *Un prophète*. 24 Dec. 2015 <www.allocine.fr/film/fichefilm-110268/secrets-tournage>.

Delcroix, Olivier. "La Bonne Etoile de Tahar Rahim." *Le Figaro*, 25 Aug. 2009: n. pag.

———. "Jacques Audiard: 'C'est mon plus gros film.'" *Le Figaro*, 26 Aug. 2009: n. pag.

Des Déserts, Sophie. "Les Gens vont comprendre nos problèmes." *Le Nouvel Observateur*, 27 Aug. 2009: n. pag.

Fontaine, David. "*Un prophète* (Une révélation)." *Le Canard enchaîné*, 26 Aug. 2009: n. pag.

Frodon, Jean-Michel. *Le Cinéma français. De la Nouvelle Vague à nos jours*. Paris: Cahiers du cinéma, 2010.

Korber, François. "Témoignage." *Le Monde*, 26 August 2009: n. pag.

Lebrun, Michel, and Jean-Paul Schweighaeuser. *Le Guide du "polar."* Paris: Syros, 1987.

Libiot, Eric. "Pourquoi tant d'amour?" *L'Express*, 20 Aug. 2009: n. pag.

Lorrain, François-Guillaume. "Dans *Un prophète*, de Jacques Audiard, Niels Arestrup est un parrain corse. Il explose l'écran. Rencontre." *Le Point*, 20 Aug. 2009: n. pag.

MacDonald, Megan C. "Humanism at the Limit and *Post-Restante* in the Colony: The Prison of the Postcolonial Nation in Jacques Audiard's *Un Prophète* (2009)." *International Journal of Francophone Studies* 15.3–4 (2012): 561–80.

Melinard, Michaël. "*Un prophète*. Audiard nous emmène au paradis." *L'Humanité Dimanche*, 20 Aug. 2009: n. pag.

Mérigeau, Pascal. "Audiard en prison." *Le Nouvel Observateur*, 20 Aug. 2009: 64–66.

Monnin, Isabelle. "C'est pas du cinéma." *Le Nouvel Observateur*, 27 Aug. 2009: n. pag.

Murat, Pierre. "Le Seigneur des barreaux." *Télérama*, 26 Aug. 2009: n. pag.

Oscherwitz, Dayna. "Monnet Changes Everything? Capitalism, Currency and Crisis in Jacques Becker's *Touchez pas au grisbi* (1954) and Jacques Audiard's *Un prophète* (2009)." *Studies in French Cinema* 15.3 (2015): 258–74.

Philippe, Olivier. *Le Film policier français contemporain*. Paris: Cerf, 1996.

Radovic, Rajko. "A Bandit Apart." *Film International* 8.3 (July 2010): 14–20.

Raspiengeas, Jean-Claude. "Requiems pour hommes seuls." *La Croix*, 18 May 2009: n. pag.

Schwartz, Arnaud. "Chronique carcérale d'une ascension." *La Croix*, 26 Aug. 2009: n. pag.

Tessé, Jean-Philippe. "Un modèle." *Cahiers du cinéma* 648 (Sept. 2009): 18–22.

Théate, Barbara. "Au bout de l'enfer carcéral." *Le Journal du Dimanche*, 23 Aug. 2009: n. pag.

———. "Naissance d'*Un prophète*." *Le Journal du Dimanche*, 23 Aug. 2009: n. pag.

"Une Evolution propre au film de prison." Secrets de tournage sur *Un prophète*. 24 Dec. 24, 2015 <www.allocine.fr/film/fichefilm-110268/secrets-tournage>.

Widemann, Dominique. "Le Cinéma doit ressembler à la vie." *L'Humanité*, 26 Aug. 2009: n. pag.

———. "Le Triomphe de l'intelligence." *L'Humanité*, 26 Aug. 2009: n. pag.

V

Personal Stories:
Dramas and Documentaries

Diane Kurys, *Coup de foudre/Entre nous* (1983)

André Téchiné, *Wild Reeds* (1994)

Agnès Varda, *The Gleaners and I* (2000)

We present in this section three films with strong personal dimensions. *Coup de foudre* (U.S. title *Entre nous*) and *Wild Reeds* (*Les Roseaux sauvages*) are fictions inspired by childhood or adolescent memories. For Kurys, it is about the passionate *coup de foudre* her mother experienced for another married woman and the effect on their family. Téchiné, for his part, bases his film on memories from his high school years, marked by the Algerian War and the discovery of his homosexuality. Agnès Varda's documentary *The Gleaners and I* (*Les Glaneurs et la glaneuse*) bears on both the phenomenon of gleaning and her profession as a filmmaker. Varda, a "gleaner of images," speaks also of herself as a human being ever more conscious of the onset of old age, an introspective view that would be completed in great depth in her autobiographical masterpiece *The Beaches of Agnès* (*Les Plages d'Agnès*, 2008).

Lesbianism and Homosexuality in the Cinema

Lesbianism was explored in the cinema long before the first film in this section of the present book, *Entre nous* (1983). In all likelihood, we meet it for the first time in 1929 in *Pandora's Box* (*Loulou*) by the German director Georg Wilhelm Pabst, then in quick succession in *Morocco* (1930) by his countryman Josef von Sternberg and in Leontine Sagan's *Girls in Uniform* (*Mädchen in Uniform*, 1931). Much later, after the strife-ridden 1930s and 1940s, we find it again in Jacqueline Audry's *Olivia* (1951), but it would not again appear in French cinema after that until the end of the 1960s in three films by male directors, Claude Chabrol's *Bad Girls* (*Les Biches*, 1968), Radley Metzger's adaptation of Violette Leduc's novel *Thérèse et Isabelle* (1968), and Guy Casaril's adaptation of Françoise Mallet-Joris' *The Wild Girl* (*Le Rempart des béguines*, 1972).

Everything changed in the 1970s when pornographic films and their omnipresent lesbianism reached their zenith: "For six months (from mid-August 1977 to February 1978), of 118 French films that were released, 51 were X-rated" (Audé 131). Writing in 1981, Audé laments that "the representation of lesbianism on the screen is appalling" (132), and her dismay is comprehensible, since one can only find in the preceding decade two French or Francophone films of any quality that feature lesbianism, both directed by women: *I, You, He, She,* (*Je, tu, il, elle,* 1974) by the Belgian filmmaker Chantal

Akerman and Nelly Kaplan's *A Young Emmanuelle* (*Néa*, 1976), although lesbianism isn't even the main focus in the latter film. The attempted "author" film by Michel Deville, *Trip on the Sly* (*Voyage en douce*, 1980), which portrays two married women who go on vacation together and is filled with lesbian coquetry and glamorous nudity, recalls the soft porno films of the 1970s. The fashion of erotic and pornographic films in France survives well into the following decade, to such an extent that one commentator speaks of a veritable "deluge" of such features in the middle of the 1980s (Quart 154).

It was not until the release of *Entre nous* that we would see a genuine French author film on love between two women become a commercial and critical success. On the international scene, however, lesbianism had become more and more common in nonpornographic films for the broad public in the 1980s with, for example, the Hungarian film *Another Way* (1982) by Kávoly Makk and János Xantus, the American films *Personal Best* (1982) by Roberte Towne, John Sayles' *Lianna* (1983), and Donn Deitch's *Desert Hearts* (1985), the British film *The Bostonians* (1984) by James Ivory, and the German film *Sheer Madness* (1985) by Margarethe Von Trotta—which, like Kurys' film, blurs the line between a close friendship between women and lesbianism (or bisexuality). During the same period, two films by female filmmakers were released in France that both treat in their own way lesbian desire, Joy Fleury's *Sadness and Beauty* (*Tristesse et beauté*, 1985) and Geneviève Lefèbvre's *Manuela's Loves* (*Le Jupon rouge*, 1987).

As Tarr and Rollet (91–92) observe, female filmmakers began to be interested again in lesbianism in the mid-1990s, although they can only cite Tonie Marshall's *Something Fishy* (*Pas très catholique*, 1994), Josiane Balasko's *French Twist* (*Gazon maudit*, 1995; see Chapter 17), and Catherine Corsini's *The New Eve* (*La Nouvelle Eve*, 1999). Nonetheless, Abdellatif Kechiche brought out in 2013 one of the most successful French films on lesbianism, *Blue Is the Warmest Color* (*La Vie d'Adèle*), which won ninety-four prizes, including the Palme d'Or at the Cannes Film Festival for both the director and the two female leads. Kechiche's film gives such a frank representation of lesbian relations, however, that a conservative organization in France requested and eventually obtained in December 2015 the cancellation of the film's screening license by the Administrative Tribunal of Paris "owing to the realistic sex scenes." The Minister of Culture appealed, and the following year the Council of State rendered a judgment in favor of the film, allowing its screening to resume.

Male homosexuality, one of the themes of the second film in this section, *Wild Reeds*, is much more widely represented on the big screen, and one may point to numerous films from the 1970s to the present period, among which are *The Boys in the Band* (Friedkin, 1970), *Death in Venice* (Visconti, *Mort à Venise*, 1971), *Birds of a Feather* (Molinaro, *La Cage aux folles*, 1978), *Querelle* (Fassbinder, 1982), *Victoria Victoria* (Edwards, 1982), *The Wounded Man* (Chéreau, *L'Homme blessé*, 1983), *Staircase C* (Tacchella, *Escalier C*, 1985), *My Beautiful Laundrette* (Frears, 1986), *Maurice* (Ivory, 1987), *My Own Private Idaho* (Van Sant, 1991), *The Wedding Banquet* (Ang Lee, *Garçon d'honneur*, 1993), *Philadelphia* (Demme, 1993), *Soft Pedal* (Aghion, *Pédale douce*, 1996), *Man Is a Woman* (Zilbermann, *L'Homme est une femme comme les autres*, 1998), *Water Drops on Burning Rocks* (Ozon, *Gouttes d'eau sur pierres brûlantes*, 2000), *The Closet* (Veber, *Le Placard*, 2001), *Brokeback Mountain* (Ang Lee, 2005), *Baby Love* (Garenz,

Comme les autres, 2008), and *Stranger by the Lake* (Guiraudie, *L'Inconnu du lac*, 2013)—not to mention the films that are also or especially about bisexuality, like *Le Conformiste* (Bertolucci, 1970), *Monique* (Brown, 1970), *The Wild Girl* (Casaril, *Le Rempart des béguines*, 1972), or slightly more recently *Evening Dress* (Blier, *Tenue de soirée*, 1986) and *Savage Nights* (Collard, *Les Nuits fauves*, 1992).

Works Consulted

Audé, Françoise. *Ciné-modèles, Cinéma d'elles*. Lausanne, Switzerland: L'Age d'homme, 1981.

Quart, Barbara Koenig. *Women Directors. The Emergence of a New Cinema*. New York: Praeger, 1988.

Tarr, Carrie, and Brigitte Rollet. *Cinema and the Second Sex. Women's Filmmaking in France in the 1980s and 1990s*. New York: Continuum, 2001.

14

Diane Kurys

Coup de foudre/Entre nous

(1983)

Diane Kurys, *Coup de foudre/Entre nous*: The relationship between Léna (Isabelle Huppert) and Madeleine (Miou-Miou) deepens.

Director	Diane Kurys
Screenplay	Diane Kurys, Alain Le Henry
Director of Photography	Bernard Lutic
Sound	Harald Maury, Claude Villand
Film Editor	Joële Van Effenterre
Music	Luis Bacalov
Art Director	Jacques Bufnoir
Costumes	Mic Cheminal
Continuity	Lucile Christol, Claudine Taulère
Producer	Ariel Zeitoun
Length	1h51

Cast

Miou-Miou (*Madeleine*), Isabelle Huppert (*Léna*), Guy Marchand (*Michel Korski, Léna's husband*), Jean-Pierre Bacri (*Costa Segara, Madeleine's husband*), Robin Renucci (*Raymond, Madeleine's first husband*), Patrick Bauchau (*Carlier, the art professor*), Jacques Alric (*M. Vernier, Madeleine's father*), Jacqueline Doyen (*Mme Vernier, Madeleine's mother*), Saga Blanchard (*Sophie, Léna's younger daughter*), Patricia Champane (*Florence, Léna's older daughter*), Guillaume Le Guellec (*René, Madeleine and Costa's son*), Christine Pascal (*Sarah, Léna's Jewish friend in the internment camp*)

Story

Léna Weber, an eighteen-year-old Jewish woman of Russian origin, is interned in a camp in the French Pyrenees in 1942. She escapes deportation to Germany and the death camps by agreeing to marry a former member of the French Foreign Legion, Michel Korski, who is also Jewish. When the Germans occupy the southern half of France, the so-called "Free Zone," Michel and Léna flee to Italy, then to Switzerland, before returning to France when it is liberated.

At the same time, Madeleine, a young middle-class woman, marries her lover, who, like her, is an art student in Paris. During a raid by Nazi-affiliated militiamen who have come to arrest their art professor Carlier, a group of Resistance fighters launches a counterattack. Caught between the two groups, her husband is killed by a stray bullet.

Ten years later, Léna and Michel are living in Lyon, where Michel owns and runs a successful garage. Madeleine and Léna meet by chance at a school event. Léna has two little girls, Florence and Sophie, while Madeleine has a little boy, René, born of her marriage with Costa Segara, a failed but amusing businessman who is trying to make money in the black market. Madeleine had met Segara during the Liberation and married him largely because he "made her laugh." The two women, both in bad marriages, bond immediately, experiencing a "coup de foudre" that will lead to a deep friendship with dramatic consequences for both of the couples.

The Director

Like little Sophie in *Coup de foudre*, Diane Kurys was born in Lyon in 1948 of Russian Jewish parents who divorced when she was five. The story of Léna, Michel, and Madeleine is the story of her parents, except that her father had a men's haberdashery in Lyon and not a garage (Tarr, *Diane Kurys* 12). Kurys was attracted very young to acting and, following the events of May 1968, abandoned her literary studies at the Sorbonne to devote herself to the stage. She acted for eight years in the theater, beginning in the Jean-Louis Barrault Company, but also doing café-théâtre and playing small roles in the movies and for television from 1972 to 1976 before giving up her career as an actress to devote herself to screenwriting and directing.

In 1977, with some support from the advance against receipts program, she made her first film, *Peppermint Soda* (*Diabolo menthe*), a full-length feature that had a highly successful run in the theaters and won the Louis Delluc Prize for the Best First Film. This was the beginning of a series of autobiographical films featuring her parents, herself, and her older sister. *Peppermint Soda* is about her adolescence, her middle school experience, and her relationship with her schoolmates and her sister, as well as with her divorced parents. We also see a fleeting suggestion of lesbian tendencies, a theme that will become much more explicit in her third film six years later, *Coup de foudre*. Renamed *Entre nous* for the American market, *Coup de foudre* met critical acclaim in France and was nominated for the Best Foreign Film at the Oscars in 1984.

Between the above two films, Kurys made *Cocktail Molotov* (1980), a much less successful film, both commercially and critically, that is related to the May 1968 events that Kurys had lived through at the age of twenty. After *Entre nous*, she made a highly popular film in English, *A Man in Love* (1987), which is about a torrid, troubled love affair between a young novice British actress and the (married) American male lead of the film in which they are both playing. In 1990 she returned to personal memories with *La Baule Les Pins* (also known as *C'est la vie*), another episode in her life as a little girl— summer vacations at La Baule—in which she again dwells on the difficulties of her parents' marriage. In this version, unlike *Entre nous*, her father physically mistreats his wife when he discovers that she is seeing another man and wants to leave him. Her parents are played this time by Nathalie Baye and Richard Berry rather than Isabelle Huppert and Guy Marchand, and the lesbian theme has disappeared completely.

In several of her following films, Kurys continues to depict somewhat embroidered aspects of her own life and, especially, intimate relationships. *Love after Love* (*Après l'amour*, 1992) recounts a year in the life of a thirty-year-old female novelist who has rather unhappy affairs with two different men, both of them married (or in another permanent relationship) and both fathers. Two years later, in *Alice et Elsa* (*A la folie*, 1994), a young artist named Alice is living happily in Paris with her husband Franck, a boxer. Her sister Elsa arrives unannounced one day, having left her unfaithful husband and their two children, and takes up residence in their home. There results a triangle in which Elsa attempts to destroy Alice's marriage. In the following two films, however, Kurys turns from the autobiographical genre to the depiction of others, in particular that of famous literary figures. She recounts first, in *The Children of the Century* (*Les Enfants du siècle*, 1999), the love affair between two literary giants of nineteenth-century romanticism, George Sand (a "scandalous" novelist) and Alfred de Musset (a poet and playwright). She then undertakes a fully biographical project, the life story of the novelist Françoise Sagan, the famous author of *Hello Sadness* (*Bonjour Tristesse*, 1954). She first shot a mini-series for television, *Sagan* (2008), in two parts, each an hour and a half long, a work that won a Globe de Cristal award for the Best Television Film or Series (2009), and a Best Actress award for Sylvie Testud. Pared down to one hour and fifty-seven minutes for the theaters, the film received three nominations at the Césars the same year.

Nearly a quarter century after *C'est la vie*, Kurys offered a final installment on the story of her parents, *For a Woman* (*Pour une femme*, 2013), with Benoît Magimel and Mélanie Thierry in the roles of Michel and Lena. This film contains two distinct episodes: her parents' life together in Lyon in 1947 just after the war and the relationship of the two girls with their dying father in the 1980s. In 2014 it was awarded a Best Director prize and a nomination for the Best International Film at the International Film Festival in Santa Barbara.

The Origin and Making of the Film

With a nine-week shoot in Cinemascope, three big stars, and a sixteen-million-franc budget (around $3 million at the time), *Entre nous* was a major production. After writing a first rough draft of the screenplay herself, Kurys spent a whole year refining it in collaboration with Alain Le Henry: "We sweat blood over it for a whole year. It was hard, but little by little the characters took form and substance. Details were recalled. People shared memories with us" (Pantel).

The memories are especially those of Kurys herself, recollections of her childhood when she was very small. She remembers the divorce of her parents and the day when her mother decided to go live with another woman, Madeleine, in Paris: "I was in Cabourg making sand castles with my sister. While we were losing Indochina, my parents were quarreling. My mother wanted her independence. My father wanted peace in the house. That evening they separated forever. Because of Madeleine. *Between Madeleine and me, it was love at first sight* ["*le coup de foudre*"], my mother said" (Jullian). Sophie, the little girl at the window at the very end of the film, is Kurys herself: "I was this little girl who is watching her parents argue at the end. I never saw them together again. And perhaps I made this film to reunite them, fictitiously, one last time . . ." (Tranchant). The film was for her, she remarks, a kind of exorcism: "You know, when divorces occur, the children often think that it's all their fault. They feel guilty. By bringing my parents back together again, showing them together both happy and unhappy, I exorcized myself. *Coup de foudre* was a way to free myself definitively from this suffering" (Baumberger). It is easy to understand why her film is dedicated to her parents and Madeleine.

What characterizes all of Diane Kurys' films is an obsessive concern with the details of the decor. In *Entre nous* the goal was to create the ambiance of a whole period, the beginning of the 1950s, in which we saw the introduction of the Renault 4CV and the Simca Aronde as well as large rounded refrigerators and Hoover vacuum cleaners, the fashion of flowery dresses, the use of amber sunscreen, certain perfumes, radio consoles, wind-up alarm clocks, and the popularity of the mambo. We find all of that and more in Kurys' film, which is striking, as the critic of *L'Humanité* says, for "the meticulous concern for the authenticity of every detail of the decor or the clothing" (Maurin). The same may be said regarding the music in the film, the "Big Band" of Glenn Miller that we hear at the Liberation, as well as the hit by Perry Como, "I Wonder Who's Kissing Her Now" (1939), released again after the war. The reconstitution of the historical period was essential for her because she wanted to fill her film with "the atmosphere, the states of mind, and the family and social relationships of an entire period" (Maurin), a period in which the place of the woman was in the home, her role to do the cooking and cleaning, raise the children, and respond to her husband's amorous desires if he were so inclined. As Kurys explains, "I used the memories people shared with me, but also the magazines from that period, and I tended to place my own 'madeleines' [in the Proustian sense] pretty much everywhere: a family painting, the dresses of the two sisters. . . . I'm concerned with details, authenticity . . . it's what produces the strongest impact. . . . I also try to control everything: the suitcases and shoes of the 3,000 extras or the form of the refrigerators of that period" (Cornuz-Langlois). Only a convincing evocation of this precise period could create the context necessary to understand what was so unusual, shocking, and—yes—revolutionary in the behavior of the two female protagonists of the film.

The Actors

Unlike her first two films, in which the actors were unknowns, Kurys was able to cast three major film stars for *Entre nous*, Miou-Miou, Isabelle Huppert, and Guy Marchand. All three of them—but also Jean-Pierre Bacri, less known at this time—were highly praised by the press for their performances in the film: "Jean-Pierre Bacri brings to life magnificently the character with the smallest role. Guy Marchand is more and more astonishing. He's always been amazing, but here he is an immense actor. Miou-Miou plays here one her best roles, perhaps the very best. Isabelle Huppert finally shows her mettle as an actress. . . . Thanks to these two *ad-mi-ra-ble* actresses, Madeleine and Léna are two women we will never forget" (Bescós).

Isabelle Huppert has become a superstar of French cinema. She began on the stage in the 1960s, winning acting awards along the way before launching her career in the movies, where she would garner some sixty acting prizes and a couple dozen nominations. She was nominated sixteen times for the Best Actress César and won this award for Claude Chabrol's *The Ceremony* (*La Cérémonie*, 1995) and Paul Verhoeven's *Elle* (*She*, 2016).

Miou-Miou ("Meow-Meow"), the stage name of Sylvette Herry given her by the famous comedian Coluche, began her career as an actress in the café-théâtre (see, on this subject, "The Comic Tradition and the Café-Théâtre" in Chapter 17 on Josiane Balasko's *French Twist*). She made her mark in a 1974 road movie by Bertrand Blier that became a cult classic, *Going Places* (*Les Valseuses*), alongside Gérard Depardieu and Patrick Dewaere. She received nominations for the Best Actress César in several films before finally winning it in 1980 for Daniel Duval's *Mémoires of a French Whore* (*La Dérobade*, 1979). She was subsequently nominated for the same award six more times in her career, including for *Entre nous*.

Guy Marchand was a boxer and singer before becoming an actor. Before playing Michel in *Entre nous*, a role that brought him a Best Supporting Actor nomination at the Césars in 1984, he was already very well known to the French public for his roles in several commercially successful and critically lauded films, Maurice Pialat's *Loulou* (1980), Bertrand Tavernier's *Clean Slate* (*Coup de torchon*, 1981), and, the same year, *The Grilling* (*Garde à vue*), a police thriller directed by Claude Miller. Nominated first for the Best Supporting Actor César for *Loulou*, he won this award for his performance in *The Grilling*. Generally restricted to supporting roles in films, Marchand was still nominated three more times for the Best Supporting Actor César during a career that went from 1966 to the present time and included roles both on the big screen and on television. He received high critical praise for his acting in *Entre nous*, as in the following comment: "But the revelation of *Coup de foudre* is Guy Marchand. Who would have suspected that this pretty-faced crooner could become this tender, touching father, this clumsy and generous husband, in short, this 'good man' in every sense of the word? But he does" (Rochereau).

Of Algerian origin and little known at the time, Jean-Pierre Bacri began playing small roles on television in 1978. He was finally noticed in *Entre nous* and has subsequently had an exceptional career as a screenwriter, working in tandem with Agnès Jaoui and sharing with her five Best Screenplay Césars for Alain Resnais' *Smoking/No Smoking* (1993), Cédric Klapisch's *Family Resemblances* (*Un air de famille*, 1996), Alain Resnais' *Same Old Song* (*On connaît la chanson*, 1997), and then for *The Taste of Others*

(*Le Goût des autres*, 2000; see Chap. 18), and *Look at Me* (*Comme une image*, 2005), both directed by Jaoui herself. As an actor Bacri acted in countless films between 1979 and 2016 and received a half dozen Best Actor nominations, including, at the Césars, for Luc Besson's *Subway* (1985) and *The Taste of Others*. He won a Best Supporting Actor César for *Same Old Song* and a Best Actor prize at the Cabourg Film Festival for his role in *The Taste of Others*. He was awarded the René Clair Prize in 2001 for his many notable contributions to cinema.

The Reception

Generally, the cinema press received Kurys' film with unabated enthusiasm, seeing in it especially—and the expression is found again and again in the reviews—the unusual story of an "all-consuming friendship" between two women, if it is not a "passionate friendship," a "friendship at first sight," or an "amorous friendship." Is this a lesbian film? There is no meeting of the minds, and the critics, with only a few exceptions, avoid any categorical judgment on this question, preferring to point out the ambiguity of the relationship between the two women. For certain commentators, in any case, it is definitely a feminist film, but here again there is no unanimity. One critic maintains, for example, that "*Coup de foudre* is perhaps, without making much ado about it, the first really feminist French film" (Gastellier), while another considers, on the contrary, that "*Coup de foudre* is not a feminist but rather a feminine film" (Baignères), an opinion that is shared by a colleague who goes even further, declaring that the film is a "chronicle bathed in women's perfume—not feminist but exceedingly feminine" (Bescós).

Nonetheless, there is a very broad consensus regarding the adeptness and finesse of Kurys' depiction of the relationship between Léna and Madeleine: "Rarely has anyone shown so justly, with such humor and also with such cruelty, feminine complicity" (Leclère); "These two difficult characters are treated with tenderness, tactfulness, and subtlety" (Jamet). There is a quasi-consensus also on the quality of the painstaking reconstruction in the film of the ambiance of the 1950s, despite the opinion of one commentator who feels that Kurys takes the "conspicuous nostalgia" too far (Pascaud). For Rochereau—and he is far from the only critic to recognize the importance of this film—"*Coup de foudre* is already a milestone" in French cinema, and Thévenon states outright that Kurys, with her third film, "moves instantly . . . to the head of the squad of the high flyers of French cinema."

Entre nous was one of the most popular films in France in 1983 and was very well received in the United States, where it was met by enthusiastic reviews in the homosexual press in particular (Powrie 64), despite the strong reservations of certain American critics put off by the rough treatment of the men in relation to the two heroines (Kael 133–34 and Simon 56, for example). During the whole decade of the 1980s, only *Three Men and a Cradle* (*Trois hommes et un couffin*, 1985) by Coline Serreau filled more seats. In November 1983 the National Academy of Cinema confirmed the critical and popular reception of the film by awarding *Entre nous* its grand prize, adding even more prestige to a film already nominated by France for the Best Film in a Foreign Language Oscar. Kurys won, moreover, the FIPRESCI Prize at the International Film Festival of San Sebastián, before her film was nominated for four Césars the following spring: Best Film, Best Actress (Miou-Miou), Best Supporting Actor (Guy Marchand), and

Best Original Screenplay and Dialogues. This is hardly a negligible achievement for a "woman's film" in this period.

"Women's Films"

Diane Kurys is among the most important female filmmakers in a country (and it isn't the only one) in which women had to fight tooth and nail to gain a foothold in the cinema industry. Generally confined to film editing, continuity ("script girl"), or, for the great majority, acting, women represented less than 6 percent of the active filmmakers in France in the 1980s (Lejeune 20). It wasn't until 1986, when the Fémis (the National Film School) replaced the IDHEC (the Institute for Advanced Film Studies), that the administrators began to encourage women to enroll in the directing track—formerly virtually reserved for men (Tarr and Rollet 6).

The tradition of woman filmmakers dates, nonetheless, from the very origins of cinema in France, beginning with Alice Guy, who made her first fiction films (for Gaumont) in 1896, the same year as Georges Méliès, the best known of the earliest pioneers of fiction films in the world. Guy made hundreds of films, in the United States as well as in France, before retiring from filmmaking in 1920 (Breton 11). She was the contemporary of another major pioneer, Germaine Dulac, who made twenty-five films between 1915 and 1929, including the famous impressionist—and feminist—work, *The Smiling Madame Beudet* (*La souriante Madame Beudet*, 1923). Another female filmmaker, Marie Epstein, would pick up the torch and direct six feature films between 1929 and 1938, in tandem with Jean Benoit-Lévy (including *Children of Montmartre* [*La Maternelle*] in 1933), followed by Jacqueline Audry, the director of seventeen feature films from 1944 to 1967, including *Olivia* (1951), one of the first French films on lesbianism.

The modern period of female filmmakers certainly begins with Agnès Varda, the "grandmother" of the New Wave for certain critics, and her indie film *La Pointe Courte* (1954), along with Marguerite Duras, who began making films at the end of the 1960s, and whose best-known works are *Nathalie Granger* (1972) and *India Song* (1975). Although Duras is a major reference in women's cinema, her films were scarcely distributed beyond the art house circuit (that is, they were not considered commercially viable), whereas certain films by Varda met both critical and commercial success: *Happiness* (*Le Bonheur*, 1964), *One Sings, the Other Doesn't* (*L'Une chante, l'autre pas*, 1976), *Vagabond* (*Sans toit ni loi*, 1985), and her documentary *The Gleaners and I* (*Les Glaneurs et la glaneuse*, 2000; see Chap. 16).

However, Duras and Varda were quickly joined behind the camera by other women. The events of May 1968 and the creation of the Women's Lib Movement in 1972 served as a springboard for women who wanted to make films, and more than one hundred films were made by women in the decade of the 1980s. The creation of the Women's Film Festival in 1974, held in Créteil near Paris since 1985, gave an additional boost to female cinema: thirty-eight woman filmmakers made at least one feature film between 1974 and 1984 (Breton 59), and no less than fifty in the final years of the twentieth century (1997–99). Nearly 14 percent of the films made in France in the 1990s were women's films (Tarr and Rollet 1), and this figure hovers around 25 percent today. Despite all the difficulties they still must overcome to take their place in the world of cinema, it is in France that the greatest number of women succeed in making films (Vincendeau 10).

Among the contemporary French or Belgian female filmmakers who have had the most success (or who are the most prolific), other than Duras, Varda, and Kurys, we should mention Nina Companeez (*Faustine and the Beautiful Summer* [*Faustine et le bel été*, 1971]), Yannick Bellon (*John's Wife* [*La Femme de Jean*, 1974]), the Belgian Chantal Akerman (*Jeanne Dielman, 23 quai du Commerce 1080 Bruxelles*, 1975), Coline Serreau (*Three Men and a Cradle* [*Trois hommes et un couffin*, 1985]), Nadine Trintignant (*My Love, My Love* [*Mon amour, mon amour*, 1967]), Nelly Kaplan (*A Very Curious Girl* [*La Fiancée du pirate*, 1967]), Josiane Balasko (*French Twist* [*Gazon maudit*; see Chap. 17]), the Martiniquaise Euzhan Palcy (*Sugar Cane Alley* [*Rue Cases-Nègres*, 1983]), Aline Issermann (*The Destiny of Juliette* [*Le Destin de Juliette*, 1983]), Claire Denis (*Chocolat*, 1988; see Chap. 3), and, more recently, Catherine Breillat (*Romance*, 1999), although the few works mentioned here are only representative of a much larger production of films by the above filmmakers and other women.

Despite the feminist movement that encouraged many woman filmmakers to try their hand at directing, very few of these films are really "feminist," and numerous women are allergic to the very term "women filmmakers." They are filmmakers, period. As Agnès Varda says, "I would like my films to be received and viewed like the films of any other cineaste and to be received by everyone; I wouldn't like to be locked up in a category reserved for a certain public only; I do not want to contribute to the creation of either an artistic or feminist ghetto…" (Breton 67). In other words, women directors consider their works to be "author" films, just like those of the best male filmmakers, and not "women's films," a term that often has somewhat negative connotations.

All the same, films by women tend to distinguish themselves rather clearly from most films made by men, and Varda herself admits it: "We are women, we have a different relationship to the world, and we make films differently" (Breton 67). Films by women are not going to foreground, for example, the male gaze—which cinema has done since the origins of this medium perpetually dominated by men, in which women are portrayed first and foremost as sex objects. As Françoise Audé observes, "In situations concerning male and female relations, the viewpoint that is highlighted is that of the woman. The relationship is established by the woman, [and] the man is the object of the woman's gaze. He is the Other" (135). This is obvious in *Entre nous*, where we see the two husbands, Michel and Costa, through the eyes of the two women—and if we haven't yet understood that, Kurys offers us the cabaret scene in which Madeleine's husband is the object of the two women's gaze and is ridiculed by them…. Moreover, the image of men in films directed by women is often unattractive, if not despicable, which is hardly surprising when one considers both the manner in which women have often been represented in films directed by men and the difficulties they have had to face to earn a place behind the camera: "Virtually banned from directing for a half century, they were demanding the liberty to create and the right to have their own language…. It is hardly surprising that the day they took up their position behind the camera, women didn't give the most flattering roles to their hereditary oppressors" (Andreu 61).

STUDY GUIDE

What Happens in This Film?

1. In what historical period does the action of this film begin? How does Léna manage to get out of the Jewish internment camp in the Pyrenees?

2. What is happening in Madeleine's life at this time?

3. Where do Michel and Lena decide to go to escape the Germans? How do they get there?

4. What happens to Madeleine's husband when the French Gestapo members arrest Carlier, the art professor?

5. Why did Madeleine marry Costa?

6. What suggests that Léna is beginning to find her personal situation difficult to bear? What does she wish to do rather than spend all of her time at home? What does she want to learn, for example?

7. What dramatic event occurs when Madeleine and Léna go looking for a space to rent for their shop?

8. What happens in the train that Léna takes to go to Paris? Why is this experience so momentous for Léna?

9. What do Madeleine and Léna do in Paris?

10. Under what condition does Michel agree to help Léna open her shop?

11. How does Michel react when he discovers Madeleine with Léna in the shop that has just opened?

12. What does Léna tell Michel when he comes to see her in Cabourg?

True or False?

If the statement is false, correct it!

1. Léna is furious when she learns Michel's real name (Isaac Mordeha Simon Korski), because his name is so difficult to pronounce.

2. At their marriage Madeleine and her husband learn that German troops have crossed the demarcation line and thus have now occupied the former "Free Zone" (the south of France).

3. Léna meets Madeleine for the first time in the Lyon railroad station.

4. At the beginning Léna doesn't like Madeleine's manner.

5. Carlier refuses to buy the Modigliani painting that Costa tries to sell him because it is a fake.

6. When Michel surprises Madeleine with Carlier in his apartment, he gets angry and kicks them out of his home.

7. Costa bought on the black market a large shipment of shirts that only had one sleeve.

8. When Michel protests that Léna's black dress is so tight that her underpants are visible, Léna changes her dress.

9. Léna took 60,000 francs from the cash register of the garage to pay for a marble headstone for her mother's tomb in Anvers (Belgium).

10. When Léna returns to Lyon, Michel is furious. He calls her and Madeleine "dykes."

11. Madeleine stops answering Léna's letters because she is working so hard earning a living.

12. It is Madeleine's parents who tell Michel that Léna and Madeleine are at their vacation home in Cabourg.

What Did You Learn in the Introduction?

1. What did Diane Kurys do following the events of May 1968?

2. What is Kurys' first film, *Peppermint Soda*, about?

3. What happened in Kurys' life when she was five?

4. Why is the authenticity of the decor so important in *Entre nous*?

5. Who are the stars of this film? Are they well known to the general public?

6. Are the film critics in agreement that *Entre nous* is a feminist and a lesbian film? What terms do they use to describe the relationship between Léna and Madeleine?

7. What great honor did France bestow on Kurys' film?

8. What percentage of French filmmakers were women in the period when Kurys made *Entre nous*?

9. What roles were traditionally reserved for women in filmmaking?

10. What particular events served as an encouragement for women who wanted to become film directors?

11. Why does Agnès Varda not want to be considered a "woman filmmaker"?

12. What do most films made by women have in common?

Exploring the Film

1. The Title of the Film

The original title of Kurys' film is *Coup de foudre* ("Love at First Sight"), but for its release in the United States, they replaced it with *Entre nous* ("Between Us"). **How would you explain this decision?** What is the effect of this change? One critic, Chris Straayer, claims that friendship between women ("female bonding") is the polar opposite of love at first sight, which is reserved for heterosexual relationships (50, 54). Do you think that this is a good explanation for the title change?

2. The Beginning of the Film

Describe briefly the structure of the film's prologue, which is set in the period of the Occupation of France by the Germans (1940–45). **What is the function of this prologue in connection with the subsequent events in the film? What do Léna and Madeleine have in common as regards their past?** What are the consequences of the war and the Occupation on the situation of the two women when they meet?

3. The Characters

✦ Léna and Madeleine

Why are the two women attracted to each other initially? **Why is Léna fascinated by Madeleine from their first meeting at the school?** *Review this scene* (Excerpt 1, 30'00–31'46). **How does their relationship evolve?** Are there stages? Why do they continue to speak to each other formally (using "vous") even when they have become close friends?

Kurys' mother described her relationship with Madeleine as "a little more than a friendship, a little less than a passion." **How would you describe the relationship between Léna and Madeleine? How far does it go, in your opinion?**

The famous *New Yorker* film critic Pauline Kael is hard on Léna and Madeleine, saying that they are bourgeois women badly spoiled by their husbands, who work hard to support them and only receive for their trouble ridicule, scorn, and, in the end, desertion. Léna, for example, is seen by Kael as a superficial and frigid woman incapable of appreciating the devotion of her husband, who feels superior to him as soon as she comes under the influence of Madeleine, a very sophisticated woman, and begins to see him through the latter's eyes (133). **What do you think? Do you agree with this viewpoint on the two heroines of the film?**

✦ The Image of the Men

Is this film critical of men in general? Are Michel and Costa detestable? Kurys said in an interview, "Contrary to the feminists, I never go after men to settle accounts with them, any more than I do with women" (Andreu 61). **Does she succeed in creating a fair and sensitive image of men in *Entre nous*?**

✦ Michel

In speaking of Michel, a critic said, "Guy Marchand seems pathetic, touching and . . . despicable" (Fournier 15). **Do you agree? In what sense is Michel, too, a victim?**

Michel clearly adores his kids. As Straayer observes, he seems to be an "ideal father," which contradicts the typically negative image of men in a woman's film in this period. **Can this fact affect one's interpretation of this film?** *Review the picnic episode* (Excerpt 2, 42'15–42'51).

4. *The Léna-Michel Couple*

Describe this couple. After Madeleine and Costa dine with Michel and Léna, Madeleine tells her new friend, "I don't think you two go very well together." **Why does Madeleine say that to her?** Do you agree? Why? *Review the scene in which Léna talks about her husband with Madeleine* (Excerpt 3, 40'50–42'14).

Why does Michel try to seduce Madeleine? What connection might this have with Michel's marriage? **How do you explain Michel's behavior (and Madeleine's) when he discovers her in his bedroom with Carlier?** *Review this scène* (Excerpt 4, 54'33–55'58).

What do you think of the scene in which Michel refuses to go out with Léna because she had put on a black dress that he found indecent (so tight that you could see her panties beneath it)? Is he wrong in your opinion? What did Léna do? (Her reaction apparently brought loud applause from female spectators when the film came out [Tarr, "Changing Representations" 234]). *Review this scene* (Excerpt 5, 1h08'55–1h10'01).

5. *The Failure of the Two Couples*

Why, in your opinion, is Madeleine so unhappy in her marriage? Is Costa mean to her? How would you describe him? **Why do the two couples fail completely?** Are the two women in no way responsible for this failure? What could we criticize in particular in Léna's behavior? Why does Léna find it more difficult than Madeleine to leave her husband? **Is this film a criticism of marriage as an institution?** Explain your point of view.

6. *The Decor and the Music*

In *Entre nous* we see Renault 4CVs, a large radio console, a Hoover vacuum cleaner, a large refrigerator, a windup alarm clock, as well as dresses, perfumes, and period hairdos, among other things. **Why are these elements so important to this film?** What connection do they have to the action and themes?

What music do we hear in this film? What is its role? Here are the words of the Perry Como song that we hear: "I wonder who's kissing her now. Wonder who's teaching her how. Wonder who's looking into her eyes, breathing sighs and telling lies." **Why are these words ironic?** *Review the scene where Michel comes home after work* (Excerpt 6, 36'00–38'32). In addition to the music, what is important in this scene? **What does it tell us about Michel's character?** We hear this song again at the end of the film. **Is the music diegetic (originating in the film's world) in both cases?** What importance might this have? **What particular effect does the repetition of this song have on the sexual ambiguity of the film?**

7. Women's Films and Narrative Viewpoint in Entre nous

What is there in the point of view, the treatment of the gaze (that of the characters, that of the spectator) that is a function of the fact that this is a film made by a woman? What observations could you make, in this respect, on the scene in the cabaret where Léna and Madeleine watch Costa do his pantomime act? *Review the following excerpt of that scene* (Excerpt 7, 1h11'20–1h12'43). In general, what happens to the male gaze in this film? Think, for example, of the two men who watch Léna and Madeleine dance the mambo together in the nightclub in Paris. How do the two women turn the tables on the men as regards the gaze? *Watch this excerpt again also* (Excerpt 8, 1h25'24–1h26'00).

8. The Maternal Instinct

What role do maternal feelings play in *Entre nous*? Is there a difference between Léna and Madeleine in this respect? Does the film make any judgment on the effect of the behavior of the two women on their children? If so, in which scenes in particular? *Review the scene in which Michel brings Sophie back home after Léna and Madeleine forget her in the street* (Excerpt 9, 1h05'18–1h05'56). One critic maintains that the continual presence of the children encourages the spectators to regard the two women simply as friends (Holmlund 152). Do you agree?

9. The Taboo of Female Eroticism

In postwar society, female eroticism (like lesbianism, of course) is still taboo. How does this taboo affect Léna and Madeleine's behavior with each other?

Is *Entre nous* about lesbianism? We know that Kurys refused to include overtly lesbian scenes despite the wishes of certain backers of the film. Why, in your opinion? Are there nonetheless scenes in the film that lead us to ponder this question? Kael suggested that the film was about "spiritual lesbianism," that is, lesbianism without sex (134). What do you think?

Madeleine is a sculptor, and her workshop is filled with statues of nude women. Are we supposed to assume that is an indication of her sexual preferences?

Much has been said (positively and negatively) about the "ambiguity" of the relationship between the two women in this film. Do you find the film ambiguous in this respect? One critic emphasizes the importance of the looks that the two women exchange, looks that could suggest either amorous desire or friendship (Holmlund 145). Could that contribute to the film's ambiguity? What is the role of ellipses (action that is not shared with the spectators) in the creation of ambiguity here? In your opinion, is the ambiguity of this film a quality or a flaw?

10. Heterosexuality

What role does heterosexuality play in this film? How does it contribute to the ambiguity that many critics see in the character of the two women and in their relationship?

In the train on the way to Paris where she is going to meet Madeleine, Léna indulges in some serious sexual activity with a soldier who happens to be in the same compartment—as his buddies watch. *Review this scene* (Excerpt 10, 1h22'18–1h23'13). **Do you agree with Straayer, who feels that "the scene in the train reaffirms Léna's heterosexuality" (55)?** When Léna describes this episode to Madeleine, she reveals that she has had an orgasm for the first time, even though she didn't "go all the way." And it is Madeleine who has to explain to her what she has experienced. **May we conclude, as Straayer later does, that Madeleine "is cinematically responsible" for Léna's orgasm?** Detail: Does the train whistle play a metaphorical role at the end of the sex episode?

11. Patriarchal Society

Straayer suggests that *Entre nous* "attacks more vigorously the patriarchal structure than individual men" (54). Although the principle of absolute equality between the sexes is written into the Constitution of the Fourth Republic in 1946, women still don't have certain rights in the 1950s (they still need authorization from their husband, for example, to open a bank account and won't receive this right until 1965). **How is this aspect of the situation of women represented in this film?** Put another way, how does Kurys bring out the patriarchal character of French society in this period? *Review the scene in the garage, then the scene at home* (Excerpt 11, 47'26–48'54). **Go online and search for information on the rights of women in France in the 1950s.**

12. The Shop

What does the shop represent for Léna and Madeleine? Ginsburg suggests that the ultimate breakup of Léna and Michel is provoked on purpose by Madeleine when she makes her presence known at the very moment that Michel arrives with a big plant to celebrate the opening of the shop. This is, according to Ginsburg, a "subversive" act intended to anger Léna's husband and drive him to the violent action that we witness (56). **Do you agree with this interpretation?** *Review this sequence* (Excerpt 12, 1h40'00–1h41'30).

Certain commentators maintain also that the close-up of Michel's bloodied hands near his crotch toward the end of this scene suggests his fear of emasculation ("castration") by the female gaze (Powrie 70) or by a world dominated by women (Tarr and Rollet 245). **What do you think of this viewpoint?**

13. The Denouement

Review the last scene of the film (Excerpt 13, 1h45'32–1h48'54). **How would you describe Léna's treatment of Michel in this scene?**

Kurys says in an interview, "I do not believe they are leaving to go live together. I think they are just going to be there for one another, just as closely, as intimately, as intensely as before" (Joecker and Sanzio 120). **Is this your impression also?**

Kurys adds that she thinks the relationship between the two women is more sentimental and sensual than sexual: "I believe that, in reality, they are each seeking a man; they probably want to reproduce the type of relationships that were ingrained in them earlier. If they have other affairs, it probably won't be with other women—but what they found together, between the two of them, is unique" (Joecker and Sanzio 121). **Do** you agree with this interpretation of the relationship between Madeleine and Léna? Kurys also said in an interview that the letters exchanged between her mother and Madeleine were "passionate," and that the two women, according to her mother, had tried unsuccessfully to have sexual relations; all it did was "make them laugh." Later, both women had love affairs with other men (Pally). **Does this knowledge have any effect on your interpretation of the film?**

At the end of the film we learn that the narrative viewpoint (at least in part) is that of Diane Kurys when she was five years old (Sophie in the film). **What is the effect of this revelation on the spectator?** How might it affect, for instance, our perception of the relationship between Léna and Madeleine or of the separation of Kurys' parents?

Diane Kurys' Filmography

1977   *Peppermint Soda (Diabolo menthe)*

1979   *Cocktail Molotov*

1983   *Coup de foudre/Entre nous*

1987   *A Man in Love (Un homme amoureux)*

1990   *La Baule-les-Pins/C'est la vie*

1992   *Love after Love (Après l'amour)*

1994   *Alice et Elsa (A la folie)*

1999   *The Children of the Century (Les Enfants du siècle)*

2003   *I'm Staying! (Je reste!)*

2005   *L'Anniversaire*

2008   *Sagan*

2013   *For a Woman (Pour une femme)*

2016   *"Cut It Out!" (Arrête ton cinéma!)*

Works Consulted

Andreu, Anne. "Ces dames se sont mises à la caméra...." *L'Evénement du jeudi*, 13 Aug. 1992: 61.

Audé, Françoise. *Ciné-modèles, Cinéma d'elles*. Lausanne, Switzerland: L'Age d'homme, 1981.

Baignères, Claude. "Bouffée d'oxygène." *Le Figaro*, 8 Apr. 1983: n. pag.

Baumberger, Jeanne. "Avec *Coup de foudre*, Diane Kurys s'est exorcisée." *Le Provençal*, 10 Apr. 1983: n. pag.

Bescós, José-M. "Coup de foudre." *Pariscope*, 13 Apr. 1983: n. pag.

Boillon, Colette. "Le Bonheur d'être comédien. Un entretien avec Guy Marchand." *La Croix*, 7 Apr. 1983: n. pag.

Breton, Emile. *Femmes d'images*. Poitiers: Messidor, 1985.

Colvile, Georgiana M. M. "Mais qu'est-ce qu'elles voient? Regards de Françaises à la caméra." *The French Review* 67.1 (Oct. 1993): 73–81.

Cornuz-Langlois, Nicole. "Diane Kurys: 'Ce sont les détails qui font un film.'" *Le Matin*, 8 Apr. 1983: n. pag.

Forbes, Jill. *The Cinema in France after the New Wave*. Bloomington: Indiana UP, 1992.

Fournier, Thérèse. "Diane Kurys: en amitié, le coup de foudre est aussi fort qu'en amour." *F Magazine*, 14 Apr. 1983: 15.

Gastellier, Fabian. "Coup de foudre." *Les Echos*, 7 Apr. 1983: n. pag.

Ginsburg, Terri. "*Entre Nous*, Female Eroticism, and the Narrative of Jewish Erasure." *Journal of Lesbian Studies* 4.2 (2000): 39–64.

Holmlund, Christine. "When Is a Lesbian Not a Lesbian?: The Lesbian Continuum and the Mainstream Femme Film." *Camera Obscura* 9.1–2 (1991): 145–78.

Jamet, Dominique. "Mais au café de Flore, y'avait déjà des folles. . . . " *Le Quotidien de Paris*, 6 Apr. 1983: n. pag.

Joecker, Jean-Pierre, and Alain Sanzio. "Coup de foudre pour Diane Kurys." *Masques* 18 (1983): 118–23.

Jullian, Marcel. "Coup de foudre." *V.S.D.*, 7 Apr. 1983: n. pag.

Kael, Pauline. "The Current Cinéma." *The New Yorker*, 5 Mar. 1984: 130–34.

Kurys, Diane, dir. *Coup de foudre/Entre nous*. Fox Lorber Home Video, 1998.

Leclère, Marie-Françoise. "Les Films-femmes." *Le Point*, 4 Apr. 1983: n. pag.

Lejeune, Paule. *Le Cinéma des femmes: 105 femmes cinéastes d'expression française (France, Belgique, Suisse) 1985–1987*. Paris: Editions Atlas Lherminier, 1987.

Maurin, François. "Une histoire d'amitié." *L'Humanité*, 7 Apr. 1983: n. pag.

Pally, Marcia. "Come Hither—But Slowly: Dessert with Diane Kurys." *Village Voice*, 31 Jan. 1984: 52, 62.

Pantel, Monique. "Pour Diane Kurys, le tournage de *Coup de foudre*, c'était le bonheur total." *France-Soir*, 7 Apr. 1983: n. pag.

Pascaud, Fabienne. "Coup de foudre." *Télérama*, 16 Apr. 1983: n. pag.

Powrie, Phil. *French Cinema in the 1980s. Nostalgia and the Crisis of Masculinity*. Oxford, UK: Clarendon Press, 1997.

Quart, Barbara Koenig. *Women Directors. The Emergence of a New Cinema*. New York: Praeger, 1988.

Rochereau, Jean. "Féminisme bien tempéré." *La Croix*, 7 Apr. 1983: n. pag.

Simon, John. "Dishonesty Recompensed." *National Review*, 4 May 1984: 54–56.

Straayer, Chris. "The Hypothetical Lesbian Heroine." *Jump Cut* 35 (Apr. 1990): 50–57.

Tarr, Carrie. "Changing Representations of Women in the Cinema of Diane Kurys." *Women in French Studies* 5 (Winter 1997): 233–41.

———. *Diane Kurys*. Manchester, England: Manchester UP, 1999.

———. "Maternal Legacies. Diane Kurys' *Coup de* foudre (1983)." *French Film: Texts and Contexts*. Ed. Susan Hayward and Ginette Vincendeau. London: Routledge, 2000. 240–52.

Tarr, Carrie, and Brigitte Rollet. *Cinema and the Second Sex. Women's Filmmaking in France in the 1980s and 1990s*. New York: Continuum, 2001.

Thévenon, Patrick. "Ce que Sophie savait." *L'Express*, 8–14 Apr. 1983: 23.

Tranchant, Marie-Noëlle. "Au bonheur de Diane." *Le Figaro*, 6 Apr. 1983: n. pag.

Vincendeau, Ginette. "Women's Cinema, Film Theory and Feminism in France. Reflections after the 1987 Créteil Festival." *Screen* 28.4 (1987): 4–18.

15

André Téchiné

Wild Reeds (Les Roseaux sauvages)

(1994)

André Téchiné, *Wild Reeds*: François (Gaël Morel) and Serge (Stéphane Rideau) go to Toulouse by moped.

Director ....André Téchiné
Screenplay .... André Téchiné, Gilles Taurand, Olivier Massart
Director of Photography .... Jeanne Lapoirie
Sound .... Jean-Paul Mugel
Film Editor .... Martine Giordano
Art Director .... Pierre Soula
Costumes .... Elisabeth Tavernier
Continuity .... Claudine Taulère
Producers .... Alain Sarde, Georges Benayoun,
.... Paul Rozenberg, Chantal Poupaud
Length.. 1h50

Cast

Elodie Bouchez (*Maïté*), Gaël Morel (*François*), Stéphane Rideau (*Serge*), Frédéric Gorny (*Henri*), Michèle Moretti (*Mrs. Alvarez*), Jacques Nolot (*Mr. Morelli*)

Story

Spring 1962, a seemingly commonplace wedding in a quiet corner of southwestern France. However, Pierre, the groom, must resume his military service in Algeria, where the OAS (*Organisation de l'armée secrète*/Secret Army Organization) has been spreading terror two months before independence, which is violently opposed by the French inhabitants. Mrs. Alvarez, his former French teacher and a communist activist, refuses to help him desert. Pierre's brother Serge, for his part, has just been rejected by Maïté, Mrs. Alvarez's daughter, who refused to dance with him. She preferred chatting with François, one of Serge's classmates whom he hardly knows.

After returning to boarding school, Serge tries to make friends with François so they can combine their strengths in order to prepare the *baccalauréat* (end of high school exam) and . . . attract girls. They also eventually exchange caresses in their dorm room, meaningless erotic games for Serge but a troubling, decisive experience for François, who is beginning to acknowledge his homosexuality. Henri, a new student, soon invites himself into their budding friendship. He is a *pied-noir* (a descendant of French settlers) and an OAS sympathizer, which pleases neither Maïté, a communist like her mother, nor Serge, whose brother has now died in Algeria, most likely a victim of an OAS attack. Thus begins a dance of desire and repulsion among the four protagonists, with Henri as the outlier and troublemaker.

The Director

A filmmaker, screenwriter, and occasional actor, André Téchiné (1943–) has made over twenty-five films since the beginning of the 1970s. Like François in *Wild Reeds*, a sort of alter ego according to the filmmaker, Téchiné was a talented high school student who had a passion for cinema. He left his native region in the Southwest—where *Wild Reeds* was shot—to study cinema in Paris, where he subsequently became a critic at the *Cahiers du cinéma* (1964–68) and an assistant director.

Téchiné has said that he made his first films as a reaction against the New Wave, even though he often praised the filmmakers associated with this movement in the *Cahiers*. He met considerable success with *French Provincial* (*Souvenirs d'en France*, 1975), a family saga with Jeanne Moreau spanning forty years, from the Popular Front of the late 1930s to the 1970s. Téchiné described his next film, *Barocco* (1976), a thriller with Isabelle Adjani and Gérard Depardieu, as "a reflection on expressionism in American cinema, which had made a strong impression on me" (Kaganski). This movie was followed by a period drama, *The Brontë Sisters* (*Les Soeurs Brontë*), in 1979.

Téchiné and critics agree that his melancholic *Hotel America* (*Hôtel des Amériques*, 1981), the story of an encounter between a young drifter and a widow who cannot cope with her husband's death, marks a turning point toward more realism in his work. It was also his first collaboration with Catherine Deneuve, who would become his favorite actress, and his first film with a (secondary) homosexual character. "More and more," he says about his trajectory as a filmmaker, "I made my films all alone in a corner, and I freed myself not only from my strong feelings about the New Wave, but also from the imaginary mentorship of filmmakers who had inspired me to make movies," among them Murnau, Tourneur, Dreyer, Renoir, Rossellini, and Demy (Kaganski).

Téchiné went on to make several well-received dramas that also revealed new talent among his actors. In 1985, *Rendez-vous*, the story of a love triangle, received the Best Director Award at the Cannes Film Festival and brought attention to Juliette Binoche. *The Innocents* (1987), another love triangle, winner of four nominations and one award at the Césars, displays Téchiné's interest in social themes—the rise of the National Front here—and features Abdellatif Kechiche, who will become a filmmaker and make *Games of Love and Chance* (*L'Esquive*, 2003; see Chap. 8), in his second movie role. *I Don't Kiss* (*J'embrasse pas*, 1991) deals with a young man from the provinces who goes to Paris with dreams of becoming an actor but ends up as a male prostitute. Manuel Blanc, who plays the lead role, received the Best Promising Actor César.

Téchiné reached his highest critical and popular acclaim in the 1990s. *My Favorite Season* (*Ma saison préférée*, 1993)—six nominations at Cannes and seven at the Césars—is about difficult family relationships, another of his favorite topics. Daniel Auteuil and Catherine Deneuve play estranged siblings who reunite around their ailing mother.

According to critics, *Wild Reeds* marks the end of Téchiné's earlier exploration of film form and his transition to a more classical yet personal style, an evolution that Lalanne compares to Truffaut's: "We can see in this trajectory a similar path [. . .]. Truffaut, like Téchiné, seemed bent on making classical films, but in a different way" (Lalanne, *Wild Reeds* 17).

Téchiné has since made around ten films that revisit some of the themes of his earlier works. Among the most noteworthy is *Thieves* (*Les Voleurs*, 1996), a film noir on family relationships featuring the Auteuil-Deneuve duo and in which Deneuve plays a lesbian philosophy teacher. Drug trafficking and illegal immigration form the backdrop of *Far* (*Loin*, 2001), set in Tangier, Morocco. In this film we reconnect with two characters from *Wild Reeds*, played by the same actors. Serge, the protagonist, has failed his *baccalauréat* and become a truck driver working the route between Europe and Morocco, where he meets up with his girlfriend and a childhood friend during layovers. François, now a filmmaker, has come to introduce a film by Renoir at the local film club.

Téchiné's next films depict encounters between middle-aged men and women, some of whom are still stuck in the past (*Changing Times* [*Les Temps qui changent*], with the mythical Deneuve-Depardieu couple in 2004, and *Unforgivable* [*Impardonnables*], shot in Venice, in 2011). They deal with social themes, like AIDS in *The Witnesses* (*Les Témoins*, 2007) and religious and ethnic tensions in *The Girl on the Train* (*La Fille du RER*, 2009), in which a young compulsive liar alleges that she was the victim of an anti-Semitic attack by black men. This film was inspired by a true story, as was the thriller *In the Name of My Daughter* (*L'Homme qu'on aimait trop*, 2014), based on the widely publicized disappearance of a casino owner's daughter. Téchiné's last film to date, *Being 17* (*Quand on a 17 ans*, 2016), deals like *Wild Reeds* with the discovery of homosexuality by adolescents, a topic close to the director's heart. In 2009, moreover, he presided over the jury of a screenplay competition against homophobia titled "How We Look at Gay Youth" organized by the Ministry for Youth and Sports and the National Institute for Prevention and Health Education.

With around seventy nominations and six important awards, including the Prix René-Clair in recognition of his life work in 2003, Téchiné ranks among the great French filmmakers. He has made genre films and personal pieces sometimes inspired by his own life and has worked with both unknowns—launching their film careers—and renowned actors (Marie-France Pisier, Isabelle Adjani, Isabelle Huppert, and Emmanuelle Béart, in addition to those already mentioned). His films express the spirit of the times and deal with social issues (drugs, AIDS, prostitution, juvenile delinquency, politics, immigration, sexual identity) without "turning into a sociological study" or delivering a moral message or lesson, as he likes to point out (Kaganski). What Téchiné loves above all is to film "moments of self-questioning when our lives partly escape us and seem strange." "If there is one common thread in my films," he adds, it is "the way we deal with change" (Roth-Bettoni 51).

The Origin and Making of the Film

Wild Reeds is the expanded version of a television film titled *The Oak and the Reed* (*Le Chêne et le roseau*) commissioned by the Arte channel. It was part of the series *All the Boys and Girls of Their Age* (*Tous les garçons et les filles de leur âge*), consisting of nine hour-long telefilms that depict the transition to adulthood in the 1960s, 1970s, and 1980s. The producers entrusted the making of the films to directors who were eighteen in these respective decades. For Téchiné, it was the beginning of the 1960s, the setting of *Wild Reeds*. Arte imposed other restrictions: the films had to be autobiographical, include a party scene with teenagers and popular songs of the time, and blend feelings of love and the political context. The shoot was to last between one and three weeks, on a limited budget.

Téchiné accepted the offer because he considered this project a welcome break after *My Favorite Season*, his hit of the previous year. He liked being free of all financial responsibility but did not particularly care for the theme, remarking that "a teenage love story sounded very boring" (Lalanne, "Pour la sortie"). The film took shape, however, when he remembered the intrusion of the Algerian war in his own life the day a *pied-noir*, an Algerian-born French student, arrived in his provincial high school. Téchiné and his collaborators wrote the screenplay, which ended with François reading one of La Fontaine's fables, "The Oak and the Reed." They subsequently expanded this piece into *Wild Reeds* by developing the narrative threads that were still hanging, blending the political and intimate aspects better, and deepening Maïté's character.

Téchiné used the Algerian War as the "underlying thread of the film." He wanted to show its impact in a "remote corner of deep France" by gradually increasing its presence in the story in order to push the characters to find themselves (Jousse 13). Even though his family and friends were not personally affected by this conflict, the event that Téchiné refers to above broadened his worldview and helped him set his plot in motion. As he explains, "I had really witnessed the arrival of a *pied-noir* student in high school, and as a result I discovered some beliefs that I didn't know existed, or rather that I had never been confronted with. They were totally alien to me. I was raised in a sort of progressive Catholic ideology [. . .] and was familiar with communist ideology—because our teachers were communists" (Roth-Bettoni 51). Techiné had already filmed a politically involved character (on the extreme right) in *The Innocents* (1987), but not in the Algerian context.

By making *Wild Reeds*, Téchiné wished to reflect on wisdom that is only acquired through experience and cannot be passed on by others: "Humans always make mistakes. Our lives are a succession of adjustments, and these adjustments are what I like to focus on, as they are the only way to learn" (Roth-Bettoni 51). Specifically he wanted to show what happens when people with opposite opinions meet: "I did not try to make a politically correct film [...]. I wanted a direct face-off with the enemy that would not go as expected, that would lead to questioning on both sides" (Jousse 13).

The film was shot in Villeneuve-sur-Lot, in southwestern France, in the middle school and landscape of his youth. The director used two 16 mm cameras that allowed him to include some improvisation and obtain a more natural performance from the actors (because the one being addressed was always in front of a camera instead of off-screen, as is the case in the classic shot/reverse shot with one camera, a technique that Téchiné wanted to avoid). Following his usual approach, he shot each scene as if it were a short film and not part of any narrative continuity (Kaganski). The actors only knew the part of the story that they were playing (Jousse 13). Thanks to this approach the shoot, as Téchiné comments, was very easy and pleasant: "[It] took place in a state of jubilation, of euphoria, with an exhilarating freedom that I had never experienced before." On the other hand, the editing lasted six months and was complicated "because we had to find a coherent form and introduce continuity at that stage" (Roth-Bettoni 50).

Téchiné finds paradoxical that a commissioned film should have become his greatest success, and he was very surprised by its reception. In his mind he had made a film on a political subject, the Algerian War, but spectators and critics mostly saw in it a story about a young man discovering his homosexuality. As he explained, "The film was screened at gay festivals in the USA; at the risk of seeming pretentious, I even became a gay idol (laughs). The story of a teenager discovering his sexual orientation was a novelty, and as a result the Algerian War was ignored (laughs). That's the way it often goes; we cannot foresee what spectators are going to remember" (Lalanne, "Pour la sortie").

The Actors

To make *Wild Reeds* Téchiné hired a group of amateurs to play the young people and a few professionals for the adult roles. As usual he was excellent at casting because his three teenage male actors were nominated for the Most Promising Actor César, and Elodie Bouchez received the Most Promising Actress César. They have all pursued careers in film.

Gaël Morel (François) has played in six films since *Wild Reeds*, including Téchiné's *Far* (2001), in which he portrays a secondary character who is a filmmaker. He stepped behind the camera in 1995 and made his first two feature films, *Full Speed* (*A toute vitesse*, 1996) and *First Snow* (*Premières neiges*, 1999) with two of the stars of *Wild Reeds* in leading roles, Elodie Bouchez and Stéphane Rideau. Morel has made around ten films to date. His fourth feature film, *After Him* (*Après lui*), a drama with Catherine Deneuve, the muse of his mentor Téchiné, won four nominations at the Directors' Fortnight at Cannes in 2007.

Stéphane Rideau (Serge) held the lead role in *Far* (2001) and has played in twenty-five films, including six of Gaël Morel's eight films. He also worked as casting director for Téchiné's *The Girl on the Train* (2009).

Frédéric Gorny (Henri) also became an actor after *Wild Reeds*. He has appeared in around thirty short and feature films and television series. He is best known for his participation in the twelve seasons of *Lawyers & Associates* (*Avocats & associés*), a crime series.

Élodie Bouchez had acted in a few films before *Wild Reeds* brought her fame. Her talent was confirmed a few years later when, after playing in another dozen films, she received three prestigious awards for her portrayal of Isa in *The Dreamlife of Angels* (*La Vie rêvée des anges*, 1998; see Chap. 7): the César for Best Actress, the Best Actress award at Cannes, and the Lumières prize for Best Actress (see the presentation of this film in Chapter 7). She has appeared in over seventy films and television series in France and the United States, including several films by Gaël Morel and the American series *Alias* and *The L Word*.

The teachers are portrayed by seasoned actors. Michèle Moretti (Mrs. Alvarez) has played in around a hundred films since the 1960s. She won the Best Supporting Actress César for *Wild Reeds*, her seventh collaboration with Téchiné. Working with the director was particularly beneficial to Jacques Nolot (Mr. Morelli), who besides acting in over sixty films is also a screenwriter, director, and writer. Like Moretti, he has appeared in seven films by Téchiné and collaborated on two others, adapting his own autobiography in *I Don't Kiss* and one of his plays in the medium-length film *La Matiouette, or the Hinterland*. Like his friend Téchiné, Nolot is a gay man born in southwestern France. Both his writings and his four movies deal with homosexuality. His film *Before I Forget* (*Avant que j'oublie*, 2007), the story of an unhappily aging gay man in Paris suffering from writer's block, was nominated in the Directors' Fortnight at Cannes and for the Delluc Prize.

Téchiné likes to follow his actors' careers and mentor them. The fact that the young actors of *Wild Reeds* have had successful film careers and continued working together is a tribute to his influence.

The Reception

Wild Reeds received broad critical and popular acclaim. It was presented in the *Un Certain Regard* selection at Cannes (featuring, for the most part, around twenty bold and original films by young filmmakers), where it received a lengthy standing ovation (Lalanne, *Roseaux Sauvages* 6). The film won the Louis-Delluc Prize in 1994 and, the following year, four awards and two nominations at the Césars (Best Film, Best Director, Best Screenplay, Most Promising Actress, a nomination for Best Supporting Actress for Michèle Moretti, and another for Most Promising Actor for the trio composed of Gaël Morel, Stéphane Rideau, and Frédéric Gorny). Abroad, *Wild Reeds* represented France at the Oscars; it won the Best Foreign Film Award from the Los Angeles Film Critics Association, the New York Film Critics Circle, and the U.S. National Society of Film Critics.

Commentators praised the spontaneity and lyricism of the film, the way it reproduces life without making a moral statement or using the characters as spokespersons. "If *Wild Reeds* is a film 'about' youth because of its origin as a television piece," Euvrard writes, "then it is also a film 'about' the provinces, 'about' the Algerian War, 'about' homosexuality.... In reality, it is not a film 'about' anything but, on a modest scale, a true work of art based on these (and other) elements that recreate life in a natural way" (31).

Critics also applauded the representation of nature: "As in Renoir's films, [nature] keeps a 'human face,' resonates with the characters, who in turn seem to grow like plants" (Kohn). In the same vein, Vatrican writes of the long swimming sequence, "Renoir-like, it conveys the flavor of life, captured in its most intimate manifestation, in its fragile beginnings" (11). Several scenes, like Maïté and François' conversation at the swing and Henri and Maïté's lovemaking by the river, bring to mind one Renoir film in particular, *A Day in the Country* (*Partie de campagne*, 1936/1946). In this film the Dufours, shopkeepers in Paris, spend a Sunday by the riverside with their daughter Henriette and their future son-in-law. They meet two boatmen, Rodolphe and Henri, who offer to take Henriette and her mother on a tour and end up seducing them on a little island in the river. Téchiné seems to refer to this film when Serge tells François that his brother used to bring girls to the river and "the beauty of the scenery made them easy prey."

In addition to the widely acknowledged connection with Renoir, some critics also mention a kinship with Truffaut, citing the "innocent maturity" of the young actors (Degoudenne 64) and the scenes where François is in front of the mirror and at the shoe shop, episodes that "are directly inspired by Truffaut's *Stolen Kisses* [*Baisers volés*]" (Horguelin).

There were also a few dissenting comments even though their authors appreciated the film as a whole. Frodon, for example, thinks that Téchiné's use of La Fontaine's fable as a frame of interpretation for the film is overly explicit, and that there is too strong a dichotomy in the characters' attitude toward the OAS: on the one hand, "hedonistic detachment" and swims in the river, on the other "narrow-minded rigidity," that is, categorical rejection or approval.

Above all, critics see in *Wild Reeds* a break with the formalism and theatricality of the director's earlier films: "The Téchiné who is emerging here is very different from the director we used to know," writes Benjo, to which Horguelin adds, "It is a true pleasure to see him stripping his work of mannerism in what is definitely his freest and most original film to date." For Murat, "*Wild Reeds* is without a doubt the most personal and accomplished film he has made in a long time. He seems totally free." Lalanne observes that the film strikes the right balance between new and familiar themes and recalls both a sonata and a symphony, "a sonata because Téchiné tries his hand again at a light production with little-known actors [. . .]. A symphony because he rearranges most of the motifs of his previous compositions" (1994).

Gaspéri, for her part, considers *Wild Reeds* a leading film on the 1960s that succeeds in depicting the impact of the Algerian War on the youth of the period. The presence of this conflict in the film, she writes, "shows how a generation that was considered lost came into its own, setting the stage for May '68."

The Historical Context: The Algerian War

The story of *Wild Reeds* takes place around May and June 1962, during the last months of the Algerian War (1954–1962) that opposed the French government and the Algerian National Liberation Front (*Front de Libération Nationale*, or FLN), ending with Algerian independence in July 1962. The time of the story can be established thanks to a few events mentioned in the film that will be explained below.

The Algerian War left a mark owing to its brutality and because Algeria, unlike other French colonies in Africa and Asia, was a settlement colony. Many French families had moved there after the invasion of Algiers in 1830 and made up between 10 and 12 percent of the population—about one million people—around the time of the period depicted in the film. The "*pieds-noirs*," (literally, black feet), as French settlers in Algeria were called, owned most of the resources of the country. The rest of the population (around 90 percent) consisted of Muslim people of Arabo-Berber origins, the great majority of whom worked for the settlers. In the film Henri is a *pied-noir* born near Constantine, a city where his parents owned a bakery.

Encouraged by the many independence movements after World War II and the example of Indochina, which had seceded from the French colonial empire in 1954 after a bloody war, Algerian nationalists created the FLN in 1954 and started to carry out attacks that were severely repressed. In the film Henri's father was killed by a bomb planted by the FLN. To counter the escalating violence, France deployed additional professional soldiers as well as young men doing mandatory military service. Pierre, Serge's brother, belongs to the latter group.

The conflict led to a political crisis in France that caused the collapse of the Fourth Republic. The French called on General de Gaulle to prepare a new constitution and solve the Algerian problem. De Gaulle initially supported the status quo regarding French Algeria. This position gave the *pieds-noirs* hope, especially when he uttered the now famous words "I have understood you"—a rather vague formula interpreted as a statement of support—during a speech in Algiers on June 4, 1958. However, De Gaulle soon determined that French Algeria was no longer viable and invited the population of Algeria and metropolitan France to participate in a "referendum on self-determination for Algeria" on January 8, 1961, in order to decide if people who lived in Algeria could choose their own future. Seventy-five percent of voters answered positively (but only 69 percent in Algeria and 28 percent in Algiers, the city with the largest concentration of French settlers). The *pieds-noirs* felt betrayed by De Gaulle and metropolitan France, a feeling expressed by Henri in the film in his composition for Mrs. Alvarez and in a conversation with Mr. Morelli, when the young man cites De Gaulle's "I have understood you" in a sarcastic tone.

Following this referendum, opponents to Algerian independence mobilized. They created a terrorist organization, the OAS (the Secret Army Organization) that launched attacks in France and Algeria starting in 1961. In Algeria a small faction of the army, led by four generals (including General Salan), carried out a failed coup attempt on April 22, 1961, to oppose negotiations. The generals were condemned to prison, except for Salan, who managed to escape and ran the OAS until his arrest the following year. He received a life sentence at his trial on May 23, 1962. In the film Henri learns this news on the radio and is so depressed that he cannot focus on his schoolwork. He tells Mr. Morelli, "[Salan] was the only person who wanted to save us, and they are crushing him, dragging him through the mud!"

The negotiations between the French government and the FLN led to the Evian Accords of March 18, 1962, that ended the hostilities and led to a referendum on Algerian independence. Independence was approved by 90.7 percent of voters in metropolitan France on April 8, 1962, and 99.72 percent of voters in Algeria on July 1. The story of *Wild Reeds* takes place after the referendum in metropolitan France, and this is why

Mrs. Alvarez tells Pierre that there is no need to desert: the cease-fire has been declared, and independence is near.

In spite of the Evian Accords, the situation remained extremely dangerous in Algeria because the OAS undertook a reign of terror, attacking both the French army and the FLN. In the film, we learn that Pierre was probably killed in an OAS-led operation.

The great majority of the *pieds-noirs* (around 800,000) chose to leave Algeria in 1962 and were taken back to France in droves, as we see in the television news that Henri is watching. One hundred fifty thousand more would follow before the end of the decade. Many of them settled in southern France, often in substandard conditions owing to insufficient accommodations. Such is the case for Henri's mother, who lives with another *pied-noir* family in Marseille.

STUDY GUIDE

What Happens in This Film?

1. Why did Pierre decide to get married, and how did he find his wife?

2. Why was Mrs. Alvarez invited to the wedding?

3. Who is the new high school student, and how does he behave in class?

4. Why did Serge and François leave the classroom during an exam and meet in the bathroom? How did Henri interpret this meeting?

5. What did François confide in Maïté when they were at the party? How did she react?

6. What happened to Henri's father? How did Henri react to this event?

7. What happened when Serge, François, and Henri found themselves in the bathroom one night after Pierre's death?

8. Why did Mr. Morelli replace Mrs. Alvarez?

9. What does Mr. Morelli think of Henri's attitude? How does he propose to help him?

10. Where did Henri go after missing his train? What did he want to do? What actually happened?

11. What store did François visit while Maïté was shopping for a bathing suit? Why?

12. What did François, Maïté, and Serge do while waiting for the results of the *baccalauréat* exam? Who joined them? What happened?

True or False?

If the statement is false, correct it!

1. Pierre and his brother Serge come from a family of rich farmers.

2. Mrs. Alvarez finds Henri's composition too narcissistic and abstract.

3. Henri criticizes the people of metropolitan France for being indifferent to the situation of the French residents of Algeria.

4. Henri has just arrived from Algeria with the other *pieds-noirs* brought back to metropolitan France.

5. François exchanged beds with Serge to be closer to Henri.

6. In the fable by La Fontaine that François reads aloud in class, the reed is destroyed by the storm but the stronger oak is able to survive.

7. Maïté went to live at François' house while her mother was away at the hospital.

8. Henri left the school because he was depressed to find out that General Salan, the head of the OAS, had been sentenced to life in prison.

9. Henri's mother chose to stay in Algeria in spite of the political situation.

10. When François goes to see Mr. Cassagne, the latter tells him that he had great difficulty accepting his homosexuality as a teenager.

11. During the outing by the river, François thinks that Maïté is interested in Henri and that she and Henri will become good friends.

12. Henri sold his father's watch to break with his past.

What Did You Learn in the Introduction?

1. What are some characteristics of Téchiné's first films, and why is *Hotel America* considered a turning point in his cinema?

2. What other award-winning film did Téchiné make in the 1990s?

3. Which of Téchiné's films deal with homosexuality?

4. Why was Téchiné asked to make the television film on which *Wild Reeds* is based?

5. What surprised Téchiné about the critical reception of *Wild Reeds*?

6. What actor or actress revealed by the film has become a big star in French cinema?

7. To what famous director is Téchiné compared in reviews of *Wild Reeds*, and why?

8. What were French residents of Algeria called, and what was their situation at the beginning of the Algerian War?

9. Why did the French residents of Algeria feel betrayed by De Gaulle and abandoned by the people of metropolitan France?

10. What was the OAS, and what role did this organization play near the end of the Algerian conflict?

11. Why did Henri revere General Salan?

12. What did many French residents of Algeria do after the 1962 referendum on Algerian independence?

Exploring the Film

1. The Beginning of the Film: The Wedding

What are the advantages of beginning the film with a celebration? What do we learn about Serge and his brother Pierre's family background? What characters are introduced?

Where would François have preferred to go? When he tells Maïté about a film that he recently watched (Ingmar Bergman's *Through a Glass Darkly*), he says that he particularly liked the heroine because "she has to choose sides, and it's an exhausting struggle." **Could this comment allude to what is going to happen to some of the characters?**

The Arte television channel that commissioned the original film requested that it include both a personal and a political theme. How did Téchiné incorporate both elements in the opening sequence? What is Pierre's personal situation with regard to the war? What does he want to do? Why does he hope that Mrs. Alvarez will be able to help him?

When Pierre, disappointed by Mrs. Alvarez's response, stops the music, the cook starts singing the chorus of an Occitan anthem, "Se Canto," that is often heard at athletic and cultural events. **What might be the connection between this evocation of the Occitan people, who often feel oppressed by the political power centralized in Paris, and the film?**

2. The Characters

+ *François*

What social class does François come from? What are his interests? Why does Serge think that he and François could be good friends?

Téchiné often says in interviews that François is his alter ego. **What elements of the story support this view, based on the introduction to this film?**

How does François discover his homosexuality? *Review the scene where François, Henri, and Serge leave class to go to the bathroom* (Excerpt 1, 16'50–19'10). Why did Serge want François to meet him in the bathroom? What personal principles do François and Serge mention in their discussion? **Why does François change his mind about the math homework?** At the end of their conversation, how do you interpret Téchiné's close-ups, first on François, who is taking the homework from Serge, then on Serge, and again on François? What is Henri's role at the end of this scene?

How does Maïté help François to recognize and accept his sexual orientation? For example, what does she say when he confides that he slept with Serge? Later, how does she explain François' sudden fascination for Henri? *Review the sequence in which François confesses that he is homosexual* (Excerpt 2, 50'00–53'25). What does François end up admitting with regard to Serge and Henri? How does Maïté reassure him?

In the scene where François is looking at himself in the mirror (end of Excerpt 2), **why does he repeat *"Je suis un pédé"* ("I am a queer") louder and louder?** How does Téchiné film the reflection of François' face in the mirrors? How can we interpret this progression, symbolically?

How does the discovery of his homosexuality affect François' principles and his ideas about people? For example, how does his interest in Serge affect his integrity as a student? At the beginning of Excerpt 2, how does his opinion of Henri change once he feels attracted to him?

What is François' role in his relationships with Maïté and Serge, Serge and Henri, and Maïté and Henri? In the case of the François-Serge-Henri trio, how does Téchiné define François' role in the staging of the beginning of Excerpt 1, when François arrives in the bathroom?

+ *Maïté*

What is Maïté's friendship with François based on? What do we learn about Maïté's ambivalence about sexual relations in the party scene? *Review this scene* (Excerpt 3, 27'30–30'30). How does Maïté react to François' revelation? What impact will this revelation have on their relationship?

When Maïté accompanies Serge to the river during Pierre's funeral, he asks her if she has had relations with boys. What does she answer? **What does she think of adolescence?** Why does she keep her distance from Serge in particular?

Review the scene in which François talks to Maïté about Henri (beginning of Excerpt 2, 50'00–50'55). How does Maïté react when François says that he would like her to meet Henri? What terms does she use to describe OAS supporters? How could her upbringing explain this attitude? **What does Maïté respond when François tells her that she is too sectarian and does not understand Henri?** Why do you think she is so upset in this scene?

Why is her mother's illness a turning point for her? *Review one of the sequences of her visit at François' house* (Excerpt 4, 1h06'05–1h07'17). What does her mother talk about when she is sick? Why is this so troubling for Maïté?

How does Maïté feel when she meets Henri at the Communist Party headquarters? For example, what compels her to offer him coffee and invite him to sleep in the building? Why does she finally change her mind, and why does she cry when he leaves?

+ *Serge*

How is Serge different from François and Maïté? How does he envision his future? **What does his sexual encounter with François mean to him?** Why is he considering marrying his brother's widow?

How do you explain Serge's animosity toward Henri even before Pierre's death?

+ *Henri*

What do we know about Henri's past? What event left a particularly strong mark on him?

Why does Henri spend his time listening to the radio? What is his position on the Algerian conflict? *Review the scenes where he is watching television and where Mr. Morelli is tutoring him* (Excerpt 5, 1h10'00–1h13'10). What do we learn about the situation in Algeria on television? Whom does the journalist blame for it? Why is Henri unable to focus when he is studying with Mr. Morelli that day? What highlights his solitude in this scene?

Why do you think Henri decided to leave the school? **What gave him the idea to set fire to the Communist Party headquarters?** How did meeting Maïté change his plans, at least for a while? During this meeting, what makes him seem a little more human?

Generally speaking, what is Henri's role in the film?

+ *Mrs. Alvarez and Mr. Morelli, the French Teachers*

What composition topic did Mrs. Alvarez assign? **Why would she have given Henri a zero on it at the** *baccalauréat* **exam?** *Review the scene where Mrs. Alvarez gives back the compositions* (Excerpt 6, 9'45–12'15). To whom does Henri compare the bourgeois people that the poet Rimbaud hated? How does he take up the defense of French colonists when Mrs. Alvarez mentions the rights of the Algerian people? What do you think of the way she judges Henri's paper?

What do Mr. Morelli and Henri have in common? *Review the scene where Mr. Morelli talks with Henri after class* (Excerpt 7, 56'05–58'30). Why does Mr. Morelli say that he understands Henri? What does he propose to him?

In what different ways do Mr. Morelli and Mrs. Alvarez treat those who, like Henri, do not share their opinions? What does their conversation about Henri reveal about their attitudes toward life? *Review the scene where Mrs. Alvarez and Mr. Morelli are at the restaurant* (Excerpt 8, 1h26'55–1h30'06). Where does Mrs. Alvarez think Mr. Morelli stands on the Algerian conflict, in your opinion? **Imagine her thoughts when she learns that Mr. Morelli's wife is Algerian (an Arab).**

According to Julie McQuinn, the rare use of background music in the film (we hear Samuel Barber's *Adagio for strings* a few times) is meant to underline moments when characters have unusual experiences that either bring them intense happiness (as when François and Serge go to Toulouse by moped) or make them question their beliefs. In other words, moments of deep reflection or feeling. **If we agree with this analysis, how can we interpret the presence of Barber's music on the soundtrack after Mr. Morelli and his wife leave at the end of Excerpt 8?** How do the camera movements also convey Mrs. Alvarez's state of mind?

Téchiné has said of Mr. Morelli's wife that she is "a little autistic, exiled, and skittish [. . .] an unforgettable figure" (Jousse 12). **Why is Mrs. Morelli so fearful and shy, in your opinion?**

3. *"The Oak and the Reed"*

What is the meaning of the fable by La Fontaine that the students must discuss in Mr. Morelli's class? *Review the scene where François reads the fable aloud* (Excerpt 9, 54'10–55'52). In this fable, what is the oak's opinion of himself and the reed? How does the fable end? What is its moral?

In naming his film *Wild Reeds*, Téchiné invites us to study the connections between the fable and the film. In fact Mr. Morelli himself draws a lesson from the fable when he tells Henri, "You act like the oak in the fable, Mariani. Be careful." **What does he mean by that? In addition to Henri, what other characters behave like the oak? What danger are they in (or what price do they pay)?**

For Lalanne ("Roseaux Sauvages") the film "is about oaks that learn to become reeds." **Do you agree with this analysis?** Does it apply to all the characters? **Who are the "reeds" of the film?**

4. A Film about the Algerian War or Homosexuality?

As we saw in the introduction, Téchiné became interested in Arte's project once he thought of building his film around the Algerian War. "But what everyone saw," he said, "was not the intrusion of the Algerian War in a remote corner of France, but the other side of the story, the discovery of homosexuality" (Lalanne, "Pour la sortie"). Assuming that the film is 'about' one of these two themes, which one seems most striking to you? How does the Algerian War intrude upon the story, and what is its role? What did you think of the representation of homosexuality?

Is there another theme that seems as important to you, if not more important? Alternatively, do you share Euvrard's opinion that "it is not a film 'about' anything at all," but simply an art form that recreates life?

5. The Spirit of the Times: The 1960s

For most critics the film depicts the atmosphere of the 1960s without turning into a historical panorama. Téchiné himself said that he wanted to avoid "fanatic attention to historical accuracy" because "it is incompatible with cinema, which is the art of the present" (Jousse 13). **What elements nonetheless place the film in the 1960s?**

Critics also agree that the film conveys the atmosphere of opposition to Gaullism and patriarchal society that would lead to May 1968. Besides Henri, **what other characters are critical of General de Gaulle, specifically his belief in the grandeur of France and the heroism of its people?**

What is the importance of family in the lives of François, Maïté, Serge, and Henri? **What do we know about their fathers, in particular?**

The 1960s saw the rise of the sexual revolution, summed up by a famous slogan of May 1968, "Jouissez sans entraves" ("Free Love"). **Do you think the film reflects the spirit of the times as regards sexuality?** Jean-Michel Frodon, a critic for *Le Monde*, blamed Téchiné for offering unsatisfactory alternative solutions to the issues of the day (including the Algerian conflict): "hedonistic detachment" on the one hand and ideology on the other. **Do you think that the adolescents of the film are indifferent to the world around them and are only interested in pleasure seeking?**

6. The Last Sequence

According to Freud, running water symbolizes sexual pleasure. Given the title of the film and the prominence of La Fontaine's fable, **how could we interpret the last sequence of the film, by the river? How does Téchiné represent Maïté's first love-**

making experience? *Review the scene of her conversation with François* (Excerpt 10, 1h39'45–1h40'35). How does François interpret Maïté's fears in this scene? **What is she afraid of, in fact?** What other scenes does this episode echo? (In what other circumstances did she admit being afraid?) *Review the scene where Henri is watching Maïté swim* (Excerpt 11, 1h42'00–1h43'15). How does Téchiné make Henri appear threatening when Maïté notices him and turns toward him? What happens to Maïté when she turns around in the water and faces Henri's gaze? **Were you surprised when she made love with him?**

How do the romantic involvements of the four young people end? *Review the sequences where the two couples are talking by the river* (Excerpt 12, 1h46'06–1h48'27). What important question does François ask Serge, and how does he respond? **What message about life does the director express through Serge?** What does their sexual encounter mean for Maïté and Henri? Why does Maïté refuse to leave home and follow Henri?

How do you interpret Maïté's running toward François and kissing him frantically at the end? *Review the end of the film* (Excerpt 13, 1h49'00–1h51'55). Why is she crying? Why does Téchiné frame Serge in a close-up at this point?

The last shot of the film (when François, Maïté, and Serge go away whistling "Se Canto" at the end of Excerpt 13) recalls both the first shot of François and Maïté at the beginning of the film (where the same whistled tune is heard) and the scene where Maïté, her mother, and François leave the wedding while the guests are singing the Occitan song. *Review this scene* (Excerpt 14, 9'10–9'45). Téchiné also uses striking panning shots in Excerpts 13 and 14. **What do you think the director wanted to convey by structuring the end of his film in this manner?**

André Téchiné's Filmography

2004   *Changing Times (Les Temps qui changent)*

2007   *The Witnesses (Les Témoins)*

2009   *The Girl on the Train (La Fille du RER)*

2011   *Unforgivable (Impardonnables)*

2014   *In the Name of My Daughter (L'Homme qu'on aimait trop)*

2016   *Being 17 (Quand on a 17 ans)*

2016   *Golden Years (Nos années folles)*

Works Consulted

Barclay, Fiona. "The Pied-Noir Colonial Family Romance in André Téchiné's *Les Roseaux sauvages.*" *Expressions Maghrébines* 12.2 (2013): 67–78.

Benjo, Caroline. "Brèves rencontres: de Cannes à Toronto, 1994." *Vertigo: Revue d'esthétique et d'histoire du cinéma* 11–12 (1994): 155–61.

Degoudenne, Laurence. "*Les Roseaux Sauvages.*" *Grand Angle* 174 (Aug.–Sept. 1994): 63–64.

Euvrard, Michel. "Quêtes d'indépendance." *Cinébulles* 14.1 (1995): 30–31.

Everett, Wendy. "Film at the Crossroads: *Les Roseaux Sauvages* (Téchiné, 1994)." *French Cinema in the 1990s: Continuity and Difference.* Ed. Phil Powrie. Oxford, England: Oxford UP, 1999. 47–57.

Frodon, Jean-Michel. "Les Roseaux Sauvages." *Le Monde*, 2 June 1994: n. pag.

Gaspéri, Anne de. "Les Roseaux Sauvages." *Le Quotidien de Paris*, 1 June 1994: n. pag.

Horguelin, Thierry. "Les Roseaux Sauvages." *24 images* 73–74 (Sept.–Oct. 1994): 55.

Jousse, Thierry, and Frédéric Strauss. "Entretien avec André Téchiné." *Cahiers du cinéma* 481 (June 1994): 12–17.

Kaganski, Serge. "Entretien André Téchiné–*Loin.*" *Les Inrocks*, 28 Aug. 2001. <http://www.lesinrocks.com/2001/08/28/cinema/actualite-cinema/entretien-andre-techine-loin-0801-11218281/>.

Kohn, Olivier. "Les Roseaux Sauvages." *Positif*, July–Aug. 1994.

Lalanne, Jean-Marc. "Pour la sortie de *La Fille du RER*, le réalisateur André Téchiné évoque sa filmographie." *Les Inrocks*, 18 Mar. 2009. <www.lesinrocks.com/2009/03/18/cinema/actualite-cinema/pour-la-sortie-de-la-fille-du-r-e-r-le-realisateur-andre-techine-evoque-sa-filmographie-1143164/>.

———. "Les Roseaux Sauvages." *Le Mensuel du cinéma* 18 (June 1994): 49.

———. *Les Roseaux Sauvages.* Coll. Lycéens au cinéma. Paris: Bifi, 1998.

Marshall, Bill. *André Téchiné.* Manchester, England: Manchester UP, 2007.

"La Master Class d'André Téchiné." <http://www.forumdesimages.fr/les-programmes/toutes-les-rencontres/la-master-class-dandre-techine>.

McQuinn, Julie. "Listening again to Barber's Adagio for Strings as Film Music." *American Music* 27.4 (2009): 461–99.

Murat, Pierre. "*Les Roseaux Sauvages.*" *Télérama*, 1 June 1994: n. pag.

Roth-Bettoni, Didier. "André Téchiné. Le dépaysement humain." *Le Mensuel du cinéma* 18 (June 1994): 50–51.

Téchiné, André, dir. *Les Roseaux sauvages.* Lions Gate, 2008.

Vatrican, Vincent. "Au seuil de la vie." *Cahiers du cinéma* 481 (June 1994): 10–11.

Wood, Robin. "*Wild Reeds*: A Film of the Past, for our Future." *Film International* 23.4–5 (2006): 20–24.

16

Agnès Varda

The Gleaners and I
(Les Glaneurs et la glaneuse)

(2000)

Agnès Varda, *The Gleaners and I*: The love of gleaning—a potato shaped like a heart.

Director .... Agnès Varda
Screenplay... Agnès Varda
Directors of Photography .... Agnès Varda, Didier Doussin,
.... Stéphane Krausz, Didier Rouget, Pascal Sautelet
Sound .... Emmanuel Soland
Film Editors.......................... Agnès Varda, Laurent Pineau
Music .... Joanna Bruzdowicz
Producer .... Ciné-Tamaris
Length... 1h22

Cast

Agnès Varda (*the narrator*), Claude M. (*the man in the trailer*), Guilène M. (*Claude's friend*), Edouard Loubet (*the chef*), Jean Laplanche (*the winegrower and psychoanalyst*) and his wife Nadine, Maître Raymond Dessaud (*the country lawyer*), Hervé (*aka VR 2000, the ragpicker*), Bodan Litnanski (*the designer of the Ideal Palace*), Louis Pons (*the painter*), Jérôme-Noël Bouton (*Etienne-Jules Marey's great-grandson*), Maître Martine Sirol (*the judge*), François L. (*the man in boots in Aix-en-Provence*), Salomon G. (*the homeless black man*), Charly P. (*the old Chinese man*), Robert M. (*the multi-gleaner*), Maître Brigitte Espié (*the town lawyer*), Alain F. (*the parsley eater*)

Story

The "I" of the title is Agnès Varda. Moved by the sight of people eating leftover produce at the farmers' market and struck by the similarities between their gestures and those of female gleaners in a painting by Millet, she is traveling around France looking for information on a practice believed to be a thing of the past: gleaning. The gleaners are the people she meets during her peregrinations; they are picking leftover fruits and vegetables that are unsold or unsalable. Some are anonymous and glean by necessity or for ethical reasons. Others, sometimes noted artists, have made gleaning the basis of their art. Behind each of them hides a character whose unexpected facets are revealed to us by Varda, like Alain, who eats leftover parsley right from the market and can enumerate its nutritional virtues—and spends his evenings as a volunteer French teacher at a hostel for immigrants. The non-gleaners of the film are equally interesting, like the congenial winegrower (and famous psychoanalyst) who recites Du Bellay's poetry to her.

Moved by her natural curiosity, Varda also gleans objects, impressions, and images that are sometimes unusual, like her own hand caught by the camera by pure chance. Her documentary on gleaning is thus also a self-portrait, in addition to a reflection on what lies outside the norm, be it a heart-shaped potato or an old woman's wrinkled hand.

The Director

With a career spanning over sixty years and almost as many films, Agnès Varda is one of the most original and talented filmmakers of her generation. Her multifaceted oeuvre includes fiction films, documentaries, hybrid films, and installations. In the words of one critic, "Her film 'career' resembles the jumble of real life: it is full of round trips, steep slopes and freewheeling, sadness, and laughter" (Assouline).

After studying art and photography in Paris, Varda was hired as a photographer in 1949 by her friend Jean Vilar, the founder of the Avignon Theater Festival and director of the Théâtre National Populaire. She found the cast of her first feature film, *La Pointe Courte* (1954), among the actors of the TNP. In this film inspired by a Faulkner novel, fictional sequences about a couple in crisis alternate with documentary vignettes on the lives of fishermen in the Pointe Courte neighborhood of Sète, the town where Varda spent her teenage years and met Vilar. This well-received, award-winning first film, shot on a small budget, would be considered in retrospect one of the first films of the New Wave and earn Varda the nickname of "grandmother" of this movement (as well as a street bearing her name in Pointe Courte). It anticipates Varda's interest for both fiction and documentary in addition to hybrid works combining the two genres, a characteristic of what she calls her "*cinécriture*."

While continuing to work as a photographer Varda made a few short- and medium-length documentaries—including *Diary of a Pregnant Woman* (*L'Opéra Mouffe*, 1958) about the old people and the homeless of the Rue Mouffetard in Paris—and associated with other short film directors, like Jacques Demy (her future husband), Chris Marker, and Alain Resnais (the editor of *La Pointe Courte*). These filmmakers would form with her and other cineastes the "Left Bank Group" ("Groupe Rive Gauche") of the New Wave. After the success of Godard's *Breathless* (*A bout de souffle*, 1960), the producer asked Godard to refer him to "guys" who could make other good films on a small budget. Varda was hired on his recommendation and directed *Cleo from 5 to 7* (*Cléo de 5 à 7*, 1962), the film that propelled her to the forefront of French cinema. This second feature—the story of a singer who strolls around Paris in real time while nervously awaiting the results of her medical tests—was selected for the Cannes and Venice film festivals and won the Méliès Prize.

The 1960s were very productive for Varda. On the fiction side, she made *Happiness* (*Le Bonheur*), the story of a happy family in an impressionist framework inspired by Auguste Renoir's "Picnic" ("Déjeuner sur l'herbe"). When the husband admits an infidelity, the wife is found drowned (accident or suicide?), and the film ends on a shot of a new family (with the former mistress replacing the wife) picnicking at the same place. This disturbing film with an ambiguous message received the Louis-Delluc Prize and a Silver Bear at the Berlin Film Festival in 1965. It was followed by *The Creatures* (*Les Créatures*, 1965), a less accomplished work that juxtaposes the story of a couple and the birth of a novel. *Lions' Love* (1969), shot in Los Angeles, is about an independent filmmaker who tries to make her first Hollywood film but cannot comply with the requirements of the studios. Half fiction, half documentary, the movie is also a story of sex and politics filmed in the hippie community that depicts American society at the time of Robert Kennedy's murder during the 1968 presidential campaign. Varda also made many short- and medium-length films in the 1960s, mostly documentaries on political themes like *Salut les Cubains* (1963), an homage to the Cuban Revolution based on 2,000 photos that she took during a trip to that country, and *Black Panthers* (1968).

In the following decade Varda made more films about women's issues. She had discovered the Anglo-American feminist movement during her stay in the United States and got involved in the French movement upon her return, fighting for abortion rights in particular. A noteworthy film of this period is *One Sings, the Other Doesn't* (*L'Une chante, l'autre pas*, 1976), an ode to female friendship and the right to choose one's life, in which both motherhood and abortion have their place.

Varda went back to Los Angeles in the early 1980s to shoot *Mural, murals* (*Mur murs*, 1980), a documentary feature on the murals of the city, then went on to make fiction films about single women. *Documenteur* (1981), also shot in California, is the story of a French divorcée who is raising her son alone during a work assignment in Los Angeles. *Vagabond* (*Sans toit ni loi*, 1985), one of her most critically acclaimed films (and the Silver Lion winner at the Venice Film Festival), paints the portrait of a female vagabond found dead in a ditch through the testimonies of people who had crossed her path. *Kung-Fu Master* (1987) is another story about a "monstrous" woman ostracized by society, this time a depressed divorcée who has an affair with a classmate of her fourteen-year-old daughter. Jane Birkin, who plays the mother, is also the subject of the documentary *Jane B. for Agnès V.* (1988), a portrait that combines short fictional pieces and conversations with Varda as well as reflections on the ability of images to convey people's true selves. In *Ulysses*, winner of the César Award for Best Short Documentary in 1984, Varda again muses on the power of images by examining a photo of a little boy that she had taken thirty years earlier.

After making a few films in memory of her husband, filmmaker Jacques Demy, in the 1990s (including *Jacquot de Nantes* in 1990, a black-and-white fiction film on his life and work), Agnès Varda focused on documentaries from 2000 on and also started working as an installation artist. *The Gleaners and I* marks a return to social cinema that reprises the theme of marginality found in *Vagabond* and also displays Varda's taste for depicting the little people, her interest in art, her reflections on static and moving images, her tendency to film herself as a woman artist, and the resistance and eclecticism that, according to Bénézet, characterize her whole work. *The Gleaners and I* had a sequel, *The Gleaners and I: Two Years Later* (*Deux ans après*, 2002), in which Varda reconnects with some of her "characters" and reflects on her film in the light of the comments she has received.

A few years later Varda made a blatantly autobiographical documentary, *The Beaches of Agnès* (*Les Plages d'Agnès*, 2008), described on her official website as a "poetic and playful auto-biofilmography." This film won the *Etoile d'Or du documentaire* from the French cinema press and the Best French Film Prize from the French Syndicate of Cinema Critics in 2009. It ends on the celebration of Varda's eightieth birthday, for which she received eighty *balais* (brooms), a most appropriate gift for this eccentric filmmaker who loves objects and words ("*balai*" is also a slang term for "year").

Varda has won an impressive number of awards and accolades for her work: an Honorary César honoring her whole career in 2001, the René Clair Prize from the French Academy in 2002, a nomination to the Jury of the Cannes Film Festival in 2005, the Honorary Henri-Langlois Prize in 2009, the *Carrosse d'Or* from the Society of Film Directors in 2010, the Honorary Prize at the Locarno Festival and the European Cinema Prize (in the category "Lifetime Achievement Award") in 2014, and an Honorary Palme d'Or at Cannes in 2015. Varda is the only woman among the six recipients of this prestigious prize awarded on an irregular basis since 1997, along with Ingmar Bergman, Woody Allen, Manoel de Oliveira, Clint Eastwood, and Bernardo Bertolucci. She was also the first female director to receive an Academy Honorary Award in 2017. At the time of this writing, Varda has just presented at Cannes her latest oeuvre, *Faces Places* (*Visages Villages*, 2017), a multiple award-winning documentary co-directed (at the age of eighty-nine) with the hipster photographer known as JR.

The Origin and Making of the Film

Varda says that her films always proceed from a strong emotion. For *The Gleaners and I*, it was the shock she felt when she saw people, especially old women, "go to market after the market," bending down to collect food that was being discarded. And when she saw a television show explaining that nothing goes to waste in the fields thanks to ultra-efficient machines, she thought, "What is left, then, for gleaners, both those painted by Millet and the ones I know?" (Piazzo). This question, together with her curiosity about the capabilities of the digital camera, led Varda to make *The Gleaners and I*. The new camera reminded her of one of her first documentaries, *L'Opéra-Mouffe*, which she had shot with a small 16 mm camera in 1957. "It's a lot of fun to find yourself in the same situation forty-five years later, with the same freedom to shoot and then take a break to edit the film," she said (Levieux).

By making this film Varda wanted to show "a terrible social reality" that she had experienced herself during the war, but also to speak about "the pleasure of finding things, whether on the street or in the fields. And about how much simple good sense it makes to glean" (Bonnaud). She began driving around France in September 1999 looking for images and witnesses according to a very fluid method that she describes thus: "I wander a lot. I don't know what I may find. Nothing is planned. I just leave, alone. I am in a receptive state of mind, so I meet people! Then I come back . . . with a camera. There are two, three, or four of us, and we shoot. Then I edit—that's when I organize things—the commentary takes shape . . . and, sometimes, calls for more shooting! I make my film . . . while making it" (Piazzo). Her crew shot a large part of the documentary with a professional digital camera, while she filmed many scenes alone with her small digital model.

To find her gleaners, she asked all her collaborators to talk about the film around them in order to single out "characters." This approach led her to François, the man in boots, "lord of the town" of Aix-en-Provence. In other cases, she had to resort to ruse, pretending to look for someone who did not exist in order to start conversations with strangers. She used this method to gain access to the residents of the trailers and speak to Claude and his friends. Some potential witnesses refused to be filmed out of modesty or to protect their territory, afraid that she might reveal the "good spots" to everyone else. Therefore she took the time to build trust with those who had agreed to participate.

Varda reveals in an interview that when she began *The Gleaners and I* she felt pity for the people whom she was filming, but the feeling subsided when she realized the richness of their lives. "These people are so extraordinary," she observes, "that they seem to come straight out of a novel. The poor are neither simple-minded nor stupid nor victimized. Often they have what others lack: common sense" (Frois). She preferred to show the practice of gleaning directly through them, without adding commentary because, as she explained in English, "the more I met them, the more I could see I had nothing to make as a statement. *They* make the statement; they explain the subject better than anyone" (Anderson 25).

Varda, who says she likes to "leave behind a few bits and pieces of [herself]" in each of her films (Piazzo), soon wanted to include herself among the gleaners. She gives several explanations for this decision: the ease of use of the DV camera that allowed her to "insert herself into the film physically" (Bonnaud), pure chance that led her to talk while filming her hand, providing a ready-made monologue she had not anticipated, and, finally, the desire to be honest with her witnesses. In her own words, "I felt that I was asking so much of these people to reveal themselves, to speak to me, to be honest with me, that I should reveal something of myself, too" (Anderson 24).

Varda spent "a winter that was both instructive and inspiring" making her documentary, appreciating in particular the fact that she could film spontaneously and shoot again as needed at the editing stage. Using digital cameras also allowed her to reduce costs, a real boon since she could only find modest funding for her project, which was considered too eccentric and was originally destined for television. Varda was thus surprised and honored when Gilles Jacob, the Cannes Film Festival director, decided to include *The Gleaners and I* in the "out of competition" section before it was even finished. Varda worked doubly hard not to miss the opportunity because, as she said, "I was delighted to be invited onto the Croisette with a potato as the star of my film" (Gasperi).

The Reception

The Gleaners and I received exceptional acclaim for an art house documentary. Following its presentation at Cannes, where it was barely noticed, it was shown in a few theaters the day after its television release. It met with applause, a rather rare occurrence in theaters according to Varda, and word of mouth did the rest. Varda began receiving screening requests and invitations at many international festivals. Thanks to the support of the Agence pour le Développement Régional du Cinéma, a few copies even circulated in small provincial towns, to the director's delight: "This is how it happened to be shown on the Aix island one day, on the Yeu island the next, in small villages in the Vendée, the Gironde, or the Massif Central. Meanwhile, big cities were waiting for a copy. That really tickles me ..." (Lequeret 33).

The Gleaners and I was also praised by critics and won the Best French Film Prize from the French Syndicate of Cinema Critics in 2000. Commentators considered the film the culmination of Varda's work, citing thematic and formal connections with her earlier films: "*The Gleaners and I* is a new gem in her rich, extensive filmography, a documentary as free and playful as *Murals, murals*, an experiment as open and random as *Daguerréotypes* [a 1974 documentary on her shopkeeper neighbors of the Rue Daguerre], a political work as strong and powerful as *Vagabond*" (Bonnaud), "another expression of her artistic principles, this time turning her vagabond approach into the subject of the film" (Mandelbaum). Adjectives such as "free," "playful," "random," "political," "vagabond" and their synonyms recur often in reviews of the film.

The documentary drew praise for its political message. It was described as "a testimony like no other on the poverty that, alas, plagues our beautiful country" (Copperman), a "social patchwork" in which Varda "successfully addresses our society's waste and overconsumption, denounces social violence, sings the praises of recycling" (Bonnaud), and opens our eyes to "an appalling reality" (Landrot) while avoiding clichés.

Critics applaud Varda's choice of witnesses and her way of filming them, with her "keen hummingbird's eye" that "excels at unearthing gems from the crowd of unknowns" and knows how to "uncover the beauty and laughter behind their ugly, grumpy looks" (Landrot). They appreciate her respect for them, her simplicity, and the fact that she "does not grant herself any rights over her characters" (Mandelbaum).

Reviewers also commend the personal side of the film and Varda's original approach, blending a social documentary with a self-portrait in portraying herself as a gleaner. Critics mention her ability to create unexpected connections, for example between gleaning and filmmaking, or between her aging body and discarded objects. They often cite the shots of her wrinkled hand and note her (obsessive) interest in the passage of time.

Critics also point out the formal originality of the documentary, describing it as "a delightful improvised trip, a sort of road movie" (Bonnaud), "a puzzle," "a patchwork," or "a UFO" (Assouline). Some, like Landrot, are pleased that the film "jumps randomly from one encounter to the next," while others note that it is more structured than it seems. Mandelbaum finds it "both powerfully coherent and deliciously random," and Bonnaud writes that, "as the film progresses we clearly see the structure of the project, we understand what holds together all these disparate fragments of lives, destinies, occupations, and places." Everyone draws different life lessons or ideas about filmmaking from the documentary. As Boujut explains, "Little by little, we can see emerging from the shapeless puzzle another way of seeing and living." Bénoliel, for his part, admires the close link between the form and content of the film: "Varda's method is also the subject of her film: she gleans shots randomly [. . .], she is always rearranging the shooting schedule, adding, and recycling." "Gleaning is like filming," he concludes (62–63).

What critics appreciate above all is the director's humor and the energy and love of life that radiate from her film. While noting that Varda titled her musical score "Aging Agnès," Landrot adds, "At the end of the screening, filled with such shared energy, we think instead of Ageless Agnès, Amusing Agnès, Animated Agnès, and we want to thank her."

A Brief History of French Documentary Filmmaking

The Gleaners and I belongs to a long tradition of French documentaries that was born with the Lumière brothers' cinematograph in 1895 and enjoyed varying degrees of popularity until its rebirth in the 1990s. After the initial success of the Lumières' newsreels, the documentary genre was soon overtaken by fiction films, starting with those of Georges Méliès. After World War I it developed primarily in the Anglo-Saxon world— *Nanook of the North* (Robert Flaherty, 1922) is considered one of the first documentary features—and in the Soviet Union with Dziga Vertov's avant-garde films such as *Man with a Movie Camera* (1929). Vertov's Soviet propaganda documentaries had a strong influence on Jean Vigo—his first film, *A propos de Nice* (1930), is a documentary about the city that criticizes social inequalities—and on postwar directors like Jean Rouch as well as militant filmmakers of the 1970s.

A French documentary tradition started to appear at the end of the 1930s with militant films on the working class made during the Popular Front, like Jean Renoir's *Life Is Ours* (*La Vie est à nous*, 1936). In the scientific arena the mountaineering documentaries of climber and explorer Marcel Ichac and those of Jacques-Yves Cousteau on marine life reached international acclaim as early as the 1940s. Cousteau earned his greatest accolades with two Oscar-winning films, *The Silent World* (*Le Monde du silence*, 1956), codirected with Louis Malle, which also won the Palme d'Or at Cannes, and *World without Sun* (*Le Monde sans soleil*, 1964), recipient of the *Grand prix du cinéma français* (a prestigious prize now extinct) in 1964. Also noteworthy are Georges Rouquier's documentaries on rural France—shorts essentially, except for *Farrebique*, a peasant chronicle that won an award at Cannes in 1946, to which Rouquier added a sequel, *Biquefarre*, in 1983. René Clément also made shorts about French rural and urban life as well as films on Africa and the Middle East. His short *The Railroad Workers* (*Ceux du rail*, 1942) raised his visibility and launched his subsequent career as a fiction film director, twice winner of the Oscar for Best Foreign Language Film.

One of the most influential post–World War II documentarists was Jean Rouch, who made many ethnographic films in Africa starting in the 1940s, including *I, A Negro* (*Moi, un noir*), recipient of the Louis-Delluc Prize in 1958. With sociologist Edgar Morin he also filmed the well-known *Chronicle of a Summer* (*Chronique d'un été*) that won the FIPRESCI Prize from the International Federation of Film Critics at Cannes in 1961. In this piece Rouch records, without their knowing, the response of ordinary Parisians asked the question "Are you happy?" This film is an example of the *cinéma vérité* ("truthful cinema") advocated by Rouch, a type of documentary without commentary or background music where the director's presence is mostly felt in the editing. This approach was made possible by the invention of portable cameras and tape recorders that could capture sounds and images at the same time and gave directors a lot of freedom for location shooting. Rouch's techniques had a great influence on the directors of the New Wave.

Filmmakers of the "Left Bank Group" of the New Wave, like Agnès Varda, Chris Marker, and Alain Resnais, adopted some of the elements of *cinéma vérité*, but they favored a more subjective approach in order to highlight the fact that life as represented on film always expresses the director's individual truths. Consequently they were more present in their documentaries, questioning their witnesses themselves, adding commentary or, more generally, treating their subject from a very personal angle, whether political, philosophical, or poetic. This was the case for Varda in her first shorts. In *L'Opéra Mouffe* (1958), for example, she filmed the residents of Rue Mouffetard à la Rouch, but also evoked her pregnancy. Marker and Resnais proceeded the same way in their "films essays," for example *Statues Also Die* (*Les Statues meurent aussi*, Jean Vigo Prize in 1954), their co-directed film on African art that also criticizes colonialism, *The Lovely Month of May* (*Le Joli Mai*, 1962), a politically engaged variation by Marker on Rouch and Morin's *Chronicle of a Summer*, and *Night and Fog* (*Nuit et Brouillard*, Jean Vigo Prize in 1956), Resnais' short film on the Nazi extermination camps during World War II.

After a decade marked primarily by post–May 1968 militant cinema and Marcel Ophüls' masterpiece *The Sorrow and the Pity* (*Le Chagrin et la pitié*, 1971) about the behavior of the French during the Occupation, the 1980s were an important period for the documentary. Following television deregulation new channels were created, some of which encouraged the creation of auteur documentary features. This triggered new vocations and led to the creation of documentaries for theaters that benefited from the funding put in place for heritage films. As a result, the number of documentaries released in theaters nearly doubled after the year 2000, some meeting resounding success at the French and international box offices. Their themes include nature and the environment, as in *Microcosmos* (Claude Nuridsany and Marie Perennou, 1996), *Winged Migration* (*Le Peuple migrateur*, Jacques Perrin, 2001), *March of the Penguins* (*La Marche de l'empereur*, Luc Jacquet, Oscar for Best Documentary Film in 2006), and *Oceans* (Jacques Cluzaud and Jacques Perrin, 2010); rural France, with *Peasant Profiles* (*Profils paysans*, Raymond Depardon, 2001–2008), *To Be and to Have* (Être et avoir, Nicolas Philibert, 2002 Louis-Delluc Prize and 2003 César for Best Editing), a film sensation about a one-room schoolhouse out in the sticks, and *Leadersheep* (*Tous au Larzac*, Christian Rouaud, César for Best Documentary in 2012); the food industry and the impact of globalization, as in *Food Beware: The French Organic Revolution* (*Nos enfants nous accuseront*, Jean-Paul Jaud, 2008), as well as the suburbs and immigration, for example in Yamina Benguigui's films, like *Mémoires d'immigrés* (1997).

Varda's trajectory as a documentary filmmaker matches the development of the genre. She began her career with short films in the 1950s and has made most of her documentary features since the end of the 1980s (see the "Filmography"). Her oeuvre also illustrates—to an extreme degree—the closer links between fiction film and documentary following the technological mutations in the postwar period.

STUDY GUIDE

What Happens in This Film?

1. What does the verb "to glean" mean? What did people glean in the past, as in Millet's painting?

2. What does Agnès Varda, the "I" of the title, glean?

3. What is the story of Claude, the man who lives in a trailer? How does he manage to survive?

4. One of the witnesses distinguishes between gleaning something from the ground, "*glaner*," and from a tree or vine, "*grappiller*." Give a few examples of these two activities in the film.

5. According to the French Penal Code, in what circumstances is gleaning allowed?

6. What did Varda glean during her trip to Japan?

7. What is "artistic" gleaning?

8. What amusing spectacle does Varda offer us when she forgets to turn off her camera?

9. What structure associated with cinema did Varda find in a vineyard?

10. What is the problem of the young people whom Varda films with their dogs in a town square in the Pyrenees Mountains?

11. Why does the man in boots of Aix-en-Provence feed himself from trash cans?

12. What is on the painting that is retrieved from a museum reserve at Varda's request? What happy coincidence provoked her enthusiasm when she first saw the painting?

True or False?

If the statement is false, correct it!

1. Claude, the man who lives in a trailer, alerted the association "Les Restos du cœur" (that provides meals for the hungry) that an industrialist had just dumped tons of unmarketable potatoes in a field.

2. Edouard Loubet, the restaurant owner, gleans primarily to offer less expensive dishes to his customers.

284 Contemporary French Cinema

3. Varda meets a winegrower named Jean Laplanche who is also a famous politician.

4. Gleaning has been allowed since the sixteenth century.

5. Varda is horrified when she notices a water stain on her ceiling upon returning from Japan.

6. Seeing Rembrandt's self-portrait makes Varda want to film herself.

7. Varda went to the "treasure store" because someone told her that she would find a painting about gleaning combining works by Millet and Breton.

8. Bodan Litnanski has a particular fascination for clocks, and they appear everywhere on his "totem towers."

9. Varda is afraid of trucks when she is driving on highways.

10. During her travels Varda meets a winegrower who descends from the Lumière brothers.

11. Salomon, the homeless black man, can hardly feed himself with the food he retrieves from trash cans.

12. Alain, the parsley eater, earns a living by teaching immigrants how to read and write.

What Did You Learn in the Introduction?

1. What are some of the links between Varda and the New Wave?

2. What film brought Varda to the attention of a broader public, and in what circumstances did she make it?

3. Name a few films that Varda has made in the United States.

4. What themes related to women are found in *One Sings, the Other Doesn't*?

5. Who was Jacques Demy, and what importance did he have in Varda's personal and professional life?

6. What does *The Gleaners and I* have in common with Varda's earlier films?

7. Why did Varda wish to make *The Gleaners and I*, and how did she find the settings and characters for her film?

8. What did Varda find out regarding her characters, and why did she decide not to include commentary in her film, breaking with a common practice in traditional documentaries?

9. Why did Varda film herself in *The Gleaners and I*?

10. Cite some aspects of the film that critics liked.

11. How did technological change affect the documentary genre after World War II?

12. What explains the renewed interest in documentaries at the end of the twentieth century, and what are some of the main themes of the most renowned among them?

Exploring the Film

1. Gleaning Yesterday and Today

How does Varda introduce the topic of gleaning? *Review the beginning of the film* (Excerpt 1, 0'20–2'13). Is the cat that appears in this excerpt related to the subject of the film? What does its presence in the shot suggest about Varda's approach to filmmaking?

How does the French title of the film (*Les Glaneurs et la glaneuse*, i.e. *The Gleaners and the Female Gleaner*) express one of the differences between gleaning in the past and the present when compared to the title of Millet's painting, *Les Glaneuses* (*The Female Gleaners*, 1857)? What are other differences and similarities between past and present when it comes to gleaning? *Review the transition between past and present* (Excerpt 2, 2'40–4'07). **How does Varda express this transition with the soundtrack?** With whom does she implicitly associate the urban gleaners through her choice of music?

Varda presents today's gleaning through a road movie around France. Why does she go to Arras first, in the North? What is the appeal of the Beauce region, where she takes us next? Later she drives to Burgundy. Why is she interested in this area? Why does she go to the island of Noirmoutier? **What do the transition scenes on the highway tell us about the director's personality?**

2. The Gleaners

+ *Claude, the Man in the Trailer*

What type of questions does Varda ask to make Claude talk? What are his present living conditions? What does she learn about his past and the reasons for his hardship? *Review her conversations with Claude* (Excerpt 3, 11'50–15'23). **What do the itinerant people who live nearby think of Claude?** Why do you think Varda includes their comments?

+ *Edouard Loubet, the Chef*

How is he different from the other gleaners of food? What does Varda like about him? In your opinion, why does she juxtapose his portrait and Claude's, using an abrupt transition between the two?

+ *François, the Man in Boots of Aix-en-Provence*

François is the man who has lived "100 percent" off of other people's discards and "garbage" for over ten years. **At whom and what is he angry?** What facet of his personality does he reveal when he says, "I'm like the lord of this town in a way; all these imbeciles are throwing everything away, and I come behind them and take it all"? Varda has filmed him walking most of the time. Why, in your opinion?

✦   *Alain, the Teacher-Gleaner*

Varda says that Alain impressed her the most, and she ended her film with his portrait. **How do you explain her preference?** *Review her conversation with Alain* (Excerpt 4, 1h10'50–1h14'10)? How does she film Alain before addressing him? Why do you think she uses voice-over when he speaks, for example when she focuses on the parsley or even on his face?

✦   *Hervé (aka VR 2000), Bodan Litnanski, and Louis Pons*

What do these three gleaners have in common? How do they resemble or differ from the other gleaners of the film? **Does their presence in the film affect your perspective on gleaning? How?**

Among the gleaners of food presented above, which one did you find the most interesting? Why? Does Varda show pity for those who glean out of necessity? **What aspects of their lives does she highlight?**

3. *The Glaneuse (I)*

Varda says in an interview that she inserted herself among her characters as a "filmer-gleaner" (Bonnaud). **By positioning herself as gleaner, what relationship does Varda establish between herself and the other gleaners of the film, and between herself and the spectators?** Is Varda's relationship with her audience different from the usual relationship between documentary filmmakers and their public? Explain your answer.

How does Varda use the digital camera to film her own body? *Review the scene where she introduces herself as a gleaner* (Excerpt 5, 4'15–5'50). What aspects of her hair and hand does she show? Why? Are these images traditional in a self-portrait? Why (not)? Does she use the capabilities of the digital camera in the same way with her other characters? Why (not)? **What does she say about old age in this excerpt?** (Note: she cites a line from Pierre Corneille's play *Le Cid* (1636): "Oh rage! Oh despair! Oh age, my enemy!")

What do we learn about Varda as a "character" in the film? *Review for example the scene where she comes back from a trip to Japan* (Excerpt 6, 31'20–33'15). In this scene, how does she signal that we are about to enter her private sphere? What elements of the scene inform us about Varda's personal and professional life? Consider for example the photos that she dumps on her desk. Why Gérard Philipe at the Avignon Festival? Why a poster of the film *Jeanne and the Perfect Guy* (*Jeanne et le garçon formidable*)? (Check the cast of this film.)

Varda films her own hand here and feels that she is being confronted with "horror." **What "horror" is she referring to?** How does she feel when the camera closes in on this part of her body? Varda said about this episode, "When I saw my hand holding the postcard of Rembrandt's self-portrait that I had brought back from Japan, I was immediately struck by its close connection with the subject of the documentary" (Bonnaud). **What is this connection, in your opinion?** Can we relate the manner in which she films her hand and the way she shoots the stain on her ceiling? How does she transition between her reflections about her hand and her visit to Hervé, the ragpicker? (What are some important motifs in the short transition sequence?)

As a gleaner of images or "filmer-gleaner," what does Varda have in common with Robert, the "multi-gleaner"? **What parallels can you find between Varda's technique and that of the other artistic gleaners?** To discuss this question, you may take into account the following remarks by Louis Pons and Hervé about reclaimed objects: "For most people, it is a pile, a pile of junk. For me it is a marvel, a world of possibilities" (Louis Pons); "Ultimately, the encounter takes place on the street. The object calls me because it belongs here" (Hervé).

4. Gleaned Images

+ *The Heart-Shaped Potatoes and the Clock*

Like the rural and urban gleaners of the film, Varda gleans food and objects. **How do the heart-shaped potatoes reflect Varda's state of mind in this film?** *Review her discovery of these particular potatoes* (Excerpt 7, 9'45–10'52). What idea came to her when she observed these potatoes at home?

Another object that Varda gleaned is a clock. How does it differ from the other clocks of the film (like the one at the Musée d'Orsay, for example)? **Why does Varda like this particular clock? Visually, how does she establish a connection between herself and the theme alluded to here?** *Review her discovery of the clock* (Excerpt 8, 1h08'58–1h10'20). How does the music of François Wertheimer (the musician with whom she collects discarded objects) reinforce this theme? What happened to the heart-shaped potatoes in this excerpt? **What parallel can you find between them and Varda?**

+ *The Last Judgement*

In general, what is the function of museum visits and scenes where Varda shows us paintings? **Do you think that Rogier van der Weyden's painting *The Last Judgement* has something to do with the subject of the film, beside the geographical connection?** (We see it in the Hospices of Beaune, in Burgundy, where Varda is filming vineyards.) *Review her images of the painting and her interview with a winegrower* (Excerpt 9, 20'46–22'54). What characters of the painting does she show one after the other? Do you think she is suggesting a parallel with the characters of her film? Is it significant that the scenes about the painting alternate with the winegrower's interview? How does the latter explain the absence of gleaners from the vineyards of Burgundy?

+ *Jean Laplanche, the Winegrower and Psychoanalyst*

Jean Laplanche is a famous psychoanalyst, co-author of the *Dictionary of Psychoanalysis* (1967), a reference book translated into many languages. Varda was unaware of his identity before asking him questions about winegrowing. **Why do you think she included his philosophical thoughts in her film**—the idea that "people find their origins in others first"? Beside his occupation, why is this character so original? *Review the interview with Jean Laplanche* (Excerpt 10, 23'30–25'32). **What does his wife talk about at the end of the excerpt, and what other digression does this introduce?** (Laplanche also gleaned ideas from his meeting with Varda. He says in *The Gleaners and I: Two Years Later* that as a psychoanalyst he is also a kind of gleaner because he "pays attention to particular words that 'fall out' of a person's discourse" and does not know in advance what he is going to find.)

+ *The Town Lawyer and the Country Lawyer*

Agnès Varda shared with us in an email dated May 2, 2017, that she was inspired by La Fontaine's fable "The Town Mouse and the Country Mouse" (without meaning to denigrate lawyers!) when she imagined the two barristers in their court robes, Maître Dessaud in the country and Maître Espié in town. Other than the amusing literary reference, why does Varda film them in the fields and on the street, respectively? **What is their role in the film?** *Review Varda eating figs, then Maître Dessaud in the cabbage patch* (Excerpt 11, 27'40–29'56). In your opinion, why does Varda juxtapose the scene with Maître Dessaud and her conversation with the man who runs the fig orchard? In the first part of the excerpt, **why does she use a close-up shot of the figs instead of showing her witness explaining that he does not allow people to pick left over fruit?**

5. A Social and Political Documentary?

✦ Poverty and Social Class

Martin O'Shaughnessy considers *The Gleaners and I* a successful example of the return of the political in French cinema at the end of the twentieth century, arguing that Varda shows several ways of resisting the violence and exclusion fostered by the social system. He adds that this documentary resembles other social films of this period by depicting local and pragmatic forms of resistance rather than ideological ones (the political films of the 1970s, by contrast, often showed class conflicts and collective action). **In what ways do the poor attempt to remedy their situation in the film? Do they opt for individual or collective solutions?** At times Varda highlights instances of solidarity among the destitute (for example, in the part devoted to Salomon, the black gleaner). What does she also suggest by showing an old woman shooing Salomon away with her cane at the market?

When the volunteers of "Les Restos du cœur" are done gleaning potatoes, Varda concludes, "On that day, they gathered around three hundred kilos, a small but important advance on the enemy." **Who/what is the enemy here? Generally speaking, do you think she passes judgment on the business owners and supervisors who appear in the film?** If yes, how does she express her disapproval or hostility?

Varda includes one scene of collective action in her documentary when she shows the *Frigo Manifestation* (Fridge Protest) and then goes on to film a demonstration organized by the Communist Party in her neighborhood, around the statue of the lion in the Denfert-Rochereau traffic circle. What is the significance of these scenes? What might be the connection with Varda's self-portrait? *Review the demonstrations* (Excerpt 12, 1h 01'00–1h 01'55). In this excerpt, analyze the way in which Varda moves from the fridge exhibit to people gleaning fruit in Provence. What elements are featured in the transition?

Varda said in an interview, "I am outraged by these supermarket managers who pour bleach on the food products they throw out. . . . There is an obvious intention to make discarded food inconsumable; it is extremely unpleasant" (Frois). **Do you feel this indignation in the scene that illustrates this practice?** How does Varda present the respective viewpoints of the supermarket manager, the young people, and the judge? Does she take sides? *Review this scene* (Excerpt 13, 50'24–53'06).

✦ Politics and Aesthetics

After filming the rotting heart-shaped potatoes in Excerpt 8, Varda made the following comment: "I like to film rot, remains, debris, mold, and waste. But I always remember that after the market some people go to market in the trash." **What does she mean by**

this with regard to her film work? What is the connection between this remark and the way she presents the "Poubelle, ma belle" (Beautiful Trash) initiative that teaches children to recycle waste?

Some critics think that Varda loses sight of her social project by making many artistic and personal digressions and by beautifying reality instead of showing its sordid side. Others, on the contrary, argue that blending the social theme with aesthetic and personal considerations allows Varda to deliver a strong message on different aspects of our society while suggesting *sotto voce* an alternative model. **Which opinion do you agree with?**

6. Life Lessons

In their great majority, critics and the people who comment on Varda's film in *The Gleaners and I: Two Years Later* find that *The Gleaners and I* teaches us how to live. What do you think they mean? **What lessons do you find in Varda's film?**

Alain, the gleaner-teacher, told Varda in *Two Years Later* that he liked her documentary, except for the parts where she talks about herself and her old age. Do you agree with him that these digressions detract from the film? **Is there a life lesson in the private portrait as well?**

Agnès Varda's Filmography (Feature Films)

1954   *La Pointe Courte*

1961   *Cleo from 5 to 7 (Cléo de 5 à 7)*

1964   *Happiness (Le Bonheur)*

1965   *The Creatures (Les Créatures)*

1967   *Far from Vietnam (Loin du Vietnam,* ensemble documentary)

1969   *Lions Love (. . . and Lies)*

1974   *Daguerréotypes* (documentary)

1976   *One Sings, the Other Doesn't (L'Une chante, l'autre pas)*

1980   *Mural, murals (Mur murs,* documentary)

1981   *Documenteur*

1985   *Vagabond (Sans toit ni loi)*

1987   *Kung-Fu Master*

1987   *Jane B. for Agnès V. (Jane B. par Agnès V.,* documentary)

1990   *Jacquot de Nantes*

1992   *The Young Girls Turn 25 (Les Demoiselles ont eu 25 ans,* (documentary)

1993   *The World of Jacques Demy (L'Univers de Jacques Demy,* documentary)

1994   *One Hundred and One Nights (Les Cent et Une Nuits)*

2000   *The Gleaners and I (Les Glaneurs et la glaneuse,* documentary)

2002   *The Gleaners and I: Two Years Later (Deux ans après,* documentary)

2006   *The Widows from Noirmoutier (Quelques veuves de Noirmoutier,* documentary)

2008   *The Beaches of Agnès* (*Les Plages d'Agnès*, documentary)
2017   *Faces Places* (*Visages, villages*, documentary)

Works Consulted

Anderson, Melissa. "The Modest Gesture of the Filmmaker: An Interview with Agnès Varda." *Cineaste* 26.4 (Autumn 2001): 24–27.

Assouline, Florence. "Agnès Varda, ne filme que les restes." *L'Evénement*, 6 July 2000: n. pag.

Bénézet, Delphine. *The Cinema of Agnès Varda: Resistance and Eclecticism*. New York: Wallflower Press, 2014.

Bénoliel, Bernard. "La main de l'autre." *Cahiers du cinéma* 548 (July–Aug. 2000): 62–63.

Bonnaud, Frédéric, and Serge Kaganski. "*Les Glaneurs et la glaneuse*, le ciné-brocante d'Agnès Varda." *Les Inrockuptibles*, 4 July 2000: n. pag.

Bonner, Virginia. "The Gleaners and 'Us': The Radical Modesty of Agnès Varda's *Les Glaneurs et la glaneuse*." *There She Goes: Feminist Filmmaking and Beyond*. Ed. Corinn Columpar and Sophie Mayer. Detroit, MI: Wayne State UP, 2009. 119–31.

Boujut, Michel. "Les beaux restes." *Charlie-Hebdo*, 19 July 2000: n. pag.

Cooper, Sarah. "Film Portraits: From Jane B. to Agnes V." *Selfless Cinema?: Ethics and French Documentary*. London: Legenda, 2006. 77–90.

Copperman, Annie. "A la recherche du grain perdu." *Les Echos*, 6 July 2000: n. pag.

Euvrard, Janine, and Michel Euvrard, "Situation du documentaire en France." *Ciné-Bulles* 15.3 (1996): 50–53.

Frois, Emmanuèle. "La cinéaste retrouve le documentaire. Une glaneuse nommée Varda." *Le Figaro*, 6 July 2000: n. pag.

Gasperi, Anne de. "La patate d'Agnès Varda." *Le Figaro*, 16 May 2000: n. pag.

Landrot, Marine. "*Les Glaneurs et la glaneuse*." *Télérama*, 5 July 2000: n. pag.

Lequeret, Elisabeth. "Le bel été de la glaneuse." *Cahiers du cinéma* 550 (Oct. 2000): 32–33.

Levieux, Michèle. "Agnès Varga, une 'glaneuse' résistante." *L'Humanité*, 7 July 2000: n. pag.

Levine, Alison Murray. "Contemporary French Documentary: A Renaissance, 1992–2012." *A Companion to Contemporary French Cinema*. Ed. Alistair Fox et al. Hoboken, NJ: Wiley-Blackwell, 2015. 356–75.

Mandelbaum, Jacques. "Biens sans maître glanés par maîtres sans bien." *Le Monde*, 5 July 2000: n. pag.

O'Shaughnessy, Martin. "Post-1995 French Cinema: Return of the Social, Return of the Political?" *Modern & Contemporary France* 11.2 (2003): 189–203.

Piazzo, Philippe. "Agnès Varda, glaneuse sachant glaner." *Le Monde*, 5 July 2000: n. pag.

Rachlin, Nathalie. "L'exclusion au cinéma: le cas d'Agnès Varda." *Women in French Studies* (2006): 88–111.

Rosello, Mireille. "Agnès Varda's *Les Glaneurs et la glaneuse*: Portrait of the Artist as an Old Lady." *Studies in French Cinema* 1.1 (2001): 29–36.

Smith, Alison. *Agnès Varda.* Manchester, England: Manchester UP, 1998.

Varda, Agnès, dir. *Les Glaneurs et la glaneuse.* Zeitgeist Video, 2002.

Witt, Michael. "The Renaissance of Documentary Filmmaking in France in the 1980s and 1990s." *Critical Studies in Television: Scholarly Studies in Small Screen Fictions* 7.2 (2012): 10–29.

VI

Comedy

Josiane Balasko, *French Twist* (1995)

Agnès Jaoui, *The Taste of Others* (2000)

Jean-Pierre Jeunet, *Amélie* (2001)

Olivier Nakache and Eric Toledano, *The Intouchables* (2011)

The comic tradition dates from the very beginnings of cinema, and during the silent film era the first great star of French comedy, Max Linder (1883–1925), was one of the models for Charlie Chaplin. In the 1930s, the "Golden Age" of French cinema, the comic genre reached dizzying heights with the delirious farces of René Clair and the southern France melodramas of Marcel Pagnol, as well as the advent, in the latter's films, of new stars like Raimu and Fernandel (*The Baker's Wife* [*La Femme du Boulanger*], *Heartbeat* [*Le Spountz*], 1938). In the 1950s the great comic actor Bourvil was celebrated for his performance beside Jean Gabin in *Four Bags Full* (*La Traversée de Paris*, 1956), but the genre was particularly marked in this period by the highly original burlesque films of Jacques Tati and his eccentric protagonist Mr. Hulot (*Monsieur Hulot's Holiday* [*Les Vacances de Monsieur Hulot*, 1953]; *Mon Oncle*, 1958). The following two decades would see the resounding box office success of classical comic films such as *Don't Look Now. . . We're Being Shot At!* (*La Grande Vadrouille*, 1966) and *The Adventures of Rabbi Jacob* (1973) by Gérard Oury (both films featuring Louis de Funès), and Edouard Molinaro's *Birds of a Feather* (*La Cage aux folles*, 1978).

The popularity of comedies persisted as well in the 1980s and 1990s, and highly talented directors such as Jean-Marie Poiré, Patrice Leconte, Michel Blanc, Josiane Balasko, Claude Zidi, Etienne Chatiliez, and Francis Veber (to mention only a few of the most prominent) made their mark on French cinema. Poiré's *Les Visiteurs*, for example, was at the top of the box office in France in 1993, and Josiane Balasko's *French Twist* (*Gazon maudit*) sold four to five million tickets in 1995, second only to the comic blockbuster *Guardian Angels* (*Les Anges gardiens*), also by Poiré. At the end of the decade, as at the beginning of the twenty-first century, Francis Veber met extraordinary success with comedies such as *The Dinner Game* (*Le Dîner de cons*) in 1998, winner of three Césars, and *The Closet* (*Le Placard*) in 2001.

The comic vein hardly subsided after the turn of the century, as we see in the following chapters on *The Taste of Others* (*Le Goût des autres*, 2000), an author comedy by Agnès Jaoui, *Amélie* (*Le Fabuleux Destin d'Amélie Poulain*, 2001) by Jean-Pierre Jeunet, and *The Intouchables* (*Intouchables*, 2011) by Olivier Nakache and Eric Toledano. These last two works reached heights of popularity throughout the world that French films had never before seen—despite the fact that the champion for a French film in France remains the comedy *Welcome to the Sticks* (*Bienvenue chez les Ch'tis*, 2008) by Dany

Boon, with more than twenty million entries. Some comic franchises, like *Taxi* (1998, 2000, 2003, 2007), *Would I Lie to You?* (*La Vérité si je mens,*1997, 2001, 2012), and the string of Astérix films (1999, 2002, 2008, 2012) brought in huge crowds, and the recent dramatic comedy by Michel Hazanavicius, *The Artist* (2011), astonished the world of cinema and filled movie houses everywhere in the course of winning five Oscars, three Golden Globes, and six Césars—150 prizes in all at international film festivals. Along with the thrillers, comedy has maintained its place at the top of the box office in France.

17

Josiane Balasko

French Twist (Gazon maudit)

(1995)

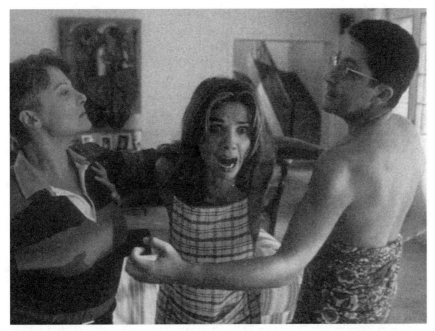

Josiane Balasko, *French Twist*: Marijo (Josiane Balasko) and Laurent (Alain Chabat) fight over Loli (Victoria Abril).

Director .... Josiane Balasko
Screenplay. .... Josiane Balasko, Telshe Boorman
Dialogue.. .... Josiane Balasko
Director of Photography .... Gérard de Battista
Sound .... Pierre Lenoir, Dominique Hennequin
Music .... Manuel Malou
Film Editor.. Claudine Merlin
Art Director .... Carlos Conti
Costumes .... Fabienne Katany
Continuity... Patrick Aubrée
Special Effects .... Jacques Gastineau
Stage Manager .... Eric Vidart-Lœb
Producer .... Claude Berri
Length... 1h47

Cast

Victoria Abril (*Loli*), Josiane Balasko (*Marijo*), Alain Chabat (*Laurent, Loli's husband*), Ticky Holgado (*Antoine, Laurent's friend and business associate*), Catherine Hiegel (*Dany, Marijo's former lover*), Catherine Samie (*the old prostitute*), Catherine Lachens (*Fabienne, the owner of Le Sopha Club*), Michèle Bernier (*Solange, Marijo and Dany's friend*), Telsche Boorman (*Dorothy Crumble*), Katrine Boorman (*Emily Crumble*), Miguel Bosé (*Diego, the seductive Spaniard at the end of the film*), Véronique Barrault (*Véro*), Sylvie Audcœur (*Ingrid*), Maureen Diot (*Christelle*)

Story

A native of Barcelona, Loli is a housewife and mother of two small children living in Provence (near Avignon) in a large, beautiful home with her husband Laurent, a real estate agent. Laurent is a highly successful businessman and no less successful with the ladies, hitting on all the available local beauties, including his kids' babysitter. In love with her husband and suspecting nothing, Loli is nonetheless aggravated at having to spend so many evenings alone while her husband tends to his "clients." When Marijo, a blatantly "butch" lesbian—stocky, short hair, male workclothes, a cigarillo between her lips—breaks down in front of her house and ends up fixing her clogged sink, Loli invites her to dinner to spite her husband, who has abandoned her once again that evening. Marijo is hardly insensitive to Loli's obvious charms and is not shy about letting her know, making Laurent furious when he realizes what is going on. Loli, however, finally becomes aware of her husband's constant philandering and goes into full revolt, refusing to give up Marijo's presence in their home. . . .

The Director

Born Josiane Balaškovic on April 15, 1952, daughter of a Parisian café owner of Yugoslavian origin, Josiane Balasko is a screenwriter, dialogue writer, actress, and film director specializing in comedies. She abandoned high school to study for the entrance examination for the Advanced School of Decorative Arts but wound up instead in the famous acting school of Tania Balachova, where she discovered that she had a talent for making people laugh with her somewhat graceless physical appearance. She began her acting career in 1973, first playing supporting roles in films directed by first-rate filmmakers like Jacques Doillon, Roman Polanski, Claude Zidi, Yves Robert, Claude Miller, André Téchiné, and Gérard Oury. In 1976 she joined a group of café comedians called "Le Splendid" (see "The Comic Tradition and the Café-Théâtre" below) which brought together a number of actors who would become some of the best known in France when they brought their comic sketches to the big screen: Christian Clavier, Michel Blanc, Gérard Jugnot, Thierry Lhermitte, Marie-Anne Chazel, and Valérie Mairesse, notably—and even Anémone for several films.

Between 1976 and 1977 Balasko's career took off, with appearances in nine films, but she really began to make her mark with the Le Splendid cast in whacky comedies produced first as café-théâtre and then brought to the screen. We are speaking here mostly of the films of Patrice Leconte (*French Fried Vacation* [*Les Bronzés*], 1978; *The "Bronzés" Go Skiing* [*Les Bronzés font du ski*], 1979) and Jean-Marie Poiré (*Santa Claus*

Is a Stinker [*Le Père Noël est une ordure*], 1982—which became a cult movie—and *Gramps Is in the Resistance* [*Papy fait de la résistance*], 1983). Short and pudgy, Balasco played the main role in another comedy by Poiré that was highly successful at the box office (two million spectators), *Men Prefer Fat Girls* (*Les Hommes préfèrent les grosses*, 1981), for which she was both co-author and co-director. Drawn to writing very young, she has been recognized as "one of the best dialogue writers in French cinema, both sexes included" (Castiel, "*Gazon maudit*" 31).

In 1985 Balasko goes behind the camera for the first time, explaining, "It was only to be able to give myself roles that I contemplated turning to directing" (Riou). She had realized, she says, that once you reach forty, if you don't want to be "reduced to ashes," you have to write roles for yourself because cinema prefers "fresh flesh" (Vincendeau, "Twist and Farce" 26). She made a first film, *All Mixed Up* (*Sac de noeuds*, 1985), about dropouts, a work for which she wrote the screenplay and in which she stars, alongside Isabelle Huppert and Jean Carmet. Although somewhat awkward, this first attempt had some success owing to its clear originality. It was soon followed by *Lady Cops* (*Les Keufs*, 1987), a police comedy in which she attacks racism, and *My Life Is Hell* (*Ma vie est un enfer*, 1991), a feminist variation on the Faust theme that she again both wrote and starred in—still without any notable commercial or critical success.

Balasko finally hit her stride as a director in 1995 with *French Twist* (*Gazon maudit*), which was France's entry for the Best Film in a Foreign Language at the Oscars the following year. The film was also nominated for the same prize at the Golden Globes and finally received it in 1996 at the Palm Springs International Film Festival. Without ever again reaching the heights of *French Twist*'s success, Balasko has had a long distinguished career as a director, actor, and screenwriter up to the present day, receiving an honorary César in 2000 for her many contributions to French cinema.

The Origin and Making of the Film

Shot over a four-month period in the summer of 1994 in the magnificent Luberon and Vaucluse countryside and in the cities of Cavaillon, Roussillon, and Avignon, *French Twist* was a result of the influence of Bertrand Blier, the "spiritual father of this comic family," who had the audacity to attack taboos (Strauss 60), but also a declaration of independence. As Balasko tells it, she had written a first version of the screenplay just after playing in Blier's *Too Beautiful for You* (*Trop belle pour toi*, 1990), at a time when she was completely under his spell: "Working with Bertrand Blier had so entranced me that I was in an alternate state. The screenplay I had written was frankly monstrous; I tossed it into a drawer" (Riou). She realized that "the challenge was to make a comedy without referring to a model, since the models for comedies were most often masculine" (Jousse 62).

Inspired surely by the example of Coline Serreau, who had dared, in *Why Not?* (*Pourquoi pas?*, 1977), to depict a happy bisexual love triangle (then a quadrangle), Balasko reinvented the traditional love triangle (a man, his wife, and his mistress) by inserting a woman—a lesbian—between a man and his wife. The filmmaker notes "a striking lack in the representation of female homosexuality," whereas "there are many good films that depict sensitively men who love other men. As for women who love women, nothing other than vaguely literary melodramas or erotic films intended to titillate the males. On the basic lesbian, the archetype, nothing" (Riou).

The great challenge for Balasko was to find a way to represent lesbians in a believable manner, to avoid the kind of caricature or burlesque that we see in *Birds of a Feather* (*La Cage aux folles*, 1978). Moreover, she wanted to avoid making a film that lent itself to voyeurism: "Voyeurism is purely masculine," she says, "and voyeurism in front of two women making love, you can find that in any porno film" (Jousse 63). To combat voyeurism Balasko gives an increasingly important role to feelings in the relationship between the characters, convinced that feelings are more "violent" and "much more disturbing" than the sex act itself (Jousse 63). She is proud, moreover, to have made, in the sequence where Laurent and Marijo have sexual relations solely to make a baby, "the first scene of non-love brought to the screen: two beings who have absolutely no desire to touch each other and are forced to do so" (Jousse 62), an "erotic" scene—according to Balasko—that refuses to cater to the spectator's voyeuristic desires.

As for the denouement of *French Twist* that offers the spectators a rather utopian take on a happy triangular family, Balasko softens her tone and attempts to forestall criticism by playing on the solid prestige of her elder colleague, Coline Serreau: "It's not a denouement that asserts, 'That's the way it should be'; it just dreams a little and says, 'Why not?'" (Tranchant).

The Actors

The four actors who play the main roles in *French Twist* are already well known to the general public in France. Josiane Balasko, who plays the role of the lesbian Marijo, had met solid success, as we've seen above, in the film adaptations of the comic sketches of Le Splendid at the end of the 1970s. Her success as an actor only grew greater in the following years, with nominations for Best Actress at the Césars for her performance in Bertrand Blier's hugely popular success *Too Beautiful for You* in 1990, where she played across from Gérard Depardieu, and in Jean-Jacques Zilbermann's *Not Everyone's Lucky Enough to Have Communist Parents* (*Tout le monde n'a pas eu la chance d'avoir des parents communistes*) in 1993. In her own films she tends to play rather weird characters, as she readily admits: "Even if the roles that I played were all more or less those of characters who were a little lost, marginalized, and abandoned, I feel that I've always played special beings" (Jousse 63).

In order to play the role of a very masculine lesbian in *French Twist*, she had observed the exterior appearance of lesbians, like their clothes and hairdo. She imitated masculine gestures, men's manner of standing and sitting, their self-confidence. As for the "inside," she says, she tried to look deep into herself, to find her masculine side, "and I found it, which was very amusing" (Vincendeau, "Twist and Farce" 26). But above all she realized, she adds, that love is the same whether it be heterosexual or homosexual: the feelings, the jealousy, the desire to possess are the same, although the technique may be different . . . (Rodgerson 44). Whatever the case may be, certain feminist critics upbraided Balasko for making this film and playing the role of a lesbian while at the same time projecting the public image of a heterosexual woman and the mother of two children; for these reasons, they could not consider *French Twist* to be a truly "gay" film (Hayward 133). To finish, Balasko received a final Best Actress nomination at the Césars in 2004 for Guillaume Nicloux's dark drama, *Hanging Offense* (*Cette femme-là*).

Alain Chabat, who plays Loli's husband Laurent, comes from television, where he was well known to the broad public for his participation in the comic sketches of "Les

Nuls" (The Zeros), a group of actors that was created at the end of the 1980s and whose form of humor was very low, to say the least. Les Nuls won several Sept d'Or (Golden 7s), a prize formerly awarded by the TV magazine *Télé Sept Jours*, for its various programs. They were especially known, however, for *Le Journal Télévisé Nul* (*The Really Lame Nightly News*), a false TV news program appearing every evening on the Canal+ channel during the 1987–88 season, with whacky portraits of an invited guest, parodies of commercials, and comic sketches (think *Saturday Night Live*).

Chabat received a Best Actor nomination at the 1996 Césars for his role in *French Twist*, as well as nominations for his roles in several other films in the following years. Like Balasko, he is also a director and screenwriter, winning a César for the Best First Work as a director for *Didier* (1977), and a nomination as well for the Best Actor César for the role of Didier, a dog turned into a man ... who continues to act like a dog. Chabat's comic film *Asterix and Obelix Meet Cleopatra* (*Astérix et Obélix: Mission Cléopâtre*, 2002), in which he also plays the role of Julius Caesar, won an award and several nominations at the Césars in 2003.

Victoria Abril was born in Madrid but has lived in Paris since 1982. Described by one critic as "the supreme cinema actor" (Brown 63), she is notorious for somewhat scandalous roles since her appearance in Vincent Aranda's *Forbidden Love* (*Changement de sexe*, 1976), in which a seventeen-year-old boy, José María, becomes María José. She was nominated for a Best Supporting Actress César for Jean-Jacques Beinex's film *The Moon in the Gutter* (*La Lune dans le caniveau*, 1983). In 1989 she played a porno film star with whom a mentally ill man falls in love in Pedro Almodóvar's film *Tie Me Up! Tie Me Down!* (¡Átame!, 1989), for which she won numerous acting awards, as well as for her role in another Aranda film, *Lovers* (*Amantes*) in 1991. Having acted in a dozen films before *French Twist*, she is known mostly for her erotically torrid roles in the works by Aranda and Almodóvar, with whom she would eventually make around fifteen films, and it was this reputation that followed her in Balasko's film. As the latter unrepentantly remarks, "I chose Victoria Abril for her past as a sex symbol" (Jousse 62).

The critics are unanimous as regards Abril's performance in *French Twist*, one of them finding her "stunning in a very tricky role" (Trémois). The three actors above, Balasko, Chabat, and Abril, thus all bring to this film a well defined on-screen identity that serves to develop and enrich their characters. And Chabat doesn't hesitate to indulge in a little wink to the public when his character Laurent says to his wife Loli, "I was *nul* (really lame) last night. I apologize."

Ticky Holgado, who plays the role of Laurent's friend and associate Antoine, had played supporting roles in the cinema and on television since the beginning of the 1980s, appearing notably in Claude Berri's great hit *Manon of the Spring* (*Manon des sources*, 1986), Balasko's *Lady Cops* (1987), Yves Robert's *Uranus* (1990), and Jean-Pierre Jeunet and Marc Caro's *Delicatessen* (1991). Although suffering from lung cancer beginning in 1992, he met his greatest success in *French Twist* (nominated for the Best Supporting Actor at the Césars) and played in Jeunet and Caro's *The City of Lost Children* (*La Cité des enfants perdus*) the same year. His last role was in Jeunet's *A Very Long Engagement* (*Un long dimanche de fiançailles*) in 2004, the year he passed away from his illness.

To finish, we need to mention the contributions of Catherine Hiegel and Catherine Samie, both veteran members of the Comédie-Française, in the roles, respectively, of Dany, Marijo's former lover, and of the philosophical old prostitute, "both remarkable" in their performances (Coppermann).

The Reception

Released on March 1, 1995, *French Twist* is one of the most popular French films of 1995, filling four to five million seats in France and making a big hit in Spain, Italy, Mexico, Quebec, and the United States. That year it was only beaten at the French box office by *Guardian Angels* (*Les Anges gardiens*), a comedy by Jean-Marie Poiré with Gérard Depardieu and Christian Clavier (another former member of Le Splendid) that is in the long tradition—no surprise here—of male comedies in which women are objects of ridicule. The following year *French Twist* won the Best Screenplay César and nominations for Best Director, Best Film, Best Actor (Chabat), and Best Supporting Actor (Ticky Holgado), as well as the Lumières Award for the Best Screenplay.

Some representatives of the film press are skeptical about this somewhat disconcerting film in which lesbianism, seldom represented in the cinema, is treated moreover in a comic vein. Some only see the "vulgar" side of the film, "banal vulgarity, routine screenplay with the salacious developments you can imagine" (De Bruyn 43), and everyone notes the clichés—"all the clichés, all the vulgar jokes you might expect on homosexuality come out" (Fontana)—as well as the stereotypical characters, whether it be the philandering husband, the housewife, or even the butch lesbian. Some critics stop there, relegating the film to the category of light comedy and vulgar farce. Others see beyond the overly trite comic situations, observing that this particular triangle, "hesitating between gross farce, worn clichés, grinding satire, and, oh yes, discreet emotion, dances before us with a certain grace" (Coppermann).

Among the more favorable critics, many cover the film with high praise, one calling it an "explosive story, *bloody well* written and right on" (Strauss 60), another chiming in with "As such, *French Twist* is already an astonishing success, a scathing response to masculine cinema and to its fantasized siliconized women, a slap in the face to the pervasive conformism. Between emotion, Gallic vitality, and gravity, Josiane Balasko demonstrates the true talent of a moralist with a sharp eye and remarkable verve" (Pascal). Riou sees the film the same way, adding, "But the art of fleshing out the characters that Balasko learned in the theater, the art of suddenly illuminating unsuspected dimensions that cause the puppets to grow, to open their eyes and heart to the point that they touch ours, turns this film ultimately into . . . an authentic, important and subtle work." Vincendeau perhaps has the last word by remarking simply that *French Twist* made a lesbian relationship acceptable to whole families at the movies, "and that's quite something" ("French Twist/Gazon maudit" 42).

The Comic Tradition and the Café-Théâtre

French Twist belongs to a long tradition of farces and light comedy in France, beginning in the nineteenth century with the plays of Eugène Labiche, Georges Feydeau, and Georges Courteline, among many other writers of lesser talent, a tradition that we rediscover in the twentieth century in the works of playwrights and film directors like Sacha Guitry. This theatrical genre specializes in relatively licentious plays, full of unexpected plot twists and caricatures of middle-class characters, in which there is often a married couple whose conjugal tranquility is troubled by the arrival of a third party, a man who courts the wife, who is always very pretty and just as fickle. The main characters of the traditional French *vaudeville* are thus the husband, the wife, and her lover, its main theme adultery. The love triangle in these comedies becomes the most common theme of "Boulevard" theater, that is, the melodramatic shows commonly offered to the middle class in the big Parisian theaters.

Balasko's film thus presents us with the situation of a traditional "vaudeville," with one exception, and it is a big one: the wife's lover is a woman, not another man. The critics are quick to note it: "*French Twist* succeeds, improbably, in combining a "vaudeville"-type comedy with author cinema on a loaded subject: feminine homosexuality" (Roy 59). As Balasko herself observes, *French Twist* is the very first lesbian comedy in the cinema, and we see here also the first husband cuckolded by a woman. One of the great originalities of the film is that we laugh about men, who are presented in a negative light, and Balasko makes no apologies: "That female filmmakers sometimes feel like being severe with masculine characters is actually a healthy reaction. We've seen so many imbecilic female roles in the movies ..." (Jousse 63). She thus indulges in a flagrant subversion of the type of comedy to which the French public is accustomed—and that public nonetheless applauded loudly. It should be noted that the public's expectations had been formed to some extent by the same comic medium that had served as a springboard for Balasko and the whole troupe at Le Splendid, that of *café-théâtre*, about which we need to say a few words.

The very first café-théâtre in Paris, created at the Café Royal by Bernard Da Costa, dates back to 1966, but this new comic vehicle owed its success especially to the events of May 1968. The number of cafés in Paris that included a little theater grew rapidly after that date, counting around twenty at the beginning of the 1970s. Among these, the most well known remain the Café de la Gare of Romain Bouteille and Le Vrai Chic Parisien of Coluche (both at Montparnasse), as well as Le Splendid (in the former neighborhood of Les Halles), where numerous actors and comic authors began their careers and later became famous, including notably (in addition to the actors of Le Splendid) Coluche, Patrick Dewaere, Miou-Miou, Gérard Lanvin, Rufus, Renaud, and, yes, Gérard Depardieu. If we are to believe Da Costa, "all the French actors, known or unknown, came from the Café-Théâtre" (151). The successful female directors Coline Serreau, Diane Kurys, and Tonie Marshall also passed through this mold.

The café-théâtre cultivates the ethics of protestation, contestation, and general radicalism in a humoristic mode, mocking, sometimes farcical and crude, and thoroughly irreverent. When Le Splendid presented its first show, *Le Nouvel Observateur* reported that the spectacle was "a burlesque piece, produced in a brand-new café-théâtre by a group of dangerous mental cases who respect nothing" (Grenier 175). Like the traditional *vaudeville*, its target is the French bourgeoisie, which is often subjected to cruel caricature, but, above all, the creed of the café-théâtre was to "go after stupidity, vanity, and inanity" wherever they were (Grenier 188–89). The café-théâtre was not concerned with "political correctness," and that worked for Balasko, who admits, "Speaking of things no one speaks of and presenting images that are normally censured has always been a source of motivation for me" (Jousse 62).

As we mentioned above, Bertrand Blier was a great source of inspiration for Balasko, beginning with *Going Places* (*Les Valseuses*, 1974), about which she said, "It was the first time that anyone spoke like that in the cinema. He liberated the medium, treating subjects that were more or less taboo, more or less shrouded in silence" (Tranchant). It was, moreover, Blier, she confesses, who had suggested to her the title of *Gazon maudit*, which won her over immediately: "I adore this image, all at once hermetic, poetic, and explicit. 'Gazon' for the pubic hair and 'maudit' like the prohibition against love between women. Reread Baudelaire . . ." (Pascal).

Following the sexual revolution of the 1960s, as well as the Women's Lib movement and the fight for the rights of homosexuals in the 1970s—not to speak of the influence of satirical publications like *Charlie Hebdo* and *Hara-Kiri*—the café-théâtre played a particularly important role in the blossoming of women in the worlds of theater and cinema. To begin with, it liberated female comic actors to speak their minds, using crude, often obscene, language. It allowed them to break the boundaries of the roles that were normally assigned to them—objects of male sexual desire or of ridicule, subjected to certain proprieties—in order to exploit their bodies in a Rabelaisian manner by emphasizing, for example, its physiological functions. They were thus able to integrate contemporary themes into their repertoire, such as feminism: "the liberation of women, the denunciation of their 'alienation,' their pregnancies, their periods, their orgasms, abortion, and birth control . . ." (Da Costa 199). In addition, the café-théâtre offered opportunities for female actors whose physique didn't correspond to the classical canons of beauty, and Balasko observed, concerning the film *Men Prefer Fat Girls*, that "it was the first time that a girl played a starring role without being a beauty queen" (Lejeune 78).

Balasko is certainly not the only nor even the first woman to make comic films in France, although the genre was completely dominated by men until after May 1968. The same year that she made her first film, *All Mixed Up* (1985), Coline Serreau recorded a stunning box office triumph with *Three Men and a Cradle* (the same year that Agnès Varda finished one of her greatest film, *Vagabond* [*Sans toit ni loi*], although this is hardly a comedy). Other women made comedies in the 1980s and 1990s, such as Tonie Marshall, Marion Vernoux, Laurence Ferreira-Barbosa, Valérie Lemercier, and Catherine Corsini, but, as Brigitte Rollet observes, Balasko is "probably the only one who nearly systematically pushes beyond the limits of behaviors that are considered socially and sexually accepted and acceptable" ("Unruly Woman?" 136). In fact, Balasko never really left the café-théâtre; she consistently maintained "its spirit of provocation, quipping, and mockery" (Baignères).

French Twist and Lesbianism

As regards lesbianism in *French Twist*, and despite the fact that Balasko was elected godmother of Gay Pride in 1994, the filmmaker consistently held herself apart from the lesbian current of cinema that was established at the beginning of the 1990s in the United States (Pascal). Intending her films for a broad public, she had no desire to screen *French Twist* at women's or gay and lesbian film festivals. Some critics espoused her position to the point of denying that it was a "lesbian film": "*French Twist* is not a film on lesbianism, but rather an offbeat *marivaudage*, a brilliant variation on a trio unlike the others. Her penchant for paradox, for reversed situations, seems to be inherited directly from Bertrand Blier. Are lesbians caricatured in this film? Of course, [but] Balasko never ridicules her heroine" (Ferenczi). In any case, it is clear that Loli's bisexuality ends up as the focus of the film, despite the insertion of Marijo into the married couple. (For a more in-depth study of lesbianism—and homosexuality in general—in French and world cinema, see the introduction to Part V—"Personal Stories: Dramas and Documentaries.")

STUDY GUIDE

What Happens in This Film?

1. Why does Marijo knock on Loli's door at the beginning of the film? What does Loli's son think when he sees Marijo? How does Marijo help Loli out?

2. How does Loli react when Laurent announces that he has to meet a client that evening? Who does she invite to dinner in his place?

3. What does Laurent finally do when Marijo dances with Loli at the restaurant?

4. What is the destination (purpose) of Laurent and Antoine's bicycle ride? What does Laurent reveal to his friend at the cafe?

5. How does Loli learn the truth about her husband's regular cheating? What decision does she make as a result?

6. What decision does Marijo announce after the night when Loli makes love with her husband?

7. What does Loli propose to Marijo and her husband to solve their dilemma? Does it work?

8. How does Loli behave the evening that they have Marijo's two friends to dinner?

9. On what condition does Marijo agree to leave Laurent and Loli's home?

10. Why do Laurent and Loli go to Paris? Where exactly do they go?

11. What is the situation in Laurent and Loli's home after Marijo has her baby?

12. What happens when Laurent goes to see the house being sold by Diego, the Spaniard from Barcelona, at the end of the film?

True or False?

If the statement is false, correct it!

1. We meet Laurent for the first time in his real estate office with a client.

2. When Laurent goes home, he behaves coldly toward Marijo, telling his wife that she is a "dyke."

3. That evening, Laurent shows a beautiful piece of property to a couple that is seeking a new home.

4. Loli and Marijo are very uncomfortable dining together; they don't know what to say to each other.

5. When Loli wants to make love with her husband that evening, he prefers to sleep.

6. Marijo returns late that evening, after dining with Loli, because she had forgotten her wallet. When Loli returns it to her, she thanks her and leaves.

7. When Laurent bends down to pick up his glasses at the restaurant, he sees that Loli has taken her shoes off.

8. When Laurent asks Marijo if she is afraid to get out of her minibus to fight with him, she comes out with a cricket bat.

9. While Laurent and Antoine go riding on their bikes, Loli asks the neighbor to watch the kids and goes shopping with Marijo.

10. Laurent decides to follow the advice of the old prostitute to try to get his wife back.

11. When the triangle arrangement goes into effect, Laurent begins taking his wife to houses that are up for sale to make love to her there.

12. When Loli finds Marijo in the lesbian nightclub, she tells her to check into a home for unwed mothers.

What Did You Learn in the Introduction?

1. What is "Le Splendid"? What tradition does it belong to?

2. Name a few comic films produced by the Le Splendid troupe.

3. What is the fourth film made by Balasko? What prize did it win at the Césars?

4. In which Bertrand Blier film did Balasko play a starring role for which she was nominated for a Best Actress award at the Césars?

5. Why was Alain Chabat such a familiar face for the public before playing in *French Twist*?

6. What role did Victoria Abril play in the Pedro Almodóvar film *Tie Me Up! Tie Me Down!*?

7. Why did Balasko want to make a film on lesbianism? What did she want to avoid above all?

8. Why are certain film critics skeptical about Balasko's film? What is Ginette Vincendeau's conclusion?

9. What is the most typical comic situation in a *vaudeville*? What is the great originality of Balasko's film in this respect?

10. What essential role did the café-théâtre play for women in both theater and cinema?

11. What important films did Coline Serreau and Agnès Varda bring out in 1985?

12. Why did Balasko not want to be identified with lesbian cinema?

Exploring the Film

1. The Title of the Film: "Gazon maudit/French Twist"

"Gazon" (literally "lawn") is a slang expression that refers to a woman's pubic hair and by extension to her vagina. **What does "maudit" ("cursed") mean in this context?** To understand this title, Balasko suggests rereading Charles Baudelaire, who devotes several poems to *femmes damnées* ("damned women") in his famous book of poetry *The Flowers of Evil* (*Les Fleurs du mal*, 1857). Find one of these poems on the internet, and explain what women he is talking about. Do you find the title "*Gazon maudit*" vulgar or, on the contrary, "poetic," as Balasko claims.

What aspect of this film is reflected in the English title, *French Twist*?

2. The Beginning of the Film

Where does the action of the film begin? What do we learn, as regards the geography of the action, during the beginning credits?

What do we learn about Marijo's character during the credits? Is her vehicle, a Volkswagen Microbus, significant in this respect? **With whom was this type of vehicle identified in the 1960s?** We hear in the background one of the big hits of Procol Harum, "A Whiter Shade of Pale" (1967), from the same period. **Look for the words to this song on the internet.** In your opinion, what connection might there be between this song and the film that is beginning?

3. The Characters

+ *Stereotypes*

At the beginning of the film, there are three main characters in extremely stereotyped roles. **What stereotypes are in play here?** *Review the first three sequences of the film after the opening credits: at the café* (Excerpt 1, 2'45–5'30), *at home* (Excerpt 2, 5'30–6'35), *and the arrival of Marijo* (Excerpt 3, 6'35–8'45).

+ *Laurent, Antoine, and machismo*

How is the machismo of Laurent, Loli's husband, established from the outset? Why does Laurent ask Antoine to call him on the telephone at seven o'clock that evening? What **chauvinistic clichés** (as regards love and feelings) do the two men use, later in the film, to justify cheating on their wives? *Review the sequence where Laurent and Antoine talk at the café during their bike ride* (Excerpt 4, 39'30–42'20). What "noble" rationale does Laurent offer to explain why he was so careful to hide his affairs from his wife?

+ *Loli and Marijo*

How are Loli and Marijo's characters established in the two sequences at the beginning of the film (see Excerpts 2 and 3 above)? How is Marijo "different" in relation to the Laurent-Loli couple? Is it simply a question of sexuality, or is there something else (on the social level, for example) that separates them?

Why does Loli like Marijo so much from the very beginning? What does Marijo offer her (contrary to her husband)?

4. The Seduction

How do you explain the rapid seduction of Loli by Marijo when she returns to "get her wallet" after her initial departure? Is there any connection to Laurent's behavior that evening? Why does he not want to (or cannot) make love with Loli as she desires? *Review the sequences where Loli meets Marijo outside her home, then returns to sleep beside her husband* (Excerpt 5, 22'30–23'15 and Excerpt 6, 23'15–23'45). **What role does the music play in the latter part of this sequence (Excerpt 6)?** When Loli goes to bed, we hear the French version of a Spanish song, "Historia de un amor" ("Story of a Love"). **What is the obvious implication for what is going to follow in the film?**

5. At the Restaurant

Describe the behavior of Laurent and Antoine as regards lesbians at the beginning of this scene. How does Laurent realize that Loli and Marijo are having intimate relations? *Review the first part of the restaurant scene* (Excerpt 7, 25'00–27'00). How does Laurent first react to his discovery? **What fundamental opposition (rivalry) is prepared here?**

6. The Love Triangle

What circumstances lead Loli to impose the presence of Marijo in her home over Laurent's opposition? **What role does the episode with the old prostitute play in the development of the love triangle?** *Review this episode* (Excerpt 8, 52'00–54'55).

Why does Loli make up with her husband afterwards? Ultimately Laurent takes Loli to make love in houses he is handling for sale. **Why is this both comical and ironic?**

7. The Dinner with Marijo's Friends

What causes problems between Loli and Marijo after the triangle is established? **What role does Laurent play in that? Why is he so charming with Marijo and her friends Dany and Solange?** How would you explain Loli's violent behavior? *Review the episode of the argument between Loli and Marijo in the kitchen while Laurent chats graciously with Dany and Solange in the living room* (Excerpt 9, 1h12'30–1h14'00). What would you say about Laurent's behavior here?

When Laurent plays tarot with Marijo and Dany after dinner, he says to the latter, speaking of Marijo, "Not to worry, we're just discussing . . . man to man." **What does this little comment indicate as regards his new attitude toward Marijo as an adversary?**

8. The Copulation Scene

What do you think of the scene in which Laurent is led to have sex with Marijo to give her a child? *Review this sequence* (Excerpt 10, 1h23'00–1h25'10). **Is this episode "erotic," as Balasko claims? How do two people who detest each other manage to have sexual relations?** How do you interpret the strange, surprised expression that comes over Marijo's face at the very end of the scene? What is she feeling? Balasko comments on it without clarifying anything: "We will never know if they took pleasure in this act; the ambiguity remains" (Jousse 63). **Do you agree with this comment?**

According to a British critic, certain English lesbians were highly critical of this episode, pointing out that Marijo could very well have done without Laurent's services by using a sperm donor (Rodgerson 44). **Do you think that Balasko could have adopted this strategy in her film without deeply changing the work? Should she have done so?**

9. The Break-Up and the Reunion

Why does Loli finally break up with Marijo? When she learns that Marijo is going to have a baby soon, she nonetheless goes to see her in Paris. **What do we note as regards the appearance of Loli now (hairdo, clothes)? What has changed? Why, in your opinion?** Has Marijo's appearance also changed at the end of the film? How?

What image does the film give of lesbians in the nightclub sequence in Paris? **Why did Balasko show them this way in her film?** Is there any connection to the way the story ends?

10. Nudity

What does Loli's frequent nudity indicate about her character? Does she use her nudity for any discernable purpose? Do you feel that this nudity contributes to the quality of the film, that it has an important thematic function? Or does it only serve to engage and titillate the spectators?

And what are we to think of Laurent's frequent nudity? What use does Laurent make of his nudity as regards Marijo? What does the French word "phallocratie" mean? Can you see any connection between Laurent's nudity in front of Marijo (the fact that he displays his genitals aggressively) and the threat that she represents for him?

11. Lesbianism

Balasko observed, regarding the success of her film in the United States, "Here people criticized me for showing lesbianism in a caricatured way. There, on the other hand, the lesbian American journalists congratulated me, saying, "We're sick and tired of the 'lipstick dykes,' that is, lesbians who are too pretty, all made up, and very feminine" (Lequeret 90). **What is the image of lesbians offered in French Twist?** Is there a uniform image throughout the film?

Why does Laurent become so baffled, so helpless, before the relationship that develops between Marijo and his wife? *Review again the sequence in which Laurent and Antoine talk at the café during their bike ride* (Excerpt 4, 39'30–42'20). Lucille Cairns recalls the consternation of Marcel in Proust's In Search of Lost Time (A la recherche du temps perdu, 1913–22) when the narrator has to compete with a lesbian, a much more formidable rival than another man, for Albertine's affections: "But here the rival did not resemble me, her arms were different, I couldn't fight on the same terms, give Albertine the same pleasures nor even imagine exactly what they might be" (231). Is this reflection relevant to Laurent's dilemma also?

12. Homophobia

How is Laurent's homophobia expressed in his first encounter with Marijo? What expression does he use in speaking of her to Loli? In your opinion, do homophobia and machismo go together naturally?

The philosopher Michel Foucault suggests that what is really shocking as regards homosexuality is the question of feelings: "I think that's what makes homosexuality so 'troubling': the style of homosexual life more than the sex act itself. Imagining a sex act that doesn't conform to laws or to nature is not what bothers people. But when individuals begin to love each other, that's a problem" (Le Bitoux et al. 38). What do you think? Is the idea of two persons of the same sex falling in love with each other more disturbing than the sex act itself (as Balasko claims as well)?

13. Comedy and Sentiment

Balasko was particularly drawn to comedies based on situations, and the principal source of the humor in *French Twist* comes clearly from the situation created when Marijo inserts herself into Laurent and Loli's marriage. But Balasko comes from the café-théâtre where vulgar comedy—of which we see many examples in the crude language of the characters of this film—and gross farce were common. **In which episodes does *French Twist* slip into pure farce, into burlesque?**

Balasko recognizes that there are clichés in her film, but she adds that in the course of the film these clichés are destroyed: "What I really like," she says, "is to take the clichés, the archetypes, and demolish them" (Lejeune 78). In order to do so, she emphasizes the *critical role of feelings*. One critic notes also that "the initial comedic stereotyping of the characters . . . doesn't survive for long" in the face of the strong feelings involved (Strauss 61), and another observes as well that "Balasko skirts around the traditional Boulevard comedy situation, which is just a departure point in the scenario, and turns her film into a true sentimental comedy, that is, a film in which feelings are preeminent" (Roy 59). Do you agree with these two critics? How does the foregrounding of human feelings contribute to the destruction of the stereotypes?

In addition, another critic recalls the famous work by Henri Bergson, *Laughter. Essay on the Meaning of the Comic* (*Le Rire. Essai sur la signification du comique*, 1940), in which the philosopher underlines the fact that the worst enemy of laughter is sentimentality and that comedy needs what he calls 'a temporary anesthesia of emotion' (Rollet, "Unruly Woman?" 129), which is to say that sentiment and comedy simply do not mix. Is the idea of "sentimental comedy" thus an oxymoron, a contradiction in terms? Is Bergson's principle relevant to *French Twist*? Does the sentimental element work to the detriment of the comic element, or are the two aspects of the film complementary in your view?

14. The Baby and the Film's Denouement

After their first dinner together, Loli asks Marijo if she had ever had the desire to have a child. Later in the film, Antoine deplores the fact that he hasn't seen his kids for twelve

years, "which is the hardest thing in the world." **Why does Balasko introduce the theme of children, here and elsewhere in her film (before the denouement)?**
In the Parisian nightclub, Loli tells Marijo that "a child needs a mother and a father." Describe the new family that forms at the end of the film. *Review the first part of the denouement* (Excerpt 11, 1h34'00–1h35'25). A critic remarks that *French Twist* only exploits lesbianism in order to reinforce "the legitimate social unit," the traditional family and the heterosexual couple (Cairns 236–37). **What do you think? Is this Balasko's real purpose?** Cairns asks, moreover, why Balsako didn't create in her film a family with Loli, Marijo, and the children without Laurent, instead of proposing an alternative family model under the aegis of the Father. **Why, in your opinion, did Balasko choose the conjugal trio we see at the end of the film? Was she wrong?**
Antoine's strong southern France accent recalls the films of Marcel Pagnol. In *The Well-Digger's Daughter* (*La Fille du puisatier*, 1940), one of the biggest successes of the Occupation period, the problem of social inequality between the two families concerned is resolved by the birth of the baby at the end of the film. **Does Laurent and Marijo's baby play the same role here?** Vincendeau observes that the denouement of *French Twist* proves that it is maternity and not love that conquers all the problems ("French Twist/Gazon maudit" 42). **What do you think? Is that the definitive "message" of the film? Otherwise, how would you interpret the denouement of *French Twist*?**
At the end of the film, Laurent tells Diego, the handsome Spaniard, that he would "always be welcome" if he ever wanted to return to the home he was selling to Laurent. Diego replies, "Careful. I could take you up on that." **What does this episode suggest in the context of the film's denouement?** If Laurent had an affair with a man, would that be less serious than with a woman?

Josiane Balasko's Filmography

1985 *All Mixed Up (Sac de nœuds)*

1987 *Lady Cops (Les Keufs)*

1991 *My Life Is Hell (Ma vie est un enfer)*

1995 *French Twist (Gazon maudit)*

1998 *Un grand cri d'amour*

2004 *The Ex-Wife of My Life (L'Ex-femme de ma vie)*

2008 *A French Gigolo (Cliente)*

2013 *Half-Sister (Demi-sœur)*

Works Consulted

Andreu, Anne. "Le Cinéma s'intéresse enfin à la femme de ma voisine." *InfoMatin*, 8 Feb. 1995: 19.

Baignères, Claude. "Sonate à trois, rire à la clef." *Le Figaro*, 8 Feb. 1995: n. pag.

Balasko, Josiane, dir. *Gazon maudit*. Miramax Home Entertainment, 2003.

Brown, Georgia. "Strange Ways." *Village Voice* 41 (23 Jan. 1996): 63.

Cairns, Lucille. "*Gazon maudit*: French National and Sexual Identities." *French Cultural Studies* 9 (1998): 225–37.

Castiel, Elie. "*Gazon maudit*." *Séquences* 178 (May–June 1995): 29–31.

———. "Victoria Abril." *Séquences* 178 (May–June 1995): 30–31.

Coppermann, Annie. "Entre grosse farce et émotion." *Les Echos*, 10 Feb. 1995: n. pag.

Da Costa, Bernard. *Histoire du café-théâtre*. Paris: Buchet-Chastel, 1978.

De Bruyn, Olivier. "*Gazon maudit*." *Positif*, Mar. 1995: 43.

Ferenczi, Aurélien. "La Femme qui aimait les femmes." *InfoMatin*, 8 Feb. 1995: 19.

Fontana, Céline. "Amours en herbe." *La Croix*, 11 Feb. 1995: n. pag.

"*Gazon maudit (French Twist)* 1995." *Lesbian Film Guide* 4th ed. Ed. Alison Darren. New York: Continuum, 2000. 83–84.

Gianorio, Richard. "Victoria Abril. Lesbienne et ménagère." *France Soir*, 8 Feb. 1995.

Grenier, Alexandre. *Génération père Noël. Du Splendid à la gloire*. Paris: Belfond, 1994.

Hayward, Susan. "Hardly Grazing," Josiane Balasko's *Gazon maudit* (1995): the mise-en-textes and mise-en-scène of sexuality/ies." *Gay Signatures: Gay and Lesbian Theory, Fiction and Film in France, 1945–1995*. Ed. O. Heathcote, A. Hughes, and J. S. Williams. Oxford, UK: Berg, 1998. 131–50.

Howze, Jennifer. "Hands Off, She's Mine." *Première* (Mar. 1996): 45.

Jousse, Thierry. "Rencontre avec Josiane Balasko." *Cahiers du cinéma* 489 (Mar. 1995): 62–63.

Le Bitoux, Jean, René de Ceccatty, and Jean Danet. "De l'amitié comme mode de vie: un entretien avec un lecteur quinquagénaire." *Le Gai Pied* 25 (Apr. 1981): 38–39.

Lejeune, Paule. *Le Cinéma des femmes*. Paris: Atlas Lherminier, 1987.

Lequeret, Elisabeth. "Pour Josiane Balasko, l'Amérique valait bien un baiser." *Cahiers du cinéma* 568 (May 2002): 90.

Majois, Isabelle, "*Gazon maudit*." *Ciné-Fiches de Grand Angle* 180 (Mar. 1995): 19–20.

Pascal, Michel. "Feydeau à Lesbos." *Le Point*, 4 Feb. 1995: n. pag.

Riou, Alain. "Lesbos people." *Le Nouvel Observateur*, 8 Feb. 1995: n. pag.

Rodgerson, Gillian. "Oo la la !" *Diva*, Feb. 1996: 42–44.

Rollet, Brigitte. "Two Women Filmmakers Speak Out: Serreau and Balasko and the Inheritance of May '68." *Voices of France. Social, Political and Cultural Identity*. Ed. Sheila Perry and Máire Cross. London: Pinter, 1997. 100–13.

———. "Transgressive Masquerades at the *Fin de siècle*? *Gazon maudit* and *Pédale douce*." *France: Fin(s) de Siècle(s)*. Ed. T. Unwin and K. Chadwick. Lewiston, NY: Edwin Mellen Press, 2000. 139–53.

———. "Unruly Woman? Josiane Balasko, French Comedy, and *Gazon maudit*." *French Cinema in the 1990s. Continuity and Difference.* Ed. Phil Powrie. Oxford, UK: Oxford UP, 1999. 127–36.

Roy, André. "*Gazon maudit*." *24 Images* 77 (Summer 1995): 59–60.

Strauss, Frédéric. "L'Empire des sens." *Cahiers du Cinéma* 489 (Mar. 1995): 60–61.

Tarr, Carrie, and Brigitte Rollet. *Cinema and the Second Sex: Women's Filmmaking in the 1980s and 1990s.* New York: Continuum, 2001.

Tranchant, Marie-Noëlle. "Josiane Balasko: 'Mon film n'est pas une provocation.'" *Le Figaro*, 4–5 Feb. 1995: n. pag.

Trémois, Claude-Marie. "*Gazon maudit* de Josiane Balasko." *Télérama*, 8 Feb. 1995: n. pag.

Vincendeau, Ginette. "French Twist/Gazon maudit." *Sight and Sound* 6 (Mar. 1996): 41–42.

———. "Twist and Farce." *Sight and Sound* 6.4 (1 Apr. 1996): 24–26.

18

Agnès Jaoui

The Taste of Others (Le Goût des autres)

(2000)

Agnès Jaoui, *The Taste of Others*: Clara (Anne Alvaro) gives an English lesson to Castella (Jean-Pierre Bacri).

Director .... Agnès Jaoui
Screenplay .... Jean-Pierre Bacri, Agnès Jaoui
Director of Photography .... Laurent Dailland
Sound .... Jean-Pierre Duret, Michel Klochendler,
.... Dominique Gaborieau
Film Editor .... Hervé de Luze
Music .... Jean-Charles Jarrell
Art Director .... François Emmanuelli
Costumes .... Jackie Stephens-Budin
Continuity .... Brigitte Hedou-Prat
Producer .... Daniel Chevalier
Length 1h52

Cast

Jean-Pierre Bacri (*Jean-Jacques Castella*), Anne Alvaro (*Clara Devaux*), Alain Chabat (*Bruno Deschamps, Mrs. Castella's chauffeur*), Agnès Jaoui (*Manie*), Gérard Lanvin (*Franck Moreno, Castella's bodyguard*), Christiane Millet (*Angélique Castella, Castella's wife*), Wladimir Yordanoff (*Antoine*), Anne Le Ny (*Valérie, the costume designer*), Brigitte Catillon (*Béatrice Castella, Castella's sister*), Xavier de Guillebon (*Weber, Castella's collaborator*), Raphaël Defour (*Benoît, the painter*), Bob Zaremba (*Fred, the bar owner*), Robert Bacri (*Castella's father*), Céline Arnaud (*Virginie, the Castellas' niece*)

Story

Mr. Castella, a business owner in the provinces, grumpy but not mean, is set in his ways and reluctant to participate in new activities imposed on him. English classes in order to utter a few words at the signing of an Iranian contract? Not for him. The first session ends early because the teacher, Clara Devaux, does not know any methods that are at least a little "fun." On the other hand, there is no escaping an evening at the theater with his wife, who, it turns out, is no more enthusiastic than he is about the idea. But their niece has a small part in the play, so. . . . To Angélique's great surprise, Castella's face suddenly lights up as he focuses his gaze on the actress who is impersonating a grieving lover. He has just recognized his English teacher, transfigured in the role of Bérénice.

From this point on, Castella the uncultivated businessman begins to show interest in the cultural tastes of Clara and her group of friends, becomes a serious student of the English language, and even dabbles in love poetry. He attends the theater in secret, invites himself to the café frequented by Clara's group after the plays, and tries his best to follow the intellectual conversations without noticing that the others are mocking him and taking advantage of his generosity.

Will Clara and her friends begin to take him seriously? This is what Bruno and Franck, Castella's chauffeur and bodyguard, are wondering. As for Angélique, she is mostly concerned with her little dog Flucky and her candy pink home decor.

The Director

When Agnès Jaoui stepped behind the camera with *The Taste of Others* in 2000, she already had a long artistic career behind her as an actress (around ten films), playwright (two plays), and screenwriter (five screenplays). She had been passionate about storytelling since her childhood, when her psychotherapist mother brought her along to group therapy sessions where she listened to life stories, and she had undergone psychoanalysis herself for several years, "the best screenplay school in the world" in her opinion (Grassin). She had taken to writing as a teenager following the discovery of the *Diary of Anne Frank*, a book that touched her deeply because her parents were Tunisian Jews who had immigrated to France. She ultimately acquired a solid knowledge of film by accompanying her brother Laurent—now a director—to a neighborhood art house theater that showed Soviet movies and, later, by going to the movies in her student days. At that time she had a particular liking for "Lubitsch, Capra, Renoir, Allen, Bergman, Kurosawa," a list that later included "Tim Burton, Pedro Almodóvar, Cédric Kahn or

Lars von Trier. 'Inventors' [. . .]. People who, like her, do not care what people think" (De Bruyn).

After brilliant studies at the prestigious Lycée Henri-IV, Agnès Jaoui took theater classes at the Cours Florent, then at the Théâtre des Amandiers run by Patrice Chéreau in Nanterre. But she found the latter a little too sectarian and refused to join his troupe when she graduated. This marked the beginning of a difficult period during which she worked at odd jobs waiting for acting gigs, an experience that ignited her desire to take charge of her own destiny.

In 1987 her meeting with the theater, television, and film actor and writer Jean-Pierre Bacri, who had already made twenty-five films, was an important milestone in her personal life (beginning a quarter century–long relationship with Bacri until their separation in 2012) and above all in her career. Indeed, the duo began co-writing plays and screenplays, which also allowed them to give themselves custom roles in addition to the ones they were offered in other films.

Two of their first screenplays, adapted from their plays and brought to the big screen under the same titles, *Kitchen with Apartment* (*Cuisine et dépendances* [Philippe Muyl, 1992]) and *Family Resemblances* (*Un air de famille* [Cédric Klapisch, 1996]), foretell the themes and the biting humor of Jaoui's later films: both films feature meals between friends or relatives that turn into a settling of scores and bring out everyone's insecurities and pettiness. *Family Resemblances* revealed them to the broad public at the Césars where it received the Best Screenplay award and a nomination for Best Actress in a Supporting Role for Agnès Jaoui. The Jaoui-Bacri couple also authored two screenplays (*Smoking/No Smoking* in 1993 and *Same Old Song* [*On connaît la chanson*] in 1997) that earned Césars for the famous director of *Hiroshima mon amour*, Alain Resnais, who affectionately nicknamed them the "Jabacs." In spite of her many successes as screenwriter and actress, Jaoui decided to step behind the camera in order to film her stories as she pleased and because she considered directing the ultimate stage of her artistic development, saying, "I've always thought that acting was like being a child [. . .]. Writing is being an adult. Directing is being a parent to the others, to the team" (Guichard).

Starting with *The Taste of Others*, the "Jabacs" thus dedicated themselves to writing screenplays for feature films directed by Agnès Jaoui. Less sarcastic and more open to differences than their earlier works, this film was a "great adventure" with "maximum risk taking" according to Lalanne, because it goes beyond the "constricting frame of caricature and sociological typing." The gamble would pay off because the movie reaped a harvest of awards and was the film event of the year in 2000.

The Taste of Others was followed by *Look at Me* (*Comme une image*, 2004), which won the Best Screenplay Award at the Cannes Film Festival. This ensemble film is centered on the difficult relationship between an insecure young woman and her writer father (played by Bacri). According to Jaoui, "the film has a lot more themes than *The Taste of Others*" and deals with "the ways we relate to ambition, climbing the social ladder, power, the body, image" (Carrière). It is also a film that expresses the director's passion for singing: we witness the rehearsals of a choir with Jaoui as choir leader. As a matter of fact, she devoted herself to music before making her next film and released an album of Latin American songs in Spanish and Portuguese, *Canta*, that won an award at the *Victoires de la musique* contest in 2007 in the World Music category.

Jaoui came back to cinema in 2008 as director, co-screenwriter, and actress for the comedy *Let's Talk about the Rain*, which is also the Jabacs' first collaboration with actor Jamel Debbouze, cast in his first adult role. Debbouze and Bacri play (amateur) reporters who fail miserably in their attempts to interview Agathe (Jaoui), a feminist candidate in a local election in Provence. In addition to Jaoui and Bacri's usual themes the film broaches racial discrimination several times through the character played by Debouzze, Karim, whose Algerian mother has spent her life as a housecleaner for Agathe's family.

In 2013 Jaoui made *Under the Rainbow* (*Au bout du conte*), another ensemble comedy co-written and co-performed with Bacri. She portrays an actress who is preparing young children to perform a fairy tale for their school celebration and at the same time helping her very sentimental niece manage her love life. This is the first film by Jaoui that features children (albeit in minor roles), whose absence in the works of the director-screenwriter had drawn criticism.

Finally the woman who considered herself "the left-wing spokesperson for French cinema, always ready to spread the word" (Guichard), got involved in film-related causes. She took up the defense of French cinema, notably through public condemnation of the way Hollywood films are marketed, which undermines the distribution of French films in the theaters (Libiot, "Agnès Jaoui"). At the time of the debates regarding the status of part-time workers in the entertainment industry (the "*intermittents du spectacle*") in 2004, she addressed the Minister of Culture during the Césars Awards ceremony and criticized his proposed bill to lower the unemployment and retirement benefits of these workers.

Agnès Jaoui is thus an eclectic artist, "a unique personality who has for some years now been pushing the envelope in French cinema" (De Bruyn). Her cinema seeks to "unearth the little flaws in our behavior and show that they are just obstacles to our freedom and to life in society" ("*Le Goût des autres*"). Hers is a cinema based on social analysis that brings out the conventionality and sexism of the day and reflects the left-wing commitment of its co-screenwriters. It is intellectual and a tad moralizing, relies on dialogue rather than mise en scène, and places great emphasis on the arts (painting, music, song, literature). Coppermann got it right, in any case, when he predicted a bounty of accolades for this "welcome addition to the small band of female directors who at the moment contribute greatly to the vitality of French cinema [...] after Tonie Marshall and her four Césars" (for *Venus Beauty* [*Vénus Beauté (Institut)*] in 2000).

The Origin and Making of the Film

With *The Taste of Others*, Jaoui wanted to talk about a subject that had been close to her heart since her years as a high school and college student, when she felt at odds with the groups around her: "The source of *The Taste of Others*, Agnès Jaoui explains, is my fierce scorn for clans, for reputations. For these cliques that are rampant everywhere, from the school yard to the adult world, and dictate their laws about how to dress as well as how to think" (De Bruyn). She wanted to talk about exclusion, which results in the fact that "99 percent of our friends, husbands, and wives belong to our own social group," and about our tendency to look down upon those who are different from us (Pliskin).

She and Bacri began to write a screenplay for a thriller but gave up after a couple of months because they could not escape the limitations of the genre and make it their own (Kelleher 20). They kept three of their characters (the chauffeur, the bodyguard, the female drug dealer) and went back to work following their usual approach: they began with the theme, then created the characters after their own experience and invented a backstory for each before including them in the fiction. Jaoui, more literary-minded, focuses more on the narrative while Bacri provides the dialogue (Baurez, Mandelbaum, "Jaoui-Bacri"). For their first original screenplay, Jaoui wished to write "a polyphonic ensemble fiction with a bunch of characters" (De Bruyn). She also insisted on shooting several scenes in cafés, as Claude Sautet does, because, she said, "I like filming these gathering places; I like the energy that radiates from them—the energy of faces" (Douguet).

The shoot took place in Rouen in the summer of 1999, except for the scenes in Clara's dressing room, filmed in Paris. Jaoui followed the screenplay to the letter and allowed very little improvisation. She minimized camera movements because, she explains, "Dialogue comes first. If you move the camera too much, you no longer hear people talk" (Alion 78). As we will see in "The Reception" below, her decision to subordinate mise en scène to the dialogue drew some harsh criticism.

The Actors

Agnès Jaoui said of her work with the cast of *The Taste of Others* that "it was like conducting first violins" (Douguet). The actors of this ensemble film are indeed among the best of their time, and, except for Alain Chabat (Bruno Deschamps), they all started their careers in theater.

Jean-Pierre Bacri has appeared in over fifty feature films since 1979. He has played in all genres and embodied characters that are sometimes grumpy and whining, never quite in tune with those around them. The success of *Family Resemblances* (1992) and *Kitchen with Apartment* (1996)—he both acted in them and co-wrote the screenplay—gave him a great amount of freedom, and he now chooses his roles based on the quality of the screenplays that he receives, in both popular and auteur films (although he prefers the latter). Like Jaoui, Bacri is politically engaged on the left, and he appreciates stories with social themes. In one of his latest films, *Looking for Hortense* (*Cherchez Hortense* [Pascal Bonitzer, 2012]), he portrays a passive, depressed man who recovers his taste for life when circumstances force him to help an illegal immigrant woman. Bacri won, among other accolades, the César for Best Actor in a Supporting Role for *Same Old Song* in 1998 and five nominations for the Best Actor César from 2000 (*The Taste of Others*) to 2016. We should mention that his father is cast as Castella's father in *The Taste of Others*.

Jaoui and Bacri chose Anne Alvaro and wrote Clara's role for her because they felt an emotion close to that experienced by Castella when they saw her act in a play by Brecht, and because they considered her one of the few actors who could portray both Bérénice and Clara. Jaoui believes that she deserves more recognition for her work: "It's as if people who like music were not familiar with Maria Callas!" (Fajardo). Passionate about the stage since her teenage years—she skipped high school to take drama lessons—Alvaro has acted in around a hundred plays since 1970, portraying the great heroines of Corneille, Racine, Shakespeare, Kleist, Ibsen, Chekhov, and other classical and contemporary playwrights. She made her movie debut in *Danton* (Andrzej Wajda,

1982) and has appeared in around thirty films. She has garnered many prizes in the theater and two Césars for Best Actress in a Supporting Role for *The Taste of Others* and *The Clink of Ice* (*Le Bruit des glaçons* [Bertrand Blier, 2010]).

Alain Chabat (*Bruno Deschamps*) is very popular in France, active in both film and television since 1984 after a stint in radio. His roles in *Fear City: A Family-Style Comedy* (*Le Film de les Nuls*) in 1994 and *French Twist* (see Chap. 17) in 1995 increased his notoriety, and he has played more than seventy roles to this day. He was nominated three times for the Best Actor César (for *French Twist*, for his own film, *Didier*, in 1998, and for *I Do* [*Prête-moi ta main*] by Eric Lartigau in 2007), and once for the Best Actor in a Supporting Role César for *The Taste of Others*. Alain Chabat is also a director, screenwriter, and producer. The four features that he directed met with great success at the box office. His first film, *Didier* (with Jean-Pierre Bacri), in which he also plays a dog, sold three million seats and earned the César for Best First Feature Film in 1998. *Astérix and Obélix Meet Cléopatra* (*Astérix & Obélix: Mission Cléopâtre*), which he both wrote and directed in 2002, is one of the most popular French films ever, with close to fifteen million tickets sold in France and twenty-five million abroad. More recently, he wore many hats as producer, screenwriter, director, and actor for the comedy *HOUBA! On the Trail of the Marsupilami* (*Sur la piste du Marchupilami*), which drew over five million spectators to the theaters in 2012. Chabat has increasingly focused on his producing ventures and his international career. He played in *Night in the Museum 2* (Shawn Levy, 2009) and *A Thousand Words* (Brian Robbins, 2012), across from Eddie Murphy.

Gérard Lanvin (*Franck Moreno*) earned a living doing odd jobs before becoming a café-théâtre actor (see "The Comic Tradition and the Café-Théâtre" in the introduction to *French Twist*). He owes the actor and stand-up comedian Coluche his first important role at the movies in one of the latter's comedies, *You Won't Have Alsace-Lorraine* (*Vous n'aurez pas l'Alsace and la Lorraine*, 1977). He has acted in many films since, portraying manly men and big-hearted macho guys in thrillers, dramas, and comedies. He won the Jean Gabin Prize (awarded to a promising actor in French or Francophone films) for his role in Pierre Granier-Deferre's *Strange Affair* (*Une étrange affaire*, 1981), the César for Best Actor in 1995 for Nicole Garcia's *The Favorite Son* (*Le Fils préféré*), and the César for Best Actor in a Supporting Role for *The Taste of Others*.

Like Anne Alvaro, Christiane Millet (*Angélique*) and Wladimir Yordanoff (*Antoine*) are better known as stage actors. Both have performed in over fifty plays with renowned directors and played many television and film roles. Before *The Taste of Others*, Yordanoff had played opposite Bacri and Jaoui in *Family Resemblances* by Cédric Klapisch in 1996.

Finally—honor where honor is due—Agnès Jaoui cast herself as Manie to take a break from her responsibilities as director because, she said, "it was reassuring to find myself again in my traditional role, to be taken care of and pampered by the crew" (De Bruyn). Jaoui likes to say in her interviews that she became an actress to race against time by living several lives. And indeed, she has played in over twenty-five films of different genres since 1983, often embodying women who are intelligent, rebellious, and a bit aggressive (Tranchant, "Agnès Jaoui"). In addition to her leading roles, Jaoui is also known for her performance in many secondary roles—including in all her own films and those for which she wrote the screenplay—which earned her the César for Best Actress in a Supporting Role (*Same Old Song*, 1998) and three nominations for the same prize for *Family Resemblances* in 1997, *The Taste of Others* in 2001, and Bruno Podalydès' *The Sweet Escape* (*Comme un avion*) in 2016.

The Reception

The Taste of Others was the film event of the year in 2000, garnering four Césars (Best Film, Best Screenplay, Best Actor in a Supporting Role for Lanvin, Best Actress in a Supporting Role for Alvaro), and as many nominations. It was selected for the New York Film Festival and the Oscars and received the *Grand Prix des Amériques* at the Montreal World Film Festival. Finally it triumphed at the box office with close to four million tickets sold and was the second French film of the year behind the popular comedy *Taxi 2*, by Gérard Krawczyk. Its success came as a surprise because the popular genres of the time were primarily action films like *Taxi 2* and *The Fifth Element* (*Le Cinquième Elément* [Luc Besson, 1997]), and farcical comedies such as *The Visitors II: The Corridors of Time* (*Les Visiteurs 2: les couloirs du temps* [Jean-Marie Poiré, 1998]), *The Dinner Game* (*Le Dîner de cons* [Francis Veber, 1999]), and *Astérix et Obélix vs. César* (*Astérix et Obélix contre César* [Claude Zidi, 1999]).

This first film by Jaoui also received outstanding critical acclaim. "First stroke, a master stroke," reads the title of an article by Royer, who borrowed from a well-known line from Corneille's seventeenth-century play *Le Cid* to highlight the importance of classical theater in the story. "A master stroke" also for Baignières, who adds, "It's funny, casual, sarcastic, gentle, sensitive, vibrant, incisive, smooth, full of energy. Everything rings true, words as well as feelings." Mérigeau is full of praise for the film: "What is extraordinary is [. . .] that it is stunningly true and inimitably witty; it exudes love for others, the actors are fantastic [. . .]. A good film, an excellent film? No, a great film."

Commentators praise the message of the film, its critique of snobbishness and cliques: it is "a brilliant satire against exclusion, parochialism, fads, ideological and sociological dictatorships" (Gouslan) that pinpoints "a typically 'French' form of exclusion that each of us has the impression of perpetrating and enduring at the same time: cultural ostracism" (Assouline). Critics appreciate the lessons that can be drawn from the film: "a tribute to curiosity" (Lalanne), "a magnificent film on tolerance" that leaves us "a little stronger, a little happier, and a little more critical toward our own narrow-mindedness" ("Le Goût des autres"), a film that reconciles lovers of television with those of high culture [. . .], "spectators of the TF1 channel with those of Ibsen" (Pliskin).

For some *The Taste of Others* breathes new life into French cinema with its polished dialogue, its unobtrusive camera that does not steal the limelight away from the text and the actors, and its humor: "She [Jaoui] goes against the tide of political correctness that is drowning French cinema in social lament and sluggish despair. In short, we couldn't be happier!" (Baignières). Jaoui is described as the heir to filmmakers like Claude Sautet in her "pertinent X-ray of French society" (Alion 2) and her group portraits (Royer). Lalanne perceives the influence of *The Rules of the Game* (*La Règle du jeu*) by Jean Renoir in the crossing of class lines in the film, an opinion shared by Mérigeau who finds a touch of "Lubitsch also, or Mankiewicz, or else Renoir" in "the gaze of humble folk" (that of the chauffeur and the bodyguard). Critics also mention a kinship with Resnais for "the elegant precision of the editing" (Tranchant, "*Le Goût des autres*"), Sacha Guitry for the respect shown to the characters ("Théâtre de la cruauté"), and Woody Allen for humor (Pliskin).

In addition to praise, the film also received some very negative reviews—in *Les Cahiers du cinéma* in particular—that recall François Truffaut's virulent attack against the films of the "French quality" tradition in this journal in 1954. As you may recall from "French Cinema: A Rapid Overview," in his essay "Une certaine tendance du cinéma français," an important text of the New Wave, Truffaut attacked the filmmakers who gave priority to the screenplay over mise en scène and to conventional craftsmanship over creative boldness and thus ensured the popular success of their films. As Leahy points out, the negative reviews of *The Taste of Others* reproduce these arguments. Burdeau, for example, speaks of the "dictatorship of the screenplay": he argues that "the characters are set before the film," that Jaoui does not show their development, and that "nothing happens: what they experience is not real life, it's already written in the screenplay, it's nothing but screenplay." Mandelbaum also criticizes "the use of dialogue and witty expressions as the essence of mise en scène" ("Que cache"), and for Loutte the film inaugurates "a new dictatorship of taste: the rule of the tepid but well-crafted film" and "disappoints with its consensual aspect, its predictable expertise."

As if to refute these accusations, some critics made a point of demonstrating the quality of the staging. Garbarz argues that "Agnès Jaoui carefully avoids the dangers of theatricality in spite of a screenplay that relies mostly on dialogue," and he cites examples of camera movements and the presence of motifs (like Deschamps playing the flute) to prove that "Agnès Jaoui, known as an excellent screenwriter and talented actress, is also a great director" (30).

It is worth noting finally that Jaoui's film gave its name to an annual screenplay competition open to middle and high school students in several regions of France, who can submit a short film project on the theme of "Living together in diversity and equality." "The Taste of Others" contest is subsidized by the Agence Nationale pour la Cohésion Sociale et l'Égalité des chances (National Agency for Social Cohesion and Equal Opportunity) and the Ministry of Culture and Communication. "The left-wing spokesperson for French cinema" no doubt appreciated this homage.

STUDY GUIDE

What Happens in This Film?

1. What does Mrs. Castella (Angélique) criticize her husband for at the restaurant? What is her opinion of Weber, the businessman who negotiates his contracts?

2. What type of play do the Castellas attend? What are Mr. Castella's reactions during the performance?

3. Why did Manie recognize Deschamps when he came to the bar during the play?

4. What bothers Moreno about Manie's lifestyle?

5. Why does Clara ask Castella to stop telling jokes when they are having dinner at the bar with her theater friends?

6. Why was everyone uncomfortable when Castella used the word "fags" to refer to the journalists who did not attend the opening reception for Benoît's exhibit?

7. Where and how does Castella declare his love to Clara?

8. What happens to Castella and his business when Clara tells him that she does not reciprocate his feelings?

9. What happened when Castella hung Benoît's painting in his living room?

10. Why did Castella go to Manie's place, and what did she think of him?

11. What does Castella order from Benoît after buying one of his paintings? Why does this put Clara ill at ease?

12. Why is Clara nervous before going onstage to play *Hedda Gabler?*

True or False?

If the statement is false, correct it!

1. The Castellas go to the theater to accompany the Japanese clients with whom Castella is about to sign a contract.

2. On the street a pedestrian gets mad because Angélique hit him as she was getting out of her car.

3. Deschamps' girlfriend left for six months to do an internship in the United States.

4. After making love with Manie, Deschamps confesses to her that he has AIDS.

5. On the stage Clara portrays a domineering woman who sends her enemy, Titus, into exile.

6. During an English lesson, Clara and Castella spend time working on the pronunciation of the word "the."

7. Moreno resigned from the police when he and his colleague, Inspector "Turtle" (Tortue), were asked to stop investigating a corruption case.

8. Castella and his wife like to watch political programs on television.

9. Castella recognizes the aria that is playing at the tea shop because he has heard it in the popular song "Juanita Banana."

10. Weber decided to resign because he found a better paid position.

11. Valérie, the costume designer, understood on the very first day that she and Fred would get along well.

12. At the end of the film, Moreno goes up to Manie's apartment to say goodbye and invite her to join him later.

What Did You Learn in the Introduction?

1. How did Agnès Jaoui develop her taste for stories and writing?

2. For what filmmakers did Jaoui and Bacri write their first screenplays, and what was their main theme?

3. What roles did Jaoui play in *Look at Me* and *Let's Talk about the Rain*, and with what Beur actor (of Maghrebi descent) who later became a star did she collaborate for the first time in the latter film?

4. Beside her work as actress, screenwriter, and director, what is Jaoui known for?

5. What are the general characteristics of Jaoui's cinema?

6. Why did Jaoui make *The Taste of Others*, and what did she particularly want to include in her film?

7. How do Jaoui and Bacri approach the writing of a screenplay? How important is the screenplay when they start shooting?

8. In what types of roles is Jean-Pierre Bacri usually cast?

9. What does Anne Alvaro have in common with most of the actors of the film?

10. What does Alain Chabat's career have in common with Jaoui's?

11. Why is *The Taste of Others* considered a "film event," and what did critics appreciate about the film?

12. How does the reception of the film recall some of the debates that marked the beginnings of the New Wave?

Exploring the Film

1. The Title of the Film

The expression "Le Goût des autres" can mean "what other people appreciate" (their taste for culture, sports, food, clothing, etc.). It can also be interpreted as "being interested in others." What meaning do you think Jaoui gives to her title?

2. The Beginning of the Film

Review Castella's arrival at the factory (Excerpt 1, 4'30–6'50). What are the couple's conversation topics? Why did Jaoui give the dog a central position between Castella and his wife?

What type of music do we hear in this scene? Is it part of the action? What theme of the film does Jaoui introduce with this choice of music?

3. *The Characters*

✦ *Castella*

What do we learn about Castella (his professional life, the way he talks, and his interests) at the beginning of the film?

What is Castella's attitude toward his collaborator, Weber, whom his wife admires so much? What issues does he have with him?

In your opinion, why did Jaoui include the scene at the park with Castella and his father and sister?

✦ *Clara*

In what types of plays does Clara act? With what kind of people does she socialize? Why does she teach English? **How does she sum up her personal and professional life?**

✦ *Angélique*

What is important for Angélique in life? What are her tastes in matters of home decorating and entertainment? *Review the scene showing the Castellas in their living room* (Excerpt 2, 36'55–39'35). What is Angélique talking about while the camera circles around the room? **Why did Jaoui choose to film the scene this way?** What are the Castellas watching on television, and what is their conversation about? **Can we speak of a *mise en abyme* here?** (Does the episode of the series they are watching have something to do with their couple?) Generally speaking, how does Angélique behave when it comes to judging other people's tastes (like her sister-in-law Béatrice's taste for wallpaper)?

✦ *Moreno and Deschamps*

What (very different) attitudes toward life do these two characters represent? Why does Moreno often talk about corruption? What did Moreno do when he and Inspector Turtle failed to catch a "big fish" suspected of corruption? **Why did he do that, in your opinion?** What do we learn on the radio about the resolution of this case (when Deschamps and Angélique are watching Flucky in a field)? **What implicit message does this outcome suggest concerning Moreno?**

How does Moreno's worldview (his relationships with others) affect his opinion of Deschamps—and even Manie? *Review the discussion between Moreno and Manie at her place* (Excerpt 3, 49'10–52'15). What do we learn about Moreno's love life when they are discussing Deschamps' sentimental difficulties? What future does he predict for Deschamps, and do you share his fears? What divisions do you notice between Moreno and Manie at the end of the scene?

Why do you think Jaoui inserts vignettes showing Deschamps playing the flute? Do they play a role in the story? Do they tell us something about Deschamps? (This point will be developed in question 6 on "The Denouement.")

✦ *Manie*

What type of life does Manie lead? **What does she guard jealously?** *Review the scene where Moreno visits her when his contract with Castella is about to end* (Excerpt 4, 1h14'15–1h15'45). Do you think Moreno and Manie are joking when they mention marriage? **How do they envision married life?** How do you explain Manie's hostile comments about the life of a stay-at-home woman given that she told Clara a little earlier that she was tired of her precarious life and was thinking about getting married and having children?

Why is Manie ambivalent about her relationship with Moreno? What does she criticize in her attitude toward him? *Review the scene where she is talking with her female friends at the bar* (Excerpt 5, 1h21'50–1h23'00). What are the opinions of Valérie, Manie, and Clara regarding the compromises that one must make in order to share someone's life? What does the director suggest by juxtaposing the scenes of the women at the bar and the men at the nightclub?

What is Manie's role vis-à-vis the other characters of the film? For example, what role does she play in relation to Clara, Deschamps, and Castella?

4. *The Relationship between Castella and Clara*

What do you think Castella and Clara thought about each other during their first meeting (the English lesson)? **When did Castella fall in love with Clara?** How do you explain his abrupt change of attitude toward her? *Review an excerpt of the evening at the theater* (Excerpt 6, 15'30–17'20). What did Castella think about the play before seeing Clara onstage? What shows that he is experiencing something very unusual for him? Why does Jaoui alternate shots showing the Castellas in the theater and the other characters outside? (Is there a thematic link between what is happening in these two places?)

How does Castella try to get closer to Clara, and what obstacles does he face? *Review the meal at the bar after a performance of* The Imaginary Invalid (Le Malade imaginaire) *by Molière* (Excerpt 7, 58'30–1h00'35). **Why does Castella suggest to Clara that she should act in comedies?** (Is it only because he prefers this type of play?) How is his suggestion received? **What jokes do Clara's friends make about the playwrights Ibsen, Strindberg, and Tennessee Williams?** Did you find this scene funny? If not, why not?

Beside the evenings at the theater, Castella shows interest in the activities of Clara's friends, and Benoît's painting in particular. **How is Castella different from most of the other guests at the opening reception of Benoît's exhibit?** (What does he do during the reception that most of the others do not do?) What does Jaoui suggest through this contrast? *Review the scene of the opening reception* (Excerpt 8, 1h06'00–1h07'05). Castella announces to Antoine a little later that he has bought one of Benoît's paintings. What does Antoine think of this decision? Why do you think Castella bought the painting?

In this scene Jaoui included the same music as at the tea shop (an aria by Verdi that Castella had recognized because he had heard it in the popular song "Juanita Banana"). **Does Verdi's music have the same (comic) effect here? Why did Jaoui create this parallel, in your opinion?** More generally, what connection(s) does Jaoui establish between classical music (often heard in the film) and Castella's inner life?

What does Castella do to become more attractive to Clara? How does he use his English lessons to that effect? *Review the scene at the tea shop* (Excerpt 9, 1h09'10–1h12'00). What has changed in his appearance and demeanor? What does he mean when he declares, "She teach me English, but that is not the only thing she teach"? How do you react to his English mistakes (when compared to the earlier lessons, for example when he practiced the sound "the")?

Outside the cultural realm, how do Castella's contacts with Clara and her friends change his perspective? For example, what does he learn about his own prejudices and way of speaking? When he apologizes to Antoine for referring contemptuously to the absent reporters as "fags," what does it show about him?

5. Clans

As we noted in the introduction, one of the inspirations for *The Taste of Others* is Jaoui's scorn for clans that divide people, and critics appreciated the way in which she expresses this feeling in her film. Gouslan, for example, described the film as "a brilliant satire against exclusion, parochialism, fads, ideological and sociological dictatorships." **What are the artistic tastes of Clara and her friends, and how do they treat people who do not share them?** *Review for example the scene where Clara, Antoine, and Benoît are visiting the art gallery* (Excerpt 10, 39'40–40'40). What is Antoine's opinion of the works exhibited at the gallery? What does he mean when he comments that "what people want is to remain asleep"? How does Benoît behave toward the man who is displaying his artwork?

How do Clara and her friends react when they come out of *The Imaginary Invalid? Review the scene where they talk about the play* (Excerpt 11, 56'05–57'10). **According to what criteria do you think they judge the play?** (What type of play is more in line with their intellectual tastes?) Compare the opinion of the group and that of the review that Clara read before seeing the play. What does this suggest as to the mindset of this group when they arrived at the theater to see the play? **And how does Castella form his opinion of the play?**

Clara (and her friends) and Castella represent the worlds of art and business, respectively. What are the primary goals in each of these areas? **What do Clara and her friends think of the business world?** Where does the mural painting ordered by Castella stand in relation to the worlds of art and business? Is it the type of art that Benoît aspires to do and that his group of friends respect? **What is Jaoui suggesting here about the opposition between art and business?**

6. The Denouement

+ *Castella and Angélique*

How does Angélique react when she finds out that her husband has replaced one of the paintings in the living room by Benoît's modern abstract piece? *Review this scene* (Excerpt 12, 1h16'30–1h17'40). What does she think when her husband tells her that he likes this painting? What does she think of her husband without his mustache? What does Angélique not understand about the painting and her husband's mustache? To whom does she offer a cookie at the end of the excerpt? Why does Jaoui include the dog in this scene? **What do you feel for Castella and Angélique here?** Are you surprised that Angélique disappears so quickly from the story and from Castella's life?

+ *Castella and Clara*

How does Clara react to the changes in Castella? What makes her finally change her mind about him? **What role do her friends (and their perception of Castella) play in that regard?** What influence does the experience of Virginie, the costume designer,

have on her? (How does Clara feel when Virginie tells her about her relationship with Fred before Clara goes onstage at the end?)

What did you think when the character portrayed by Clara committed suicide? How can we interpret this action symbolically as far as Clara is concerned?

Do you think that the couple formed by Castella and Clara is likely to last?

+ *Manie and Moreno*

In your opinion, why did Moreno decide not to ring the bell at Manie's at the end? Just before this scene, he had learned from Deschamps that Inspector Turtle had finally managed to bring to justice the man whom they had been pursuing earlier. How do you interpret the juxtaposition of the scene about Turtle and the one where Moreno leaves without Manie?

Symbolically, how can we interpret the fact that Moreno is frozen in place as Castella's bodyguard in the film?

What do you think of the outcome for Manie, who remains alone at the end whereas Valérie and Clara seem to have found their soulmates?

+ *Castella and Weber*

What is the significance of the last scene between Castella and Weber toward the end of the story? How is this scene related to the main themes of the film? Do you think Weber will come back on his decision to resign?

+ *The Last Scene: Deschamps and the orchestra*

The film ends on the melody of a famous song performed by Edith Piaf in the 1950s, "No, I Regret Nothing" ("Non, je ne regrette rien"). Look up the lyrics of this song. **How do they apply to the characters of the film?**

How do you interpret this last scene? Why did Jaoui end her film that way? We saw quick shots of Deschamps playing the flute at different points in the film. Is there a connection between these shots, the fact that Deschamps now plays with an orchestra, and the themes of the film?

7. Some Critical Perspectives

In his book *Distinction: A Social Critique of the Judgement of Taste* (*La Distinction. Critique sociale du jugement*, 1979), sociologist Pierre Bourdieu argues that tastes are determined, even unconsciously, by social origins rather than the natural inclinations of individuals. Jaoui seems to endorse Bourdieu's thesis when she says, "I read Pierre Bourdieu's *Distinction* after making *The Taste of Others*, and I was delighted to find in it what I had developed in my story, albeit as concepts" (Guichard). Academic critics have mostly analyzed *The Taste of Others* from the angle of Bourdieu's ideas, often to conclude that the film offers a less deterministic viewpoint. **How do you understand the notion that Jaoui's film is "less deterministic" than Bourdieu's theory?**

According to Lalanne, *The Taste of Others* is very moderate in its criticism compared to Bacri and Jaoui's prior screenplays: "Otherness was not really the strong point of their earlier successes," he writes. "The world was divided into two distinct categories: on the one hand, the characters on the winning side, portrayed by Agnès Jaoui and Jean-Pierre Bacri; on the other, the ones that were mocked, in a word: everybody else." **How**

is this film different in this regard? What characters does Jaoui feel sympathy for? Toward which ones is she most critical? On what grounds?

A commentator said about the film, "After seeing it we feel a little stronger, a little happier, and a little more critical toward our own narrow-mindedness" ("*Le Goût des autres* d'Agnès Jaoui")? What does he mean by "a little more critical toward our own narrow-mindedness"? Did the film have the same effect on you as on the commentator?

Agnès Jaoui's Filmography

2000 *The Taste of Others (Le Goût des autres)*

2003 *Look at me (Comme une image)*

2008 *Let's Talk about the Rain (Parlez-moi de la pluie)*

2013 *Under the Rainbow (Au bout du conte)*

2018 *Public Square (Place publique)*

Works Consulted

Alion, Yves. "*Le Goût des autres*, un film d'Agnès Jaoui." *L'Avant-Scène Cinéma* 493 (2000): 1–92.

Assouline, Florence. "Le film qui dynamite le snobisme culturel." *L'Evénement du jeudi*, 24 Feb. 2000: n. pag.

Baignières, Claude. "Etourdissant! *Le Goût des autres* d'Agnès Jaoui." *Le Figaro*, 2 Mar. 2000: n. pag.

Baurez, Thomas. "Agnès Jaoui, Jean-Pierre Bacri: 'Au départ, *Le Goût des autres* devait être un polar.'" *L'Express*, 7 Mar. 2013: n. pag.

Burdeau, Emmanuel. "L'Affaire du Goût." *Cahiers du cinéma* 545 (Apr. 2000): 4–5.

Carrière, Christophe. "L'une Jaoui, l'autre pas." *L'Express*, 20 Sept. 2004: n. pag.

Coppermann, Annie. "L'amertume des préjugés. *Le Goût des autres* d'Agnès Jaoui." *Les Echos*, 1 Mar. 2000: n. pag.

De Bruyn, Olivier. "Portrait [Agnès Jaoui]." *Le Point*, 25 Feb. 2000: n. pag.

Douguet, Gwen. "*Le Goût des autres*. Agnès Jaoui a bon goût." *Le Figaroscope*, 1 Mar. 2000: n. pag.

Fajardo, Isabelle. "Belle de scène." *Télérama*, 1 Mar. 2000: n. pag.

Garbarz, Franck. "*Le Goût des autres*. Le dégoût des autres." *Positif* 469 (Mar. 2000): 29–30.

Gouslan, Elizabeth. "*Le Goût des autres* d'Agnès Jaoui." *L'Evénement du jeudi*, 24 Feb. 2000: n. pag.

"*Le Goût des autres* d'Agnès Jaoui." *Le Monde*, 1 Mar. 2000: n. pag.

Grassin, Sophie. "Agnès Jaoui. *Le Goût des autres*." *L'Express*, 24 Feb. 2000: n. pag.

Guichard, Louis. "Agnès Jaoui: 'Etre actrice, c'était être une enfant. Réaliser, c'est être le parent.'" *Télérama*, 2 Mar. 2013: n. pag.

Jaoui, Agnès, dir. *Le Goût des autres*. Comstar Home Entertainment, 2002.

Kelleher, Ed. "A Taste for Comedy: Actress-Director Agnès Jaoui Offers Gallic Treat." *Film Journal International* 104.2 (2001): 18–20.

Lalanne, Jean-Marc. "Le bonheur, c'est les autres." *Libération*, 1 Mar. 2000: n. pag.

Leahy, Sarah. "A (Middle-) Class Act: Taste and Otherness in *Le Goût des autres* (Jaoui, 2000)." *France at the Flicks. Trends in Contemporary French Popular Cinema*. Ed. Darren Waldron and Isabelle Vanderschelden. Newcastle, UK: Cambridge Scholarly Press, 2007. 117–29.

Libiot, Eric. "Agnès Jaoui: 'Je pense que le goût s'éduque.'" *L'Express*, 6 Sept. 2001: n. pag.

———. "Jean-Pierre Bacri 'fait ce métier pour ne pas se raser tous les jours.'" *L'Express*, 10 Sept. 2016: n. pag.

Loutte, Bertrand. "*Le Goût des autres*." *Les Inrockuptibles*, 29 Feb. 2000: n. pag.

Mandelbaum, Jacques. "Jaoui-Bacri: 'On bouge, on caricature moins.'" *Le Monde*, 5 Mar. 2013: n. pag.

———. "Que cache la moustache de Jean-Pierre Bacri? *Le Goût des autres*." *Le Monde*, 1 Mar. 2000: n. pag.

Mérigeau, Pascal. "Grand bonheur." *Le Nouvel Observateur*, 2 Mar. 2000: n. pag.

Messu, Michel. "La Critique sociale du jugement de goût revisitée." *Le Goût dans tous ses états*. Ed. Michel Erman. Bern, Switzerland: Peter Lang, 2009. 69–85.

Nettelbeck, Colin. "Regardez-moi: Theatre, Performance, and Directorship in the Films of Agnès Jaoui." *Australian Journal of French Studies* 45.1 (2008): 3–15.

Pliskin, Fabrice. "La guéguerre du goût." *Le Nouvel Observateur*, 24 Feb. 2000: n. pag.

Reynaud, Patricia. "*Le Goût des autres* d'Agnès Jaoui: de l'adaptation de P. Bourdieu au cinéma à sa subversion." *Stealing the Fire: Adaptation, Appropriation, Plagiarism, Hoax in French and Francophone Literature and Film*. Ed. James Day. *French Literature Series* 37. Amsterdam, Netherlands: Rodopi, 2010. 157–75.

Royer, Philippe. "Chez Jaoui, chacun cherche l'autre." *La Croix*, 1 Mar. 2000: n. pag.

"Théâtre de la cruauté." *L'Express*, 24 Feb. 2000: n. pag.

Tranchant, Marie-Noëlle. "Agnès Jaoui: 'Le malaise, c'est fécond.'" *Le Figaro*, 2 Mar. 2000: n. pag.

———. "*Le Goût des autres*. Castella, Bérénice, le chauffeur et la serveuse." *Le Figaroscope*, 1 Mar. 2000: n. pag.

19

Jean-Pierre Jeunet

Amélie
(Le Fabuleux Destin d'Amélie Poulain)

(2001)

Jean-Pierre Jeunet, *Amélie*: Amélie (Audrey Tautou) finds the little tin box—now it begins.

Director ....Jean-Pierre Jeunet
Screenplay ....Jean-Pierre Jeunet, Guillaume Laurant
Dialogue ....Guillaume Laurant
Director of Photography ....Bruno Delbonnel
Sound ....Jean Umansky, Sophie Chiabaut
Music ....Yann Tirsen
Film Editor ....Hervé Schneid
Art Director.......................................Aline Bonetto
Costumes ....Madeline Fontaine
Lighting ....Darius Khondji
Continuity ....Anne Wermélinger
Special Effects ....Duboi, Les Versaillais
Producer...Claudie Ossard
Length...2h02

Cast

Audrey Tautou (*Amélie*), Mathieu Kassovitz (*Nino Quincampoix*), Rufus (*Raphaël Poulain, Amélie's father*), Lorella Cravotta (*Amandine Fouet, Amélie's mother*), Serge Merlin (*Raymond Dufayel, the painter*), Jamel Debbouze (*Lucien, the grocer's assistant*), Claire Maurier (*Suzanne, the café owner*), Clotilde Mollet (*Gina, the waitress*), Isabelle Nanty (*Georgette, the hypochondriac tobacconist*), Dominique Pinon (*Joseph, the rejected lover*), Artus de Penguern (*Hipolito, the writer*), Yolande Moreau (*Madeleine Wallace, the concierge*), Urbain Cancelier (*Collignon, the grocer*), Maurice Bénichou (*Dominique Bretodeau, the adult owner of the box of boy's treasures*), Ticky Holgado (*the man in the talking portraits*), Michel Robin (*Collignon's father*), Andrée Damant (*Collignon's mother*), Claude Perron (*Eva, the stripper*), Flora Guiet (*Amélie as a little girl*), Marc Amyot (*the photo booth repairman*), André Dussollier (*the narrator, voice-over*)

Story

Amélie grows up in the Paris suburbs with a severely introverted doctor for a father and an exceptionally eccentric mother. Suffering from a lack of attention, Amélie's heart quickens at her father's touch when he listens to her chest, leading him to conclude that she has a heart murmur. Believing her to be too fragile to go to school, her parents decide to homeschool her. Still very little, she loses her mother when she is crushed to death by the body of a suicidal tourist who has thrown herself off the top of the Notre-Dame cathedral. Living alone with her depressed widowed father, friendless, Amélie escapes from her situation by creating a whole world in her exceedingly lively imagination. At twenty-four she is living alone in an apartment in Montmartre, where she works as a waitress in a brasserie (café restaurant), *Les Deux Moulins*.

One evening, at the very moment that she learns of Princess Diana's death on television, she discovers hidden behind her bathroom wall a small metal box containing the childhood treasures of a boy who had lived in her apartment in the 1950s. Having observed the joy of the owner of the box when she manages to return to him these souvenirs of his youth, she devotes her life to making the people around her happy, albeit anonymously. . . .

The Director

Born in 1953, Jean-Pierre Jeunet grew up in Nancy, the capital of the Lorraine region. He left school at seventeen to take a job at the post office (where his father was employed), while spending the end of his afternoons at the movies. Fascinated by the cinema, Jeunet moved to Paris in 1974 to study animation at the Cinémation Studios. He began making film shorts, as well as video clips and commercials. Virtually an autodidact, he crossed paths in 1974 with Marc Caro, a graphic artist specializing in satirical animations, and they made two animated films together, *The Escape* (*L'Evasion*, 1978) and *The Carousel* (*Le Manège*, 1980), both of them prizewinners, including a Best Animated Short Film César for *Le Manège*. After a year of hard work, the duo finished in 1981 *The Bunker of the Last Gunshots* (*Le Bunker de la dernière rafale*), a science fiction film short about a squad of soldiers hunkered down in an underground bunker, terrified by an invisible enemy whose existence is rather nebulous. Winning awards in numerous festivals, it became a cult film (running for six years straight!), launching both Jeunet and Caro into careers as recognized filmmakers.

Each of them would work primarily on his own during the remainder of the 1980s, meeting only sporadically to do a project together. Jeunet continued to make video clips and commercials, as well as a short, *Things I Like, Things I Don't Like* (*Foutaises*, 1989), which won a multitude of prizes, including a second Short Film César. This film was the beginning of a long association with the actor Dominique Pinon, and with its "I like, I don't like" motif, an important source for *Amélie*.

The two filmmakers immersed themselves completely in the world of the big screen by directing together in 1990 their first feature film, *Delicatessen*. Both a horror film and a black comedy, *Delicatessen* takes place in a dystopian post-apocalyptic universe in which the absurd is only outdone by the grotesque. It features a butcher who assassinates the tenants in his apartment building in order to have a source of meat for his clients. . . . Winning four Césars (Best First Work, Best Screenplay, Best Production Design, and Best Editing) and becoming a cult film, *Delicatessen* thrust the two filmmakers into the forefront of French cinema.

Jeunet and Caro soon directed a second film together, *The City of Lost Children* (*La Cité des enfants perdus*, 1995). As for their first feature film, Jeunet was responsible for the directing, while Caro devoted his energies to the set design and the visual effects. Greeted enthusiastically by the critics, this new science fiction film offers a surrealistic and nightmarish world whose protagonist is a sage who lives on a platform in the ocean, and who is aging rapidly because he has lost the power to dream. To prolong his life, he has children kidnapped to steal their dreams. . . . *The City of Lost Children*, which astonished everyone by the multitude and ingeniousness of the special effects, was nominated for the Palme d'Or at Cannes and won the Best Production Design César, despite the fact that the critical and popular reception was modest in France and abroad. Nonetheless, the seven months of postproduction necessary to edit the 144 shots and 40,000 digital images was a valuable experience for Jeunet, an experience that he would put to good use in the making of *Amélie*, after perfecting even more, in an American film adventure, the art of special effects.

Now famous owing to the success of his two first films, Jeunet was invited by Hollywood to direct *Alien: Resurrection*, the fourth film in the series. This is the only film that Jeunet ever made for Hollywood. A modest success, *Alien* was released in 1997 with Sigourney Weaver, Winona Ryder, and Jeunet's perennial actor, Dominique Pinon, whom he had brought with him from France. Pinon, whom we saw much younger in the role of the assassin "Curé" in *Diva* (1980, see Chap. 11), also played in Jeunet's following film, *Amélie* (2001), the first feature film that he made in France without Marc Caro as co-director.

The Origin and Making of the Film

After two years of work in Hollywood, with all the constraints of the American production system, Jeunet was eager to "return to a universe in which he could express himself in complete liberty" (De Bruyn 121). He especially wanted to make a film in Paris and, above all, in the very neighborhood where he lived, Montmartre, one of the most picturesque (and therefore most touristic) in the city. He worked an entire year on the screenplay of his new film, struggling with a mass of potential subjects before managing to define his project, which would be, he said, "a fairytale," "a film on the victory of imagination" (Delassein). This was followed by nineteen weeks of shooting on location in the shadow of the Sacred Heart Basilica, in the streets and shops of the Abbesses neighborhood, such as the grocery of the Rue des Trois Frères, "Au Marché de la butte" (rebaptized "Maison Collignon" since the film came out), the brasserie Les Deux Moulins in the Rue Lepic, or the Rue Saint-Vincent and the Boulevard de Clichy (with its sex shops). Since it was a Franco-German coproduction, certain indoor scenes (in particular the apartments in Amélie's building) were nonetheless shot in a studio in Köln (Cologne), Germany.

In any case, this was the first time in his career that Jeunet had filmed on location, and it was an enormous challenge for a director like him who felt the need to control absolutely everything in each shot (Deydier and Libiot 59). The brasserie on the Rue Lepic stayed closed to the public for the three weeks of filming there—a situation that did not discourage some longtime customers of the cigarette counter: "Isabelle Nanty, who played the role of the tobacconist, tried to explain to them that she was an actor, and that she couldn't sell them cigarettes. They invariably replied, 'That's OK, here's the money, just give me my pack'" (Ageorges 13).

Since Jeunet was filming in the spring, rain was often a problem (twenty days of rain in May), which forced him to make compromises: "If the weather was too gray, we simply added rain or fog to accommodate the circumstances. In postproduction, thanks to digital techniques, we were able to add color when the sky wasn't quite blue enough" (Ageorges 13). In fact, Jeunet digitized the entire negative during the six weeks of postproduction, which allowed him to add a multitude of special effects, often inspired by comic strips or cartoons, some of which are spectacular (for example, the liquefaction of Amélie, rendering literal the metaphor according to which one "dissolves into tears" when one's heart is broken . . .). The digitizing of the film also enabled Jeunet to bathe his whole film in a golden greenish hue, a color that evokes hope for the French and adds to the film's poetic, fantastical, and retro atmosphere (Silberg 20).

Following unabashedly in the footsteps of Georges Méliès, the originator of the very first special effects in films, Jeunet admitted that everything in *Amélie* "is a matter of stylizing. We worked minutely to eliminate from the frames cars, graffiti, and posters that we didn't like" (De Bruyn 121). Insisting on putting at least one original visual idea in each shot, Jeunet massaged digitally every image to obtain exactly the effect he was seeking, still a very new practice in France at this time. Despite his modest $10 million budget, his attention to detail was simply extraordinary: "Although shot on location, every shot of *Amélie* is entirely artificial, reworked with a graphics palette, decorated like a candy box, dripping with colors and accessories" (Lalanne and Péron 31); "Like his preceding works, *Amélie* shows a quasi-maniacal attention to phantasmagorical colors, to camera angles that deform reality, to sets that bring out the magical side of daily reality, to the special effects—seldom ever so well utilized in French cinema—to the unbelievable close-ups of faces, to the soundtrack, and to the score" (Garbarz 30). The proliferation of close-ups in the film is striking, especially since Jeunet often used wide-angle lenses, combined with very rapid zooms in, to deform faces and exaggerate them as is done in cartoons.

The Actors

The close-ups of the faces also foreground the remarkable quality of the acting, especially that of Audrey Tautou in the role of Amélie. It has been calculated that there is a close-up of Tautou's face every two minutes on the average (Peters 1048) that, with the frequent direct looks into the camera by Amélie, creates a deep complicity between her and the spectators. Destined by all indications to have an exceptional career as an actor, Tautou had already won the Most Promising Actress César in 1999 for her role in Tonie Marshall's *Vénus Beauté (Institut)*, and Jeunet had chosen her to play Amélie after seeing her on a poster for that film.

For her performance in *Amélie*, Tautou garnered rave reviews from all sides, one critic, clearly under her spell, declaring that she was not only "Venus beauty" but also "Venus candor, Venus affection, Venus seduction, Venus delight" (Alion 126). She becomes the incarnation of "la Française," of everything French, including French cinema, and some saw in her the next model for Marianne, the very symbol of France, following Brigitte Bardot, Catherine Deneuve, Mireille Mathieu, and Laetitia Casta, among others (Vincendeau 25). In 2004 she made a second film with Jeunet, *A Very Long Engagement (Un long dimanche de fiançailles)* and became the highest-paid French actress at that time. A few years later, in 2006, she was chosen to star beside Tom Hanks in the film adaptation of Dan Brown's blockbuster novel, *The Da Vinci Code*.

Tautou is strongly supported in the film by Mathieu Kassovitz (the director of *Hate*, Best Film César in 1995; see Chap. 5), in the role of Nino Quincampoix, the young man with whom Amélie falls in love. According to Jeunet, Kassovitz is, like Tautou, "the type of actor with which a camera falls in love; he is even better on-screen than in person" (Campion). Kassovitz's acting talents had already been recognized, in fact, well before *Amélie*: he won the Most Promising Actor César for Jacques Audiard's first feature film *See How They Fall (Regarde les hommes tomber)* in 1995.

Jeunet demonstrates a certain boldness in casting Jamel Debbouze, a well-known television and theater comic (three weeks at the Olympia in 2000) and a notorious clown, in the role of Lucien, the North African grocer's helper who is a little slow-witted and handicapped (like Debbouze himself, who lost his right arm in a train accident in 1990). Despite the strongly stereotypical character of most of the characters in *Amélie*, the ensemble acting of the cast—a swarm of talented actors, some of whom have worked on previously films with Jeunet and Caro (Dominique Pinon, Ticky Holgado, Rufus, Serge Merlin)—guaranteed the success of the film. The originality, the unbounded imagination, and the ingeniousness of Jeunet, combined with a brilliant cast, bore their fruits: the "fabulous destiny" of *Amélie* was to enjoy an extraordinary worldwide reception.

The Reception

The officials in charge of the Cannes Film Festival of 2001 gave Jeunet's film the cold shoulder. Its exclusion from the official selection of French films—owing in part to the absence of André Dussollier's voice-over narration when they screened the film in February—was like a slap in the face to the two million spectators who had filled the cinemas to see the film since its release two weeks before the opening of the festival.

Amélie was a smash hit at an unprecedented level, and the media began to speak of the "scandal" of its non-selection. At the top of the French box office for a month, it recorded three million entries in France in three weeks, more than eight million at the end of December 2001, more than seventeen million throughout the world at the beginning of January 2002, and more than thirty million by the end of 2003. As Jeunet remarked, "It's a hit in Poland, Greece, Finland, and Hong Kong. . . . In the United States it's already made $12 million. . ." (Lefort and Péron 21).

Ultimately *Amélie* was not only the greatest success of the year in France: it sold the highest number of seats in the United States—as in Great Britain and Japan—in the whole history of French cinema up to that time, more even than Edouard Molinaro's *Birds of a Feather* (*La Cage aux folles*, 1978). Its success in the United States was attributed, at least in part, to the Americans' need to get over the traumatic shock of the terrorist attacks of September 11, 2001, *Amélie* being released scarcely a few weeks after this catastrophe (Vanderschelden 87). Whatever the case may be, *Amélie* was nominated for five Oscars (Best Original Screenplay, Best Art/Set Direction, Best Cinematography, Best Sound, Best Foreign Language Film) and won four Césars: Best Director, Best Film, Best Music Written for a Film, and Best Production Design. The extraordinary success of Jeunet's film served to prime the French film industry in 2001, its market share rising to nearly 50 percent at one point, as opposed to the usual 30 percent maintained against the irresistible growth of American cinema in France and throughout the world.

A large majority of film critics agreed that *Amélie* was a masterpiece and praised the extraordinary mastery of Jeunet. The titles of the articles speak for themselves: "The Delights of Amélie," "Mathematical and Sentimental, An Irresistible Romance," "Jeunet: A Filmmaker's Destiny," "Audrey Tautou, A Pure Joy," and so on. As one of the commentators says, "Full of visual and narrative inventiveness, *Amélie* combines comedy, tenderness, and emotion with consummate art. Jean-Pierre Jeunet proves here, if it were necessary, the full extent of his talent, taking his place as one of the most promising directors in the panorama of French film" (Taillibert 40). Another critic is even more emphatic: "Between heaven and earth, a dazzling demonstration of the technical mastery of Jeunet. . . . In short, a film you only dream of, a perfect film" (Alexandre 35). The spectators are charmed by this fairytale in which modest people, despondent for the most part, are led to experience a little happiness in their very ordinary lives thanks to Amélie's anonymous but salutary interventions—although Amélie sometimes has recourse to vigilante methods (à la Zorro).

Since the presidential elections were approaching (2002), the politicians did not want to be left out: President Chirac organized a screening at the Elysée Palace, inviting Jeunet and his whole crew; and the Prime Minister Lionel Jospin, while pointing out that he had seen the film in a cinema in town, also organized a screening for the members of his cabinet. Even the mayors and vice mayors felt compelled to add their praise in published interviews, provoking the ironic observation by a critic of *Le Monde* that *Amélie* had "become not only a commercial triumph but a social phenomenon, and all the politicians who wanted to spruce up their images as someone 'close to the people' had jumped on the wagon" (Frodon 18).

A few discordant notes were sounded, however, in this vast symphony of praise. Some critics were severely irritated by this image of happy little people in a Parisian neighborhood inhabited by stereotypical white people, devoid of any racial or sexual diversity (other than the grocer's little North African whipping boy), with no graffiti or trash or anything unattractive—a postcard Paris, sugar-coated to the hilt. Some would go so far as to speak of "ethnic cleansing" and of "EuroDisney in Montmartre" (Lançon 5, Bonnaud). As in the case of *Diva* and of the "cinéma du look" twenty years before, some of the elites of film criticism inveighed against the film, accusing Jeunet of dazzling the public with flashy visual effects, of using commercial aesthetics to cover up a lack of serious content.

But they did not stop there: they took Jeunet to task for the very image that he was projecting of France, and especially for the underlying right-wing ideology that they thought they could detect there. For some of them, there is "something nostalgic here that plays into the hands of the National Front" (Martin-Castelnau and Bigot 6). Martin-Castelnau and Bigot do not agree with this opinion and, among many others, balk at the scorn exhibited by the "elites," noting that "this film portrays very modest people with tenderness and respect," that it "shows amiable people, damaged by life, disenchanted, sometimes petty, but who are nonetheless going to experience this form of redemption that is called happiness," adding ironically, "Therein lies the rub. Little people that are not mocked or lambasted? . . . The people depicted without sarcasm or condemnation? What an inadmissible scenario. . . . Jeunet devotes to this rabble an irresistible ode" (6).

That's just too much for Serge Kaganski, the film critic at the weekly cultural magazine *Les Inrockuptibles*. He responds sharply to his two colleagues, castigating *Amélie* ferociously, reproaching Jeunet for having made a film that is not "a source of knowledge of the world, of discovery of reality, and of experience of time that is passing, but only a simple technical way of recreating the world as he sees it" ("*Amélie* pas jolie" 7). He condemns Jeunet's "desire to master and control absolutely the images" and his "ultra-formalistic bias that produces a stifling form of cinema, animated taxidermy, a Grévin Museum with wax figures that move" (7). It is understandable to accuse Jeunet of lack of realism and of formalism, but Kaganski goes much further, calling *Amélie* a "major populist film" and criticizing Jeunet for having turned Montmartre into a "village"— and everyone knows, he says, that "the ideology of the villages is deeply reactionary" (7). It's just a short hop from there to call Jeunet's film an extreme right-wing work that would not be out of place in a video clip promoting the National Front, especially given that Jeunet carefully cleaned up his Montmartre, as we've already noted, of the very diverse population that is normally seen there: "But where," Kaganski asks, "are the West Indians, the North Africans, the Turks, the Chinese, the Pakistanis, etc.? Where are those whose sexuality is different? Where are the Parisians who populate the capital in 1997 [the year in which the film is set]?"

The public, indignant and outraged, reacted immediately. Insults rained down, and Kaganski was amazed to see himself called "Stalinist" and "fascist" ("Comment je me suis disputé" 17). Other readers offer more measured objections: "If a film that takes place in Paris smells of Pétainism simply because it doesn't have its quotas of Pakistanis, gays, and others, *Amélie* sure has a lot of company" (18)! Or this rather sarcastic comment: "But to say that Jeunet is juggling with fascist ideas, that he is flirting with Le Pen, and that his people (myself among others), while they're nice enough, very 'sincere,' are basically idiots (since they are so unaware) and willing objects of Pétainist propaganda! . . . I think that as a result of trying to hold yourself above everyone else you have entered the sphere of delusion, egocentrism (they're all lame but me), and scorn" (18).

As if that were not enough, the right-wing press joined in, a journalist with *Le Figaro* comparing Amélie to Arlette Laguiller, the far-left Trotskyist firebrand of French politics: "The happiness of the people, by the people, and for the people, that's her thing" (Baret). With Baret's diatribe against Laguiller, for which "Amélie-the-Red" was only a pretext, the political recuperation of *Amélie* was complete. As for Jeunet's reaction to the accusation of populism, he simply answers, in an interview among the bonuses on the DVD (Disque 2, 2000), "Forget the New Wave; that was fifty years ago. Today we try to make films for the public, not for ourselves."

Amélie and Poetic Realism

Although the period of reference in *Amélie* is clearly the 1950s (beginning with the little box of boyhood treasures), many critics, in their comments on the film, evoke the "poetic realism" movement of the 1930s. They are referring, of course, to the films of René Clair (*Under the Roofs of Paris* [*Sous les toits de Paris*, 1930]), Jean Renoir (*A Day in the Country* [*Partie de campagne*, 1936]), and especially Marcel Carné (*Port of Shadows* [*Quai des brumes*, 1938]; *Hôtel du Nord*, 1938; *Daybreak* [*Le Jour se lève*, 1939]), the latter a filmmaker greatly admired by Jeunet. The universe of Carnet and his favorite screenwriter, the poet Jacques Prévert, is inhabited by modest people, workers or simple employees from the lower middle classes. The pairs of lovers in their films are always doomed to meet a tragic fate, owing either to their socioeconomic condition or simply to the sordidness of the world (which is far from the case in Jeunet's film, we would remark).

The films in the poetic realist mode are usually marked by the presence of stereotyped, picturesque secondary characters (especially those of René Clair) and by the abundance of metaphors and symbols that accompany a very witty dialogue (primarily the films of Carné and Prévert). We rediscover this panoply of social types, sharply caricatured, in Jeunet's film: the grocer, the concierge, the café owner, the writer, the waitress, the painter, the tobacconist, the beggar, and the hypochondriac, among others. What Jeunet's film has most in common with poetic realism, however, other than its characters, is the iconography, the folkloric image of Paris that it presents: "cobbled streets and steep steps, corner shops and street markets . . . postcard views of Notre-Dame, the Sacré-Cœur and the Pont des Arts alternate with Parisian roofscapes, cafés and art-nouveau metro stations. . . . And inhabiting these locations are the 'little people' of Paris who filled the films of Renoir, Carné and René Clair" (Vincendeau 23). In short, animated postcards, stereotypes in motion.

The title of the film is a clear reference to a work by Sacha Guitry, *Le Destin fabuleux de Désirée Clary*, from the same period as Carné (1942), which, like *Amélie*, uses voice-over narration. Guitry's film begins, moreover, with a photo album, one of the sources of inspiration, perhaps, for the photo album in Jeunet's film (along with the authentic album of a press photographer, Michel Folco, that served as the direct model). In Guitry's film this album provides a series of images, page by page, that evoke scenes (narrated in voice-over by the director) resembling precisely the storyboards that Jeunet likes to use in the preparation of all of his films—and serves, in addition, as an ellipsis between Désirée as a little girl and the young lady she becomes, just as the ellipsis at the beginning of Jeunet's film does for Amélie.

The evocation of the cinema of the 1930s added to the nostalgia that is a primary characteristic of Jeunet's film and that constituted much of its charm for numerous spectators. The nostalgic side of the film is reinforced by the (intentional) resemblance of its images with those of a close friend of Carné's, the famous photographer of the 1930s Robert Doisneau, whose touristic shots of Paris were known throughout the world. A well-known saying by Doisneau suggests clearly the influence he may have had on Jeunet as regards the representation of Paris: "I do not photograph the city as it is but rather as I would like it to be." Jeunet wanted the action of his film to take place, precisely, in the "postcard Paris" for which he was criticized, a fairytale Paris permeated with the nostalgia of his childhood and of the childhood of millions of other French people. Since he announced his intention unambiguously and repeatedly, accusing his film of "lacking realism" is a curious criticism.

STUDY GUIDE

What Happens in This Film?

1. What is the purpose of the beginning credits? Is it simply a matter of introducing the actors and the crew? What aspect of each character is revealed?

2. Why do Amélie's parents take her out of school? Who takes over her education?

3. How does Amélie lose her mother the day they go to light a candle at Notre-Dame?

4. What technique (that we have already seen) does the narrator use to introduce the people around Amélie (Suzanne, Gina, Joseph, Georgette, and Hipolito)? What characterizes Joseph and Georgette in particular?

5. Why has her neighbor Dufayel, the painter, not left his apartment for twenty years? (Why is he referred to as "the glass man"?)

6. What event turns Amélie's life upside down on August 30, 1997, at the very moment that the death of Princess Diana ("Lady Di") is announced on television? What does she find hidden behind the wall?

7. What has Raymond Dufayel been painting for twenty years? What character always escapes his grasp, always seeming to be "in the center but still outside"?

8. What resolution does Dominique Bretodeau make in the café after recuperating his box of boyhood treasures from forty years before? What overwhelming desire invades Amélie after observing Bretodeau's newfound happiness?

9. How does Amélie begin to put into practice her new vocation when she spots the blind man on the sidewalk? Why is the fact that it is a blind person particularly relevant to Amélie's project? Whose funeral does she see on television afterwards? Why are there millions of people weeping for her own passing?

10. What project does Amélie put into effect as regards Joseph and Georgette? What fruit does her stratagem bear?

11. How does Amélie get in touch with Nino? Where does he work? Where is he every Wednesday (where she goes to meet him)?

12. Why do Nino and Amélie not become acquainted at the "Deux Moulins" café? What does she write in the note that she has Gina, the other waitress, put in Nino's pocket? What spectacular thing happens to Amélie when Nino leaves the café?

True or False?

If the statement is false, correct it!

1. Amélie's father is very extroverted, while her mother is very calm and serene.

2. Amélie's only friend is her goldfish, who is suicidal. Her mother gets rid of it and gives her a Kodak camera to console her.

3. At the age of eighteen Amélie leaves home to enroll in the university.

4. Amélie exhorts her father to go back to work as a doctor rather than staying at home all the time.

5. Amélie enjoys small pleasures like skipping stones on the Canal Sant-Martin.

6. Collignon, the grocer, regularly abuses his assistant Lucien.

7. Amélie fails at first in her search for Dominique "Bredoteau" because he no longer lives in Paris.

8. Amélie picks up in the street the album of discarded photos that Nino dropped from his moped.

9. Amélie changes the time on Collignon's alarm clock so that he awakes very late the next morning.

10. Amélie's father regularly receives postcards that show his garden gnome traveling all over the world.

11. Amélie makes the concierge Mado happy again by leading her to believe that her husband is not dead.

12. Amélie settles Collignon's hash once and for all by leading him to believe that he is going mad.

What Did You Learn in the Introduction?

1. With whom did Jeunet make his first films?

2. What is the subject of their first feature film, *Delicatessen*, in 1990? What awards did it win?

3. What is the subject of their second feature film, in 1995? What was astonishing for the spectators who saw this film?

4. Jeunet always shot his films on sound stages in studios. How is *Amélie* different in this respect? Where was it shot?

5. What allowed Jeunet to put an extraordinary number of special effects in his film?

6. For which film did Audrey Tautou win the Most Promising Actress César in 1999?

7. Who plays the role of Nino Quincampoix in *Amélie*? What award did he win for his performance in the Jacques Audiard film *See How They Fall*?

8. What record did *Amélie* hold in the United States? How did it fare at the Césars in France?

9. What did certain commentators criticize about the content and form of Jeunet's film?

10. What does *Amélie* have in common with poetic realism of the 1930s as regards its characters and iconography?

11. How does the narration of *Amélie* recall that of Sacha Guitry's film *Le Destin fabuleux de Désirée Clary*?

12. What connection is there between the images in *Amélie* and the photographs of Robert Doisneau?

Exploring the Film

1. The Beginning of the Film

What is the purpose of the prologue of Amélie as regards the style and tone of the film? What fundamental opposition is introduced by the last two parts of the beginning of the prologue, before the beginning credits? Is this opposition important for the rest of the film? Explain. What connection is there between the presentation of the crew at the beginning of the film and Amélie's games? **Review the beginning of the film and the beginning credits** (Excerpt 1, 0'50–3'30).

The narrator tells us in the prologue what the characters do not like, then what they do like. **Why does he do that?**

The images of the prologue are commented in voice-over by an omniscient narrator who intervenes subsequently at various moments of the film. The narrator announces, for example, two days before the death of Princess Diana (at the end of the twenty-minute prologue), "August 29. In forty-eight hours Amélie Poulain's destiny is going to change. . . ." **Who does this narrative voice represent, in your opinion: God? The Director? Both?** In what sense might we compare the director to "God"?

What role does the death of Diana (August 31, 1997) play in the establishment of the temporal frame of the film? Is this in fact a film about that period, or is the temporal register determined differently?

2. The Characters

+ *Amélie as a child*

What aspect of Amélie's childhood is expressed through her games during the be-ginning credits of the film? *Review the last part of Excerpt 1* (2'00–3'30). What role did her parents play in the development of her character? How would you describe her character? How would you explain the striking development of her imagination? How is her unbridled imagination highlighted when she is waiting for Nino to arrive at the café?

+ *Amélie as an adult*

Describe Amélie's life after she goes to live in Paris. What sort of pleasures does she especially like? How is Lady Di's death going to change her life? *Review the sequence where Amélie discovers the treasure box* (Excerpt 2, 14'15–16'00). **Why is Amélie's plan to help others find happiness so important to her?** (Does Amélie live vicariously?)

What does Amélie's identification with the Zorro character mean? What role does she play in this respect? Do you find her intervening (meddling?) in the life of others admirable or reprehensible?

How do you explain the attraction that Amélie's character holds for so many spectators? A female politician from that period remarks, in reflecting on the film, "The phenomenon of identification is powerful and explains the huge success of the film" (Bresson, Dely, and Hassoux 3). Does the proliferation of close-ups of Audrey Tautou's face, as well as her looks directly into the camera and remarks directed to the spectators, play a role here? What is the effect of the latter on the spectators?

Paraphrasing a famous statement by Flaubert concerning Madame Bovary, Jeunet declared, "Amélie Poulain, c'est moi!" ("I am Amélie Poulain.") **On what is Jeunet basing this identification with his heroine, in your opinion?** (What does he have mostly in common with her as a filmmaker?) Do you feel that you can identify with Amélie? Explain.

+ *Collignon and Lucien*

Why do you think Jeunet created the antipathetic character of the grocer Collignon who abuses his employee Lucien? What function does he have in the film?

+ *Raymond Dufayel*

Why is Dufayel called the "glass man"? What are the consequences of his handicap on his personal life? **From what point of view does Amélie resemble Dufayel in the way she lives?**

Why has Dufayel reproduced every year for the last twenty years the same painting by Renoir, *The Boatmen's Lunch* (*Le Déjeuner des canotiers*)? **What is the importance of**

Dufayel's reflections on the girl that he has trouble grasping? *Review the first meeting of Amélie and Dufayel* (Excerpt 3, 27'40–30'40). What are his conclusions about this girl? Why does he say, later in the film, "She likes stratagems. In fact, she's a little cowardly"?

What essential realization is suggested in the sequence of the televised film with Stalin (in Russian), after the scene in which Dufayel makes his observations about "the girl with the glass of water"? (This scene follows the episode in the café where Amélie lacks the courage to introduce herself to Nino.)

Dufayel helps Amélie change her life, but she returns the favor with her videos and their montage of excerpts from American television shows. What do we note as regards the style of the current version of *Le Déjeuner des canotiers* that he is working on near the end of the film? What is the connection with Amélie's cassettes? Or is it simply the example of Amélie (who finally dares to take a risk in her life) that is relevant here?

+ *Nino*

Nino works in a sex shop (Video Palace) and at the Throne Carnival (Foire du Trône). What image do we have of him? Does he have anything in common with Amélie? Why is she attracted to him? **What might the album of bad photos, which seems so important to him, represent?** How would you interpret the narrator's remark when Amélie leafs through the album for the first time: "What a family album!"?

What strategy does Amélie use to return the album to Nino? *Review this sequence* (Excerpt 4, 1h12'55–1h17'20). Describe how Jeunet films and edits this whole sequence, ending with the close-up on Amélie's face and her look into the camera.

Does the use of the photo album in the end credits, with the photos of the actors, add anything to the significance of this object?

+ *Joseph and Georgette*

What do these two characters have in common (as regards their personality)? Amélie succeeds in getting them interested in each other and becoming lovers. Why does their relationship go sour?

3. Montmartre

Why did Jeunet choose Montmartre as the main setting for his film? Why, in your opinion, did he digitally remove all the graffiti and posters (that he didn't like) from the walls and eliminate all of the cars that normally fill the streets in Paris? What effect was he trying to achieve?

Jeunet was criticized by certain commentators, as we've seen above, for having created a "postcard Paris" for tourists. **Do you agree with this criticism?** Do you consider the image Jeunet presents of Paris to be a negative aspect of his film? Where do we see actual postcards in *Amélie*? What do they represent? What might that suggest as regards the image of Paris throughout the world, whatever the reality might be?

4. A Utopian, Euphoric Vision?

As we've also seen, a certain number of critics accused Jeunet of offering a utopian vision of life in Paris, of only showing its positive, indeed euphoric side. What do you think about this? **Does Jeunet depict a perfect world?** Are all these "little people" who inhabit Jeunet's universe happy as clams?

Is the theme of childhood relevant here? **Is childhood connected to the theme of happiness in *Amélie*?** What image does Jeunet give of childhood in his film (Amélie, Nino, Bretodeau)?

5. A Propaganda Film?

Many commentators have observed that *Amélie* gives a reassuring image of traditional French values. For some of them, this could be perceived as a suspicious attempt to freeze the French in an anachronistic national identity that is a product of pure nostalgia and official anti-communitarianism (refusal of diversity). For them, Jeunet's film is a piece of reactionary (extreme right-wing) propaganda in which the solution of social problems is a return to a mythical sentimentalized past that recalls either Pétain's populism or the xenophobia of Jean-Marie Le Pen's National Front party. **What do you think about this? Is this interpretation of the film viable?**

6. Means of Transportation

Since Jeunet has virtually eliminated cars from the streets of Paris, all that are left are the subway, the train—and Nino's moped. **How should we understand this aspect of the film?** In general, who takes the subway (or rides a moped) as opposed to those who get around in a personal vehicle?

What interpretation could we give to the final scene of the film in which Amélie and Nino ride around Paris on his moped (in fast motion, with a wildly jiggling camera, blurred images, fast jerky editing, and Godardian jump cuts)? What opposition does Jeunet seem to create in his film between movement and immobility?

7. Technology

What role does technology play in this film? Think especially of the means of communication, representation, and reproduction: telephones, cameras, television, videos, movies, telescopes, photocopy machines, and photo booths, for example). **What importance does the problem of communication have in *Amélie*?** And the mediation of the relationships between people (as opposed to direct contact)? How does Dufayel succeed, for example, in persuading Amélie to take the risk of meeting Nino and finally engaging directly in life?

According to one critic, the film is about the power of technology to change the world (Moore 12). **What do you think about that, especially as regards *Amélie*'s actions?** Might this idea also apply to the use of new digital technologies by the filmmaker?

8. Cinematography, Special Effects, Sound, Colors

Why does Jeunet often place the camera at ground level? Why does he often use down shots from high above in the railroad station scenes? What feeling is he trying to convey, for example, with the towering down shot on Amélie alone in the main hall of the Gare du Nord toward the end of the film, when she fails to meet Nino?

What are the most surprising special effects? Where do we see fast- or slow-motion shots? Describe the editing of the sequence where Amélie helps the blind man in the street. What is striking here? *Review this sequence* (Excerpt 5, 35'15–36'25). How can we interpret the shot in which Amélie literally melts into a puddle of water on the floor of the café?

There is often accordion music in *Amélie*, beginning with the prologue. Accordion music is one of the great popular traditions in France. Why does Jeunet use it in his film? **What feeling is he trying to provoke?** Is there a connection between this waltz music and Amélie's character? **What kind of visual and auditory effects accompany the scene where Amélie steals the garden gnome from her father?** *Review this sequence* (Excerpt 6, 39'05–39'50).

Jeunet's camera is extremely mobile, sometimes imitating the movements and the viewpoint of a human being, as in the scene where Nino loses the briefcase with his photo album in the street, and Amélie comes and picks it up and (in the following scene) leafs through it. *Review this scene* (Excerpt 7, 40'30–42'30). **Discuss the camera movements here.**

The television programs are always in black and white. What role does that play in Jeunet's narrative strategy in the film? In addition, what historical period is evoked in this manner?

It has been observed that the dominant colors in *Amélie* are red and green (Vanderschelden 52), especially red, beginning with Amélie's clothes and her apartment, as well as the facade of the café, the beating heart, the sex shop, the gnome's hat, etc. Do these two colors seem to have a particular meaning in the film?

9. Animation

Before making films with actors, Jeunet made cartoons. He has admitted being strongly influenced by Tex Avery, the great master of American cartoons in the 1930s and 1940s whose well-known motto was, "In a cartoon, you can do anything." **Where do we see the influence of cartooning in this film? What is the effect sought by Jeunet?**

10. Mise en abyme

When a painter represents the act of painting in one of his or her paintings (for example, *Las Meninas* by the Spanish painter Vélasquez [1656], where we see the painter at work in a corner of the canvas), it is referred to as a *mise en abyme*. By analogy, the same term is often used to describe a play in a play or the depiction of the act of writing in a novel. **May we speak of a *mise en abyme* of the act of making a film in Amélie, literally or metaphorically—or both?** How might we interpret, for instance, the sequence in which Amélie fabricates the phony love letter from the husband of the concierge? What role does the use of fast motion play here? *Review this sequence* (Excerpt 8, 1h22'35–1h23'15).

As everyone knows, a director is responsible for the staging of the film. Is the "staging" subject to a *mise en abyme* in Jeunet's film also? **Who does staging here** (think of the manner in which Nino's album is returned to him, for example)?

In *Amélie*, we often see characters who watch or blatantly spy on other characters (with binoculars, for example), without their knowing it. What is the subject of a *mise en abyme* in this case?

Amélie imagines the "kidnapping" of Nino while she waits for him to arrive at the brasserie. Again, what is the obvious subject of a *mise en abyme* here?

Jean-Pierre Jeunet's Filmography

1978   *The Escape* (*L'Evasion*, short animation, with Marc Caro)

1980   *The Carousel* (*Le Manège*, short animation, with Marc Caro)

1981   *The Bunker of the Last Gunshots* (*Le Bunker de la dernière rafale*, film short with Marc Caro)

1989   *Things I Like, Things I Don't Like* (*Foutaises*, film short)

1991   *Delicatessen* (with Marc Caro)

1995   *The City of Lost Children* (*La Cité des enfants perdus*, with Marc Caro)

1997   *Alien: Resurrection*

2001   *Amélie* (*Le Fabuleux Destin d'Amélie Poulain*)

2004   *A Very Long Engagement* (*Un long dimanche de fiançailles*)

2009   *Micmacs* (*Micmacs à tire-larigot*)

2013   *The Young and Prodigious T. S. Spivet*

2015   *Casanova* (film for television)

Works Consulted

Ageorges, Sylvain. "Les Abbesses nous font leur cinéma." *A Nous Paris*, 16–22 Apr. 2001: 12–13.

Alexandre, Grégory. "Le Fabuleux Destin d'Amélie Poulain." *Ciné Live*, Apr. 2001: 35.

Alion, Yves. "La Liberté à tout prix." *L'Avant-Scène Cinéma* 502 (May 2001): 124–26.

Amar, Marlène. "Travail à l'ancienne." *TéléCinéObs*, 11 Dec. 2003: 59.

Andrew, Dudley. "Amélie, or Le Fabuleux Destin du Cinéma Français." *Film Quarterly* 57.3 (2004): 34–46.

Baignères, Claude. "Valse à mille temps." *Le Figaro*, 25 Apr. 2001: n. pag.

Baret, Guy. "Amélie Laguiller et Arlette Poulain." *Le Figaro*, 5 June 2001: n. pag.

Bonnaud, Frédéric. "The *Amélie* Effect." *Film Comment* 37.6 (Nov.–Dec. 2001): 36–38.

Bresson, Gilles, Renaud Dely, and Didier Hassoux. "La Classe politique analyse le succès du film: 'Un besoin de bonheur simple.'" *Libération*, 2–3 June 2001: 3.

Campion, Alexis. "Jean-Pierre Jeunet, le miracle d'Amélie et 'le goût de chiotte absolu.'" *Le Journal du dimanche*, 12 Aug. 2001: n. pag.

De Baecque, Antoine. "Trois absents de taille." *Libération*, 9 May 2001: 31.

De Bruyn, Olivier. "Les Délices d'Amélie." *Le Point*, 20 Apr. 2001: 121.

Delassein, Sophie. "Le Fabuleux Destin de Yann Tiersen." *Le Nouvel Observateur*, 14 June 2001: n. pag.

Delerm, Philippe. *La Première Gorgée de bière et autres plaisirs minuscules*. Paris: Gallimard, 1997.

Deydier, Catherine, and Eric Libiot. "Jeunet: un destin de cinéaste." *L'Express*, 19 Apr. 2001: 58–59.

Durham, Carolyn. "Finding France on Film. *Chocolat, Amélie* and *Le Divorce*." *French Cultural Studies* 19.2 (June 2008): 173–97.

Ezra, Elizabeth. "The Death of an Icon: *Le Fabuleux Destin d'Amélie Poulain*." *French Cultural Studies* 15.3 (Oct. 2004): 301–10.

Frodon, Jean-Michel. "Une chevauchée fantastique sans pareil." *Le Monde*, 1 Jan. 2002: 18.

Garbarz, Franck. "Le Fabuleux Destin d'Amélie Poulain. La 'recolleuse' de morceaux." *Positif* 483 (May 2001): 29–30.

Gorin, François. "Amélie, Loana, Jean-Luc et moi." *Télérama*, 25 July 2001: 30–32.

Guitry, Sacha. *Le Destin fabuleux de Désirée Clary*. <http://www.telerama.fr/cinema /films/le-destin-fabuleux-de-desiree-clary,24966.php>.

Gural-Migdal, Anna. "Paris comme parc d'attractions à la Disney dans *Le Fabuleux Destin d'Amélie Poulain*." *Journal of the Australasian Universities Language and Literature Association* 108 (Nov. 2007): 131–48.

Haun, Harry. "Fantasy in Paris." *Film Journal International*, Nov. 2001: 14–16.

Jeunet, Jean-Pierre, dir. *Le Fabuleux destin d'Amélie Poulain*. Miramax Home Entertainment, 2002.

Kaganski, Serge. "*Amélie* pas jolie." *Libération*, 31 May 2001: 7.

———. "Comment je me suis disputé à propos d'*Amélie Poulain*." *Les Inrockuptibles*, 12 June 2001: 16–19.

Lalanne, Jean-Marc, and Didier Péron. "Un coup de Jeunet." *Libération*, 25 Apr. 2001: 31–33.

Lançon, Philippe. "Le Frauduleux Destin d'Amélie Poulain." *Libération*, 1 June 2001: 5.

Larcher, Jérôme. "Le Cabinet de curiosités." *Cahiers du cinéma* 557 (May 2001): 112.

Lee, Mark D. "*Le Fabuleux Destin d'Amélie Poulain*." *The French Review* 76.5 (Apr. 2003): 1061–62.

Lefort, Gérard, and Didier Péron. "Je ne suis pas près de revivre un tel miracle." *Libération*, 26 Dec. 2001: 21–22.

Lucien, Guillaume. "Pourquoi tant de haine pour Amélie?" *Libération*, 3 June 2001: 4.

Martin-Castelnau, David, and Guillaume Bigot. "Le Secret d'Amélie Poulain." *Libération*, 28 May 2001: 6.

Moore, Rick Clifton. "Ambivalence to Technology in Jeunet's *Le Fabuleux Destin d'Amélie Poulain*." *Bulletin of Science, Technology & Society* 26.1 (Feb. 2006): 9–19.

Mulard, Claudine, and Thomas Sotinel. "Amélie Poulain, un tour du monde en 17 millions d'entrées." *Le Monde*, 1 Jan. 2002: 17–18.

Oscherwitz, Dayna. "Once Upon a Time That Never Was: Jean-Pierre Jeunet's *Le Fabuleux Destin d'Amélie Poulain* (2001)." *The French Review* 84.3 (Feb. 2011): 504–15.

O'Sullivan, Charlotte. "*Amélie*." *Sight and Sound*, 11 Oct. 2001: 40–41.

Parra, Danièle. "Entretien avec Marc Caro et Jean-Pierre Jeunet. Rencontre avec deux tronches de l'art." *Revue du cinéma* 471 (May 1991): 42–45.

Péron, Didier. "Quatre millions d'adhérents." *Libération*, 3 June 2001: 2–3.

Peters, Jeffrey N. "Tautou's Face." *Publications of the Modern Language Association of America* 126.4 (Oct. 2011): 1042–60.

Riou, Alain. "Amélie jolie." *Le Nouvel Observateur*, 19–25 Apr. 2001: 129.

Scatton-Tessier, Michelle. "Le Petisme: Flirting with the Sordid in *Le Fabuleux Destin d'Amélie Poulain*." *Studies in French Cinema* 4.3 (2004): 197–207.

Séguret, Olivier. "Cannes, son délit d'Amélie." *Libération*, 9 May 2001: 30–31.

Silberg, Jon. "A Magical Paris." *American Cinematographer* 82 (Sept. 2001): 20–22.

Sotinel, T. "Quand Georges Perec rencontre Marcel Carné." *Le Monde*, 25 Apr. 2001: n. pag.

Taillibert, Christel. "*Le Fabuleux Destin d'Amélie Poulain*." *Jeune Cinéma* 268 (May–June 2001): 39–40.

Vanderschelden, Isabelle. *Amélie. Le Fabuleux Destin d'Amélie Poulain (Jean-Pierre Jeunet, 2001)*. Chicago: U of Illinois P, 2007.

Vincendeau, Ginette. "Café Society." *Sight and Sound*, 11 Aug. 2001: 22–25.

20

Olivier Nakache and Eric Toledano

The Intouchables (Intouchables)

(2011)

Olivier Nakache and Eric Toledano, *The Intouchables*: Driss (Omar Sy) takes Philippe (François Cluzet) for a wild ride in his wheelchair.

Directors .... Eric Toledano and Olivier Nakache
Screenplay .... Eric Toledano and Olivier Nakache
Director of Photography .... Mathieu Vadepied
Sound .... Pascal Armand, Jean Goudier, Jean-Paul Hurier
Music .... Ludovico Einaudi
Film Editor .... Dorian Rigal-Ansous
Costumes .... Isabelle Pannetier
Art Director .... François Emmanuelli
Continuity .... Nathalie Vierny
Producers ..... Nicolas Duval Adassovsky, Laurent Zeitoun, Yann Zenou
Length.. 1h53

Cast

François Cluzet (*Philippe*), Omar Sy (*Driss*), Anne Le Ny (*Yvonne*), Audrey Fleurot (*Magalie*), Clotilde Mollet (*Marcelle*), Alba Gaïa Kraghede Bellugi (*Elisa*), Thomas Solivéres (*Bastien, Elisa's boyfriend*), Cyril Mendy (*Adama*), Salimata Kamate (*Fatou, Driss' mother*), Grégoire Oestermann (*Antoine, Philippe's friend*), Christian Ameri (*Albert, the gardener*)

Story

Philippe is an elegant, immensely rich quadriplegic man who lives in a nice neighborhood of Paris and loves modern art and classical music. He is looking for a caregiver. Driss is a Senegalese-born fellow who lives in the suburbs and has recently come out of prison. For him, Berlioz is the name of a neighborhood rather than a composer, and his musical preference goes to Earth, Wind & Fire. He must prove that he is looking for a job to remain eligible for unemployment benefits.

These two men who live in radically different worlds meet for a job interview. Driss impresses Philippe with his casual attitude, his jokes, and especially his genuine character and lack of pity for the disabled person in front of him. To his great surprise he is hired on a trial basis. He hesitates a bit but cannot resist the prospect of living in a luxurious environment and under the same roof as Magalie, Philippe's attractive secretary.

Philippe and Driss will get to know each other gradually, confide in each other, and learn about their respective tastes and needs. Together, these two people hurt by life will become . . . the "intouchables."

The Directors

Eric Toledano and Olivier Nakache were born in 1971 and 1973, respectively, and grew up the first in Versailles, the second in a suburb of Paris. They met as teenagers and were united by their passion for cinema, especially Italian comedy. They began making small films for an association that helps autistic children, followed by pieces around the theme of friendship often inspired by their own experience. They made a name for themselves with their second short film, *Little Shoes* (*Les Petits Souliers*, 1999), about the adventures of four Arab and Jewish friends who have been hired as Santas for one night. The roles are played by the directors' friends Jamel Debbouze, Gad Elmaleh, Atmen Kelif, and Roschdy Zem, most of whom have since become stars in French cinema. Their first feature, *Let's Be Friends* (*Je préfère qu'on reste amis*, 2005), examines the development of a friendship between a thirty-year-old single man who is unlucky at love (Jean-Paul Rouve) and a divorced fifty-year-old who is full of life but also bruised (Gérard Depardieu). *Those Happy Days* (*Nos jours heureux*, 2006) tells the story of a summer camp (the two directors were camp counselors in their youth) during which life in a group leads to self-discovery and allows both the children and the young adults to accept themselves better. *So Close* (*Tellement proches*, 2009) treats the themes of family life and fatherhood, a new stage in the personal lives of the directors at the time.

With *The Intouchables* Nakache and Toledano ventured into an area unknown to them, that of disability, and for the first time they drew inspiration from a true story that was unrelated to their own lives. They made the film to give a first leading role to their actor friend Omar Sy, who had already played in some of their shorts and feature films and whose comic potential they admired. As they note, "The longer we shot with him, the more obvious it was that he was headed for stardom" (Rouchy).

They also cast Sy as the lead in their next film, *Samba* (2014), the story of a difficult love between an undocumented Senegalese man who is struggling to make ends meet and a French executive—played by Charlotte Gainsbourg—who is recovering from a nervous breakdown by working for an organization that helps illegal immigrants.

The Origin and Making of the Film

In the course of their search for a story that could showcase Omar Sy, Nakache and Toledano remembered a documentary that had made a particularly strong impression on them about the life of Philippe Pozzo di Borgo, a rich aristocrat and the former CEO of the Pommery champagnes, who had become quadriplegic after a paragliding accident. This documentary, inspired by Pozzo di Borgo's autobiographical narrative *A Second Wind: A Memoir* (*Le Second Souffle*, 2001), described his disability, the death of his wife two years after his accident, his despair, and his life-changing meeting with Abdel Sellou, his caregiver. The directors paid him a visit in Morocco and were struck by his charisma, humor, and unswerving optimism. Pozzo di Borgo agreed to have his story serve as the basis for the film and made this one request: "If you make this film, it has to be funny. This story must be told through humor" (Gandillot).

Following their usual approach, Nakache and Toledano worked with three producers and eliminated the parts of the project on which their colleagues could not reach a consensus. They and their interpreters met with Pozzo di Borgo several times to get to know his daily life and consult him about the screenplay. Pozzo di Borgo also helped convince Mathieu Vadepied, the Director of Photography, who had previously worked as Art Director for filmmakers Jacques Audiard and Maurice Pialat, to come back to work. Vadepied was attracted by the presence of Omar Sy, one of the rare black actors ever to play a leading role in French cinema, and by the challenge of making a comedy on a serious topic.

The shoot took place at the Hôtel d'Avaray, the headquarters of the embassy of the Netherlands in the seventh *arrondissement* of Paris, and in a low-income apartment block in Bondy, north of the capital. Everything went smoothly even though the directors could sense some tension among the residents the day they shot a scene with police officers.

In May 2011 the film created a buzz at the Cannes Film Festival, where an eight-minute excerpt was screened before film professionals. Distributors from around twenty countries bought the rights to the film, including the very influential American producer and distributor Harvey Weinstein (now disgraced), who had ensured the success of films like *Amélie* and *The Artist* in the United States. This boded well for the film six months before its theatrical release.

The Actors

Omar Sy (Driss) was the great revelation of *The Intouchables*. Born into a modest family of West African origin—his mother was Mauritanian and his father Senegalese—in Trappes, a suburb of Paris, he was planning to become an air-conditioning technician before he met actor Jamel Debbouze, the older brother of a childhood friend, who hired him for his television show on the Canal+ channel. Subsequently Omar Sy and Fred Testot formed the comic duo "Omar and Fred" that appeared on the stage and on television starting in 1997, and notably in the comic television series *SAV* (*Service après-vente/ Customer Service*) on Canal+ from 2005 to 2012. His friends Toledano and Nakache convinced him to play in their first short and then gave him prominent roles in their second and third features. He portrayed a summer camp counselor in *Those Happy Days* and a hospital intern in *So Close*.

The Intouchables marked a turning point in Omar Sy's career. Because he was never trained as an actor he felt like an impostor in his first films, but he felt like a true actor in this new role: "With this film, *The Intouchables*, I overcame my reservations about myself. For the first time . . . I wasn't just following my instincts. I had prepared my game" (Rouchy). The film also earned him the César for Best Actor—a rare honor for a comic actor—and critical acclaim. For Rouchy it was the "Birth of a giant": "Overflowing with contagious energy and caustic humor, touching, sometimes poignant, intelligently directed, hysterically funny, he jumps off the screen." *The Intouchables* launched Omar Sy to the forefront of the French and international film world. He has since played in a dozen films, including Nakache and Toledano's latest feature *Samba* (2014) and the Hollywood blockbusters *X-Men: Days of Future Past* (2014) and *Jurassic World* (2015).

The character of Philippe is portrayed by François Cluzet—Daniel Auteuil was approached for the role but ultimately refused. A theater and film actor, Cluzet has appeared in around seventy films by renowned directors, including Diane Kurys, Bertrand Tavernier, Tony Gatlif, Claire Denis, Bertrand Blier, and American directors Robert Altman and Lawrence Kasdan. He worked the most, however, with Chabrol, his favorite director, on films such as *The Proud Ones* (*Le Cheval d'orgueil*, 1980), a family chronicle in Brittany, the drama *Story of Women* (*Une Affaire de femmes*, 1988), and the thriller *Hell* (*L'Enfer*, 1994), in which he plays a jealous husband. Cluzet has received around ten nominations at the Césars for Most Promising Actor, Best Supporting Actor, and Best Actor, and earned his first César for Best Actor in 2007 for his role in *Tell No One* (*Ne le dis à personne*) by Guillaume Canet, with whom he has collaborated several times since. Earlier (1984), he had won the Jean Gabin Prize awarded to a promising actor in French or Francophone films. Cluzet is a versatile actor who is sometimes compared to Dustin Hoffman. He is able to play tormented characters in thrillers as well as people from different social backgrounds in dramas and comedies. He appears in two other films featured in this textbook, *Coup de foudre* (Kurys, 1983)—very briefly—and *Chocolat* (Denis, 1988).

Cluzet was won over by the screenplay of *The Intouchables* and accepted the role right away. As he remembers, "I immediately thought of a circus duo and saw its potential for success. I understood that Omar would be the Auguste, the clown that makes people laugh, and that I would portray the white clown, the one that wields some authority, that sets the tone. This tandem reminded me a little of a father and his son"

(Giordano 165). On the set he served as a mentor to Omar Sy, who appreciated his advice and generosity. Cluzet found his role difficult for several reasons, beginning with the fact that he was unable to move in his wheelchair and felt that he was playing "a lazybones role" (166). In addition he experienced deep loneliness and suffering while portraying a handicapped man, especially since he felt ostracized by some members of the film crew: "They reacted the way some people do toward a person with disability, who frightens them a little" (167). Cluzet admitted that "*The Intouchables* is to this day the only film in which I acted that made me cry" (167).

Among the supporting actors, Anne Le Ny (Yvonne) has played in many movies and television films and series, including *The Taste of Others* (*Le Goût des autres*) by Agnès Jaoui (2000), in which she portrays Valérie, the theater dresser (see Chap.18). She stepped behind the camera in 2007 and made a well-received feature, *Those Who Remain* (*Ceux qui restent*), starring Vincent Lindon and Emmanuelle Devos, followed by two comedies—*My Father's Guest* (*Les Invités de mon père*) in 2010 and *The Chef's Wife* (*On a failli être amies*) in 2014—and a drama, *Cornouaille*, in 2012.

Audrey Fleurot (Magalie) had her first role in a movie in 2007. *The Intouchables* revealed her talents, and she has played in around fifteen films since.

The Reception

The Intouchables broke all records: best film at the French box office in 2011 and second-best film of all time in France after *Welcome to the Sticks* (*Bienvenue chez les Ch'tis* [Dany Boon, 2008]); French-language film that sold the most seats worldwide, dethroning *Amélie* (*Le Fabuleux Destin d'Amélie Poulain*, Jean-Pierre Jeunet, 2001), the record holder for over ten years; most profitable non-English language film of all times; film with the longest number-one streak at the French box office (ten weeks in a row, like Francis Veber's *The Dinner Game* [*Le Dîner de cons*, 1998]), etc.

The film garnered sixteen prizes and over thirty nominations, including nine nominations at the Césars in 2012, the César for Best Actor for Omar Sy, the Critics Special Prize at the ColCoa French film Festival in Hollywood, and a nomination at the Golden Globes in the Best Foreign Language Film category. It was even honored with a private screening at the White House and at the Elysée Palace in Paris.

Given the interest of the distributors early on, at the screening of an excerpt from the film at the Cannes Film Festival in May 2011, *The Intouchables* was highly anticipated. It received rave reviews, as well as a few negative comments that could be expected because the film is a popular comedy, a genre considered too "commercial" and frowned upon by the most intellectual critics. Surprisingly, some of the latter, like Carrière, had nonetheless no qualms in voicing their enthusiasm: "Sorry, this time we like this film"; or Libiot, who does not refrain from speaking of his "pleasure" in seeing the film: "A word that sounds like a swear word," he says, "so rarely is it used by critics." For this critic, who had been following Toledano and Nakache's film career, *The Intouchables* confirms that "they have reached (near) maturity." Jacques Mandelbaum, who considered their earlier films "one step above the brackish gruel that is served to the good people under the name of French comedy," writes that with *The Intouchables* they have moved up to "the next level."

Press articles evoke the resounding success of the film at the box office, a feat all the more remarkable in that it treats "a risky subject-matter, disability, in an equally high-risk genre, comedy" (Emery). Critics appreciate its transgressive humor and the story of a friendship that transcends social divisions, while noting that the plot is rather implausible, even if it is based on a true story. Pagès speaks of a "beautiful utopia," Gandillot of "a hymn to joy, an ode to friendship, a modern fairy tale" that leaves viewers "in high spirits, aware that they have witnessed for two hours an exemplary and exceptional reconciliation between social classes." Writing in the communist newspaper *L'Humanité-Dimanche*, Ethis also sees in the film "a great social synthesis, a multicultural encounter" in tune with the "aspirations of the public, eager for more solidarity, hope, and humanity." Mandelbaum goes even further with a political interpretation that drew the ire of Jean-Marie Le Pen, the founder and former president of the notoriously xenophobic extreme right National Front political party: "The film spins out a generous social metaphor that shows the many benefits to be drawn from the encounter between Old France, paralyzed by its privilege, and the vital strength of young people of immigrant descent."

The Intouchables also received some very negative comments criticizing clichés and suggesting that the good feelings of the film hide inequalities and the reality of class relations. Lalanne describes it caustically as an "evy-hay ["heavy"], demagogical fable on interclass fraternity" and "a rather repulsive film" built on "the story line of a TF1 soap opera, spiced with humor à la Canal" (TF1 and Canal+ are private television channels) ["Intouchables"]. For Péters, too, the film deadens the spectators' ability to rail against inequalities: "In the flat land of the Bisounours/Kissybears [a children's television program], the good feelings of the film, an example of the same trend in society at large, lead to a completely anesthetized critical mind." Iacub contends that fraternity in the film is an illusion, and that poor people like Driss remain a dominated class: Driss must return to his normal life, give back the Fabergé egg, and submit to an unjust social order. Delfour sees in *The Intouchables* "a perfectly reactionary" remake of Cinderella whose message is simple: "Instruction, culture, the desire for emancipation, rebellion are useless; cosmetic beauty and chance alone have some power. Driss is a lesser Cinderella, beautiful but in banal duds and unemployed; however, he chances upon a prince charming who takes a liking to him, dresses him in a suit, and lifts him out of the social nothingness in which he was wallowing." An opinion that drew the following retort from his colleague Granotier (a good example of the sparring occasioned by the film in the newsrooms): "I liked *The Intouchables*, and what's wrong with that? [. . .]. I don't like to be considered stupid enough, along with seven million fellow spectators, to confuse a fairy tale with reality. My taste for reality doesn't prevent me from liking fairy tales." This is reminiscent of the strong responses to critics who panned *Amélie* (2001) because they, too, objected to the fairy tale side of the film that the broad public liked so much.

While many French reviews focused on class relations, American commentators were more offended by Driss' portrayal. Journalists from the *New York Times* and the *New Yorker* expressed opinions similar to those of Weissberg in *Variety*, denouncing racial stereotypes and arguing that Driss was an Uncle Tom whose duty it was to amuse his master, like slaves in the past. To prevent these critics from lowering the appeal of the film in the United States, distributor Harvey Weinstein organized screenings for the black community and black intellectuals and even encouraged Barack Obama to show the film at the White House. Thanks to his efforts *The Intouchables* was a hit in the United States and even received the African-American Film Critics Association Prize, among other awards.

As a result of this success, the band Earth, Wind & Fire enjoyed renewed popularity and went on a new European tour after the release of the film. A new edition of *A Second Wind: A Memoir* by Philippe Pozzo di Borgo came out in 2011, and the author wrote a sequel, *The Guardian Devil* (*Diable gardien*), in which he gives additional details about his relationship with his caregiver Abdel Sellou. Finally, the success of the film benefited associations for people with disabilities because the directors requested that they receive a percentage of the proceeds.

More than a great film event, *The Intouchables* is seen by many as a "social phenomenon," a triumph of humanism and solidarity in times of crisis that allows people to forget "rating agencies, failing banks, and soaring unemployment" (Rouchy). In addition to the economic crisis, Giordano explains its impact by the conflictual political context (the rise of the National Front and the infighting among candidates in the primaries of the presidential election in the fall of 2011), and by anxiety linked to the commemorations of the tenth anniversary of 9/11 (148).

Disability on the Big Screen

People with disabilities have appeared in movies since the beginnings of cinema, but their representation has changed considerably as their place in society has evolved. One of the first notable films that featured invalids was the horror movie *Freaks* (Tod Browning, 1932), in which people suffering from physical malformations portrayed monsters being exhibited at a circus. As in this film, handicapped people often played negative and secondary roles in movies. Piéral, for example, the most famous dwarf actor in French cinema, mostly embodied malevolent characters in his career of fifty years, starting with *The Devil's Envoys* (*Les Visiteurs du soir* [Marcel Carné, 1942]) and *Love Eternal* (*L'Éternel Retour* [Jean Delannoy, 1943]). He also acted in *The Hunchback of Notre Dame* (*Notre-Dame de Paris* [Delannoy, 1956]), a film adapted from Victor Hugo's novel in which we meet many monstrous and repulsive characters in the Court of Miracles, a den for criminals and undesirables where "normal" people only ventured at their own peril.

Disabled and incapacitated people are also cast as vulnerable characters, like the young blind woman in *City Lights* (Charlie Chaplin, 1931), as innocent victims, as is the case of the deaf-mute in *Johnny Belinda* (Jean Negulesco, 1948), or as wise and saintly people, as in *The Heart Is a Lonely Hunter* (Robert Ellis Miller, 1968) [Pris]. Starting in the 1970s they are seen more and more in high-profile dramas that garnered prestigious awards. They embody war-disabled characters, as in *Johnny Got His Gun* (Dalton Trumbo, 1971) or *The Deer Hunter* (Michael Cimino, 1978); victims of congenital malformations, like the protagonist of *The Elephant Man* (David Lynch, 1980); psychiatric patients as in *One Flew Over the Cuckoo's Nest* (Miloš Forman, 1975); autistic people, as in *Rain Man* (Barry Levinson, 1989) and *Forrest Gump* (Robert Zemeckis, 1994), among other films.

Francophone cinema is not far behind in the representation of people with disabilities, even if its signature films on the topic are more recent than those across the Atlantic. *The Eighth Day* (*Le Huitième Jour*) by Belgian director Jaco Van Dormael marked a turning point when it came out in 1996. Like *Rain Man*, the film tells the story of a friendship that develops between an able-bodied man and a mentally disabled one. However, for the first time one of the leading roles is played by an actor with Down syndrome, Pascal Duquenne. His performance, as well as Daniel Auteuil's in the other leading role, earned them a joint Best Actor Award at the Cannes Film Festival, a prize that changed the way we look at disability and difference.

The number of fiction films and documentaries featuring disabled actors in leading roles has increased markedly since 2000. The filmmakers depict their characters as normal human beings, with their strengths and weaknesses, without hiding the difficulties of their daily lives, and by avoiding voyeurism. They appear in dramas like *The Diving Bell and the Butterfly* (*Le Scaphandre et le papillon* [Julian Schnabel, 2007]) and documentaries—including Sandrine Bonnaire's piece on her autistic sister, *Her Name Is Sabine* (*Elle s'appelle Sabine*, 2007)—but also in screwball comedies like *Aaltra* (Benoît Délépine and Gustave Kevern, 2004), a Belgian road movie in which the two protagonists are in wheelchairs as a result of an absurd farm accident. In these comedies, humor (usually of the dark kind) and transgression are used to broach taboo subjects, like sexuality. The hero of *Uneasy Riders* (*Nationale 7* [Jean-Pierre Sinapi, 2000]), for example, is a fifty-year-old muscular dystrophy patient. Wanting to make love before his disease worsens, he requests to have prostitutes brought to him.

When *The Intouchables* was released in 2011, disability was thus a rising theme on the big screen, a fact confirmed by the creation in 2009 of the *Festival Cinéma and Handicap*, an annual event dedicated to short films, and the huge success, just a few months after Nakache and Toledano's film, of Jacques Audiard's *Rust and Bone* (*De rouille and d'os*, 2012), about the psychological recovery and new love life of a young female amputee. Still, Eric Blanchet, General Manager of the Association for the Integration of People with Disabilities (Association pour l'insertion des personnes handicapées/ADAPT), considers the release of *The Intouchables* "a true turning point." "The presence of disabled characters in comedies, action films, even horror films, makes it possible to rise above the usually depressing image of disability," he adds (Pris).

Indeed, *The Intouchables* has set a precedent. The second film at the French box office in France in 2014 was *La Famille Bélier* by Eric Lartigau, a comedy about a family in which the daughter alone is not hearing impaired, and where communication is in sign language. This film is inspired by a true story and counts disabled people among its actors—born deaf, specifically—two characteristics that are found in a growing number of recent films. An example of this trend is *The Finishers* (*De toutes nos forces* [Nils Tavernier, 2014]), a film financed by the APAJH Federation (an association that helps adults and young people with disabilities), in which a seventeen-year-old paraplegic—in real life as well as on the screen—challenges his father to compete with him in the Ironman triathlon in Nice. This tendency is not specific to French cinema. In Canada, for example, director Louise Archambault met with solid success with her film *Gabrielle* (2013), whose protagonist and the young woman who portrays her are both suffering from Williams syndrome.

As a final note, the theme of disability is also more and more popular in romantic comedies. The heroes of two films released in 2015, *The Sense of Wonder* (*Le Goût des merveilles* [Eric Besnard]) and *A Steady Balance* (*En Equilibre* [Denis Dercourt]), are respectively a young man with Asperger syndrome and a former horse stuntman in films now confined to a wheelchair.

STUDY GUIDE

What Happens in This Film?

1. What happened when the police arrested Driss for speeding?

2. Why did Philippe hire Driss as his caregiver? What convinced Driss to accept the position?

3. What does Antoine think of Driss' presence at Philippe's house? When they met at the café, what did he reveal to Philippe about the six months that Driss spent away from his family?

4. How does Magalie react when Driss hits on her (when he invites her to take a bath, for example)?

5. What did Driss do to alleviate Philippe's phantom pains one night?

6. Why does Philippe cherish his Fabergé eggs so much? What happened to one of these eggs?

7. What type of relationship does Philippe have with Eléonore? What does Driss think about this, and what advice does he give Philippe?

8. During Philippe's birthday party, what do the classical music pieces remind Driss of? If you have seen the film *The Taste of Others* (*Le Goût des autres*) by Agnès Jaoui, does this scene from *The Intouchables* remind you of something?

9. Who are Elisa and Bastien? What influence did Driss have on them?

10. Why did Driss leave his position at Philippe's house? What happened to Philippe when he left?

11. How was Driss' job interview with the representative of a trucking firm? Compare this interview with the one at Philippe's house at the beginning of the film.

12. Where did Driss and Philippe go after the episode with the police? What had Driss organized there?

True or False?

If the statement is false, correct it!

1. Driss had a job interview with Philippe because he was looking for his first real job. He wore a suit to make a good impression.

2. Berlioz is the name of a low-income neighborhood in a suburb of Paris.

3. Driss was born and grew up in a low-income neighborhood in a suburb of Paris with his many siblings.

4. Alice, Philippe's wife, died in the paragliding accident that left Philippe paralyzed.

5. Driss discovered an interest in opera through contact with Philippe.

6. On Driss' advice, Philippe sent Eléonore a photo of himself in his wheelchair.

7. When she saw Driss wearing a suit at the birthday party, Magalie compared him to Michael Jordan.

8. Philippe did not see Eléonore at the café because she arrived twenty minutes late.

9. Driss took his first flight when he accompanied Philippe to the mountains.

10. Philippe managed to sell Driss' painting to Antoine for a hundred euros.

11. Yvonne started a relationship with Magalie when Driss left.

12. Driss had fun shaving Philippe in the likeness of Charlie Chaplin.

What Did You Learn in the Introduction?

1. What are some of the important themes in the films of Nakache and Toledano?

2. What is the story of *The Intouchables* based on?

3. Who is partly responsible for the success of the film?

4. What did Omar Sy do before acting in Nakache and Toledano's films?

5. What did Cluzet find difficult in portraying Philippe?

6. What aspect of the film received different interpretations from French critics?

7. What political interpretation of the film offended the ex-president of the National Front?

8. To what aspect of the film were American critics particularly sensitive?

9. How did the success of *The Intouchables* benefit associations that help people with disabilities?

10. Why is this film considered by some a "social phenomenon"?

11. In what types of roles was the actor Piéral cast? Why?

12. Before *The Intouchables*, what Francophone film marked a turning point in the representation of disability? Explain why and give examples of later films in which the same characteristic is found.

Exploring the Film

1. The Title of the Film

Why is the film called *The Intouchables*? What is an "untouchable" in India? Think of other meanings of this word. How can Driss and Philippe be considered "in/untouchable"?

2. The Beginning of the Film

What did you think about the relationship between Philippe and Driss when you saw the scene of the police chase? What type of film does the beginning of the film seem to introduce? How does this first scene already announce some of the themes of the film? Which character dominates? First we hear classical music, and then rock music when the police escort the car. Why do the directors use these two very different musical genres?

3. The Setting: The Suburbs and the Upscale Neighborhoods

What contrasts do the directors establish between the suburbs and the swank neighborhoods of Paris? What do the buildings and individual homes look like? What means of transportation are associated with each space? **Compare the two following scenes** (Excerpt 1, 17'22–18'53 and Excerpt 2, 19'20–21'22). In your opinion, why did the directors choose such vastly different living environments?

What clichés on the suburbs and its residents do some of the characters voice, like Philippe's friend Antoine and his adopted daughter Elisa? Is Antoine right in worrying about Philippe? **Review the scenes with Antoine** (Excerpt 3, 34'36–36'25) **and Elisa** (Excerpt 4, 58'16–58'41).

4. The Characters

+ *Philippe and Driss*

Philippe and Driss form a rather unlikely duo. Make a list of the physical, social, and cultural oppositions between the two men.

What is there about Driss that impresses Philippe? How does their relationship evolve? What influence do they have on each other? What are some key moments in the development of their relationship?

The growing intimacy between Philippe and Driss also allows them to discover similarities between each other. What do they have in common?

Beyond the individual stories, what symbolic interpretation can we give of the friendship between Philippe and Driss?

+ *Philippe, Driss, and Women*

Compare Philippe's and Driss' seduction techniques. What is the directors' point of view on these two approaches? How do you explain the approach chosen by Philippe?

Female characters are often secondary and objectified in the male buddy movie. Is this the case in *The Intouchables*? What roles do women play in Philippe's and Driss' lives?

5. Cultural Oppositions

When it comes to painting, how do Driss and Philippe react differently when they look at a piece of modern art or the painting of a nude woman seen from the back? Review the scenes at the museum (Excerpt 5, 32'35–33'35) and at Philippe's house (Excerpt 6, 1h26'45–1h27'09). If you have already seen *Hate*, what parallels can you draw with the scene in which the three protagonists from the suburbs crash the opening of an art gallery?

Why does Driss start to paint, and why does Philippe sell one of Driss' paintings to Antoine? **Can this be interpreted as a comment on modern art?** Lalanne, a commentator for the cultural magazine *Les Inrockuptibles*, criticizes the treatment of modern art in the film. He writes, "This obsessive focus on contemporary art as a big scam that should be exploited in order to make a quick buck is surely the only touch of real malice in the film," adding, "It is a shame that social criticism, when it finally appears, takes aim at the wrong target" ("Briser les classes"). Do you share his opinion?

As regards music, how does Driss react at the opera and while listening to the orchestra at Philippe's birthday party? What type of music does Driss prefer, and why? **Does the confrontation of different music styles in the film have a particular meaning?**

Cultural differences are a favorite theme of comedy (we find the same contrast between popular and intellectual culture in *The Taste of Others* [*Le Goût des autres*], for example). **Is one type of culture presented as superior to the other in *The Intouchables?*** What effect does popular culture have on Philippe? And intellectual culture on Driss? In particular, why is Driss successful at his second job interview? *Review this interview* (Excerpt 7, 1h37'42–1h39'10). According to this scene, what facilitates the integration of young people from the suburbs? Is Driss' experience a model that these youths can follow?

6. Disability

How do the job candidates at the beginning of the film look upon physical disability? How is Driss different in that regard?

Overall, spectators with disabilities reacted positively to the film, appreciating its refusal to elicit pity. For the president of APAJH (the association that helps adults and young people with disabilities, mentioned above), the humor in the film is borderline, but it is "a way to make disability move into the realm of the ordinary" (Rocfort-Giovanni)—and as a matter of fact some of the "politically incorrect" episodes were suggested by Philippe Pozzo di Borgo himself. **What examples of "borderline" humor did you notice in the film?** Did some of Driss' jokes shock you? **For example, what did you think of *the following scene at the Museum of Modern Art*** (Excerpt 8, 33'36–34'28) in which Driss refuses to give chocolate to Philippe and says, "Pas de bras, pas de chocolat" ("No handy, no candy," or, literally, "No arms, no chocolate!")? (This French saying originated in a funny story and is used in commercials, films, video games, politics, music, etc. to point to the absurdity of a situation.)

What other types of disabilities are presented in this film?

7. Comedy

The film displays different types of comedy. Give some examples of comedy based on words, gestures, and situations. **What is the purpose of comedy in the film? Who/What is its target?**

A critic wrote about *The Intouchables*, "The challenge was to have a fruitful encounter between two completely opposite worlds: popular comedy on the one hand [...]. On the other, a darker, high-brow cinema, very demanding as regards both form and content" ("De Pialat et Audiard à Nakache et Toledano"). **What aspects of the film belong to popular comedy? To a more intellectual cinema?**

A characteristic of comedy is to solve conflicts and restore individual and social harmony. **Besides issues in the relationship between Driss and Philippe, what other conflicts are resolved in the film?** What types of reconciliation occur? What positive impact does Driss have on the other characters?

8. Staging (Mise en Scène)

The directors use **parallel scenes** that highlight oppositions in order to show the characters' motivations and evolution. **Analyze the following examples:** Driss in his bathroom in the suburb and his discovery of the bathroom at Philippe's; Driss' two job interviews; the two scenes where Driss scolds a man who has parked his car illegally in front of Philippe's house; Philippe's two dates with Eléonore.

9. Philippe's Birthday Party

What important themes of the film appear in this scene? What is the most important impact of Driss' music and dancing on the guests? *Review excerpts of this scene* (Excerpt 9, 1h04'20–1h05'37, and Excerpt 10, 1h11'26–1h12'30).

As we noted earlier, the birthday scene elicited virulent reactions from American critics that almost compromised the success of the film in the United States. Do you agree with Weissberg's comment that this scene reinforces social and racial stereotypes and represents Driss as a servant in charge of amusing his master? **Can you find some of the stereotypes associated with black men in this scene and elsewhere in the film? Which ones?**

Eric Toledano and Olivier Nakache's Filmography

1999 *Little Shoes (Les petits souliers, film short)*

2005 *Let's Be Friends (Je préfère qu'on reste amis)*

2006 *Those Happy Days (Nos jours heureux)*

2009 *So Close (Tellement proches)*

2011 *The Intouchables (Intouchables)*

2014 *Samba*

Works Consulted

Carrière, Christophe. "*Intouchables*. Chronique d'un succès annoncé." *L'Express*, 3 Nov. 2011: n. pag.

Delfour, Jean-Jacques. "*Intouchables*: Cendrillon des temps modernes." *Libération*, 29 Nov. 2011: n. pag.

"De Pialat et Audiard à Nakache et Toledano." *Marianne*, 12 Nov. 2011: n. pag.

Dubois, Régis. *Les Noirs dans le cinéma français.* Lille: The Book Edition, 2012.

Emery, Elodie. "Deux millions et demi de Français ont déjà vu la comédie signée Nakache et Toledano." *Marianne*, 12 Nov. 2011: n. pag.

Ethis, Emmanuel. "*Intouchables* est une proposition de réconciliation." *L'Humanité-Dimanche*, 24 Nov. 2011: n. pag.

Gandillot, Thierry. "*Intouchables*, imparable." *Les Echos*, 2 Nov. 2011: n. pag.

Giordano, Isabelle. *Dans les coulisses d'*Intouchables. Paris: Grasset, 2013.

Granotier, Sylvie. "J'ai aimé *Intouchables* . . . et alors?" *Libération*, 5 Dec. 2011: n. pag.

"Harvey Weinstein trouve 'répugnant' l'avis de Jean-Marie Le Pen sur *Intouchables*." *L'Express*, 2 Mar. 2012. Web. 3 Jan. 2016. <www.lexpress.fr/culture/cinema/quand-harvey-weinstein-trouve-jean-marie-le-pen-xenophobe-et-raciste_1089021.html>.

Iacub, Marcela. "*Intouchables*: la preuve par l'oeuf." *Libération*, 11 Dec. 2011: n. pag.

Lalanne, Jean-Marc. "Briser les classes." *Les Inrockuptibles*, 23 Nov. 2011: n. pag.

———. "*Intouchables*, une fable relou et démagogique." *Les Inrockuptibles*, 1 Nov. 2011: n. pag.

Libiot, Eric. "Comme dans un fauteuil." *L'Express*, 3 Nov. 2011: n. pag.

Mandelbaum, Jacques. "*Intouchables*: derrière la comédie populaire, une métaphore sociale généreuse." *Le Monde*, 2 Nov. 2011: n. pag.

Michael, Charlie. "Interpreting *Intouchables*: Competing Transnationalisms in Contemporary French Cinema." *SubStance* 43.1 (2014): 123–37.

Nakache, Olivier, and Eric Toledano, dir. *Intouchables*. Sony Pictures Home Entertainment, 2013.

Pagès, Frédéric. "*Intouchables*." *Le Canard enchaîné*, 2 Nov. 2011: n. pag.

Péters, Sophie. "Au plat pays des Bisounours." *La Tribune Desfossés*, 17 Nov. 2011: n. pag.

Pris, Frédérique. "Les handicapés, nouveaux héros des comédies." *Le Soleil*, 25 Dec. 2014. Web. 29 Dec. 2016. <www.lapresse.ca/le-soleil/arts/cinema/201412/25/01-4830962-les-handicapes-nouveaux-heros-des-comedies.php>.

Rocfort-Giovanni, *Bérénice*, and Elsa Vigoureux. "*Intouchables*: radiographie d'un succès foudroyant." *Le Nouvel Observateur*, 1 Dec. 2011: n. pag.

Rouchy, Marie-Elisabeth. "Naissance d'un géant." *Le Nouvel Observateur*, 3 Nov. 2011: n. pag.

Weissberg, Jay. "Review: *Intouchable*." *Variety*, 29 Sept. 2011: n. pag.

APPENDICES

The Films in Historical Context

Major Milestones in Recent French History 1980–2017	French Films Presented in This Book
	1980 François Truffaut, *The Last Métro*
1981 François Mitterrand (socialist) elected President of the Republic.	1981 Jean-Jacques Beinex, *Diva*
	1983 Diane Kurys, *Coup de foudre/ Entre nous*
1984 Creation of SOS Racism to fight against racism.	
1985 Creation of SOFICAS (Societies for the Financing of Cinema, Audio-visual Projects).	
Creation of the Fête du Cinéma (annual event).	
Schengen Convention permitting free circulation in the countries of the European Union.	
1986–88 Jacques Chirac (conservative) Prime Minister.	1987 Louis Malle, *Goodbye Children*
1988 François Mitterrand reelected President of the Republic.	1988 Claire Denis, *Chocolat*
1989 Jack Lang, Minister of Culture, creates new subsidies for super-productions of films bearing on the French patrimony.	
The "headscarf affair": three middle school students in Creil are suspended for refusing to remove their Islamic veil (*hijab*) in school.	

1990 Broadening of the financing of French cinema by television channels (3 percent of gross sales).	
1991 Rioting of youths in Mantes-la-Jolie in the Paris suburbs.	
	1992 Régis Wargnier, *Indochine* André Téchiné, *Wild Reeds*
1993 General Agreement on Tariffs and Trade (GATT): France granted a "cultural exception" to the free trade agreement as regards films.	
The Pasqua Law of 1993 stiffens the conditions for foreigners entering and residing in France.	
1993–95 Edouard Balladur (conservative) Prime Minister.	
1994 Rioting of youths in the suburbs of Avignon.	
1995 Jacques Chirac elected President of the Republic on the theme of inclusion; Alain Juppé Prime Minister.	1995 Josiane Balasko, *French Twist* Mathieu Kassovitz, *Hate*
Summer: violent riots in the Paris suburbs; angry youths burn cars. In autumn the Juppé Plan on the reform of retirement plans and medical insurance provokes strikes that paralyze the country for weeks.	
1996 Police remove undocumented people from the Saint-Bernard Church in Paris; media firestorm.	
1997 Early legislative elections; the left wins: Lionel Jospin (socialist) Prime Minister.	1997 Bruno Dumont, *The Life of Jesus*
	1998 Erick Zonca, *The Dreamlife of Angels*
1999 Opening of a reception center for immigrants at Sangatte near Calais.	
Same-sex civil unions (PACS) become legal in France.	

	2000 Agnès Varda, *The Gleaners and I*
	Agnès Jaoui, *The Taste of Others*
	2001 Jean-Pierre Jeunet, *Amélie*
2002 Jacques Chirac reelected President of the Republic against Jean-Marie Le Pen of the National Front (extreme right).	
Nicolas Sarkozy, Minister of the Interior, closes the immigrant center at Sangatte, creating the "Calais jungle" (makeshift dwellings). The euro replaces the French franc.	
	2003 Abdellatif Kechiche, *Games of Love and Chance*
2004 Law forbidding the wearing of "ostentatious" religious signs (*hijab*, Jewish *kippa*, large crucifixes) in public schools.	
2005 Autumn: Violent riots in suburbs in Paris and throughout France; thousands of cars and buildings are burned. Sarkozy calls the youths of the suburbs "rabble" and threatens to "hose down" the Cité des 4 000 in La Courneuve.	2005 Michael Haneke, *Caché*
2006 The Article L622-1 of the Code governing the entrance and residence of foreigners and the right of asylum is voted into law: anyone helping illegal immigrants risks five years in prison and a fine of 30,000 euros (referred to as the "crime of solidarity") by its opponents.	
2007 Nicolas Sarkozy (conservative) is elected President of the Republic against Ségolène Royal (socialist), the first women candidate to make the second round of voting in a presidential election in France.	
	2008 Laurent Cantet, *The Class*

	2009 Philippe Lioret, *Welcome* Jacques Audiard, *A Prophet*
2010 Law forbidding hiding one's face in public (targets the wearing of *la burqa*, the complete Islamic female garment, in public).	
	2011 Olivier Nakache and Eric Toledano, *The Intouchables*
2012 François Hollande (socialist) elected President of the Republic.	
2013 The "crime against solidarity" is abolished. Homosexual marriage becomes legal in France.	
2015 Terrorist attacks in Paris against the magazine *Charlie Hebdo* (Jan.), then at the Bataclan show venue, at the Stade de France football stadium, and other places in the center of Paris (Nov.).	
2016 Terrorist attack in Nice (July 14, Bastille Day).	
2017 Emmanuel Macron (center, founder of the "La République En Marche" political party) elected President of the Republic against Marine Le Pen (National Front).	

Contemporary French Films: Award Winners 1980–2016

The following pages contain a list, year by year, of French films that have won prestigious French or international prizes, as well as the top box office success each year. Given the great number of awards given overall, we have limited ourselves here to the prizes presented below, given in the order that we have chosen for the winners' list: (a) French prizes outside of festivals, (b) prizes won in festivals, and (c) foreign prizes outside of festivals.

The **Césars** are the most prestigious national prizes awarded to French films each year. They are given in around twenty different categories, but we will include only the following major awards: **Meilleur film** (Best Film), **Meilleur premier film** (Best First Film), **Prix de la mise en scène** or **Meilleur réalisateur** (Best Director), **Meilleur scénario original ou adaptation** (Best Original Screenplay or Adaptation), **Meilleur film documentaire** (Best Documentary), **Meilleur film d'animation** (Best Animated Film, awarded since 2010).

Le Prix Louis Delluc (the Louis Delluc Prize) is awarded each year to the best film. Since 1999 **Le Prix Louis Delluc du premier film** (the Louis Delluc Prize for the Best First Film) has also been given.

Le Prix Jean Vigo (the Jean Vigo Prize) goes normally to a young film director who demonstrates unusual independence of mind and stylistic originality.

The Prizes at the Cannes Film Festival. Among the numerous awards given at the Cannes Film Festival, we will retain the following, generally considered to be the most prestigious:

+ **La Palme d'Or** (The Golden Palm), awarded to the best of festival;

+ **Le Grand Prix** (1995–)/**Grand Prix du Jury** (1989–94)/**Grand Prix Spécial du Jury** (1967–88), awarded to the second best film;

+ **Le Prix de la mise en scène** (internationally known as the "Best Director Award"), given to the filmmaker considered to be the best director among those in competition that year;

+ **Le Prix Un Certain Regard**, awarded since 1998 to the best film in the parallel selection (a group of films told in particularly innovative ways);

+ **La Caméra d'Or** (Golden Camera), awarded to the best first film among those in the Official Selection, the Quinzaine des réalisateurs (Directors' Fortnight—largely for independent filmmakers on the fringes), and the Semaine de la critique (the Critics Week—new young talents in particular).

Le Lion d'Or (the Golden Lion) is the prize for the Best Film at the Venice International Film Festival (la Mostra).

L'Ours d'Or (the Golden Bear) is the prize for the Best Film at the Berlin Film Festival.

For the **Oscars** and their British equivalent (**the BAFTA awards**), we have restricted ourselves to the same categories as for the Césars, only adding the **Oscar du Meilleur film en langue étrangère** (Best Foreign Language Film) and the **BAFTA du Meilleur film non anglophone** (Best Non-Anglophone Film).

*The film titles below are all in French, but English versions of any particular title can be found quickly online in the Internet Movie Database at http://www.imdb.com/.

1980 François Truffaut, *Le Dernier Métro* (Césars du Meilleur Film: du Meilleur réalisateur et du Meilleur scénario original ou adaptation)
Alain Cavalier, *Un étrange voyage* (Prix Louis Delluc)
René Gilson, *Ma blonde, entends-tu dans la ville?* (Prix Jean Vigo)
Alain Resnais, *Mon oncle d'Amérique* (Grand Prix Spécial du Jury à Cannes)
Jean-Pierre Denis, *Histoire d'Adrien* (Caméra d'or à Cannes)
Louis Malle, *Atlantic City* (BAFTA du Meilleur réalisateur)
Claude Pinoteau, *La Boum* (film français en tête du box-office)

1981 Jean-Jacques Annaud, *La Guerre du feu* (Césars du Meilleur film et du Meilleur réalisateur)
Jean-Jacques Beineix, *Diva* (César du Meilleur premier film)
Claude Miller, *Garde à vue* (César du Meilleur scénario original ou adaptation)
Pierre Granier-Deferre, *Une étrange affaire* (Prix Louis Delluc)
Jean-Pierre Sentier, *Le Jardinier* (Prix Jean Vigo)
Alain Tanner (Suisse), *Les Années Lumière* (Grand Prix Spécial du Jury à Cannes)
Francis Veber, *La Chèvre* (film français en tête du box-office)

1982 Bob Swaim, *La Balance* (César du Meilleur film)
Andrzej Wajda, *Danton* (César du Meilleur réalisateur; Prix Louis Delluc; BAFTA du Meilleur film non anglophone)
Daniel Vigne, *Le Retour de Martin Guerre* (César du Meilleur scénario original)
Pierre Granier-Deferre, *L'Etoile du Nord* (César de la Meilleure adaptation)
Philippe Garrel, *L'Enfant secret* (Prix Jean Vigo)
Romain Goupil, *Mourir à 30 ans* (César du Meilleur premier film; Caméra d'or à Cannes)
Gérard Oury, *L'As des as* (film français en tête du box-office)

1983 Ettore Scola, *Le Bal* (Césars du Meilleur film et du Meilleur réalisateur)
Maurice Pialat, *A nos amours* (César du Meilleur film, ex-aequo avec *Le Bal*, et Prix Louis Delluc)
Euzhan Palcy, *Rue Cases-Nègres* (César du Meilleur premier film)
Patrice Chéreau, *L'Homme blessé* (César du Meilleur scénario original)
Jean Becker, *L'Eté meurtrier* (César de la Meilleure adaptation; film français en tête du box-office)

Gérard Mordillat, *Vive la sociale* (Prix Jean Vigo)
Robert Bresson, *L'Argent* (Prix de la mise en scène à Cannes)
Jean-Luc Godard, *Prénom Carmen* (Lion d'or à Venise)

1984   Claude Zizi, *Les Ripoux* (Césars du Meilleur film et du Meilleur réalisateur)
Richard Dembo, *La Diagonale du fou* (Prix Louis Delluc; César du Meilleur premier film)
Bertrand Blier, *Notre histoire* (César du Meilleur scénario original)
Bertrand Tavernier, *Un dimanche à la campagne* (Prix de la mise en scène à Cannes; César de la Meilleure adaptation)
Michel Blanc, *Marche à l'ombre* (film français en tête du box-office)

1985   Coline Serreau, *Trois hommes et un couffin* (Césars du Meilleur film et du Meilleur scénario original ou adaptation; film français en tête du box-office)
Michel Deville, *Péril en la demeure* (César du Meilleur réalisateur)
Mehdi Charef, *Le Thé au harem d'Archimède* (César du Meilleur premier film; Prix Jean Vigo)
Claude Miller, *L'Effrontée* (Prix Louis Delluc)
André Téchiné, *Rendez-vous* (Prix de la mise en scène à Cannes)
Agnès Varda, *Sans toit ni loi* (Lion d'or à Venise)

1986   Alain Cavalier, *Thérèse* (Césars du Meilleur film, du Meilleur réalisateur et du Meilleur scénario original ou adaptation)
Régis Wargnier, *La Femme de ma vie* (César du Meilleur premier film)
Leos Carax, *Mauvais sang* (Prix Louis Delluc)
Jacques Rozier, *Maine-Océan* (Prix Jean Vigo)
Claire Devers, *Noir et Blanc* (Caméra d'or à Cannes)
Claude Berri, *Jean de Florette*, (Prix BAFTA du Meilleur film; film français en tête du box-office)
Eric Rohmer, *Le Rayon vert* (Lion d'or à Venise)

1987   Louis Malle, *Au revoir les enfants* (Césars du Meilleur film, du Meilleur réalisateur et du Meilleur scénario original ou adaptation; Prix Louis Delluc; Lion d'or; BAFTA du Meilleur réalisateur; film français en tête du box-office)
Serge Meynard, *L'Œil au beur(re) noir* (César du Meilleur premier film)
Jean-Luc Godard, *Soigne ta droite* (Prix Louis Delluc, ex-aequo avec *Au revoir les enfants*)
Maurice Pialat, *Sous le soleil de Satan* (Palme d'or à Cannes)
Laurent Perrin, *Buisson ardent* (Prix Jean Vigo)

1988   Bruno Nuytten, *Camille Claudel* (César du Meilleur film)
Jean-Jacques Annaud, *L'Ours* (César du Meilleur réalisateur)
Etienne Chatiliez, *La Vie est un long fleuve tranquille* (Césars du Meilleur premier film et du Meilleur scénario original ou adaptation)
Michel Deville, *La Lectrice* (Prix Louis Delluc)
Luc Moullet, *La Comédie du travail* (Prix Jean Vigo)
Marcel Ophüls, *Hôtel Terminus* (Oscar du Meilleur documentaire)
Luc Besson, *Le Grand Bleu* (film français en tête du box-office)

1989   Bertrand Blier, *Trop belle pour toi* (Césars du Meilleur film, du Meilleur
        réalisateur, et du Meilleur scénario original ou adaptation; Grand Prix du Jury
        à Cannes; film français en tête du box-office)
        Eric Rochant, *Un monde sans pitié* (César du Meilleur premier film; Prix
        Louis Delluc)
        Dai Sijie, *Chine ma douleur* (Prix Jean Vigo)
        Bertrand Tavernier, *La Vie et rien d'autre* (Prix BAFTA du Meilleur film
        non anglophone)

1990   Jean-Paul Rappeneau, *Cyrano de Bergerac* (Césars du Meilleur film et du
        Meilleur réalisateur)
        Christian Vincent, *La Discrète* (Césars du Meilleur premier film et
        du Meilleur scénario original ou adaptation)
        Jacques Doillon, *Le Petit Criminel* (Prix Louis Delluc)
        Patrice Leconte, *Le Mari de la coiffeuse* (Prix Louis Delluc, ex-aequo avec
        Le Petit Criminel)
        Patrick Grandperret, *Mona et moi* (Prix Jean Vigo)
        Yves Robert, *La Gloire de mon père* (film français en tête du box-office)

1991   Alain Corneau, *Tous les matins du monde* (Césars du Meilleur film et du
        Meilleur réalisateur; Prix Louis Delluc; film français en tête du box-office)
        Marc Caro et Jean-Pierre Jeunet, *Delicatessen* (Césars du Meilleur premier
        film et du Meilleur scénario original ou adaptation)
        Eric Brazier, *Le Brasier* (Prix Jean Vigo)
        Jacques Rivette, *La Belle Noiseuse* (Grand Prix du Jury à Cannes)

1992   Cyril Collard, *Les Nuits fauves* (Césars du Meilleur film et du Meilleur
        premier film)
        Claude Sautet, *Un cœur en hiver* (César du Meilleur réalisateur)
        Coline Serreau, *La Crise* (César du Meilleur scénario original ou adaptation)
        Christine Pascal, *Le Petit Prince a dit* (Prix Louis Delluc)
        Olivier Assayas, *Paris s'éveille* (Prix Jean Vigo)
        Régis Wargnier, *Indochine* (Oscar du Meilleur film en langue étrangère; film
        français en tête du box-office)

1993   Alain Resnais, *Smoking/No Smoking* (Césars du Meilleur film, du Meilleur
        réalisateur et du Meilleur scénario original ou adaptation; Prix Louis Delluc)
        Tran Anh Hung, *L'Odeur de la papaye verte* (César du Meilleur premier film;
        Caméra d'or à Cannes)
        Anne Fontaine, *Les Histoires d'amour finissent mal* (Prix Jean Vigo)
        Krzysztof Kieslowski, *Trois couleurs: Bleu* (Lion d'or à Venise)
        Jean-Marie Poiré, *Les Visiteurs* (film français en tête du box-office)

1994   André Téchiné, *Les Roseaux sauvages* (Césars du Meilleur film, du Meilleur
        réalisateur et du Meilleur scénario original ou adaptation; Prix Louis Delluc)
        Jacques Audiard, *Regarde les hommes tomber* (César du Meilleur premier
        film)
        Raymond Depardon, *Délits flagrants* (César du Meilleur film documentaire)
        Cédric Kahn, *Trop de bonheur* (Prix Jean Vigo)

Pascale Ferrand, *Petits Arrangements avec les morts* (Caméra d'or à Cannes)

Hervé Palud, *Un Indien dans la ville* (film français en tête du box-office)

1995   Mathieu Kassovitz, *La Haine* (César du Meilleur film; Prix de la mise en scène à Cannes)

Bernard Campan et Didier Bourdon, *Les Trois Frères* (César du Meilleur premier film; film français en tête du box-office)

Claude Sautet, *Nelly et Monsieur Arnaud* (César du Meilleur réalisateur; Prix Louis Delluc)

Josiane Balasko, *Gazon maudit* (César du Meilleur scénario original ou adaptation)

Xavier Beauvois, *N'oublie pas que tu vas mourir* (Prix Jean Vigo)

Tran Anh Hung, *Cyclo* (Lion d'or à Venise)

Bertrand Tavernier, *L'Appât* (Ours d'or à Berlin)

1996   Patrice Leconte, *Ridicule* (Césars du Meilleur film et du Meilleur réalisateur; BAFTA du Meilleur film non anglophone)

Bertrand Tavernier, *Capitaine Conan* (César du Meilleur réalisateur, ex-aequo avec *Ridicule*)

Sandrine Veysset, *Y'aura t'il de la neige à Noël?* (Prix Louis Delluc et César du Meilleur premier film)

Cédric Klapisch, *Un air de famille* (César du Meilleur scénario original ou adaptation)

Pascal Bonizer, *Encore* (Prix Jean Vigo)

Gabriel Aghion, *Pédale douce* (film français en tête du box-office)

1997   Alain Resnais, *On connaît la chanson* (César du Meilleur film et du Meilleur scénario original ou adaptation; Prix Louis Delluc)

Alain Chabat, *Didier* (César du Meilleur premier film)

Luc Besson, *Le Cinquième Elément* (César du Meilleur réalisateur et film français en tête du box-office)

Robert Guédiguian, *Marius et Jeannette* (Prix Louis Delluc, ex-aequo avec *On connaît la chanson*)

Bruno Dumont, *La Vie de Jésus* (Prix Jean Vigo)

Gilles Mimouni, *L'Appartement* (BAFTA du Meilleur film non anglophone)

1998   Erick Zonca, *La Vie rêvée des anges* (César du Meilleur film)

Bruno Podalydès, *Dieu seul me voit* (César du Meilleur premier film)

Patrice Chéreau, *Ceux qui m'aiment prendront le train* (César du Meilleur réalisateur)

Francis Veber, *Le Dîner de cons* (César du Meilleur scénario original ou adaptation; film français en tête du box-office)

Cédric Kahn, *L'Ennui* (Prix Louis Delluc)

Claude Mourieras, *Dis-moi que je rêve* (Prix Jean Vigo)

1999   Tonie Marshall, *Vénus Beauté (Institut)* (César du Meilleur film, de la Meilleure réalisatrice, et du Meilleur scénario original ou adaptation)

Emmanuel Finkiel, *Voyages* (César du Meilleur premier film et Prix Louis Delluc du premier film)

Otar Iosseliani, **Adieu plancher des vaches!** (Prix Louis Delluc)
Noémie Lvovsky, **La Vie ne me fait pas peur** (Prix Jean Vigo)
Luc et Jean-Pierre Dardenne (Belgique), **Rosetta** (Palme d'or à Cannes)
Bruno Dumont, **L'Humanité** (Grand Prix à Cannes)
Claude Zidi, **Astérix et Obélix contre César** (film français en tête du box-office)

2000   Agnès Jaoui, **Le Goût des autres** (Césars du Meilleur film et du Meilleur scénario original ou adaptation)
Laurent Cantet, **Ressources humaines** (César du Meilleur premier film et Prix Louis Delluc du premier film)
Dominik Moll, **Harry, un ami qui vous veut du bien** (César du Meilleur réalisateur)
Claude Chabrol, **Merci pour le chocolat** (Prix Louis Delluc)
Patricia Mazuy, **Saint-Cyr** (Prix Jean Vigo)
Orso Miret, **De l'histoire ancienne** (Prix Jean Vigo, ex-aequo avec *Saint-Cyr*)
Gérard Krawczyk, **Taxi II** (film français en tête du box-office)

2001   Jean-Pierre Jeunet, **Le Fabuleux Destin d'Amélie Poulain** (Césars du Meilleur film et du Meilleur réalisateur; BAFTA du Meilleur scénario original; film français en tête du box-office)
Danis Tanovic, **No Man's Land** (Oscar du Meilleur film étranger; César du Meilleur premier film)
Jacques Audiard, **Sur mes lèvres** (César du Meilleur scénario original ou adaptation)
Patrice Chéreau, **Intimité** (Prix Louis Delluc; Ours d'or à Berlin)
Eugène Green, **Toutes les nuits** (Prix Louis Delluc du premier film)
Emmanuelle Bourdieu, **Candidature** (Prix Jean Vigo)
Alain Guiraudie, **Ce vieux rêve qui bouge** (Prix Jean Vigo, ex-aequo avec *Candidature*)
Yves Caumon, **Amour d'enfance** (Prix Un Certain Regard à Cannes)

2002   Roman Polanski, **Le Pianiste** (Césars du Meilleur Film et du Meilleur réalisateur, Palme d'or à Cannes; BAFTA du Meilleur Film et du Meilleur réalisateur)
Costa-Gavras, **Amen** (César du Meilleur scénario original ou adaptation)
Nicolas Philibert, **Etre et avoir** (Prix Louis Delluc)
Zabou Breitman, **Se souvenir des belles choses** (César du Meilleur premier film)
Rabah Ameur-Zaïmeche, **Wesh, wesh, qu'est-ce qui se passe?** (Prix Louis Delluc du premier film)
Charles Najman, **Royal Bonbon** (Prix Jean Vigo)
Julie Lopes-Curval, **Bord de mer** (Caméra d'or à Cannes)
Alain Chabat, **Astérix et Obélix: Mission Cléopâtre** (film français en tête du box-office)

2003   Denis Arcand (Canada), **Les Invasions barbares** (César du Meilleur film, du Meilleur réalisateur, et du Meilleur scénario original ou adaptation)

Julie Bertuccelli, ***Depuis qu'Otar est parti . . .*** (César du Meilleur premier film)

Noémie Lvovsky, ***Les Sentiments*** (Prix Louis Delluc)

Lucas Belvaux (Belgium), ***Un couple épatant /Cavale/Après la vie*** (Prix Louis Delluc, ex-aequo avec *Les Sentiments*)

Valeria Bruni Tedeschi, ***Il est plus facile pour un chameau . . .*** (Prix Louis Delluc du premier film)

Jean-Paul Civeyrac, ***Toutes ces belles promesses*** (Prix Jean Vigo)

Abdellatif Kechiche, ***L'Esquive*** (César du Meilleur film, du Meilleur réalisateur, et du Meilleur scénario original ou adaptation)

Gérard Krawczyk, ***Taxi 3*** (film français en tête du box-office)

2004   Arnaud Desplechin, ***Rois et reine*** (Prix Louis Delluc)

Yolande Moreau, Gilles Porte, ***Quand la mer monte . . .*** (César du Meilleur premier film et Prix Louis Delluc du premier film)

Patrick Mimouni, ***Quand je serai star*** (Prix Jean Vigo)

Tony Gatlif, ***Exils*** (Prix de la mise en scène à Cannes)

Christophe Barratier, ***Les Choristes*** (film français en tête du box-office)

2005   Jacques Audiard, ***De battre mon cœur s'est arrêté*** (César du Meilleur Film, du Meilleur réalisateur, et de la Meilleure adaptation, BAFTA du Meilleur film non anglophone)

Hubert Sauper, ***Le Cauchemar de Darwin*** (César du Meilleur premier film)

Radu Mihaileanu, ***Va, vis et deviens*** (César du Meilleur scénario original)

Philippe Garrel, ***Les Amants réguliers*** (Prix Louis Delluc)

Antony Cordier, ***Douches froides*** (Prix Louis Delluc du premier film)

Jérôme Bonnell, ***Les Yeux clairs*** (Prix Jean Vigo)

Michael Haneke, ***Caché*** (Prix de la mise en scène à Cannes)

Luc Jacquet, ***La Marche de l'empereur*** (Oscar du Meilleur documentaire)

Cédric Klapisch, ***Poupées russes*** (film français en tête du box-office)

2006   Pascale Ferran, ***Lady Chatterley*** (César du Meilleur film et de la Meilleure adaptation; Prix Louis Delluc)

Guillaume Canet, ***Ne le dis à personne*** (César du Meilleur réalisateur)

Isabelle Mergault, ***Je vous trouve très beau*** (César du Meilleur premier film)

Rachid Bouchareb, ***Indigènes*** (César du Meilleur scénario original)

Karl Zéro et Michel Royer, ***Dans la peau de Jacques Chirac*** (César du Meilleur film documentaire)

Jean-Pierre Darroussin, ***Le Pressentiment*** (Prix Louis Delluc du premier film)

Laurent Achard, ***Le Dernier des fous*** (Prix Jean Vigo)

Bruno Dumont, ***Flandres*** (Grand Prix à Cannes)

Patrice Leconte, ***Les Bronzés 3*** (film français en tête du box-office)

2007   Abdellatif Kechiche, ***La Graine et le Mulet*** (Césars du Meilleur film, du Meilleur réalisateur, et du Meilleur scénario original; Prix Louis Delluc)

Marjane Satrapi et Vincent Paronnaud, ***Persepolis*** (Césars du Meilleur premier film et de la Meilleure adaptation)

Barbet Schroeder, ***L'Avocat de la terreur*** (César du Meilleur film documentaire)

Mia Hanson-Løve, *Tout est pardonné* (Prix Louis Delluc du premier film)

Céline Sciamma, *Naissance des pieuvres* (Prix Louis Delluc du premier film, ex aequo avec *Tout est pardonné*)

Serge Bozon, *La France* (Prix Jean Vigo)

Olivier Dahan, *La Môme* (film français en tête du box-office)

2008   Martin Provost, *Séraphine* (Césars du Meilleur film et du Meilleur scénario original)

Jean-François Richer, *Mesrine, l'instinct de mort, Mesrine, L'ennemi public n° 1* (César du Meilleur réalisateur)

Philippe Claudel, *Il y a longtemps que je t'aime* (César du Meilleur premier film; BAFTA du Meilleur film non anglophone)

Laurent Cantet, *Entre les murs* (César de la Meilleure adaptation; Palme d'Or à Cannes)

Agnès Varda, *Les Plages d'Agnès* (César du Meilleur film documentaire)

Raymond Depardon, *La Vie moderne* (Prix Louis Delluc)

Samuel Collardey, *L'Apprenti* (Prix Louis Delluc du premier film)

Emmanuel Finkiel, *Nulle part, terre promise* (Prix Jean Vigo)

2009   Jacques Audiard, *Un prophète* (Césars du Meilleur film, du Meilleur réalisateur, et du Meilleur scénario original; Prix Louis Delluc; Grand Prix à Cannes; BAFTA du Meilleur film non anglophone)

Riad Sattouf, *Les Beaux Gosses* (César du Meilleur premier film)

Stéphane Brizé, *Mademoiselle Chambon* (César de la Meilleure adaptation)

Serge Bromberg et Ruxandra Medrea, *L'Enfer d'Henri-Georges Clouzot* (César du Meilleur film documentaire)

Léa Fehner, *Qu'un seul tienne et les autres suivront* (Prix Louis Delluc du premier film)

Olivier Ducastel, Jacques Martineau, *L'Arbre et la forêt* (Prix Jean Vigo)

Laurent Tirard, *Le Petit Nicolas* (film français en tête du box-office)

2010   Xavier Beauvois, *Des hommes et des dieux* (César du Meilleur film; Grand Prix à Cannes)

Roman Polanski, *The Ghost Writer* (César du Meilleur réalisateur et de la Meilleure adaptation)

Joann Sfar, *Gainsbourg (Vie héroïque)* (César du Meilleur premier film)

Michel Leclerc, *Le Nom des gens* (César du Meilleur scénario original)

Jacques Perrin, Jacques Cluzaud, *Océans* (César du Meilleur film documentaire)

Sylvain Chomet, *L'Illusionniste* (César du Meilleur film d'animation)

Rebecca Ziotowski, *Belle Epine* (Prix Louis Delluc)

Katell Quillévéré, *Un Poison violent* (Prix Jean Vigo)

Mathieu Amalric, *Tournée* (Prix de la mise en scène à Cannes)

Guillaume Canet, *Les Petits Mouchoirs* (film français en tête du box-office)

2011   Michael Hazanavicius, *The Artist* (Césars du Meilleur film et du Meilleur réalisateur; Oscar du Meilleur film et du Meilleur réalisateur; BAFTA du Meilleur Film, du Meilleur réalisateur, et du Meilleur scénario original)

Sylvain Estibal, *Le Cochon de Gaza* (César du Meilleur premier film)

Pierre Schoeller, *L'Exercice de l'Etat* (César du Meilleur scénario original)

Roman Polanski, *Carnage* (César de la Meilleure adaptation)

Christian Rouaud, *Tous au Larzac* (César du Meilleur film documentaire)

Joann Sfar, *Le Chat du Rabbin* (César du Meilleur film d'animation)

Aki Kaurismäki, *Le Havre* (Prix Louis Delluc)

Djinn Carrénard, *Donoma* (Prix Louis Delluc du premier film)

Rabah Ameur-Zaïmeche, *Les Chants de Mandrin* (Prix Jean Vigo)

Olivier Nakache et Eric Toledano, *Intouchables* (film français en tête du box-office)

2012   Michael Haneke, *Amour* (Césars du Meilleur film, du Meilleur réalisateur et du Meilleur scénario original; Palme d'Or à Cannes; BAFTA du Meilleur film non anglophone)

Cyril Mennegun, *Louise Wimmer* (César du Meilleur premier film et Prix Louis Delluc du premier film)

Benoît Jacquot, *Les Adieux à la reine* (Prix Louis Delluc)

Jacques Audiard, *De rouille et d'os* (César de la Meilleure adaptation)

Sébastien Lifshitz, *Les Invisibles* (César du Meilleur film documentaire)

Stéphane Aubier et Vincent Patar, *Ernest et Célestine* (César du Meilleur film d'animation)

Héléna Klotz, *L'Age atomique* (Prix Jean Vigo)

Alain Chabat, *Sur la piste du Marsupilami* (film français en tête du box-office)

2013   Guillaume Gallienne, *Les Garçons et Guillaume, à table* (César du Meilleur film, du Meilleur premier film et de la Meilleure adaptation)

Roman Polanski, *La Vénus à la fourrure* (César du Meilleur réalisateur)

Albert Dupontel, *9 mois ferme* (César du Meilleur scénario original)

Pascal Plisson, *Sur le chemin de l'école* (César du Meilleur documentaire)

Eric Omond, *Loulou, l'incroyable secret* (César du Meilleur film d'animation)

Hélier Cisterne, *Vandal* (Prix Louis Delluc)

Jean-Charles Fitoussi, *L'Enclos du temps* (Prix Jean Vigo)

Abdellatif Kechiche, *La Vie d'Adèle* (Palme d'Or à Cannes)

Pierre-François Martin-Laval, *Les Profs* (film français en tête du box-office)

2014   Abderrahmane Sissako, *Timbuktu* (César du Meilleur film, du Meilleur réalisateur, et du Meilleur scénario original)

Thomas Cailley, *Les Combattants* (César du Meilleur premier film et Prix Louis Delluc du premier film)

Olivier Assayas, *Sils Maria* (Prix Louis Delluc)

Volker Schlöndorff, *Diplomatie* (César de la Meilleure adaptation)

Karl Zéro et Michel Royer, *Dans la peau de Jacques Chirac* (César du Meilleur film documentaire)

Thomas Szabo et Hélène Giraud, *Minuscule, la vallée des fourmis perdues* (César du Meilleur film d'animation)

Jean-Charles Hue, *Mange tes morts* (Prix Jean Vigo)

Marie Amachoukeli, Claire Burger et Samuel Theis, *Party Girl* (Caméra d'or à Cannes)

Philippe de Chauveron, *Qu'est-ce qu'on a fait au Bon Dieu* (film français en tête du box-office)

2015   Phillipe Faucon, *Fatima* (César du Meilleur film et de la Meilleure adaptation)
Arnauld Desplechin, *Trois souvenirs de ma jeunesse* (César du Meilleur réalisateur)
Deniz Gamze Ergüven, *Mustang* (César du Meilleur premier film et du Meilleur scénario original)
Cyril Dion et Mélanie Laurent, *Demain* (César du Meilleur film documentaire)
Mark Osborne, *Le Petit Prince* (César du Meilleur film d'animation)
Nicolas Pariser, *Le Grand Jeu* (Prix Louis Delluc)
Damien Odoul, *La Peur* (Prix Jean Vigo)
Jacques Audiard, *Dheepan* (Palme d'Or à Cannes)
Arthur Benzaquen, *Les Nouvelles Aventures d'Aladin* (film français en tête du box-office)

2016   Paul Verhoeven, *Elle* (César du Meilleur film)
Claude Barras (Suisse), *Ma vie de courgette* (Césars de la Meilleure adaptation et du Meilleur film d'animation)
Houda Benyamina, *Divines* (César du Meilleur premier film et Caméra d'or à Cannes)
François Ruffin, *Merci Patron!* (César du Meilleur film documentaire)
Stéphane Brizé, *Une vie* (Prix Louis Delluc)
Maud Alpi, *Gorge cœur ventre* (Prix Louis Delluc du premier film)
Albert Serra, *La Mort de Louis XIV* (Prix Jean Vigo)
Olivier Assayas, *Personal Shopper* (Prix de la mise en scène à Cannes)
Olivier Baroux, *Les Tuche 2 – Le Rêve américain* (film français en tête du box-office)

Index